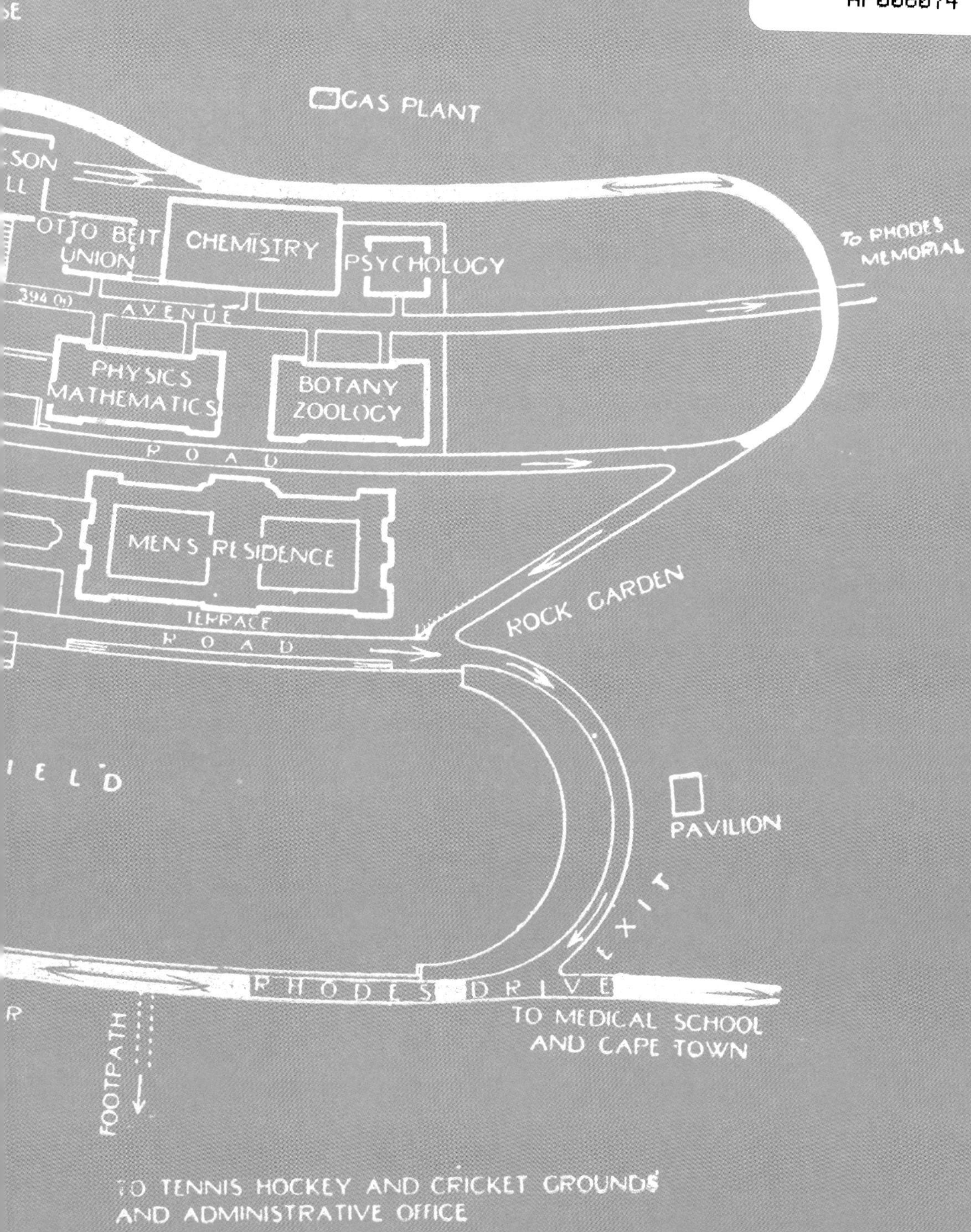
GAS PLANT
OTTO BEIT UNION
CHEMISTRY
PSYCHOLOGY
To RHODES MEMORIAL
AVENUE
PHYSICS MATHEMATICS
BOTANY ZOOLOGY
ROAD
MEN'S RESIDENCE
ROCK GARDEN
TERRACE
ROAD
PAVILION
EXIT
RHODES DRIVE
TO MEDICAL SCHOOL AND CAPE TOWN
FOOTPATH
TO TENNIS HOCKEY AND CRICKET GROUNDS AND ADMINISTRATIVE OFFICE

# UCT UNDER APARTHEID
## PART 1

### 1948–1968

From Onset to Sit-in

# UCT UNDER APARTHEID
# PART 1

## 1948–1968

### From Onset to Sit-in

## HOWARD PHILLIPS

First published by Fanele, an imprint of Jacana Media (Pty) Ltd in 2019

10 Orange Street
Sunnyside
Auckland Park 2092
South Africa
+2711 628 3200
www.jacana.co.za

© Howard Phillips, 2019

All rights reserved.

ISBN 978-1-928232-85-8

Editing by Russell Martin
Proofreading by Lara Jacob
Cover design by publicide
Set in Garamond MT 11/14pt
Printed by ABC Printers, Cape Town
Job no. 003588

See a complete list of Jacana titles at www.jacana.co.za

# CONTENTS

| | | |
|---|---|---|
| Foreword | | vii |
| Preface: To the Readers | | viii |
| 1. | UCT and the World in 1948 | 1 |
| 2. | Running UCT | 3 |
| 3. | Building a Second UCT | 24 |
| 4. | Teaching, Learning and Researching: UCT's Academic Project | 40 |
| 5. | Pure Science: The Faculty of Science | 47 |
| 6. | The Applied Sciences: Engineering and Medicine | 83 |
| 7. | The Professional Faculties: Commerce, Law, Education, Architecture and Social Science | 146 |
| 8. | The Arts: Musical, Liberal and Fine | 183 |
| 9. | Reaching Out: UCT and the Wider Community | 240 |
| 10. | Colliding and Colluding: UCT and the Apartheid State | 259 |
| 11. | Learning in (and out of) Class: Student Life | 278 |
| 12. | UCT and the World in 1968 | 337 |
| Note on Sources | | 341 |
| Notes | | 343 |
| Index | | 393 |

# FOREWORD

When I became Vice-Chancellor of the University of Cape Town (UCT) in July 2018, universities across South Africa were contending with student protests. They began in 2015 with the #RhodesMustFall movement, which addressed the influence of persistent colonialism in our physical space, followed at UCT by #FeesMustFall in the admission space and #OutsourcingMustFall in the employment space. In other universities, #AfrikaansMustFall addressed the intellectual and symbolic space. All of these issues have their roots in our past, which was overshadowed first by colonialism and then by apartheid. In both cases, a white minority of European origin sought to impose their political will, their languages and their culture on a majority population that represented many different traditions, languages, cultures and even geographies, in the case of the slaves who were brought from other continents and the migrant workers who left their homes in search of work.

The publication of this book, *UCT Under Apartheid, 1948–1968: From Onset to Sit-In,* reminds us that the academic space is one of different views, which can lead to controversy, disagreement, resistance and, when necessary, protest. It is a space where we need to uphold and exercise the freedom to examine ideas and what they mean for our practical lives. This narrative has relevance for our lives today because the past and the present are connected. It is in understanding that connection that we become able to dissect our history, untangle the different perceptions, improve our understanding, seek restoration where it is needed, and work towards the kind of future we want for those who come after us.

Professor Mamokgethi Phakeng<br>
Vice-Chancellor<br>
University of Cape Town

# PREFACE: TO THE READERS

This preface is deliberately addressed to 'The Read**ers**' and not 'The Reader' as I conceive of the readership of this volume as being quite diverse, wanting rather different things from the text. In my mind I can identify at least nine possible categories of reader, viz.

- current UCT administrators whose primary interest is in the history of the structure and operation of the University, the better to understand how and why the infrastructure and procedures which they have inherited came about and how knowledge of this could inform policy-making now;
- current UCT public relations and alumni officers concerned with how UCT's past might impact on its image now and in the future;
- current and former members of UCT's academic staff who are curious about the history of their own departments and how and why these did or did not change under the influence of people whose names still echo around the corridors for good or for ill;
- former members of the non-academic staff who wish to recall their years in the employ of 'Varsity';
- former UCT students who are now at a more reflective stage of their lives in which nostalgia about and memories of their student years feature prominently;
- current UCT students curious about the backstory to the present;
- Capetonians who did not attend UCT but whose lives in the Peninsula were touched in some way by 'Varsity' and its students, whether through SHAWCO, Varsity sports teams, Rag, Summer School, the Little Theatre or performances by College of Music and Drama School students;
- those interested in the history of apartheid-era South Africa, of which UCT constituted a microcosm, reflecting acutely and eloquently many of the processes, divisions and tensions of the larger society;
- historians of universities and of education locally and abroad who see a history of UCT as providing a valuable case study within these sub-disciplines, especially for comparative purposes; indeed, given the recent publication of histories of several South African universities,[1] it is becoming possible to contemplate writing a comparative history of the university in South Africa.

# PREFACE: TO THE READERS

To satisfy such a diverse array of wants, this book seeks to straddle at least some of them, making it a holistic, multi-sided examination of UCT, which tries to give voice to a wide range of historical actors on and off the University's three campuses in the first twenty years of South Africa's apartheid era. It aims to avoid providing a one-dimensional, prof-down, administrator-centred view of UCT's past in which students are largely offstage, 'only of narrow interest, a chronology of events of a largely administrative nature and committee decisions by old academics long forgotten', as one scholar has dismissively described the genre of university history.[2]

Accordingly, the book concentrates on the primary actions by which the University, in all its diversity, functioned as a tertiary educational institution in apartheid-era South Africa – hence the action-based titles of the chapters between its contextualising opening (chapter 1, 'UCT and the World in 1948') and closing (chapter 12, 'UCT and the World in 1968') chapters. As Goethe has Faust say, 'In the beginning was the Act'.[3]

The central chapters begin by investigating the two structural frameworks within which UCT operated, the institutional-administrative (chapter 2, 'Running UCT') and the physical (chapter 3, 'Building a Second UCT'), before examining at length the institution's core business, teaching and researching (chapters 4–8). To make the latter chapters easier to navigate, they focus on teaching and researching in general (chapter 4) and then systematically on associated clusters of disciplines, usually as they were housed within those human constructs, faculties. Starting with the pure sciences (chapter 5) and the applied sciences, engineering and medicine (chapter 6), they then go on to investigate the professional faculties, Commerce, Law, Education, Architecture and Social Science (chapter 7) before looking at those departments loosely clustered under the label 'The Arts: Music, Liberal and Fine' (chapter 8).

Having examined the inner working, as it were, of the institution, the book shifts to its relations with the world beyond its walls. Chapter 9 ('Reaching Out') deals with its outreach activities off campus, while chapter 10 ('Colliding and Colluding') probes its increasingly fraught relationship with its statutory overseer and financier, the apartheid government. Finally, recognising all too well that the other side of the teaching coin is learning, something which chapters 4–8 make clear by their attention to students' perspectives on what they were taught and how, chapter 11 ('Learning in (and out) of Class') looks at both the formal and informal learning process – widely interpreted – through students' eyes. It is possible to identify exactly who these students were by consulting the full list of UCT graduates, diplomates and certificants between 1948 and 1968 at http://www.alumni.uct.ac.za/uctgrads-1948to1968

In what follows, racial labels are used not because they are objectively accurate but because they reflect the political and social reality of a time when they (or their contemporary equivalents) became even more decisive than they had been before 1948 in shaping South Africans' lives. In sum, this volume seeks to provide a history of UCT in the round during the first phase of the apartheid era, providing a bifocal history which views UCT equally well from close up and from a distance. This is necessary not just to cater for the wide interests of the anticipated readers listed above. As it begins the second century of its existence as an independent institution of higher learning and at the same time reaches the 190th anniversary of its existence as an educational institution too – its forebear, the South African College, was founded on 1 October 1829 – UCT must face up to its record under apartheid, of which it might be both proud and ashamed in 2019. In this regard there are similarities with the kind of historical reckoning with the past that German universities had to undertake after the Nazi era. In a label characteristic of the German language's tendency to join words to create a new concept, this is known as *vergangenheitsbewältung* – in English 'coming to terms with the past' and in isiXhosa *ukujamelana nexesha elidlulileyo*. Moving forwards requires a knowledge of how the present was reached, bearing what baggage.

Ideally, a history of UCT under apartheid would span the whole apartheid era, from 1948 to 1994. There are, however, two main reasons why this volume does not do so and stops in 1968. Firstly, the archives of government departments for the years after 1989 are not readily accessible because of the 30-year closed period for official records; secondly, perspective on events and actors of the more recent years is still lacking, and we may still be too close to them to be able to provide an adequate assessment. To misquote Francis Bacon, historians who follow too closely on the heels of history may have their brains kicked out.

The year 1968 is thus the terminal point of this volume because it marked a watershed in student–administration relations – the sit-in of that year – and because it was the first year of a new principalship, that of UCT's fifth Vice-Chancellor, Sir Richard Luyt.

Consequently, a second volume on UCT under apartheid, covering the years 1969 to 1994, should follow this one sooner rather than later. Maybe it should be titled 'UCT under Apartheid, 1969–1994: Degrees of Discontent'.

The author of such a volume will be fortunate indeed if that project is as helpfully supported as this one has been in terms of finance, personnel and data access. For these, my sincere thanks to the following are more than due:
- the Council of UCT for funding the project and for ensuring that two Registrars and their secretariat headed by Marius Lund provided the necessary administrative support;

## PREFACE: TO THE READERS

- Council member, Mr Justice Ian Farlam, who ensured that the project did not fall off the Council agenda and judiciously backed it through thick and thin;
- the heads of UCT's Department of Historical Studies for providing me with accommodation and resources for the duration of the project;
- the ever-willing and richly knowledgeable archivists in UCT's Administrative Archives, Lionel Smidt and Stephen Herandien, the always-prepared-to-assist Eric Nosilela and his team in the UCT Registry Office, the most helpful and resourceful staff of UCT Libraries' Special Collections, Digital Library Service and Government Publications Divisions, UCT's Oppenheimer Library, the National Archives of South Africa in Pretoria, and the Cape Town campus of the National Library of South Africa;
- my three committed research assistants, Ms Lesley Hart, Dr Farieda Khan and Dr Neil Overy, who combined persistence with imagination in tracking down information in ways which benefited the project immeasurably. For two years our monthly report-back meetings were highlights of the project, allowing all four of us to share our findings to the obvious interest and delight of one another;
- the almost 200 former staff and students of UCT who willingly shared with us their memories of the University, to the enormous benefit of the project, as will be readily apparent in the text;
- my family, Juelle, Laura and Jeremy, who, in countless ways, facilitated the project's progress directly and indirectly and who, once again, paid the high price of having a single-minded historian as husband or father;
- those readers of part or all of the text whose sharp eyes and in-house knowledge and perspective helped improve the contents of the volume;
- Bridget Impey and her team at Jacana Media for their speedy efficiency in turning my text into this handsome book, and my editor, Russell Martin, whose meticulous eye benefited the text immeasurably and made Spell Check and Grammar Checker appear hit-and-miss and amateurish in comparison.

Howard Phillips
2 April 2019 (UCT's 101st birthday)

# CHAPTER 1

# UCT and the World in 1948

For the world, South Africa and the University of Cape Town, 1948 was a watershed year.

In Europe, the Cold War, which was to frame the world's history for the next four decades, was gathering pace; in Asia and the Middle East, decolonisation was well under way, with the independence of Burma, Malaya and Israel following that of India and Pakistan the year before; in the United States, President Truman was beginning the slow rollback of entrenched racial discrimination by ordering the desegregation of the armed forces and the Federal civil service; in Latin America, Peronism was pioneering the path of post-war import-substituting industrialisation, which was to become an especially appealing policy in that continent; and in Africa, fledgling nationalist movements were starting to gain traction as they questioned the continuation of colonial rule, particularly in North and West Africa.

In New York the brand-new United Nations Organisation was setting up a host of organs to co-ordinate international initiatives for a better, safer world. Along with the General Agreement on Trade and Tariffs, which came into force in that year, these were all concrete manifestations of the accelerating process of globalisation. In every sphere its pace was quickening. For instance, in that year globalising devices like the transistor, the long-playing record and the Xerox photocopier all came onto the market, while the first commercial jet aeroplane flew from London to Paris in just 34 minutes.

In South Africa, 1948 was a red-letter year too, for it saw the accession to government of D.F. Malan's National Party, with its recently devised policy of apartheid. Within weeks of becoming Prime Minister in May, Malan was declaring portentously in Parliament, 'We want apartheid as far as our educational institutions are concerned, more particularly in our universities.'[1]

UCT, one of the two universities he had in mind when making this statement – the University of the Witwatersrand (Wits) was the other – was also under new leadership in 1948, with Dr T.B. Davie having assumed the position of Principal

*Changing of the guard. The new Principal, T.B. Davie, confers an honorary degree on his predecessor, Dr A.W. Falconer, in December 1948.*

and Vice-Chancellor at the beginning of the year. In his formal installation address in March he had already committed himself to the maintenance of 'an atmosphere of absolute intellectual freedom' at the University, an insistence which signalled that UCT and the apartheid government would soon be in collision on matters of principle. That this would be a collision in practice too is evident from Davie's further declaration of his 'absolute dedication to the welfare of his charge [as] the minimum that is expected of a principal'.[2]

The 4258 students to whom these words were directed included some 1200 who had seen military service in the recent war, making them a significant but soon-to-dwindle minority on campus. In fact, their number in 1948 was, for the first time, smaller than in the two preceding years, indicating that, with regard to their presence and influence on campus, 1948 was a turning point too.

'I think you will find the work interesting, but not without its difficulties', Davie's predecessor, Dr A.W. Falconer, had told him when his appointment was announced in 1947.[3] Falconer was not wrong.

# CHAPTER 2

# Running UCT

Institutional analysts today widely recognise that the framework of an institution's operations consists of the interaction between top decision-makers (acting in concert or in competition) and what they call 'the basic building blocks of institutions' – structures, rules and procedures.[1] Accordingly, this chapter will focus on these elements within UCT so as to lay the groundwork for understanding the whole University's history in this period. To this end it will explore the character of the top decision-making bodies and the individuals responsible for its broad policies, as well as their modus operandi, along with that of those who administered these policies. The broad policies themselves and their execution on campus will be investigated in later thematic chapters, with one exception: that pertaining to finance, which will be dealt with at the end of this chapter, for funding underpinned every decision taken by the University.

As in the ancient Scottish universities on which UCT was modelled, in 1948 the upper-level operation of the University remained divided into the same two adjacent spheres, which had been demarcated by UCT's founding Act back in 1916 – the academic and the administrative. Ultimate responsibility for the former rested with its 50-member Senate chaired by the Principal,[2] which devolved this responsibility to ten separate faculties which, in turn, oversaw the 59 departments undertaking the university's core business, the day-to-day teaching of students. For its part, the administrative sphere which facilitated this academic enterprise fell under the supreme authority of the University's elected Council, which bore primary responsibility for all financial affairs. It was chaired by one member chosen from its ranks and was serviced by the Registrar, the University's chief administrative officer. To assist him he had a financial and clerical staff of nineteen.

The titular head of both of these arms of UCT was the Chancellor, who was, at the beginning of 1948, the Prime Minister, Jan Smuts, who had filled this honorific post since 1937.[3] After his death in 1950, he was succeeded by South Africa's new Chief Justice, the tough-minded Albert van der Sandt Centlivres, an old-fashioned

Cape liberal and South African College old boy with a deep, more-than-armchair commitment to the rule of law and academic freedom, which he labelled 'the very life-blood of every university'.[4] Increasingly during the fifteen years of his chancellorship, as state policies made inroads on individual and institutional freedom, this commitment was tested – and not found wanting, as the titles of two of his public speeches, 'The Time to Speak Out Has Come' and 'Blundering into University Apartheid', testify. On his death in 1966 the president of the SRC lamented that 'We students have lost a revered friend … the epitome of a Chancellor … he had become the very embodiment of our ideals.'[5]

By 1966 the political atmosphere had become so charged that the question of who should succeed Centlivres was no longer an issue above party politics, and the three contenders in the first-ever race for the chancellorship drew their core support largely along party political lines. A Progressive Party bloc in UCT's Convocation, the body of staff and graduates which elected Centlivres's successor, was eventually able to carry the day for Harry Oppenheimer, South Africa's supreme mining magnate, who, perhaps paradoxically, stood on the mildly liberal side of white politics in the country. But, as he mused with self-awareness, 'In the South African context I may seem to be a liberal but at heart I'm just an old-fashioned conservative.'[6]

Initiating what became a mutually beneficial relationship with UCT, which brought very substantial material benefits to it and academic lustre to him, Oppenheimer associated himself with its formal call for academic freedom to be respected, but added, with characteristic pragmatism, 'When we insist on freedom for the university, we must also ask ourselves what we should do with it … We need not only Academic Freedom but Academic Wisdom too.'[7] As he was to show in his 32 years as UCT's Chancellor, such academic wisdom meant, for him, quiet, behind-the-scenes backing and lobbying to bolster the University's official stance on academic and personal freedom. As he saw it, it was his primary duty 'to give any support and encouragement I can to the Principal in carrying out his important and desperately difficult work'.[8]

In fact, to a large degree, Oppenheimer's conception of his role vis-à-vis UCT's Principal reflects the nature of all Chancellor–Principal relations throughout this period. It is perhaps best understood as being akin to that between the Patron and the CEO of a non-government organisation.

Not surprisingly, the four men who filled the position of Principal or Acting Principal and Vice-Chancellor in these years – T.B. Davie (1948–55), R.W. James (1955–7), J.P. Duminy (1958–67) and Sir Richard Luyt (1968–80) – took full advantage of such chancellorial support as they sought to steer UCT through the increasingly choppy political seas of South Africa in the 1950s and 1960s.

For this hazardous task the 51-year-old Thomas Benjamin Davie was well fitted.

A bilingual South African born in Prieska, who was educated at Victoria College, Stellenbosch, before taking a medical degree at Liverpool, he had held two different professorial posts in England before becoming Dean of Medicine at Liverpool in 1945. In this position he demonstrated 'a great deal of tact and skill in negotiation and … a judicious exercise of firmness … there are very few such persons available anywhere', judged one of the two vice-chancellors under whom he served there. To this the other added, 'He has a way of getting the best work out of people and welding them into a team.'[9] Such attributes proved very important in UCT selecting him as its third Principal.

Even though, as Principal, Davie was increasingly handicapped by acute rheumatoid arthritis which began to afflict him, limiting his mobility from soon after his arrival in Cape Town, his large personality, upbeat vision and enthusiastic demeanour suffused the whole University. Recognising how far UCT's natural development had been arrested by World War II and the need to accommodate the temporary surge in student numbers as a result of the influx of ex-servicemen and ex-servicewomen, he aimed to make up this backlog by raising funds to expand the University systematically across all fronts. His ambitious Development Fund Appeal in 1950, the acquisition of the Rosebank Showgrounds alongside UCT to construct new buildings, the prodigious increase in medical staff through the introduction of the joint staff appointment scheme with financial buy-in from the Cape Provincial Administration, the enlargement of the University's footprint beyond campus through adult education and a student-run community welfare scheme, and the promotion of cross-disciplinary fields like oceanography, microbiology, geochemistry and chemical engineering were all part and parcel of what he called 'my policy'.[10]

Not that 'my policy' ended there. Davie's treatment of students (and their leaders in particular) as maturing and responsible individuals marked a sharp change from Falconer's high-handed style. 'It is a fundamental principle of the whole of my dealings in this University to get students to discipline themselves and manage their own affairs in a dignified and efficient manner', he explained to a worried parent.[11] In line with this thinking, he set up the student-dominated Student Amenities Financial Council to handle the funding of all key student bodies and the Students' Health and Welfare Centres Organization (SHAWCO) to run the already-existing students' community clinics and social welfare bureaux in a more systematic and effective manner. To help orientate incoming students academically and socially, in 1953 he initiated Freshers' Week into which he drew senior students for the experience they could offer; he also involved them in the tutoring of first-year students who were having difficulty with their studies.

Indeed, Davie went out of his way to make himself accessible to all students by holding open-house teas on Sunday afternoons during term, while student leaders were told to 'take it for granted that I shall always be at your disposal both in the office and at other times for the discussion of matters of common interest. I hope, in fact, that you and your principal officers will make a habit of coming to see me at regular intervals in order that we might keep each other in touch with all developments of common interest in our respective spheres.'[12]

Staff of all grades were similarly welcomed. 'He had an almost boyish enthusiasm for social contact and good company', noted one professor, 'so that even junior members of his staff felt that he enjoyed entertaining them. But he entertained not simply for pleasure; it was part of his method of work. He was essentially a builder of a university team and he delighted in the opportunity to bring his staff in contact with each other and with visitors from overseas.'[13] Little wonder that Davie ruefully warned a friend about to take up a university principalship, 'You may look back with regret occasionally to the days when you could call your soul your own and when you were still entitled to some private life.'[14]

Yet, it is clear that Davie's charisma, gusto and effective direction of university affairs won him wide support on campus, even when his hold on the tiller was deemed to be too tight. 'In his way he was an autocrat', observed *Varsity*, but 'his autocracy was both rational and kindly and no request of the SRC was ever refused by him but that reasons were given which were both understood and accepted by the SRC.'[15] One SRC president spoke of 'the happy spirit which has existed … between staff and student … at our university. The example has always been set from the top', while his successor openly told Davie, 'Sir … your stature in the eyes of all Cape Town students is undoubtedly unique in South African University circles.'[16]

Certainly the main source of this high stature on campus was Davie's increasingly forceful stand on academic freedom as the attacks on it from Government circles grew year by year.

When Davie arrived at UCT in 1948 his ideas on academic freedom were still inchoate, much influenced by the fate of this freedom in the universities of Nazi Germany and the Iron Curtain countries. 'A University flourishes only in an atmosphere of absolute intellectual freedom', he told the audience at his inaugural lecture.[17] By 1950, however, two years of apartheid, combined with vigorous debates with liberals (who included his wife Vera) on and off campus, had sharpened his conception of intellectual freedom appreciably, encouraging him to formulate his ideas in a characteristically succinct and memorable way as 'freedom from external interference in (a) who shall teach, (b) what we teach, (c) how we teach and (d) whom we teach … Our lecture theatres and laboratories shall be open to all who … can show that they are intellectually capable of benefitting by admission to our teaching …'[18]

Two more years of apartheid and exposure to the American liberal establishment during a long visit to the United States toughened his ideas even further, prompting him to declare in 1954 that a university in a multi-racial society should 'reflect in the composition of its student body the multi-racial picture of the society it serves'.[19] A year later he went even further, telling freshers at UCT (if his speech notes did indeed become his spoken words) that staff and students alike should 'rise up in arms if [their] freedoms [were] threatened. The Univ[ersity] is dead where students fail to fight for these rights both for themselves individually & for their student associates in other universities.'[20]

Some professors believed that Davie's increasingly powerful statements on academic freedom reflected his growing recognition that his rapidly deteriorating health made a challenge to the crystallising state policy of university apartheid a matter of urgency.[21] Indeed, barely a fortnight before his death in December 1955, his dinner guests found that 'the only discussion he would permit was the discussion … of the open and closed universities. And try as we might we could not turn the discussion away from something that engaged his mind and even his whole body so passionately … At the end of our dinner … he stood up with his gnarled hand on the cane … and said: "I will fight this. I will not give in."'[22]

'Worn into the ground'[23] by his ailment, by copious doses of cortisone to counter it and the weight of the multifarious responsibilities he had taken on – it was often said that, even in his impaired condition, he did the work of three men[24] – Davie's death at the age of 60 left UCT stunned and leaderless at a critical moment. Its colours firmly nailed to the mast of academic freedom but now without a captain, it was unsure of how to proceed along the course on which Davie had set it. 'How we are going to miss his great wisdom and statesmanship', sighed one senior professor.[25]

Appreciating that no suitable successor to Davie could be found at short notice, UCT appointed an Acting Principal, Reginald William James, its 64-year-old professor of physics[26] who had already stood in as Principal twice before, once when Davie was abroad and once when he was seriously indisposed. Widely respected on campus as a scientist of international calibre – he had been elected a prestigious Fellow of the Royal Society earlier in 1955 – and as a good-tempered, even-handed and clear-sighted Dean of Science and head of Physics, James 'radiated decency and integrity'.[27] With the recently retired Registrar, A.V. Carter, at his side as special consultant, James largely followed Davie's policies for the next two years, though in a lower-key, more restrained fashion. It did fall to him, however, to give UCT the lead in opposing the official introduction of legislation in 1957 to turn it into a 'whites only' institution. Rising to this high-profile public role as best he could, he drew on his personal experience at Leipzig University in 1932 to echo Davie in warning a jampacked public meeting at the City Hall that it was 'but a small step' from giving a government the power to decide whom a university should admit, 'to decide what shall be taught, and who shall teach it … I assure you that we must not take this threat lightly.'[28]

A month later, along with Centlivres and the chairman of UCT's Council, he led a solemn march through central Cape Town to demonstrate the University's opposition to the Separate University Education Bill – in vain, for the Extension of University Education Bill (as the bill was paradoxically retitled) was passed into law in 1959. By then UCT had a new Principal, a man of very different stripe from Davie and James, Jacobus Petrus Duminy.

Duminy was an anglicised Cape Afrikaner who had won a Rhodes Scholarship to study mathematics at Oxford after gaining his first degrees at the SA College and UCT.[29] This made him the first UCT graduate to head his alma mater, an achievement of which both he and the University were justifiably proud. After Oxford he had spent eighteen years on the staff of the Department of Mathematics at the Transvaal University College and its successor, Pretoria University – twelve of these as professor – before moving into full-time academic administration as Principal of Pretoria Technical College in 1942. This position had drawn him more deeply into higher education affairs, giving him a familiarity with the field sufficient to impress UCT's selection committee and to offset the fact that he would turn 61 in the year he became Principal of UCT, 1958.[30]

In this position he quickly realised how far UCT's staffing, facilities, equipment and administrative structure were falling short of meeting the needs of the burgeoning student body, and so set to work to overcome these deficiencies with the organisational will, planning foresight and readiness to speak on public platforms, which were his forte. He gave high priority to the task of a Principal 'to draw the community into the affairs of his University, to be its Chief Public Relations Officer, to stimulate interest in its activities and to gain financial support for it',[31] and was at his best in doing this for UCT. He became widely known for his sententious speeches on education, citizenship, political and social values, and service to society; not surprisingly, he was a very keen member of Rotary of which he became international vice-president.

However, in his dealings with UCT's students, his touch was less deft. Stand offish, stiff and formal in his interactions, with a very strong sense of propriety, he did not easily connect with a generation of students over forty years his junior, even when he opened his house to all students for tea on Sunday afternoons. 'He heard what students said – he was always very courteous – but he did not listen', recalled an SRC president trenchantly,[32] while another student explained tellingly that it came as a shock to find UCT, having been 'presided over by a Principal [i.e. Davie] … suddenly ruled by a Headmaster [Duminy]'.[33] 'He cannot expect students to behave like adults until he treats them as adults', warned the student newspaper.[34] That that was always going to be unlikely is indicated by his private view that, in general, students were 'immature, idealistic and over-zealous, and should not be flattered by having too much attention paid to their views and outbursts'.[35]

This disconnect between Duminy and UCT students became even wider when it came to social and political matters. Steeped in the paternalist social relations of the farm on the outskirts of Cape Town where he had grown up and the traditional Christian values he had imbibed there, he was conservative in his social and moral outlook and politically a strong believer in the priority of getting Boer and Brit to work together, not least to guide the evolution of those whom he, with unwitting condescension, labelled 'our Non-White peoples'.[36] Although he could not accept the overbearing rigidity and compulsion of apartheid or its lack of Christian compassion, he was not averse to racial and social hierarchies, provided they did not interfere unduly with the right of all 'to live happy and contented and useful lives, and to enjoy the fullest opportunity to use their time and their talents for the common good of their community'. If these were infringed on by 'our measures of discrimination', he argued, 'then it is surely our duty to take these measures into review and put them into effect with greater respect for the feelings of those against whom we discriminate and with greater caring for their comfort and well-being'.[37]

Such benevolent paternalism, allied to the public school values he had soaked up at the South African College and Oxford – his vocabulary was rich in words like 'sportsmanship', 'loyalty', 'dignity', 'honour', 'courtesy' and 'gentlemanly' – put him at increasing odds with politically and socially progressive students on campus. Time and time again he railed in public against 'a casualness and slackness in thought, speech and writing, as well as in manners, dress and morals … a lack of self-discipline, a tendency to confuse freedom with licence, to compromise between good and evil'.[38] To him, the sexual revolution of the 1960s, even in its mild manifestation in Cape Town, was sheer anathema. 'I deplore and detest the amorality, vulgarity and depravity abroad in the world of today', he declared with vehemence. 'We of the older generation are looked upon … as eccentric old squares meddling in circles where our gratuitous interference should not be tolerated. This, we are told, is the age of autonomy of the student!'[39] As far as he was concerned, there were too many 'campus drones' at UCT[40] who 'are set on throwing off the shackles of restraint, on taking the fullest advantage of their new found freedoms of life … including opportunities to indulge in speed, sex and drink; a community which coolly claims the further indulgence to be as slovenly spoken, as shabbily dressed, as boorishly behaved as it jolly well pleases'.[41]

His moderate political conservatism alienated progressive students equally, especially when its mild edge was reduced to a sliver after 1964, when he moved further to the right after junior staff and students whose innocence he had vouched for were in fact found guilty of involvement in sabotage inspired by the African Resistance Movement. People who knew Duminy spoke of him as 'a shaken man' after this, who felt he had been seriously misled by those for whom he had gone out on a limb.[42]

His commitment to academic freedom – 'it is the duty of a university to welcome to this fountain-head all those who can with profit come and drink at it – including those of Non-White origin, so that they will presently be able to go out into their several spheres of living as standard-bearers of Western learning', he had proclaimed in his inaugural address in 1958[43] – became increasingly insipid, and action to back it up more cautious and tip-toe in character. 'The students of today', he told an old SA College friend in 1966, 'entertain very strange ideas about the functions of a University, the rights and obligations of students, and (most of all) about what they call "Academic Freedom".'[44] He therefore sought to avoid public confrontation with the Government over this or security laws threatening freedom of speech and information, preferring instead to intercede with cabinet ministers and senior officials behind the scenes. 'It is not the function of a university to be a platform or even provide one for party politics or some kind of unofficial opposition to the government of the country which it serves', he insisted.[45]

Of such an attitude politically aware students despaired. 'I cannot but tell you how frustrated we sometimes are when we emerge from seeing you, not so much because we invariably end up in a deadlock, but because you do not seem to have a plan or ideology for this University or our country', lamented one SRC president. 'Things are not going well, Sir.'[46]

Almost inevitably, therefore, the longer Duminy remained in office – he retired at the end of 1967 aged 70 – the deeper the rift grew between him and a swelling number of alienated students. 'I find myself wondering what measure of good our fiery young reformers finally achieve', he mused aloud.[47] As they challenged the content and style of his Principalship, so his responses became more and more intolerant. As a result, 1967 ended with racially integrated student dances and dinners forbidden, a nominated Interim Students' Council in office in place of an elected SRC, and *Varsity* suspended and its editor effectively expelled. 'Support Our Principles but Not Our Principal', ran one telling student slogan then current on campus.[48] The public verdict of the president of the Interim Students' Council on Duminy at the time of his retirement was damning: 'Men gain respect by their actions, and if the SRC has failed to show respect [for him], the fault is not necessarily its!'⁴⁹

In the light of this breakdown of relations between Duminy and the student body, it was fortunate for UCT that the attitude to students of his successor, the 53-year-old Sir Richard Luyt, was closer to that of Davie. The one SRC president whose term of office straddled the principalships of both Duminy and Luyt, Duncan Innes, recalled how differently the two men had treated him: Duminy would address him from the other side of his large desk, while Luyt would sit around a table with him and chat. 'Communication between us was very good. We came to trust one another; there had been no trust between Duminy and me. Luyt was good at handling difficult issues by talking about them; with Duminy there was nothing to talk about … Also, Luyt had a sense of humour, unlike Duminy.'⁵⁰

Richard Edmonds Luyt was an English-speaking Capetonian by birth who won a Diocesan College Rhodes Scholarship after graduating in economics at UCT. He joined the British colonial service soon after the outbreak of World War II, but, for the next five years, saw active service in Ethiopia, ending up as a lieutenant-colonel and military adviser to Emperor Haile Selassie. After the war he spent 21 years back in the colonial service in Northern Rhodesia, Kenya and finally in British Guiana as Governor, for which he was knighted in 1964. Unprecedently for UCT, therefore, its new Principal was not an academic, but a professional administrator, a man who was wholly at ease in handling people of all ages, races and ranks. 'You'll like him, and will find him an attractive person, strong and straightforward', forecast Harry Oppenheimer, who had interacted with him on the Copperbelt. 'He's a man of genuinely liberal ideas and an appealing person. He's not a man to allow himself to be messed about.'⁵¹ Indeed, Luyt thought that being labelled liberal might count against him: 'I will be surprised if the UCT Council find the courage to offer appointment to a suspected Liberal,' he confided wryly to a friend after his interview at UCT. 'A Government under Vorster and a University under Luyt are hardly likely to excel in team work.'⁵²

But neither his non-academic background nor his purported liberalism was a barrier to his easing the atmosphere on campus. 'You brought peace to the University at a time when it was ready to explode', a contemporary reminded him years later. 'The feverish temperatures of that time rapidly cooled down as soon as you made it your business to find out what was troubling students … You also restored dignity to your office and to the University.'⁵³ Indeed, by the end of 1968, Luyt's first year in office, the foremost liberal professor on campus, Monica Wilson, was telling a fellow academic with relief, 'We like our new Principal very much indeed and it is quite a different proposition from working [here] a year or two ago.'⁵⁴ Such a conclusion would surely have owed much to Luyt's public delineation of his own position, like his avowal that he 'was not one of those who says that while students are at university they must keep their noses in their books and leave politics to the acknowledged politicians'.[55]

Luyt's outgoing personality and personal affability, his ready ear and engaging smile, and his 'almost boyish enthusiasm and optimism' (as a member of Council put it[56]) certainly go some way to accounting for why people warmed to him, but what also won him support on campus was his tolerance, tact and patent even-handedness and magnanimity. 'I personally almost always prefer to supplement … correspondence with a talk with the person concerned in an endeavour to generate maximum goodwill', he told a senior professor who had rebuked the president of the SRC for a minor misdemeanour.[57]

Politically aware students also liked what they heard from the new Principal and even more what they saw of his actions. For instance, unlike his predecessor, he became an honorary vice-president of the National Union of South African Students (NUSAS), he joined the Civil Rights League and confidently announced in his inaugural address in March 1968 that a university 'needs the right to employ the best staff it can attract and the right to teach the best students who offer themselves'.[58] It is a mark of how far his other traits appealed to students that, when later in that year he effectively backtracked on this commitment in the Mafeje Affair,[59] students did not turn on him as they had on Duminy. So much so, that the last SRC president to serve under him, Sarah Cullinan, readily labelled him 'an unwavering friend of students and their representative institutions'.[60]

The right-hand men – and they were all men – who supported UCT's Principals administratively in this period were of two kinds, Deputy Principals and Registrars. Until 1960, UCT had no Deputy Principals, and both Davie and James had had to shoulder the full weight of providing executive leadership alone. Indeed, it was this very fact and how much it was felt to have contributed to Davie's early death which decided Council to lighten the new appointee's administrative load by creating a full-time position of assistant to the Principal. To fill this post (which was titled Deputy Principal), in 1960 Duminy chose the long-serving professor of French, Donald Inskip, a man who had shown himself dexterous at chairing committees and skilled at handling people.[61] Referring to what he called Inskip's 'creative and constructive temperament', a local editor predicted that this would create 'a happy partnership' between 'the Duminy dryness and your own fruitfulness'.[62]

It did. Sharing similar political views, the two of them worked together smoothly, with the new Deputy Principal being given particular responsibility for planning and development, two of UCT's highest priorities in Duminy's eyes. So heavy a demand did these two portfolios put on Inskip's time – the construction of a second UCT was at its height in the 1960s[63] – that in 1967 a second long-experienced professor, Ben Beinart of Law, was appointed to share the administrative burden. A year later, with UCT still expanding apace, Luyt appointed him and a third professor, Walter Schaffer of Physics, as full-time Assistant Principals alongside Inskip, who continued energetically in his post until his retirement in 1971. In the space of eight years (1960–8), therefore, UCT's executive leadership had quadrupled in size, although the number of students and staff had not even doubled. A trend was beginning.

The number of staff in the UCT Administration Office grew in like fashion in this era, from 19 to 60, under the two Registrars, Albert Carter (1939–55) and John Benfield (1956–71). Carter had been in this post since 1939,[64] so was well experienced in the art of oiling the University's administrative wheels efficiently but unobtrusively and executing decisions of the executive loyally, without question – James described him as 'that sheet-anchor for Principals in administrative difficulties'.[65] His successor, Benfield, not unexpectedly, followed suit, for he had been Assistant Registrar to Carter since 1946 and knew all about the executive's need for well-informed, reliable and prompt administrative backing. This he and his staff provided in a quiet, efficient and unassuming manner, which accurately reflected his own personality.

The high-level decisions that they had to implement emanated ultimately from the two university bodies, which bore responsibility for UCT's administrative and academic matters – Council and Senate.

Consisting of the Principal and nineteen others chosen by the Senate and five outside constituencies with a vested interest in UCT,[66] the Council was UCT's supreme governing authority on whose agenda all non-academic matters (and several academic, if finance was involved) appeared. Of the 65 individuals who sat on Council between 1948 and 1968, 60 were men and 5 women; all were white. Of the total, 82% were English-speaking, 18% Afrikaners who were fully bilingual, for proceedings were conducted solely in English. Eight of the 65 were Jewish, the rest Christian. Lawyers, professors (current or retired) and medical doctors made up the largest professional groups on the Council, though the few businessmen who were members were very influential because of their financial nous. Indeed, all three men who headed Council as elected chairmen in this period, the level-headed Duncan Baxter (1945–60), the cool-headed Allan Stephen (1960–6) and the hard-headed Clive Corder (1966–72), came from business or investment backgrounds. Given the predominantly staid outlook of the bulk of Cape Town's white establishment from whom the 65 were drawn and the fact that most on Council were over 55 years old, it is no surprise to find that Council was inclined to take a conservative stance on most matters, especially those of a political or social hue. One liberal academic complained to a colleague at Witwatersrand University in 1967 that UCT was an institution 'which contains so high a proportion of verkramptes'.[67]

Compared to the Council, UCT's Senate (which usually had a fair sprinkling of those under 55 as members) often took a less conservative line, especially under Davie and Luyt and when outspoken liberals were present in some number. Of the 161 individuals who sat on Senate between 1948 and 1968, only 14 were not current UCT academics, viz. three Principals, the two Council members appointed to Senate every second year, and the University Librarian, who became a member of Senate in 1967. The rest were either full professors – 127 of them – or lecturers or associate professors appointed by their fellows to represent their particular interests on this, the highest academic body at UCT. Until 1955, the two lecturers' representatives on Senate were only assessor members with no right to vote, but in that year they were granted full membership, as were the two associate professors' representatives who were elected to Senate for the first time in the same year.[68]

All 161 Senate members were white, and of these 156 were men; the five women members were two lecturers' representatives, two Council appointees and the only female professor at UCT throughout these years, Monica Wilson of Social Anthropology.

When Wilson first arrived at UCT in 1952, Senate had 56 members; by the time she was approaching retirement in 1968, this figure had risen to 79 because of the growth in the number of chairs, with most of the increase having occurred in the 1960s, UCT's and South Africa's decade of multi-sided growth. Of the 85 professors appointed by UCT between 1948 and 1968, 48 were South African (23 of these were UCT graduates) and 27 from the United Kingdom. However, if these totals are broken down chronologically, the result is revealing: between 1948 and 1958, 18 professorial appointments were of South Africans and 20 of British men, yet between 1959 and 1969 South Africans outstripped British appointees by 30 to 7.

This was not only because there was a growing supply of chair-worthy South Africans that UCT was able to draw on (in striking contrast to the situation earlier in the century[69]), but also because, after 1960, the political situation in the country made it a less attractive destination for academic job-seekers from abroad. In 1960–1, a spate of resignations left seven chairs and sixteen lectureships or senior lectureships vacant, prompting the *New York Times* to trumpet, 'South African Professors Flee Posts'.[70] Gravely, the chair of Senate's committee on salaries and conditions warned, 'We are in danger of sinking to the level of a second-rate university.'[71] Efforts to avoid such a situation by undertaking recruitment tours abroad, by using personal networks to draw up-and-coming scholars to UCT posts or by creating appealing fellowships were only partially successful. One senior professor even urged the University to make its conditions of employment more appealing by including, in effect, what he called a 'risk premium to cover, firstly, the fear that white South Africa is doomed; and secondly, the more realistic fear that freedom of thought and expression may not long survive under White or Black Nationalism'.[72]

Such radical advice UCT did not take, however, for the post-Sharpeville resurgence of the economy and consequent increase in the state's annual grant to universities allowed it to improve salaries across the board in the 1960s. Having learnt its lesson in the 1950s about the need to ensure that the differential in salary scales between professors and lecturers was equitable – in 1953, 66 angry lecturers had returned their salary increase cheques because they felt that this was not the case when their increments had been fixed and that consequently their status had been demeaned – in the 1960s UCT ensured that it consulted the Lecturers' Association fully and listened to its views closely when new salary scales were under discussion. As a result, the University's outlay on academic salaries grew to 48.2% of its total expenditure in 1968 compared to 40.1% twenty years earlier. What with raising the retirement age to 65 for both male and female staff in 1963, the addition of subsidised medical aid and housing in 1964, and group life assurance cover and more generous leave conditions in 1968, UCT's 893 academics were significantly better off in 1968 than their 521 predecessors had been in 1948. Though some of UCT's academic staff might have opposed academic apartheid in these years, none objected to receiving the benefits of the apartheid state's white welfare policy every month.

Although full-time black non-academic staff like laboratory attendants, library stack attendants, artisans, janitors, messengers, cleaners, labourers, gardeners and kitchen and serving staff enjoyed only some of these fringe benefits such as housing loans and fee rebates for their children at UCT; and although their leave conditions were inferior to those of their white-skinned counterparts; and although they had to use toilets on campus designated 'Non-Europeans', oral and written evidence suggests that in apartheid South Africa, UCT was generally perceived by these employees as a more benevolent employer than most. That 30–40% of its more than 450 black workers were in its employ for over five years and that at least two generations of the same family often worked for it – for example, the Dryding, the De la Cruz, the Francis and the Jacobs families – point in this direction, as do the records of the Non-European Staff Association (established in 1959 and soon renamed the UCT Workers' Association), which have little to say about disputes and confrontations with the University. Indeed, from its organ, the *Janitors' Staff News*, the Workers' Association appears to have enjoyed amicable relations with both the all-white UCT Staff Association and with the University's Administration, which helped it financially. It was delighted when Chancellor Centlivres accepted its invitation to its annual ball in 1966 and when UCT approved its design of a

UCT Workers' badge for its members. Probably the members of this acquiescent and compliant organisation would have had little time for the non-collaborationist stance of the Unity Movement, which dominated 'coloured' student politics then.[73] For all this deference to the powers that be, the UCT Workers' Association enjoyed no representation on any statutory forums at the University. In these years the only presence which its members had at Senate or Council meetings was when they brought in tea while deliberations proceeded slowly through the long afternoon.

The fact that Senate meetings did not adjourn for tea points to the fact that, as the size of that body had increased, so its proceedings became more and more unwieldy, not only because there were more speakers, but also because a growing student body translated into longer and longer agendas. Afternoon meetings stretched on beyond dusk, major issues were less than thoroughly discussed for lack of time, and unfinished business piled up, causing it to be referred to hastily created sub-committees. There was an 'increasing sense of stress in meetings', noted one professor, and 'increasing uncertainty and indecisiveness in the functioning of the [administrative] system'.[74]

Ad hoc remedies, like getting the General Purposes Committee of Senate to vet all would-be Senate items first or starring those items deemed really discussion-worthy, proved in vain, and by 1958 Senate was (in its own words) 'perturbed by the apparent decline in the administrative functioning of the University'.[75] It therefore instituted a thorough inquiry into UCT's ailing, forty-year-old administrative system which, it rapidly became evident, was being swamped by a rising tide of undifferentiated business and uncoordinated decision-making. To overcome these required an administrative revolution, which is exactly what the chair of the inquiry, Professor Batson of Social Science and Social Administration, prescribed.

Encouraged by Duminy, whose strength was organisational planning, the organogram-minded Batson proposed a radical overhaul of UCT's top decision-making processes: a mass of routine, uncontroversial business should be stripped out of the Senate's agendas and instead published in a monthly Principal's Circular, the contents of which would be accepted unless it incurred a written objection; an Expenditure and Development Committee should be set up by Senate to co-ordinate financial planning of academic matters across the University; and a Committee of Deans should be created to act as a 'committee-of-first-reference' for all matters destined for the General Purposes Committee; these it would first digest and collate before sending them on. The trimming of Senate and General Purposes Committee business which Batson intended to bring about in this way would, he argued, make possible a halving of the number of Senate meetings held every year, a reduction in their length and a sharpening of their immediate relevance by the introduction of two standing items, 'Matters of Urgency' and 'Question Time'.

So desperate was Senate to free itself of the weight of paper before it that it readily accepted Batson's proposals, which were implemented with unaccustomed speed from September 1960. Moreover, with the reformist bit between his teeth, Batson pushed the administrative transformation even further, persuading Senate's main committees and each Faculty Board to follow Senate's lead in how they operated. Soon their meetings were also halved in number by the appointment of Deputy Deans to deal expeditiously with routine matters, while a template was introduced to standardise the minuting of meetings and the procedure for appointing temporary staff was streamlined. By the end of 1960 already, a grateful Senate was praising Batson for his well-researched planning 'which has formed the foundation for the reorganisation of the Senate administrative system'.[76]

Duminy was equally pleased with the result of the Batsonian revolution. In 1965 he proudly commended its key features to the University of the Witwatersrand, which 'appears to have reached the stage which the University of Cape Town reached in 1959/60'.[77] He spoke particularly highly of the Principal's Circular as 'a very useful and time-saving instrument of administration',[78] as it served to 'absorb a host of items which would normally have found their way to one or other board or committee.'[79]

Yet, while Duminy and the professors may have enthused at the outcome of Batson's administrative revolution, lecturers were less taken with the result. The Lecturers' Association complained that its members felt even more excluded from academic decision-making – now in the hands of an even smaller coterie of professors – or even the distribution of information, for the Principal's Circular was available to professors and Council members only. Lecturers felt 'treated as mere pawns and cogs in the machine with little knowledge of University policy and virtually no voice formulating it', they grumbled. The Principal's Circular may have speeded up administration, 'but it has been at the cost of virtually freezing the lecturing staff out of the vital decision making and administrative system'.[80] To remedy this it called for an immediate increase in the number of lecturers' representatives on Senate – this had remained at two ever since 1918 – but it was to be eight more years before this call was even partly heeded.[81]

Although Batson's administrative revolution may have cut the number of meetings on campus, it did not trim the number of administrative staff required to service it. Quite the contrary: having increased gradually from 19 to 30 between 1948 and 1958, the number of office staff jumped to 53 in 1964 and to 60 in 1968. 'Universities have grown into large business organisations', the Chief Financial Officer explained.[82] It is no coincidence that a state-of-the-art administration block, Bremner Building, was

*State-of-the-art technology 1965-vintage. UCT's ICT 1301 computer in a refurbished room in the Mathematics Block, which served as UCT's first Computer Centre*

opened in 1963. Nor was it out of keeping with this growth trend in administration that many of the new positions were of a specialist nature: in 1967 eight dedicated senior positions were created in areas like committees, management, finance, salaries, staffing and residences.

Computer services did not yet feature as an administrative speciality for, at this early stage in UCT's use of computers – it hired its first computer, an ICT 1301 which used punch cards, in 1964 – only limited use was made of this facility by Administration staff, mainly for fee records and accounting. But by 1968 plans were in train to add salaries and staff records to this, requiring more than the two punch operators appointed in 1964. With hindsight, it is clear that another revolution in UCT's administrative system – even more fundamental than Batson's – was in the wings.

No less under strain from the ongoing growth in student numbers were UCT's finances. In the immediate wake of World War II this fact had been masked by the special subsidies given to the University to cater for the nearly 1500 ex-servicemen and ex-servicewomen who suddenly descended on the campus in 1946. But from 1948 their numbers began to diminish rapidly, graduation ceremony by graduation ceremony, thereby reducing UCT's overall income, but not as quickly as its complement of extra staff specially hired in 1946. Adding further pressure on its

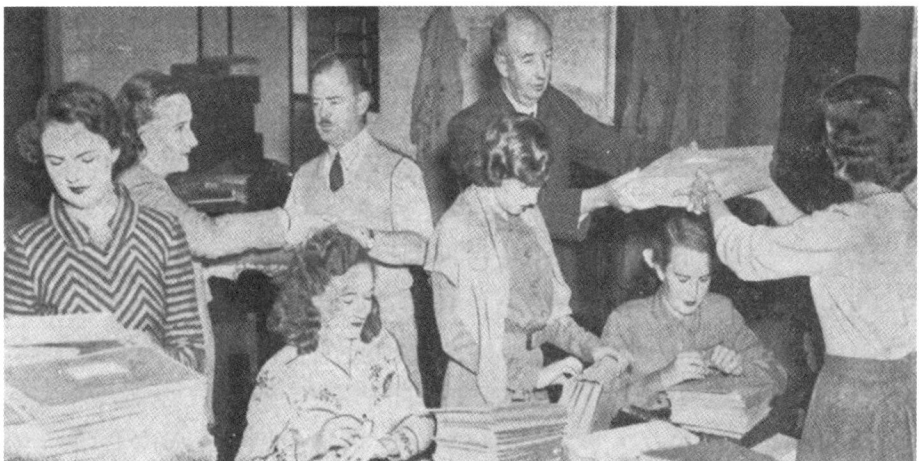

*An appealing sight. Staff in the UCT Development Fund Appeal office preparing brochures for despatch in July 1950. The jacketed organising officer of the appeal, the professor of accountancy, Harold Greenwood, is on the right* (Cape Argus, 3 July 1950).

financial resources was the Smuts Government's removal of the wartime freeze on salaries and cost of living allowances but without providing a commensurate grant to pay these. By 1949, with an accumulated deficit touching £120,000 (i.e. a quarter of UCT's total annual income),[83] UCT was 'in a precarious position', Davie admitted.[84]

With the new National Party Government slow to decide on its funding policy for universities, UCT was forced into cutting back on appointing staff and leave substitutes, into cancelling subscriptions to some journals and purchasing back numbers of others, and into trimming the number of extra-mural lectures it offered, while at the same time raising revenue by increasing fees – the source of a third of its income – and launching a special Development Fund Appeal in 1950. Faced by a similarly dire financial scenario, all of South Africa's universities were in 'state of disquiet, of gloom', Davie told the Minister of Education.[85] Yet, UCT's economy measures, its tight rein on expenditure, its raised fee income (which made it, with Witwatersrand University, the most expensive university to attend in South Africa), a yield of £400,000 from its Development Fund Appeal, and the Government's adoption of a more adequate funding formula for universities (raising its contribution to UCT's income to just over 60%) as the country's economy finally benefited from the global post-war boom, all eventually eased the University's financial plight, but at the cost of seriously arrested development. Accordingly, when in 1957 the Government indicated that it would not be able to meet even half of UCT's backlog of applications for building funds, the University not only raised fees yet again, with the justification that it did not favour 'public utility pricing',[86] but also embarked on a radical departure in its financial policy, that of seeking loans from the private sector instead of relying on state funding to put up new buildings as in the past.

With its credit good, its reserves replenished and the members of Council's Finance Committee well respected and well connected on the local financial scene, UCT began to take out large, long-term loans from companies like Southern Life, Old Mutual and Colonial Mutual. Of course, as the bulk of these loans were intended for the construction and equipping of new teaching and residential buildings, they were underwritten by the state, which also subsidised part of their repayment. Over the next ten years UCT contracted loans of this type totalling R9.08 million (about R1.9 billion in 2019 terms), which certainly gave it a heavy debt to repay for the rest of the century, but which did leave it, in return, with an enviable array of large, well-equipped, state-of-the-discipline buildings in which to conduct its academic project.

Given his penchant for development planning, Duminy had quickly taken the helm in driving the project ahead. In 1960 he announced a 25-year Development Plan for UCT 'to maintain the leadership which it holds in Africa … [as] we are at present in great danger of lagging behind in the field of university education in Africa'.[87] As he did not feel that private sector donations would be sufficient to make this possible, in 1961 he launched a new fund-raising campaign, to secure R5 million to 'make up the leeway we had lost over the lean years in respect of buildings, staff and equipment'.[88] To steer this campaign and then become the University's permanent fund-raising arm, the UCT Foundation was created. Initially guided by a firm of professional fund-raisers, it soon developed a slick and systematic modus operandi of its own and by 1969 had raised R5.13 million. Prudently, more than two-thirds of this was invested in the stocks and shares recommended by UCT's new professional investment managers, Syfrets Trust, which had been appointed in 1965 to replace the 'casual advice [hitherto given] from individuals'.[89]

Nor was it long before the wisdom of such financial prudence became manifest. UCT's nest egg made it possible to meet the escalating construction and building maintenance costs and interest rates of the late 1960s up to a point, but that point was reached when, late in 1968, the Government unexpectedly put a ceiling on its subsidy to universities while it devised a new funding formula. With an echo of Davie's lament almost twenty years earlier, Deputy Principal Inskip acknowledged that 'our present position is bad!',[90] for UCT, like most of South Africa's universities in these boom years, had been caught right in the middle of a costly building programme. With a deficit – and consequential cutbacks – again looming, UCT's diminished reserves had to be further tapped just so that 'the whole machinery of the University should not break down', explained the chair of its Finance Committee defensively.[91] Rather more melodramatically than Davie in 1950, Luyt told a government commission inquiring into university affairs in 1969, 'We are … frankly stony broke at the moment! We've exhausted all our reserves – by the end of 1969, we haven't got a penny left – a cent left.'[92]

Unbeknown to it, UCT was gaining a foretaste of its lot in the coming decades of financial instability and uncertainty, when the boom years of 1954–68 were to become a vanishing memory.

## Chancellors and Vice-Chancellors

*UCT's third Chancellor, Albert van der Sandt Centlivres (right), being congratulated on his installation in April 1951 by the Principal, T.B. Davie.* (Cape Argus, 6 April 1951)

*The fourth Chancellor, Harry Oppenheimer, delivering the address at his installation in May 1967. On his right sits the chair of Council, Clive Corder, and on his left, only just visible, the Principal, J.P. Duminy, and the Deputy Principal, Professor Donald Inskip.*

*T.B. Davie's installation as UCT's third Principal and Vice-Chancellor in March 1948. Davie is on the right; to his right are J.H. Hofmeyr, the Minister of Education, General Jan Smuts, UCT's Chancellor from 1937 to 1950, and W.D. Baxter, chair of UCT's Council from 1945 to 1960.*

*J.P. Duminy (right) being installed as UCT's fourth Principal and Vice-Chancellor by Chancellor Centlivres, March 1958.*

*Sir Richard Luyt (right) being installed as UCT's fifth Principal and Vice-Chancellor by Chancellor Oppenheimer, March 1968.*

# CHAPTER 3

# Building a Second UCT

One very visible product of the University's structures, rules and procedures discussed in the previous chapter – what were there called 'the basic building blocks' of the institution – was its buildings and they, in turn, exercised a deeply formative influence on life at UCT. As Winston Churchill put it insightfully, 'We shape our buildings; thereafter they shape us.'

Ever since its move to Rhodes's Groote Schuur estate in 1929, UCT has been justifiably proud of its location there and of the way in which the elegant, restrained neoclassical design of its buildings by J.M. Solomon took full advantage of this mountainside site. In 1948 its prospectus spoke with obvious pride of how UCT had been 'endowed with one of the most lovely sites in the world, on Cecil Rhodes's estate at Groote Schuur'.[1]

By that year only one permanent building had been added to Solomon's original twelve, the Bolus Herbarium in 1938, and it was in the same architectural style as those around it. Over the next twenty years, however, it was joined by nineteen new buildings and several additional storeys, wings and annexes,[2] erected on an ad hoc basis to meet the needs of a swelling student body, giving what an architect member of UCT's Council called an 'impression that the immediate needs of the users of the new buildings had been met on individual merit without sufficient regard for the composition as a whole'.[3]

This chapter will examine how and why this construction of what amounted to a second UCT, partly surrounding the first, took place. The buildings constituting this second UCT were very different in architectural character from the first, exemplifying the fact that most older universities, by dint of their longevity, space and the pressure on them to accommodate more and more students and facilities after World War II, became stylistically heterogeneous, akin to many post-World War II townscapes in their accumulative architecture. The very concrete results of this process are evident to this day.

For all its visual grandeur, the Groote Schuur campus was not an easy site on which to build. Situated on a steep, wet slope down which mountain streams ran, it was also subject to a clause in Rhodes's will which prescribed harmony with the style of his Groote Schuur homestead as the only acceptable form for buildings on this land. Feeling that Solomon's first UCT buildings had not met this condition adequately – 'more respect might have been paid to the wishes of the late Mr. Rhodes', they believed, 'which, without any great effort or trouble, might well have been faithfully observed both in letter and in spirit'[4] – the Rhodes Trustees now intended to ensure closer adherence to these conditions.

Yet, if UCT was, literally, between a rock and a hard place when it came to building on the Groote Schuur estate, the Rhodes Trustees were in a similar position, figuratively speaking, when it came to sitting in judgement on architectural designs. Since they were most unwilling for the Trust to be thought of as a dog in the manger obstructing UCT's development, they proceeded to bark rather than bite. For example, not only did they allow the Modernist-style New Science Lecture Theatre to be built in 1948–9 out of recognition for UCT's urgent need for a large venue to accommodate first-year Medical and Science students,[5] but they also repeatedly extended the deadline for UCT to remove from its campus the unprepossessing ex-army huts hastily erected in 1945–6 as a short-term measure to meet the residential and tuitional needs of ex-soldiers. (Astonishingly some of these still remain in use today in 2019 as University House Men's Residence.)

With equal pliancy, they did not long sustain their opposition to UCT's plans for Baxter Hall Women's Residence (1958[6]) when Davie obdurately insisted that the plans were not 'a flagrant breach of good taste or even run counter to the general spirit of the requirement of the will',[7] nor did they long oppose the design of the new Medical Library (1953) even though it was not in the Groote Schuur homestead style but was, they accepted, 'in harmony with the remainder of the buildings' on the Medical School campus.[8] Their rejection of the style of the extension to the Geology Building was as short-lived, and they accepted a face-saving compromise in 1958,[9] while during UCT's building boom over the next ten years they practically turned a blind eye to the proliferation of variegated, non-Groote Schuur-style buildings on the campus. One, the Anatomy Block on the Medical campus, which the Cape Provincial Institute of Architects described as 'radically different in appearance [even] to the existing buildings of the Medical School', they approved with the requirement of only superficial changes, most of which the architect dismissed anyway.[10] It therefore comes as little surprise to discover that by 1967 local architects were twitting the Trustees' representative that UCT had obviously decided unilaterally that 'Groote Schuur style' could be interpreted as meaning no more than 'qualitatively of a high order'.[11] Well might one conclude that the frenzy of construction which produced a second UCT bulldozed (in more than one sense) almost all aesthetic constraints aside.

Of the nineteen new buildings erected or started between 1948 and 1968 on the Groote Schuur campus and the three on the Medical School campus, thirteen were tuitional in function, three residential (Baxter Hall, Driekoppen Residence and Tugwell Hall), two library-related and one administrative. Three of the nineteen – the Child Guidance Clinic (1957), Baxter Hall (1958) and Driekoppen (1965) – were located on the ex-Rosebank Showgrounds section of the Groote Schuur estate, which UCT had acquired so expectantly in 1952.[12] Although it was intended to build a students' community centre there too, this did not happen and the rest of the large site was developed only after 1968 into UCT's so-called 'Lower Campus', which secured for the University its long-cherished goal of easy access to and from a long stretch of the Main Road in Rosebank.

That eight of the thirteen tuitional buildings were for three faculties, Science, Engineering and Medicine, emphasises how far the space requirements of these rapidly burgeoning disciplines had fallen behind their needs in an increasingly technocratic age. Indeed, J.P. Duminy confessed that when he returned to his alma mater as Principal in 1958, he was shocked to find the temporary wooden structures that had been put up on the Hiddingh campus before World War I still in use, 'machines that were doing duty in the engineering workshops when I was a student … still rattling their way along, and the recording machines installed in the Department of Physiology … still rattling on their axes'.[13] Moreover, the situation on the Groote Schuur campus was even worse: 'temporary war-time hutments erected to serve as lecture-rooms, laboratories and offices were falling to pieces; buildings everywhere were overcrowded to distraction.' The 'all too obvious signs of the financial starvation' which UCT had endured since World War II were, he concluded, everywhere to be seen.[14]

The nineteen buildings which constituted the 'second UCT' were not part of a single architectural vision of the Solomon variety, but were disparate structures designed by 28 different architects or architectural partnerships working independently of each other. What these particular architects did share, however, was a training that stressed Modernism in building design, in which form followed function and materials were left as is, so as to reveal their natural essence in accordance with the axiom 'truth to materials', an approach then much favoured by UCT's own School of Architecture and its first professor, Leonard Thornton White.[15] The fruits of this Modernist style at UCT were increasingly stripped-down, relatively unadorned blocks which ranged from the sleek to the Brutalist.

While for those buildings at the centre of University Avenue the need for uniform height was grudgingly accepted – Thornton White grumbled about 'the somewhat [*sic*] severe architectural restrictions (externally) laid down by the Rhodes Trustees nearly forty years ago'[16] – away from the heart of UCT's central thoroughfare such constraints were regarded very lightly. There, Senate's Building Advisory Committee insisted, the conditions imposed by Rhodes's will did not apply at all. In the case of the Brutalist and grossly over-scaled Chemistry Building (1969–72), it declared that its character did not have to be 'imitative of those of other buildings', while 'some architectural features, if the purpose for which the building is designed demand it … would present a pleasing variation to what might otherwise be regarded as a monotonous and uniform sky line'.[17]

Indeed, so strong was the Modernist dominance of architectural and artistic thought on campus that when, in 1959, plans were accepted for a two-storey block with a quadrangle in the Solomon style, to house UCT's Administration Office, 22 members of the Faculty of Fine Art and Architecture pilloried it as 'neither scholarly, humanitarian, liberal nor forward-looking … Its character … [was] authoritarian and undemocratic.'[18] As a result of this outcry, which the Faculty Board echoed *nem. con.*, the commission was withdrawn and a new architect, Brian Mansergh, a sometime member of the School of Architecture, appointed. From his drawing board the sleek Bremner Building (1963) emerged.[19]

In fact, five of the 28 architects involved in the design of the 'second UCT' were or had been full-time or part-time staff of its School of Architecture – Thornton White, Owen Pryce Lewis, Jock Sturrock, Hugh Floyd and Mansergh – an ethically delicate situation which dated back to 1940 when Thornton White had persuaded UCT to make the firm of Thornton White, Pryce Lewis and Sturrock its first-choice architect.[20] Between them, the five designed ten of UCT's buildings in this period, the New Science Lecture Theatre, the original Chemical Engineering Building and the Centlivres Building (Thornton White), the R.W. James Physics Building (Pryce Lewis), the Child Guidance Clinic and the Chemical Engineering Extension Building (Floyd), Bremner Building (Mansergh) and three buildings on the Medical campus, the Medical Library, the Falmouth Building and the South African Mining Industry Centre for Organ Transplantation and Heart Disease Building (Sturrock). Another seven of the buildings were designed by men who had been trained at UCT. It was thus not just on its students but on the fabric of its own university that the School of Architecture cemented its mark. Referring to his Centlivres Building (1959), Thornton White told a friend, 'It fits in with the older buildings, though it is an entirely modern concrete structure … I put everything I know into it, designing and detailing everything of importance personally.'[21]

At the height of this building boom from 1958 to 1968, the construction of

UCT's second ring of buildings comprehensively disrupted activities across the Groote Schuur and Medical campuses. Noise and dust made lecturing, tutoring and even concentration difficult, while bulky builders' bulldozers, bakkies and trucks blocked roads and parking spaces. 'It almost looks as if someone is … building a double carriage-way up to Rhodes memorial', quipped a *Varsity* columnist,[22] to whom it seemed that building operations were akin to 'the removal and reorganization of a large part of Devil's Peak'.[23] To add to this tumult, in 1961–2 Rhodes Drive, which ran between the upper and lower parts of the Groote Schuur campus, was rebuilt into a freeway which decisively split the two parts, save for a subway linking them.[24]

Demands for noise reduction were loudly voiced by several academics, but usually to little effect because of the cost involved. Nor was the builders' task made any easier by the interference of academic staff who, believing that they knew more on technical matters than the architect, instructed contractors on site to make last-minute changes to the plans. The head of the Department of Electrical Engineering, for instance, was told to ensure that his staff refrained from 'hampering the progress of electrical installations' in this way.[25]

However, the greatest interference with building operations came not from overweening academics but from overstretched finances when, in 1967, both interest rates and the cost of building material rose sharply, putting the building programme under severe financial strain. Forced to cut its coat according to its cloth, the University economised on fitting out the interior of its Chemistry Building then under construction so as to save it just under R1 million, thus rendering only parts of the building functional when it was opened. Having learnt the risks of financial overcommitment so dramatically, UCT determined to write into its future building contracts the right to vary its tender specifications by as much as 30% of the price should its financial circumstances suddenly alter. It also realised that it should have had a far more rigorous and detailed financial feasibility plan for the new building on the table before the architects had been appointed, a deficiency which it hastily sought to remedy. Both of these learnt-the-hard-way provisions were to stand it in good stead in the financially volatile 1970s and 1980s.

Not that all oversight of its building programme had been absent up to this point. Already in 1959, as a consequence of the Bremner Building brouhaha, Senate had set up a Building Advisory Committee to give it a formal voice in the planning of buildings, while three years later it commissioned a survey of the University's land, buildings and space requirements to inform its future physical planning. The resultant *UCT Redevelopment Survey* (undertaken by fifteen final-year Architecture students under Sturrock's supervision) concluded that the layout of buildings on the Groote Schuur campus had become haphazard 'and there is urgent need for the preparation of a comprehensive redevelopment plan … [to] be reviewed every three years, if the land still available for building purposes is to be used effectively'.[26]

By the time of the *Survey*'s publication in 1964, UCT had already begun to move towards more comprehensive planning of its buildings by creating a five-man Building Committee to co-ordinate planning across the University and to oversee all construction, and by appointing Thornton White as its dedicated, full-time architectural consultant. 'We have weekly meetings and make decisions in a matter of hours, cutting out months of the sausage machine', he explained to a friend.[27] Belatedly, he spelt out height, scale, roofing and exterior norms for future buildings on University Avenue and insisted that the building line on it follow the general curve of the Avenue. After his death in 1965, his son-in-law and de facto successor in the post, Wynand Deyzel, tried to uphold this framework, but with only partial success.

Away from University Avenue he had even less success constraining his fellow architects, much to the dismay of students and staff. For example, the Staff Association objected in writing to the way in which the buildings were being erected 'in such a way as to eliminate trees and open ground which previously enhanced the appearance of the University and provided places for those who wished to sit or stroll out of doors … Vistas have been blocked so that windows in many buildings open only onto other buildings.'[28] A similar feeling of loss at 'pines and oaks going down left, right and centre before bulldozers' prompted one student to alter a sign on the campus warning 'Danger – Construction Ahead' to 'Slow – Destruction Ahead'[29] and the College of Music to threaten not to play at Graduation in protest against 'what is regarded by some of us as the ill-advised and unnecessary destruction of a group of trees in the grounds of the College'.[30]

It was this kind of concern that finally persuaded the University Council that its Building Committee needed a more up-to-date and professional assessment of where UCT was going. Accordingly, in 1968 it commissioned a new planning survey from a team led by the professor of urban and regional planning, Julian Beinart. Two years later the work of this planning survey was incorporated into the programme of UCT's permanent Planning Unit, which had just been set up to draft an ongoing development plan for the University.

More immediately, however, the Building Committee had to consider three feasibility studies for new buildings, undertaken in 1967–8 in accordance with UCT's new preliminary assessment policy. One, for a seventeen-storey women's residence on Main Road, Rosebank, it referred back to the architect, Christiaan Strauss Brink (Thornton White's successor as professor of architecture and his former student), when local residents objected vehemently to such a structure looming over them. The second study, questioning the merits of erecting a sports centre below Smuts and Fuller Halls, was readily approved, not least because it strongly advised against such a building infringing on UCT's rugby fields, held so dear by thousands of Ikey players over the years and perhaps by a dozen architectural planners. Like its UCT-trained architect, Roelof Uytenbogaardt, they saw in it 'one of Solomon's finest realisations in the design of our University', the large expanse of green above which the University's buildings ascended the mountainside in tiers.[31]

The third, for an extension to the College of Music and a concert hall and theatre, it embraced with delight – and no little relief – for this promised to resolve its longstanding problem of how to carry out the wish of the former chair of its Council, Duncan Baxter (who had died in 1960), that his bequest of just over R500,000 be used to erect a theatre open to all Capetonians. For eight years this matter had been batted back and forth because a suitable site in the city could not be found and because the apartheid-minded Cape Provincial Administration refused to partner with UCT in constructing a performing arts facility which would not be racially segregated. Finally, in 1968 UCT decided to erect the concert hall and theatre by itself on its own property in Rosebank, as a performing arts complex which would serve the College of Music too. The open land below the College of Music was 'ideally suited for a complex of this type and size', enthused the feasibility study. 'Not only is it adequate physically, but its general character and setting and its general traffic approaches render it ideal for a Performing Arts Centre, serving both the University and the public of Cape Town.'[32] Nor was the author, Jack Barnett, another UCT-trained architect, mistaken in his assessment, as he was to show all too well in the award-winning design he produced for the Baxter Theatre, which was erected there after he won the commission in 1969.

UCT thus entered the 1970s with three stand-out buildings in the pipeline, a high-rise women's residence in Rosebank (opened in 1974 as Tugwell Hall), a stark, all-concrete, low, Lego-like Sports Centre, opened in 1977 alongside its rugby fields, and the brick-enclosed, castellated, russet-coloured Baxter Theatre (1977) below the College of Music. In all senses of the phrase, literally and aesthetically, the three buildings represented the highs and lows of UCT's architectural legacy of this period.

Ten years of such runaway construction on the Groote Schuur campus completely overwhelmed the simple road system there, which, by 1958, was still as it had been thirty years earlier when the University had moved to the site. However, as the first new buildings began to appear on the slope above Jameson Hall in that year, so too did a makeshift gravel road to reach them. Its inadequacy was soon apparent and so in 1963 a ring road was built beyond the highest buildings on the slope, linking up into a single system the main exit and entry roads to the campus.

Even more sweeping was the transformation of Rhodes Drive in 1961–2 as part

**"Currently, of course, all our faculties are directed at solving our traffic problem."**

*1962 Cape Argus cartoon referring to the traffic problems on the Groote Schuur campus caused by the widening of Rhodes Drive, which channelled general traffic through the Groote Schuur campus for nearly a year.*

of Cape Town's highway revolution driven by the City Engineer, Solly Morris,[33] which changed it from a single-lane country drive to a high-speed motorway. The fragmenting effect of this on the Groote Schuur campus has already been referred to;[34] however, what it also did was to put paid to the thirty-year-old student practice of hitch-hiking on Rhodes Drive, causing deep resentment among students of the day and stoking their disaffection with Duminy and the University Council for not supporting their protests.[35] The provision of hitching bays on the main exit road from the campus was a poor substitute. As for pedestrians, now barred from crossing Rhodes Drive, the new subway beneath it became the principal route for those walking to and from the Main Road.

Another factor driving the expansion of UCT's road system and the formal naming of its roads – Sports Avenue, Residence Avenue, University Avenue, North Road and South Road[36] – was the swelling number of cars and motorbikes coming onto UCT campuses daily, as these vehicles became more affordable during South Africa's boom years, while the bus service to the difficult-of-access Groote Schuur campus remained poor. Whereas in 1951 no more than 170 cars arrived on the latter campus every morning,[37] in 1964 nearly 800 did so just between 8 am and 9 am.[38] What this meant for parking can easily be imagined by anyone arriving on this campus at peak time during any term weekday in the last sixty years – congestion, contention, indignation and parking rage. As early as 1949 a khaki-uniformed traffic cop was employed part-time to ensure that only cars bearing an 'S' sticker (signifying that the driver was a senior member of the academic staff) parked on University Avenue, a regulation extended to other choice parking areas on this campus by the newly formed University Parking Committee in 1952, to the chagrin of more junior academics who labelled it 'unnecessary public discrimination between grades of teaching staff … which runs counter to the democratic spirit of this University'.[39]

Students too began to complain of the unavailability of parking places after 9 am, which, by the late 1950s, was causing a rising incidence of illegal parking on and alongside the Groote Schuur campus. In response, UCT raised the status of its traffic cop to 'University traffic officer' – though this promotion was undermined by students ironically dubbing him 'Speedy' – and gave the Registrar authority to impose a more than nominal fine for traffic offences, but both without marked effect. Nor did levying a 50 cent fee (today the equivalent would be about R115) on those wishing to park on the campus reduce demand significantly, though it did evoke a petition by 180 academics against the principle involved – in vain.

The only realistic answer to the escalating demand for parking space was to provide more parking, and this it was finally able to do to a degree in 1964, with the laying out of large parking areas to the north and south of the rugby fields. This allowed the University, from 1965, to require all cars coming onto the Groote Schuur campus to display a parking disk; cars without a disk were ticketed by one of the four traffic officers it now employed, and their drivers summonsed to appear before the newly established UCT Traffic Court. Temporarily, these steps had the desired effect, but the underlying motor of the demand for parking space remained in place, often driving the drivers of each vehicle to desperation, an increasingly common experience at UCT for the motorised minority as they arrived on campus each morning.

On UCT's much smaller campuses at its Medical School and Hiddingh Hall in town, there was even less room for manoeuvre when it came to addressing parking problems, although these emerged somewhat later than on the Groote Schuur campus as these campuses were more easily accessible by foot and public transport. By 1963, however, both found it necessary to have a traffic officer on duty to control traffic and to monitor parking. Yet his presence was clearly not enough, for soon the word 'chaotic' was being employed to describe both situations.[40] In the case of the

*Desperation parking on the car-filled Groote Schuur campus* (Varsity, 8 April 1970).

Hiddingh Hall campus, it was the simultaneous arrival of part-time Law, Commerce and Accountancy students at 5 pm which produced the sudden congestion; at the Medical School it was the surge in student numbers in the late 1960s as UCT endeavoured to meet the Government's wish that it produce more doctors. In both cases the result was a spillover of student traffic into surrounding streets, much to the annoyance of nearby residents.

Where the two smaller campuses differed markedly from each other, however, was in the availability of teaching accommodation. On the Hiddingh Hall campus the congestion in the parking area outside the buildings in no way resembled the spacious situation within the buildings. Even before UCT 'bought' the former buildings of the South African College School (SACS) for £1 in 1960 when the school moved to Newlands, the campus had tuitional space to spare, as only Drama and Fine Art students had classes there during the day, while part-timers attended before 9 am or after 5 pm. After 1960, the acquisition of the SACS buildings[41] added appreciably to this abundance of space. Thus, the only building activity necessary there was maintenance of the old buildings.

On the Medical School campus, however, so limited was the space for new buildings that, apart from Sturrock's Medical Library (1953), most additional teaching space was the product of ad hoc annexes, extensions, wings and extra storeys. Very fine co-ordination of the different projects was required. 'To keep the School as a going concern we shall have to play a gigantic game of draughts,' mused Thornton White, 'trying to get each department into its final place with the least number of moves.'[42] His successor as architectural consultant for the Medical School, Sturrock, addressed the problem by taking on most of the architectural work himself, and so it is his mildly Modernist hand which is most visible in the additions made from 1959 to 1966 and in the two new buildings which he was able to squeeze onto the site, the Falmouth Building, which grew by stages (1959–66), and the Centre for Organ Transplantation and Heart Disease Building (1971), donated by the South African mining industry to mark the high point of the Medical School's achievements, the first heart transplant in 1967.

Only two Medical campus buildings approved in this period were not from his hand, the box-like Faculty Lecture Theatre (1971) and the equally unadorned, towering office-block-like Anatomy and Radiology Building (1971) adjoining it. Their architect, Hannes van der Merwe, a former student of Thornton White's, prided himself on his advanced Modernism and, like many of the buildings constituting the second UCT, these two structures did not hold back in brazenly proclaiming their functionalism.

Yet, while a contemporary guide to South African architecture might have praised such buildings at UCT as 'an advance on the kind [of architecture] which had been executed in the past' and 'a precedent for more contemporary planning and presentation',[43] lay people on campus were not quite as taken with the results of ten years of Modernist architecture at UCT. Indeed, in 1969, in a telling judgement on these buildings, UCT's Council went as far as to lay down that no further building should take place on the Groote Schuur campus until it had considered written reports on all proposed buildings 'indicating the aesthetic effect, if any, that the proposed development would have on the appearance of the main campus, the dignity of its setting and the grace and charm of the University property generally'.[44] By then, however, as subsequent generations of staff and students were to discover, the runaway second building of UCT had already shaped the University in concrete ways.

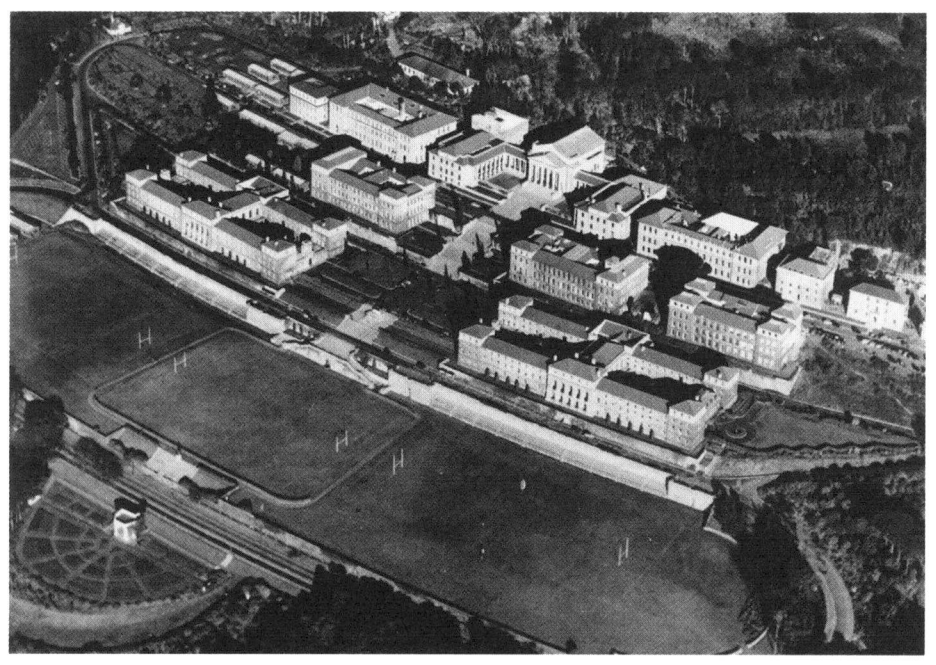

*The growth of UCT's Groote Schuur campus is evident from these two aerial photographs taken in 1949 and 1967. Moreover, as the right-hand side of the 1967 photograph clearly shows, construction of buildings and roads was still in full spate then.*

*When gown makes way for town. The conversion of Rhodes Drive into a dual-carriage highway in 1961 required UCT to give up some of its frontage on the Drive, including its boundary walls which were demolished, as shown here. Not only did this require the statue of Cecil John Rhodes to be moved from there to a site above the rugby fields (where it was to remain for 54 years), but it also put an end to hitch-hiking on Rhodes Drive, to the anger of many a student (see chapter 11).*

*UCT Medical School, c. 1967, located, ironically, between Groote Schuur Hospital and Mowbray Cemetery*

*The missing link. The extension of Woolsack Drive to the upper campus in 1963, as shown here, facilitated the University's connection with its developing Lower Campus, which became its residential hub.*

*Lady Elizabeth Beattie, widow of UCT's first Principal and Vice-Chancellor, Sir Jock Beattie, formally opens the Beattie Building in 1964. To her immediate right sits Beattie's successor-but-three, J.P. Duminy, and to her immediate left the chair of Council, A.F. Stephen, and Deputy Principal Professor Donald Inskip.*

*Beware of oncoming bulldozer! Library staff stare transfixed by the excavations under way right next to their building, 1964.*

*Chancellor Centlivres opens the custom-designed Medical Library, 1954. Seated alongside him are (from left to right) the University Librarian, R.F. Immelman, the Principal and Vice-Chancellor, T.B. Davie, and the chair of the University Library Committee, Professor H.C. Baldry.*

*Acting Principal R.W. James speaking at the laying of the foundation stone of the Centlivres Building in 1957. At the right, readying himself to respond, stands Centlivres himself.*

# CHAPTER 4

# Teaching, Learning and Researching: UCT's Academic Project

The ideal of the unity of teaching and research, first developed by Wilhelm von Humboldt in the 19th century and revered by all Western universities in the 20th century,[1] was one towards which UCT gradually began to edge from the mid-1930s, as it recovered from the dire impact of the Great Depression.

By 1948 research had started to appear in pockets around the University as a significant ancillary to teaching, especially in the Faculties of Medicine, Science and Arts. This development, along with the institution's support for it, was evident in, for instance, the establishment in 1944 of a standing University Research Committee to oversee all research matters, its compilation of an annual research report from 1947, the quadrupling of the Staff Research Fund to £2000 annually, the introduction of special research leave, the creation of junior research posts in three department with active research projects,[2] and the 117% increase in the number of postgraduate degrees awarded in the 1960s compared to the 1950s.[3] As early as 1950 senior academics had begun flying a kite in the interests of research, saying out loud that UCT's staff ought to be able to devote a third to a half of their time to research.[4]

As at the University of the Witwatersrand and the University of Natal, research grew markedly in the next two decades as academics and postgraduates at UCT responded positively to the research needs of – and the financial incentives offered by – industry, commerce and the state while the country's economy boomed. By 1965 the Staff Research Fund had almost quadrupled to R15,000 annually and sixteen dedicated research units had been set up in UCT departments, funded by the state's Council for Scientific and Industrial Research (CSIR), the Atomic Energy Board and the Medical Research Council, the mining and fishing industries, and the US Department of Health. Eight of these units were in the Faculty of Medicine and six in Science. Of the 34 CSIR-funded research units at all of South Africa's universities in 1965, 10 were at UCT.[5] Moreover, to make the fruits of this burgeoning research widely available, university grants in aid of publication were increased year by year, while in 1957 UCT agreed to pay 50% of the page costs of articles by its staff appearing in any approved journal. To help academics carry out research abroad and attend conferences while there, from 1961 funds from the generous Bremner Bequest were earmarked to help finance such travel.[6]

In comparison to the innovative thrust of the research being carried out at UCT, its teaching in these two decades remained, in the main, tradition-bound, as indeed was the case in other universities in South Africa and beyond.

Formal, didactic lectures in the Oxbridge style were the chief mode of delivering the contents of undergraduate courses, based on the principle that lecturers alone possessed the required knowledge, which had to be conveyed to an audience of students waiting to take it down in their notebooks. This one-way flow of information – from the full jug to the empty mug, as it has been wittily characterised[7] – assumed that learning took place primarily by listening attentively. This was 'the quickest way in which a student can get a grasp of a set of facts and an interpretation of them', explained one UCT lecturer,[8] and to this end every feature of the lecture was geared: the fixed seating in serried rows so that all students focused on the lecturer, the discouragement of questions during the lecture, and the formal, hierarchical atmosphere which was cultivated by lecturers wearing academic gowns, their use of 'Mr' and 'Miss' when addressing individual students, and the requirement, especially in big classes, that students sign an attendance register. 'You sat there as a meek student and listened to the experts, so-called', remembered an Arts Faculty student. 'They behaved in a very formal manner, in a very formal system, so one didn't get to know the lecturers well.'[9]

Such an environment allowed uninspiring chalk-and-talk lecturing to be accepted as usual – dictated notes, blackboards covered in graphs, formulae and calculations to be copied down, disorganised content and poor delivery. One student spoke critically of the 'muffled monologues euphemistically called "lectures"'.[10] In extreme cases lecturers eschewed even eye contact with students. 'He came in, put down his notes [from his textbook], read them and walked out', recalled two students about the same lecturer, though twenty years separated their experience of him.[11]

In the absence of systematic course evaluations (which were introduced only in 1979), students grumbled among themselves about lecturers, but usually this went no further. 'The average student soon learns how to cope with the tasks required of him by his lecturer, without seriously challenging his own values', lamented a vice-president of the SRC.[12] However, in 1969, taking a leaf out of an Education Reform Programme at Wits, UCT's SRC conducted a comprehensive survey of student opinion about the state of education on campus. The results, based on a 30% response, do provide a taste of where UCT's teaching practices pinched students most. Representative opinions included sentiments like 'Lecturers are not interested in their students', that there was too much spoonfeeding and parrot learning, that 'We are not schoolchildren, but students', that lectures should be more 'illuminating and above all stimulating', and that all prospective lecturers should attend a course on lecturing.[13]

On the other hand, when a lecturer did enhance a lecture with slides, films or images from an overhead projector or did display spark and passion and did give good, well-structured notes, students warmed to him or her. Memories like 'He used to get carried away with his subjects',[14] his lectures were 'like a performance',[15] 'You *wanted* to listen to him',[16] he 'was very inspiring – within a week he knew the name of everyone in the class',[17] his lectures were 'always meticulously prepared and he made excellent use of the blackboard',[18] are samples of rather different memories of the teaching at UCT, which make it clear that it had another, more positive side to it too. And when a handful of lecturers like Jack Simons in Native Law and Administration and Martin Versfeld in Philosophy deftly utilised Socratic question-and-answer methods instead of didactic lectures to teach their small classes, the response of students was overwhelmingly positive. Simons 'directly involved his audiences, whom he encouraged to participate', recalled one student of his classes,[19] while another admitted that his lectures were 'a revelation … a mind-opening experience'.[20] A third student taking Simons's course confessed to a classmate after a year in Simons's interactive class, 'You know, for the first time I am no longer afraid to think!'[21]

Simons would have found such evidence of the success of his pedagogy as heart-warming as did a lecturer in mathematics, Kathleen Pay, who used a student-centred approach in her didactic lectures to get her class to understand her subject matter. 'Seeing the light that comes when understanding dawns, when they see how something works, that is so rewarding,' she mused in her retirement. 'I enjoyed teaching.'[22] For their part, her students felt that their understanding was 'enhanced by her concern for us … to pass the course … everything is well illustrated by use of examples which leads altogether to a very comprehensive and understandable presentation of each topic within the subject.'[23]

In the Faculties of Arts and Social Science, lectures were complemented by the discussion of related topics in small-group tutorials, which became a standard part of the teaching in all their departments in 1951 – until then, only a handful of departments in these faculties had offered them.[24] Medicine too ran tutorials from 1951, but only in its clinical departments where the focus was solely on discussing individual cases which had been assigned to students.

A few years later the Faculty of Science introduced a third type of tutorial, one-on-one meetings between each first-year and a designated member of staff who, like an Oxford moral tutor, would give advice on general academic matters like note-taking, study methods and assignment writing. To provide subject-specific help too, every lecturer in first-year Science courses was required to fix a time when she or he would be available to answer course-related questions in private, so as to overcome the 'hesitancy of students to consult their lecturers'.[25]

Of course, lectures and tutorials were not the only modes of teaching at UCT. Especially in the Faculties of Science, Engineering and Medicine, afternoon practicals in departmental laboratories put the accent on learning by doing, while hands-on training of a different sort was central to instruction in Fine Art, Drama and Music. In Medicine, ward rounds loomed large in the clinical years, allowing senior medical students to feel the pulse (literally and figuratively) of hospital work.

For students in departments like Botany, Zoology, Geography, Geology, Oceanography, Archaeology and Social Work, fieldwork provided comparable occasions for hands-on learning. Such opportunities to apply the knowledge and skills gained in lectures or by reading were generally popular among students, not only for the training they afforded through guided engagement with actual issues off campus, but also for the social interaction and collegiality they offered with fellow students and staff. 'Going to places such as Langebaan, Tsitsikamma, the Koue Bokkeveld and Bain's Kloof gave me my first exposure to real world ecology – it was inspirational', reflected a former Zoology student who went on to head that department himself.[26]

Yet, for all such complementary teaching, it is clear that in 1968 didactic lectures still overbore all other modes of instruction at UCT and that most of them remained lecturer-centred, promoting passive learning.

Reasons for the endurance of such lecturing methods included many first-years' lack of more than a superficial background in a subject because of the unspecialised nature of South Africa's matriculation curriculum; the pedagogic conservatism of most lecturers, who sought to replicate the teaching methods they had encountered as students; and the absence at UCT of credible alternative models of teaching – teaching methods in higher education began to become a subject of academic inquiry only in the 1960s, and UCT did not establish its own Teaching Methods Unit until 1977.

More broadly, it is also open to question whether those other than, say, the top 20% of South Africa's matriculants really were adequately equipped in terms of literacy and numeracy to cope with more than a simple didactic lecture. Certainly UCT's Senate minutes of the 1950s are filled with complaints about the lack of preparedness of first-years. They were not 'sufficiently prepared for exercising the individual control of study and work which distinguishes the university atmosphere from that of the high school', UCT told an official commission of inquiry in 1952. 'Generally speaking, they are unable to organise their work, to use books of reference, to draw sound and independent conclusions from individual study and investigation, and to communicate these in clear and correct language to others.' The reason for this, it suggested, was the overemphasis on examinations at school, which produced 'excessive taking and memorising of dictated notes to spoonfeeding and cramming in the schools'.[27] As a result, too many UCT students were, in the words of one professor, 'perfectly content to remain sponges, soaking up what they are told and having it squeezed out of them, drop by drop, in final examinations'.[28] For some, even this was beyond them: in a sample study of 90 UCT students in 1958, 15% were found to have the reading skills of twelve-year-olds.[29]

Not that such experiences deterred UCT from committing itself to examinations as the chief measure of students' academic competence. Despite students grumbling about the shortcomings of examinations as a fair test of such competence – the 1969 Education Survey noted that 'Very few admitted to any merit whatsoever in the exam system', even citing one angry opinion that 'Exams prostitute education'[30] – end-of-year examinations remained a fixed feature of UCT's academic year. In student folklore, the appearance in October of new buds on the creepers entwining the buildings on the Groote Schuur campus was taken as a sign that swotting for final examinations should commence – 'a warning ... ignored by the foolish', *Varsity* called it[31] – and that student societies and the SRC would have copies of old exam papers for sale. 'Our whole educational set-up is held back by being based on the Scottish tradition where examinations are the only aim', lamented one senior academic.[32]

That so many students, especially first-years, failed these examinations and dropped out of UCT – in 1965, 45.8% of all its first-years failed, a figure higher than the already high figures at South Africa's other universities,[33] despite UCT enjoying one of the best staff–student ratios in the country – raises the deeper question whether, given the low admission requirements for most degrees in South Africa – in the majority of cases a modest matriculation pass was all that was needed – more students from the white community were attending the country's universities than would normally occur in a population of comparable size. Certainly statistics showing that 16% of white South Africans were at university in 1960 were among the highest in the world; in Britain the equivalent figure was 4.1%.[34] 'This dipping deep into the intellectual barrel' in the interests of creating a white professional class 'meant a lowering of average general ability at the universities', a student newspaper concluded damningly.[35]

Having sketched the broad framework within which UCT's academic project of teaching and researching took place, this history will deepen this examination by focusing in the next four chapters on the contents of this project at the level of the primary locales of such activity, faculties and their constituent departments based on disciplines which were the product of Europe's attempt to classify knowledge. It will be useful, but by no means definitive, to group them according to four broad terrains, the pure sciences as in the Faculty of Science, the applied sciences as in the Faculties of Engineering and Medicine, the professional field spanning the Faculties of Law, Commerce, Education, Architecture and Social Science, and the arts and humanities as embodied in the Faculties of Music and Arts and the School of Fine Art. The accompanying table provides an indication of the changing size of these faculties, using as a criterion that key factor in all university decision-making, student numbers. The table is a revealing companion to the next four chapters.

*Table 1: Students registered in each faculty in 1948, 1958 and 1968 by number and (in brackets) as a percentage of the total number of students registered at UCT in that year.*

|  | 1948 | 1958 | 1968 |
|---|---|---|---|
| Arts | 665 (15.6) | 934 (18.8) | 1312 (17.7) |
| Commerce | 425 (9.98) | 710 (14.3) | 1257 (17) |
| Education | 82 (1.9) | 186 (3.8) | 288 (3.9) |
| Engineering | 641 (15.1) | 606 (12.2) | 783 (10.6) |
| Fine Art & Architecture | 478 (11.2) | 443 (8.9) | 658 (8.9) |
| Law | 26 (0.6) | 116 (2.3) | 123 (1.7) |
| Medicine | 1128 (26.5) | 697 (14.1) | 1105 (14.95) |
| Music | 376 (8.8) | 610 (12.3) | 730 (9.88) |
| Science | 366 (8.6) | 592 (11.9) | 905 (12.27) |
| Social Science | 70 (1.6) | 66 (1.3) | 231 (3.1) |

*Source*: Annual UCT reports in Attachments to Minutes of UCT Council meetings, 14 November 1949, 3 June 1959 and 4 June 1969

Reading these chapters will make very clear how powerful the professoriate was in determining UCT's academic project, as in these years professors were formally responsible to Senate for the content and conduct of teaching in their department, for examinations there, 'and for the proper conduct and administration of the department' as long as they headed it, i.e. until they retired. Or as a sometime lecturer put it flippantly, 'The professor was Mr Big.'[36] Rotating headships were introduced only in the 1980s. Consequently, in what follows, professors loom large, but not so as to block out due attention to other academics on their staff, to what was taught and how, and to student perspectives on this. If the histories of faculties and departments that follow are not wholly in the round, they aim to provide studies that are at least semi-circular.

# CHAPTER 5

# Pure Science: The Faculty of Science

Throughout the twenty years from 1948 to 1968 the Faculty of Science remained one of UCT's middle-sized faculties, containing 9–12% of all UCT's students in its fourteen departments. It was able to do this because, as the country's economy boomed from the mid-1950s, the need for scientific and technical expertise increased apace. Not only did the existing departments expand their intake to meet this demand for more science graduates, but five new departments (Biochemistry, Mathematical Statistics, Microbiology, Geochemistry and Oceanography) were added to their number to cater for new specialisms. Another consequence of this accelerating economic development was an increase in students registered in other faculties – in particular Engineering, Medicine and Commerce – taking basic science courses in subjects like physics, chemistry, pure mathematics and applied mathematics.

However, offering these service courses to 'outsiders' came at a cost, viz. teaching a large number of first-years, many of whom were ill prepared to cope with mathematics and science at a level significantly higher than that required for matriculation. Not surprisingly, therefore, the Faculty of Science, along with Engineering, recorded the highest first-year failure rates at UCT in the 1950s, of over 60%.[1] In the 1960s it sought to address this by introducing small-group tutorials and raising its entry level to require at least good matriculation passes in mathematics and a science subject. Presumably it is a measure of the relative success of these measures that in the 1960s the failure rate in Science fell below what it had been in the preceding decade.

Evidence of a greater throughput of its students is the growth of the number of BSc degrees awarded relative to the total number of students in the faculty (from 5.8 in 1948 to 6.1 in 1968) and the surge in postgraduate students (one MSc awarded in 1948, sixteen in 1968), trends which the first permanent Dean of Science, Frank Warren, actively encouraged by lobbying for more staff after his appointment in

1965. The Faculty was 'shockingly understaffed', he warned, and thus was not keeping up with the rapid advances made in most scientific fields since the end of World War II.[2]

Nowhere was such understaffing more evident than in one of the Faculty's largest departments, Physics. There the staff–student ratio remained above 1:50 all through these years, lecture halls bulged at the seams and additional laboratory practicals had to be run on Saturday mornings to accommodate first-year classes of over 400. 'The relative economy in teaching courses for large numbers of students has ... reached (and passed) its optimum', complained its new head, Walter Schaffer, in 1957.[3]

He had taken over the headship when the long-serving R.W. James stepped into the breach as Acting Principal upon the sudden death of T.B. Davie.[4] By then Schaffer had been on the staff for eleven years[5] and, like several of his colleagues, had been drawn into James's research field of crystallography.[6] However, it was not as a researcher that he made his name in the department, but as an adept and fair-minded administrator who was keen to encourage up-to-date teaching and research by his colleagues. To that end he convinced UCT to establish two new chairs in the department, in theoretical physics and in nuclear physics, secured special funding to purchase UCT's first electron microscope and to equip a dedicated nuclear physics laboratory, created a separate first-year course requiring advanced mathematics and calculus for those intending to go on to Physics II, and pushed for the undergraduate syllabus to be updated by the inclusion of topics in modern physics like ionisation, radioactivity, and atomic and nuclear physics. Until then, recalled a bright student of that era, the syllabus was one which suggested that the staff were 'uncomfortable with everything that had developed [in physics] after 1930. Their attitude [was] that you were lucky if you ever got to really understand quantum mechanics.'[7]

Such innovation was facilitated by his appointment of several young physicists who had received their training at top institutions like Cambridge's Cavendish Laboratory, Oxford, Utrecht and Indiana. They were now keen to replicate this learning at UCT. Men – and they were all men – like Robin Cherry (who succeeded Schaffer as professor in 1972) and Peter Barrett were appointed as they more than met Schaffer's principal criteria – 'they must know Physics and their personalities must be right ... [and] not ... quarrelsome'.[8]

Some of these new appointees pursued research in the field in which James had made his (and the department's) name internationally, X-ray crystallography, thereby following the path taken in 1945–6 by two precocious MSc students, Alan Cormack and Aaron Klug, both of whom taught briefly in the department before going abroad to make careers for themselves, which culminated in Nobel Prizes for both. James had not been wrong when in 1954 he described the young Cormack as 'the man we should keep our eye on'. He was 'undoubtedly the best of the younger members of the physics staff from the point of view of ability and willingness to apply that ability to do good research work', he told the Principal.[9]

Other young lecturers in the department were attracted by research opportunities in newer fields like plasma physics, radioactivity detection and nuclear physics. Work in the last-mentioned area became especially appealing from 1964 when the joint UCT–Stellenbosch University Southern Universities Nuclear Institute, boasting a new Van de Graaff accelerator, was opened at a site between the two universities, and the 33-year-old Frank Brooks arrived from Harwell to assume UCT's new chair of nuclear physics. Although he lacked a doctorate, he was soon drawing postgraduates in numbers by virtue of his reputation for dedicated supervision and his willingness to spend hours with them in the laboratory, 'never shying away from doing all-nighters at the lab', as one recalled.[10] By the time he retired in 1996, 37 MSc and PhD students had benefited from this commitment.

The other professorial newcomer in 1964, the 38-year-old Wilhelm Frahn, may not have been the first occupant of UCT's chair of theoretical physics – it had been briefly occupied by John Irving in 1959–60 – but he was the man who, in effect, turned a subject which existed only in theory in the department into a reality. His rigorous mathematical training in Aachen and practical experience as a nuclear physicist at the Council for Scientific and Industrial Research (CSIR) and Stellenbosch University provided ideal preparation for the position. The head of Physics at Witwatersrand University had little doubt that he would offer 'a better training for research students in theoretical nuclear physics than … any other man in South Africa'.[11] Quickly gathering postgraduates around him eager to engage with the natural world mathematically, he became, to all intents and purposes, 'the father of theoretical physics in South Africa',[12] for he trained most of the first generation of locals in that most abstract of specialities which, one of its foremost practitioners believed, was 'actual philosophy [since it] has revolutionized fundamental concepts … about space and time … about causality … and about substance and matter'.[13]

Not surprisingly, only a handful of the students in the department actually encountered theoretical physics head-on, for most went no further than the Physics I course required for engineering and medicine. Lectures to these big classes, which Schaffer regretted were filled with 'rather mediocre students who are uninspired and therefore uninspiring to teach',[14] were the preserve of more experienced members of the department, each of whom had his own way of handling the often boisterous, largely male audience: James and Schaffer through displaying their mastery of the subject and their pedagogic skill by deftly explaining difficult-to-comprehend concepts, Cherry by showing what one student described as 'his human touch in conveying his research' to those before him,[15] and John Juritz by lacing his well-constructed lectures with dry wit and beguiling practical demonstrations, not the least of which was playing the bassoon in his lectures on acoustics. In the Physics II and III classes the lecturers found it less necessary to play to the gallery as there were fewer students and most were more committed to the subject.

That the total number of students taking physics courses in 1968 had risen to over 950 from the 549 of twenty years earlier, that the number of those teaching them material which now at least had 'the flavour of modern physics'[16] had doubled to sixteen, and that the ranks of technicians and laboratory attendants had grown to nine from the six of 1948 made the department's move into a new, state-of-the-art building in 1967 more than timely. Appropriately, it was named the R.W. James Building.

Fittingly, perched atop the building was a domed mini-observatory containing a 10″ telescope,[17] for, since 1958, Physics had strongly supported the teaching of astronomy on campus by the newly appointed honorary professor of astronomy, Richard Stoy, who was also Her Majesty's Astronomer at the Royal Observatory in Cape Town. Indeed, so keen was Schaffer to see astronomy take off at UCT – 'great tracts of vital research are crying out for attention' in the 'relatively unworked southern skies', he argued[18] – that he assigned one of his lecturers with a doctorate in astrophysics, John Fernie, to assist Stoy. Together they mounted the first university courses in astronomy in South Africa at Honours and Master's levels, while at the same time seeking to popularise the subject by offering a short, non-technical introductory course for all-comers.

Yet, few students ventured to commit themselves exclusively to the new field and the bulk of astronomy teaching took place within special astrophysics or field astronomy options in the Physics, Land Surveying and Applied Mathematics Departments. Consequently, by the time that Stoy resigned in 1968, only seven students had taken the BSc course in astronomy, while Physics was still providing one of its staff to co-teach with him. If the sub-department of Astronomy remained a satellite of the Physics Department, the prospect of it escaping from the former's pull was, however, dawning, for in 1969 UCT's Committee of Deans urged the University to replace Stoy's honorary position with a full-time professorial post, especially in the light of the probability of the creation of a modern observatory in the Karoo. They clearly were a far-seeing group of men.

In many ways the history of another very large department in the Faculty, Chemistry, parallels that of Physics. For both disciplines the 1950s and 1960s were decades of runaway expansion and innovation; in chemistry these new fields ranged from atomic energy, synthetic materials, petrochemicals, fertilisers and pesticides to food preservation and, after the discovery of DNA in 1953, biochemistry. Fuelled by such developments, secondary industry in South Africa mushroomed, increasing demand for trained chemists hand over fist.

This translated into swelling student numbers in Chemistry departments around the country. At UCT enrolments rose by 50% between 1950 and 1960 to 790, but thereafter slowed because of the constraint of limited accommodation, as in Physics, until the opening of a giant new Chemistry Block in 1971, the featureless P.D. Hahn Building. As in Physics too, over half of these students were from other faculties, in particular Engineering and Medicine, and took the specially geared Chemistry I course, delivered by dedicated teachers like Willie Campbell and Jack Elsworth. Elsworth's dynamism at the lectern was complemented by his affable personality as he made a point of introducing himself to each and every student at the first laboratory practical. 'He circulated widely,' recalled a first-year medical student appreciatively, 'giving advice and helping sort out difficulties. This continuum from theory [in lectures] to practice [in the laboratory] was a major contributor to his popularity.'[19] The handful of Engineering students who did go further – most were doing chemical engineering – were seen in the department as a necessary burden. It was difficult to hold their interest in a general chemistry class, grumbled one professor, and as a result the class was, 'as it were, diluted by the foreign population'.[20]

But, providing service courses to non-Science Faculty students did keep student numbers high, though the price was, as in Physics, a heavy teaching load for staff. On average, the staff–student ratio stood at 1:60, prompting the head to lament in 1963 that 'it simply cannot be upheld that we are teaching the students in first-year classes … at a proper university level'.[21] Research by staff was compromised as a result as they and student demonstrators struggled to arrange sufficient laboratory sessions for everyone. Accordingly, practicals had to be held on Saturday mornings too, while apparatus suffered through overuse. The department's technicians and its long-serving glassblower, Bill Lewis, were consequently fully occupied in maintenance and repair work all year round.

The sheer weight of teaching also meant that revision of the syllabus lagged in keeping up with rapid developments in the discipline. Practicals, complained a senior student in 1966, were 'a rehash of practicals done 30 years ago – with the same apparatus'.[22] The contents of the first-year courses for engineering and medical students were, understandably, more descriptive than analytical, but the smaller, more specialised Chemistry II and III courses, which sought to emulate courses at top universities in Britain, struggled to do so because of a lack of specialists in the new fields. Such specialists were all too readily snapped up by the chemical industry as soon as they graduated. At UCT this meant that the teaching of new branches like biochemistry, analytical chemistry and geochemistry was left largely in the hands of non-specialists until the 1960s.

What altered this situation significantly was outside intervention, either by the mining industry, which offered to fund dedicated posts in geochemistry, or by the pharmaceutical and food industries, which pressed strongly for a distinct chair of biochemistry, or by UCT itself, which, in 1968, finally acknowledged the plight of the Chemistry Department with its heavy load of first-year teaching by granting it R10,000 per annum to improve its first-year courses by increasing its staff and overhauling how courses were taught.

Such initiatives facilitated more research by staff, which was also boosted by the acquisition in 1967, thanks to a special grant, of a nuclear magnetic resonance spectrometer, only the second such instrument in the country. It was 'crucial in bringing us up to the mark with what was happening in top universities in Europe and the USA' and in the 'inclusion of instrumental analysis in the syllabus', judged a later UCT chemistry professor.[23] This helped make the department the leader in South Africa of minute spectroscopic investigation of substances for the next twenty years as some of its members applied the techniques which had been developed by James and his team in Physics. Prominent in doing so was one of the department's three professors, the dexterous Cecil Leisegang (professor of inorganic and theoretical chemistry, 1962–78), while his fellow professor from 1966, the astute former Harwell research fellow, Ernest Prout (professor of physical chemistry, 1966–85), concentrated for his part on solid state kinetics.

Others in the department trained their microscopes on larger molecules. Alistair Stephen, who joined in 1951 as a 29-year-old lecturer holding doctorates from UCT and Oxford, focused on carbohydrate chemistry, eventually establishing a CSIR-funded research unit in this area in 1965, soon after assuming the department's chair of organic chemistry. His predecessor in the chair, Fred Holliman, had also started out ploughing a rather lonely furrow after his arrival from Cambridge in 1947, but had then turned his attention to microbiology at the behest of the then head. As a result, by 1962 when he left South Africa for Leeds University for political reasons, he was teaching microbiology both within the Chemistry Department and without, always displaying what his old chief at Cambridge described as his 'gift for clear, vigorous exposition'.[24]

His departure made the need for the dedicated teaching of microbiology and biochemistry pressing enough to overcome the turf wars between several departments over which of them should teach these subjects, and in 1966 they accepted a proposal to set up a fully-fledged department of biochemistry as the discipline, in the words of a Senate sub-committee, 'occupies a central place in modern biological sciences'.[25] Once the uncompromising, 42-year-old Hamburg graduate, Claus von Holt, had assumed the chair in 1967, his new department carved out a clear place for itself between other departments with an overlapping interest and, as the first independent biochemistry department in the country, proceeded, under his 'Teutonic management' (a student's words), to place 'South African biochemistry firmly on the map'.[26]

Another emerging field located on the borderline between disciplines and therefore caught up in an academic tug of war was geochemistry. The Department of Geology had raised the need for a dedicated post in this area as early as 1950, but it was not until several mining houses had indicated their willingness to provide funding that a dedicated senior lecturer was appointed. From 1959, therefore, a New Zealander with Indiana and Oxford training, Ross Taylor, offered a single course in geochemistry within the Department of Geology embracing both geology and chemistry and an Honours course in pure and applied geochemistry.

However, in 1961 the geochemical pendulum swung away from the Geology Department when, thanks to the Chamber of Mines, a full chair in an independent Department of Geochemistry was endowed and filled by the man who had been UCT's professor of inorganic and physical chemistry since 1956, the 43-year-old Louis Ahrens. Internationally renowned for his cutting-edge geochemical research while on the staff at MIT and Oxford University between 1946 and 1956 – 'at present there is no English-speaking geochemist with a higher and more deserved reputation', wrote Oxford's professor of geology[27] – Ahrens was appointed Chamber of Mines Professor of Geochemistry by UCT without advertisement. Nor did he disappoint as head of the new department, for he was soon attracting large funds for research from the CSIR and a mining industry eager to exploit South Africa's mineral wealth beyond gold. With the former's backing, a state-of-the-art X-ray fluorescence spectroscope was purchased and in 1965 the CSIR went even further by sponsoring the creation of the Geochemistry Research Unit in his department, while the Anglo American Mining Corporation followed suit by funding two research posts in economic geochemistry.

A thorough and perceptive researcher himself, Ahrens inculcated these traits in his students, along with a healthy dose of critical curiosity. He 'always sought to understand the basic science behind … data, reminding his students of Darwin's precept: "six samples are enough for a scientist"', recalled Ross Taylor.[28]

At a time when academics from South Africa were being increasingly shunned on the international circuit, Ahrens was feted in geochemical circles far and wide, even in the Soviet Union. Such was his reputation that in 1972 he was elected president of the International Association of Geochemistry and Cosmochemistry. With no little accuracy, an article in *New Scientist* referred to him as 'that star of

Capetown University'.[29] This was doubly appropriate a description, for in 1969 he was appointed one of thirteen principal scientific investigators by the US National Aeronautics and Space Administration to analyse the composition of rocks and soil recently brought back from the moon by American astronauts. This was a 'worthy distinction … which enhances, too, the international reputation of the university', observed a Cape Town newspaper proudly,[30] a sentiment which it was to echo two years later when Ahrens's laboratory was asked to analyse pieces of two meteorites which had fallen to earth in the USSR. Truly his reputation was stellar.

As the preceding paragraphs suggest, research was the department's primary focus. All through the 1960s it usually had more postgraduate students than undergraduates. Thus its staff remained small: Ahrens and his protégé (and eventual successor as professor), Tony Erlank, who shared the teaching of its one undergraduate course, which covered topics similar to those that Ross Taylor had taught. Only at postgraduate level did research and teaching begin to meld directly, the Honours syllabus from 1967 listing, for example, topics like meteorites and the origin and composition of the mantle, stable isotope geochemistry, and practical training in fluorescence techniques for analysis of rocks and minerals.

The department's size made it close-knit, fostering good rapport between staff and students, which was enhanced by the approachability of both Ahrens and Erlank. Ahrens, in particular, readily socialised with colleagues over a drink and easily won the confidence of students. Not surprisingly, therefore, for several years running he was chosen as the SRC's representative on the Senate, being labelled by them 'A friend of the students'.[31]

Although the department under whose auspices geochemistry had made its debut at UCT, Geology, also began to draw an increasing number of postgraduates in the 1960s – from 12 in 1960 to 28 in 1968 – unlike Geochemistry, its undergraduate intake far outnumbered these, almost topping 200 by 1968. This was the result of the post-war growth in demand for civil engineers, land surveyors and geologists, the last by South Africa's booming mining industry. Geologists were 'an integral part of the mining industry and the mining engineer will continue to seek their aid in the most economic way to mine', declared the president of the Chamber of Mines encouragingly in 1963.[32]

Under both Fred Walker (1939–56)[33] and his protégé, Eric Simpson (1957–74), state-of-the-art equipment was acquired by the department to analyse rocks and minerals more thoroughly, student laboratories were supplied with better-quality microscopes, and lectures were enhanced by the use, from 1958, of UCT's first overhead projector, which, the department enthused, 'virtually replaces the blackboard as a lecturing device'.[34]

But it was in expanding the department's profile as a centre of research that Simpson left fewest stones unturned. Described by Walker as 'a first-rate organiser',[35] this 33-year-old UCT- and Cambridge-trained geologist set up the Pre-Cambrian Research Unit with a large grant from the Chamber of Mines to explore the mineral potential of the little-known western side of the subcontinent, while he also initiated a big project to probe the geology of the seabed around South Africa. That he himself had served in the navy during World War II might explain his fascination with marine geology. In short measure a 12-foot dinghy was purchased to carry out an investigation of the inshore sea floor, specialised equipment was acquired to measure the undersea magnetic field, equipment was installed aboard UCT's new oceanographic research ship to conduct deep-sea marine geological research, and in 1967 a dedicated Marine Geological Research Group was established in the department.

As Simpson's involvement in marine geology grew, so too did his international reputation in the field. His trips to conferences and symposia abroad multiplied by the year, prompting colleagues at UCT to refer jokingly to him as 'our visiting Professor' when he appeared on campus.[36] Behind his back too, some even dubbed him 'a geopolitician'.[37]

In this situation, a senior colleague, Morna Mathias,[38] often had to hold the geological fort for him, which she did with aplomb. 'She ... had a great presence and authority in the lecture hall,' noted a former student, 'which she quickly established over even the rowdiest of classes', which were 90% male.[39] It might be suggested that in doing so, she displayed the durability and lustre of mathiasite, the mineral which was named after her for her ground-breaking research on this alkaline rock.

Some of the findings of the escalating research in the department fed directly into its revamped Honours course, but undergraduate courses remained focused on teaching the rapidly evolving techniques of geological investigation and analysis to would-be geologists and basic geology to would-be civil engineers and land surveyors.

In one sense, the greater impact on the department of its burgeoning research was on its accommodation capacity. By 1968 researchers attached to the department outnumbered the lecturers by seven to five, and additional floors and wings had to be added to house them and their equipment. They were active in seven major research programmes thanks to funding from the state's Department of Mines, the CSIR, mining houses, the Atomic Energy Board and the Geological Survey. By playing to its locational strengths, especially under Simpson, the department had struck gold, figuratively speaking that is.

Even more effective in taking advantage of its location in Cape Town was the brand-new Department of Oceanography. A composite scientific study of the ocean through a variety of disciplinary lenses, oceanography had begun to appear in universities in Europe and North America between the wars. But in South Africa it was not until the new Principal, T.B. Davie, started to push for such a department at UCT in 1948 that lobbying began in earnest.[40] Cape Town's proximity to three oceans and the country's main fishing grounds and the presence in the Peninsula of marine research expertise and facilities made UCT 'the ideal spot for the establishment of a school of oceanography', he argued.[41] His call brought the fledgling Oceanographic Division of the CSIR's National Physical Research Laboratory, which concentrated on marine data collection, to a rented room at UCT in 1954, but it was not until 1958 that the Government eventually approved the creation of the country's first chair of oceanography at UCT, to lead the co-ordination of marine research on campus.

In anticipation of this, UCT's marine scientists had already secured and equipped a wooden ex-trawler as a research vessel – it was named *John. D. Gilchrist* after UCT's founding marine zoologist[42] – and set up a loose umbrella body, the grandly named Institute of Oceanography, to allow everyone with an interest in matters marine to share ideas and resources. But focusing these interests proved difficult in the face of competing disciplinary agendas from fields like marine biology, marine geology and marine geochemistry and UCT's inability to find a suitable candidate to fill the new chair.

Finally, it was decided to appoint a visiting professor to get the new department off the ground, a task which both incumbents, Leopoldo Trotti (1959–61) and Jack Darbyshire (1961–2), found problematic because of the competing ambitions of the other departments. In its early years, therefore, the new department was very much an instrument for existing marine disciplines; indeed, Darbyshire was succeeded by the empire-building Eric Simpson as acting head of Oceanography until 1965. One of the most powerful marine scientists at UCT, John Day of Zoology, put it bluntly when he said that he believed that oceanography was 'not a "Department" in the ordinary sense of the word, but supplies research facilities in Botany, Civil Engineering, Electrical Engineering, Geology, Land Surveying and Zoology'.[43]

Since the CSIR held a similar view of the new 'department', it was not slow to give it substance by providing funding for three research units to be located there, one to examine a range of oceanographic questions from different disciplinary perspectives, one on marine effluents and one specifically on South Africa's oceans. By 1968, fifteen researchers from several disciplines were employed in these projects, all under the auspices of the Department of Oceanography whose own research direction was determined by a steering committee made up of heads of 'marine' departments, a CSIR representative and, from 1966, the captain of the *John D. Gilchrist*'s successor, the custom-built *Thomas B. Davie*. It was not a situation calculated

*In-depth research. UCT's oceanographic research vessel, Thomas B. Davie, leaving Table Bay, circa 1966.*

to give the department a distinctive role, direction or character of its own, except as a convenient location for and administration of the marine research of others. Indeed, not until 1966, when the chair was finally filled by a permanent appointee for the first time, the 52-year-old Captain John Mallory, a former head of the South African Navy's Hydrographic Research Unit, did the department begin to emerge out of the shadow of other departments.

Calm and unflappable, Mallory started to carve out a research niche for the department itself by concentrating on waves and tides, especially 'rogue waves' off the south-east coast and wave action, and effluent pollution at possible sites for a nuclear power station on the west coast. He also undertook to add teaching to the department's activities. A CSIR oceanographer, Sandy Harris, was appointed senior lecturer in 1967 and the first undergraduate course in oceanography in the country was offered to 22 eager students. The ascent from being a backwater of oceanography to being in the mainstream of the subject had begun.

As already indicated, John Day, professor of zoology from 1946 to 1974, was a deeply committed marine biologist.[44] 'His life was zoology', observed a colleague accurately about this single-minded workaholic.[45] Because the loss of a leg in World War II more or less ruled out continuing the intertidal research he had been doing in the 1930s, when he assumed the chair in 1946 he turned his attention to estuaries and their ecology. With the assistance of the CSIR, he began an ambitious survey of South Africa's 43 estuaries, and from then on sought to press every new member of his department to become involved in either this project or another with marine connections. Given his position as head of the department and his forceful personality – postgraduates spoke of dreading sessions with him as they were 'like the Inquisition'[46] – few were able to resist, with the result that the department not only consolidated its longstanding reputation as a centre of marine biology, but also made estuarine ecology a recognised field of study. Out of his project many of the basic concepts of estuarine ecology were formulated thanks to his sharp insights, making his (and UCT's) name known among marine biologists 'from Vladivostok to Valparaiso', as a fellow biologist put it.[47]

As his own primary research was done early on, when data-gathering and taxonomy were the priority, it tended to be descriptive in character; thereafter, however, he steered the project in a more analytical direction, insisting that his students and colleagues adopt a rigorously quantitative approach to the bank of data accumulated by then. By doing so he put his indelible stamp on estuarine ecology locally and beyond, summed up in his 1981 synthesis, *Estuarine Ecology, with Particular Reference to Southern Africa*. His other major work, a monumental monograph on aquatic worms, had been published in 1967.[48] As an obituary judged, 'His work will be quoted as long as there are marine scientists and his findings referred to in textbooks as long as there are students of the subject.'[49] Fittingly, he was hailed as 'South Africa's leading marine biologist' on his death in 1989;[50] equally fittingly, UCT named its new Zoology Building after him soon thereafter.

Complementing his estuarine work were the studies of sandy beach ecology by his erstwhile research assistant and eventual successor as head of the department, Alec Brown. Although Brown was overshadowed as a scholar by his mentor, whom he found 'quick to criticise, sparing in praise'[51] and 'dictatorial and inflexible',[52] he did outdo Day as a lecturer, displaying a flair for delivering lectures which were fluent, engaging, challenging and witty. He 'stimulated debate and was a great encouragement to me to try and think outside the box', recalled one of his students.[53] He challenged us 'to think beyond the facts to the history, concepts and philosophies that underpin science', added another.[54] It comes as no surprise, therefore, to find that he was selected as one of the first recipients of UCT's Distinguished Teacher Award, the student nominators declaring that it was 'a privilege to attend' his lectures.[55]

Not all of Zoology's staff succumbed to the call of the sea, however. Gerry Broekhuysen, whose Leiden doctorate had indeed been in marine biology, switched his attention to birds, establishing a reputation as an ornithologist who was equally at home talking to students, avid amateur birdwatchers or radio audiences.[56] From 1960 he was joined in his avian enthusiasm by three researchers in the new Percy FitzPatrick Institute for African Ornithology, which had been endowed by the FitzPatrick Trust[57] at the behest of Percy FitzPatrick's daughter. Though independent of the Zoology Department until 1973, the Institute was accommodated, very appropriately, in a wing added to the Zoology Building in 1960.

Even more averse to marine research was Broekhuysen's fellow Dutchman Bob Krijgsman, for he was an experimental physiologist interested in terrestrial invertebrates, a speciality which he made the basis of a separate undergraduate course in 'General Physiology' in the department in 1960 and on which he published dozens of papers. Indeed, a colleague believed that 'the whole subject of invertebrate physiology would have been the poorer had he turned his talents elsewhere'.[58]

What this did mean was that, for all its focus on marine research, the Zoology Department was able to offer comprehensive undergraduate courses which effectively covered creatures on land, sea and air. This fact the syllabus reflected well: students were required to dissect worms, snails, cockroaches, dogfish, frogs, rabbits and pigeons – animal ethics only began to emerge as a consideration in the late 1970s – in order to understand their anatomy, physiology, histology and morphology. It was like 'almost all the Ten Plagues', quipped one undergraduate,[59] before going on to study elementary genetics, embryology, animal behaviour and ecology. This broad range of topics was necessary because over half of all first-years in the department were medical students or would-be medical students trying to get into the Faculty of Medicine by taking a BSc first. Few of either had an interest in non-human creatures as such. Perceptively, however, one noticed that 'Along the way we … [were] learning the basic medical way of thinking: studying living systems from simple to complex, small to large, part to whole'.[60]

Medical students and aspiring medical students aside, the department's first-year classes consisted mainly of Science students with a bent for nature. As environmental awareness began to develop around the world in the 1960s, creating job opportunities in this field, so their number grew. By 1969 there were as many non-medical students taking Zoology I as medics – twenty years earlier the latter had outnumbered the former by almost three to one – while the 27 majoring in Zoology in that year were nearly three times the 1949 figure. Pointing in the same direction was the growth of postgraduates in the 1960s, most of whose research was, not unexpectedly, marine in nature.

The common maritime focus and the camaraderie it engendered, especially during field trips to sites like Langebaan Lagoon, fostered good staff–student relations, what one described as 'a social and an academic nexus'.[61] On John Day's instructions, every senior undergraduate was given her or his own bench in the laboratory, a staff–student tea club was organised, and 'every effort' was made 'to connect with each of us in the class'.[62] It was, reflected an erstwhile student, 'a discipline-based enculturation process'.[63]

The *esprit de corps* which such initiatives produced gave the department an excellent reputation among its students who felt it cared about them, and generated 'a real buzz'.[64] In 1966 it was the only department in the Science Faculty to build a Rag float. 'The bar was set high in our Department', reflected a high-achieving student of the time, but 'an extraordinary … level of support [was] provided … We were co-operating, not competing.' As a result, he concluded, 'there were rich benefits for us and the department.'[65]

In short, it is clear that the department's international stature rested, ultimately, on very effective teamwork marshalled and directed by John Day in a most congenial environment, in all senses of the phrase.

Equally favoured by its location on the south-western tip of Africa was the Department of Botany, which had made the flora of the Cape Peninsula its primary focus of research during the long tenure (1923–50) of Robert Adamson as Bolus Professor of Botany.[66] This culminated in the publication in 1950 of *Flora of the Cape Peninsula*, which he co-authored and to which seven members of department and the Bolus Herbarium contributed, making it a landmark in the history of both the department and of botany itself in South Africa, just as the Cape floral kingdom was being identified as one of the six floral kingdoms of the world.

Perhaps it was awe at Adamson's achievement and the magnitude of the task of extending it to the rest of the Cape kingdom that made his two successors, William Edwyn Isaac (1951–61) and Wilhelm Lütjeharms (1962–71), avoid keeping the department on the same, single-minded path after 1950, instead leaving the further investigation of Western Cape fynbos largely to the Bolus Herbarium across the road, to the Kirstenbosch National Botanical Garden and to the avid amateurs of the Botanical Society.

Isaac, a 46-year-old Cardiff graduate who had been professor at Rhodes University, was mainly interested in marine algae like seaweed, while the 55-year-old Lütjeharms had spent a quarter-century specialising in soil microbiology at the University of the Orange Free State before coming to UCT in 1962. Neither was a dynamic lecturer nor a drawcard as a researcher around whom students eagerly clustered. The department now 'needs someone at the head who can restore discipline and provide inspiration for both staff and students', commented a departmental insider after Isaac left for Nairobi in 1961,[67] while Lütjeharms, a leading South African botanist advised UCT, was not 'somebody who would put your Botany Department on the map, after having been unable to do so for more than 20 years in Bloemfontein'.[68] He did not show 'any marked interest outside his specialized field of research', warned another botanist, who doubted 'the degree to which he inspires students and junior staff'.[69]

Consequently, in the absence of leadership, drive and a clear idea of the direction in which the department should be gearing its research, in the 1950s and 1960s botanical research at UCT lost focus and wilted. Isaac justified this by arguing that the department's activities had become 'more diversified'.[70] The contrast with its neighbour in the building, the Department of Zoology, could not have been more marked. MSc and PhD numbers levelled off and collaboration with Kirstenbosch declined. The formal contribution to the department by Kirstenbosch's director, Brian Rycroft (who was simultaneously Pearson Professor of Botany at UCT), was limited to six hours' teaching per week, while most of the non-professorial staff appointed to the department in these years were not inclined to turn such individual research as they did into large research projects which attracted postgraduates. The one significant exception to this was the 'bright spark in the department',[71] the ebullient and charismatic Ted Schelpe, who made a botanical mark for his work on ferns, mosses and orchids, but whose potential to expand this into something much bigger was limited by his appointment as curator of the Bolus Herbarium in 1956, in succession to the formidable 'Ma' Bolus.[72] Even so, until his death at the age of 61 in 1985, Schelpe and the Herbarium staff did offer some guidance to the few keen postgraduates working on plant taxonomy, especially once the Herbarium was amalgamated with the department after Schelpe became its curator. Teatimes there generated rich and lively discussion led by the high-spirited Schelpe –'it was more like being in a seminar', recalled one postgraduate participant enthusiastically. 'It made up for the disappointing [Botany] Department.'[73] As a result, in the 1960s Schelpe and the assistant curator, Anthony Hall, supervised nearly a third of all postgraduate theses in botany at UCT.

Schelpe and Hall also contributed to undergraduate teaching in the Botany Department's senior courses, Schelpe's 'sink or swim' approach to his students (drawing on his Oxford experience) causing dismay among those not up to scratch. One remembered 'the tall, lanky figure of Professor E.A.C.L.E. "Ted" Schelpe striding through Kirstenbosch or the Caledon Wild-Flower reserve plucking flowers from bushes and flinging them back to some hapless student with the demand that the specimen be identified, at least to Family if not Genus level'.[74] Other lecturers in the department were more sedate in how they taught, offering less memorable fare in ways which ranged from the solid but laboured to the dense. The impression left lastingly on a senior student was that they were 'uncaring and indifferent as both lecturers and researchers. The department was a disappointment to me.'[75]

What did remain in students' memories, however, were two things: the variety of fresh botanical specimens always laid out for them in the laboratory, courtesy of the department's long-serving laboratory attendant, Abel Jacobs, who had collected them either from the slopes above UCT's main buildings or from his own garden; and the department's field trips for senior students who, rhapsodised one, were thus 'brought face to face with an incredible range of adaptive strategies as well as divergent communities, all in a stimulating convivial atmosphere'.[76] Clearly, as in the case of Zoology's camps, these trips, whether to the department's research stations in Bain's Kloof or Cape Point or to a hut in Namaqualand or the Little Karoo, all fostered congenial staff–student relations and opened the eyes of many a student to the wider biome. They were 'fundamental to getting me to see the bigger picture and in thereby changing my direction', reflected a professor in the department who had studied there 35 years earlier.[77] Another student of this era recalled that the botanical changes she saw on ecological and taxonomic trips to Bain's Kloof from year to year 'made quite an impression on me'.[78]

The contents of the department's courses for Science students aimed to equip them with theoretical and practical knowledge of the key elements of plant science, with a special emphasis on taxonomy, not surprisingly, given UCT's location in what a Canadian botanist enviously described as 'the floristically most unique corner of the world'.[79] To this, genetics and ecology at a very basic level were added in the 1960s, in keeping with the developing interest in these areas internationally.

For the sake of the 100–150 first-year medical students who took the special half-course in botany, the contents of that course excluded most taxonomic matter and instead placed emphasis on floral anatomy, physiology and microbiology. The lecturer concerned hoped that doing this would overcome medical students' perception that botany was 'merely a nuisance, a subject which ... had to be taken and ... passed before they could proceed to the real business which had brought them to the University'. It did not and, for the said lecturer, the medics remained 'as something of a challenge' to teach,[80] not least because of their adolescent pranks in class, which often produced 'a barrage of paper darts, from the back rows!'[81]

Yet, however burdensome such service teaching might be to the department – 'only an infrequent [medical] student ... [had] a real love of the subject', lamented one lecturer[82] – it was essential, for only a handful of the 100–160 Science students taking Botany I went on to Botany II and III. In 1968, for example, only six of the first-year intake of 151 two years previously enrolled for Botany III. The department was not blooming.

Yet, one member of the Botany Department, Dorothea Olivier, did teach in a budding sub-department in these years. Flowing from watershed inventions like the electron microscope and discoveries like antibiotics, viruses and DNA, microbiology had emerged in the 1930s as an exciting cross-disciplinary field of study globally. World War II accelerated its development and, recognising this, in 1947 UCT became the first university in the country to introduce a distinct course in microbiology. Conceived, very unusually for UCT as a composite course[83] for third-year students only, it initially consisted of a quarter each of bacteriology, mycology, protozoology and chemistry, taught by academics from those departments. In 1958 chemistry was replaced by sections devoted to virology and the ecology of micro-organisms as these were deemed to be closer to the career paths of most students.

Along with these changes in the course's content went a tightening of its structure so as to co-ordinate its separate components better. Olivier was officially appointed the one lecturer in the department and gradually began to extend her microbiological knowledge beyond that of fungi to the other areas covered by the course so that she could make connections between them more effectively and even teach the full course if need be. But further bypassing of UCT's formal structures was not permitted and, on paper at least, the shadow department had to have a professorial head. Lütjeharms readily assented to assuming this position as acting head, for he was first and foremost a soil microbiologist; indeed, this may have been the deciding factor in his selection as professor of botany despite the negative comments about his capacity to lead research.

Once he was in his position, his intentions were clear: to turn microbiology into a fully fledged department with its own professor and to develop a graduate school in the subject. To his mind, 'a subject in which no doctor's degree can be awarded should, therefore, in principle, not belong in a university'.[84] Given the rising number of students taking the course – 29 by 1967 – he was able to achieve the latter aim when Honours and Master's degrees in microbiology were introduced; his former goal he accomplished in 1970 when he was himself appointed as the first full-time professor of microbiology at UCT. Personal ambition and scientific development had thus worked together to turn a cross-disciplinary field of study into an academic discipline in its own right at UCT.

In some ways geography followed a similar path to academic acceptance at UCT. For over a dozen years before a chair of geography was finally established at UCT in 1936, its claim to be a respectable academic discipline and not just a subject taught at school had been debated back and forth on campus. Thus, when the 28-year-old

*How a subject grows on you. A cartoonist's view of ardent Botany students and staff* (Varsity, 5 August 1964)

Bill Talbot took up the chair in 1936, both he and his subject were, in a sense, on probation.[85] By 1948 both had passed the scrutiny of his fellow professors with flying colours.

In effect the one person in a one-person department until 1946, Talbot buried himself in his teaching, as, gradually and without grandstanding, he extended his department's base and, critically, its student intake. In many ways he moulded a department in his own image, unobtrusive, hard-working, politically innocent and frugal, while his wife, Anne-Marie, herself a Berkeley graduate in geography, was often inspanned at short notice to help with teaching.

To bolster student numbers, Talbot eventually persuaded four Science departments to accept geography as one of the auxiliary subjects to be taken by students majoring in their disciplines, while a new course in economic geography was introduced to draw in BCom students. Even though he did not build up a graduate school about him, he persisted in what a history of the department calls 'his gentle but relentless cultivation of a rich and fertile foundation on which his Department grew and, eventually, flourished'.[86]

His own research, pursued with the same single-minded zeal, reflected his holistic, regional view of geography, best demonstrated in his painstakingly compiled magnum opus, *Atlas of the Union of South Africa*. In 598 hand-drawn maps it mapped the country in physical, demographic and economic terms. Modestly funded by the state's National Council for Social Research, which welcomed the fact that Talbot 'likes to do a job of work for the job's sake and not for the remuneration he may receive' and that by getting him to do 'the donkey work, the Government have saved a considerable sum of money',[87] the atlas appeared with a telling green-and-gold cover in 1960, just in time for the Union's 50th anniversary. 'The Department is purring with satisfaction' at its publication, reported the Students' Science Society.[88] Seen by a senior civil servant as a ready tool 'of incalculable value'[89] to inform state policy-making, it offered a visualised, official view of apartheid-era South Africa.

Perhaps it is an indication of Talbot's lack of pushfulness on behalf of his staff that only three of the eight lecturers appointed between 1948 and 1968 stayed there for more than five years. 'We need some stability – men [*sic*] who will not too soon be attracted by higher salaries, family ties, or other considerations elsewhere', he sighed unreflectively at one point.[90]

Not surprisingly, all three shared Talbot's conception of geography and his commitment to teaching. Jack Mabbutt (1948–56) viewed the geography of the world through a holistic, regional lens, as is evident in the multidisciplinary volume on *The Cape Peninsula* which he edited in time for the 1952 Van Riebeeck Tercentenary Festival. David Hywel Davies (1955–65), an Aberystwyth graduate, applied an even tighter lens, focusing specifically on Cape Town's central business district, before leaving UCT in 1966 to take the chair of geography at the new University of Zambia, where his competence, conscientiousness and cartographic skill matched that of his mentor, Talbot. A similar knack as a teacher, both at the lectern and in the mapping laboratory, was the hallmark of the longest-staying lecturer in the department, Laurence Impey. 'Work which other instructors made a chore [for students], Impey has made a pleasure', enthused Talbot.[91] This Impey continued doing ever reliably until his retirement in 1983, 27 years after joining the department.

In a syllabus devised by Talbot to provide a broader conspectus of physical, human and economic geography in Europe and its colonies than at any other South African university, cartography – both reading and drawing maps – featured prominently. 'You would go out into the field with your surveying instruments … to plot where things were in the landscape,' recalled a colleague of Talbot's, 'then come back and give it to the [department's two professional] cartographers [to draw]. Otherwise you'd work from aerial photographs.'[92] For classroom teaching a very extensive map collection was built up and on this Talbot did not stint. The collection was used by several departments besides Geography. 'Lecturers would come to the map unit [from all over the University] to book out great big, hanging wall maps. If you were giving a lecture on China you'd want the wall map of China, if you were a visiting lecturer from America, you'd want the map of the United States.'[93] Indeed, so large did the map collection become that, before the department could move from its cramped quarters in the Geology Building to a spacious home on the top floor of the Beattie Building in 1965, the whole of that top floor had to be strengthened to bear the weight of all the maps in their steel cabinets.

Maps were thus synonymous with Talbot's department. Talbot's 'enthusiasm for maps rubbed off on me', observed a former student. 'I can remember drawing map projections and also learning to plane-table survey on Rondebosch Common. This prepared me well for work as an assistant map research officer, my first graduate job in the UK.'[94] The map collection itself was under the watchful eye of a man whose official position of laboratory attendant bore little relation to what he actually did in the department. The Talbots aside, Samuel Johnson was the longest-serving member of the department (1939–82), a stalwart in the laboratory, the map unit, the darkroom, the departmental library and the meteorological instrument section. A 'Who's Who in the Geography Department' distributed to students in 1974 described him as 'guide, philosopher, and friend' to all students and 'the most indispensable member of the staff'.[95]

In a small, homely department whose student enrolments did not top 100 until 1955 and 200 until 1967 – one student called it 'the poor relation' of the Faculty[96] – relations between the three to four academics and students were close and, generally, cordial. A lively Students' Geographical Society was established in 1958, in which staff were equally welcome, a camaraderie which the introduction of field excursions in 1966 only enhanced. Moreover, since most of the students planned to become geography teachers in schools, the bond between them and the department lasted beyond their departure for the Faculty of Education. Only in the 1970s, with the growth of environmental awareness worldwide, did the character and size of the department's student body begin to alter, along with the very conception of geography and its purpose. Talbot's retirement in 1973 marked the end, not just of his academic career, but also of an era of modest, make-do geographical studies at UCT.

If the Geography Department enjoyed the benefits of being small and close-knit, Mathematics had to confront the costs of being by far the biggest department in the Faculty of Science, servicing a very wide range of students. At its maximum size when its two components, Pure Mathematics and Applied Mathematics, were loosely combined into a single Department of Mathematics (1949–61) because one of the chairs could not be filled on a long-term basis, its student enrolment topped 1400. Some 60% of these were from Engineering and Land Surveying, 10% from Commerce and 30% from the Faculties of Arts and Science. Almost all were male.

With an academic staff of 22, plus 8 to 10 student demonstrators, teaching 31 distinct undergraduate and postgraduate courses, it was unwieldy to administer and difficult to keep in line, especially as the two departments retained a significant degree of autonomy. One head of the department recalled how 'responsibilities, distractions and crises … almost hourly beset the person who is bearing the strain as head'.[97]

Therefore, almost as soon as two new professors, Keith Househam and Dennis Parkyn, had been appointed in 1961, the composite department was again divided into its two components, Pure Mathematics and Applied Mathematics, because, as one of them explained, 'the combined department was found to be too large to administer efficiently'.[98] From then on the two departments were independent of each other, although their disciplinary kinship meant that they liaised on matters of common interest. In 1966 this binary existence was expanded to accommodate a third mathematical offshoot, Mathematical Statistics, which had mushroomed from a single course in the Pure Mathematics Department to an autonomous department in its own right as a result of UCT's belated recognition that statistics was not just another application of mathematics, but a discipline in its own right, the wave of the future in science, social science, business, medicine and engineering. It had become far more than just 'the grammar of science', as Karl Pearson called it in 1892. Clearly demonstrating this, by 1969 the three-year-old Department of Mathematical Statistics (as it was called until 1991) had nearly 700 students from the Faculties of Engineering and Commerce in its six courses. In that year too, its first professor, the 33-year-old wunderkind Cas Troskie set up a Statistics and Operations Research Laboratory in the department, where his staff and senior students dealt with an escalating number of requests for advice on statistical problems from all over the University. There has been a 'phenomenal increase in the demand for courses in Statistics', noted the Science Faculty approvingly.[99]

Unlike Troskie, an Afrikaner with degrees from Pretoria University and Unisa, whose father was dismayed to see his son take a chair at 'liberal' UCT, three of the four men who occupied the other mathematics chairs at UCT before 1961 had been trained in the Oxbridge mathematical tradition in Britain. This was evident from the inclusion of stodgy, Cambridge-style topics in the pure mathematics syllabus and of classical mechanics in the applied mathematics syllabus, from their ongoing preference for an instruction-by-demonstration mode of course delivery – 'lecturers in Mathematics use more chalk and more square feet of blackboard than any other class', it was observed wryly[100] – and from the use of tutorials to learn by doing, in which students had to solve dozens of problems by themselves, with a senior student available to help if necessary. With deliberate ambiguity, one student dubbed them 'regular problem classes'.[101]

Of the four professors, the two applied mathematicians, Anton Hales (1949–54) and Dennis Parkyn (1962–71), were respectively Cambridge and Oxford graduates.[102]

It was while at Cambridge that Hales's interest in geophysics had been kindled by his supervisor, the theoretical geoscientist Harold Jeffreys, an interest which proved to be the lodestar for a career which took him from the chair at UCT to the directorship of the Bernard Price Institute for Geophysical Research at the University of the Witwatersrand, and then to head geoscience centres in Dallas and Canberra. While he was at UCT, however, he was hard put to do much work in this field as his time and energy were consumed by a heavy teaching load (which included his new option in theoretical geophysics) and by having, as its first head, to weld together the new, composite Department of Mathematics and simultaneously rebuild its Pure Mathematics division after its ten years under a professor ill-suited to headship.[103] One of the ways Hales sought to achieve this was by drawing the staff together over tea, a simple but effective strategy for social and intellectual bonding. But he left UCT before this initiative could bear significant fruit. By the time that his 36-year-old successor, Parkyn, was eventually appointed, the composite Mathematics Department had been split in two again, restoring the formal division between them. This remained in place until their re-merger in 1995.

That it took eight years before Parkyn was appointed indicates the difficulty that UCT had in filling the chair, for it had made several attempts before this to do so, all in vain. Indeed, appointing Parkyn – who lacked both a doctorate and what a senior colleague called 'stature as a mathematician'[104] – underlines how desperate UCT had become, for his own research on elasticity was peripheral and his publication record thin. In his favour, however, was a good reputation as a teacher and a keen interest in two then-emerging topics, satellite orbits and computers. It was in the latter field that he was soon making a name for himself at UCT, introducing a course on 'Numerical Analysis and Computation' as 'an introduction to the analysis of numerical problems and their solution by means of high speed digital computers'[105] and advising the University on the acquisition of its first computer. He was, acknowledged a fellow professor, 'one of the University's officers best informed on the technicalities of computer matters'.[106] Not surprisingly, in 1971 he was offered UCT's new chair of computer science without it being advertised. He accepted.

In Pure Mathematics (or Mathematics, as it was titled from 1964 since its proud head believed, 'It is in no need of a rather absurd little adjective to save it from confusion with something else'[107]), both professors, Douglas Sears (1950–61) and Keith Househam (1961–84), had gained their first degrees at the University of the Witwatersrand before studying further abroad, Sears at Oxford and Househam at Princeton. At Oxford Sears had blossomed under the influence of the renowned mathematical analyst E.C. Titchmarsh, who drew him into the world of differential equations, a field on which he continued to focus for the rest of his career as both researcher and teacher. As a teacher, he was known for being able to pitch his lectures at the right level for the audience before him, be they first-year engineers or third-year mathematics majors. A bright tutor in the department praised him for teaching not only mathematics, 'but also how to be mathematicians'.[108] Titchmarsh felt that 'He has much originality and infinite patience',[109] the latter trait standing him in particularly good stead during the years he headed the joint Department of Mathematics (1954–61) in succession to Hales.

The 43-year-old Househam's ascent to the chair of pure mathematics was much slower than that of his predecessor, the 32-year-old Sears. Househam had returned from Princeton without a doctorate, a lack that he did not remedy during the 36 years (1948–84) that he was on the department's permanent academic staff. 'He has the capacity for good research', noted Sears, 'but needs to be pushed into it.'[110] However, in a department hard pressed by teaching demands, he was not, and had to admit in his application for the chair in 1961, 'I do not as yet have any publications to my credit.'[111]

Instead, it was into teaching that he poured his energies, delivering elegant and well-crafted lectures in courses spanning all years. He is 'most thorough and sound and he teaches systematically, so that students do not get bewildered', enthused one student. 'The discipline of his classes was always excellent.'[112]

To this commitment to teaching he added an even greater commitment to administration once appointed to the chair in 1961. Determined to rebuild a languishing department – five posts were vacant in that year, the first-year failure rate was over 40% and the number of postgraduates tiny – he set about doing so by improving the quality of thesis supervision so as to develop an attractive postgraduate school from which he could recruit a new generation of staff, a pressing necessity given the chronic shortage of suitable staff in the country and the difficulty of drawing foreigners to UCT because of the political situation in South Africa. It was necessary, he argued, 'to attract young men [*sic*] into the posts. To direct them, inspire them, train them and let them mature.'[113] To address the high failure rate, he secured a large grant from the UCT Foundation to overhaul the tutorial system so as to allow more one-on-one contact between weak students and tutors, while elsewhere in the department his imperious, hyper-meticulous approach to administration became ubiquitous. 'He is not an easy person to work with, either for those above or those below him', commented a senior colleague. 'In exercising authority he seems to antagonise people very easily.'[114] A colleague labelled him simply as 'a martinet'.[115]

For Househam himself, the end – of reviving his department – justified the means, even if the personal cost he had to pay was high. Thus, even though he was not especially interested in computers, he agreed to become the first director of UCT's new Computer Centre in 1964,[116] so that UCT (and thus his own department) would not lag behind other universities in this respect. So as to be able to perform this role effectively, he withdrew his application for study leave in that year, explaining, 'the welfare of the department means more to me'.[117]

Paradoxically, therefore, it was as steered by two doctorate-less, publication-thin professors, Parkyn and Househam, that the two recently sundered departments were recast. In this formative task the two powerful professors were assisted by three long-serving associate professors, all of whom were fine as teachers but unproductive as researchers. In (Pure) Mathematics, the veteran number theorist Stanley Skewes[118] continued to deliver challenging but clear lectures laced with puckish humour; in Applied Mathematics Martin Pollard[119] followed a similar path until his early death in 1960. But, for the third associate professor, Michael Whiteman, it was not a lack of research that was a barrier to promotion, but doing research of the wrong sort, for he was entranced by psychical research and mysticism on which he wrote two books and numerous articles before his retirement in 1971. 'If this work had been in a mathematical field', admitted Sears, 'I should have had no hesitation in proposing that Dr Whiteman be promoted ... I am however incompetent to judge the value of these publications as academic work.'[120] Yet, though disappointed by the failure of their numerous applications for promotion, the three of them remained stalwarts of the teaching arm of mathematics at UCT.

Not that good teaching was confined to the upper rungs of the academic ladder. Lecturers appointed specifically for their teaching ability like Christie Feros, Ian McArthur, David Allison and three of the four women on the permanent staff before 1970, Johanna Alma, Helene Kipps and Kathleen Pay, enjoyed a deserved reputation for their skill in implanting a grasp of mathematics into struggling first-year engineering students. 'My lecturing style was more one of [school] teaching', reflected Pay. 'You taught them how to pass. I think my methods were effective as in one year we had seven firsts!'[121]

From the mid-1960s their ranks began to be supplemented by UCT-trained mathematicians who were not only teachers, but keen researchers too, for example Ronnie Becker, John Webb, Stephen Schach and Douglas Butterworth. Since three of these were to spend their entire careers at UCT after returning with higher degrees from abroad, it is clear that Househam's 'grow your own timber' policy was beginning to bear fruit.

But, Househam knew, some diversity of training was equally necessary if the department was to raise its reputation nationally and attract postgraduates. Accordingly, between 1963 and 1965, he appointed three young lecturers with no prior contact with UCT, Hartmut Schlagbauer, Wesley Kotzé and Guillaume Brummer, graduates respectively of Frankfurt, of Stellenbosch and McGill, and of Stellenbosch and Amsterdam. Since all three had a research interest in the same broad area, topology, and since this coincided with that of a slightly older non-UCT graduate who had been on the staff since 1958, Keith Hardie, a common research focus for at least four members of the department began to crystallise, to very good effect. In 1966 Hardie started a Topology Research Seminar, which grew into a formal Topology Research Group six years later, and which set him on a path to national and international recognition in the 1970s.

It is therefore not a surprise to discover that topology featured prominently in postgraduate coursework in the 1960s as part of what the prospectus proudly labelled 'modern mathematics' to distinguish it from the stolid Cambridge-style mathematics taught in the department between the wars.

The undergraduate pure mathematics syllabus showed similar modernisation, largely thanks to the influence of modern American math. The adoption as textbooks of several volumes from the Van Nostrand University Series in Higher Mathematics published in New York points in the same direction.

Not that keeping up to date was contingent on the staff reading the latest American textbooks. Subscriptions to the leading mathematical journals kept those who read them abreast of their subject, while, on paper at least, there were enough mathematicians and physicists on campus who had studied abroad to develop what an advert for a post in the department optimistically termed 'a lively corporate mathematical life'.[122] Pure mathematics research was purely abstract and required neither equipment nor fieldwork – there were 'no local problems to be done', acknowledged Sears[123] – while most projects in applied mathematics required little more than 'paper, pen and ink in large quantities together with a still larger amount of patience', observed Parkyn.[124] The only significant costs were for electric desk calculators and a computer, both of which were paid for by the University. Moreover, staff enjoyed priority in using them. As a student in the Numerical Analysis and Computing course in 1968 ruefully recalled, he was allowed two minutes a day on UCT's new ICL 1301 computer to feed in his punch cards. 'If you succeeded, you would print out the result; if you didn't, come back tomorrow.'[125] Staff, however, were permitted a second attempt on the same day if their first failed.

Yet for the majority of students encountering difficulty in one or both of the mathematics departments – most were from the Faculty of Engineering – it was not privileged access to calculators and computers that was the obstacle, but the issue of what they felt was the inappropriateness of some of what was taught, especially the theory of statics and dynamics and the mathematical analysis of problems. On occasions, a combination of a particularly high failure rate, rumblings among students and questions from the Faculty of Engineering as to whether it should take over the teaching of engineering mathematics brought this unhappiness to a head, prompting Parkyn to revise the applied mathematics courses so as to make them more pertinent to the needs of Engineering Faculty students. Even so, he admitted that he could not discover 'what the engineers in fact really want'.[126] Househam, on the other hand, roundly rejected any such reorientation of the pure mathematics courses, declaring, 'The argument that engineering students should be taught only what is relevant is a dangerous one … A university must teach broad scientific principles from which the practising engineer himself should adapt and apply what is relevant from time to time … I would suggest that it is wiser to leave the teaching of pure Mathematics to the pure mathematicians.'[127] It was a response entirely in character, and one whose like would be heard many times in the next twenty years in the Faculty of Science and beyond as he sought to safeguard the interests of his cherished department against all-comers.

Only one department in the Faculty of Science serviced a wider range of other faculties than did Mathematics, and that was the Department of Logic and Psychology, as it was known until 1951, when Logic was moved both in name and content to the Philosophy Department. Both its pre-1951 title and its location in the Faculty of Science stemmed from the department's origin in the escalating captivation by the subject of its first professor, the philosopher-turned-psychologist Hugh Reyburn.[128] By 1920 the persuasive Reyburn had convinced UCT that Logic should be excised from Philosophy and combined with his new love, psychology, into a novel Department of Logic and Psychology, making it the second university psychology department in South Africa. Adroitly he ensured that it had a building of its own which included laboratories, a clear sign to all that the new discipline was a fully fledged science. Its location in the Faculty of Science, where allocating funds for equipment was standard practice, was an obvious, desirable corollary.

The growing recognition in the academic world of psychology as a respectable university subject meant that, by the 1940s, five UCT faculties had incorporated it in some form into their curricula. Thus, its standard courses were taken by students from the Faculties of Arts, Science and Social Science, while its staff also taught special courses in the Faculties of Education and Medicine. Given this range of students, it is not surprising that one head of the department complained that most of the students taking courses in psychology lacked even elementary scientific training and were 'therefore seriously handicapped by having to acquire the basic habits of scientific thinking before they can begin to grasp the subject'.[129]

Scientifically unprepared they may have been, but their steadily growing number helped the department put down firm roots and rid itself of the perception that it was a soft option, far removed from the real world. Indeed, to some it seemed to have the potential to help fashion a fresh foundation on which a more secure post-war world might be built. As one such student recalled this mood, 'Old moral certainties were being exposed as dangerous delusions, and if one was young enough, the challenge of "year zero": building a better world could be experienced as very real.'[130] By 1955 the department was teaching 200 undergraduates from five faculties, a figure which rose to 312 ten years later and to 460 in 1970. A significant growth in the number of postgraduate students began only in the early 1960s, as the demand for clinical and industrial psychologists began to grow and psychology itself became a recognised profession in South Africa. As Reyburn would have hoped, the subject was at last being transformed 'from a marginal academic discipline to a fully-fledged profession whose technical expertise was in great demand'.[131]

Reyburn's own interest in his later years was largely in human personality and in determining its foundations by multiple factor analysis. Although his ability to pursue research in this field was curtailed by a serious stroke in 1937, during the next thirteen years until his death in 1950 he co-authored six scholarly articles applying factor analysis to personality. Notwithstanding this achievement, he was but a shadow of the dynamic lecturer and researcher he had once been.

It was not until 1955 that UCT was able to find a suitable successor, for the salary it could offer during the years of financial stringency until then was uninviting compared to professorial pay scales in Britain and North America. Not surprisingly therefore, the appointee, the 38-year-old Kenneth Hall, came from a lecturer's post at Bristol, although this was supplemented by considerable clinical experience at the local mental hospital where he headed the Department of Experimental and Clinical Psychology.

At UCT his interest turned from abnormal psychology to primate behaviour and ecology as he became fascinated by interaction within the baboon packs of the Peninsula. An anthropologist who briefly joined him in his fieldwork was filled with admiration for his determination, single-mindedness and perceptiveness. 'We spent the whole day among the baboons, like herdboys with a flock of sheep', she reported. 'His success in persuading the pack to accept him in this way was a very great achievement. I came home after ten hours' watching, but he was still seeing the pack to bed. That is typical … All the time he has been with the packs detailed notes have been made and these have to be collated. The observations are not haphazard but directly related to hypotheses about primate behaviour … [He] is one of the foremost scholars in the field of primate behaviour because he has both a first-rate theoretical understanding and exceptional ability for field work.'[132]

Unfortunately for UCT, the writing up of this landmark research by a psychologist occurred after Hall had returned to Bristol in 1959 to take up the chair of psychology there. From his Peninsula field notes emerged several pioneering articles in primatology, a field in which his name is still held in high esteem today.

A major reason for his departure from UCT was his concern at what effect the state's proposed policy of university apartheid might have. His successor, Kurt Danziger, soon discovered that Hall's foreboding was more than justified. Despite being only 34 when he took up the UCT chair in 1960, Danziger had already taught at three very different universities (Melbourne, Natal and Yogyakarta in Indonesia) after training at UCT and Oxford. That he had spent the first twelve years of his life in Germany before his family's flight to South Africa to escape Nazi rule only added to his unusually wide experience of the world. Equally wide were his forays into different areas of psychology and his interest in arts and science. 'It is this breadth of interests which makes him … a first-rate psychologist', wrote his former head at Melbourne. 'His lectures are models of lucidity and brevity. He can explain complex and abstract theories with precision based on understanding and on sharp, critical insight.'[133]

Convinced that in apartheid South Africa psychology had to be of practical value to justify its existence, he concluded that for him this meant 'working towards the kind of knowledge that would be part of the movement for social emancipation'.[134] Accordingly, soon after he arrived at UCT, he initiated a project to tap into the social consciousness of the coming generation by getting students and school pupils of all races to write histories or autobiographies covering the next fifty years. The very different views of the future which these yielded, depending on the racial classification of the author, made clear the close correlation between social identity and social consciousness. Where such consciousness was wholly at odds with historical trends, he warned, 'as in the case of the ideology of apartheid there arises the spectre of a totally "false consciousness" whose every cognition must necessarily be wrong'.[135]

Nor did Danziger challenge apartheid only in the pages of recondite scholarly journals. As the apartheid government increasingly resorted to holding political prisoners in solitary confinement, not only did he testify in court about the deleterious effect of such conditions on the reliability of any evidence such a prisoner might give – one of those on whose behalf he testified was UCT graduate Neville Alexander – but he also initiated a protest among university academics against solitary confinement. 'It was one of the few avenues of legal protest left', he recalled, 'and therefore had to be used even though there was no expectation that it would have any effect on the powers then in control.'[136]

But it did have an effect on the powers then in control, and this was to render him persona non grata in government circles. A Cabinet Minister labelled him 'an Australian communist'[137] (though he was neither), his house and car were attacked, and his passport revoked. Reading the writing on the wall accurately, he resigned and left UCT for York University in Toronto in August 1965. To remain in South Africa, he was reported as saying, 'meant that one would either "die on your feet or live on your knees"'.[138] UCT issued no public statement on his forced departure, though it did waive the usual notice period and request the Principal to ascertain the reasons for the state's action against its professor. To their credit, his colleagues in the department did at least issue a public statement protesting against the government's action and calling for 'the publication of any unpublished facts, if these existed, which would throw light on the decision'.[139]

At York University, his inquiring mind again took his psychological interest in new directions, in one of which, the history of psychology, he earned international acclaim as a masterly pioneer and, consequently, entries in at least two encyclopedias of psychology.[140] But it was not for these achievements alone that in 2004 a remorseful UCT awarded him an honorary doctorate. 'An honorary degree at this point represents for me a form of closure', he told a reporter.[141]

The appointment of Peter Radloff (1967–73) as Danziger's successor seemed to herald a shift away from social psychology and political controversy, for the new professor was more interested in the physiological underpinnings of human behaviour than in that very behaviour itself. 'He appears sometimes to be more interested in the paraphernalia of research than research itself', judged his head at Witwatersrand University.[142] In the event, Radloff had little opportunity to demonstrate his academic predilections at UCT, for his time was filled with controversy over a host of non-academic matters like favouritism, inappropriate behaviour to students, and maladministration. UCT therefore compelled him to resign in 1973, even barring him from the department in the months until his resignation took effect. That 'He tore the department apart, leaving it in tatters for the rest of the 1970s'[143] has now been encoded as part of the department's own self-memory.

Radloff's departure left the department yet again under an acting head, in this case the psychologist of language use and acquisition and of identity Peter du Preez, who had joined the department as a lecturer in 1964 and who was eventually to be appointed to succeed Radloff in 1976.

Earlier caretaker heads, in 1950–5 and 1965–6 respectively, had been the department's stalwarts, James Taylor and Vera Grover.[144] Even though Taylor had been in the department since 1924, his tardiness in publishing his findings on the behavioural basis of perception – 'I have worked on this problem at intervals over the past 25 years, but have refrained from publication until I should have satisfied my own standard of proof', he explained in 1952[145] – counted against him when it came to filling the chair in the 1950s. He had not 'done anything yet substantially to advance knowledge of the subject … [and] does not appear to have lived up to his early promise', concluded a selection panel.[146] In fact, it was not until 1962, the year of his retirement, that his magnum opus finally appeared.[147] That it won him a DSc from his alma mater, Aberdeen University, and an entry in a leading biographical dictionary of psychology published in 1997[148] suggests that it was worth waiting for.

Vera Grover, on the other hand, was never an applicant for the chair as her chosen speciality, developmental psychology – her 1947 doctorate was on the relationship between mental ability and learning to read – saw her take over as director of the Child Guidance Clinic after Reyburn's death.[149] For the next nineteen years, until her retirement in 1971, she poured herself into its operation, turning it into a full-time diagnostic, remedial, teaching and research unit loosely linked to the Psychology Department. By 1968 it was seeing over 300 children a year and offering clinical instruction to students from three departments, Psychology, Social Science and Psychiatry. The public service which it provided, UCT recognised, 'has added very considerably to the prestige of the University' while at the same time creating 'a new type of training' for students.[150]

As if this extra-departmental activity was not enough, Grover's interest in learning disabilities drew her into the wider field of mental handicap in which she gained a national reputation as a public intellectual and campaigner. She served on the National Council for Mental Health for 30 years, was its president in 1967–8 and helped found its Division for Mental Handicap. The fact that in 1992 UCT accepted her endowment of a chair in mental handicap[151] in the Department of Psychiatry and named it after her underscores her standing in the eyes of her peers.

Given that the Department of Psychology had seven heads between 1948 and 1968, four permanent and three acting, and that this too was a period of runaway expansion and innovation in the discipline itself, it is not surprising to find that the syllabus was in a state of constant flux, especially in the upper-level courses. Thus, while basic topics like thinking, learning, memory, perception and motivation remained at the core of Psychology I, and child psychology (Grover's speciality) loomed large in Psychology II, the contents of Psychology III and the Honours courses changed regularly, in part reflecting some of the predilections of whoever was head of the department at the time: problems of personality and temperament and the elements of factor analysis under Reyburn; the theory of perception under Taylor; principles of animal behaviour under Hall; social psychology under Danziger; and psychophysiology under Radloff. Unchanging from 1956, however, when Hall introduced it, was the requirement that students undertake practical work in the department's laboratories at least once a week; these were usually experimental in nature, involving tests on rats, pigeons and fellow students.

Although many students found Taylor's dry formulation of human behaviour in mathematical terms abstruse –'that was hard on us students', remembered one[152] – most of the teaching in the department was tailored, perhaps somewhat reluctantly, to the fact that only a small proportion of undergraduates intended to major in the subject. For instance, only 10% of the first-year class of 114 in 1953 went on to Psychology III, a percentage which did not rise markedly until the mid-1960s when careers in clinical psychology began to open up: to illustrate, 13% of the 1963 Psychology I class went on to Psychology III, but of the 1966 class, 24% did.

The content of the junior courses was thus solid and informative rather than sparkling – they 'provided quality information', judged a senior student.[153] But this did ensure that students gained a sound foundation in the discipline. Looking back on his training at UCT from a distance of fifty years, a professor at an English university was struck by the 'excellent grounding in psychology [he had received there in the mid-1960s], much broader and more interesting than most courses in the UK and the US today. We graduated with a better grasp of the subject as a whole than people from those countries.'[154] Clearly, learning was not just a theoretical subject in the department's syllabus. As Reyburn had insisted in his book *An Introduction to Psychology*, the first psychology textbook published in South Africa, in 1924, 'Form and content in education are indissolubly connected.'[155]

If applied to teaching in the Science Faculty as a whole in this era, a period that UCT's Principal, J.P. Duminy, saw as one which 'the applied sciences and technology have been running away with',[156] Reyburn's observation might raise the question whether, with a few notable exceptions, the enormous expansion of Science syllabuses had not overwhelmed the form in which they were delivered. As at least one Honours complained in 1966, 'half the lecturers re-hash book knowledge instead of teaching attitudes and reasoning methods'.[157]

# Teaching

*Distance learning. John Juritz lecturing with his usual stylishness to a large Physics I class in the New Science Lecture Theatre in 1961.* (Cape Times, 31 August 1961)

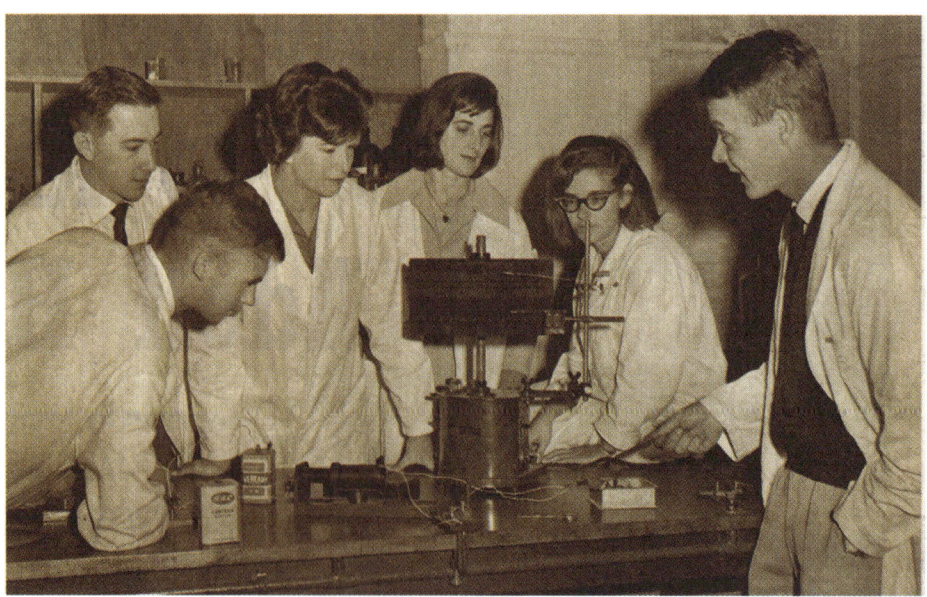

*The heart of the matter. A junior lecturer in the Zoology Department, Robin Bolt, demonstrates to a group of Zoology I students how to record the heartbeat of a frog, 1964.* (Cape Times, 25 July 1964)

*A postgraduate student demonstrates an experiment to first-year Physics students, c. 1965*

*Down to bedrock. Students pore over the specimens in the Geology Department's well-stocked museum in 1949.*

# Fieldwork

*Dr Ted Schelpe of the Botany Department leads a group of his third-year students on a botanising trip in Bain's Kloof in 1955.* (Cape Argus, 1 October 1955)

# Research

*Keeping a close eye on matter. Awed by the power of UCT's new R40,000 electron microscope in 1968 are (standing from left to right, behind the manufacturer's representative who is looking through the lens) Professor Claus von Holt of Biochemistry, J.G. Benfield (the Registrar), Associate Professor Max Lamchen of Chemistry and Professor Roland Guelke of Electrical Engineering.* (Cape Argus, 22 August 1968)

*Professor Louis Ahrens and a postgraduate student, Catherina Fullard, check the data produced by the Department of Geochemistry's CSIR-funded X-ray spectrograph, 1968.*

*Distant relations? Professor Kenneth Hall of the Psychology Department closely observes a baboon at the Cape Point Reserve as part of his inquiry into the social behaviour of primates.* (Courtesy of Stephen Peet)

*Professor John Day (extreme left, standing) and his third-year Zoology students about to set out to test the waters of Langebaan Lagoon, 1953.*

# CHAPTER 6

# The Applied Sciences: Engineering and Medicine

The two disciplines examined in this chapter, engineering and medicine, could as appropriately be included in the next chapter on the professional disciplines, for the training that engineering and medical students received at UCT equipped them no less for professional careers. That they are not in that chapter is more a reflection of the common 'hard' scientific basis which underlay them compared with that on which law, commerce, education and architecture rested, and a reminder that academic disciplines are, as a leading educationalist has explained, very much 'socio-historical constructs of a particular time',[1] and thus fluid.

## Engineering

No faculty at UCT was more directly affected by South Africa's post-war economic boom than Engineering. The rapid expansion of the mining industry on the back of a steadily rising international gold price and the West's demand for uranium during the Cold War, along with the runaway growth of infrastructure and secondary industry in the country in the 1950s and 1960s, put a premium on engineering skills. For instance, the construction of new national roads, bridges and dams required civil engineers aplenty, the growing number of factories mass-producing anything from clothing to kitchenware needed mechanical and electrical engineers, while the burgeoning fertiliser and petrochemical industries called for chemical engineers in numbers. Indeed, in 1961 a member of a government-appointed inquiry into the shortage of engineers, the Straszacker Commission, had the distinct impression that 'The engineering field is expanding [in South Africa] as nowhere else'.[2]

The effect of this escalating demand for engineers was apparent at UCT, as in the four other engineering faculties in South Africa, in increasing student numbers, congested lecture rooms, laboratories and workshops, overused equipment and staff hard pressed to cope with very heavy marking loads. There was 'an appalling

*Meeting the demand. An African Explosives and Chemical Industries Ltd. advert in* Varsity, *2 September 1964.*

lack of accommodation', warned UCT's architectural consultant. 'Most of their rooms ... are so full of machinery, apparatus, etc. that there is virtually no room for students (except sitting on and in dangerous contact with machines).'³ Not until the Department of Civil Engineering moved into the new Snape Building in 1965 and the old Engineering Block was enlarged for the two remaining engineering departments was this overcrowding eased.

The pressure of students on the Faculty and facilities before this was intense. Their number rose by 35% between 1955 and 1965 and then, once the new accommodation was available, by another 27% to total 783 in 1968. Not that the number of graduates produced by the Faculty increased by the same proportion, for the failure rate among first-years often topped 45%, of whom a percentage then dropped out of engineering (or indeed university) entirely. Nonetheless, between 1948 and 1968 UCT turned out just on 1600 engineering graduates or 25% of all new BSc (Engineering) graduates in South Africa in this period. Of the UCT graduates, just over 45% were trained as civil engineers, almost 20% each as electrical engineers and mechanical engineers, and nearly 15% as chemical engineers. Given the emphasis on infrastructural projects in this phase of South Africa's development and the fact that all aspects of these projects had to be undertaken locally, it is no surprise that civil engineers outnumbered other engineers at UCT, as they did in all of South Africa's engineering faculties then.

That UCT concentrated on just four branches of engineering – unlike the other faculties of engineering, which included two or three additional branches in their curricula – suggests a decision to limit itself to its existing strengths as long as it was so hard pressed for space, equipment and staff. Mainly because of this, large donations from the private sector were required for a dedicated building and new equipment before chemical engineering was given the status of an independent department in 1965.

The curriculum for the BSc (Eng) degree in these four departments retained the structure adopted when the faculty was formed in 1918. Following the English civic university model, it divided the four-year degree in half: years one and two were devoted to providing the scientific underpinnings of engineering through courses in physics, pure maths and applied maths and mastery of basic engineering skills like engineering geometry, workshop practice and design, while years three and four focused on whichever of the four branches a student had opted to pursue, culminating in a design thesis requiring the student to come up with a solution to an original engineering problem. How critical this was to passing or failing is well captured in the warning given by a lecturer to a final-year civil engineering student about his design for a structure, 'If it will fall, so do you.'[4]

Practically minded students wanting hands-on experience at once found years one and two 'grim and disheartening', grumbled one, 'mainly maths with hardly a sight of anything resembling real-life engineering problems'.[5] 'The course does not start as an engineering course until the third year', complained another.[6]

To staff in the Faculty the reason for this was quite clear: if a student had a solid theoretical grounding in the basic sciences, he (and the handful of she's) could apply this basic knowledge to master all manner of engineering specialisms. Or, in the metaphorical reply by a doyen of the Faculty to the question 'whether to give the student a toolbox to carry on his back all his life or to give him teaching to enable him to make his own tools', the answer should be 'produce thinking toolmakers'.[7]

Students who received more of the 'toolbox'-type education spoke critically of the 'parrot fashion learning' it produced',[8] in striking comparison to those who were trained to become 'toolmakers', one of whom enthused, 'We were challenged to apply our minds to see alternatives. UCT produced "thinking engineers", as opposed to more "technical engineers", as at Stellenbosch. Problem-solving and applying the mind … [made] students think and question … We were taught to think beyond our academic training.'[9]

Together, the two approaches gave UCT students a broad introduction to the discipline, including some exposure to branches of engineering other than their chosen field. All were taught by means of a mixture of lectures, laboratory and drawing office sessions, and practical work on and off campus. Indeed, so much store did the Faculty set on practical work that it made it compulsory for its students to spend part of their vacations working in engineering workshops or factories or on projects. 'The best training for civil engineering students', declared a lecturer in that department, 'is on the job doing actual work under trained civil engineers.'[10]

Given the foundational character of the BSc (Eng) degree, the syllabuses in civil, electrical and mechanical engineering did not change much in these years or deviate from the mainstream topics taught at British universities of this period – materials, structures, soil mechanics and hydraulics in civil engineering, electrotechnics and electronic communications in electrical engineering, and machines and engines in mechanical engineering. Tellingly, all final-year students did a short course in economics to help them grasp the economics of practice.

Where additions were made to the syllabuses in the 1950s and 1960s, these were usually because of the emergence of new fields of engineering (like industrial engineering, control engineering and public health engineering), the invention of new machines (like electronic devices and air conditioners) or the recognition of an altered environment in which engineering had to be practised, such as the emergence of enormous factories which made necessary the introduction in 1951 of a fully fledged course in Industrial Administration for mechanical engineers.

Only in the chemical engineering syllabus were the innovations more than add-ons, for the subject itself underwent a fundamental change of character during these years. Having started out in the early 1920s as applied and chemical engineering under the auspices of the Department of Mechanical Engineering, in 1956 this sub-department was shifted to the Department of Chemistry, which had just appointed an applied chemist to its staff.

But by then the subject was already in the throes of a significant reorientation under the impact of the rapid expansion of the local chemical industry, which was diversifying its products and services apace as the application of chemical processes grew and became more sophisticated. Recognising this, in that year Applied and Chemical Engineering was renamed Chemical Engineering and the longstanding entry in the prospectus that the course sought to produce 'a man [*sic*] who is essentially a chemist, but who has a sound working knowledge of the elementary principles of engineering'[11] was replaced by a statement that the course 'aims at producing a man [*sic*] who, apart from a thorough knowledge of chemistry, is familiar with the principles of chemical engineering, chemical plant design, industrial stoicheiometry, corrosion, etc.'.[12]

A wholly new syllabus was consequently drafted from scratch to reflect this rather different emphasis. Soon students began to flock into the course so, that in 1960 a limit was placed on new enrolments for want of staff and facilities. A move into a dedicated Chemical Engineering Building later that year eased the situation and by 1964 there were 130 undergraduates in the department, eager to take advantage of the jobs offered by the burgeoning chemical and metallurgical industries. 'Every graduate has three offers of work', boasted a lecturer. 'They tend to move to management …'[13]

Recognising the particular needs of such a career path, in that year the sub-department rejigged its senior courses to cater for two types of graduate, those aiming for a practical or managerial job in industry (for whom subjects like business administration and applied economics were added to the standard curriculum) and those inclining to chemical engineering science and research (for whom more theoretical and mathematical subjects were prescribed). The effect was as hoped – the creation of a flourishing research group in the sub-department, the inflow of funds from the private sector for research and, in 1965, the creation of UCT's first chair in chemical engineering, which, at last, was accorded autonomous departmental status within the Faculty of Engineering. The man appointed to the chair was the senior lecturer who had piloted the discipline's ascent, the 41-year-old Donald Carr.

A UCT graduate who had worked in the chemical engineering industry in Scotland and South Africa, he had quickly become the mainstay of the sub-department after joining it as a lecturer in 1956. A deft researcher in the field of heat transfer, he had a keen eye for innovation both in the laboratory and in the lecture hall. An external examiner of his course spoke of how his capacity 'for critical review of established techniques and his readiness to implement modifications [of his own teaching] … has resulted in an undergraduate course which is stimulating, comprehensive and completely modern in its approach'.[14]

With the assistance of Heinrich Buhr, a bright ex-student of his who had joined the sub-department in 1961, Carr continued to build up a vigorous research arm in areas like fluid mechanics, liquid metal heat transfer and applied reaction kinetics with support from the private sector. It was funding from this source too – in this case, the liquor and baking industries – which was responsible for the creation of a lectureship in biochemical engineering in 1969 and the introduction of a fourth-year course in the subject. Like 'yeasts', which formed part of the syllabus, the new department was rising.

Elsewhere in the Faculty, however, research did not enjoy the same priority, staff explaining repeatedly that the demands of teaching and marking consumed all of their time. 'Not always', the head of Civil Engineering admitted frankly when asked by the Straszacker Commission if his department encouraged postgraduate research,[15] while a colleague of his told the Commission, 'There is an overemphasis on research ... The yardstick for assessing a teacher should be how much work does he put into his students...'[16]

Certainly teaching in the largest department in the Faculty, Civil Engineering, went well beyond the lecture hall and tutorial room to encompass instruction in the drawing office, the laboratory, in the field and the survey camp, and at project sites too. Until 1965, when the department moved into the state-of-the-art Snape Civil Engineering Building (named after its founding professor, Alfred Snape[17]), its 150–220 students per annum were squeezed into increasingly cramped quarters. This gave it little scope to introduce into its syllabus some of the new sub-branches then developing in the discipline; only two were added in this period, consequently, traffic engineering and public health engineering.

The training received by the 742 civil engineers the Faculty turned out between 1948 and 1968 was therefore broad in character, especially as Snape's successor as professor, Reginald Robertson (head, 1949–65), was strongly opposed to specialisation at undergraduate level. He believed that this would cause 'another implementation of Parkinson's Law. Everyone ... [will be] in a watertight compartment.'[18] As far as he was concerned, undergraduate training was chiefly about 'inculcating fundamental principles'.[19]

This he did ably enough, bearing out the opinion of the selection committee that he 'should be an excellent teacher, but not necessarily a stimulus to research at an advanced level'.[20] Appointed at the age of 49 because UCT had become desperate to fill Snape's chair after two unsuccessful attempts to do so, this Oxford-trained structural engineer came to Cape Town from a post at Nottingham University College where his wide practical experience had offset his lack of zeal for research.

Not surprisingly, his hands-on conception of the discipline was shared by the seven men whom he appointed to the department. All had worked on civil engineering projects or as consulting engineers, but, tellingly, five of them, like Robertson himself, did not have doctoral degrees. Not that Robertson was much bothered by this; typical was his comment up-front that one of his senior lecturers had been so occupied in planning a new laboratory for the department that there was 'little time available from teaching duties so that the preparation of publications cannot be expected during this period'.[21]

Very different was the outlook of Robertson's successor, the 50-year-old Maurice Kaplan (head, 1966–71). Having practised as a private civil engineer for eight years before going on to head the Civil Engineering Division of the Council for Scientific and Industrial Research (CSIR) in Pretoria and then Britain's Civil

Engineering Research Council, he straddled the practical and the academic spheres of engineering training with unusual ease. A CSIR journal spoke of his 'research approach' to engineering problems,[22] a trait reflected in his 30 published articles. With two engineering doctorates from UCT on top of undergraduate degrees in civil engineering, commerce and economic history, he had what one of his referees referred to as 'a broader background than most engineers have … and is aware of what goes on in his own professional field and much beyond'.[23]

Not unexpectedly, UCT appointed this high achiever without hesitation, convinced that he would be able to lift the Civil Engineering Department's sights beyond the workshop and the laboratory. Nor were these hopes disappointed: by the end of 1967 Kaplan had introduced an array of MSc courses which were so appealing to both new graduates and practising engineers that, within five years, they and doctoral students in the department numbered 77, an almost tenfold increase since 1965, Robertson's last year at UCT.

A significant number of these enrolments were of aspirant water and sanitation engineers, for in 1966 Kaplan had also persuaded UCT to set up a chair in water resources and public health engineering in the department. Its first incumbent, the effervescent Gerrit Marais (1968–92), wasted no time in introducing both undergraduate and postgraduate courses in the subject and in establishing a research unit on water quality with the support of the state's Water Commission. From this base in Civil Engineering, Marais's international reputation as a waste water engineer was well and truly launched.

If, under Kaplan,[24] what was taught in Civil Engineering became less narrowly focused on practical training – he believed engineers needed 'high intellectual ability and a considerable knowledge of many sciences'[25] – in the Department of Mechanical Engineering the more limited conception remained firmly in place. Until 1954 two technically skilled artisan-engineers with no university degrees, Duncan McMillan and William Weaver (both of whom had been appointed by the South African College before World War I[26]), dominated the department, while McMillan's successor as professor, the 48-year-old George Elliott (head, 1957–61), might have held a BSc (Eng) degree from UCT, but remained predisposed to the McMillan–Weaver approach to mechanical engineering. For instance, before the Straszacker Commission he argued that increasing the academic contents of the syllabus 'results in practical matters being dropped … Employers expect practical professional knowledge … In the old times there was an opportunity to talk to graduates on diesel plants etc. [for instance]. These things are now thrown out because of [having to include] control systems in theory of machines.'[27] The echo of the Civil Engineering Department in the pre-Kaplan era is clear.

The innovations Elliott did make to the curriculum were thus practical responses to the escalating growth and mechanisation of South African industry – greater coverage of physical metallurgy, the creation of a metallography laboratory, and the introduction of a special course in refrigeration and air conditioning at the behest of the South African Institute of Refrigeration. Research and attracting postgraduates were not high priorities for him. 'Sound, good teaching. No real research', noted a member of the selection panel after interviewing him,[28] an assessment which might justifiably be applied to most in the department in this era.

As in Civil Engineering, the staff appointed by McMillan and then Elliott had extensive experience of working in industry for firms like Vacuum Oil, General Motors and Hubert Davies Industrial Equipment, but only a few had more than a first degree in mechanical engineering, among them the creative experimental engineer Reino Stegen, who had an MSc in thermodynamics from Birmingham University, and the motor vehicle engineer Peter Metcalf, a senior lecturer in the department who succeeded Elliott as professor at the age of 43 in 1962.

While not a researcher of Kaplan's stature, Metcalf did not want for research experience. He had spent five years on the staff of the British Motor Industry Research Association in the Midlands after adding Oxford degrees to his UCT BSc (Eng). Its director described him as 'extremely competent in basic science and technology … [showing] much initiative in the organisation and execution of research work'.[29]

His ability as a teacher matched this. In a comment which reveals as much about Elliott as about his then senior lecturer, the former expressed surprise that Metcalf did not 'repeat the same thing [in his lectures] year after year. This attitude to teaching takes up a tremendous amount of time', he remarked, but it had certainly seen him make 'a wonderful success of design'.[30] The laboratory report that his students had to write up 'helps one to sort out one's ideas', acknowledged one of them with satisfaction. 'It is in the write-up that one learns.'[31]

Another mark of the currency of Metcalf's thinking was his awareness that the growing sophistication of industrial technology in South Africa meant that a more scientific track was needed in the curriculum for those students attracted to the careers then emerging in engineering research and development and design. To meet what he described as the 'widening scope of Engineering Science',[32] in 1968 he introduced a 'Mechanical Sciences' option containing more physics and applied and pure mathematics than in the standard curriculum. Elliott had forecast that Metcalf had 'originality and enough to keep things moving' as a head of the department.[33] He was not wrong, for Metcalf quickly began to shift the department into a higher gear.

The Department of Electrical Engineering had already been in high gear for twenty years by then, ever since its dynamic and innovative professor, Brian Goodlet,[34] had returned from war service and continued the modernisation of the curriculum which he had begun before World War II. Having witnessed the effect of research in overdrive during the war, he introduced a 'B' stream to the electrical engineering curriculum, which included more pure and applied mathematics and physics for those wanting to go into research and development, while light-current electronics was given more attention in the standard syllabus, especially in the field of electronic communications and systems, which had made such strides during the war.

Nor did this modernising momentum flag when Goodlet left for a senior post at the Harwell Atomic Research Station in 1950, for he was succeeded by his admiring deputy, the 46-year-old Roland Guelke (head, 1951–69), who had joined the department as a lecturer in 1938. The fact that he was a research physicist first and an electrical engineer only second[35] did not endear him to hands-on engineers like McMillan and Robertson, but it did equip him very well to ensure that the department kept abreast of the electronics revolution of the 1950s and 1960s in both teaching and research. Fuller treatment of transistors and analogue computers in the syllabus signalled this clearly.

Guelke's own research was in electro-acoustics in which he mounted a postgraduate course which fully utilised the well-equipped acoustic laboratory in the department and which, unexpectedly, also drew him into collaboration with departments usually far removed from engineers' ken, viz. Music, Architecture and Otolaryngology (ENT). Indeed, his contact with the Faculty of Music saw him appointed as its interim Dean in 1966, while his work on how sound was received by the cochlea led him into the rapidly developing specialism of medical electronics. Deservedly, his sound research won him the accolade of being 'the father of acoustics in South Africa'.[36]

Although Guelke insisted that all appointees to his department should have practised as electrical engineers professionally, he was equally adamant that, once in the department, they should undertake research. 'A department that is not doing research is not worth its salt', he maintained. 'Teaching imposed a strain, but not research.'[37]

Appointing individuals possessing both practical and research experience thus became the aim already in the 1950s, giving the department a profile rather different from Civil and Mechanical Engineering. It is indicative of the ethos which Goodlet and then Guelke created that the two senior lecturers who best fitted this mould, the electrical machinery engineer Nicholas Enslin and the medical electronics engineer Louis Besseling, both went on to become professors in the department after Guelke's retirement in 1969, while the senior lecturer whose strength lay in teaching and administration, Gilbert Webster, rose no higher than the rank of associate professor, and that only in the year before his retirement in 1976. He was 'essentially a practical engineer', judged Guelke, 'and his contribution to … the department … represented a very useful balance to the more academic approach of others'.[38]

However, ability as a researcher and a more academic approach were no guarantee of effective teaching. 'The method by which Electrical Engineering is put across is very poor', grumbled one student to the Straszacker Commission. 'You must do a lot of your own thinking.'[39] This, explained another, was the result of lecturers' inability to come down to the average student's level. 'The lecturer suddenly comes in and just gives odd points', added a third. 'When it comes to studying for exams the student has to go to the library and make his own notes', he concluded reproachfully.[40]

On the other hand, practical sessions in the laboratory seem to have been far more successful as a mode of instruction. The department's technical assistants were conscientious in setting up experiments beforehand, most students arrived well primed, and demonstrators were on hand to resolve difficulties and provide advice. 'The total time devoted [to practicals] was most worthwhile', concluded one enthusiastic student. 'Through laboratory work he gained most of his knowledge of electrical engineering, particularly electronics … Doing laboratory reports drive[s] points home.'[41]

By a pragmatic combination of ability, diligence, lecture notes, textbooks, mutual coaching and guided laboratory practice, 315 students (314 of whom were male) secured BSc (Eng) degrees in Electrical Engineering at UCT between 1948 and 1968. This constituted just over 25% of all such engineers trained in South Africa in this period. However, the total of 315 was also less than half of the total number of students who had originally enrolled for the degree at UCT. As the Dean of the Faculty observed rather clinically, 'They weed themselves out.'[42]

The long-serving Dean who made this sharp remark, George Menzies, was the even longer-serving head (1946–76) of the smallest department in the faculty, Land Surveying. It had become an independent department under him only in 1946,[43] before then having fallen under the Department of Civil Engineering.

By 1948 the strong opposition in the profession to the training of land surveyors at a university had begun to ebb, as both the University of the Witwatersrand and the University of Natal had set up courses of their own too. Nevertheless, until 1959 it was still possible to qualify as a land surveyor through pupillage and an examination conducted by the profession, which made university departments wary of incurring criticism from the Institute of Land Surveyors by watering down the practical side of their syllabuses.

The UCT department therefore offered a broad training which combined theory, experiment, hands-on fieldwork and practical training at the Trigonometrical Survey

Office in Mowbray or with a land surveyor with three-week survey camps during the vacations. Between 1948 and 1968 this training yielded 158 students with the degree of BSc (Land Surveying).

Their practically oriented training reflected Menzies's own hands-on inclination, for research held little appeal for this capable teacher, administrator, committee man and residence warden. Active in professional land-surveying bodies locally and abroad, he did, however, seek to keep his department abreast of the wave of electronic equipment which was transforming his profession in the 1950s and 1960s, like photomappers, tellurometers and analogue computers. With no little accuracy Menzies forecast in 1959 that the land surveying profession 'may undergo enormous change within a comparatively few years'.[44]

Menzies's recognition of the importance of these innovations is apparent too in the changing level of training which he expected in staff whom he appointed. Like him himself, those appointed before the early 1950s were practising professionals with no more than a first degree. Of one such a referee wrote, 'He has very quickly developed into a very practical Land Surveyor without forgetting the more scientific side of his training as evidenced by the usual talks and arguments that take place in a large survey office.'[45] On the other hand, those appointed after the mid-1950s usually had higher degrees and specialist training in fields like photogrammetry. About one of these a referee judged, 'His interests … tend to be oriented more towards the academic and theoretical spheres, than those of the professional cadastral surveyor.'[46]

What did not change in the Department of Land Surveying or elsewhere in the Faculty of Engineering throughout the 1950s and 1960s was the character of the student body. With very few exceptions, it was made up of white males, close to 4000 of them during the twenty years if those who dropped out before graduating are included. The bulk of these were English-speaking South Africans as the Afrikaner presence of earlier decades had begun to wane after the opening of a faculty of engineering at Stellenbosch University in 1944. However, one distinctive minority did remain within the English-speaking student body, viz. students from the then Rhodesias whose A-level mathematics gave them a decided advantage, especially in the first year of the degree course. The fact that almost all of them stayed in a UCT residence only strengthened their sense of a common identity.

This 'Rhodesian' identity was over and above a wider identity as engineering students which strongly pervaded the whole student body of the Faculty. The existence of an engineering students' association and council, a monthly newsletter and an engineering students' journal bear testimony to this. An editorial in the journal spoke of the Faculty as 'an organic unit … [whose] students hold ideas, interests and opinions which are fairly uniform'.[47]

Aware that an engineering degree was a guarantee of a well-paid job in industrialising South Africa – 'The belief was that "You were made for life if you got an engineering degree"', recalled a student of this era[48] – most of these students saw themselves as an elite in the making, a feeling which the Faculty fostered through presenting engineering as a tough discipline, only 'for clever people', as one student described it. 'You don't go into engineering unless you are very bright. Weak students went to the softer subjects, such as sociology, history, religious studies … We did think of ourselves as rather special.'[49]

This self-perception as a rugged, masculine class apart, of being practical doers rather than talkers, was given ostentatious outer form in their conduct – heavy beer-drinking, rumbustiousness in lectures, Rag and Intervarsity – and their casual, supposedly manly dress, from open-necked shirts and flannels in the 1940s and 1950s to shorts and sandals in the late 1960s. Interest in wider social and cultural issues was not encouraged – 'the engineer's interests extend only as far as the cursor on his slide rule', scoffed a non-engineer[50] – and, if politics were discussed, conservative opinions dominated. One of the few students not to subscribe to this ethos described the average engineering student disparagingly as 'parochial in his education and naïve in his political views',[51] to which he attributed a lack of participation in wider student affairs, what the student journal called being 'notoriously negligent in this respect'.[52] That a very full timetable of lectures and practicals, occupying five mornings and at least four afternoons per week, precluded such involvement, the author rejected as a mere excuse to cover the narrowness of engineering students' interests. Students, like the one who graphically portrayed his four years in the Faculty as akin to having 'a rope round his neck and … being pulled by a winch through a mill',[53] would not have agreed.

## Medicine

If the Faculty of Engineering was the greatest direct beneficiary of the economic boom of the 1950s and the 1960s, the Faculty of Medicine benefited to a large extent too, but less obviously. More evident were the effects on it of a series of scientific, technological and organisational revolutions during the same period, which lifted much of what happened within its walls to a world-class level, best epitomised by its key contributions to the first heart transplant operation in December 1967. Cumulatively, they made these years golden ones for UCT's Medical School, which were fostered in rather different ways by its three Deans, the judicious Ben Ryrie (1941–53), the imaginative Marinus van den Ende (1953–7) and the diligent and clubbable Bromilow Bromilow-Downing (1958–77).

The scientific and technological revolutions mentioned above themselves wrought a medical and pharmacological revolution which ranged from the therapeutic (e.g. antibiotics, dialysis, chemotherapy, and restorative and replacement surgery) to the diagnostic (e.g. CT scans, MRI scans and ultrasound), spawning a host of new medical specialties in the process, which jostled with one another for a place in the School's hierarchy, then still headed by the Departments of Medicine, Surgery, and Obstetrics and Gynaecology. The 22 departments and sub-departments in the Faculty in 1948 increased to 30 in 1968, while the number of qualifications they offered rose from 6 to 23. The most momentous of these new qualifications were the MMed degrees introduced in 1954 as medical training in South Africa matured, for they effectively opened a broad path to specialisation locally in over fifteen medical disciplines for the first time. The creation of the College of Physicians, Surgeons, Obstetricians and Gynaecologists (which subsequently became the Colleges of Medicine of South Africa) in the same year to validate such specialisation professionally was the coping stone for the system of medical specialisation in South Africa.

The innovations at undergraduate level broke new ground too, but in a different way, by accepting a discipline ancillary to medicine, physiotherapy, into the Faculty of Medicine for the first time. This, however, involved fewer than 150 students in total. The overwhelming majority of students in the Faculty were those registered for the MBChB degree, which remained a six-year programme, just as it had been since its inception at UCT in 1920, though from 1949 the South African Medical and Dental Council (SAMDC) required all new graduates to complete a compulsory intern year at an approved hospital after graduation so as to gain hands-on clinical experience under close professional supervision. In the words of a senior academic, this was to prevent their being 'let … loose on the public without preliminary hospital training'.[54]

The undergraduate MBChB curriculum was divided into three parts: a first, pre-medical year in which four purely scientific subjects (physics, chemistry, botany and zoology) were taken; two pre-clinical years focusing on medical sciences (physiology, anatomy, pathology and pharmacology); and three clinical years devoted to a host of practical clinical subjects. It was in this last category in particular that the largest increase in departments and sub-departments took place after World War II, mainly as a result of the revolutions mentioned already. The result was to place even heavier pressure on an already overloaded curriculum to accommodate the newcomers adequately. 'It is becoming increasingly difficult in the six years at present available … to deal effectively with the rapidly growing volume of general, scientific and medical knowledge', complained a worried Faculty committee in 1955.[55]

But accommodated in the curriculum they had to be if the Faculty was to remain abreast of the post-war explosion in medical knowledge. Therefore, even though, as one Dean expressed it, 'It is easier to move a cemetery than to change a curriculum',[56] the 1950s and 1960s were filled with much chopping and changing of the curriculum while trying to maintain its overall coherence, logic and flow. Finding a happy medium was not easy. Although an official report on the facilities needed for medical training might confidently assert, 'The day of watertight compartments for each subject, theoretical as well as clinical, has gone',[57] the reality in departments, wards and hospital corridors was more akin to that wryly described by a Glasgow professor of surgery who faced similar issues then: 'Medical Schools are not designed for change', he explained. 'They are feudal kingdoms where every baron is all-powerful in his castle. Every Professor agrees in principle with the need for pruning the curriculum, but prestige and a genuine belief in the importance of his own subject impel him to demand extra lecture time for his own department.'[58]

Adding or expanding disciplines in UCT's School of Medicine was only possible because the increased personnel and resources required were available as the result of a third revolution in the 1950s. This was primarily organisational in nature and injected both staff and funds into the Faculty in unprecedented quantities through the landmark Joint Staff Agreement which UCT concluded with the Cape Provincial Administration (CPA) in 1951. The CPA was responsible for operating the six teaching hospitals then used by UCT: Groote Schuur Hospital (GSH), the Somerset Hospital, the Peninsula Maternity Hospital, the Mowbray Maternity Hospital, St Monica's Home and the Lady Michaelis Orthopaedic Hospital.[59]

The roots of this Agreement lay in reformist official attempts after World War II to address the dire state of health in the country, a situation most manifest in its teeming hospitals. Putting their faith in the highly promising curative brand of medicine, provincial authorities in the Cape and Transvaal took over direct responsibility for hospitals from faltering local hospital boards and made access to them free. The resultant surge in patient numbers was met by significantly increasing the number of paid, full-time doctors on the hospitals' staffs, at the expense of the system of honorary appointments which, an inquiry into GSH in 1948 judged, 'has reached its breaking point'.[60]

For the Faculty of Medicine, this increase of medical staff – by 27 full-time clinical posts in 1949 alone[61] – at its main teaching hospital, GSH, in 1947–9 was a godsend, coming as it did just as the wave of ex-soldiers registered for the MBChB degree reached the hospital years of their training. It therefore hastened to put this favourable situation on a permanent footing, an outcome which it achieved in 1951 with the signing of the Joint Staff Agreement. In terms of this, UCT and the CPA would share the cost of all clinical and pathological appointments at GSH, with UCT having authority over their academic duties and the CPA over their purely medical responsibilities. The solid, guaranteed income from what was now becoming a relatively well-funded, well-equipped hospital made such positions attractive, and in the first year of the Joint Staff Agreement over a hundred additional full-time and sessional clinicians and pathologists were jointly appointed by UCT and the CPA. Indeed, such was the surge in the size of its staff that in 1953 the Faculty of Medicine revised downward the basis on which its Board was constituted so as to prevent its decision-making becoming too unwieldy. 'We never had to ask twice for posts', recalled one physician, while a colleague in the Department of Surgery remembered the period as 'dynamic – there was money. [We could] order anything, including pigs [for research], and the Province paid.'[62] Little wonder that the professor of surgery, writing in the heyday of the Agreement, described it as 'one of the greatest steps forward in the development of the UCT Medical School … [which was] largely responsible for the "Blossoming Out" [of the School] after 1951'.[63]

A second stimulus to this 'blossoming out' was the increasing availability of funding for research from public and private sources locally and abroad. That this was a necessity for a 'proper' medical school in the post-war era the Faculty did not doubt. Already in 1948 it was nailing its colours to the mast in this regard, declaring forcefully that research should not be looked upon 'as an additional activity of the school, but as a natural and fundamental duty. The idea of research as an extra, for which special grants must be begged, is an absurdity in modern medicine.'[64]

The Joint Staff Agreement did not bring benefits to whole of the Medical School at once. Until 1957, three of the four pre-clinical departments in the Faculty, Physiology, Pharmacology and Anatomy, were not included in its ambit because their staff were not engaged in clinical work. This rankled with them, for it meant that they were not eligible for the better staffing and equipment funding which the Agreement brought to their clinical and pathology colleagues. The material consequences of this – a fixed number of posts, uncompetitive salaries and outdated equipment – made it difficult to recruit and then retain staff in these departments. Their indignant lobbying against this 'arbitrary division' between the clinical departments and themselves[65] eventually bore fruit in 1957 when they secured most – but not all – of the benefits of the Joint Staff Agreement too. In 1968 they were still complaining that their staff were not eligible for merit awards on the same terms as their clinical colleagues; if they were, the departments suggested meaningfully, 'it may well be an inducement for them [the current incumbents] to remain [in their posts]'.[66]

The long tenure of Archie Sloan, the professor of physiology from 1955 to 1980, and of his even longer-serving deputy, Harry Zwarenstein, from 1926 to 1965, appear to belie such notions of a high staff turnover, but only two of the other twenty full-time academics in that department between 1948 and 1968 stayed there for more than half-a-dozen years. Both Sloan and Zwarenstein were ardent researchers in a department with a strong research tradition going back to its establishment in 1911,[67] which probably goes a long way to explain their abiding presence there.

The 38-year-old Sloan, a physiologist with a medical degree, continued the research on exercise physiology which he had begun while a lecturer at his alma mater, Glasgow University. At UCT this eventually grew into an investigation of the physiological basis of physical fitness at a time when sports medicine as a distinct field still lay far in the future in South Africa. Thousands of students and schoolchildren whose fitness levels he assessed in relation to their body composition thereby became aware of the negative correlation between fatness and fitness which he postulated. Or, as he expressed it more academically in his UCT doctoral thesis on the topic in 1966, 'The maintenance of a satisfactory degree of physical fitness demands regular physical exercise and avoidance of obesity.'[68]

As for Zwarenstein, his innovative hormonal research for pregnancy testing and the study of endocrine glands had already peaked by the 1940s, though without securing him the promotion this achievement merited.[69] His subsequent research was not of the same calibre, however, being more of the 'interesting observations that led nowhere on further scrutiny' variety, as one of his top students put it with regret.[70] But no student of his was disappointed by his teaching of biochemistry in these years, for this retained all the zest, wit and clarity which had made him so popular a lecturer and supervisor of practicals before the war. These traits 'make it difficult to sleep in his lectures', remarked a student magazine wryly but tellingly.[71] Confirming the affection that students felt for him is the fact that, after he retired in 1965, they paid for a bust of 'Zwarrie' to be sculpted, which was then placed in the Physiology block.

Until the department could benefit from the Joint Staff Agreement's largesse after 1957, the number of Zwarenstein's fellow full-time lecturers remained small – in that year they totalled but four. Nevertheless, Sloan was reluctant to create a single departmental research project to pool their skills and, as a result, research followed the bent of those individuals who remained in the department long enough to begin projects of their own, which ranged from the haematological to the nutritional to the enzymological.

Where Sloan was prescriptive, however, was in requiring students to carry out experiments themselves. 'Physiological knowledge is founded on experiment', he averred, and so all students should 'learn the discipline of experimental technique … To teach an experimental science without experiments is like teaching a language without grammar.'[72] To this end even senior staff were deployed to the department's laboratories to supervise practical classes in the three main areas of teaching, biochemistry, human physiology and histology.

By 1959 these subjects were being taught in this way in several courses, to an array of students ranging from second- and sixth-year medics and BSc (Medicine) students to intending physiotherapists and nursing sister tutors. Postgraduate students were, however, few and far between until the 1980s.

What all of them received was a good grounding in human physiology, which provided a sound foundation for their subsequent careers. 'It stood me in very good stead when I was being interviewed for the Royal College of Surgeons Fellowship in Dublin', recalled a cardiologist who had taken a BSc in physiology at UCT. 'I was able to answer the questions posed confidently and correctly. Professor Zwarenstein would have been proud of me.'[73]

What would have pleased 'Zwarrie' even more was the way in which, after his retirement in 1965, the subject which he had championed since the 1940s, medical biochemistry, gained in stature on the foundation he had created for it. Recognising this, in 1966 the department was rebranded Physiology and Medical Biochemistry as the latter could 'no longer be regarded as an adjunct of physiology'.[74] Yet, because of the existence of an overlapping department in the Faculty, Chemical Pathology, it took a dozen more years for medical biochemistry to be accorded independent departmental status such as the discipline had long enjoyed at other medical schools in the English-speaking world.

In the case of Pharmacology, another 'adjunct' of the Physiology Department, independent departmental status took even longer to accomplish, which was paradoxical as Pharmacology had existed as an independent department at UCT from 1918 to 1941.[75] Because its second professor, John Gunn, had died during World War II, the chair was not immediately filled, leaving all teaching in the hands of Gunn's assistant, Norman Sapeika. His junior status made it necessary for the department to be placed under the wing of the Physiology Department, a temporary arrangement which was made official in 1948 because of renewed doubts in the Faculty about the merit of having a free-standing department of pharmacology with no clinical side to it within a clinically dominated Faculty of Medicine.

Incorporation of pharmacology into a composite Department of Physiology and Pharmacology (to cite its official name from 1948 to 1965) was supposed to produce integration of the two components, but no such process occurred. 'Pharmacology is an academic discipline quite distinct from physiology and with no more common ground than there is between any other pair of medical sciences. A lecturer in Pharmacology cannot be expected to give adequate teaching in Physiology nor can a physiologist give any but the most elementary instruction in Pharmacology', argued Sloan,[76] but in vain.

Not until the post-war pharmacological revolution (Sapeika called it 'the drug explosion'[77]) had strengthened the complementarity between clinical medicine and pharmacology through the creation of clinical pharmacology – which emerged as an academic discipline in the United States in the early 1950s – did the Faculty's attitude towards the subject alter sufficiently for it to be accepted as meriting a department of its own. A doctor with only a superficial knowledge of pharmacology, warned Sapeika, 'will be in certain respects the equivalent of a potentially harmful drug'.[78] In 1965, therefore, a separate department was re-established after 24 years, with the enduring Sapeika as professor. Blithely the Dean of the Faculty declared that the chair did not have to be advertised as Sapeika 'is eminently suited for appointment to the Chair'.[79] After 32 years in the department, the new professor, now 56 years old, must have grimaced when he heard this.

Diligent but uninspiring, he continued to give dull lectures which differed little from the contents of the textbook he had written, *Actions and Uses of Drugs for Medical Students and Practitioners*, which went through seven editions between 1943 and 1966. Student comments about lectures by 'Soporific' (as they dubbed him) were scathing.[80] For all their painstaking detail and systematic coverage of how drugs affected the body (and vice versa), they left students 'bogg[ed] down in a morass of bland indifference', complained one,[81] which tutorial demonstrations did little to ameliorate.

On the other hand, research clearly excited Sapeika far more than did teaching, as is clear from his steady output of narrowly focused articles on the effects of drugs and poisons, which eventually totalled 170. Among his colleagues his name was a byword for diligently ploughing his own precise furrow alone and for organised and efficient research. That he was able to produce so many papers attests to his single-minded zeal, for, aside from two technical assistants, he bore the brunt of the formal teaching in his sub-department alone until 1963 when a recent medical graduate was appointed as a lecturer. However, like his successors, this lecturer did not remain in the department long before leaving for a position in a livelier, more supportive department. That Sapeika's successor in the chair described the department he inherited as 'an orphan'[82] is a telling comment on Sapeika's long-running one-man show.

Pharmacology's neighbour in the building, the Department of Anatomy, also had a long-serving man at its head – Matthew Drennan was its de facto founder and occupied the chair from 1916 to 1956 when he retired aged 71 – but there all similarity ended. Students' attention was as captivated by his superb, hand-drawn anatomical illustrations on the blackboard as by his Scottish-accented repetition of key terms during lectures. Moreover, team-led research in the department was given a vigorous thrust by the discovery in 1951 of abundantly rich fossil beds near Hopefield, about 150 kilometres north of Cape Town. These Drennan, his colleagues and senior students proceeded to excavate in a rough-and-ready way shocking to archaeologists, unearthing what one called a 'very prolific graveyard of prehistory'[83] containing ancient mammalian remains, hand tools and even a fossilised human skull and jaw, which Drennan believed came from an extinct human species which he named *Homo saldanensis*.[84] As a result, in the 1950s his engaging lectures were further enhanced by the inclusion of evidence from this world-famous site at Hopefield. 'All of us feel relaxed in his lectures and enjoy the clarity and vividness of his delivery', reported a medical students' magazine appreciatively.[85]

Drennan's closest collaborator in the excavations was an up-and-coming senior lecturer in the department, Ronald Singer. A UCT medical graduate, Singer threw himself into excavation with characteristic gusto and soon began to author or co-author with Drennan several articles on *Homo saldanensis*. By 1958 thirteen articles by members of the department on the Hopefield fossil finds had appeared, giving it, briefly, a high profile in physical anthropology circles internationally. When Singer was a visiting professor at the University of Illinois in 1960, he was feted as being on the cutting edge of studying 'man [*sic*] as an animal and man as a human'.[86]

By then he had expanded his anthropological gaze far beyond *Homo saldanensis* to sites elsewhere in Africa as he sought to piece together the evolution of early humans through archaeology, genetics, serology and analysis of the biological make-up of the current indigenous populations of Africa. No wonder students found his lectures exciting or that in 1962 he was offered the chair in anatomy and anthropology at Chicago University. The appeal of this position and his distaste for apartheid led him to accept.

Perhaps another reason for his move was that he had not been appointed to succeed Drennan in 1955. Instead, a 47-year-old reader in physical anthropology from Edinburgh University, Lawrence Wells, had followed Drennan in the chair. A Witwatersrand University graduate who had been at Edinburgh since 1951, Wells was attracted back to South Africa because he felt it was 'a growing point from the anthropological angle',[87] which it certainly was, given the recent rich discoveries at Hopefield and in the then Transvaal at Makapansgat and Sterkfontein. His prior experience was broad-ranging, to be sure – human and comparative anatomy, physical anthropology and palaeontology – and his research record under Raymond Dart at Witwatersrand was impressive. His doctoral thesis there in 1946 on 'Muscular Variation in the Human Leg and Foot, with Special Reference to the South African Native' tellingly brought together his anatomical and physical anthropological interests within the racialised framework then so common among white scientists in South Africa.

To Drennan's typological lectures in Anatomy I on 'race characters, as found in the skeleton of various types of mankind [*sic*]', Wells thus added a human genetics component, though given his shyness and obvious lack of ease before large classes – 'he would not make eye contact with his class', remembered one of his students[88] – it is doubtful if what he said made a lasting impression. 'You learnt anatomy at the [dissecting] table, not in his lectures', judged another student bluntly.[89]

For almost every second-year MBChB student, their initial entry into the dissection rooms, with their all-pervading, sickly sweet smell of death and formalin, was an unnerving landmark in their training as, for most, it marked their first encounter with death. 'Rows of silent figures swathed in thick plastic sheets lie in long parallel rows around us …', recalled one graphically, 'like a subterranean tomb filled with ancient mummies … Using our scalpels, we are gradually turning the human body into … a *Gray's Anatomy* spread out before us.'[90]

But for the handful of students who were not white-skinned, entry into the dissection rooms constituted a second landmark too, their first experience of UCT as an officially segregated institution. Not only were the rooms separated along gender lines (as they had been since 1911), but also according to students' skin colour, as had been the case since the mid-1940s. There were thus three separate dissection rooms in the department, a large one for white male students, and two smaller rooms, one for all 'non-white' students and one solely for white women students.[91] The shock of being formally segregated by race for the first time at UCT is still evident in the following recollection by a 'coloured' woman doctor 49 years after that watershed moment: 'When they first split the class along gender lines, and the females from our ['coloured'] group followed [the white women students to the female dissection room], they [the laboratory assistants stopped us and] said, "No, not you."'[92] Instead, they were directed to the 'non-white' dissection room.

Even the choice of cadavers reflected the department's exaggerated racial sensitivities on behalf of whites, for no white cadavers were laid out in the 'non-white' dissection room, so as to ensure that the students there did not lay a hand on a white body and so surreptitiously infringe the country's racial order. Cadavers assigned to white students were not, however, subjected to such posthumous segregation, presumably because the department did not feel that black bodies being dissected by white-held scalpels posed a threat to the racial status quo. A similar hyper-sensitivity, this time on behalf of all female students, ensured that only women's corpses were allocated to them for dissection. In the South Africa of those decades, race and gender regularly topped science and logic. A candid aside by a clear-eyed laboratory attendant, 'When the skin is off, they all look the same',[93] would therefore not have gone down well with the powers that be in the department.

The academic powers that be in the department included an unusually large number of men who went on to occupy chairs elsewhere, two at the University of Natal Medical School, one at Witwatersrand, and Singer at Chicago. Of the professors at Natal, one, Ted Keen, eventually returned to UCT in 1974 to succeed Wells. This meant that the UCT Anatomy Department came to have a significant influence, both good and ill, on anatomy training well beyond its walls.

The rest of the academic staff between 1948 and 1968 consisted of nine men and two women, all of them white-skinned. The appointment of the women was deemed necessary so that a woman would supervise dissections in the room used by female students. Preparing the cadavers and laying them out were, however, the responsibility of the department's technical assistants led by the taciturn Archie Lamb and the gregarious giant of a man, Daan Coetzee, whose room became a regular haven for students in need of emotional support, a plaster for a scalpel cut or an aspirin. Especially in the week when dissections began, there was usually a queue outside his office in the basement.

One floor up, in the Anatomy lecture theatre, the contents of the syllabus for second-year students changed little between 1948 and 1968, modelled as it was on that at Edinburgh University, Drennan's alma mater and Wells's most recent home. Its basic topographic approach to the body remained as that set out in Cunningham's classic *Textbook of Anatomy*, first published in 1902 and eventually to run into fifteen editions, to two of which Drennan contributed. Gross human anatomy, embryology and physical anthropology formed the core of the syllabus, complemented by visits to the Anatomy Museum on the same floor, with its 'rich and growing collection of human skeletal material of different racial origin', as a departmental job advertisement proudly put it.[94] A trimmed-down version of this course was also given to physiotherapy and nurse-tutor students from 1957. The only significant changes to the MBChB syllabus were the addition of radiographic anatomy in 1953 to take advantage of the perspectives offered by X-rays and Wells's inclusion of human genetics soon after he arrived. When an Anatomy II course was introduced in 1967 as part of a revived BSc (Medicine) degree, it elaborated on these topics and gave a wider view of the discipline as a whole.

Medical students in their clinical years received refresher courses along the lines of the Anatomy I course, though with a more applied bent, most obviously in the section on surgical anatomy. Similarly practical, though for a very different purpose, were the short courses in basic anatomy which the department gave to speech therapy and fine art students. Once a week the latter group of students introduced an unaccustomed air of levity into its gloomy corridors redolent of what Coetzee pungently described as 'meth, death and formalin'. 'You are the queerest crowd', he told one such carefree group. 'We have to be, you know,' came the reply, 'after all, we're artists!'⁹⁵

But such high-spiritedness was not the norm among students in the building. Most were weighed down by the sheer volume of anatomical data which they had to memorise and the number of bones they had to be able to identify. Those who did so successfully were left with a good working knowledge of anatomy, to be sure, but also with the idea of immutable racial differences and fixed racial typologies strongly endorsed both by what they had been taught in the department and how they had been taught. Once in place, such racialised lenses were not easily removed. Nor did they prompt any questioning of the racial ideas underpinning apartheid. Quite the opposite.

Not that the main third-year course for medical students, pathology, did anything but reinforce such racialised conceptions, for its post-mortems were also segregated by race, with students of a hue different from that of white cadavers not permitted to attend on pain of being 'dismissed at the stroke of a pen', as Dean Bromilow-Downing made abundantly clear.⁹⁶ In some years, therefore, they had to 'peep through a crack in the swing doors [of the mortuary] first to see whether it was a white body [being brought in] in order to know whether we could go in or not', recalled one such student bitterly.⁹⁷ In other years they took their seats in the mortuary, but were then instructed to leave if the corpse about to be brought in was white. With bizarre logic, however, 'non-white' students were allowed to see organs from white cadavers once these had been removed. Paradoxically, not one of the upholders of this white racial sensitivity seems to have taken note of the fact that all bodies had already been washed and prepared for the autopsy by a black African mortuary attendant. Almost all of these 'upholders' were white academic staff from the Department of Pathology, who seem to have implemented this crude maintenance of the racial order in South Africa without a second thought, so ingrained had it become in them.

Between 1947 and 1960 the Department of Pathology was part of a larger Division of Pathology, which included the Departments of Bacteriology and Chemical Pathology too. To all intents and purposes, however, the divisional structure was no more than a means to facilitate co-ordination among the three departments so that they would more easily fit within GSH's organisational structure, where their interests would be more effectively represented if they were conjoined. Academically, however, they were virtually autonomous.

From 1948 to 1971 the Department of Pathology was headed by Jim Thomson, an Aberdonian by schooling, medical training and accent. A dexterous pathologist with seventeen years' experience in four universities and some 2000 post-mortems to his credit, he came to UCT from the University of Durham's Medical School in Newcastle, aged 42. A man of strong personality, choleric temperament and brusque manner, he quickly restored the department to the traditional path of post-mortems, specimen reports and tutorials among the bottles on the shelves of the Pathology Museum, from which it had begun to veer towards active clinical pathology in Ryrie's last years as head.[98] Naturally, Thomson's lectures reinforced his more conservative conception of his subject, which he presented in a rambling manner punctuated by sallies against views with which he disagreed. He was 'most dogmatic – there were no shades of grey as far as Thomson was concerned and he was prone to lay down the law. He would say, "This is the diagnosis, it cannot be anything else!" and of course this inevitably led to friction in certain areas', recounted a close colleague.[99] For their part, students were taken aback to hear him proclaim, 'Everybody else believes this and therefore I believe that this is nonsense', as he paced up and down in front of them.[100] It was a lecturing style which 'grew on one', admitted a senior student wryly.[101]

Less idiosyncratic was his teaching at the autopsy table and in the laboratory where his attention to detail drove home the need for sharp-eyed observation in making a post-mortem diagnosis, while his rapid-fire questioning, sharp wit and conspicuous, raised eyebrows ensured that those attending had prepared themselves well. Those whom he considered to be fools he did not suffer gladly.

His second-in-command and eventual successor, Dirk Uys, was definitely no such person. 'I may well have subjected … him to greater stresses than usual,' acknowledged Thomson, but it 'has left his co-operation and loyalty quite unaffected'.[102] Indeed, Uys, a UCT and Witwatersrand graduate who joined the department in 1955 as a senior lecturer, was known for his unruffled and equable temperament, in striking contrast to his head. His clear, concise and logical lectures also contrasted markedly with Thomson's fare, yet as diagnostic histopathologists both men were equally accomplished. Unlike Thomson, however, Uys was an active researcher, especially in the field of comparative pathology, which, in the South Africa of those years, invariably meant the investigation of diseases 'whose incidence and presentation', he explained, 'are significantly altered in the Bantu and other racial groups'.[103] His Witwatersrand MD thesis on 'Renal Pathology in the Bantu Race' (1954) well illustrates this contemporary fixation on racial difference in every aspect of life – and death.

In the 1960s, however, prompted by the rise in organ transplantation at GSH, he began to explore the pathology of transplanted organs and the techniques for investigating their tissues. In this, as in all his research projects, he collaborated easily and productively with his fellow researchers. He was, one of them predicted accurately, 'a colleague with whom his associates would have the happiest of relationships'.[104]

Of the other long-serving members of the academic staff, only Golda Selzer made her mark as a researcher, working in the fields of virology and immunology rather than pathology. This won her a UCT fellowship in 1966, although to several generations of students she was much better known for her pioneering forays into clinical pathology in her teaching (despite Thomson's disapproval), the counselling, encouragement and academic support she readily gave to all medical students, especially if they were struggling with pathology, and her pivotal role in the creation and operation of the Students' Health and Welfare Centres Organization (SHAWCO). Appropriately, the citation which accompanied UCT's award of an honorary doctorate to her in 1987 did not miss the opportunity to liken her to 'another kind of selzer that also bubbles and that also deals effectively with acidity'.[105]

Yet, for most of her colleagues in the Pathology Department, the time required to conduct biopsies of thousands of specimens from UCT's main teaching hospital (a commitment dating back to the department's inception in 1918) left little opportunity for research. Even Thomson bemoaned the fact that, though head of the department, he had to spend 'more of his time in matters concerning the hospital histopathology and autopsy service … than in academic affairs'.[106] While such behind-the-scenes work certainly generated additional income and thus additional staff and resources for the department, it did little to improve its teaching and research record.

This was initially the case too in the Department of Chemical Pathology, which began to be accepted in its own right as not just a branch of the Pathology Department in 1949 when Ryrie's former assistant in pathological chemistry, Geoffrey Linder, was appointed UCT's first professor of chemical pathology.[107]

Under him, the new department shared his own preferred low profile – his mentor at Bart's in London had spoken of him as 'a careful and … wise investigator … [with] a retiring personality'.[108] His teaching, research, routine biopsies and running of the department thus proceeded without fanfare, but also without much growth. His successor, James Kench, thus inherited a department in 1958 with a staff of just two technologists besides himself, a budget which was tiny, and no more equipment than 'a rusty centrifuge counterpoised by [three] sandbags'.[109] For the forceful, forthright and ambitious Kench – one of his referees described him as 'somewhat abrupt and unpolished'[110] – fresh from the well-endowed University of Manchester, this was an intolerable situation which he quickly set about transforming.

Himself possessing doctorates in both chemistry and medicine, he had no doubt that his department should have a more chemical orientation in all that it did. He therefore appointed two medical biochemists to his staff, revamped the syllabus to include more organic chemistry, required students to sit in on biopsy tests by his staff, and insisted that the department have a distinct entry in the Faculty of Medicine prospectus and that a separate examination be introduced in the subject for fourth-year medical students. Lacking the necessary foundation in chemistry and biochemistry, they struggled to follow his intricate, detailed lectures, which were delivered, to boot, with a heavy Mancunian accent; but they were awed by his commitment to remaining on the cutting edge of his subject, which he publicly demonstrated by tearing up his lecture notes after each lecture 'since he hoped that they would be out of date by the next year'.[111] On one memorable occasion he even made his class rip up their notes taken at his previous lecture as an article in the latest *Nature* had disproved what he had taught them the week before.

His commitment to his own research on disorders of protein metabolism was equally zealous. In 1963 the Council for Scientific and Industrial Research (CSIR) recognised the quality of his work by establishing a Protein Research Unit under him in the department. This added further staff to a complement already growing to meet the teaching hospitals' need for biopsy investigations. These had increased from 50,000 per annum in 1959 to 236,600 in 1967.

These figures point to the escalating demand for such biopsies as routine by the medical profession in general, which accordingly made private sector pathology an appealing career for new graduates. A growing number of postgraduates in the department from the 1960s bore testimony to this fact and to the reputation Kench had created for it as a hotspot of medical science.

In supervising them Kench was assisted by two of his best MMed (Path) students, Gideon Potgieter and Mervyn Berman, both of whom he appointed to his staff and both of whom subsequently went on to fill chairs in the subject, the former at the University of the Orange Free State and the latter as his own successor at UCT from 1977. Determined to follow intellectually but not temperamentally in Kench's footsteps, in his inaugural lecture Berman did add one wry reservation about his mentor's approach to his job, 'namely that he set and expected too high a standard from both students, [and] postgraduates and of medical practice in general'.[112] That Berman himself was rated in the Faculty as 'an excellent teacher at both undergraduate and postgraduate level'[113] suggests that his tongue may not have been entirely in his cheek when he made the above remark.

The third department making up the Division of Pathology, Bacteriology, was headed from 1946 by Marinus van den Ende, a 34-year-old whizz-kid who returned to his alma mater fresh from doing state-of-the-art research at the National Institute for Medical Research in London during World War II.[114] Convinced that bacteriology's future lay in virology – 'that's what is going to take over', he told a rapt class[115] – he overhauled the syllabus to give virology a more prominent place and backed up his words by setting up a CSIR-funded Virus Research Unit in his department.

To his lectures he brought a currency and an engagement which students found exciting. 'Drawing upon his own research experience,' recalled a colleague who sat in on his lectures, 'he presented his subject as living and vital.'[116] Students marvelled at the ease with which he was able to reduce complex material 'to basic ideas quickly' and make them accessible.[117] These traits were equally evident in the charismatic leadership he provided in the numerous projects which he initiated in the Virus Research Unit, on diseases like influenza, polio, rabies, Rift Valley fever and bluetongue in sheep. Indeed, *Lancet* spoke of him as 'a born research-worker, both in the laboratory and in the field, with a highly critical mind and amazing energy',[118] while medical and scientific members of his unit alike 'looked to him for an unfailing supply of the van den Ende drive and inspiration', reported the *British Medical Journal*.[119]

Within a short time his reputation as a dynamic research leader soared, giving him and his department an ascending profile locally and internationally. The CSIR, the Poliomyelitis Research Foundation, the Cape Blood Transfusion Service, the South African Bureau of Standards and the new World Health Organisation appointed him to their committees, and in 1956 the Swiss pharmaceutical giant CIBA invited him to participate in its international symposium on the nature of viruses, along with the likes of Crick and Watson of DNA fame. Three years earlier UCT had appointed him as full-time Dean of the Faculty of Medicine; characteristically, he had accepted only if he was allowed to retain his chair in bacteriology and continue his beloved research after hours. Yet his many-sided talents were unable to reach full flower, for he died of lymphoma in 1957, aged 45.

His was certainly a very hard act to follow. The man chosen to do so was his former deputy, the 44-year-old Arthur Kipps, also a UCT medical graduate, who had worked in the department since 1947. Mentored by Van den Ende – his MD thesis was on the bluetongue virus – he continued to give virology equal exposure in the department's teaching and research, ensuring that the Virus Research Unit continued to be a prolific source of scholarly publications. More than forty of these bore his name as author or co-author, while he received high praise in the acknowledgements section of many a postgraduate thesis for the quality of his supervision.

Like Van den Ende's, Kipps's virological expertise was sought after by many local and foreign bodies and, like his mentor's too, his lectures were models of lucidity and enthusiasm. 'He dramatized his material so that he often had us sitting on the edge of our seats', enthused a student of his who went on to occupy a chair himself. 'I remember his waving a copy of *Scientific American* at us while expounding on an early review of interferon with such effect that we were convinced that this was the most important discovery made during our life-time.'[120]

Though less dramatic in their pedagogic technique, others in the department were equally able to impress students with their teaching, Walter Becker by his brisk, straight-to-the-point style, Andy Naudé by his meticulously prepared lectures and willingness to go the extra mile to help those struggling with the subject, and Arderne Forder by what students labelled the 'verve and academic joyousness' with which he lectured[121] and his affirming use of the title 'Dr' to every one of them, even though they were only in the third year of their MBChB degree programme. That all three of them went on to fill chairs of their own – the first at Stellenbosch and the last two at UCT – speaks of their ability as scholars. Moreover, that Naudé and Becker, as professors, followed the virological path which Van den Ende had blazed attests to their mentor's ongoing influence far beyond the grave. At UCT this culminated in the creation in 1978 of a separate chair in clinical virology on a par with that of bacteriology.

Although the curriculum planners tried to ease the transition from the pre-clinical to the clinical subjects by a degree of mutual intercalation, it is evident that to students, entry into the clinical years was a big step up to where 'real medicine' began. 'Medicine at last,' enthused one new fourth-year excitedly, 'at last the vast amount of knowledge … can be applied, the scientific approach to healing of sickness practised.' Another felt that this entry to the clinical years and to GSH was like 'a first graduation'.[122]

For the clinical departments the quarter-century after 1948 was a harvest time in which they reaped the fruit of the investment which they had made in research, training and resources in the preceding decade. On the tide of a thriving economy and the Joint Staff Agreement and research funding which this made possible, these departments swelled in terms of staff, postgraduates, laboratory facilities and research output. For example, between 1950 and 1970 the number of full-time consultants in the Department of Medicine rose from 4 to 29, the number of registrars from 4 to 26, and the number of publications per annum from 6 to 155. It was, indeed, a golden era for the department.

The two men who laid the foundation for this efflorescence of the Department of Medicine had jointly led it since 1938, Frank Forman as professor in clinical medicine and John Brock as professor in the practice of medicine.[123] Their respective skills complemented each other neatly. Forman was a superb clinician and teacher by example, combining diagnostic ability of the highest order with gentleness of manner towards patients, which became the stuff of legend and emulation among several generations of undergraduates, interns and registrars.[124] One of his students paid him the supreme accolade of declaring, 'If you were sick as a student, you would go to Forman.'[125]

Brock, for his part, could not hold a candle to Forman in the wards, but was a researcher and project leader of international calibre, his particular field being nutritional diseases. His undoubted talent in these two roles secured him funding from the CSIR to found a Social Medicine Research Unit in the department in 1950 (it was renamed the Clinical Nutrition Research Unit in 1952 to reflect its thrust better), which became his vehicle for conducting pioneering research into kwashiorkor and the connection between dietary fat, cholesterol and coronary heart disease. Since South Africa, with its diverse disease profile and racial composition, offered extensive opportunities to investigate both diseases of poverty and wealth, Brock was able to attract substantial funding to his unit from US foundations, the American National Institutes of Health, pharmaceutical firms and the World Health Organisation, which made the unit a thriving research hub within what a contemporary called 'a fertile intellectual environment'.[126]

Yet, unlike Van den Ende, Brock carried little of his innovative research into his undergraduate lectures, which were broad in scope but largely derived from Davidson's *Textbook of Medicine*. His attempt to introduce social medicine into the syllabus – in 1951 he still believed it 'to be the greatest contribution I can make to our University and Medical School'[127] – had very limited success and remained marginalised from mainstream clinical training, constituting, in the eyes of most students and staff, 'an idealistic distraction'[128] on the road to professional qualification because of its equal attention to a patient's social and psychological circumstances along with the physical. In the words of a student of the time, 'We wanted real, exciting pneumonia, a proper stroke, real myocardial infarction. We wanted real medicine, pukka disease, not theory.'[129] Even with Brock's support as sole professor in medicine, a position he assumed in 1954 when Forman gave up his chair, the three men who filled the dedicated senior lectureship in social (or, as it was relabelled from 1961, 'comprehensive') medicine between 1954 and 1969 were unable to integrate their approach into the syllabus in the face of what an ally of Brock's described as 'the conservative clinical approach of his peers and the explosion of technical advances and therapeutic expertise that occurred between 1940 and 1980'.[130] The most they could manage was to organise 'comprehensive' ward rounds once a week, in which a consultant physician's firm was expanded to include a GP, a social worker, a physiotherapist and a dietician. All the same, with Brock's retirement in 1970, even wishful mention of comprehensive medicine in the department's prospectus entry vanished. Its approach was to find a more congenial home in the new Department of Community Health two years later.

Foremost among Brock's clinical peers – Forman apart – were a host of very able clinicians-cum-researchers, each one of whom made his name in a distinct field of medicine: Lennox Eales (who in 1964 followed Forman in the chair of clinical medicine) won international fame for his pioneering research into porphyria, which convinced the CSIR to co-fund his Renal Metabolic Research Group in the department; Peter Jackson whose investigations into diabetes and pre-diabetes drew him into endocrinology, then a fledgling field in which he and his former house physician, Raymond Hoffenberg, were pioneers in South Africa as leading members of the department's Endocrine Research Group; and Velva Schrire, a world-class cardiologist who founded not only a cardiac clinic at GSH in 1951 despite the opposition of his seniors, who disapproved of so narrow a specialty, but who also went on to gain the backing of the CSIR to establish a fourth research unit, on cardio-vascular pulmonary diseases, in the department in 1960.

While only Eales and Hoffenberg possessed matching pedagogical skills – in both cases students spoke of their ability to make even complex matters intelligible to undergraduates, a tell-tale sign of a good teacher – the department did not rely on them alone to provide good-quality teaching. Two up-and-coming physicians, Stuart Saunders and Eugene Dowdle,[131] began to win praise from students for their bedside teaching from soon after their return to UCT in 1960, while over twenty physicians in private practice, acting as part-time consultants or clinical tutors, effectively taught senior students the clinical ropes from their own accumulated experience rather than from textbooks. About one of the best of these, the long-serving Helen Brown (the only woman on the department's academic staff), a former student wrote, 'Her clinical acumen, experience, theoretical knowledge and simple approach to solving problems have left their mark on everyone.'[132]

Her mark was of a piece with that which the department as a whole sought to leave on its students, viz. how to approach a patient properly, how to take a full case history systematically before making an examination – 'we used to have little tape recordings [of the questions to be asked, in the right order so as] … to learn things like that', recalled a student of the 1960s[133] – and how to respect a patient. This close contact between students and patients amazed a German exchange student as it was so different from the situation in his home country, where students only rarely examined a patient themselves. Teaching at UCT was 'from a rather practical outlook', he reported, 'the stress is put on the teaching of the different signs and symptoms and how to come to a correct diagnosis. It is the patient who is at the centre of your thoughts, and not only his disease.'[134] From this and other contemporary accounts, it is clear that, notwithstanding the escalating revolution in medical technology then under way, the old style of hands-on medicine it had inherited from its Scottish forebears was still common at UCT.

Yet, it is unlikely that the proclaimed ideal of dealing with patients courteously and respectfully was always fully observed, whether because of students' gaucherie or their over-eagerness to examine especially interesting cases or because, in the racialised social order of apartheid South Africa, white doctors might quite unthinkingly patronise patients of a different skin hue. Such patients 'were stripped and lay there exposed, without apology [by the white physicians], while with white patients they were polite, exposing only that part of the body that was to be examined', recalled a 'coloured' medical student of the early 1960s indignantly.[135] Nor was this all that embittered 'coloured' students during their clinical years; in particular, they objected to the way in which they were deliberately excluded from seeing any white patients, be it in wards, in outpatient departments or in clinical presentations. In practice this translated into their halting and staying behind when a clinical firm crossed from 'non-white' to the white wards of GSH or the four other teaching hospitals, or their leaving the lecture room if a white patient was wheeled in for a clinical demonstration. 'We darkies sat in a corner [of the lecture room] so that a rapid exit could be made when a "European" patient was brought in', remembered an Indian student of the 1950s.[136] Rare attempts by progressive lecturers to ignore these standard discriminatory practices at GSH were, until the 1970s, rebuffed by ward sisters acting, literally, as gatekeepers. Forman's characteristically non-confrontational response to this situation was to opt to present only 'non-white' cases in his clinical demonstrations so that no students would be excluded. As for UCT itself, for all of its lip-service opposition to academic segregation, it did not formally challenge these overtly discriminatory, non-statutory practices, citing what it believed to be 'the legal limitations of our position'.[137]

These practices, in the view of some 'coloured' and Indian students of this era, rendered the clinical teaching which they received 'seriously flawed in theory and practice', as one put it.[138] For instance, a 'coloured' student trained in the 1960s admitted years later that being limited to 'Non-European' wards gave her the impression that white women did not get genital tract infections. To her it seemed that 'non-white' women were 'the only ones who get [Fallopian] tubal infections. [And] only black women … do not use family planning.'[139] A contemporary of hers felt that he had been exposed to only half the cases white students were, 'yet [was] expected to perform as well'.[140] More poignantly, over fifty years after graduating, an Indian doctor reflected, 'I often wonder what real student life would have been like if there was no segregation at that time.'[141]

Such racially discriminatory teaching practices were as much the norm in the Department of Medicine's equally eminent clinical peer, Surgery, prompting a few 'coloured' and Indian students to boycott surgical ward rounds on occasions, in exasperation at being denied access to unusual cases in white wards. '[We] would adjourn to the medical library', recalled one, to study textbooks instead,[142] which only intensified their sense of receiving an inferior training.

THE APPLIED SCIENCES

*Student dissection of Medical School staff (1): Professor Jannie Louw*

What they missed out on was full exposure to the accelerating post-war revolution in surgery, in the vanguard of which stood UCT's Department of Surgery. Regular visits to the United States and Western Europe, extensive subscriptions to international journals and weekly journal club meetings kept the staff abreast of the latest developments in the discipline so that innovations like intravenous fluid therapy, using antibiotics in lung surgery, improved anaesthesia, inserting prostheses like pacemakers and shunts, and open-heart surgery were introduced soon after their first use in First World hospitals. For example, the first open-heart operation in Africa using a heart-lung machine was performed by a member of the department at GSH in 1958, just five years after it was pioneered in Philadelphia.

Of the three professors to head the department after the retirement of its founder, Charles Saint, in 1946, two were steadfast disciples of his, Marcus Cole Rous (1947–9)[143] and Jannie Louw (1955–80); unsurprisingly, they adhered closely to his approach to surgery and how to teach it.[144] Posters bearing his aphorisms hung on the department's walls and his little red book, *An Introduction to Surgery*, was 'our bible during surgical clerkships', recalled a student of the late 1950s.[145]

The professor not from the Saint school, Jan Erasmus (1950–5), was a Witwatersrand graduate with an unusually holistic view of surgery for the time. His meticulously prepared lectures were thus stronger on explaining how surgical interventions should restore the functioning of the whole body system – so-called surgical physiology – than on the practical surgical techniques required to do so. The dissatisfaction that this caused among his colleagues and scalpel-minded undergraduates, along with his growing personal preference for the highly specialised field of neurosurgery, led him to resign in 1955, though only 44, so he could pursue his favoured specialty full-time.

By contrast, his successor, the 40-year-old Jannie Louw, was a hands-on medical generalissimo who stamped his dictatorial personality on everything he did. His systematic lectures to undergraduates were clear, richly illustrated and thoroughly didactic, allowing for no questions from his students. Yet few missed them, for such was his grasp of his subject that 'if one followed the system and the rules [he outlined], surgery became simple', opined a top student.[146] With the benefit of a different angle of vision, Erasmus judged Louw's teaching 'forceful, precise and at times somewhat dogmatic'.[147]

His ward rounds were models of bedside teaching by instruction and intimidation. On anyone – undergraduate, intern, registrar or consultant – who was not a hundred per cent prepared when presenting a case, his sharp tongue and short temper were unleashed. 'He could demolish you … if you weren't up to speed', attested a former intern ruefully. 'You'd have to have your results at your fingertips … no use scratching,

THE APPLIED SCIENCES

*Student dissection of Medical School staff (2): Professor Chris Barnard*

looking through notes … You had to know them … God, did he crack the whip!'[148]

Yet, as overbearing as he was in dealing with his juniors and subordinates, so was he caring towards his patients, whose well-being was uppermost in his priorities – he treated them 'essentially as human beings', noted Erasmus.[149] This was particularly so with child patients of whom he had many as he specialised in paediatric surgery. Woe betide any junior doctor if the file of any of these patients was not wholly up to date when Louw paid an unexpected visit or made a late-night phone call to his ward. 'His forte lay at the bedside, and one thing he taught us was how to look after a patient, since the welfare of his patients always came first', confirmed three of his colleagues.[150] Certainly his style was abrasive, but it did hammer home to his students his intended lesson, that assiduous patient care was a non-negotiable.

Nor is it surprising that a perfectionist's attention to detail characterised his conduct before, during and after an operation. A neat, adaptable surgeon who could think on his feet, he pioneered paediatric surgery as a specialty in South Africa, turning a 90% mortality in neonate operations into a 90% survival rate. 'Virtually single-handedly [he] revolutionized surgical care for children', judged one of his successors,[151] an achievement which won him honours locally and abroad. 'In the USA, to say one has had part of one's training under Jannie Louw is to be rewarded immediately with a nod of approbation and some envy', acknowledged a former colleague of his there.[152]

Under his iron rule for 25 years, UCT's Department of Surgery certainly lacked neither direction nor an ethos exactly like Louw's. As Erasmus observed drily with reference to both its past and its future, 'The tendency towards dogma is … very strong in the Cape Town Surgical School.'[153]

Although Louw's own research – apart from his forays into Cape Town's medical history[154] – was largely case-driven, empirical and narrowly focused, he was enough of a general surgeon to appreciate larger-scale experimental research in his department too. Thus, when the innovative vascular researcher Robert Goetz left the department for another surgical research post in New York in 1958,[155] Louw ensured that the funding which Goetz's unit had received was directed into a wider range of surgical research fields. In 1958, therefore, he appointed to a new post of Director of Surgical Research his protégé, a go-getting UCT graduate who had just returned from two years at the state-of-the-art surgical research and training centre at the University of Minnesota, the 36-year-old Chris Barnard.

Barnard's own specialty, cardio-thoracic surgical research, was quickly at the front of the funding queue. With characteristic energy and determination, he 'galvanized his unit into crescendo activity', to use Louw's words,[156] and within a few years it was internationally known for its pioneering open-heart and prosthetic heart valve surgery and for the wide disciplinary range of clinicians, medical scientists and postgraduates attracted to its vibrant laboratories, lectures and seminars. A newcomer from the Mayo Clinic found its atmosphere 'one of great excitement'.[157] Not surprisingly, four of the department's six ChM graduates between 1960 and 1967 worked on cardio-thoracic topics under Barnard. Undergraduates, however, saw little of him, save for an occasional lecture, or on a ward round with a tail of interns and registrars streaming behind him 'like a comet' (as one student observed graphically[158]), or when he delivered a memorable inaugural address on being promoted to the rank of associate professor in 1962. The address began dramatically as he proclaimed to his wide-eyed audience, 'The heart is just a pump!'[159]

Five years later he proved this assertion by exchanging one heart for another in the world's first heart transplant operation, performed at GSH, 'the surgical equivalent of the ascent of Everest', as *Time* magazine described it.[160] This was indeed the culmination of his methodical preparation over the preceding nine years of both himself and his surgical, scientific and technical team drawn from UCT and GSH. 'Teamwork', averred Louw proudly, was the 'sine qua non', and this had been made possible by close interdepartmental co-operation and co-ordination within the Faculty of Medicine and by UCT's Joint Staff Agreement with the CPA. 'The surgeon, although an essential and indeed a major cog in the wheel, is no longer the only one.'[161] Accurately, the *South African Medical Journal* described Barnard as 'the conductor of an orchestra of medical and nursing and technical personnel'.[162]

Nonetheless, the Department of Surgery and the Faculty of Medicine generally basked vicariously in the global acclaim for Barnard which followed. Not only did he hold his jampacked post-operation press conferences at the Medical School where awestruck students jostled to catch a glimpse of him, but just eleven days after the operation, he received an honorary DSc from UCT, the only serving member of staff ever to be so honoured. It was a high point not only in Barnard's career, but also in the history of his department, his faculty and his university. As he explained, 'We have grown up together, as it were, and have gained most of our experience together.'[163]

By then the Department of Surgery, with 36 academic members, was twice its pre-Joint Staff Agreement size. As in all the clinical departments, the Agreement had transformed the department's staffing situation by permitting part-time staff, in particular, to be increased significantly in number. It is telling of the unashamedly masculine ethos which the discipline exuded at UCT – as elsewhere in the world – that this increase included no women. The mixture of new ideas and fresh approaches which younger, part-time consultants like 'Helmie' Madden, Bill Silber and Bill Schulze added to the breadth of experience of long-serving general surgeons like George Sacks, Robert Forsyth and Jack Heselson reinforced the department's clinical teaching. Combined with Louw's exemplary lectures, this meant that, in all senses of the phrase, surgery at UCT in the 1950s and 1960s was at the cutting edge.

Even before the 1951 Agreement came into force, several consultants had developed specialties (like orthopaedics, urology, otorhinolaryngology, ophthalmology, plastic surgery, thoracic surgery and neurosurgery) alongside their practice of general surgery, even to the point of having GSH recognise these specialties and specifically allocate beds to them. With the growth in academic staff after 1951, UCT also formally acknowledged this escalating world-wide trend towards surgical sub-specialisation by creating seven parallel academic sub-departments with their own heads, but under the broad authority of the Department of Surgery when it came to teaching.

Four of these (Urology; Diseases of the Ear, Nose and Throat, which was given the more professional name Otorhinolaryngology in 1958; Neurosurgery; and Plastic Surgery, which was broadened into Plastic Surgery and Maxillo-Facial Surgery in 1966) were still finding their feet academically for most of this period. Headed and, in the main, staffed by part-timers who simultaneously ran busy private practices, these consultants had to balance their private work with their teaching and their clinical commitments at GSH. This was not easy to do, however diligent a practitioner was. 'No matter how devoted a person is in the academic department', observed one part-time consultant with long experience in a similar department, 'I don't think a part-time head can ever compare with a full-time head.'[164] This meant that these fledgling sub-departments had to accept the handful of teaching slots allocated to them in the MBChB programme, that their disciplines barely featured in final examinations or orals, and that they generated very little research. Between 1950 and 1968 all four sub-departments together produced only four MD, six MMed and six ChM graduates. Most were in otorhinolaryngology. A neurosurgeon could have been speaking for all four sub-departments when he put the absence of research in his department down to the fact that 'neurosurgery has, to a large extent, been service-oriented due to the demands made by a large population in need of expert care … [and it also] had to establish itself in the academic sphere to gain acceptance in student training programs'.[165] Echoing him, a urologist explained, 'Research was difficult because of the heavy clinical load and virtual absence of fulltime staff.'[166]

The two, long-in-the tooth part-timers teaching dental surgery, a distinct section within Plastic Surgery, did not even apologise for their lack of research, for they were purely practical in orientation. Indeed, they even eschewed lecturing to medical students, basing their teaching instead only on clinical demonstrations and practical instruction at the chair-side. Even after the extraction of their section from Plastic Surgery in 1965 and the creation of a new sub-department called Oral and Dental Surgery, this approach persisted, intensifying the feeling of most medical students that the subject was an unnecessary burden in a South Africa in which GPs were less and less likely to be called upon to perform even elementary dental surgery. Eventually, in 1999, dental surgery returned to its vestigial place in Plastic Surgery.

Two other sub-specialties within the Department of Surgery, orthopaedic surgery and ophthalmology, followed a rather different trajectory, as by 1968 both had full chairs and numerous full-time staff thanks to large donations from outside UCT. In Orthopaedic Surgery the Pieter Moll and Nuffield Chair[167] was filled from 1955 by the dexterous Witwatersrand and Liverpool graduate, the 41-year-old Colin Lewer Allen, 'a large man with large hands and a rough, carpenter-like approach to his type of surgery', as a student saw him.[168] Within a short time he had introduced more hands-on training for students, like that at the mecca of orthopaedic training, Liverpool University,[169] and had increased the number of orthopaedic beds available for doing this by having the Princess Alice Orthopaedic Home in Retreat accepted as a teaching hospital and significantly expanded in capacity. However, his primary interest was in the mechanism of impaired gait rather than its surgical correction, which led him to develop a 'UCT Artificial Limb', a novel prosthesis for patients who had lost a leg. When news of this invention reached the press in 1959, letters from disabled people all over the world flooded the department, 'a fan-mail which would have pleased any Hollywood film star', joked Allen.[170] But his hopes that this would become a lucrative source of funding for further prosthetic research were disappointed when the CSIR raised doubts about the efficacy of the artificial limb. Disheartened, he withdrew into clinical work and unenthusiastic teaching. His sub-department consequently entered a period of drift, attracting very few postgraduates as it staggered under the weight of trauma surgery at GSH, a situation which continued until his early retirement for health reasons in 1976.

In this unpromising situation, the best teachers were usually those who had a clinical base outside the department in private practice, men like Teddy Sarkin, Martin Singer and George Dall, all of whom drew on their experience in the polio epidemic of 1956–7 to inform their teaching.

The other sub-department to secure a full chair in this period, Ophthalmology, was able to do so only because of a large endowment in 1968 by the Mauerberger Foundation, a local philanthropic trust set up by a successful Cape Town businessman. As this open-handedness had been preceded the year before by a not insubstantial donation to the sub-department by a grateful patient to help fund research, the purchase of specialised equipment, academic travel and the augmentation of staff salaries, Ophthalmology was well set to upgrade its academic side, which had languished as long as it had been staffed only by part-time consultants. In 1967 a full-time head was appointed for the first time and two years later the position was elevated into the Morris Mauerberger Chair of Ophthalmology, to which UCT appointed a Witwatersrand and London graduate, David Sevel. Only the third professor in the subject in the country, he was, at 35, also the youngest professor in the Faculty.

Even with this injection of vigour, the course given to fifth-year MBChB students (which was modelled on that given at London, Oxford and Manchester universities) was still regarded as marginal by most of them. 'We were told if we spelt it [ophthalmology] correctly we would pass', quipped one unimpressed student.[171] As for postgraduates, as only four students had gone on to gain MMed (Ophthalmology) degrees since they had been introduced in 1954, Sevel clearly needed to add vision to his vigour. Happily for the sub-department, he did.

As with all the sub-departments under the Department of Surgery (which were often lumped together dismissively as 'minor subjects'), Ophthalmology was allocated no more than fifteen lectures in the MBChB programme, along with a bi-weekly ward round and a limited number of Outpatients attendances at GSH. In the eyes of a consultant in the sub-department, this was 'completely inadequate',[172] a view which his colleagues in the other sub-departments would have endorsed. How to accommodate the burgeoning 'minor subjects' in the MBChB curriculum was a problem that the Faculty still believed in 1968 could be addressed by the lengthened academic year introduced in 1960. It would be another two decades before it recognised that this was not a viable solution.

One of the reasons for the difficulty in finding teaching time for 'minor subjects' in the curriculum was the unwillingness of the three dominant clinical departments, Medicine, Surgery, and Obstetrics and Gynaecology, to give up any of their allocation, a defence of their turf going back to the Faculty's earliest days. 'There was always an enormous competition for time', pointed out the professor of obstetrics and gynaecology, 'physicians wanted more time, surgeons wanted more time, and new disciplines wanted more time'.[173]

For itself, Obstetrics and Gynaecology was determined to maintain a ring-fence around its eight-week residency at a maternity hospital during the Practical Obstetrics block in fifth year. These students were warned to 'devote their whole time to the subject of Obstetrics while engaged in their practical work – except that they may attend systematic lectures, provided such attendance in no way interferes with instruction at the Maternity hospital'.[174]

During this time, all fifth-year students had to deliver at least ten babies themselves (this number was raised to fifteen in 1965) and to be present at or on standby for several more births. The frank recollection of one such student after attending his first birth doubtless captures the awestruck feelings of many – it 'was probably the most miraculous thing I had ever seen. The sudden coming to life of a bloodied ball of human flesh really illustrates the miracle of creation. I shall never forget the experience.'[175] Echoing this sentiment, a second student spoke of obstetrics as 'exciting – there you get your hands dirty'.[176]

Until GSH opened a maternity division of its own in 1963, clinical obstetrics was taught at the Somerset Hospital and at the three maternity homes dotted around the Cape Peninsula, the Peninsula Maternity Home in District Six, St Monica's in Bo-Kaap and the Mowbray Maternity Home. This geographical dispersion hampered efficient teaching, with staff and students having to travel back and forth for clerking and instruction. 'A certain degree of chaos in teaching ... now necessarily exists, because of the distances', complained one head of the department,[177] while students lacking cars were forced to rely on public transport. Latecomers to classes found little sympathy among the teaching staff.

Besides clinical obstetrics, undergraduate obstetrics and gynaecology training included nearly 100 systematic lectures, two-thirds on obstetrics and a third on gynaecology. In the former, the emphasis (at least until the mid-1960s) was on preventing maternal deaths in childbirth as many births still took place at home. Haughtily, surgeons referred to obstetricians as being no more than 'physicians with scissors'.[178]

However, with the introduction of foetal heart monitors, Apgar scores and refined methods of amniocentesis in the 1960s and with the importation of the first ultrasound machine to South Africa in 1967, the well-being of the foetus and the neonate began to attract more attention. Not unexpectedly, the word 'foetal' appears with growing frequency in the list of publications by members of the department from 1967. What is equally clear from this list is that gynaecology held far less appeal for the staff than did obstetrics. Between 1948 and 1968, only 30% of all scholarly articles they produced dealt with gynaecological topics, as against 70% with obstetrical topics. The gynaecological health of non-pregnant women was obviously still largely a Cinderella subject.

With but two notable exceptions, the meticulous obstetrician Patricia Massey and the unassuming gynaecologist Ruby Sharp, the staff in the department were all men, 8 of them in 1948, 14 in 1956 when Sharp left UCT, and 36 in 1970 when Massey retired. The department's founding father, Cuthbert Crichton, had retired in 1950,[179] but his surgical approach remained dominant in the department's teaching for the next decade and a half. Indeed, in the time of his successor, his former student and sometime first assistant, James Louw, the department was criticised by the South African Medical and Dental Council's inspector for paying 'too much attention … to major surgical procedures such as hysterectomies and Caesarian sections … One only has to know what a small percentage of those who qualify in medicine are ever called upon to undertake operations of this nature, to realise how teaching time could be better utilised.'[180]

In both the delivery room and the operating theatre Louw was the model of a deft, exact obstetrical and gynaecological surgeon whom students and registrars sought to emulate, but in the lecture theatre it was a different story: he was a rigid martinet who barred latecomers, talking and even note-taking, telling undergraduates, 'You must listen to me carefully',[181] as textbooks would provide the basic information needed. The contents of his lectures were consequently exiguous, to the point of some students even asking, 'Does this man merit his position and name?'[182]

Nor was he a prolific researcher – his private practice, very reluctantly approved by UCT in 1958, took up part of his every day – but he was an excellent organiser in the interests of his department. He set up an effective, Peninsula-wide obstetrical 'flying squad' which included two of his students; he established a cytological service in his department for all of Cape Town's maternity homes and clinics; he persuaded UCT to appoint his top student and the department's first MD graduate, Harold Jordaan, as an honorary lecturer in the department even though the CPA would not follow suit at a provincial hospital because he was not white-skinned;[183] and he successfully lobbied both UCT and the CPA to add a state-of-art Maternity Block to GSH in 1962. With wry humour, some students painted the teasing name 'St Jame's Palaace [*sic*]' above its entrance when it was almost complete. This 104-bed block at last gave the department what Louw called a 'central core' from which to run its multifarious activities.[184] Undoubtedly it was his greatest contribution to the department before his sudden death in 1964, at the age of 50.

His successor, the 40-year-old Dennis Davey, had a broader view of obstetrical and gynaecological training. His own student years at St Mary's Hospital Medical School in London and the Royal Postgraduate Medical School in that city had culminated in a PhD and convinced him that research should be as much part of his new department's brief as clinical work drawing on neonatology and the latest technology and techniques.

He therefore insisted on the construction of departmental laboratories, the recognition of cytology as a distinct sub-specialty, and the revamping of tutorials so that students were more closely involved in actual patient care. To follow through on these innovations, in 1967 he invited the pioneer of ultrasound, Ian Donald of Glasgow University (who was himself a UCT Arts graduate), to spend a few weeks in the department. Donald's riveting lectures and dynamic personality did just this. A student who was present remembered how he 'shook everything up' by arguing for a more interventionist approach to labour instead of 'wait and see' obstetrics.[185] That his words had an effect was quickly apparent in the change in obstetrical thinking adopted by several consultants working in the department's teaching hospitals.

Until Davey assumed the chair, almost all of the consultants were part-timers who ran private practices alongside their academic positions. In fact, Massey used to quip that she had 'born [*sic*] about half the people in Cape Town'.[186] Wanting a deeper commitment to both teaching and research, Davey slowly began to supplement these part-timers with young full-timers like the promising Herman de Groot, Peter Baillie and Wulf Utian. Already by 1968, therefore, nearly a quarter of the staff were full-time academics, a fact reflected in the lengthening list of books and articles by members of the department, the institution of an annual departmental research day, and the publication of an annual clinical report. The department was well set for a rebirth in a new form as the revolutionary age of the contraceptive pill dawned.

As indicated above, one of the midwives to this rebirth was neonatology, a sub-specialty of paediatrics, which itself was accorded full specialty status at UCT only in 1953. Until then, 'Diseases of Children' (or 'Sick Kids' as it was known to students) had been wholly ancillary to Medicine, its practitioners (tellingly listed in the Faculty's prospectus as 'paediatric physicians') all part-timers and its teaching restricted to lectures 'at times convenient to the class' and its ward rounds and demonstrations offered 'at times to be arranged'. Until the 1950s, 'paediatric physicians' were called in only if babies had a feeding problem or gastroenteritis, hence the colloquial tag for them, 'baby feeders'. 'Paediatrics was a despised, derided, and more or less neglected branch of Medicine which was barely tolerable within the same building as "The Big Three" [Medicine, Surgery, and Obstetrics and Gynaecology] to which paediatricians were expected to – and did – make humble obeisance', fulminated an outspoken campaigner for the discipline's independent status.[187]

By 1949, however, UCT had decided in principle to take the first step in this direction. Recognising how far new modes of treatment, nutritional knowledge and ideas on preventive and social medicine had advanced the concept of child health – UCT was 'far behind comparable schools elsewhere', observed the Dean[188] – and aware that plans to build the Red Cross War Memorial Children's Hospital in Rondebosch were under consideration, it decided to create a chair of child health, though within the Department of Medicine.

When he arrived in 1953, its first incumbent, the feisty, Glasgow-trained Findlay Ford, was appalled at what he found passing for paediatrics, lambasting it as 'a poor Uriah Heep kind of organisation, without any real organisation … the kickabout of anyone who chose to kick it or tramp on its face'.[189] In keeping with his forthright and combative personality, this crusty 39-year-old set about asserting the autonomy of his sub-department wherever he could, even if this meant challenging head-on the physicians' overarching, inhibiting dominance and belief in the traditional unity of Medicine.

As soon as he could, he began to expand the scope of his subject to include premature babies and neonates and dedicated clinics in fields like paediatric nephrology, paediatric haematology, paediatric cardiology, child psychiatry and paediatric endocrinology, while simultaneously creating several full-time positions to give his sub-department a fully committed core of specialists whom he encouraged to do research which would help mark out exclusively the terrain of paediatrics. By 1958 four of his twelve, all-male staff were full-timers.

In the area of teaching, he pushed for more time for his subject in the undergraduate curriculum timetable and gave it a distinctly social medicine orientation, emphasising nutrition, infectious and congenital diseases, child growth and development, and living conditions. He insisted that Child Health be made a 'must-pass' component of the final examination in Medicine, with an external examiner of its own, so that students would take it seriously, and demanded that the sub-department have dedicated paediatric interns assigned to it and not just a few hours' duty from medical or surgical interns each week. 'We are going to fight for our rights and for other departments similarly affected', he proclaimed. 'We touch our professional caps to no man in or out of South Africa.'[190]

Such pugnacious plain-speaking – in striking contrast to his gentleness towards his patients – by this 'stormy petrel' (as the Dean described Ford[191]) did in fact meet with considerable success. By his retirement in 1969, Child Health, though still nominally part of Medicine (it remained so until 1981), had a full-time staff of nine, a part-time staff of ten and was training ten registrars, one of whom was female. Undergraduates received 300 hours of paediatric instruction compared to 120 hours in 1953, visits to patients' homes and immunisation clinics were arranged regularly, a social worker accompanied ward rounds, research by staff and postgraduate students was flourishing – 41 MD and MMed degrees in the subject had been awarded – and the work of men like John Hansen on kwashiorkor and infantile malnutrition, Pat Smythe on neonatal tetanus, Malcolm Bowie on neonatal sugar intolerance, and 'Boet' Heese on neonatal respiratory distress syndrome had put the sub-department on the international paediatric map. Proof of this was the stream of students from abroad coming to do an elective term there and the appointment of seven of its staff or graduates to chairs at other universities in South Africa or beyond. Appreciatively, one of them recalled how 'Those of us who were the "Young Turks" with him [Ford] … were given full freedom to develop our interests and skills, and he was always there to back us and assist us when difficult clinical or research decisions had to be made. It was this special quality that nurtured the department in its phenomenal growth during the 1950s and 1960s.'[192]

Yet, if Ford was the man who, through the creation of a de facto Department of Child Health at UCT, in effect 'established paediatrics as a major clinical discipline in South Africa', as his obituarists concluded,[193] he was also a man who recognised the need not to be bound to a limited definition of his burgeoning subject either in name or compass. For example, on the eve of his retirement he was finally able to persuade UCT to widen the title of his chair to 'Paediatrics and Child Health', as paediatrics included the development and care of children too, and not just their health. This change was wholly in keeping with his ongoing lobbying for the establishment of a multidisciplinary Institute of Child Health as a co-ordinating centre for child-related initiatives by medical, paramedical and social welfare practitioners and bodies. The Institute was finally opened alongside Red Cross Children's Hospital in 1974, and remains concrete evidence of Ford's simultaneously far-sighted and wide-angled conception of his field.

A second discipline to emerge from the shadow of the 'Big Three' clinical departments in this period was anaesthetics. Although it had been recognised as an independent teaching department in 1937, it was not until 1948 that it gained its first full-time appointee, the 58-year-old Tom Fuller, as a stopgap head of department. Even so, this did not mean that overnight surgeons accepted anaesthetists as more than medical technicians; they were still treated as 'the stooge and butt of the surgical profession,' remembered one anaesthetist ruefully, 'bullied and chastised at will',[194] as they were largely dependent on surgeons' goodwill for their engagements and payment.

However, as had been happening elsewhere in the world since the mid-1930s, over the next ten years the standing of anaesthetics at GSH and UCT grew markedly as a result of the introduction of more refined anaesthetic agents and more sophisticated techniques which lowered the high number of anaesthetic deaths appreciably and because surgeons were embarking on increasingly complex operations for which the services of a specially trained anaesthetist were essential. A veteran anaesthetist expressed his delight at this turn of events, declaring, 'What the surgeon dares to do depends on what he knows anaesthetists can do.'[195] Even as haughty a surgeon as Jannie Louw was constrained to concede that 'The art of anaesthesia was being replaced by the science of anaesthesia'.[196]

As in paediatrics, a sure sign of the increasing stature of anaesthetics in these years was the inflow of postgraduate students. Between 1955 and 1968, under Fuller's successors, the American-trained 'Buck' Jones (1953–61) and Arthur Bull, 29 MMed (Anaes) degrees were awarded, 24 to men and 5 to women eager to specialise in the rising discipline. The department 'has grown out of all recognition compared to my previous remembrance of it in 1950', concluded one of its graduates after a return visit in 1961.[197]

Nor was it long before the South African Society of Anaesthetists began to urge UCT to create a chair of anaesthetics as three other universities in the country had already done, in order to raise the level of teaching and research in the subject and to keep up with the accelerating needs of a number of specialties beyond general surgery which it now served too, like obstetrics, intensive care and gross trauma. To this request UCT finally acceded in 1965, appointing as its first professor the 45-year-old Arthur Bull, a UCT graduate who had also been trained in Oxford's cutting-edge Department of Anaesthesia by the foremost British anaesthetist of the day, Robert Macintosh. 'Anaesthetics can no longer be regarded as ancillary, but must be treated now as a subject in its own right', observed UCT's Principal, J.P. Duminy, accurately.[198]

The occasion on which Duminy made this statement was one which solidly consolidated the newly enhanced standing of anaesthetics at UCT. He was speaking at a function in 1966 to thank the Anglo American Corporation and De Beers for a large grant to the sub-department for research. Together with another large donation that year from a grateful patient, these sums helped Anaesthetics establish its first research laboratory in 1967.

Of this rising tide, Bull, who was an excellent organiser and an accomplished researcher, took full advantage. By 1968 he had expanded the staff by a third to 33 (19 full-timers and 14 part-timers), added the Somerset Hospital to the five hospitals already being used for teaching anaesthetics, arranged access to a computer for rapid analysis of the results of an investigation into anaesthetic techniques used on babies delivered by Caesarean section, and brought to a successful conclusion his joint project with the Department of Electrical Engineering to construct an electronic blood warmer for massive blood transfusions. With characteristic wit, he named the machine (which Plessey then manufactured and sold commercially under licence) the 'Taurus Blood Warmer'. *Taurus* is Latin for 'bull'.

His sense of humour and of perspective served him well in the operating theatre where he 'eschewed histrionics and radiated an air of purposeful calm', according to colleagues.[199] Students and staff alike found him approachable and wise in his advice. Nearly sixty years after being told by him in an undergraduate lecture that 'eternal vigilance is the price of safety' in the operating theatre, a surgeon reflected that this aphorism had 'stood me in good stead … throughout my … career'.[200]

Bull set a good example in theatre, ward and lecture room, and his fellow anaesthetists readily gave him their support. Of them all, Gaisford Harrison came closest to emulating his chief as a lecturer and researcher possessing what two former colleagues described as 'the ability to turn a mundane anaesthetic into an exciting [pedagogic] event'.[201] Nor was his research any less significant. Indeed, his longitudinal analysis of the incidence and causes of deaths due to anaesthesia at GSH since 1956 was a benchmark study internationally in pinpointing the risks associated with anaesthesia, while his preliminary investigation into a rare syndrome in which an anaesthetic triggered a soaring temperature in a patient, usually with fatal results –'the anaesthetist's nightmare', he called it[202] – was so widely quoted in the medical literature that it achieved the enviable status of a 'citation classic'.[203] Harrison himself went on to succeed Bull in the chair in 1981 and to be elected a Life Fellow of UCT.

Though not flying as high as Bull or Harrison, the other full-timers in the department taught more by hands-on example and demonstration than by didactic lectures, for usually the former conveyed appropriate anaesthetic skills more effectively than the latter. For instance, one fifth-year recounted how he watched wide-eyed as a patient on the operating table stopped breathing as she was being anaesthetised with nitrous oxide. 'My supervisor … pumped oxygen into her lungs and … administered a couple of hefty blows to her sternum. She resumed breathing and apparently recovered completely. At that time I admired his aplomb but decided that I would always see to it that I administered at least 20% oxygen whenever I had to use nitrous oxide.'[204]

More polished was the key role that a member of the department, Joe Ozinsky, played in the first heart transplant operation in 1967. His cool head, deep knowledge of anaesthetic agents and their likely effect on a patient were the epitome of the high level of practice in the department, lessons which it ensured were not lost on students or the rest of UCT. 'This event served to highlight the careful research and development of anaesthetic care … which has been in progress since the inception of cardiac surgery … and which has in no small part contributed to the success of the cardiac surgery team', declared Bull with a justifiable sense of achievement.[205] No less a surgeon than Chris Barnard confirmed this, maintaining, 'The anaesthetist had become a major figure in modern surgery. He protected the patients from surgical trauma and damage, using as few drugs as possible – checking blood pressure, venous pressure, control of respiration, acid level, pulse rate, urine output and cerebral reflexes. In effect, he was both caretaker of the sleeping body and its physiological bookkeeper. Without an anaesthesiologist such as Dr Ozinsky, no transplant or major heart operation would be possible.'[206]

As indicated above, formal lectures played only a limited part in the training given to undergraduates – no more than a dozen lectures were given in the fifth year on the theory and practice of anaesthesia. These were followed by practical instruction in the administration of anaesthetics which, until 1960, culminated in each student having to administer at least twenty anaesthetics personally, under the watchful eye of a member of staff. Yet, giving twenty anaesthetics hardly offset their inexperience in an increasingly complex field; accordingly, it was just as well that in 1961 the South African Medical and Dental Council laid down that all interns had to administer fifty anaesthetics during their internship year. Unlike their patients, they had to remain wide awake throughout every one of these operations.

A third discipline to come of age in the 1950s and 1960s, also on a wave of technological advance, was radiology. A generous, twelve-year endowment in 1935 had seen a chair in radiology created and filled until 1947,[207] but thereafter the department's academic side had waned, as, under two GSH-based lecturers, its focus became primarily clinical. That there were two heads signals that already radiology was being refined by technological innovation into a diagnostic arm (diagnostic radiology or radiodiagnosis) and a therapeutic one (radiotherapy or radiological therapy), the latter primarily targeting cancer by means of new, high-energy X-ray machines and a better understanding of radiobiology. In 1948 the South African Medical and Dental Council recognised each as a specialty in its own right, but it was not until 1962 that UCT elevated them to the rank of separate departments.

It took this step because of the need to turn them into more than just clinical departments which did a little teaching on the side. 'There has been very little, if any, advance and, in relation to the general forward progress of medicine, it has fallen very severely behind', lamented the acting Dean of Medicine in 1965. A professorial appointment, together with the academic influence this would bring, 'was necessary to lift the routine hospital and teaching services of the department out of the rut into which they had fallen.'[208]

In fact, there had briefly (1956–8) been a professor in the department before this, the diagnostic radiologist Jack Jacobson, but he had returned to private practice too soon to have tackled its academic shortcomings, while his temporary successor, the perennial acting head, Leslie Werbeloff,[209] put higher store on meeting the needs of those patients seen by his department than those of students taught there. After all, he argued, the former constituted a seventh of all patients admitted. Not surprisingly, the new professor in radiodiagnosis appointed in 1964, Philip Palmer, judged the quality of the teaching he found on his arrival to be below 'the minimal acceptable level'.[210]

The 43-year-old Palmer was a London-trained radiologist whose experience in hospital-based radiodiagnosis stretched from Westminster and Cornwall to Bulawayo. He held a broad view of his discipline, believing that the head of a university department should be 'not only a competent interpreter of X-ray films', but also someone who recognised 'that it is necessary to be a good physician to be a good radiologist, and that his task lies in educating through all that radiology can offer'.[211] As far as he was concerned, 'there is no department in a hospital which can fulfill its functions without radiology'.[212]

To enable his department to take on such a large commitment, he first convinced UCT and the CPA to quadruple his staff to sixteen and then deployed the new personnel to expand the department's dual functions of teaching and patient diagnosis across the board. State-of-the-art equipment replaced outdated machines, a reference library of radiology films and teaching material was built up with funds from a firm manufacturing X-ray machines, and the administration of the department was rationalised to allow for a degree of regional specialisation. 'Nothing was sacrosanct – he changed everything', recalled a then junior member of his staff.[213]

Teaching moved up the scale of importance from Werbeloff's time. The department's function was 'not only to X-ray clinical patients',[214] but equally to ensure that every MBChB graduate gained a basic understanding of what she or he saw on an X-ray image. Consequently, a radiological dimension was added to the second-year courses in anatomy and physiology to introduce students to this perspective; small-group tutorials were begun where students could question their teachers in detail; and clinical teaching sessions given by Palmer became 'notable for a buzz of interest and sometimes controversy', as two former attendees reported.[215]

From this strengthened foundation Palmer was able to extend his departmental dominion outwards, in keeping with his wide view of his subject. He reserved to himself the sole right to decide who would be X-rayed and in what order; physicians and surgeons trying to jump the queue on behalf of their patients were barred from the X-ray room; and he laid down that copies of all X-rays, no matter for which GSH department they had been done, were henceforth to be kept in a central registry run by his department. The benefits to teaching of this autocratic realignment were quick to appear: supervision of students, interns and registrars was streamlined, X-rays of patients became more promptly available, and a spirit of dynamism and innovation enthused staff and students alike. 'He instilled a strong measure of decorum and pride in the department', judged one of his registrars.[216]

Within a few years the department's structure had in this way been comprehensively overhauled and modernised, and well geared to take on board the next wave of transforming technology in the 1970s and 1980s, computers. By then Palmer had long since departed for greener pastures in the United States, first to the University of Pennsylvania in 1969 and then to the University of California at Davis, where his energy and creativity won him first place in 2003 in the 'Four Most Influential Teachers in Global Radiology' Award by the well-respected professional journal *Diagnostic Imaging*. It would not be far-fetched to say that this would have come as no surprise to those who knew him at UCT thirty-five years earlier.

Radiotherapy was slower to take off as an academic subject, for it was still emerging as a discipline in its own right in the 1950s. The department's focus (in all senses of the word) was on treating people with cancer, to which all academic activity was adjuvant, comprising no more than a lecture a week for one term and periodic instruction in clinical radiotherapy to fifth-year students. Research was rare. By 1968 only five MMed (Radiotherapy) degrees had been awarded; in comparison, thirteen MMed (Radiodiagnosis) degrees were awarded in the same period.

Until 1964 the small department was run by the Glasgow-trained radiotherapist James Muir Grieve whose preferred terrain of activity was the hospital, not the lecture room. However, his deputy from 1961 was an independent-minded, 34-year-old graduate of Cambridge and UCT, Rossall Sealy, who, even then, was showing a more academic leaning than his head of department, with four articles in the *South African Medical Journal* already to his credit.

Once he succeeded Grieve as head in 1964, this more academic inclination was given greater scope in the department too. The training of radiographers was improved, laboratory research commenced for the first time and academic staff were encouraged to present the fruits of their research at international conferences. By

1969, 23 papers by members of the department had been published since 1964, eight of them by Sealy. This research stood him in very good stead indeed, for, when UCT finally created a chair of radiotherapy in 1980, Sealy was appointed as its first incumbent. Paradoxically, however, it was Grieve who prompted the single most significant piece of research linked (indirectly) with the department. In 1956 he had raised the question of how to calculate the different X-ray dosages to employ on malignant tumours and surrounding tissue with a nuclear physicist who was temporarily assisting the department. The young physicist was Allan Cormack, who, once he moved to the United States, solved the problem mathematically, thereby providing the theoretical underpinning for the invention of the CT scanner. Doing so co-won him the Nobel Prize for Physiology and Medicine in 1979. Later, Cormack was to express his gratitude to Grieve 'for pointing out the necessity for a solution to the absorption problem'.[217]

The extent to which the fourth department to come of age in this period, Psychiatry, flowered is abundantly clear if one compares its situation in 1948 with that twenty years later. In 1948 it was a small department bracketed with Neurology under the authority of the Department of Medicine and run by three part-time lecturers and two part-time demonstrators. Headed by Gordon Key, the superintendent of the Valkenberg Mental Hospital, its teaching allocation amounted to a block of lectures and classical demonstrations only in the fifth year of the MBChB curriculum. The clinical material for these demonstrations was drawn from the ten beds assigned to Psychiatry in the Neurology ward at GSH and from the wards at Valkenberg whence, typically, a chronic patient would be brought to the lecture theatre and asked pointed questions to reveal his or her disorder. This psychiatry course was 'totally inadequate by modern standards', concluded a Faculty sub-committee, in that it was given 'almost solely by members of the staff of the [Valkenberg] Mental Hospital', which meant that its focus on psychoses and committal under the Mental Disorders Act was far too narrow.[218] Of research, there was little sign.

Compared to this, the Department of Psychiatry in 1968 was unrecognisable. Separate from Neurology since 1962 (though still nominally part of the Department of Medicine), it had a staff of seventeen psychiatrists (four of them full-time), seven registrars and two clinical psychologists. In the wards their activities were complemented by three social workers, three occupational therapists and several nurses with special psychiatric training. The department's teaching in the MBChB curriculum now spanned all three clinical years and included lectures, tutorials, clinical demonstrations, clinical clerking and attending consultations in GSH's Outpatients Department and Psychiatric Emergency Unit, in both of which sixth-year students in effect acted as junior interns. At postgraduate level it offered two diplomas (in

# THE APPLIED SCIENCES

*Student dissection of Medical School staff (3): Professor Lynn Gillis*

psychiatric medicine and psychiatric social work), one certificate (in psychiatric nursing) and training for the newly created fellowship of the Faculty of Psychiatry of the Colleges of Medicine in South Africa. The clinical material for all of these activities came from its 80 beds at GSH, from its adjacent Psychiatric Day Hospital and from the William Slater Rehabilitation Hospital in Rondebosch. Research was in full spate too, two major departmental projects funded by state bodies having recently been completed. Reflecting the racialised view of the world predominant in that era of high apartheid, both had focused on those officially designated 'coloured' at the time, probing possible connections between mental ill-health and alcoholism among them and the reasons why chronic schizophrenics did or did not seek hospitalisation.

Buoyed up by its rapid, multi-sided growth, the department confidently described itself in 1968 as having become 'a fully fledged clinical and academic subject of high standing' in the Faculty, and 'one of the major resources of trained psychiatric personnel in South Africa'.[219] This sea change in its status rested on several factors: the development of new and effective psychotropic drugs like lithium, imipramine and chlorpromazine, which made a number of psychotic and depressive conditions manageable and thus analogous to other disease conditions treated in general hospitals by physicians; the clearer, less subjective diagnosis of these conditions by their precise, detailed description in the World Health Organisation's definitive *International Classification of Diseases* in 1949 and the American Psychiatric Association's *Diagnostic and Statistical Manual of Mental Disorders*, first published in 1952; and the recognition, in the light of the preceding, that psychiatry was about treating not just acute psychological disorders in mental hospitals, but also less florid, everyday conditions like anxiety and depression, at a range of therapeutic sites, depending on patients' particular needs. As in the case of Medicine, these ranged from general and day hospitals to extra-hospital clinics and even patients' own homes within the community. 'For so many cases there are so many cures', explained an exponent of this 'new' psychiatry, 'and today we realise it matters where, as well as how, the patient is treated'.[220]

As a consequence, psychiatry was increasingly seen in the Western world as a hard and exact science like medicine, and so came to be regarded by UCT's Faculty of Medicine and state health authorities too as part of mainstream medical science, with all the funding benefits that this brought with it. The Dean himself declared that psychiatry was 'no longer a somewhat esoteric subject mostly dealt with in the confines of mental hospitals ... [and that it] now has wide ramifications in the body of medicine – in hospitals, in general practice, and in the life of the community'.[221]

The psychiatrists responsible for inculcating this transformed conception of psychiatry at UCT were all South African medical graduates who had trained at the Maudsley Hospital in London, where such ideas had flourished after World War II. Henry Walton, a gifted lecturer, began to spread these ideas enthusiastically as soon as he returned to UCT in 1958, while simultaneously holding students 'spellbound with his lectures and tutorials, crammed with sex and sin', as one of them remembered.[222] Isaac Sakinofsky took charge of running a key feature of the 'new' psychiatry, the department's Psychiatric Day Hospital in Observatory. The intensive, daytime service which it afforded was 'particularly valuable', explained his head of department, 'as it allows patients the benefits of full psychiatric treatment without being dislocated from their ordinary daily life'.[223] That he was thereby pointing up that this day hospital had much in common with the medically based day hospitals then being planned for the Peninsula is clear.

The said head of department was the 38-year-old Lynn Gillis, who had trained not only at the Maudsley Hospital but had also been on the staff of the kindred Tara Hospital for Nervous Diseases in Johannesburg for seven years before coming to UCT in 1962. With this background, he put his mind and body into reshaping the Psychiatry Department into a model of 'modern' psychiatry, a task for which his great organisational and people skills equipped him well. Tara's head described him as 'a man of creativity and initiative',[224] while a physician colleague aptly characterised him as forward-thinking and sure of his direction, but 'with an eclecticism which reveals his profound knowledge of psychodynamics tempered by what I can best and rather colloquially call horse sense'.[225]

It therefore was not long before transforming initiatives began to flow from his office with the aim of expanding the nature and ambit of psychiatry as practised at UCT and GSH and gearing it better to meet the diverse needs of different categories of patients. By 1968 the policy had produced more staff, multidisciplinary therapeutic teams, new courses to train the non-psychiatrists in these teams, the establishment of the Emergency Psychiatric Unit and the Psychiatric Day Hospital already mentioned, a psychiatric social club run by former patients under the department's aegis, domiciliary visits within the wider community, and a decentring of Valkenberg from UCT's psychiatric terrain. Its attempt to continue operating autonomously as a Department of Mental Disorders did not last long in the face of Gillis's determination to provide a modern, comprehensive psychiatric service.

Word and deed were creatively employed to instil this modern version of psychiatry into the next generation of GPs, for some of whom the notion that psychiatry was 'odd' and 'not a serious medical discipline' still prevailed.[226] From lectures and small-group tutorials on patients' psychological reaction to illness, how to interact with patients and the nature of mental health and illness, students were introduced in their senior years to full-on clinical psychiatry at GSH. Here every effort was made to locate the subject firmly within the broader medical context, not only academically but also physically. At GSH, 'I deliberately located my department in the corridor between the Medicine and Surgery wards', explained Gillis, 'so that doctors and students could see psychiatric patients behaving quite normally, playing cards, to make them see that these patients were little different from their own. There had to be a lot of re-education to open their eyes.'[227]

It is a mark of his success in having psychiatry accepted by his colleagues in the Faculty as well within the medical fold that in 1964 they unanimously approved the creation of UCT's first chair in the subject (and South Africa's third), though Gillis was not appointed to this until 1969 because of the need for complex negotiations between UCT, the CPA and the central government's Department of Health, all of which shared responsibility for mental health. As he himself acknowledged with typical modesty years later, 'I was the beneficiary of being born into an exciting, bubbling time for psychiatry.'[228]

Much less effervescent in these years was Psychiatry's alter ego, Neurology. Although headed by the meticulously professional Sam Berman for twelve years until his death in 1963, Neurology (or, as it was briefly known, Neuropsychiatry) did not in the 1950s and 1960s take advantage of the kind of pharmacological or technological breakthroughs, like electroencephalography and electromyography, which boosted the standing of the Departments of Psychiatry, Anaesthetics or Radiology in these decades. Thus, its staff complement never rose above three, it was able to attract precious few registrars, and its teaching slot in the MBChB curriculum remained small. The fact that the sixteen beds it was assigned at the new GSH were dotted all round the hospital reflected its marginal position.

Even though by 1949 this number had grown to thirty beds now located in two dedicated Neurology wards (one for whites and one for 'non-whites'), the department remained on this plateau, unable to excite undergraduates or draw many postgraduates. Perhaps the unfamiliarity and daunting nature of the discipline – often referred to as 'neurophobia' among students – played a part in putting them off, but perhaps so too did Berman's painstaking precision in speech and behaviour and austere personality. He 'demanded a high standard of reasonableness and logicality in method from all about him and in particular from students', an intern commented, so he was 'not … very easy … to get on with if one was not on one's toes and alert'.[229]

Yet, even the independence of Neurology from Psychiatry in 1962 – the two had been joined into one department since 1958 – and the appointment of the less forbidding and more colourful Jim MacGregor as Berman's successor in 1963 did not improve the department's appeal. That would have to wait until the 1970s and 1980s, when the CT scan and MRI gave it powerful new diagnostic tools, and the inspiring clinician and teacher Frances Ames succeeded MacGregor as head.

Another Cinderella department in the years after 1948 was Dermatology. Though a few lectures in what was then deemed a 'special subject' had been part of the MBChB curriculum since 1919, it still remained a marginal sub-specialty in 1948, as its approach was felt by many in the Faculty to be only skin deep and concerned primarily with cosmetic conditions. As late as 1979, a standard dermatology textbook concluded glumly that the subject 'does not occupy an important place in the curriculum of most medical schools, possibly because patients rarely die from skin diseases'.[230]

Staffed by four part-timers who also had private practices, as a minor component of the Department of Medicine from 1951 it was responsible for just eighteen lectures in the fifth-year programme, along with practical instruction in the Dermatological Clinic at GSH. Even though the Clinic focused on common dermatological conditions likely to be seen by GPs (like eczema, acne and fungal infections), students found the teaching 'very sketchy'[231] and unimaginative – 'the lecturer would just drone on, reading from his notes and you didn't see any illustrations of any kind', recalled a top student.[232]

Nor was its already limited appeal helped by the personality and style of its head from 1954 to 1964, Richard Lang. A vain and arrogant man who prided himself on being 'the best dermatologist in Africa' (hence his nickname among students, 'Lang of Africa'), he delighted in publicly disparaging colleagues and humiliating students. 'He would kick students out of the Outpatients [Dermatological Clinic] if they could not answer his questions', remembered one unhappily.[233] Moreover, when it came to students who did not share his white skin pigmentation, crass racism was added to his disrespect for those whom he taught. 'You, non-white, get out!' he once shouted at a 'coloured' student who had inadvertently entered the lecture room where a white patient was being demonstrated,[234] banishing him to an outside corridor where 'non-white' students had to gather on such occasions to be shown a patient who was not white-skinned. A better illustration of the importance of the skin in South African society and its social implications could hardly be asked for.

But such questions were not even raised in the department by its staff, nearly all of whom were busy running their private practices alongside their part-time teaching engagements. Neither Lang nor his successor as head, Jack Jacobson (1965–7), spent time doing research, an activity actively encouraged only by Walter Gordon, the department's first full-time head from 1967 to 1982. Little wonder that, shortly before his retirement, Lang should have bewailed the fact that 'so few young candidates have come forward to be trained in dermatology'.[235] By 1968 only one MD but not a single MMed (Dermatology) had been awarded, while of the six registrars in the department between 1960 and 1968, only two finally completed their specialisation. Clearly, a thicker skin than most possessed was needed to train under Lang.

If dermatology was a Cinderella subject in the Faculty, public health in this era was an 'ugly duckling'. Looked down upon by clinicians and students as barely a member of the medical family – some dismissed its practitioners as 'latrinologists',[236] while others were nonplussed by its emphasis on maintaining good health rather than treating ill-health – the department was tolerated largely because of its pivotal role in training medical officers of health.

Its staffing ever since its inception in 1919 reflected this fact, for its head was *ex officio* Cape Town's Medical Officer of Health and its lecturers members of his and allied departments. This meant that its entire staff consisted of part-timers for whom teaching was a secondary activity and research a luxury. When, to this was added the fact that the course given to the fifth-year MBChB students included visits to a water purification plant, a sewerage works, the abattoir and a municipal housing estate, it can be understood why many undergraduates felt that public health was a 'pleasant distraction … taken in lighthearted spirit'.[237] That these students were at the same time deeply immersed in their own clinical training only drove home public health's very different character from the clinical subjects.

These visits and inspections were of a piece with the general tenor of the department's syllabus, for both its course in the MBChB programme and its diploma in public health course emphasised traditional, statutory public health topics like sanitation, water supply, nutrition, ventilation and vital statistics. That these were much the same as the topics that the two men who headed the department after 1948, Fred Fehrsen (1944–52) and Ed Cooper (1952–72), had studied when they had taken their diploma in public health courses between the wars suggests that, under them, the department was not bursting with innovation. In fact, aware that it had a potential rival in the course in social medicine given in the Department of Medicine,[238] it became increasingly unsure of its own terrain, as is apparent from its change of name in this period, as it sought to define itself more distinctively: in 1953 'Public Health' gave way to 'Public Hygiene', which in turn was replaced by 'Promotive and Public Health' in 1962. Appointing a full-time lecturer to a department with the last, clear-cut name would, hoped the Dean, 'assist in formulating a new attitude towards the preventive aspects of Medicine, and stimulating more interest and enthusiasm into student thinking'.[239]

That this would happen under Cooper was wishful thinking, however, and it was not until 1972, when the department was merged with social medicine (by then labelled 'comprehensive medicine') into a wholly new Department of Community Medicine, that the 'ugly duckling' began its transformation into a swan.

Five very particular minor or special subjects were also taught in the Faculty on a similar basis, i.e. by heads of municipal or state institutions, in addition to their principal occupations: infectious diseases by the superintendent of the City Infectious Diseases Hospital; medical jurisprudence by the senior state pathologist; vaccination by the district surgeon of Cape Town; venereology by the city's venereal disease officer; and leprosy by the superintendent of the Pretoria Leper Institution. Save for the last subject (which was optional until the course was discontinued in 1959), all of them continued to be taught thus until the 1970s, though medical jurisprudence was renamed 'forensic medicine and toxicology' in 1966.

As in public health, the teaching of these subjects was very practical, drawing on years of hands-on experience, but usually no longer informed by the latest thinking in the field or inclined to foster research in it. Moreover, as a practitioner in one of these subjects acknowledged, there was always the added risk of 'inflicting on the students that greater and, for the student, unnecessary detail which his own interest and curiosity may have led him to pursue'.[240]

Equally hands-on (in this case literally as well as figuratively) was the first of the so-called 'professions allied to medicine' (PAMS) to be given university status, physiotherapy. However, as the descriptor PAMS indicates,[241] the demarcation line between the medical and the paramedical was very firmly drawn. Nor in these years was it challenged by the latter group. 'When we physiotherapists attempt to teach medical specialist subjects we … do not know what to teach the students', the first head of the Department of Physiotherapy at UCT freely admitted. 'In our ignorance and lack of background we are unable to select the important points.'[242]

A profession with such an avowedly inferior self-image did not seem to merit a place in a university faculty and UCT said so. The Faculty of Medicine 'does not make itself responsible for the training of auxiliary personnel', it told the CPA haughtily in 1948 in response to a request to provide such training,[243] while as late as 1964 a Witwatersrand University anatomist put into words what several of his UCT counterparts were still thinking: 'Until these paramedical disciplines can demonstrate that they are active fields of research they have no place in a university.'[244]

Yet, by then, UCT had yielded to pressure from the CPA for more physiotherapists to be trained to meet the needs of public hospitals, a pressure which had been intensified by the frightening impact of the polio epidemics of 1947–8 and 1956–7, which had struck white children in particular. In response to this insistence, in 1957 UCT had softened its earlier stance and agreed to offer a diploma course in physiotherapy for a trial period, as a compromise between what those calling for a full degree course wanted and the position of those who argued that physiotherapy should be taught in a technical college, not a university. Accordingly, a tiny Department of Physiotherapy was set up in 1958 (the third at a South African university) and a diploma in physiotherapy offered, taught by the widely experienced, 57-year-old Margaret Roper, who was seconded to UCT for that purpose by GSH. In 1959 she was joined by two other seconded physiotherapists, appointed partly to help her introduce a further course which aimed at producing physiotherapy teachers. However, by 1968 only two students had gained this Certificate in Teaching Physiotherapy. On the other hand, 139 Diplomas in Physiotherapy had been awarded, more than confirming the success of the trial as the subject began to be deemed a worthy (if 'other') part of the Faculty of Medicine. In 1973 the medical superintendent of GSH acknowledged that the survival of more patients thanks to greater medical knowledge and technology 'has led to a greater need for intensive care units – and for paramedical staff, particularly physiotherapists, with a wider knowledge of disease, therapy and machinery'.[245] What with the creation in 1960 of a small, medically staffed Physical Medicine Department (the forerunner of the Department of Rheumatology), 'PAMS' was almost beginning to give way to the term 'paramedical professions'. For their part, male medical students were readier to embrace the newcomers on campus and sought 'a closer liaison with our feminine colleagues in a very important paramedical service'.[246]

The syllabus for the Diploma in Physiotherapy followed the British model closely, i.e. extensive teaching of both the theory and practice of physiotherapy, built upon a foundation of basic sciences taught in the first year of the three-year programme. To these the Certificate in the Teaching of Physiotherapy syllabus added courses in educational method and theory and the psychology of education. Both qualifications included a large clinical component.

Every one of the 139 recipients of the Diploma in Physiotherapy (as well as the two who received the Certificate in the Teaching of Physiotherapy) was a woman – indeed, from 1964 to 1969 entry was officially restricted to women only – which made the department a wholly female island in a male-dominated Faculty, thus feeding the impression that physiotherapy was not cut from quite the same cloth as medical departments. Unusually, it is also possible to add that all 139 diplomates were 'of good physique and ... interested in human relationships' as these were requirements for admission to the course.[247] Indeed, so determined was UCT to ensure that the former requirement was met that, initially, applicants were asked to attach to their application a photograph of themselves in a bathing costume as visual evidence of their capacity to lift and strenuously massage patients. Only when parents and hospital authorities objected was this requirement withdrawn.

It is also possible to conclude, thanks to oral testimony, that almost all of the 139 diplomates were white-skinned. In fact, 'coloured' and Indian students were so few and far between that the usual ban by UCT and the CPA on 'non-whites' seeing white bodies dead or alive was only sporadically enforced. 'I was not separated from the rest of the class in the Anatomy class or while doing dissection', recalled one such student. 'I was the only black person, but I think I was just treated as an honorary white ... I was not excluded from being part of the class when the white patients were being treated, and although the white nursing sisters would look at me a bit askance, no one said anything. I was not allowed to treat white patients myself though.'[248] In contrast, a 'coloured' student a few years earlier found the doors to all 'white' rooms or wards closed to her. Accordingly, when she was offered a post at GSH after qualifying, she turned it down, saying that she did not wish to work 'in half a hospital for half the pay'.[249] Such overtly discriminatory practices were quietly shelved only in the late 1970s when individuals in the Faculty itself began to ignore them.

Physiotherapy was not in fact the only all-female department in the Faculty. An even smaller department was that of Nursing Tuition, which came into being at the same time as the Physiotherapy Department, with the intention of turning out professionally trained nurse tutors. Again the pressure came from the CPA, anxious to be able to train up more nurses for its hospitals.

Accordingly, the two-year Diploma in Nursing Tuition, which, the prospectus explicitly noted, was 'open to men as well as women' who were already registered nurses, included both medical and pedagogic courses 'to fit the holder to undertake the teaching of medical and surgical nurses'.[250] It was clearly the fact that Paddy Harrison had already lectured for nine years at the Carinus Nursing College, in addition to her extensive nursing experience in different hospitals, that saw her seconded from Carinus to head the small, new department in 1958, and then taken onto UCT's staff as a lecturer two years later. The interaction with the wider Faculty which this afforded stood her and the academic claims of nursing in very good stead, and in 1982 she was appointed UCT's founding professor of nursing.

By then, the Diploma in Nursing Tuition had been discontinued for want of numbers. Instead, a BSc (Nursing) degree had been instituted in 1972 to offer nursing training which was more scientifically informed. With a similar aim in mind, a BSc (Physiotherapy) was also introduced in that year. In parallel with the burgeoning profession of physiotherapy, the diploma course had been a runaway success, 164 students — all female — being awarded this qualification by 1970. This evidence of strong demand and the department's ongoing wish to enhance its standing (and that of the physiotherapy profession) within the Faculty had convinced it to upgrade its qualification to degree status.

No such doubts about the standing of their profession or their qualification assailed the 2356 students who received MBChB degrees from UCT between 1948 and 1968. By 1950 the surge of ex-service students, which had so strained UCT's resources and staff in the preceding five years and required stopgap measures to meet, had begun to ebb — the 1194 students registered in the Faculty in 1946 had dropped to 976 — and in the next two decades fell even further, to a low of 647 in 1956, before moving upwards from the mid-1960s, in response to the Government's request that more doctors be produced to meet the acute shortage anticipated. By 1968, as a result of this pressure, total enrolments in the Faculty had risen to 1017, a 14% increase since 1963.

Of the 2356 MBChB graduates, some 70–75% were officially classified as white males, about 15% as white females and about 10–12% as 'coloured' or Indian males and females. Among white students, two ethnic groups continued to constitute significant minorities, Jews and, until Stellenbosch University's Medical School opened in 1956, Afrikaners.[251] This made the student body of UCT's Medical Faculty more diverse than that at any other South African medical school of the period, fuelling ethnic and racial cliquishness among its members over and above that imposed on them by the official policy of racial segregation.

Whatever their skin pigmentation or ethnic differences, however, they did share a sense of superiority vis-à-vis non-medical students, what an SRC member (himself a medical student) labelled a 'snob attitude' towards other students.[252] The source of this was the escalating esteem which medicine enjoyed internationally, especially after World War II, as a result of a slew of discoveries and inventions which empowered it immeasurably in its battle against disease. 'The swollen-headedness and unrestrained arrogance of medical students has now reached a point where a stethoscope and a white coat have become symbols of the unfounded presumptuousness of a crude, bantam-cock mentality', railed an infuriated *Varsity* columnist.[253] To many non-medical students, medical students, isolated from the rest of UCT on their own campus two kilometres away, seemed blind to a world beyond medicine. They were the 'most confirmed "shop-talkers"' at UCT, complained one, wittily advising them to read Grey's *Elegy* 'with as much relish as Gray's *Anatomy*'.[254] Their decisions to have their own Medical School tie in 1957 and blazer and badge in 1960[255] were taken as proof of their wish to have a separate identity of their own. No one asked what female medical students were to do with such male emblems.

Not surprisingly, medical students' self-perception was rather different. Unique among students in their encounter with death – 'very few other students knew about human vulnerability as we did', observed one[256] – in their own eyes they epitomised zeal and commitment and were determined, despite a swamping workload, to master the complexities of medicine in the interests of humanity. Life for them, remarked one, was 'one whirl of Patients, Pathology and Post-mortems'.[257] Initiatives by the Medical Students' Council to widen medical students' intellectual and cultural horizons through promoting experimental theatrical productions on campus and staging recitals, debates and art competitions rarely attracted more than a minority. Students were too busy 'rushing off to lectures, afterwards straight up to Hospital, or if still a sophomore, straight into the dissecting laboratory', explained a senior medical student.[258]

Yet, the outcome of this zealous pursuit of their studies was notable: 2356 doctors (or 36% of all doctors trained at South Africa's medical schools in this period), the majority of whom possessed, thanks to their training at UCT, the skills of a sound GP oriented to clinical diagnosis and practice and the confidence to employ these skills to good effect. The aim spelt out by Van den Ende as Dean, that UCT should turn out a 'basic doctor' who could then move in any desired direction,[259] had been achieved.

Against this background, it is easy to understand Jannie Louw's sense of pride when he noted in the preface to his history of the UCT Medical School, published just after that *annus mirabilis* for the Faculty and GSH, 1967, the year of the first heart transplant, that in the golden era since World War II, the School had 'matured to a degree that has established for itself international recognition as a major centre of teaching and research'.[260] Or, as Raymond Hoffenberg put it more succinctly after returning to Cape Town from a sabbatical in the United States and Britain in 1965, 'If I were sick, I am sure I would rather be treated here!'[261] On the other hand, Hoffenberg would also have recognised how much the School's First World pedagogic and therapeutic excellence owed to the abundance of clinical material available at GSH from the poorer, Third World-like communities of the Peninsula, yet how little its research focused on the pathologies affecting them. Apartheid may have brought restrictions to the School, but it is clear that it brought blinkers and benefits too, however indirectly.

# Engineering

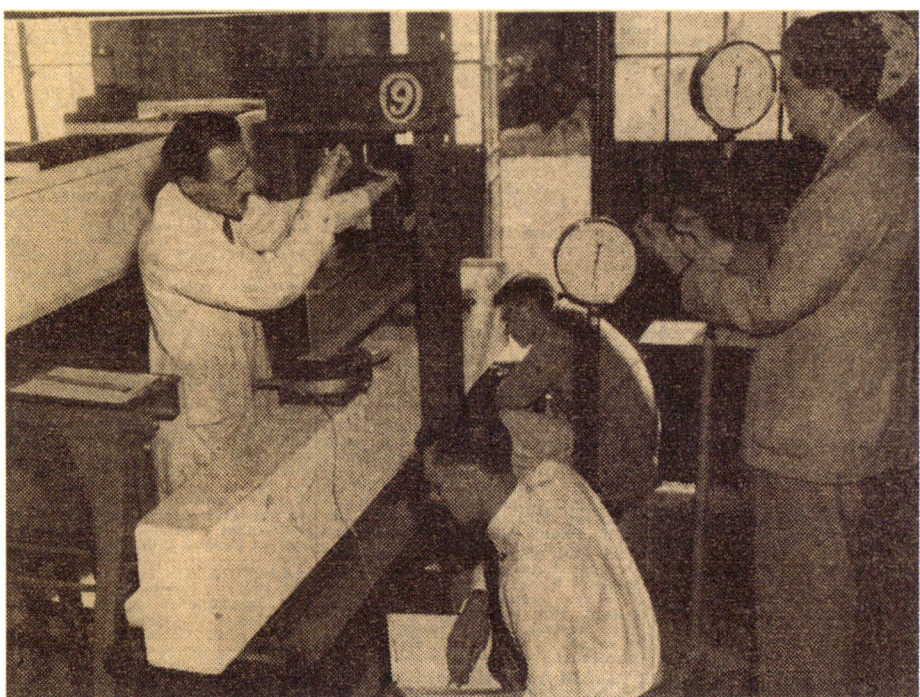

*Highly stressed. Third-year Civil Engineering students monitor the pressure being put on a concrete beam by senior lecturer W.H. King in an experiment to establish its breaking point, 1953.* (Cape Times, 9 October 1953)

*The long-serving, impeccably dressed Dr Heinz Einhorn lecturing Electrical Engineering students on electrical circuits, 1941*

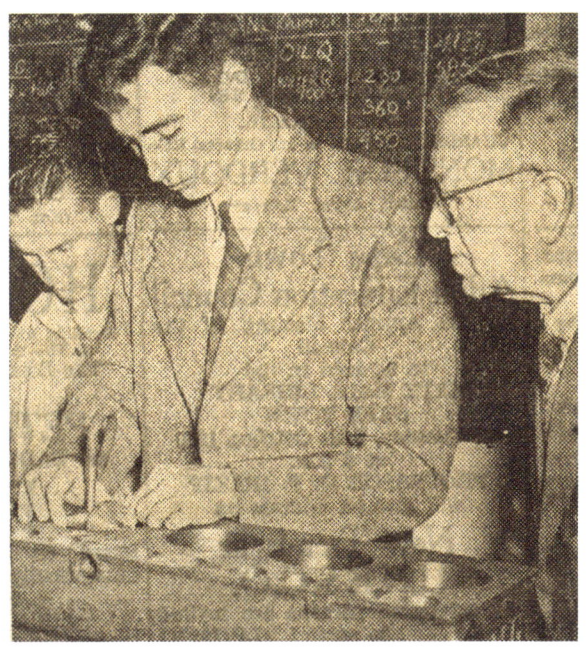

*Precision engineering. Professor Duncan Macmillan of Mechanical Engineering (on the right) watches two undergraduates measure the bore of a car cylinder to a hundred-thousandth of an inch.* (Cape Argus, 21 October 1950)

*Precision measurement. Land Surveying students using a state-of-the-art tellurometer c. 1960, soon after its invention at the CSIR in Pretoria.*

# Medicine

*All ears. Dr Joan van der Horst of the Anatomy Department demonstrates the working of the inner ear to Diploma in Nursing students, 1961.* (Cape Times, 31 August 1961)

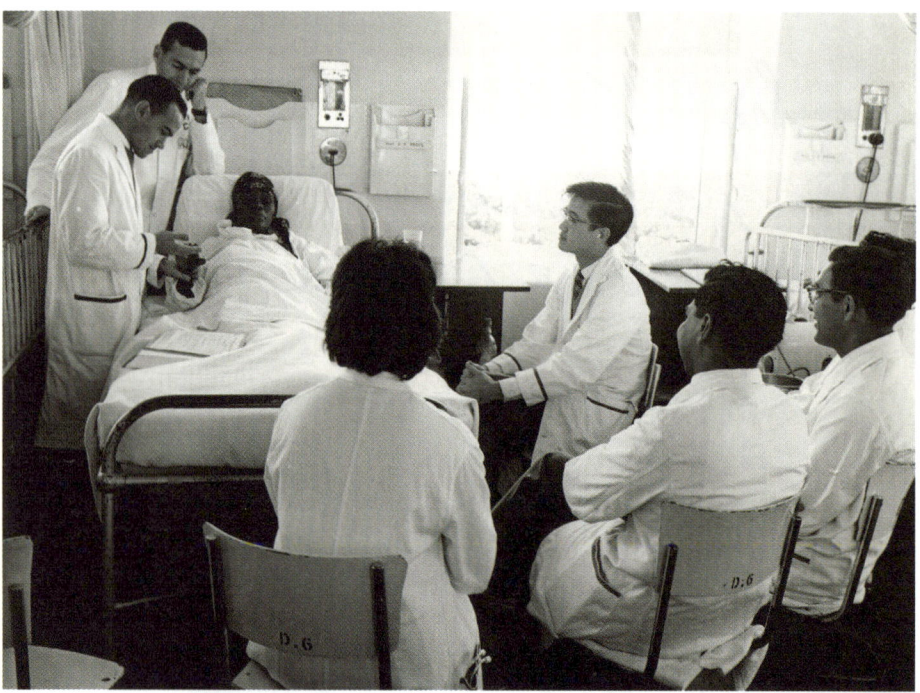

*Clinical segregation. A bedside tutorial for 'Non-European' students only in a 'Non-European' ward at Groote Schuur Hospital in 1961. Watching his student closely as he carries out an examination of a patient for signs of clubbing is the physician Dr Eugene Dowdle.*

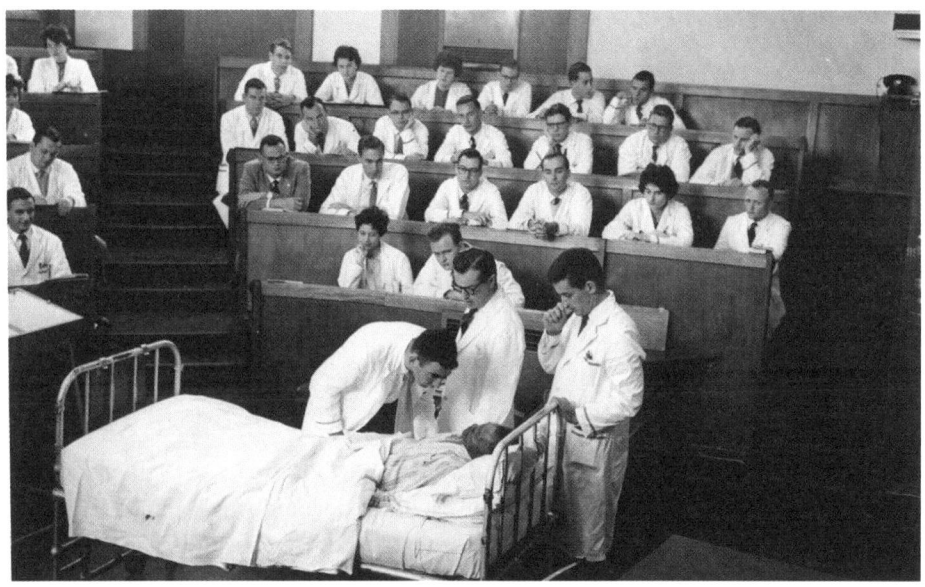

*Clinical demonstration. Senior lecturer Dr Hymie Gordon (centre) watches two final-year students, Peter Folb (left) and Gerald Levine, examining a patient intensively before making a differential diagnosis at Groote Schuur Hospital in 1961. Folb later became professor of pharmacology at UCT.*

*Taking it to heart. Professor Chris Barnard deep in concentration as he listens to the glowing citation for the award of the honorary DSc degree awarded to him for performing the world's first heart transplant operation just 11 days earlier on 3 December 1967. On his left are the chair of Council, Clive Corder, and UCT's Chancellor, Harry Oppenheimer, and on his right Deputy Principal Donald Inskip, and a member of the University Council, the Rev. A.J. van der Merwe.*

# CHAPTER 7

# The Professional Faculties: Commerce, Law, Education, Architecture and Social Science

As much the beneficiaries of South Africa's economic boom of the 1950s and 1960s as the pure and applied sciences were the faculties devoted single-mindedly to the training of future professionals (like accountants, auditors, business, industrial and financial managers, stockbrokers, lawyers, teachers, architects, quantity surveyors and social workers), many of whom were required to service the multi-sided needs of the country's expanding mining and manufacturing sectors. 'Was there [even] sufficient potential student material to fill this need?' asked the state's National Bureau of Education and Social Research with concern in 1963, assuming as it did that most 'student potential material' would be white-skinned.[1]

Encouraged by generous state subsidies and private sector donations to meet this pressing demand, UCT, like other South African universities, did not hesitate to allow its relevant faculties to expand. The results of this are a dominant theme in the histories of the Faculties of Commerce, Law, Education, Architecture and Social Science which constitute this chapter.

## Commerce

Of the five faculties providing such dedicated professional training, Commerce grew the most, tripling its intake between 1948 and 1968, which made it into UCT's second-biggest faculty after Arts in 1968; twenty years earlier it had been the fifth-largest faculty.

This increase in student numbers came in two distinct surges. In 1952 its enrolment rose by 53% to 600 since the previous year as a result of UCT (along with other South African universities) taking on full responsibility for the training of local articled clerks. This was a step taken in response to the accounting profession's

# THE PROFESSIONAL FACULTIES

*Ready for business. A student cartoonist's view of Accountancy students* (Varsity, 20 May 1964)

desire to raise the standard of its future practitioners whose preparation, until then, had consisted largely of ad hoc, how-to-do-it coaching classes run after hours by practising accountants.

The second increase was less a single surge than an accumulating swell starting in the early 1960s and continuing into the 1970s on the back of South Africa's economic boom. This had prompted commerce and industry to expand and diversify, thereby increasing the need for better-trained accountants, auditors and business managers. 'Modernization of the whole economy appears … to be merely a matter of time, for a stage has been reached when economic progress is self-generating', wrote a leading economist buoyantly in the late 1960s.[2] Not only did this escalating demand for accounting, financial and management skills raise the numbers in the Faculty by 46% between 1962 and 1967 to 1257, but in 1966 it also added to the two existing departments in the Faculty, Accounting and Commerce, what was, in effect, a third department, the Graduate School of Business, even though the GSB behaved as if it were practically autonomous.

As implied above, the first surge in enrolments in 1952 occurred mainly in the Department of Accounting where eight part-time lecturers and fourteen tutors had to be recruited hastily to cope with the influx of articled clerks after 5 pm. Yet, part-time staff (including the professor) teaching large numbers of part-time students after hours was not a recipe for good quality education, especially as, in the said professor's opinion, 'the standard of general education among C.T.A. [Certificate in the Theory of Accounting] candidates is very low'.[3] For their part, academic staff were hard pressed to prepare students adequately for the profession's Chartered Accountant (CA) examination – the syllabus was 'so extensive', complained one, 'that the lecturer can only deal with the subject on the broad principles',[4] while most part-time lecturers had little time between their business activities and teaching to keep up with recent developments in the discipline.

The training which the Department of Accounting provided for most of the period was thus narrow, very practical and exam-directed, with minimal encouragement given to exploring beyond these bounds.[5] Unsurprisingly, the Library held few books on accounting beyond textbooks and practically no accounting journals. Perhaps a sense of the mindset which such training fostered among these career-focused students is best summed up in the words of a top student who also tutored in the department before becoming one of Cape Town's foremost accountants: 'Accountancy is a very practical subject', he explained. 'The academic or theoretical side of the discipline hasn't amounted to much.'[6]

The part-time professor who headed this exam-oriented department from 1948 to 1968 was, of course, a practising accountant himself, the 45-year-old Herbert Greenwood, a senior partner in a large local accounting firm. His statement in his application for the post, that he saw accountancy as more than 'merely … figure-work' and as involving research too,[7] overcame UCT's concerns about his lack of a university degree and perceived unfamiliarity with modern theories of accountancy. But in fact, for most of his twenty-year tenure, his words remained words and he was a stranger to academic research.

The one new development to which he was alive was in how office and factory automation would relieve accountants of essentially bookkeeping tasks. 'The machine is going to take care of the "how" and the Accountant will need to know more of the "why"', he forecast.[8] He anticipated that, increasingly, accountants would have to advise management on issues like taxation, statistical analysis and investment strategies. Yet, it was not until shortly before his retirement that he actually acted on these insights by widening the range of courses to be taken by CTA students so as to include economics, English and management accounting, disciplines which he described as offering 'a University background in mind-training'.[9]

Perhaps his tardiness in pursuing his ideas owed something to the fact that it was not until 1960 that his department was granted its first full-time position (alongside its sixteen part-time posts), which was filled by Jan Langhout, a UCT BCom graduate who saw accounting more as an applied science than as a subject for technical instruction. It is possibly a mark too of how Greenwood viewed the future of his discipline that the two men and one woman whom he thereafter appointed as full-time lecturers all held university degrees in addition to their CA qualifications.

A rather different path to a rather different type of accounting career was indeed beginning to emerge at UCT in the late 1960s, which culminated in 1968 with the transformation of the existing BCom degree into a preliminary qualification for entering the accounting profession. That the profession itself approved of this graduate route to accountancy is evident from the fact that its Public Accountants' and Auditors' Board supplemented the salaries of all full-time staff in Accounting by 5%.

While articled clerks formed a significant component of the second surge in student numbers in the Faculty too, making up nearly 60% of its 944 students in 1965, the other 40% had a different career path in mind, being primarily students registered for the BCom degree in the Department of Commerce with the aim of going into fields like business, industry, insurance, banking, local government administration and the actuarial profession. The scope of the degree was consequently wide, offering a broad training in subjects 'which have direct practical utility in business; a survey of the structure of the economic world, and of principles underlying its working; and a study of methods of applying this knowledge of economic and other principles in dealing with problems … of business and public administration'.[10]

This sweeping conception of the ambit of the degree reflected the distinctive stamp of the man who headed both the Department and the Faculty of Commerce from 1932 to 1964, Bill Hutt. By 1948,[11] Hutt's extensive spoken and written words had gained him a deserved reputation as a doughty champion of free enterprise, vehemently opposed to Keynesian economic policies and trade unions and ever ready to take issue with anyone supporting them. Cast within this framework, his lectures offered a probing analysis of economic and business issues from an avowedly neoclassical economics perspective, his enthusiasm sweeping students along with him. 'He taught the dangers of Keynesian economics … in direct opposition to what was being taught in the Department of Economics', recalled a member of that department. 'The end result was a body of students … who … got into the habit of thinking for themselves.'[12] One of them was Raymond Ackerman, the founder of the Pick n Pay supermarket chain, who found Hutt's teaching 'absolutely riveting', and decisive in opening his eyes to the working of the market and the important role of what Hutt termed 'consumer sovereignty' in it. 'That has stayed with me and had a huge influence on my life', Ackerman judged in retrospect.[13]

Hutt's unwavering views on economics, his forceful personality and his long tenure as head of department meant that neoclassical economics suffused the entire

BCom syllabus, with books by Hutt himself (four of them) and by his erstwhile LSE colleagues, Arnold Plant, Friedrich von Hayek and Lionel Robbins, prominent on its reading lists. Not that any of his appointees to UCT was otherwise inclined ideologically – four of them had studied only at UCT under him, while two others were products of the LSE. Of one, Ben Gurzynski, Hutt had a 'high opinion of his powers';[14] the other, John Hampton, Hutt felt, was 'a useful, loyal and greatly valued colleague'.[15] Hutt's imprint on his department was thus all-embracing and, aided by his general bonhomie – except if Keynes or trade unions were mentioned – created a group of like-minded academics who shared a strong *esprit de corps*.

Although several of them applied to succeed Hutt as professor of commerce, his successor was chosen from well outside his and the LSE's network, to allow the department to be comprehensively overhauled after his 34 years as its head. Hutt's wide-ranging BCom syllabus was dated in conception in an era of greater specialisation; its content was thin on recent developments in the science of management, operational research and the use of computers; postgraduates were rare; and closer relations with the business sector were needed. In short, noted UCT's Principal as chair of the selection committee, 'The Faculty must become identified with the changing needs of society' and its new head 'must ... combine attention to [business's] needs, with [the] preservation of acad[emic] standards'.[16] These requirements the 38-year-old Bob Boland met to a T.

A London-born accountant who had gained practical experience of financial management before moving into teaching the subject in new management schools in Britain, Ireland and France, Boland was also well versed in the ideas of the Harvard Business School, where he had recently spent a year. No sooner had he arrived at UCT in August 1965 than he was introducing tutorials and essays into the teaching programme and calling for a new type of undergraduate degree to replace Hutt's old BCom. With its emphasis on the latest management and business methods – the prospectus entry now spoke of a 'scientific approach to management problems and the use of current quantitative and computer techniques in those areas in business management formerly considered to be largely matters of opinion and judgement'[17] – the new degree was given the novel title of Bachelor of Business Science (BBusSc) to drive home its scientific basis. 'It is designed to meet the needs of tomorrow rather than those of yesterday', announced the Faculty self-assuredly.[18]

This four-year BBusSc degree was introduced in 1968, along with a thesis-based MBusSc; at the same time, the old three-year BCom degree was recast more narrowly as a qualification for would-be accountants only. Two year later, the Department of Commerce was itself renamed the Department of Business Science. Clearly it was under new management.

Yet, modernising the Department of Commerce was not Boland's sole – or even primary – objective. In his interview with UCT's selection committee in 1964, he had 'sold them the idea of founding a business school at UCT', he recalled,[19] and on this he was determined to deliver as quickly as possible.

In fact Hutt had tentatively begun a Postgraduate School of Business Administration and Applied Economics in that very year, to offer a part-time Master of Business Administration (MBA) degree to 'potential senior executives … to develop more rapidly those managerial skills which can be learned through decision-making in practice'.[20] But this initiative was still feeling its way in 1965 when Boland arrived.

One of Boland's referees from the Harvard Business School had described him as 'in a very nice way … an aggressive sort of person and … ambitious',[21] traits which were very much to the fore as he set about establishing at UCT, in an appropriately business-like fashion, a fully fledged business school offering the country's first full-time MBA course. His strategy of first securing 'cash and contacts'[22] through a personal approach paid off handsomely and, by the end of 1965, the nascent Graduate School of Business (as it was named) had generous start-up funding from Old Mutual, ad hoc accommodation in the old Protem hutments,[23] a country-wide student recruitment network thanks to the co-operation of Shell South Africa and several supportive businessmen, and four core staff, appointed in a flurry by a hastily constituted Action Committee independently of UCT's usual staff appointment procedures. From its official authorisation by UCT's Council to its opening in February 1966, the new Graduate School of Business (GSB) took five months to come into being. 'My motto was, "It's impossible, let's do it"', mused Boland in retrospect.[24]

Predictably, dynamism and innovation were hallmarks of Boland's teaching and he made his brand of participatory teaching the norm at the GSB. Students were divided into teams of five or six who then discussed in depth a particular business case which each member had studied closely the night before. 'The whole theory of the School is that you teach each other', explained one of its teachers.[25] This was followed by a plenary session led by the lecturer, who drew key principles and insights out of students' contributions. At this 'autonomous group learning' (as Boland labelled it), he excelled. He 'darted around the classroom and kept everyone on their toes by asking questions left, right and centre', remembered a student in his first class.[26] Those attending his courses on accounting and finance 'hung on the [very] words he used', recalled another.[27]

Boland's high-powered and inclusive pedagogy was complemented by that of several visiting lecturers from Europe and North America whom he brought out, courtesy of the School's start-up funding, for short stints to teach their specialities. Attracted by the prospect of a working-cum-tourist trip to Africa, they added a level of expertise to the School which put it in a class of its own in South Africa. In a School which unashamedly aimed to be 'a little Harvard Business School in Africa' (the description is Boland's[28]), they felt entirely at home. Local content began to enter the syllabus only later.

In every way, therefore – syllabus, case material, prescribed books and pedagogy – the GSB modelled itself on the Harvard Business School, 'the gold standard', as a student called it,[29] even to the extent of requiring a suit-and-tie dress code to be followed by male students, aimed, as it was, at instilling a sense of being members of a select group of smart young men – 35 of the first class of 36 full-timers were male and all 23 of the part-time class. All were white-skinned.[30]

Most students were graduates with several years' work experience behind them and looked upon the MBA (or the Advanced Diploma in Business Administration if they were non-graduates) as an effective means of career advancement. All lived in hutments adjoining the School and ate in a common dining room in a nearby UCT residence, so as to foster a strong sense of being part of a tight-knit family of comrades-in-learning. 'Learning came from close relationships in small groups', believed Boland.[31] Working on common tasks far into the night and over weekends just to keep up with the gruelling 29-week schedule mapped out for them only strengthened such camaraderie. 'The nervous intensity of the programme is meant to simulate the modern business atmosphere, in which problems and attendant decisions are strictly enveloped by a time limit', observed a student perceptively. 'These conditions force one to either make the time, or simply fall by the wayside.'[32] In fact, seven full-time students dropped out of the first course within a month, while an eighth tried to commit suicide.

Leisure time was a luxury – except for the annual sports day aimed at boosting the *esprit de corps* – and those wives living in hutments with their student spouses were warned that they would probably be neglected. 'It was monastic', recalled one husband with a sigh.[33] In fact, wives were not entirely neglected, as Boland set up a Wives' Club to make them aware of the pressure their husbands were under and how best they could support and motivate them. Unequivocally displaying the sexist assumptions of the time, the GSB's programme co-ordinator told the *Cape Times* that 'wives play an important part in their husbands' careers. They should and must help them reach the top.' To that end, at the club's weekly meetings they were 'taught how to entertain the boss, and to judge whether it would be more advantageous to give cocktail or dinner parties to enhance their husband's prospects … Like their husbands, they are given case-studies which they must work on at home.'[34] Boland certainly did not believe in half-measures when it came to requiring students' total immersion in and commitment to the MBA programme.

Not that he spared himself or his own family from such a commitment. They lived across the road from the GSB and he made sure he was available to students after hours and over weekends. His wife worked in the GSB office.

Aware that the start-up funding would run out after three years and determined that his GSB should itself be a model of good business enterprise, Boland also offered short courses for business executives and professional bodies to create an independent funding stream and to publicise the School, set up a GSB advisory board containing a number of top local businessmen, invited several of them to give guest lectures at the School, and allowed companies to undertake recruitment among the students. As he put it in the GSB's first annual report, 'The long-term success of such a School is directly related to the acceptance of its graduates by the business community.'[35] Though he did not teach marketing, he clearly knew more than a little about it in practice.

The proof of the success of his multi-pronged sales technique and imaginative administration both within the classroom and without came in 1969, when UCT formally made the GSB a permanent part of the Faculty of Commerce, no longer dependent on outside funding for its existence. In another way its success is also apparent in a tribute by a member of the first class (which was echoed by many of his peers), that the course he took at the GSB had been the 'open sesame' to a high-flying career in business.[36]

Between the bustling Boland and Greenwood's assertive successor, Leon Kritzinger (who arrived in 1969), the Faculty of Commerce would clearly mean business at UCT and beyond.

**Law**

Although at almost opposite ends of the UCT scale in terms of their size, the Faculty of Law and the Faculty of Commerce shared a number of features. Both taught full-time students during the day on the Groote Schuur campus and part-timers on the Orange Street campus after 5 pm; both provided little by way of postgraduate training, deferentially assuming that top students would rather further their studies abroad; both had to find a happy medium in what they taught in undergraduate courses between the technical and the academic; both employed only a few full-time lecturers but a large number of part-timers from their respective professions; and both increased their intake of undergraduates prodigiously in the decades after 1948.

On top of this, between 1945 and 1950 Law underwent not only a complete change of professorial personnel, but, as a consequence, also an expansion of its primary objective. Whereas the triumvirate of professors who had launched it as a faculty employing full-time academics in the 1920s, Wille, Wylie and Emmett,[37] had concentrated on providing academically respectable legal training for intending advocates, their trio of successors, Denis Cowen, Tom Price and Ben-Zion Beinart, wanted to go further than this by giving their students a wide legal education. 'The lawyer of the future ... should have some ideas beyond the mere earning of as large an income as possible', proclaimed Price in his inaugural lecture in 1947. 'There is a great deal to be said in favour of the principle of giving every would-be lawyer both a comprehensive academic training and a thorough practical grounding.'[38] With this sentiment Beinart B-Z concurred, citing in his inaugural address US Supreme Court judge Oliver Wendell Holmes's injunction that law should be taught '"in the grand manner", which I interpret to mean as a system of concepts and ideas, in ever-continuing development, and not as rules of thumb and *dicta* of authority'.[39] Their intention to give substance to spoken words was soon evident in their founding in 1954 of *Butterworth's South African Law Review* (which became *Acta Juridica* in 1957) as 'a journal which emphasises the importance of the academic study of law ... [so as to put] the products of basic investigation and research ... before the legal public'.[40]

A tension between the not wholly compatible aims of providing both legal training and a legal education consequently runs through the Faculty's history after 1950, becoming particularly marked when it rejected a proposal from the Law Society for the introduction a three-year LLB degree as it felt its scope would invariably be too narrow, and when the differing pedagogic requirements of would-be advocates and would-be attorneys and government law clerks came into direct competition. In both cases the wish to provide a legal education was given priority.

The three men who piloted the Faculty along this broader pedagogic path all held South African LLB degrees (Beinart and Cowen from UCT and Price from Natal), but two of them (Beinart and Price) had also gone on to take higher degrees, the former at the LSE and the latter at Cambridge. Tellingly, after interviewing Price in England, UCT's chief adviser on overseas appointments had reported that Price was 'an ambitious scholar who will with certainty take the steps necessary to make his name known in the learned world'.[41] This he did not achieve as professor in Roman-Dutch law at UCT from 1946 to 1966, however, not only because of his early death at the age of 51, but also because his diverse interests drew him onto many UCT committees and into the wardenship of a residence and local politics.

These extensive extra-academic commitments showed in his teaching. His lectures on his speciality, delict, were often identical to dense journal articles he had written. 'It was [often] not clear what he was getting at', remembered one of his students,[42] while a second recalled Price's unwillingness to discuss issues raised by students in class, preferring instead to dismiss them with a sharp riposte. 'He gave the impression of not being interested in students', concluded a third.[43]

The very opposite was true of Ben-Zion Beinart, the professor in Roman law from 1950 to 1974, when, at the age of 59, he left UCT for a chair at Birmingham University. Steeped in the writings of the old Continental legal authorities, whether in Latin, Dutch, German, French or Italian (all of which he could read), he drew heavily on these in his lectures to 'breathe life into the law', as one of his top students described it, 'and show it … not … operating in a vacuum but as a living system designed to deal with practical human problems'.[44] Though his delivery lacked spark, students were impressed by his obvious learning, his critical approach to law, and his general affability and approachability. His 'humanity as much as his scholarship … created … an indelible impression', judged a sometime student of his who rose to the Bench.[45]

More a legal scholar than a scholarly lawyer, he devoted much of his time to research, translating and annotating works of old authorities to reveal the legal foundations of individual liberty, of which he was a staunch defender. Indeed, such was his commitment to this project that, even when he was appointed Assistant Principal of UCT in 1974, he kept up his research. 'The task of the teacher of law … is to examine the sources of Roman law', he insisted, 'and … to indicate the direction it was taking and should be taking, and the lessons that could be learnt therefrom.'[46] Accordingly, he utilised his familiarity with these sources to inform, behind the scenes, a number of legal teams challenging apartheid legislation, especially the National Party Government's attempt to remove 'coloured' voters from the common electoral roll in 1952.

On all fours with this was his membership of liberal organisations like the Liberal Party, the Civil Rights League and the South African Institute of Race Relations. He was a middle-of-the-road liberal who sought to resolve problems by even-handed, well-informed and good-humoured negotiation. But by the late 1960s, such traits were being scorned by more radical students – one referred to 'Big Ben' as too committed to compromise, 'the man for peace in our time'.[47]

Very different from Beinart in temperament and background was the third member of the trio of post-war professors, Denis Cowen. Only 29 when appointed professor in commercial and comparative law in 1946, he brought two years of wide-ranging, active practice at the Bar to the position, unlike Price and Beinart who had very little experience of the inside of a courtroom. This fact showed in everything he tackled while on UCT's staff during the next fifteen years.

His lectures were 'like a performance', declaimed in 'rich, orotund language', remembered a sometime student of his in 2016.[48] He 'strode into the room with an air of excitement that captured me then, and still lingers with me now. He wasn't just coming to transmit legal knowledge; he was meeting to share with us the delight he had in the coherence of deep concepts. The texture of his thought reverberated inseparably from the bravura of his presentation ... What could have been flat pieces of data and dull propositions of logic were transformed into formidable intellectual narratives.'[49]

On other occasions he set aside his rhetorical flourishes and taught by the Socratic method, questioning students about a case they had read and then skilfully weaving their answers into a larger whole to drive home key legal principles. Unlike Price, he enjoyed this interactive approach, rarely brushing aside what students said and actually encouraging them to formulate their own ideas clearly, cogently and logically. 'He taught us to think and write like lawyers', reflected another ex-student approvingly.[50]

Given the centrality of the spoken word to any university, Cowen's mastery of speech, language and argument rapidly saw him appointed University Orator, a Senate representative on UCT's Council and a member of several UCT committees and boards. Not that his sharp analytical skills were limited to the spoken word. His legal writing was elegant, rigorous and closely reasoned – one of the country's top jurists described Cowen's co-authored *Law of Negotiable Instruments in South Africa* as 'one of the major achievements in South African legal literature',[51] while a former Dean of Law at London University believed it was 'the best work on the subject in English'.[52] Moreover, his written arguments on the issue of the removal of 'coloured' voters from the roll were decisive, at least in the short term. In what South Africa's Constitutional Court, nearly fifty years later, called a 'seminal essay [written in 1951] by Professor D.V. Cowen',[53] he challenged the accepted legal wisdom on the entrenched clauses in the Union constitution and 'step by step, in clear, simple language and with impeccable logic', repudiated it.[54]

He also took a prominent part in UCT's attempt to stave off university apartheid, opposing it alongside T.B. Davie before an official commission of inquiry into the issue, rejecting it at mass meetings on and off campus, and co-convening a combined UCT–Witwatersrand University conference in 1957, which put the case for the 'open universities' in a booklet in which he had a major hand.[55]

Deploying his legal nous and rhetorical ability in this very public way obviously came naturally to him and fed his growing reputation as an incisive and erudite legal scholar at home and abroad. In 1952 he was briefed as a consultant to the legal team opposing the Government on the 'coloured' vote case; soon after this he was appointed adviser to the protectorates of Basutoland and Swaziland on constitutional reform and the introduction of representative government; and in

1961 he was offered a chair at the University of Chicago, which he accepted. At the acme of his career he was judged to be 'one of South Africa's leading academic lawyers' by a distinguished member of South Africa's Law Revision Committee. His contributions to this committee's high-level discussions were 'of the highest quality, backed by thorough research and expressed with a clarity achieved only by those who are gifted with intellectual qualities of a very high order'.[56]

On the other hand, when Cowen turned his high-powered courtroom skills on colleagues at UCT with astringency, he invariably alienated many of them, including even the usually imperturbable Beinart. A number were thus not sad to see him leave for Chicago. As a friend put it tactfully, he was an individualist, probably 'not greatly motivated by "team spirit"'.[57] As a result, when, five years later, he sought to return to a chair at UCT, he was discreetly advised by the Principal to withdraw his application to prevent embarrassment, which he did. 'I … became one of the University of Cape Town's "rejects"', he remarked bitterly thirty years later.[58]

Although the man who succeeded Cowen when he left for Chicago, the 36-year-old Wouter de Vos, had been teaching Roman-Dutch and Roman law as a senior lecturer in the Faculty since 1954, he easily shifted his legal focus to the different array of subjects which his predecessor in the chair had taught, though these were now bracketed together under the label 'South African Private Law'. Trained at Stellenbosch and Leiden, De Vos was the antithesis of Cowen: single-minded and undemonstrative, he was known for his methodical and precise legal mind, which was manifest in his lucid writing and word-perfect, didactic lectures which replicated the roneoed notes that students had in front of them. It is a mark of the quality of these notes that many graduates continued to refer to them long after they had left UCT.

Bookish and industrious, but not overtly political in his outlook, De Vos made his name in enrichment law. His book on unjust enrichment became the standard text on the subject in South Africa. 'Hardly any decision of the Supreme Court [in this field] since 1958 has gone by without a reference to it [or to a related article by him]', noted two legal academics 34 years later.[59] Even when he moved to the chair in Roman-Dutch law in 1966, after Price's death, enrichment law remained the forte of this epitome of a legal academic for his next 26 years on the staff.

The man who was appointed to the new chair in public law, which Cowen had hoped to secure on his return to South Africa in 1967, was by then a pale shadow of the man he had once been. In his heyday at the Cape Bar, the 59-year-old Donald Molteno had been a QC, president of the Cape Bar Council, a 'Native Representative' in Parliament and a member of the legal team which had challenged the Government on the 'coloured' franchise issue. In fact it was his team which had appointed Cowen

# UCT UNDER APARTHEID

*Lecturing by the clock. The punctual, punctilious Professor Wouter de Vos as seen by one of his students.*

its legal consultant back in 1952.

By 1967, however, Molteno's practice had long since waned, he was demoralised and his health was failing. Occasionally, his old legal acumen shone through these impediments and he would reveal Molteno the incisive constitutional lawyer of yesteryear, but, for the most part, he stuck to dully reading the roneoed course notes which he handed out to the class. Poignantly, one student recalled how, now and then, Molteno 'lit up his mediocre lectures with comments like "Oh, I was in that case."'[60]

Teaching alongside these five male professors in this period – the first woman joined the full-time staff only in 1979 – were a handful of senior lecturers, four of whom subsequently occupied chairs at UCT,[61] and up to a dozen part-time lecturers, who took off time from their practices to lecture after 5 pm. What they taught may have been very specific, but this was underpinned by hands-on experience of the courtroom and the legal office, which well complemented what the full-time academics offered. Cowen called their contribution 'indispensable',[62] especially in subjects like commercial law, company law and administration of estates in the BCom and Certificate in the Theory of Accountancy curricula. Not surprisingly, it was such a part-timer, Jimmy Gibson, the author of the standard textbook *South*

# THE PROFESSIONAL FACULTIES

*A legal foundation for success. A student cartoonist's view of the Law student* (grrr! Magazine: Art Students' Ball, 1958)

*African Mercantile and Company Law*, who became the first professor in commercial law in 1972.

The curriculum for the LLB degree itself still revolved around the Roman and Roman-Dutch law axes, informed, in places, by English law, especially with regard to civil liberties. Until 1965, the limited number of staff and the rigidity of the curriculum allowed for no additions to it. However, in that year the pooling of several part-time posts made it possible to appoint more full-time staff, while Price's death the next year necessitated the rethinking of what was taught and by whom. From this easing of the curricular logjam flowed the introduction of several new courses like administrative law, tax law, conveyancing and immaterial property law. What did not appear in the revised curriculum is equally telling of the priorities of the Faculty in the high-apartheid era. Among the subjects not included in this makeover, which also saw distinct departments demarcated for the first time, were labour law, environmental law and African customary law – presumably the compulsory Arts Faculty course in Native Law and Administration (which was relabelled Comparative African Government and Law in 1960) was deemed to cover this.

Criticism of these lacunae in the curriculum came from two very different directions. A left-inclined student pointed to its lack of attention to social and economic rights, what he called a disconnection 'between his courses and the situation on the ground on the shanties [on the Cape Flats]'.[63] From the opposite end of the political spectrum, the director of the Cape Chamber of Industries complained that Law students were 'uninstructed in the … pressing field of management-labour laws … which I see as a practical necessity' in industrial relations.[64]

Whatever new courses were introduced into the curriculum, the mode of teaching them as well as existing courses changed little throughout the 1950s and 1960s. Formal lectures remained the norm, with no small-group tutorials to complement them; essays were rare; visits to witness courts in action were not organised; and moots were unknown, save as part of the annual Law Intervarsity with Stellenbosch University (begun in 1964) or if arranged by the UCT Law Students' Council. In short, the Faculty provided a solid, conservative and book-centred legal education. Very few of the 397 students[65] (the bulk of whom were male) who left the Faculty's twin premises, on the Hiddingh campus and in the Arts Block on the Groote Schuur campus, with LLB degrees between 1948 and 1968 would have felt that they lacked a sound foundation on which to build, in time, a legal practice at the Bar or Side-Bar.

Readier to get into full practice immediately were the 168 candidate attorneys and legal civil servants who gained a Diploma in Law from UCT in these years. Introduced at the request of the Cape Society of Attorneys in 1954 to raise the quality of the training such legal practitioners received in preparation for sitting the Attorneys' Admission Examination or the Public Service Law Examination, the diploma's curriculum consisted of purely utilitarian legal subjects, without significant theoretical, historical or philosophical dimensions. This made it difficult to teach these students and LLB students in the same class. When the shortage of staff made this unavoidable, the result was dissatisfaction all round. This was 'a totally unsatisfactory procedure', grumbled one full-timer, 'as one virtually had to lecture on two different levels'.[66] Pitching the lecture at the LLB students confounded most Diploma students, while doing the opposite bored the LLB students.

From this it is clear that some LLB students' sense of constituting an elite group on campus began within their very own faculty. As a member of staff with experience of Stellenbosch Law students remarked, 'at Stellenbosch you simply taught students; at UCT, you had to convince them'.[67] UCT Law students' prominence in student politics (for which courtroom skills like oratory, interrogation and mounting a coherent argument were a boon) and as authors in the UCT–Stellenbosch Law students' journal, *Responsa Meridiana*, only fuelled this sense, particularly as there were hardly any postgraduates in the Faculty to whom to defer. Indeed, in this period, the Faculty awarded only two LLM and three LLD degrees. Adding postgraduate training to the undergraduate legal education and legal training which it already offered would take another twenty years.

## Education

Like UCT's Faculty of Law and in common with most Education faculties or departments in Commonwealth universities in this period, UCT's Faculty of Education had two functions which were not wholly compatible, however much they may have seemed to be so on paper.

On the one hand, being part of a university, the Faculty was expected to focus on the academic study of education, posing big questions about its purpose, its context and its underlying philosophy; on the other hand, its task was also to train teachers in very practical ways, introducing them to what theorists today call 'pedagogical knowledge' but what among students then was light-heartedly referred to as 'tips for teaching'. The tension between these two functions was apparent in key areas like the content of syllabuses, staffing and teaching methods. Ultimately, however, the fact that it was to qualify as teachers that almost all students had enrolled in the Faculty usually weighed most heavily in the decisions made on these issues. It would therefore not be inaccurate to describe the Faculty in this era as primarily a teacher training institution which, for historical reasons, was located within a university.[68]

Not that in 1948 the Faculty was doing well in attracting such students. It was still one of UCT's minnows, with just 82 students on its books, a figure little different from its annual enrolment all through the 1930s and 1940s. This failure to grow is a mark of the lack of appeal which teaching held for many young white English-speaking South Africans after the Great Depression of the early thirties had ebbed. Especially for young men, growing opportunities in business, industry and clerical work were far more attractive. Not until the mid-1950s, when state bursaries for intending teachers became more freely available and the demand for school teachers was increasing as new schools for whites and 'coloureds' opened in the Cape, did the Faculty begin to grow in size by leaps and bounds: in 1958 its enrolments stood at 186 and ten years later, in 1968, at 288. The fact that it offered some courses in both English and Afrikaans (as it had done since its inception), making it easier for students to gain the bilingual teaching qualification required for appointment to a government school after 1947, helped widen this appeal.

About 60% of all its students between 1948 and 1968 enrolled for a Secondary Teacher's Certificate (or Diploma as it was rebranded in 1962), which qualified them to teach in a high school, about 30% for a primary school teaching qualification, about 6% for a BEd degree, which was meant to be a qualification in education rather than in teaching, and the rest for certificates or diplomas in specialist fields like teaching 'problem children in European primary schools', 'children handicapped in speech and hearing' or 'special classes' (to use contemporary labels). A one-year 'Diploma in Native Education' was also offered from 1938, but was withdrawn in 1957 for want of takers. Until 1960 all of these courses were held during the day, but from 1961 the BEd was offered after hours too, quickly drawing a not insignificant number of working teachers keen to advance their careers. Given the Faculty's focus on teacher training, post-BEd study received little encouragement, as is evident from the tiny number of MEd (two) and PhD degrees (six) awarded in twenty years.

Over two-thirds of all undergraduates were women,[69] with their heaviest concentration being in the courses for primary school teachers, for which virtually no men registered. In fact, one lecturer spoke of the 'appallingly low intake of men', not only in these courses but more generally in the Faculty.[70] In part, the low number of men was because, until 1957, the highest primary teaching qualification was restricted to women only, in an attempt to steer those men interested in an educational career into pursuing the qualification for teaching in a high school, where, it was argued, a male presence was essential. Accordingly, men made up 45% of all recipients of Secondary Teacher's Certificates/Diplomas between 1948 and 1968. Even so, the bulk were not judged to be of the highest academic calibre. 'We get lots of third-class people', complained one Dean of the Faculty, 'and many of them are quite happy with that class. For example, I spoke to one and said to him, "You nearly got a second class mark with your paper." His reply was, "Oh, I only aimed at a third anyway!"'[71] An official inquiry into the training of white teachers at this time lamented, 'If the teaching profession enjoyed a higher status, greater numbers of a better type of student would be attracted to education.'[72]

In all courses white students far outnumbered those not so classified, constituting some 89% of all securing a qualification in the Faculty during these twenty years. Yet, despite their being so outnumbered on campus, off campus the more radical of the 200 or so 'coloured', Indian and African holders of a UCT educational qualification exercised a powerful political influence on generations of school pupils, far beyond their actual number. At politically aware schools like Trafalgar, Harold Cressy, Livingstone and South Peninsula these ardent cadres of the Teachers' League of South Africa and the Non-European Unity Movement 'constituted a collective forum which molded a process of historically aware learning among pupils', to use the measured words of one such pupil years later.[73]

Not that these teachers' training at UCT was responsible for raising their political consciousness in the first place, except perhaps as a reaction to it. Most of what was taught in the Education Faculty in the 1950s and 1960s was little different from what had been taught there twenty and more years earlier. A historian of education characterised it as 'essentially a colonial variant of what was taught in teacher training courses in Britain' between the wars.⁷⁴ Syllabuses were primarily Eurocentric in content. When they did turn to education in South Africa, it was almost solely to the education of whites. A question from the 1958 Post-graduate Primary Teacher's Certificate examination unwittingly displays exactly this tunnel vision. Candidates were asked to 'Describe the education which a youth on a farm in the interior of the Cape Colony was likely to receive in the late 18th century'. As the marking matrix makes clear, the assumption was that the youth was both white and male.⁷⁵ In addition, textbooks prescribed and exam questions posed in the 1950s and 1960s were practically identical to those of the 1930s, despite the revisionist winds then sweeping through history teaching elsewhere in the English-speaking world. About the decisive Bantu Education Act of 1953 and its implications, practically nothing was said.

Neither, for the most part, were the subjects that were in the syllabuses imaginatively taught, nor was the teaching in the Faculty geared to 21- and 22-year-olds. Dictated notes, mandatory and pedantic instruction in blackboard technique, formal dress regulations and compulsory attendance at lectures all made the Faculty appear to be what *Varsity* scoffed at as 'a glorified high school'.⁷⁶ 'We should … be expected and encouraged to express and ask questions', complained disgruntled Secondary Teacher's Diploma students in 1962. What was needed, they went on, was 'more time for discussion, which surely ought to be characteristic of university education'.⁷⁷

Students also criticised the disconnect between what they were taught in the Theory of Education course and the reality they encountered in their twice-weekly practical teaching stints in Peninsula schools. Tellingly, a graduate of the Faculty declared that, after a few years as a practising teacher, 'I was still to meet "the child" that had been talked about in the [educational] psychology classes.'⁷⁸

In short, in the twenty years after 1948 the Faculty of Education was found wanting in both the content and the mode of delivery of its teaching, though not in the assiduity of its staff. In diligent fashion, they put in long hours year in, year out to turn out nearly 1300 high school teachers and some 625 primary school teachers, i.e. about 10% of all newly qualified, university-trained teachers in the country. Nonetheless, many of these students – and not a few academics in other faculties – judged Education to be a lightweight faculty, 'a bit of a bore and laughed off as a joke', as *Varsity* put it in 1958.⁷⁹ Six years later the student newspaper was even more trenchant in its criticism, labelling it 'that orchard of ordinariness, that practical and almost living proof of the power of Parkinson's Law'.⁸⁰ On campus it was widely referred to as 'the Loafers' Course' by students⁸¹ because of its undemanding content and spoonfeeding mode of teaching. One student admitted that he used to say he was taking '"only Education" … in the same way as people used to apologise for having read Geography at the university'.[82]

Along with the prioritisation of teacher training, such academic ossification and mediocrity owed much to the Faculty's professorial heads in these years. Of the seven men who filled its two chairs after 1948 (an English- and an Afrikaans-medium chair in education existed from 1930 to 1969 to ensure bilingual teaching was offered), two, Willie Grant and Johannes Burger, each spent over twenty years as professors with their thinking on education still echoing that of the 1920s, until their retirement in 1952 and 1956 respectively;[83] a third, Eddie Pells, had been in the Faculty for 22 years before succeeding Grant for a short-lived tenure of the English-medium chair;[84] two occupants of the Afrikaans-medium chair after Burger, viz. Stephanus Olivier and Gideon Smit, remained in the post only briefly before going on to higher positions in the field of education beyond UCT;[85] and two, Reg Lighton and Ockert Erasmus, became the English- and Afrikaans-medium professors in 1961 and 1965 respectively, by which time their approaches to education had already been comprehensively shaped by their prior careers, as a school inspector and head of a teacher training college in the case of Lighton, and as a strongly theory-inclined professor of the philosophy of education in Erasmus's case.

The 58-year-old Lighton was an avid committee man and a deft administrator, capable of resolving problems quietly behind the scenes, but certainly not well abreast of new currents in educational thinking abroad. Indeed, as a minor novelist, translator and anthologist, he was more interested in literature – several of his works were prescribed for schools – and went on to serve on the state's Publications Control Board after he retired in 1969.

The 47-year-old Erasmus came to UCT from education departments at Pretoria University, the University of the Orange Free State and Unisa, where the intellectual environments were conducive to his interest in Continental European philosophies of education, especially phenomenology and fundamental pedagogics. But so arcane was this speciality and so rigid his commitment to it that even the usually unruffled Lighton grumbled in private about his fellow professor's 'utter conviction that pedagogy is as exact a science as physics … [and about his] partiality for words such as "scientistic" and "scientistically"'. This amounted to a 'virtual rejection of what is in effect our approach [in the Faculty] … [the] endeavour to keep theory and practice reciprocally relevant'.[86] For their part, Afrikaans-speaking students, faced with Erasmus's airy philosophising in his 'Teorie van die Onderwys' course, voted with their feet and switched to Lighton's more down-to-earth, parallel 'Theory of Education' course.

Almost without exception, the rest of the older permanent staff in the Faculty –

which began to grow beyond the five of 1948 only in the 1960s, to reach ten in 1968[87] – usually followed the professorial line, for, as 'stuffy lecturers of the old school' (as one student perceived them[88]), they too were steeped in the interwar school culture of accepting decisions from above and not rocking the boat.[89] Close to being a stereotype of such lecturers was William Ferguson, who was appointed senior lecturer in the history of education and the method of education in 1957 aged 46, after 21 years as a school teacher. Lighton commended him as 'a man completely dedicated to the cause of education … prompt, thorough and dependable. As a lecturer he is always well prepared and competent.' Year in and year out he shouldered the onerous task of drawing up the Faculty's lengthy list of books for inclusion in the prospectus, while, as an organiser, he was 'keen and competent … to get things done'.[90] A regular book reviewer for the journal of the South African Teachers' Association (of which he was a stalwart), he was also the author of a junior school textbook.

On the other hand, Professor Smit felt Ferguson lacked the know-how to supervise postgraduate research adequately – Ferguson himself did not have a doctorate. 'I found his knowledge of the sources and the techniques of historical research to be rather limited', Smit reported.[91] Clearly his capacity for hard work was not enough to turn him into an academic educationalist. Moreover, in UCT's lecture rooms his habits as a school teacher died hard. Students who 'misbehaved' were sent out of the room, while a young man who took off his jacket without first seeking Ferguson's permission was also told to leave the class. Little wonder that students who already held a BA or BSc degree felt that they were 'going back to school' after their first week in the Faculty.[92]

The one lecturer not in this mould was Isak 'Tinkie' Heyns, an educational psychologist with postgraduate degrees from Chicago University and several years' lecturing experience in UCT's Department of Psychology. Appointed a lecturer in education at UCT in 1960 at the age of 36, he added a novel statistical dimension to courses in methods of educational research. Lighton described him as 'a popular lecturer, bright, animated, lucid, invigorating, likeable',[93] and as a man who 'keeps himself abreast of modern findings in his fields and [who] continually revises and develops his approaches to his work'.[94]

Such a combination of abilities had been rare in the Faculty since 1930 and must have contributed significantly to his ascent to the chair of education and the deanship of the Faculty in 1970. But it was moot whether he was prepared to trim his extra-mural activities – he was a passionate rugby coach and referee and a devoted school housemaster – or had the inclination to take on the time- and energy-demanding commitment to transform the Faculty.

## Architecture

On almost every score, the School of Architecture in the Faculty of Fine Art and Architecture stood in sharp contrast to the Faculty of Education. One professor, Len Thornton White, headed it for seventeen of the twenty years under examination – indeed, he was its first professor from 1937 already;[95] all of its students were long-stayers, spending at least five years taking the same courses in the same building; and the contents and style of its teaching self-consciously sought to emulate the latest trends in the top architectural schools in Britain and the United States. Proudly, TW (as Thornton White was widely known) described the School as 'forward-looking and capable of development to meet almost any changes in architectural thought (as distinct to fashion)'.[96]

Steeped in the Modernist, socially aware ethos of the Architectural Association School in London, where he had been Vice Principal in the mid-1930s, TW purposefully fashioned UCT's infant School of Architecture in its mould from the moment of his arrival. A senior architect from outside UCT spoke accurately of 'the dominant personality of the School's head'.[97] The affinity with the London School meant that central to the training instituted at UCT were teamwork among the students, a heavy emphasis on the art of drawing neatly, clearly and accurately, extensive use of studio tutorials for instruction in which staff–student interaction was prominent, allowing the students to learn 'a good deal … without knowing it',[98] a veneration for the style and the work of Modernist architects like Frank Lloyd Wright, Le Corbusier, Gropius and Mies van der Rohe, and at least lip service to a philosophy that architecture should be 'a basic social service for people of today and tomorrow', as TW put it. Structure should be employed 'as a servant and not as a master'.[99]

TW was adamant that, in line with the requirement by the Royal Institute of British Architects for recognition of any architectural school in the Commonwealth, all lecturers had to be active in the profession so as to keep abreast of latest developments and not become armchair architects. To that end, written into every contract with staff was a requirement to 'engage in private practice or undertake research or other form of personal work, but such work must not interfere with his [*sic*] University duties'.[100]

Of such engagement TW was himself a prime exponent, not least on UCT's own campus, where he designed or co-designed the New Science Lecture Theatre, the original Chemical Engineering Building and the School's own Centlivres Building,[101] while further afield he undertook town planning commissions for towns in South Africa, Kenya, the then Rhodesias and Mauritius. The almost free rein UCT gave him to build up an architectural school he put to good effect to create one of the two leading institutions for architectural training in the country. Indeed, UCT's Principal believed that it had become 'an educational centre of world-wide repute' under TW.[102]

The men (no woman was appointed to the staff until 1976) whom he selected to implement his vision were broadly Modernist in architectural outlook, but not narrowly so. TW believed that there was virtue in variety – approaching architecture from different perspectives yielded 'a wider and deeper understanding of architecture as a University discipline', he assured one UCT Principal.[103] However, such variety was not infinite: just over half the permanent staff appointed between 1948 and 1968 were products of either the Architectural Association's School or UCT.

Among the former were TW's ultra-reliable second-in-command, Owen Pryce Lewis, whose deft artistic skill in drawing historic buildings on the blackboard to illustrate the history of the discipline offset his less-than-riveting lectures. His drawings were 'magic. It was as if you were there in the building', recalled an admiring ex-student. 'You could have heard a pin drop in the class while he drew', so rapt were its members.[104] He 'influenced me greatly because I used his classroom methodology when I became a lecturer', acknowledged another former student.[105] Another mainstay of the School out of the Architectural Association School stable was Jock Sturrock, who was better at fashioning buildings than lectures, if student opinion is to be believed; he did the former for UCT very successfully, designing three buildings on its Medical campus.[106] A third Architectural Association School product, Bill Taute, appealed to TW because he 'thoroughly understood all the developing isms', which he discussed with his students 'in a most sympathetic way, leaving them with some constructive criticism on which to base their further studies'.[107]

TW's acceptance of some variety of approach in his staff is evident in the appointment of lecturers like Hugh Floyd, whose work TW felt to be 'realistic and derivative rather than original or scholarly',[108] yet whose draughtsmanship and grasp of theory underlying structures were impressive. Floyd was one of the very few architects in South Africa able 'to grasp the inner implications of the teachings of Buckminster Fuller', judged one of his colleagues.[109] Similarly, while TW was taken by the novel psychological perspective which Douglas Pett brought to his teaching of architecture, he also recognised that 'half the students thought of him as the best man on the staff, while the other half hated him and at times avoided him'.[110]

The tolerance of this diversity of approach among the staff – thirteen full- and part-timers in 1948, rising to eighteen in 1968 – made the School an appealing home even for 'perhaps the most talented designer we have ever graduated out of this school' (to use the glowing words of the head of the City Planning Department at the University of Pennsylvania[111]), the 28-year-old UCT and Pennsylvania graduate and follower of Louis Kahn, Roelof Uytenbogaardt, who took up an assistant studio mastership at his alma mater in 1963. From here his academic career took off prodigiously, monumentally overshadowing those of others in the School as it did so. One of these was no less a figure than TW's successor, Christiaan Strauss Brink.

When TW became UCT's full-time architectural consultant in 1965 – a position he filled until his death later that year – he vacated his chair and the headship of the School, to be succeeded by the 45-year-old Brink. Trained in architecture at UCT and in civic design at Liverpool, he had been encouraged to apply for the UCT chair by the Principal, J.P. Duminy, who had known him in Pretoria, where he had been on the staff of the local university's School of Architecture since 1950. His buildings on its campus and in and around the city bore clear testimony to his Modernist vision – TW described one as 'architecturally the most progressive University residence in the Country'.[112] This brand of Modernism had been embraced by Afrikaner cultural nationalists of that era, as they saw it as another way of asserting their identity by turning their backs on English-style Victorian and Edwardian architecture.

Coming from this Pretoria context as he did, Brink discovered that several of his new colleagues at UCT perceived him as representing such nationalism in concrete, which affronted their cultural and political values. He was looked upon as 'a nobody, [a] non-descript', recalled the then chair of the Architectural Students' Council. Even before he arrived, 'the daggers were already drawn and no quarter was given'.[113] Thus, from day one Brink faced hostility from staff, which quickly snowballed and spread to students too, especially as it was aggravated by his lack of a grand vision for the School in the post-TW age, his administrative slackness, his pedantic pedagogy, the alterations he made to TW's magnum opus, the Centlivres Building, and his not unsympathetic attitude to the redevelopment of District Six after it was proclaimed a white Group Area in terms of apartheid policy.

Within a short time a significant number of staff and students were engaged in what Brink's son (who was himself a student in the School from 1970) called 'psychological warfare' against his father,[114] employing snubs, open challenges and put-downs. The School became paralysed, a situation which, understandably, produced a negative assessment by a visiting team from the Royal Institute of British Architects. This 'cold war' took its toll on Brink and he resigned in 1974, giving as his reasons a wish to expand his private practice and to be free of the burden of administration.

His only innovation to find favour in the School was his organisation of a three-month study tour of Italy for seventeen Architecture and Fine Art students, which he led in 1968–9. His rationale for the tour epitomises the narrow colonial mindset then the norm on campus: 'Not only in Rome, but the whole of Italy is the source from which our most fundamental beliefs spring, and it is just because we who live in the "new" countries have moved further away that we, especially, need to return. So much becomes clear to us then. The Republic of South Africa could not have been possible had it not been for that other [i.e. Roman] republic.'[115]

In keeping with such views, the School's curriculum under both TW and Brink closely followed those of the better British schools of architecture of the day, the activities of which were reported in the professional journals to which UCT subscribed. UCT's training combined theory and practice by means of studio work and, to a lesser extent, lectures. The art of drawing was central to this training, memorably summed up in a former student's graphic statement that 'Drawing was our language'.[116] Each year's courses were taught by a distinct year-team of studio masters headed by a year-master of senior lecturer rank. Local and foreign visiting lecturers provided specialist input on particular topics. Given the requirement that all full-time academic staff had simultaneously to practise as architects, the result was that the courses were neither academically narrow nor far removed from daily practice. Reinforcing the latter feature was the inclusion in both the BArch degree and the Diploma in Architecture[117] of a year's work in an architect's office. From 1959, when the length of the degree and the diploma programme was extended from five to six years to accommodate the swelling content of the subject, this 'external experience under the supervision of the University' (to use the prospectus's formal phraseology[118]) was set for the fourth year of study.

Modernism suffused the syllabus. 'It was rammed down our throats', remembered a student of the 1960s.[119] '"Form" and "function" were the buzz phrases', recalled another.[120] A third remembered being introduced to 'New Brutalism' in the early 1950s, with the Festival Hall on the South Bank of the Thames being cited as a worthy example.[121] Indeed, in 1951 TW used his London connections to secure places for sixteen UCT students with architectural firms in that city so they could do their 'office year' amid the state-of-the-art architecture of the Festival of Britain.

Closer to home, the Centlivres Building, the School's new home from 1959, had been tailor-designed by TW not only as a practical demonstration of Modernist architecture on a difficult site, but also, imaginatively, as an example of research in progress, for its roof and walls were covered with different materials to ascertain which best withstood the Cape weather. 'The new building will be an object lesson in construction and finishes', forecast an in-house UCT magazine.[122]

The local political climate also left its mark on the School, in the form of spatial apartheid. With no obvious reservations on their part, staff expected students doing exercises in the design of public buildings to ensure that these provided racially separate entrances and toilets. Dismayed, one politically conscious student reflected

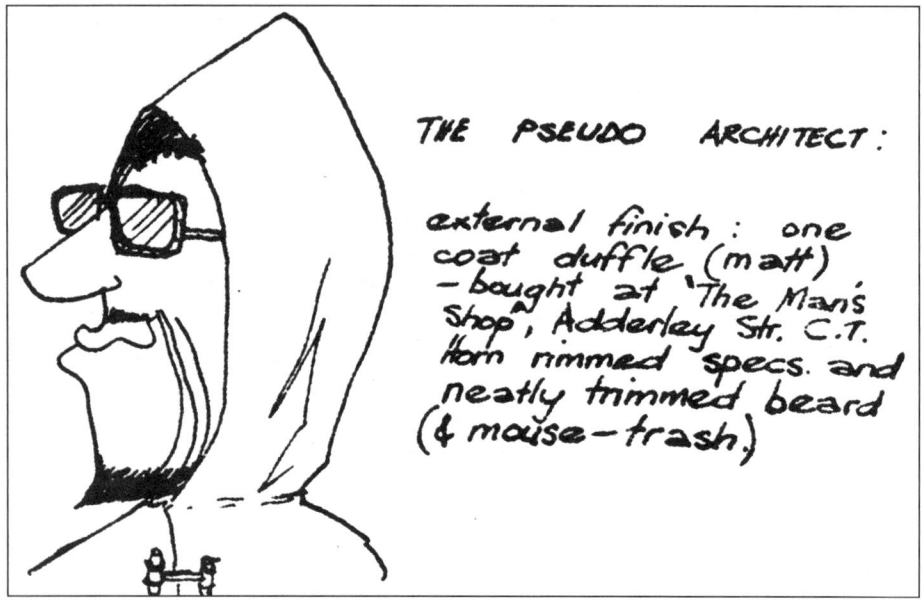

*A designer architect. A student cartoonist's cynical view of 'The Pseudo Architect'* (TAT, c. 1960)

years later that 'We, as the School of Architecture facilitated apartheid – I had to come to terms with the fact that becoming an architect meant that you were actually structuring apartheid.'[123]

However, in the 1960s few white students jibbed at such a segregatory requirement, so normative had apartheid become. Moreover, the physical and academic isolation of the School from the rest of UCT – until 1958 its home was in a rudimentary, ex-army hutment at the southern end of the rugby fields – meant that its students were at a remove from wider student politics and affairs. 'We were in a world of our own', felt one student, 'leading to a lack of engagement with the social and political events taking place on campus then.'[124]

What this isolation did breed, however, was a very strong sense of identity and *esprit de corps*, which were manifest in the biennial 'Opus' pantomime (copied from the London Architectural Association School), an annual exhibition of student work, and a lively Architectural Students' Society, which published its own magazine from 1954 and organised regular film shows, lectures, social functions and an annual Rag float. Along with these went a generally laid-back ethos among students, 'unconventional, free spirited … bohemian', as one of them characterised it.[125] To outsiders, however, these students gave a rather different impression, one student journalist describing them as 'long-haired cranks and misfits'.[126]

Yet, occasionally, this casual atmosphere was overtaken by a surge of idealistic passion, frustration or indignation, usually triggered by some in-house event, which produced mass meetings, resolutions and earnest petitions. For instance, in 1962 third-year students objected en masse to 'destructive' critiques of their work by their studio masters as, they claimed, this undermined their creativity, 'producing dull, narrow-minded architects',[127] while two years later, a visit by an Institute of South African Architects assessment team prompted a mass meeting which criticised the 'state of stagnation [in the School], resulting in the acceptance of mediocre architecture'.[128] A year later fifth-year students, stirred by critiques they had read of artificial, minutely planned cities, went as far as staging a 'pens down' protest, boycotting classes for a week and arranging an alternative programme which called into question the School's slavish adherence to the Modernist style. Not surprisingly, in Brink's time, the level of students' protest reached a new height – Brink's son called it a 'serious student insurrection' against his father.[129]

The second department within the School, Quantity Surveying (QS), was a good deal more down to earth in character. Not only was this because of the very practical nature of the subject itself, but also because, ever since its inception in 1939,[130] the department was very dependent on the local profession for teaching its courses. Until 1951 all specifically QS courses were taught by part-time lecturers who were in practice, while even after that date these men (and, like the student body, they were all men) remained essential to the teaching programme.

Accordingly, when, in 1948, the profession's Chapter of South African Quantity Surveyors complained that UCT's QS programme as a whole contained too many architectural courses and also lacked a practical component supervised by a member of the profession, the University scrapped its short-lived, five-year BSc in QS, as the Chapter had requested it to do. This degree was not reintroduced until 1964, by when, the Chapter recognised, the growing technical complexity of QS made a degree necessary for adequate qualification. QS was 'no longer confined to measuring and accounting', explained a lecturer in the subject. 'Today's quantity surveyor has become more of a building economist and cost adviser.'[131] Shortly after this, a similar argument by the building industry persuaded UCT to introduce a five-year BBSc (Bachelor of Building Science) degree too, aimed mainly at producing project managers.

Between the disappearance and the reappearance of the BSc (QS), the only QS qualification offered by UCT was a part-time Diploma in QS, spread, initially, over five years, but later extended to five and a half years to accommodate the final-year thesis adequately. From 1952, under the experienced eye of UCT's first full-time appointee in

QS, the well-qualified quantity surveyor, civil engineer and architect Jack Butt, the QS courses were taught in an appropriately hard-headed manner to ensure the approval of the Chapter. Moreover, when, in 1961, changes to the Architecture curriculum shifted architectural students out of the QS courses which they had taken jointly with the QS students until then, the syllabuses in these courses were reformulated to increase the quantity of purely QS material in them. 'Balance and progression through the years could now be considered', rejoiced Butt.[132] QS was maturing, although it was not until 1973 that it gained a chair of its own. Fittingly, the first incumbent was one of the recently retired Butt's first students at UCT, James Rabie.

The same factor which drove the escalating demand for architects and quantity surveyors from the 1950s – South Africa's flourishing economy in which new industrial, commercial, residential and public buildings were required in large numbers – also lay behind the creation of the School's third department in 1965, Urban and Regional Planning, as the boom also produced a need for new towns and townships to be systematically laid out and for existing towns, cities and regions to be redeveloped.

The introduction of a town planning qualification had been in the UCT pipeline since 1937, when a diploma course in the subject had been approved in principle. However, a lack of funding from the state meant that it was not until three other South African universities had set up such courses that the South African Institution of Town Planners was finally able to convince UCT that it should follow suit. Accordingly, in 1963 UCT secured a special, five-year grant from the new UCT Foundation to create a chair in town and country planning. The successful applicant, the 32-year-old Julian Beinart, was a whizz-kid with training as an architect at UCT and MIT and as a city planner at Yale. 'He has a brilliant brain', acknowledged TW, and a 'really strong character', but was not averse to using 'blitz tactics on a very wide scope of problems … [yet] his imagination is such that he rarely sticks to one project for more than a few weeks'.[133]

Evidence of the former traits was not slow to appear, for Beinart told UCT's selection committee that he did not approve of the chair's title ('Town and Country Planning'), preferring instead the American-style 'Urban and Regional Planning'. Somewhat taken aback, Senate nonetheless accepted the standpoint of the young professor, and in 1966 42 students enrolled for UCT's part-time, postgraduate, three-year Master in Urban and Regional Planning (MURP) degree or its diploma equivalent. By 1968 Beinart's 'outstanding imaginative power, strong commitment to ideals, and … impressive intellectual discipline' (to cite the opinion of his supervisor at MIT[134]) had attracted 26 more students, while in that year, too, the first batch of fifteen graduates received UCT's inaugural MURP degree.

These graduates in the School's newest discipline apart, by that year the School had also turned out in its older disciplines 708 architects and 151 quantity surveyors since 1948,[135] or almost 40% of all architects trained at South Africa's universities and about 25% of all quantity surveyors in those years. UCT's contribution to the structuring of South Africa in its apartheid years was not inconsiderable.

## Social Science

Even more dominant in his faculty than TW was in Architecture was Professor Edward Batson in Social Science from 1935 to 1971. By 1948 his standing in his one-department faculty and, more widely, within UCT, Cape Town and Africa was at an all-time high.[136] Not only had he recently persuaded UCT to create a separate Faculty of Social Science as an independent home for his Department of Social Science and Administration (which doubled as the grandly named School of Social Science and Social Administration in a bid to make the tiny faculty look more layered), but he was also widely known on campus as the punctilious and always well-briefed chair of several key university committees. T.B. Davie initially thought him to be 'one of the clearest thinkers in this University'.[137] Beyond UCT his name was in the headlines too, as the innovative director of pioneering social surveys of Cape Town and other southern African cities, which had employed the cutting-edge sociological gauge, the poverty datum line, to telling effect. Nor did he miss an opportunity to talk up his fledgling discipline, telling an eager reporter, 'The world is the real laboratory of the social scientist … His purpose as a scientist is to provide a base of knowledge upon which social policy may rest … The administrator who builds a social plan upon a social survey is free of the evil of ignorance.'[138] A Cabinet Minister wrote 'in the highest terms' of Batson's 'strong sense of public duty and … knowledge of the world … I can say, without exaggeration, that not only the Department of Social Welfare, but the Government itself, is much in … [his] debt for … helpful and constructive contributions towards the Union's social planning.'[139]

However, his reputation was by itself not enough to draw a large number of students to his infant faculty. Not until the second half of the 1950s, when the development of state, NGO and private sector welfare services (especially, but not exclusively, for whites) increased the demand for social assistance and counselling services by the Faculty's main product, social workers, did student enrolments begin to grow appreciably. Probably also contributing to this growth then was a greater public awareness of the profession as a result of the creation of the first professional association of social workers in South Africa.

To ensure that it benefited from these changing circumstances, in 1959 the Faculty expanded its offerings in social administration (as social work was then termed at UCT) so that it could meet the official statutory requirements for full recognition of social work qualifications more exactly. At the same time, in its zeal to grow, it sought to take advantage of a burgeoning demand for general social science graduates generated by the booming economy in new fields like market research, personnel and organisational management, and advertising. To this end, it replaced 'social science' courses with 'sociology' courses in 1958, Batson declaring that the Faculty's primary qualification, the BSocSci degree 'is by no means aimed particularly at the teaching of social workers, that is only incidentally one of its functions now … The young and expanding Faculty of Social Science … has already far outgrown its original association with social work only.'[140]

The effect of these changes on the number of undergraduates registered in the Faculty was marked. Whereas between 1950 and 1957 this did not top 60, in 1960 it reached 113 and more than double this figure in 1968. As Batson was quick to point out, while the University's intake had increased by about 4% per annum over the ten years since 1957, registrations in his faculty had increased at over 16% annually. Moreover, students from other faculties taking one or two of the new courses helped swell the numbers in individual courses even more: in 1967 a new Sociology course containing an industrial sociology component drew 350 students, necessitating the use of Jameson Hall for lectures. Well might Batson, as Dean of the Faculty, Director of the School, Professor and Head of the Department, have felt a sense of considerable achievement at his transformation of a small department training social workers into a full-blown Department of Sociology and Social Administration with its own faculty, housed since 1959 in the Centlivres Building and equipped with dedicated facilities like a social science laboratory, interview rooms, a briefing room and a socio-drama stage. His faculty/school/department now stood on a crowning height as the largest English-medium social science training institution in South Africa.

Yet, despite this outward appearance of success, all was not well in the Faculty. By 1967 Batson was 61 and had been in his post for 32 years. His innovative zest had ebbed, his teaching had ossified, his management style had become pernickety and irritating, and his reputation had waned. He had 'lost his spark', recalled a lecturer in a kindred department,[141] while another believed that Batson had become 'a bit of a joke' among his fellow academics.[142]

The long-brewing storm of student discontent broke on 30 March 1967 when *Varsity* published an exposé of the Faculty under the heading 'Something's very wrong in the Sociology Department'. This was followed by several more articles claiming that the content and manner of teaching in the Faculty were shoddy and outdated, that this promoted rote learning, that the department's rigid, rule-bound administration was pettifogging, and that its staff were generally unapproachable.

Particular objection was taken to Batson's insistence that every student taking his Sociology II course had to have a copy of the idiosyncratic statistical gazetteer which he had written, *Contemporary Dimensions of Africa*, and had to produce it before being permitted into the lecture. The Faculty 'has discouraged scientific thinking – in fact, any thinking at all', charged *Varsity*.[143] As grievances by current and former students began to appear in the daily and Sunday press, Batson felt as if his faculty was in a 'state of siege'.[144] His deputy reported that she had been met by 'a howling, booing, hissing mob [in the Sociology I class], brandishing copies of *Varsity* all over Beattie Theatre'.[145]

In the face of such an outcry, to Batson's chagrin UCT rapidly appointed a commission of inquiry into his Faculty. The wide-ranging evidence which it heard was enough to convince his fellow professors in the Committee of Deans and Senate that teaching in his Faculty was well below par and had to be revamped, preferably by creating a separate department to teach social work. Even more humiliating for Batson was the suggestion that his Faculty of Social Science should be abolished and that the one department it contained should be reincorporated into the Faculty of Arts.[146] UCT's Council 'is very dissatisfied with conditions in the Department of Sociology and Administration', it adjured him, 'and ... it proposes to effect changes as from 1968'.[147]

This it did. Small-group tutorials were hastily instituted and additional staff appointed to supervise fieldwork more thoroughly, while in 1969 a separate Department of Applied Sociology in Social Work was established to teach social work only, thereby bringing UCT into line with all other South African universities, where sociology and social work had already been split. In 1970 Brunhilde Helm, Batson's former deputy, was appointed as the first professor in the new department, he himself retaining the chair of sociology and administration until his retirement a year later. A *Varsity* columnist drolly compared the rejigged Faculty to 'the Bourbons who have learnt nothing and have forgotten nothing, [and] are back in the saddle again'.[148] Yet, despite this apparent return to the status quo ante, Batson had been deeply wounded by the very public censure of him and his Faculty. One sign of this was his decision after he retired to donate the unique record cards from his Social Survey of Cape Town to the University of Stellenbosch.

Given the fact that Helm had been nurtured by Batson ever since her student years under him in the mid-1940s, her approach to her subject differed little from his. Like her mentor in his later years, she was a commanding and orotund lecturer, but one who did little to update her material from one year to the next; like him too, when she was not teaching, she devoted much of her time to committee work both on and off campus; and like his later publications, hers were mainly short, statistical compilations. Her approach 'tended to be more empirical [than theoretical]', observed one of her referees.[149]

The rest of the permanent staff was, with very few exceptions, female, the longest-serving exception being the Faculty's loyal factotum, Bill Francis, whose formal job-title of 'laboratory attendant' gives no hint of the multiplicity of tasks which were assigned to him in his 39 years on the staff. He 'makes it possible for the Department to function smoothly because of the manner in which he administers the departmental facilities', concluded one of Batson's successors.[150]

Of the 28 women on the academic staff between 1948 and 1968, Helm aside, only five stayed more than three years, one of them being Helen Batson, the professor's wife. This high turnover suggests that working conditions or job prospects in the Faculty were not attractive, especially once the demand for social workers in society at large began to grow.

The courses which they taught closely reflected the imperious Batson's conception of social science as a science akin to the 'hard' sciences and of social work as simply applied social science. To him social science was a scientific discipline, impartial, authoritative and resting, ultimately, on verifiable evidence, in particular statistical data. He firmly believed in what one historian has called 'quantitative objectivity',[151] a conviction cultivated in him by his mentor at the LSE in the 1920s, the economist and social statistician Arthur Bowley.

Consequently, social economics, the statistical study of poverty, social pathology and demography featured prominently in the Social Science syllabus at first. A typical exam question in 1950, early in the apartheid era, did not hide its racist premise by bluntly asking students to 'Explain the effects biological traits have upon poverty'. By the late 1950s, however, with progressive students calling for 'more straight sociology' instead of the existing 'rather social-welfarish' material,[152] these subjects were being pushed to the edge of the syllabus by a growing examination of social concepts based on a structural-functionalist analysis of social processes, emanating from the work of American sociologists like Talcott Parsons. Issues like personality dynamics, socialisation, deviance and social stratification began to receive more attention, though only rarely were these examined through a South African lens.

The social work syllabus changed far less from its ameliorative, social welfare orientation in these years, retaining general subjects like social legislation, social administration and casework theory at its core throughout the period. However, a degree of specialisation became possible at postgraduate level in the 1960s with the introduction of advanced diplomas in social administration (covering fields like housing management, medical social work and personnel management) and in psychiatric social work. These, Batson hoped, would be first steps towards the creation of a graduate school in social work.

Though statistics and social theory may have been his métier, Batson recognised that training as a social worker had to be practical too, and he thus made fieldwork in poor areas a compulsory part of the social work syllabus from day one. The co-operation of numerous social welfare institutions and associations was inspanned to enable students to undertake weekly visits of observation or longer-term placements. 'We were given addresses to go to … and just had to knock on the door and explain to the residents that we had come to gather social data like income, number of children, expenditure, etc.', recalled a student of the early 1960s.[153] She remembered no objections to such intrusions from residents wherever she went in the Cape Peninsula or any reluctance to provide the information she sought. This information was entered in carefully prescribed fashion on a fieldwork report form, which was then submitted for marking by special assessors in the Faculty. With characteristically Batsonian over-attention to detail, the prospectus warned that students were 'required to correct and improve such of their reports as receive low classification symbols in the light of such indications of errors in them as may be given by the Assessors and with the aid of standard works of reference. Students who require further guidance in fulfilling this requirement are advised to submit a notification to that effect.'[154]

For most middle-class white students these visits were an eye-opener. 'That was when I discovered Windermere … which was totally flooded in winter, when people had to live in water up to their knees', recalled one who went on to become a social and political activist. 'These experiences were a turning point for me.'[155] Others, however, felt that by compiling these reports they were merely acting as Batson's foot soldiers, doing data collection for him so he could use it to update his annual poverty datum line calculations and add a new pamphlet to his ongoing series, 'Documentation of a Sociological Survey of Greater Cape Town'. 'They are required to assemble data,' complained one, 'but they are never permitted to share in the utilization of the data and see research carried through to its conclusion!'[156] Whether the connection was as linear as this is difficult to know, but certainly the publications in this series continued to appear regularly until Batson retired. A charge that they were made possible only by surveying methods that turned 'the Cape Flats into a zoo', he ignored.[157]

About three-quarters of the postgraduate theses which Batson supervised fed, directly or indirectly, into this project too. How active he was in promoting such research – in some years he even ran evening seminars for postgraduates – is evident from the fact that between 1948 and 1968 33 Master's and 2 PhD degrees were awarded to students from his one-department faculty, statistics which mark it out as the most prolific English-medium social science faculty in the country in terms of postgraduate research. Its 33 MSocSci degrees constituted almost 30% of all such degrees awarded in South Africa in these years. In the same period the Faculty awarded 405 BSocSci degrees, 61 diplomas and 7 certificates. The recipients were overwhelmingly (83%) white women who became social workers. Less than 1% were not white.

Batson thus played a decisive role in making UCT a significant source of social workers and, in so doing, shaped the profession in its foundational years. But, as shown above, by the 1960s his teaching had declined in quality and was, in addition, being seriously marred by what the head of the commission of inquiry called 'over sedulous discipline'[158] and the 'almost too meticulous application of rules'.[159] Paradoxically, therefore, it would seem that the very single-minded, perfectionist zeal which had enabled him to create the Faculty of Social Science became his and its undoing, and was largely responsible for what a professor in a kindred department called its 'parlous state' by 1971.[160] A comprehensive overhaul was urgently needed.

Whether outmoded and in need of an overhaul, like Social Science and Education, or on the cutting edge of their disciplines, like Commerce, Architecture and Law, UCT's career-geared faculties together contributed significantly to the creation of South Africa's largely white professional elite in the first two decades of the country's apartheid years. As chapter 10 will underscore, this was part of the paradox which was UCT under apartheid.

# Professionals in training

*A new commercial venture. Leading a seminar in the new Postgraduate School of Business Administration and Applied Economics (subsequently the Graduate School of Business) in 1964 is its founding director, Professor Bill Hutt (centre). On his left and right respectively are lecturers Ben Gurzynski and Ralph Horwitz, while a third lecturer, John Hampton, is closest to the camera. The names of the two students are not known.*

*Uniformly driven. Similarly clad young executives in a Graduate School of Business MBA course in marketing are put through their paces by a young lecturer (and later director), Meyer Feldberg, in 1967.* (Cape Argus, 9 December 1967)

*Laying down the law. Professor Denis Cowen lecturing to a senior Law class on the Hiddingh campus, c. 1949.*

*Survey data analysis. Professor Edward Batson examines a survey form in 1951 while his team of data analysts (including his protégé, Brunhilde Helm, second from left) inputs data from hundreds of other such forms for his ongoing social survey of Cape Town.* (Cape Times, 14 November 1951)

*Practical class in blackboard technique in the Faculty of Education in 1967.*

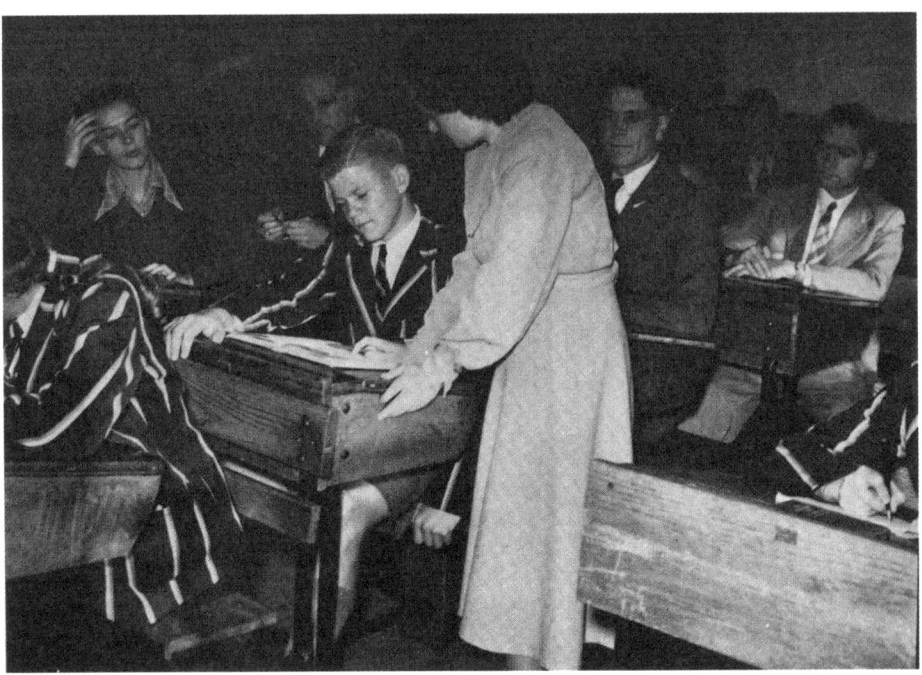

*Practice teaching. Watched by her supervisor, Professor J.F. Burger, and two fellow students, a student teacher assists a pupil in a Cape Town high school in 1949.*

*Not model architecture. The inside of the cramped home of the School of Architecture between 1946 and 1959, a wooden military hut at the southern end of UCT's rugby fields.*

*A model campus. Senior studio master, Jock Sturrock, elucidates the layout of UCT's Groote Schuur campus to a senior Architecture class in 1964.*

# CHAPTER 8

# The Arts: Musical, Liberal and Fine

From soon after UCT's inception as an independent university in 1918, its Faculty of Arts had, like the Scottish universities on which it modelled itself, included a wide array of humane disciplines from the fields of language, social science, music, fine art and architecture. Courses in a selection of these were meant to provide students with a broad, general education before they embarked on the path to a more professional qualification. In the opinion of UCT's first Principal, Sir Carruthers Beattie, South African undergraduates lacked a 'wide culture' and so a wide-ranging BA degree ought to be 'the end of a general education which I should like every one to have, after that comes the professional training'.[1]

Yet, even within this collection of humane disciplines the ideal did not survive for long in the face of pressure from the professions for early specialisation. By 1929 Music, Fine Art and Architecture had hived off into independent faculties of their own, to be followed in 1945 by Social Science. Shorn organisationally of these kindred but more professionally oriented disciplines, the liberal arts now constituting the Faculty of Arts still shared a humane foundation with them, which is why the two closest to it, Music and Fine Art, are bracketed with it in this chapter. Not that the disciplines left within the Faculty of Arts were untouched by such pressures for its students to specialise with an eye on their future professions; indeed, this is one of the themes running through its history in the period set out below.

## Music

Like Architecture and Social Science, Music was a faculty which marched to the beat of one dominant head, Erik Chisholm, who held treble sway there as Dean, Director of the South African College of Music (SACM) and Professor of Music from 1946 until his death at the age of 61 in 1965.

By 1948[2] the 'animating energy' generated by this Scotsman's 'ardent temperament' (to cite the words of one of his referees[3]) was in full swing in the College. He had replaced ten part-time teachers past their prime with four, better-qualified full-timers, had introduced new courses and advanced musical skills classes, and placed performance firmly at the heart of students' training. In pursuit of this he had founded two orchestras at the College, which gave regular concerts under his baton, and had even breathed life into the moribund Opera Department by staging three operas featuring staff and students on stage and in the pit. In his determination to take full advantage of the SACM's unusually wide scope as a home for both theoretical and practical training in Western music, opera and ballet, and to raise the standard of this training to the level of that in good British or North American music schools, 'He turned the College of Music upside down and inside out', noted a fellow professor, but in so doing gave it 'a vitality and creativity it had not known on such a scale before' as he executed 'his authoritarian steeple-chase'.[4]

Opera was one of the genres he favoured most, for he was, among other things, an opera composer in his own right. Not only did he soon introduce a Performer's Certificate in Opera, but in 1952 he revived the College's Department of Opera, which had languished since the retirement of its founder, Giuseppe Paganelli, in 1944.[5] Central to this revival was the appointment of an accomplished Italian opera singer, the 37-year-old Gregorio Fiasconaro, as part-time Director of the ambitiously renamed UCT School of Opera. Notwithstanding (or because of) their shared passion for this genre, the two clashed frequently over productions, 'and the resulting verbal duel could be heard all over the College', remembered a colleague. Yet, within an hour, the heated exchange was a thing of the past and 'they were again discussing the next season or concert perfectly amiably'.[6]

The combustible relationship between these two highly charged men may have generated heat, but it also proved to be extremely fruitful as each learnt something from the other in these encounters. 'I am not an intellectual', Fiasconaro freely admitted, but 'an instinctive actor/singer … [yet] I began to think about my productions more and more and to explore every aspect of the opera with which I was busy, in ever-increasing depth'.[7]

Students caught up by the two artistes' fervour and passion accepted the long hours and firm discipline they imposed. 'Papa [Fiasconaro's affectionate name for Chisholm] and I measured everyone's strength by his, which was immense', the opera singer acknowledged,[8] which meant that the bar for students in classes, rehearsals and performances was set very high. Indeed, for some time final-year opera students actually had to produce a one-act opera for their final exam.

The results of this high-quality training were quickly apparent in the glowing reviews which the Opera School Company's productions in Cape Town and far beyond received. 'Praise, gratitude and aesthetic satisfaction were the emotions that held sway in the audience', wrote a Port Elizabeth newspaper after a performance there,[9] while a production of *Turandot* in Johannesburg prompted the *Rand Daily Mail*'s musical critic to 'doubt whether we have ever seen anything better or grander'.[10] The schedule on these up-country tours was very demanding. 'Everyone sang almost every night', explained a soprano. 'It was tough but wonderful training because you simply had to learn a superb technique on which you could rely come hell or high water.'[11] Even hyper-critical reviewers in London were very positive when, in 1957, the School's Company visited that city and staged three operas there, one by Chisholm himself.[12] 'The young forces under Dr Chisholm's command are inspired by a spirit of adventure that is sorely lacking in our own music schools', opined one; '…they contain artistic material potentially as good as we turn out ourselves, and in one or two instances superior'.[13] It is not surprising, therefore, that, when in 1965 a Government-funded opera company was established in the Cape Province as CAPAB (Cape Performing Arts Board) Opera, it drew heavily on the Opera School for its chorus and resources like costumes, sets and equipment, much as it had already done in the case of ballet with UCT's Ballet Company.[14] This collaboration with the Opera School yielded well-funded, large-scale joint productions of grand operas like *Tosca*, *La Bohème* and *Turandot* until 1970, but by then CAPAB Opera could stand alone and so decided to go its own, well-funded way, leading to the effective demise of the School's Opera Company.

But opera was only one of the strings in the versatile Chisholm's bow. A fervid champion of contemporary classical music by composers like Bartók, Janáček and Martinů, he included such music in the BMus syllabus and established a branch of the avant-garde International Society for Contemporary Music in Cape Town to spread the sound of this music to unfamiliar local ears. He also introduced dedicated courses in conducting and, bearing in mind that most SACM students went on to teach music in schools, expanded the offerings in this unheralded field, including new techniques like melodic percussion and the Carl Orff approach to music education, 'of which our students know nothing', he acknowledged.[15]

Even after his purge of veteran part-time music teachers soon after his arrival in 1946, the bulk of instrumental teaching was still done by part-timers. In 1948 they outnumbered full-timers by eleven to seven; by 1965 the figures were 23 part-timers to 12 full-timers. Not that Chisholm would have hired part-timers in such numbers had funding permitted the appointment of full-timers. More than once he judged teaching by the former to be, 'I regret to say … of a rather indifferent quality',[16] while the competence of members of the Cape Town Municipal Orchestra who taught part-time at the College was not infrequently offset by their having to miss classes at short notice

*Music to my ears! A pleased-looking Professor Erik Chisholm accompanies Malcolm Forsyth, a trombone student who subsequently joined the Cape Town Municipal Orchestra before immigrating to Canada where he became a prominent composer* (Cape Argus, 22 October 1960).

because of their commitments to the Orchestra. But the European model of individual teaching which the SACM followed required many teachers, so there was no alternative.

As full-time members of staff Chisholm's preference was for overseas-trained musicians, as he regarded local talent as largely second-rate. 'Our standard can only be maintained if we can attract musicians to the Union', he announced with characteristic bluntness.[17] Thus, among the permanent teachers whom he appointed were the internationally renowned Hungarian pianist 'with taste, skill and heart'[18] Lili Kraus, the highly strung Welsh piano virtuoso Harold Rubens, the German musicologist Gunter Pulvermacher, and the award-winning American pianist with the delicate touch Lamar Crowson, who soon reorganised the College's piano classes, raised examination standards and gave a weekly master class open to all students. He approached music 'from both the intellectual and the emotional side,' judged a world-ranked fellow pianist, 'and ... makes both ends meet and fit'.[19]

When Chisholm did appoint South Africans, they were invariably musicians who had studied abroad too, like the lecturers in harmony, counterpoint and composition Arnold van Wyk, Blanche Gerstman and Stanley Glasser, and the pianists Laura

Searle and Helena van Heerden.

The effect of assembling this array of local and foreign musical talent at the SACM was to allow it to add to its standard European-style syllabus several specialities rare in South African musical schools, like chamber music, church music, school music and accompanying, and to give students the opportunity to play in chamber ensembles and to sing in one of the two SACM choirs. Beyond the Western classical musical canon it did not usually venture, however.

To this there were two notable exceptions: Stanley Glasser, whose interest in indigenous African music – he had collected traditional African folk music in the field in the 1950s – led him to refer to this genre in his lectures on harmony,[20] and Gunter Pulvermacher, who had studied Indian culture when a musicology student in Breslau in the early 1930s. This had widened his appreciation of music significantly and added a novel comparative dimension to the lectures on the History of Music and General Musical Knowledge which he gave after being appointed to the College's permanent staff in 1952. 'Pulvie' (as students referred to him) 'brought weird and wonderful musicological facts within reach of the average music student', enthused one. 'I, for one, will never forget my excitement when he showed us films of Japanese Noh theatre. It had a lasting effect on me.'[21]

Besides being an erudite and engaging lecturer who provided what one student described as 'very sophisticated' teaching,[22] which skilfully linked music to other art forms, at the SACM Pulvermacher increasingly filled another role too, that of foil to Chisholm – 'that is to say', explained a professor in the know, 'he had to spend a vast amount of his time soothing the feelings of people who had been ruffled by Professor Chisholm's rather brusque manner. In fact he became his musical alter ego.'[23] Not surprisingly, therefore, Pulvermacher acted as Director of the SACM when Chisholm was on leave and again on the latter's sudden death in June 1965.

This experience and his track record as a lecturer saw Pulvermacher appointed as Chisholm's successor as professor and Director of the College at the age of 58 in 1966,[24] despite objections by two professors that he held no degree nor had published any scholarly work or composed any music.

His leadership style was quite different from Chisholm's. In the opinion of one of the College's external examiners, he was 'gentle yet firm in his dealings with colleagues and students'.[25] However, he did maintain Chisholm's emphasis on students performing as often as possible. Thus, early in his seven-year headship, a UCT string quartet was formed to provide students with playing experience at an advanced level, and a novel diploma in orchestral playing was introduced as well as, at Fiasconaro's urging, a teacher's diploma in opera. This meant that by 1969 the SACM had increased the qualifications it offered to four degrees (all in music), seven diplomas (three in music and two each in opera and ballet) and five certificates (three in music and two in ballet); in 1948 it had offered four degrees in music, but only four diplomas and four certificates. During these twenty years it awarded 434 degrees, diplomas, certificates and endorsements, of which just over 51% were in school music teaching, 23% in ballet, 23% in music as such, and a mere handful in opera.

However, these figures are misleading because they take no account of the very large number of students not registered for a formal university qualification but who had enrolled part-time at the SACM to learn ballet or how to play a particular instrument. Ranging between 450 and 550 each year (compared to the 80–110 full-time registered students per year), they took advantage of the College only in its role as a conservatoire. Nonetheless, they appeared on its roll, which had the effect of making the SACM–Faculty of Music one of UCT's middle-sized faculties, though one in which most of its students – even full-time ones – felt very little connection to the university at large. Music students hardly ever stood for election to the SRC, while a College float in Rag was extremely rare. 'Everything I had to do and was required of me was on the College of Music campus or Hiddingh Hall or … at the Little Theatre', explained a former student.[26] As far as students on the main campus were concerned, the sound of the Music Faculty was always distant.

Of the part-time students, some 45–50% were taking practical classes in the College's third department, Ballet. Ever since its foundation in 1934 as the only ballet school attached to a university in South Africa,[27] the UCT School of Ballet (as it became known in 1950) had *ipso facto* been a magnet for students from throughout the subcontinent seeking top-flight ballet training for a career in dance.

Sharing their practical classes was a smaller number of full-time students enrolled for the Teacher's Certificate in Ballet – a Performer's Diploma/Certificate was added only in 1969. The 101 recipients of this qualification between 1948 and 1968 (of whom 94 were female and all but three or four white) emerged with training that went well beyond the purely practical, which distinguished them from other dancers on the South African ballet scene. As UCT had expressly made the point that teaching ballet at a university was justified 'only in so far as it provides students of music or dance with a field of academic study, not as a training in a particular technique',[28] the School of Ballet ensured that the course included theoretical and contextual subjects like the history and theory of ballet, the relationship between music and art relating to ballet, and General Ballet Knowledge. This broad conception of balletic training was very much the brainchild of the School's founding mother, Dulcie Howes. 'It is not enough for a dancer to jump up and down and point her toes', she insisted.[29] Dancers had to understand the music, the period style of a ballet, and the historical and social context of the roles they filled.

But providing such wider perspectives always remained secondary to the School's core business, practical training every morning in classical ballet strictly according to the Cechetti method. In one student's memory, ballet training was 'all practical, work, work, work. All the certificates in the world are not going to make you a dancer.'[30] A grande dame (tagged by her students as 'the Big White Chief'), Howes presided over the School and her classes imperiously. A hard taskmaster with a very strong and awe-inspiring personality, she was 'a strict disciplinarian who taught discipline', policing her students closely. 'God help you if you put on an ounce of weight', remembered one of her students with feeling.[31] No one, not even her colleagues on the staff, was spared sharp words if they stepped out of the line she had drawn. She herself was not a top-class ballerina. 'I don't have a talent, but I do have the ability to spot talent', she declared.[32] She should have added that she also had the very real ability to nurture such talent in dancers, convincing them that they were of critical importance in the bigger production picture. As a former student put it, 'She made you feel you were part of what made it all happen.'[33] Another paid tribute to her 'phenomenal capacity for generating enthusiasm and energy in all who came into contact with her. Her own, seemingly limitless appetite for hard work either inspired or shamed others into putting that extra effort into whatever task she assigned to them.'[34]

Howes's emphasis on the need for practical experience in training went far beyond the studio. Students also had to assist the staff coach children's ballet classes three afternoons a week and had to participate in the ballet productions staged by the School's UCT Ballet Company each year. Staff, invited dancers and promising students filled the lead roles in these, with the corps de ballet drawn from the rest of the School's students. Often these ballets were taken on tour to the rest of the country or to the then Rhodesias too. Not only did such tours allow dancers to develop the characters they were portraying, but they also ensured that they learnt every aspect of stagecraft, for Howes was adamant that everyone should pitch in behind the scene too, painting scenery, repairing costumes, setting lighting and sewing up torn curtains. She brooked no shirking, remembered one student with a sigh. 'It was no good making an excuse – for some task which had not been accomplished with total success – that "I did try my best". This would only elicit the implacable response: "Then your best is not good enough."'[35]

The result of this driven, single-minded approach was that UCT's School of Ballet consistently turned out a number of high-class ballet dancers who were readily taken up by local and overseas ballet companies. One of them, Johaar Mosaval, spoke for many of his distinguished peers when he said that, when he left for the Sadler's Wells Ballet School in 1951, he was confident that the basic training he had received at UCT meant 'that I could do justice at any ballet school in the world'.[36]

Howes's singular approach to teaching ballet meant that she was keen to recruit graduates of her own School to teach there once they had received further training in Britain. As she appositely phrased it, they went overseas 'as cygnets and came back as "swans"'.[37] Equally aptly, one of these 'swans' observed that, by the mid-1950s, the School 'rather reflected a dovecote – pigeons coming and going; some eventually returning home to roost'.[38]

Among the 'homing pigeons' were Howes's first lieutenant, the self-sacrificing Pamela Chrimes, the specialists in Spanish dance Jasmine Honoré and Marina Keet, the innovative choreographer Richard Glasstone, and Howes's eventual successor as head of the School, David Poole, who joined the staff in 1959 after twelve high-flying years at Sadler's Wells Ballet and the Ballet Rambert. His creativity and deftness as a producer and his ability to inspire students as a teacher – his obituary spoke perceptively of his 'empathy with the person behind the dancer'[39] – produced what Howes herself described as 'a lively, meaningful and exciting theatre performance',[40] which marked him out as her heir apparent. Indeed, when CAPAB effectively took over the UCT Ballet Company in 1963, she appointed him as its ballet master. He subsequently followed her as its artistic director in 1969, combining this with the directorship of the School after he succeeded her in this position too in 1973.

The CAPAB takeover of the UCT Ballet Company was the result of a political initiative by the National Party Government to promote 'white' culture in the recently created Republic of South Africa. CAPAB was one of the four provincial arts councils set up to implement this policy. To accomplish this in the field of dance, it set its sights on the already-functioning, highly esteemed UCT Ballet Company, offering to turn it into a paid, fully professional company in return for its know-how, skills and facilities, in particular its brand-new, tailor-made Ballet School Building on Woolsack Road, near to the SACM.

After a hand-to-mouth existence for almost thirty years, Howes and UCT found this too appealing an offer to reject and so agreed to merge the UCT Ballet Company (but not the School of Ballet, which remained part of the Faculty of Music) into CAPAB Ballet in 1963, though retaining the right to use the UCT name for performances at the three venues in Cape Town then still open to all races, the City Hall, the Little Theatre and the Luxurama Theatre, where CAPAB would not perform. This apartheid-circumventing loophole allowed ballet performances by the temporarily resurrected UCT Company to continue before multi-racial audiences until the 1970s, when the City Hall and the Luxurama were declared racially exclusive. With the closure of these venues to all races, UCT gave up its ad hoc liberal masquerade and disestablished its Ballet Company. Henceforth, its students and staff would only perform in 'whites-only' venues as part of CAPAB Ballet.

The material (if not moral) benefits of collaboration with CAPAB were not inconsiderable. Students forming the corps de ballet were now paid an allowance by CAPAB, the teaching skills of full-time professional CAPAB dancers could now be readily tapped, and the quality of sets, costumes and equipment was improved markedly. Yet, if the experience of student involvement in CAPAB Opera is anything to go by, the effect on them was not without drawbacks for UCT. Opera students requested to sing in small-scale UCT productions now asked if they would be paid for doing so, just as they were by CAPAB, 'and if the answer is negative', complained Fiasconaro, 'they vanish into the undergrowth'.[41] However, perhaps Howes's iron rule, the tight-knit nature of the Ballet School and the general isolation of its students from the rest of the SACM gave such mercenary instincts less play. For staff, however, the CAPAB connection was a boon since their conditions of employment improved significantly as part-time contracts were in many cases replaced by full-time ones. By 1968, therefore, the injection of state funds via CAPAB meant that the School of Ballet was *en pointe*, and would remain so as long as the country's economy did not lose its balance.

When Chisholm died in 1965, Howes (who had had a love-hate relationship with him) graciously described him as 'a man of great vision, determination and drive'.[42] Apart from the opening noun, these would not be inappropriate words to characterise her too.

## The Liberal and Fine Arts

In 1955, when the post-war bulge of medical and engineering students finally vanished with the graduation of the last significant batch of ex-servicemen students, the Faculty of Arts regained its pre-war status as UCT's largest faculty. Its 769 students in that year made it bigger than Medicine (678) and Commerce (668), a position which it maintained until 1982, when four of its departments left to join the Faculty of Social Science.

Notwithstanding this numerical superiority, which was largely due to the fact that it drew both profession-destined students (e.g. would-be lawyers, teachers, librarians and economists) and those seeking a general liberal arts education, a popular perception persisted among non-Arts students that the BA degree was a soft option, the preserve of students (especially women) who were more interested in social than academic pursuits – women outnumbered men in the Faculty by 30–50% in these decades – and a haven for what the editor of a student magazine labelled starry-eyed *luftmenschen*, 'beardless youths with long-stemmed pipes, bearded youths in corduroy pants and trailing scarves, wide-eyed damsels with flowing hair and undesirable attire. Such individualists, all so different, all so empty'.[43]

Twenty years later, in 1969, this stereotype had changed little. For example, a quip attributed to Engineering students had it that raising the entrance qualifications to UCT 'will virtually eliminate the Arts Faculty'.[44] As with most stereotypes, this crack showed no awareness of the Arts Faculty's bid to give the instruction it offered a more professional focus, in keeping with the escalating trend towards profession-oriented education at UCT. In 1954, for instance, it had introduced a one-year junior postgraduate Honours degree to allow a student to specialise in one subject after completing a general, multidiscipline BA, while in 1968 it dropped the requirement that all BA candidates had to take at least one 'social science' course, though it did retain (until 1972) the regulation that they all had to take at least a single course in a 'foreign' language. The degree would still be 'wide', UCT insisted, but now it would be 'sufficient in depth for secondary school teaching or a … background for administrative work'.[45] 'Insight and comprehension' and a modicum of 'brightness' would remain the minimum hallmark of its Arts graduates.[46]

The administration of the Faculty was slower to take on a more professional look. In 1951 a fixed procedure was at last agreed upon to regularise what had until then been a random method of choosing a dean – the deanship would henceforth rotate through all the Faculty's professors, who would each serve one two-year term. It took another nine years, however, for the Faculty to accept that the professor filling this post should do so full-time and be eligible for relief from all teaching and departmental administration. Nor was the incumbent given any assistance in the job until 1958, when part-time positions of student adviser (to be held by a senior academic) and dean's temporary secretary were created. The latter post was made permanent only two years later after the then dean had protested that 'the faculty would risk chaos should the post be abolished'.[47]

Of the seven language and nine social studies departments constituting the Faculty of Arts in 1968 – two more than the total of fourteen in 1948 – by far the largest was the conjoint Department of English Language and Literature, an academic division which went back to the universities of Oxford and London in the 19th century. By the 1960s, 70% or more of students in the Faculty were taking at least one of the department's composite Lang–Lit courses, a sign of the subject's centrality to UCT's BA degree. It was as important to students in the Faculty of Arts as 'mathematics is … to the sciences', argued a member of the department.[48] In 1966 this percentage translated into 1018 students; only 17 of them were postgraduates, however, in keeping with the colonial mindset that advanced studies in English could be adequately or properly pursued only in the metropole.

The downside of having so many students in the Department of English was that this compromised its teaching. For example, a significant number of Law students, compelled to take English I, showed their dissatisfaction at this by behaving rowdily in lectures – a keen Arts student doing the course spoke of how the lecturers suffered 'the persecutions of the law students in silence, hoping they would grow tired and relent'.[49]

Large classes also meant that small-group tutorials had to be limited in number and frequency. As a result, until 1966 tutorials were held only once a fortnight. However, in that year a special grant from the UCT Foundation made it possible to triple the number of Language tutorials. By providing more regular and more intensive tutorials, the new English Language Tutorial Scheme (ELTS) decreased failures appreciably and increased first- and second-class passes. The beneficial effect was quickly evident. Commenting on the improved results in the 1966 examinations, the external examiner was impressed by 'the unusual superiority of the marks gained in the language papers … The many lapses of syntax, concord, tense and word-choice that have marred students' writing in the past were largely absent. It seemed to me that command of vocabulary had also improved.'[50] Not surprisingly, therefore, when the scheme's funding expired in 1971, these special tutorials became an integral part of the department's teaching programme, though later they were hived off to become the responsibility of a new Professional Communications Unit quite separate from the Department of English.

ELTS was the brainchild of Dorothy Cavers, the second-in-command in the Language division of the English Department, who came up with the idea in response to ongoing complaints from the Faculties of Law and of Commerce about the poor writing skills of their students, despite their attendance of English I or a half-course in the language. A veteran lecturer who had been teaching phonetics in the department since 1937,[51] she had a very good sense of how effective carefully devised tutorials could be in inculcating basic skills in language and composition. In Alan Lennox-Short, a senior lecturer in English Language, she found a capable and knowledgeable organiser for the scheme, as his experience as a journalist, broadcaster and editor had equipped him well to teach effective expression. As he explained in his book of the same name, the nature of the problem was that 'None of us can afford to write as we speak; none of us can afford to speak as we write. There are few who sin in the second way; there are far too many who cripple themselves by writing much as they speak.'[52] This is what ELTS was meant to address.

Standing aloof from such elementary teaching was the head of English Language, Leslie Casson, who had succeeded the founding De Beers professor of English language at UCT, William Mackie, in 1951.[53] A 47-year-old Australian with degrees from Adelaide, Oxford and Edinburgh, he specialised in Middle English philology and literature, which he taught as if he were still in Oxford. Though his mastery of

*Take note! English literature students in a lecture in Beattie Theatre, 1964* (Cape Times, 25 July 1964).

the phonology of Middle English dialects might have enthralled a student like John Coetzee, most students found him personally forbidding and his subject arcane. He is 'exact rather than exciting', noted one of his referees accurately.[54]

Even within just the Language division of the department he kept to his irascible self, devoting much of his time to researching medieval English manuscripts in the Grey Collection at the then South African Public Library. By 1968, when he retired, he had published fifteen articles explicating these manuscripts. Clearly he subscribed whole-heartedly to the conviction he had expressed early in his tenure, that 'It is essential for the mental health of a University Department's staff that they should have ample time for adding to recorded knowledge in their subject; the senior members are best equipped for this work, though' – he graciously conceded – 'the needs of junior members, with scholarly reputations to establish, must not be overlooked'.[55]

Stand-offish Casson may have been to students, but with his fellow Australian professor in the department, Guy Howarth, who filled the Arderne chair of English literature from 1955 to 1971, he was certainly not best mates. Indeed, such was the their mutual antipathy (recalling that between their respective predecessors, Mackie and Doughty[56]) that they averted their eyes if they passed each other in the corridor and were said to communicate only by notes left in the departmental secretary's office.

The source of their animosity seems to have been personal, not ideological. Perhaps it had something to do with the fact that both were middle-aged Australians (Howarth was three years younger than Casson) with Oxford BLitt degrees, who came to UCT disappointed at having been overlooked for promotion. Unlike Casson, however, Howarth seized the opportunity offered by his new post to innovate creatively in a bid to revive a Literature division which had languished under Doughty.

Firmly convinced by his own academic experience in Australia that local literature should be included in the syllabus of local universities, he expanded the library's holdings of South African literature and tentatively included some of this in the syllabus under the heading of 'Commonwealth and Comparative Literature'. Reflecting his own passion for poetry (of which he was minor practitioner himself), in 1956 he pioneered the inclusion of an anthology of South African poetry on the prescribed reading list for English I. To this he added Pauline Smith's novel *The Beadle* in 1960. To build support for this initiative he also convened two conferences at UCT on 'South African Writing in English' in 1959 and 1960, but found that these had little effect on English Department syllabuses country-wide. As late as 1976 a local author was still bemoaning the fact that 'he and his colleagues [are] being admitted into campuses by the servants' entrance … The universities are bastions of colonial mentality.'[57]

Howarth's second innovation stemmed from his academic visit to the United States in 1957–8, which had driven home to him how far that country's authors and critics led the field of English literature globally. 'The true vitality had begun to pass from Europe to the US', he told an audience at UCT, 'yielding American literature, that enormous, thriving, pulsing issue that we know today'.[58] With this in mind, he persuaded the Cold War warriors in the US State Department to fund nine visits to UCT by American professors of American literature to teach this subject for a term, thereby giving his department an air of being in close touch with the very latest ideas in English literature.

His third innovation was even more avant-garde, a voluntary, non-credit-bearing imaginative writing class (as at several US universities) which was open to any students who wished to try out in public poetry or prose they had written. This experiment, Howarth explained, was aimed at developing students' creative side 'equally and in association with the critical … by allowing him [*sic*] scope for original imaginative writing … to be critically analysed and appraised, while at the same time explaining the mysteries of the craft of authorship'.[59] Even more radical was Howarth's decision to allow these original pieces to replace essays set in any of the English Literature courses.

Student response was limited but promising, for it gave an opportunity to the likes of John Coetzee, Jonty Driver, Stephen Gray, Vernon February, Geoffrey Haresnape and Perseus Adams to gain what Coetzee called 'the encouragement always needed by beginners unsure of themselves'.[60] Indeed, Howarth went even further by having the best of these pieces published in *A Literary Miscellany*, a little roneoed magazine he started in the department. With no little justification he felt that thereby he had facilitated 'a slight contribution to the life of literature … [for] there are some South African writers in the making'.[61]

This was just as well, since, as a lecturer, Howarth was less than captivating, as the paper planes launched by bored students in his lectures testified, while Leavisites judged his 'life and letters' volumes and his many articles on his literary finds to be 'the embodiment of a benighted and deadening scholarship'.[62] It is perhaps revealing both of his approach to literature and its unfashionableness by the 1970s that what was to be the magnum opus of his later years, 'The Life, Work and Character of John Webster, with New Attributions of Literary and Dramatic Material', could not find a publisher.

The best lecturing in English Literature at UCT in these years thus came not from UCT's professor in the subject, but from two men who went on to become professors at the University of the Witwatersrand in the mid-1960s, Philip Segal and Anthony Woodward. The effervescent, eloquent Segal had been enthusing class after class at UCT since 1941 with his passion for English authors from the Elizabethans onwards.[63] 'You just wanted to listen', remembered one Law student[64] of a man who did not hesitate to put his talent as an actor to full use. When lecturing on his beloved Shakespeare, for instance, he would often clear the front of the lecture room 'and turn his podium into a stage', recalled a student of his. 'Then he would talk about Shakespeare, and get students to come up and show them how to do this. He was brilliant, and of course you get to love the theatre and Shakespeare.'[65]

His embrace of the spoken word did not extend to its written form, however, and he produced no book-length literary study, only a few essays and articles. A review of a collection of these published after his early death aged 55, four years after leaving UCT for Wits, captured the nature of his genius exactly. He was 'at his best in spoken engagement with a subject and an audience', wrote the reviewer (who had been in his class at UCT). 'He was essentially an impassioned, discriminating mirror between books and students.'[66] Another ex-student couched his admiration simply, declaring that Segal was 'the living centre of the English Department for us'.[67]

Although seventeen years Segal's junior, Tony Woodward showed a similar ability to hold students' attention, 'wowing the class with readings from Austen to Lawrence', as one phrased it.[68] A Leavisite like Segal, he skilfully taught them how to interrogate a text closely. His Oxford tutor had been right when he stated that Woodward 'has the great ability to communicate his knowledge and his enthusiasm to others'.[69] Recognising in him the traits of an excellent academic, Wits appointed him to its second chair of English in 1965 when he was just 33. Its gain of both Segal and Woodward in successive years was certainly UCT's loss.

To support the department's lecturers, temporary junior staff and tutors were appointed in growing numbers, especially after the ELTS came into being. Among them were several young UCT graduates who went on to reach the top of the academic ladder at their alma mater, like the gentle poet Geoffrey Haresnape; the witty, anecdote-filled historical linguist, proficient in Old and Middle English and Old Icelandic, John van der Westhuizen; and the future Nobel Prize winner John Coetzee, whose tutorials, a former student in his class remembered, took the form of 'graceful monologues, exquisitely worded, but addressed to the wall above our heads … The students froze in pity for his shyness – or was it contempt? We were not sure …'[70]

With or without successful tutorials, the undergraduate curriculum in these years – while maintaining the historical division between language and literature until 1972 – provided a solid if somewhat dated introduction to the history and philology of English and a taste of its Anglo-centred literature. Works in the Great Tradition dominated the latter – 'I was steeped in the drama of Shakespeare and the fiction of Jane Austen and Charles Dickens', recounted a 1970 graduate[71] – though by then a few modern works by authors like J.D. Salinger, F. Scott Fitzgerald and E.M. Forster were tentatively being added to reading lists. 'Tentatively' is the operative word here: when in 1959 James Joyce's *Ulysses* was prescribed for English III, students were advised, according to John Coetzee, that they might be excused from reading it and attending lectures on it if they produced a note from their parents requesting such an exemption.[72]

With its largely metropolitan content and Leavisite-style Practical Criticism the favoured mode of analysis, the Department of English Literature was a 'patchy imitation of Oxford', scoffed Coetzee.[73]

Paradoxically, such Anglophilia which suffused academic life at UCT in these years did not deter a number of prominent Afrikaans scholars from taking posts in the University's Department of Nederlands and Afrikaans. Probably the attraction lay in the less onerous teaching load than at Afrikaans universities as a result of smaller student numbers, and in a working environment which was not as regimented and which recognised the need for staff to have ample time for research and writing.

Perhaps too, felt a student with a good grasp of the Afrikaner cultural landscape, UCT offered a congenial home then for the 'freer spirits of Afrikaans literature'.[74]

Thus, the staff of the Department of Nederlands and Afrikaans in these years included the country's foremost historian of the Afrikaans language, the austere Johannes du Plessis Scholtz (nicknamed 'Canis' since boyhood), who headed the department from 1950 to 1965;[75] one of the three best Afrikaans poets of the 20th century, D.J. Opperman, admiringly tagged '*die dolosgooier van die woord*' ('the magician of the word');[76] I.W. van der Merwe, who, as 'Boerneef', wrote richly evocative folk poetry and short stories about rural life;[77] the pioneer of linguistic analysis of Afrikaans literary texts, Merwe Scholtz, who succeeded his namesake as head of the department in 1966; and John Kannemeyer, a leading Afrikaans literary historian and biographer.

As practising and prolific authors themselves, these men – the only women on the permanent staff were the anthologist Marie Bax-Botha and 'Canis' Scholtz's meticulous linguistic disciple Edith Raidt – brought to their teaching hands-on insight and experience. Opperman, for instance, emphasised the need to 'get the feel of the language in all its nuances and variations, its speech rhythms, the shadow beneath the word', recalled a student of his,[78] while 'Canis' Scholtz's role as literary adviser to Nasionale Pers kept him abreast of the very latest Afrikaans writing. For his part, Merwe Scholtz delivered passionate, polished lectures that already 'sounded like the essays in [one of] his volumes'.[79] These essays, enthused a Stellenbosch professor, clearly demonstrated 'his ability to read a literary text so penetratingly and in such a novel way that you feel as if you are looking for the first time at a text which you have [actually] known for years already'.[80]

Given the immersion of the staff in contemporary Afrikaans literature and *taalgeskiedenis* (language history), it is not surprising that the combined language–literature syllabus reflected these strengths. Accordingly, *taalgeskiedenis* loomed even larger after 'Canis' Scholtz took the chair, his empirically based argument that the origin of Afrikaans did not lie in Creole admixing but in 'the everyday language of Holland south of the IJ'[81] dominating all lectures in the department on the topic. In the field of literature, verse epics and dramas by Van Wyk Louw and Opperman were prescribed soon after their publication, while in 1968 they were joined on the list by novels by avant garde authors like Etienne Leroux, André P. Brink and Breyten Breytenbach. Encountering works by such contemporary authors surprised most English-speaking students, whose prior exposure to Afrikaans literature had been only to very traditional setwork books in high school.

On paper, the Dutch language and literature taught in the department's three Nederlands and Afrikaans courses was equally up to date, but, in practice, students taking these courses struggled, for even Afrikaners found Dutch hard going. The change of the department's name to 'Afrikaans and Nederlands' (in place of 'Nederlands and Afrikaans') in 1967 confirmed the already de facto situation, that Dutch had become a distant second to Afrikaans in the department. As Merwe Scholtz explained, the change provided 'a truer reflection of the contents of the courses given by us'.[82]

Students taking Nederlands and Afrikaans I, II and III constituted less than a third of all students in the department. The majority of students were English-speakers from the Faculties of Law, Commerce and Education, who were compelled to take a course or half-course in Afrikaans only for professional purposes. The negative associations which that language elicited from most of them on political grounds were all too readily transferred to courses in the subject and to those teaching them. For example, as opposition to the Afrikaner-dominated state's exclusion of black students from UCT began to mount from 1957, D.J. Opperman increasingly perceived there to be an 'offensive anti-Afrikaans feeling at the University … with its overwhelmingly English student body and its inability to grasp the Afrikaans world',[83] while one of Merwe Scholtz's friends spoke of how he, like other Afrikaners at English-medium universities in South Africa, 'had to bear the stigma of being called a "rock spider"'.[84] Unsurprisingly, both Opperman and Merwe Scholtz subsequently left UCT for Stellenbosch University.

'Coloured' students, alienated from the department by the exclusion of any but white Afrikaans authors from the syllabus and by witting or unwitting expressions of Afrikaner racial superiority by the staff, did not, however, have the option of moving to a more congenial university environment.[85] Many bit their lips, hiding their indignation from public view, but now and then a few demonstrated their rejection of such attitudes creatively. For example, when one was asked to read aloud in class a passage containing pejorative terms like 'boy', *kleinmeid* and *kleinjong*, he did so, but omitted every one of these words. 'And so', recalled a classmate hyperbolically, 'one of the best Afrikaner writers had his passage destroyed by us as an act of revolution on that day at the University of Cape Town'.[86] Teaching – and learning – Afrikaans at UCT in these years was certainly not a politically neutral activity.

Less obviously political – though a deeper analysis of what it taught shows that this was not so – were the courses given in the new Department of Nederlandse Kultuurgeskiedenis (Netherlands Cultural History). Established in 1950 at the initiative of a Dutch-South African cultural foundation which funded it for its first five years, it aimed to give South African students a fuller grasp of the cultural roots of Dutch South Africa. Adopting a 'high art' definition of culture, the department focused on Dutch painting, sculpture and architecture from 1500. This it subsequently broadened when UCT took over the primary funding of the department in 1956 and insisted that the scope of what was taught be widened so as to contextualise Dutch culture within a West European context and to trace its influence in South Africa.

Taking full advantage of Cape Town's museums and art galleries, the department made visits to these part and parcel of the two courses it taught, a feature which only added to their reputation as 'soft' options because, in both, roneoed notes were also supplied to students, on which the entire examinations were set. 'It was boringly taught as a rote subject', recalled a dissatisfied student years later, 'incredible!'[87] This – and the fact that UCT permitted the first course in the subject to be offered after hours at the Hiddingh campus too – goes some way to explain the rise in its enrolments over the years, from 30 in 1952 to 114 in 1967. However, most of its students took the courses as fillers, the 9.25 am lecture slot for Nederlandse Kultuurgeskiedenis I and the fact that the subject was a two-course major adding to its appeal.

This favoured treatment by UCT was supplemented, even after 1956, by generous grants to the department from Holland and Belgium to buy books and periodicals, which explains why, to this day, UCT's Library is unusually well stocked with lavishly illustrated works on Dutch art. Yet, probably the greatest beneficiary of this largesse was the department's sole permanent member, Dirk Bax, who filled the chair from 1950 to 1972.

An Amsterdam- and Nijmegen-trained cultural historian with a particular interest in fine art – his book on Hieronymus Bosch was widely cited in its day – Bax applied this background knowledge to his examination of Dutch artefacts at the Cape, like buildings, artwork, furniture and silverware. The results of this research he in turn fed into his teaching, creating a well-resourced and self-contained department with a narrow, inward-looking focus. But beyond its confines, to the University at large, neither he nor his one-man department contributed much. Only among the local expatriate Dutch community in Cape Town did this gentle, reserved man ever feel at home. Throughout his career in South Africa he could see his surroundings only through colonial eyes.

The eyes of the Faculty's three, small, foreign-language departments – French, German and Hebrew – were also primarily fixed abroad. Of these, only French acquired a new professor between 1948 and 1968 in the person of Mitchell Shackleton, who succeeded the ambitious Donald Inskip, whose growing administrative commitments outside the department had made teaching and research less and less his primary interest.[88] Thus, when Inskip resigned in 1960 to become UCT's first Deputy Principal,[89] Shackleton inherited a rather directionless department.

An erudite and retiring Oxford-trained literary scholar who was equally well versed in the history of the French language – he had taught both at the University of the

Witwatersrand before coming to UCT in 1962 – Shackleton immediately identified most students' lack of proficiency in spoken French as a major impediment in the department's teaching. Even in French II and III, he noted, very few 'can express themselves at all fluently in French; most cannot make themselves understood at all'. This meant that they could barely participate in tutorials and were often hard put to follow lectures, all of which were given in French. This 'lamentable' oral proficiency 'affects not only the quality of their studies but also the reputation of the department and hence of the University', he regretted.[90]

Accordingly, his first step was to introduce compulsory conversation and pronunciation classes for students in the department's junior courses, making extensive use of audio tapes provided by the local French embassy. Nor was he slow to take advantage of this official French presence in Cape Town in other ways too to benefit his department: this good relationship secured books and films for the library, visits by French academics, bursaries for top students, and study opportunities in France for staff.

Two beneficiaries of such official favour besides Shackleton himself were the debonair, long-serving Kees Greshoff and the flamboyant Marie Whitaker, both of whom spent time in France studying further and doing research, which eventually yielded books on the works of Malraux and Rimbaud respectively. For his part, Shackleton devoted whatever time he could find free of his heavy load of teaching, supervision and administration to complete his much-delayed doctorate on Gide in 1976. How heavily this load weighed on him is evident from his uncharacteristic *cri de coeur* ten years earlier, that he had 'no hope of time for research, and though I usually work until midnight and sometimes into the small hours – not to mention weekends – I am not even able to meet the whole of my teaching commitments in a manner which I can consider satisfactory'.[91]

The heaviest part of the department's teaching load was generated by its two junior courses, French Elementary and French I, which together contained 75% of its 200–250 students, many of them taking French I only to meet the Faculty's requirement that there should be at least one foreign-language course in every BA degree it awarded. While Greshoff and Whitaker, unlike the reserved Shackleton, excelled as lecturers to big classes – a colleague spoke of Greshoff as 'a compelling communicator who awakened a keen interest in literature in generations of students'[92] – tutorials, marking and conversation classes were left largely to junior lecturers, who also gave some lectures. In 1968 the three of them – all women – made up 50% of the staff. The other 50% were responsible for teaching senior and postgraduate courses, which changed little in content from the standard literary fare and prose composition in Inskip's time, though the inclusion of works by Gide, Malraux and

Rimbaud presumably reflected the particular interests of Shackleton, Greshoff and Whitaker.

Given the transient nature of most students' stay in the department, a distinctive *esprit de corps* among the student body was slow to develop. It was not until the number of students majoring in French began to grow in the late 1960s that a Students' French Society was set up and not until the 1970s that joint activities with the local Alliance Française du Cap, like play readings and social functions, were arranged.

That, in contrast, a Deutscher Studentebund had already been in existence at UCT for over fifteen years by then probably owes much to the ongoing presence at the University of a number of German-speaking students from then South West Africa (only a few of whom were actually taking German courses but for whom the Studentebund had a special cultural appeal) and to the will to raise the department's standing by the professor of German since 1938, Joachim Rosteutscher.[93]

Able to adopt a higher profile on campus after the highly charged war years, Rosteutscher built up the Jagger Library's holdings of German books with the help of the West German Government, gave public lectures and a UCT Summer School course on his own speciality, Romantic German literature and aesthetics, which won him wide recognition in Germany,[94] and took the lead in forming the South African Association of Germanists.

Although the Department of German's undergraduate enrolments were half of those in the French Department, its reputation as 'the focal point of German studies in this country', as *Varsity* described it,[95] saw it draw more postgraduates than its Gallic neighbour: between 1960 and 1968 it awarded 17 postgraduate degrees as against 16 by French.

Most of its undergraduates were, however, not native German-speakers, which necessitated special conversation classes for all German Elementary and German I students. Yet these did not continue beyond German I, as the senior courses in the department were optimistically intended to be on a par with equivalent, high-level courses in Germany. Thus, on paper, the list of reading prescribed for these courses resembled those in German universities – classics by Goethe, Schiller, Mann and, even in the late 1960s, works by Brecht and Kafka. This meant that students emerged from German III speaking a high-flown, literary German. Indeed, one of the department's best graduates recalled that, 'when I actually got to Germany, it took me quite a few weeks to understand what people were saying and to come to grips with the actual spoken German'.[96]

Of the teachers in these courses only one stood out as a particularly able lecturer, the Austrian Karl Tober, whose accent easily gave away his country of birth. Many years later, long after he had left UCT for Witwatersrand University where he became a professor and eventually Principal, one of his former students praised the 'combination of analytical and inspirational dimensions' in his lectures,[97] while another had warm memories of how he 'took us through Faust with great enthusiasm'.[98] On the other hand, Rosteutscher, for all his deep literary and cultural learning and aesthetic sensitivity – he was a devotee of a wide-ranging German version of the history of ideas, *geistesgeschichte* – was not a lecturer with many student admirers. Aloof and impatient with his students – one described him as 'a grumpy old bugger'[99] – he was irascible and autocratic in his dealings with them, as he often was too with the staff in his own department, which he ruled with a rod of iron. With characteristic understatement, Shackleton, from whose office 'tremendous rows' could frequently be heard emanating from the German Department up the corridor, referred to Rosteutscher's 'poor reputation in human relations'.[100]

In sharp contrast, in the environs of the smallest foreign-language department, Hebrew, a pin could be heard dropping, which accurately reflected the quiet, restrained personality of its scholarly professor, Rabbi Israel Abrahams, who filled the chair in a part-time capacity from 1938 to 1968.[101] What he and his one part-time assistant taught – the department had no full-time staff until after he retired – changed little in these years, viz. Biblical and post-Biblical Hebrew language, grammar and literature, stretching from the Old Testament to the 20th century. What did change, however, was the size of the class once the new Jewish high school in Cape Town, Herzlia, began to turn out pupils who had taken Hebrew as a matriculation subject. As a result, between 1960 and 1962 student enrolments doubled to 80, which swamped the existing teaching capacity of the department. Temporary staff had to be hastily engaged, but it was clear that this could be no more than a stopgap measure. Thus, even before Abrahams formally left UCT to settle in Israel in 1968 with a corpus of erudite articles, books and Biblical translations and commentaries to his credit, the University had begun to investigate ways of securing endowments to upgrade the chair into a full-time one, perhaps to be 'named after some eminent Hebrew scholar', a Senate sub-committee suggested hopefully.[102]

The one foreign-language department which did not have to worry about keeping up with a stream of new texts in its languages was Classics, in which both Classical Greek and Latin were taught. By 1948 the primacy of these one-time pillars of all European higher education – Thomas Jefferson had called them 'indispensable to fill up the character of a "well-educated man"'[103] – had been in decline for over a generation already in the face of the advance of science and technology. But, at South African universities like UCT, this erosion was slowed by the legal profession's regulation that all LLB students had to pass Latin I. The consequence was that students compelled to take Latin I made up some 60% of the department's total enrolment of 200–300 in this period, requiring teaching 'on a mass scale', as two professors deplored.[104] Many Law students were equally dismayed at having to do the course and did not hide their feelings in lectures. A non-Law student wrote of a lecturer 'stoically bearing the restlessness of the Law students [there] … under duress'.[105]

The other five language courses in the department (Latin II and III and Greek I, II and III) contributed less than 15% of enrolments. The remaining 25–30% of students in the department were those taking courses in Classical Culture, which were taught solely in English and which ranged imaginatively over Classical literature, philosophy, religion and history in a bid to introduce South African students to the many sides of Greek and Roman civilisation.[106] Reading the writing on the wall correctly, one of the professors proclaimed that doing so had become 'one of the main functions of a Classics Department in a modern university'.[107]

Far less imaginative was what was taught in the language courses, and how. Here the standard, Victorian-era emphasis on translating and parsing classical texts and on prose composition and translation persisted, while a literary appreciation of what was translated barely featured. Even the most diligent student found the diet of doing a long translation every week hard going; almost certainly the group of Smuts Hall residents who 'worked as a co-op, dividing up the week's load into equal portions for translation … before putting together [and submitting] a joint translation'[108] was not unique. Nor were those who tracked down a published Loeb or Penguin Classics translation (which, in such instances, were condemned as 'cribs' by staff members) and used it to assist them.

Of the five men who occupied the two chairs in the department in this period – originally one in Greek and one in Latin, but from 1955 one in language and one in literature and culture – only three, William Rollo (1934–53), Anton Paap (1954–81) and Maurice Pope (1957–68), occupied their chairs for more than five years. The other two, Harold Baldry (1948–53) and George Goold (1955–7), left UCT for political or family reasons, the former for a position at Swansea and the latter for one at Manitoba.[109]

The 38-year-old Anton Paap was appointed to succeed Rollo when the latter became interim Principal of the University College of Rhodesia and Nyasaland in 1953.[110] A Utrecht- and Oxford-trained specialist in Classical Greek texts on papyri, he brought to the painstaking transcription and translation which this required a single-mindedness that relegated teaching to a distant second in his academic life. Perhaps it was this love of precision and his mastery of minutiae which made him willing subsequently to accept lengthy spells as Dean of the Faculty.

Although he and his fellow professor, Maurice Pope, may have had similar surnames, they could not have differed more in personality. In contrast to Paap's low-key reserve, the Cambridge-trained Pope wore his enthusiasm on his sleeve. 'I have always tried to maintain a lively and humane attitude [in teaching]', he averred,[111] a fact borne out by student recollections of him as a lecturer. He 'imbued in me a lifelong ambition … to visit the walls of windy Troy and tread in Schliemann's footsteps', testified one,[112] while colleagues spoke of his sharp intellect and his 'always [being] ready to initiate discussion'.[113] One product of his fertile mind was the compilation of a novel anthology of Latin texts for undergraduate teaching, its novelty lying in the fact that it included extracts not only from Classical-era authors, but also from writings well beyond the Classical period.[114]

Even more path-breaking was his work on the decipherment of Bronze Age Cretan script, a cutting-edge project in Classical studies in the 1950s and 1960s. Characteristically, his ardour for this research often spilled over into his lectures. A student recalled how his lecture on Homer easily shifted into an account of his sheer thrill 'at the discovery of Hector's name in Linear B tablets'.[115] The class was enthralled.

Only one of his colleagues, Lydia Baumbach, a senior lecturer from 1965, shared his interest in script decipherment, though in her case it was of ancient Mycenaean Linear B script, which earned her the nickname 'Lydia B' and, in 1976, one of the Classics chairs at UCT. An adept and caring teacher, she 'fully understands the meaning of Humanitas', judged a veteran classicist.[116]

The research interests of the other lecturers in the department in this period focused more on literature than language, most aiming to produce edited translations of works by lesser-known Classical authors. For them, however, teaching – given the make-up of the students in the department – was a grind. Latin I 'is, frankly, not of university standard', lamented one of the professors, but 'the only realistic policy is for us to continue teaching from the [low] point at which the schools have stopped'.[117]

Only in the Classical Culture courses was there more scope for innovative teaching, especially from 1959 when the two existing courses were converted into two, open-to-all, first-year courses all in English: Greek and Roman Literature and Philosophy, and Ancient History and Political Thought. As John Atkinson, a newly appointed Classical historian, discovered to his delight when joining the department in 1965, he had 'a fair amount of freedom' to alter the contents of the syllabuses,[118] as history and politics were outside the ambit of both the professors. Heeding Horace's injunction to 'seize the day', he did not let this opportunity slip.

On the other hand, until the 1960s, innovation in the syllabuses of the Department of History's five undergraduate courses – History I, II and III, and Constitutional

History and Law I and II – was very limited, largely because of the conservatism of the head since 1937, Harry Mandelbrote,[119] and his own vested interest in maintaining unchanged his two courses on constitutional history and law so as to retain the department's link with the Faculty of Law, which had made at least one course in the subject compulsory for its 100 or so LLB students. These constituted some 25% of all students in the History Department. Only once Mandelbrote retired at the age of 67 in 1958 was the teaching of constitutional history and law downscaled, with the law component being taken over by the Faculty of Law itself in 1964 and the remaining constitutional history section being offered as a course on its own until 1972.

This opened the way for the introduction in 1964 of the first course in African history at a South African university, a field which had emerged in Britain and the new universities in West and East Africa as decolonisation gathered pace in the continent from the 1950s. Mandelbrote's immediate successor as King George V Professor of History, the 43-year-old Leonard Thompson,[120] had advocated initiating such a course even before he assumed the chair in 1959, but his tenure as professor was too brief to achieve this – he left UCT for the University of California in 1961, as he saw little future in the country for liberals like him after Sharpeville and the state's clampdown on anti-apartheid organisations. Despondently he told a visiting historian that 'any liberal stance was doomed to failure in his lifetime'.[121] It was therefore only three years later that his successor in the chair, Eric Axelson, introduced 'An Outline of African History' as a free-standing senior course, one which, paradoxically, explicitly excluded South Africa so as not to infringe on the History II course on South Africa and, perhaps, because South Africa was deemed to be so different from the rest of the continent. That Axelson conceived of the new course himself and taught it largely alone meant, however, that it focused disproportionately on the history of Europeans in Africa rather than on that of Africans in Africa. This was because he was a specialist in the history of the Portuguese in the continent, having by 1960 written two chronicle-like books and gained a reputation as an eloquent speaker and broadcaster on the topic, to set alongside his famous discovery of the remains of three stone crosses erected by Portuguese explorers on the southern African coast in the 1480s.

Thus, though his lens on Africa's past was narrow – a colleague spoke of its 'marked colonialist flavour'[122] – the fact that African history had been accepted into the academic canon at UCT when, in many academic circles in and far beyond apartheid South Africa, it was scorned as a non-subject[123] was a decisive breakthrough as it meant that other, less blinkered historians could subsequently transform it into a more Afrocentric course, as Robin Hallett was to do in the 1970s. Its appeal, especially to progressive students wanting to understand an Africa from which apartheid had isolated them, grew rapidly then; by 1973 nearly 120 students were taking the course, almost a fivefold increase since 1964.

Except for the addition of an immediately topical component on 'The Twentieth Century to 1939' in History III in 1954 to replace a historiography and method section shifted to the new Honours degree, the rest of the undergraduate syllabus remained as it had been in 1948. History I's vast survey, 'Outline of the History of Western Civilisation', continued to provide a very broad sweep of European history 'from Adam to Adolf', as one wit put it – glumly, one former student recalled compiling a list of 'some 1400 dates that should be remembered' in a bid to get on top of the contents, which piled up relentlessly week by week[124] – while the two courses on South Africa and 'Colonisation' in History II and on medieval and modern Europe in History III remained heavily political, focusing on the actions of Europeans at home and abroad.

If, apart from the South African history course, what was taught differed little from the syllabuses in many a provincial British university of the day, the intensity with which it was taught was unusual, and not just in South Africa. Weekly small-group tutorials in which topics related to that week's lecture material were closely discussed were the norm in History I already in 1948 and were extended to History II and III as the size of their classes grew, while every term at least two essays had to be written in each year-long course. Assiduously marked and discussed one-to-one, they were integral to the department's courses, contributing significantly to its reputation for committed teaching. The critical thinking, argument and writing which this multi-pronged teaching fostered stood its students in good stead in professions like journalism and school teaching into which many of them went, thanks to the availability of state bursaries for would-be school teachers. In the years of South Africa's economic boom in the 1960s, enrolments just in History I, II and III topped 300, while thirty students were awarded Honours degrees, six MAs and three doctorates. Even the Honours dissertations bore the stamp of UCT's distinctive training in handling primary sources, which postgraduate students were required to consult, a feature that prompted more than one external examiner to comment that they were more like MA theses.

Unlike in most of the larger departments in the Faculty of Arts, History employed full-time junior lecturers to tutor its first-year students. Pre-eminent among them were two women, the dynamic, chain-smoking Marie Williams (later Maud) and the acute but more restrained Clodagh O'Dowd, both Honours graduates of the department. Their careers revolved around their teaching, neither undertaking much by way of research. In contrast, several of their colleagues led academic lives which permitted both teaching and research, though sometimes in two far-removed fields.

Jean van der Poel[125] spent over twenty years calendaring and then editing the voluminous papers of the statesman Jan Smuts in seven volumes, all the while austerely delivering incisive and authoritative lectures on everything but South African history, which, in the opinion of one impressed student, married 'just the right amount of detail with clear assessment of the processes of change'.[126] Paradoxically, though the two monographs she wrote were on South African history topics, in her retirement she insisted that she had never found South African history 'important or really interesting'.[127]

Leonard Thompson was better able to align his teaching with his primary research topic of the 1950s, the making of the Union of South Africa, as he was able to draw several postgraduates into working on aspects of this subject for their theses. Among undergraduates, however, he was known as an inspiring and lively lecturer who 'radiated a depth of knowledge; if he was not yet a world authority in his field, it was clear he was going to be', concluded one.[128] Nor was he wrong because, even before he left UCT for California, his eyes were opening wide to the Africanist thrust in the continent's historiography, which was to inform the second half of his career in the United States.

His successor in the UCT chair after Van der Poel had turned down the offer of this position, the 49-year-old Axelson, was a highly polished lecturer too, but solely in his own field. Beyond this he went only with great reluctance, devoting little effort to such tasks – and it showed, as in student assessments of him as 'a low investment teacher with little interest in students'.[129] Probably it was as well for both him and the Department of History that he was increasingly drawn into university administration from 1972 and eventually left the department to become a deft, full-time Deputy Principal in 1975.

A world away from Axelson in his commitment to teaching across the board was Rodney Davenport, who spent six years as a conscientious stand-in for different colleagues who were away on leave. Despite the ongoing mastery of new material that this required – Mandelbrote praised his 'high sense of duty' and spoke of being 'amazed at the amount of work he can get through'[130] – Davenport firmly believed that 'history teaching at all levels should be a person-to-person business'[131] and put this into practice. Former students recalled his 'absorbing' lectures[132] and how he 'won the unstinted respect of all those who have had contact with him'.[133] When he applied (unsuccessfully) for the UCT chair in 1962, one of his academic referees declared, 'He has it in him to become our leading historian.'[134] His subsequent career at Rhodes University from 1965 to 1990, and particularly his thoroughgoing, one-volume *South Africa: A Modern History* (now in its fifth edition), confirmed the referee's well-informed prescience.

Davenport was one of three former members of the UCT History Department to contribute to what was the epitome of liberal Africanist historiography on South Africa in the 1970s, the two-volume *Oxford History of South Africa* (published in 1969 and 1971), of which Thompson was co-editor. The third departmental contributor was May Katzen, who was on the staff for a short time before leaving the country in 1964 after being detained by the police. The three of them and their chapters in the *Oxford History* represent best the most prominent and notable strand in history writing and teaching as practised at UCT in this era.

Not that History was the only department in the Faculty of Arts where history was taught. Apart from Classics, where ancient history was part of the curriculum, the Department of Economics had been offering at least one course in economic history since 1925. Yet no formal collaboration or cross-disciplinary pollination took place across these three departments, for divisions within the field of history were deep. Doubtless more than one member of the History Department would have echoed an adaptation of a contemporary aphorism, that economic history brought quantitative rigour to history, but, unfortunately, it also brought mortis.[135]

Although the head of the Department of Economics and Jagger professor from 1950 to 1969, H.M. Robertson, was himself an economic historian 'by inclination and by reputation', as he himself expressed it,[136] economic history in this period was very much secondary to economics in the department's priorities. Students in the two courses in economic history (which were repeated on the Hiddingh campus after 5 pm) made up about 35% of all the department's students, a large percentage of them part-time BCom or BBusSc students anxious to get a qualification rather than question the content of the syllabus.

There was thus neither the incentive nor the resources to innovate and alter the three-quarter European, one-quarter South African syllabus in economic history in this period. Only in 1969 was a third course in the subject introduced, increasing its South African component and finally according economic history formal recognition as a full academic discipline in its own right and not just an adjunct to economics.

Robertson's many articles in the *South African Journal of Economics* contributed to this maturation of the discipline in South Africa – 'he had [thanks to his] historian's training, the power to sift … [documents] and [thanks to] an economist's understanding, the capacity to interpret them', judged a leading economist[137] – but as a teacher, though clad in his Cambridge academic gown, he was unremarkable. His pedestrian lectures were 'as dry as dust', remembered one of his students, though their content was 'precise and immaculately constructed'[138] and 'challenged the mind'.[139] Such features also characterised the rather rigid lecturing of Robertson's assiduous former student Marcus Arkin, who spent nineteen years on the staff before taking up a chair at Rhodes University in 1967.

In this situation, the most engaging teaching in economic history came from the 'inspirational livewire' of a lecturer (to quote one of her students[140]), Marcelle Kooy. Though this zest was not apparent when it came to research, her fluent manner and persuasive personality saw her take over the running of economic history courses from her mentor, Robertson, on his retirement and eventually lead the division's secession from the Economics Department in 1980 to create an independent department of Economic History with her as its first head.

Given the size of the three undergraduate courses in economics – nearly 300 students were taking them either in the morning or after 5 pm in 1958 and over 700 in 1968 – all three economic historians had to help teach this kindred discipline too, as well as offer options in the Economics Honours course, which attracted rising numbers in the 1960s as the country's economy boomed. 'I do not regard myself as sufficiently expert in all the fields in which I am having to dabble', admitted Robertson with characteristic honesty,[141] but in vain.

Their teaching supplemented that of the seven to ten dedicated economists on the staff in the 1960s, like Robertson's long-serving deputy, Sheila van der Horst;[142] the Keynesian monetary economist Joubert Botha, who went on to fill chairs at the universities of Port Elizabeth and Witwatersrand; the transferee from UCT's Department of Commerce and Robertson's eventual successor in the Jagger chair, Ben Gurzynski;[143] and the two rising stars of the department in the late 1960s and future professors there, Francis Wilson and Brian Kantor.

The first three of the above-mentioned economists were not known for their ability as dexterous lecturers to undergraduates, Botha, Van der Horst and Gurzynski all having difficulty in rendering their theoretical material less than abstruse to students. Botha, Robertson commented, 'lacked the capacity for "significant simplification"',[144] while between Van der Horst and the 100 or so students in Economics II there was, a colleague observed, 'mutual incomprehension'.[145] She was unable to pitch her lectures on international trade at a level appropriate for them and they, in turn, became inattentive and disruptive. She was far better as a rigorous, probing teacher of senior students, inculcating in them what another colleague described as 'the uncompromising standards of evidence and reasoning to be found in her own work'.[146] This work, starting with her own pioneering *Native Labour in South Africa*, originally published in 1942 and reprinted in 1971, focused on the employment of African labour in South Africa and on the deleterious economic effects of apartheid, which complemented her own anti-apartheid activities off campus for the South African Institute of Race Relations.

As unhandy as Van der Horst was in teaching large classes, so adept at this was her junior colleague Myra Mark. 'She should have been professor of lecturing', suggested a fellow lecturer in all earnest.[147] Possessing the knack of making her material comprehensible even to tyros, she commanded the attention of her classes from the moment she began speaking, thus removing any chance of indiscipline. She also overhauled the tutorial system in Economics I, increasing the frequency of tutorials and ensuring that they articulated better with lectures. Notwithstanding this and her flair for teaching, her lack of interest in research meant that she remained on the temporary staff for nine years and that, after she finally received a permanent appointment in 1970, she was never promoted again.

The brand of economics that she, her forerunners and her contemporaries taught all through this period was thoroughly neoclassical in character, as is evident from the presence of textbooks like Samuelson's *Economics* and Marshall's *Principles of Economics* on the department's list of recommended works. Left-inclined students found such a free market approach fundamentally conservative, as it portrayed capitalist economies and their operation as the norm and eschewed consideration of any other economic systems. As one put it disdainfully, 'The textbooks claimed to teach their subjects "scientifically" by looking at reality "as it is" and not "how it ought to be".'[148]

Few of his fellow students shared this view, however. Destined for business or the financial sector or for government or semi-government institutions, all of which grew enormously during the country's boom years, most students were more intent on gaining a qualification than in critically interrogating the course's contents. Students had 'a mania for taking down verbatim notes', lamented one lecturer.[149] Learning may have been largely by rote, acknowledged one BCom student, but 'it taught [us] the fundamentals thoroughly'.[150]

Far more diverse in disciplinary background were the students who took courses in what in 1952 was renamed the Department of Philosophy after the merger of the existing Department of Ethics and Politics with the Logic and Metaphysics section of the Department of Logic and Psychology.[151] Drawing its students not only from the Faculty of Arts, but also from Law, Science and Social Science, the department's courses in political philosophy, ethics, and logic and metaphysics probably attracted many of them because these were appealingly advertised as offering 'an introduction to Philosophy as well as … the philosophical background to the subjects studied at university'.[152]

As first-year students were discouraged from taking any of these courses – these subjects thus constituted two-year majors – total undergraduate enrolments never rose above 230 in this period, with the Political Philosophy and the Ethics sections contributing the largest shares. The relatively small number of students majoring in these subjects suggests that, for most, these courses were supplementary to their main focus and that, as yet, specialisation in these fields was not seen as a viable career path, a conclusion strengthened by the fact that just 26 postgraduate degrees were awarded across all three areas in the twenty years after 1948.

Throughout the entire period – indeed from 1937 to 1970 – the head of the department was the professor of political philosophy, Andrew Murray.[153] A clear and systematic lecturer on Western political thought and the nature of the modern state, in his classes he usually managed to contain his personal support for apartheid and opposition to socialism and communism, insisting that 'My lectures on Marxism are open and objective. A professor should … never use his chair to propagate any kind of doctrine.'[154] Out of class, however, his political preferences were very evident as, from a politically pluralist position, he argued firmly against communism and in favour of political and racial separation.

In the context of the Cold War and apartheid South Africa, this public stance appealed to the National Party Government; consequently, he was appointed to official commissions of inquiry, to the Publications Control Board, to the position of consultant to the South African legal team in the South West Africa case before the International Court of Justice; and to give expert evidence in several high-profile political trials and hearings. The last-mentioned role required him to be away from the department for long stretches at a time – 'The lawyers seem to be afraid to be without someone who knows the theories involved', he explained immodestly[155] – but his absence did hamper the functioning of his department and produced objections from members of UCT's Council. Eventually UCT decided to bill the state for the salary of the substitute lecturer who taught Murray's classes while he was engaged in what he light-heartedly termed 'judicial peregrinations'.[156] Given that his evidence in the biggest of these trials, the Treason Trial of 1956–61, and his professional proficiency were trenchantly derided by the defence counsel, the authorities may well have concluded that this was not money well spent.

Off campus, Murray's public speeches, articles and broadcasts attracted critical attention too. An address he gave at a public meeting was punctuated by vigorous heckling from an audience containing several 'coloured' UCT students, while he was taken to task in the press by several of his fellow UCT professors for arguing that a state could legitimately impose segregation on universities.[157] On campus he was shunned by some academics despite his restrained behaviour as a teacher and his polite manners. A 'gentlemanly collaborator with apartheid' is how a biographer has, not inaccurately, described him.[158] As will be suggested below, however, the effects of his collaboration were not only academic.

The casually dressed philosopher in the office next door to his could not have offered a sharper contrast to the prim, methodical Murray. Also appointed in 1937, Marthinus Versfeld had been solely responsible for teaching the two courses in ethics since then.[159] Eclectic in approach, his thinking drew on a wide range of moral philosophical traditions like Classical Greek, Christian, Confucian and Zen Buddhist to explore the ethics of human and environmental existence, which he then wove into his own composite whole, infused by his deep Catholicism. 'One could be Christian and [a] thinker', he averred.[160] In the words of one of his best students, 'He connected things' as he sought 'to integrate different dimensions of life, and to think intellectually about that kind of integration'.[161]

His lectures continued this intellectual quest but aloud, giving them spontaneity and immediacy as he shared with his students new ideas as they struck him. Although unsystematic, this was exhilarating, even revelatory and revolutionary for them as an example of the critical interrogation of ideas in operation. 'I learnt from him that the truth is relative and not absolute', reflected a sometime student nearly half a century later, '[that] there is no right or wrong, just positions … I was looking for people who would make me think … and found them in Versfeld and [the junior lecturer, Willem] van Ryswyk.'[162]

Punctuated by humour and an earthy wisdom and employing the Socratic method gently, his teaching, like his idiosyncratic lifestyle and his conduct, reflected his deeply held philosophical beliefs, as when his rejection of Auguste Comte's positivism saw him fling to the floor of his lecture room all three volumes of that author's *Système de Politique Positive*.

Readers of his extensive writings were as stimulated as his students, especially since, in several of his works, he raised fundamental philosophical questions about everyday objects like houses, food, wine, pots and rocks. His more serious books and articles – a label he would have disavowed vehemently as he insisted, 'I have fought a long duel with seriousness … [so] there is no need to take me seriously'[163] – on philosophers like St Augustine and St Thomas Aquinas elicited qualified praise from reviewers. One captured the essence of his peculiar approach to philosophy when he wrote that Versfeld's *Mirror of Philosophers* was marked by 'a learning that is wide but not ordered, an intelligence that is strong but not assiduous, [and] an imagination that is rich but not refined'.[164]

Notwithstanding such double-edged judgements and his 62 years, Versfeld followed Murray as professor in the department from 1971 to 1975. His right-hand man until 1974 was S.I.M. du Plessis, who had single-handedly taught the two courses in logic and metaphysics since his appointment in 1952. Steeped in modern Continental European philosophy – his three doctorates dealt with Max

Scheler, several 19th-century French philosophers and Kant – he tried to leaven his subject matter by practising dialectics and close textual analysis in class, but his grave demeanour and rigidity of mind rendered these attempts less than successful. Instead, he was perceived by the small number of students in his courses as 'a rather puritanical philosopher'.[165]

His contribution to the discipline of philosophy in South Africa was more notable for his major part in helping to organise the country's first philosophical congress, held at UCT in 1952, and for assisting Murray to launch the first scholarly journal devoted to philosophy in South Africa, the *Bulletin of the Department of Philosophy, UCT*, which later grew into the *South African Journal of Philosophy*, on the editorial board of which Du Plessis served for many years.

Apart from this trio of male philosophers – unusually for UCT, all were Afrikaners[166] – the department's student intake remained too small to allow its complement of permanent posts to be augmented. Thus, graduate assistants did much of the marking – there were no small-group tutorials – even though Murray felt that, in most cases, 'the requirements of the Department go beyond their competence'.[167] To this statement there were at least two striking exceptions, the Edinburgh- and Oxford-trained Dolores Wright, 'the antithesis of Du Plessis', one student was relieved to discover,[168] and the sharp-witted radical thinker Rick Turner. Paradoxically, having employed Turner as a graduate assistant in 1963, the year he completed an Honours degree in the department, ten years later, when Murray was asked as one of several 'connoisseurs in the field of political and social science' (to use the South African Police's Security Branch description of him) to assess his former junior colleague's political outlook, he pronounced him 'a Marxian revolutionist'.[169] On this basis Turner was banned by the Government. In this situation both Turner and Murray would have recognised the verity of Kierkegaard's dictum 'Once you label me, you negate me'. That Murray and Turner represented the opposite ends of the wide intellectual and pedagogic spectrum spanned by UCT's Philosophy Department in these years, no one would doubt.

Rick Turner was not the only member of UCT's staff with whom Murray contended at arm's length, for a key adviser to the defence team in the same Treason Trial in which Murray testified for the prosecution as an 'expert' witness was his near neighbour in the Arts Block, the head of the sub-department of Native Law and Administration, Jack Simons. Native Law and Administration was just one component of the School of African Studies, which had served as a loose administrative frame containing emerging Afrocentric disciplines ever since its inception as the School of African Life and Languages in 1920. This name had been broadened to that of African Studies in 1935.[170]

Yet, until 1960, African studies amounted to no more than the sum total of the individual activities of the four departments or sub-departments under the School's umbrella, viz. Social Anthropology, Bantu Languages or (as it became in 1963) African Languages, Native Law and Administration or (as it was renamed in 1959) Comparative African Government and Law (CAGAL), and Ethnology and Archaeology or (as it was relabelled in 1961) Archaeology. Indeed, so uncoordinated was what they taught that in 1954 the nominally cross-disciplinary MA in African Studies was scrapped.

By 1960, however, such was the recent surge in African studies internationally that several progressive UCT academics were prompted to set up a monthly seminar 'to discuss common problems in African History, Institutions, Government and Law, and Language'.[171] The convenor was Professor Monica Wilson of Social Anthropology, and early presenters included Simons, Rodney Davenport, Leonard Thompson, Denis Cowen, A.C. Jordan, Sheila van der Horst and the then Chief Secretary of Northern Rhodesia, Richard Luyt, who, five years later, was to become Principal of UCT.

However, going further than this by creating a cross-disciplinary Honours degree in African Studies proved impracticable on both academic and staffing grounds, and by the mid-1960s the School's administrative frame had become, in the words of one of its professors, 'a shell',[172] whose now adult components were keen to go their separate ways. Grouping these departments under 'School of African Studies' in the Arts Faculty handbook 'only made it difficult for an outsider to find the entries for the four departments in the alphabetically arranged handbook', quipped a senior administrator.[173] On her side, Wilson was sure that the School's demise appealed to the powers that be at UCT for more than just administrative reasons – 'it is as plain as a pikestaff', she told a colleague, 'that various people in the University would like a School of African Studies to disappear altogether (and be absorbed by Social Science) or/and to be … very different in approach … [Vice-Chancellor] Duminy … detests African Studies …'[174] Not coincidentally, the School was abolished on her retirement in 1973.

Social Anthropology was the largest of the School's four constituents; in fact, until 1969 Archaeology and CAGAL were both sub-departments falling under Anthropology's departmental authority. In the case of CAGAL, this continued until 1983 when it was merged into the new Department of Political Studies.

From 1952, when she succeeded Isaac Schapera as professor of social anthropology at UCT, the 44-year-old Monica Wilson used her lectures to open the eyes of her predominantly white students to the structure and functioning of African societies. The subject 'had the verifiable immediacy of the local scene', enthused a student. As Wilson and an African postgraduate student of hers explained the intricate network of obligation and sharing in African societies, so 'the black majority came into focus'.[175]

Although she did not eschew use of then standard Western terms like 'primitive' and 'more advanced' communities, Wilson's immersion in rural African life and language – she had grown up in the Ciskei, had done two years of research for her Cambridge doctorate in Pondoland, and had spent four years doing fieldwork near Lake Tanganyika – helped give her an insightful feel for and grasp of African culture and society, on which her well-organised and precise lectures drew. As one of her undergraduate students vividly recalled, 'On the dot of eight in the morning she would glide into the lecture hall … with her black gown flapping. Her stern demeanour silenced us all, even the newspaper readers at the back … I was mesmerised by her absorption in her subject … and … fascinated by the clarity and confidence of her exposition. There was no obvious attempt to entertain and little interaction with us. She presented her political views, imbued as they were in her topic, without prevarication or apology. Her scientifically objective account of race was formative in my understanding of the world for it revealed the rickety structures on which ideologies are so often founded.'[176]

Into her senior students and handful of MA and PhD students – top students she encouraged to do postgraduate degrees abroad – she inculcated the need for empathy, factual accuracy, an awareness of social change, and a precision of thought and expression. 'Think about every word you write', she told them.[177] To her, writing essays was 'parallel to practicals in the natural sciences … To teach this, within the social field, is our main business.'[178] 'It is impossible to teach social anthropology without giving regular essays to each student.'[179]

This typically Cambridge approach yielded of course a very heavy marking load, especially as the department's tenured staff did not exceed three. 'I, myself, feel absolutely defeated by the amount of teaching to be done', Wilson complained in 1963, the year that undergraduate enrolments topped 150 for the first time. 'We go on teaching to the best of our ability but are absolutely overwhelmed.'[180]

Given this situation, her academic output between 1952 and her retirement in 1973 is astonishing: seven books, ten chapters in books, eight journal articles and five published lectures. This spoke volumes about her self discipline, her well-informed perspective and her capacity for research and writing. Accurately, one of her referees described her as 'an indefatigable worker', impressive for her 'clarity of mind'.[181] It was this combination of high-achieving traits that won her international stature as an anthropologist whose fieldwork-rooted ethnography 'played a part in re-orientating the functionalist tradition [in anthropology] away from the tribal study written in the ethnographic present towards the study of social change in Africa'.[182] This cemented the department's already high standing in the discipline in the English-speaking world[183] and countered still prevalent ideas in some circles at UCT that social anthropology was 'a queer subject engaged in by some eccentrics'.[184]

Not least among Wilson's allies in opposing such views was Leonard Thompson in the Department of History, which is not surprising since she saw herself as an anthropologist concerned with 'how it [the present] becomes – that is with an analysis of process' over time.[185] With a shared conviction that South African history had to be decolonised so that it encompassed the historical experience of all inhabitants and not just whites, in 1963 the two of them initiated a project to produce a new, all-inclusive history of the country, in which co-operation and conflict would be the overarching theme. Their jointly edited, two-volume *Oxford History of South Africa* was the result, to which Wilson contributed five chapters and an introduction. Although the volumes attracted sharp broadsides from both the left and the right of the ideological spectrum, to many its contents were a revelation, especially in the face of the distorted history long taught in state schools. 'I remember even somebody like Nelson [Mandela] was absolutely fascinated by … [its use of] sources that we didn't even know about, and the book had a major influence on the way people saw their history', recalled a fellow prisoner of his on Robben Island.[186]

In short, Monica Wilson stood out at UCT in these years not only because she was the University's first and only female professor and dean until 1969, but more so because she was a world-ranked anthropologist.

That her two senior colleagues in the department in the 1950s and 1960s, Peter Carstens and Mike Whisson, privately referred to her as, respectively, 'Lady Monica'[187] and 'The boss'[188] is indicative of the aloof authority with which she ran her department. More outgoing and 21 years her junior, Carstens interacted with students more easily, but his research on a rural 'coloured' community in Namaqualand emulated her fieldwork methods meticulously. That he continued to follow this approach in the manner that he had been trained at UCT for the rest of his post-1965 career in Canada, where he eventually occupied a chair in Toronto, is borne out by his retrospective admission that he was not certain he had got the theory right in his Namaqualand study, 'but he was confident that the data was strong and accurate, and that was what was most important to him'.[189]

Whisson also went on to occupy a chair – at Rhodes University in 1978 – after ten years of incisive lecturing at UCT and empathetic fieldwork among Cape Town's 'coloured' community. Not only was he good at 'bringing abstract discussion back to realities of the ethnographic and sociological data', observed his Cambridge professor, but he was also morally committed to putting his scholarship and teaching 'to wider social use in the interests of community wellbeing … [which meant] espousing the cause of socially disadvantaged groups'.[190] Yet he was thrice passed over as a successor to Wilson in the chair, probably because of his sharp tongue. 'If Michael continues to set everyone by the ears he obviously would not be appointed to the chair of social anthropology', forecast Wilson. 'A professor simply must be able to keep staff.'[191]

The man whom Wilson would have liked to succeed her was her former disciple, teaching assistant and collaborator in *Langa: A Study of Social Groups in an African Township*, Archie Mafeje. Following her lead, UCT had chosen him as its new senior lecturer in social anthropology in 1968 – 'here for the first time we would appoint someone who was an insider [to African society]', Wilson explained[192] – but pressure from the South African Government forced the University to annul its decision, triggering the so-called Mafeje Affair and a student sit-in in protest.[193] Paradoxically, therefore, UCT's first attempt to Africanise the staff of the chief department in the School of African Studies was scotched as un-(white) South African and as 'tantamount to flouting the accepted traditional outlook of South Africa', as the Minister of National Education phrased it.[194]

Even more politically suspect to the apartheid government was Jack Simons's sub-department of Native Law and Administration or CAGAL. When introduced in 1938,[195] its two courses were intended to provide training for would-be 'native' administrators and missionaries,[196] but in his hands they turned, first, into a probing sociological examination of the bases of Western imperialism and colonial 'native' policies north and south of the Limpopo, and then, from the uhuru year of 1960 onwards, into a study too of the government of newly independent states on the continent. The Law component in the courses, which focused on African customary law and its relationship to Western law, was retained as it had become critical to the sub-department's viability, for from 1952 it had ensured its inclusion in the LLB curriculum as a compulsory course. The effect on enrolments in Simons's courses had been dramatic: in 1951 only 33 undergraduates were registered for Native Law and Administration I and II; in 1952 this figure more than tripled to 109, around which it continued to hover until the late 1960s.

Save for left-leaning, transient junior lecturers and tutors like Stanley Trapido, Neville Rubin, Adrian Leftwich and Alan Brooks, Simons did the bulk of the teaching himself. Although a lifelong Marxist and a member of the South African Communist Party until it was banned in 1950, he did not carry this ideology into the lecture room. His objectivity was as legendary as his interactive, Socratic style of teaching and his personal charisma. Not only did he bring 'African customs and culture to life in a way that directly involved his audience, whom he encouraged to participate', as one of his students put it,[197] but he prodded them into thinking clearly and critically about the ideas and arguments they put forward. Students were taught 'how to think, not what to think … [in lectures which were] amongst the most informative and thrilling experiences of my University career', testified another.[198] Not for nothing did T.B. Davie describe him as 'a particularly brilliant lecturer'.[199] 'I'm a teacher – this is my trade', as Simons summed himself up,[200] spelling out his pedagogic philosophy with characteristic clarity: 'The object of a class is to get the students to study, and not to give the teacher an opportunity to exhibit his wisdom and eloquence. The students, not the teacher, should do most of the talking.'[201] Overtly political activities he left by and large for when he was off campus.

However, this scrupulous separation of his pedagogy from his ideology was lost on a police informer in his class who reported the contents of his lectures so one-sidedly that the Commissioner of Police warned the Minister of Justice that 'Dr Simons does not hesitate to try and preach his doctrine in his lectures'. Moreover, according to another informer, Simons had told a Summer School audience that in Africa 'the native is held back as a result of the policies of Whites'.[202] On the evidence of such 'radical' statements, a senior civil servant damningly told the Minister of Education that 'suspicions exist about Dr Simons who, after inquiry, [was found] to be rather liberalistically inclined'.[203] The training that Simons gave to his students on the need for precision in note-taking and the use of labels had clearly passed all the informers by.

In the light of such reports and the increasing climate of political oppression in South Africa, Simons was barred from attending all save academic gatherings in 1954, jailed during the state of emergency in 1960, and then banned, briefly in 1961 and for five years in 1965. The last restraint effectively prevented him from teaching at UCT, which he left later that year for exile in Britain and then Zambia. Twenty-nine years later, after his return to Cape Town, UCT awarded him an honorary doctorate.

His political and journalistic activities off campus and the restrictions imposed on him by the apartheid state limited his writing to a host of short, mainly topical articles and pamphlets. Only in exile was he able to complete a major study on *African Women: Their Legal Status in South Africa* and, with his wife, the trade unionist Ray Alexander Simons, *Class and Colour in South Africa, 1850–1950*.

Both books were immediately banned in South Africa, which raised the knotty question for Simons's successor as head of the CAGAL sub-department, his urbane and eloquent mentee, David Welsh, as to whether *African Women* and its author might even be mentioned by name in a lecture. Monica Wilson, as head of the overarching department, forbade this, but did permit the book's contents to be anonymously drawn on for lectures. Characteristically, Simons urged (from abroad) that students' interests should be paramount – 'use the material without acknowledgement rather than banish the topic … a procedure that would merely keep the students ignorant of the way in which censorship operates'.[204] Even in exile, therefore, Simons put students' need to be exposed to a variety of views first, so that they could weigh them up critically for themselves.

Even smaller than CAGAL was the other sub-department under Anthropology, Ethnology and Archaeology, which dated from 1929.[205] Also what Wilson called a 'one-man specialism,'[206] until 1959 it was headed by John Goodwin, an expert on the Stone Age in South Africa and the man who had conceived of the basic periodisation of the region's archaeology in his jointly authored 'ur-text of South African prehistory', *The Stone Age Cultures of South Africa*.[207]

Yet, doubts on campus as to whether South African archaeology was a wholly academic subject inhibited its development. The fact that UCT was the only South African university to offer a major in the subject until the 1960s and that enthusiastic amateurs vastly outnumbered the three to four professional archaeologists in the country meant that, even in the 1950s, it still lacked what Goodwin's successor called 'the cloak of respectability'.[208] Thus, an attempt to found a chair at UCT in 1948 failed, while Goodwin was comprehensively sidelined from the high-profile Hopefield excavations by members of UCT's Anatomy Department, whose 'quick-dig' approach appealed to UCT's T.B. Davie. 'All the Principal seems to want is newspaper publicity to draw local funds to the University coffers', snorted Goodwin,[209] who was appalled by the manner in which the anatomists 'are carrying on quite unscientifically, by the best hit-and-miss processes'.[210]

These disappointments did nothing for Goodwin's teaching, which became fossilised within an intellectual framework dating back to the 1920s, when the ideas of the American cultural anthropologist Alfred Kroeber, that ethnology held the key to archaeology, were widely influential. Not surprisingly, therefore, by the 1950s Goodwin was apparently feeling that 'archaeology is moving away from me',[211] while students were finding his lectures 'boring – it was all theory'.[212] By then too, he was a very sick man (he died in 1959, aged 59) and his sub-department was faltering.

His successor, the 33-year-old Cambridge graduate Ray Inskeep revitalised the sub-department, comprehensively reshaping its syllabus and its ethos so that they reflected the more scientific methods being applied to archaeology internationally by advocates of the so-called New Archaeology. The existing syllabus might provide 'a good general course', he argued, but it did not offer 'an adequate training for research workers, or personnel fit to fill professional posts'.[213] He 'was more than a new broom sweeping clean', wrote the same student who had been bored by Goodwin's lectures. 'It was a vacuum cleaner.'[214] In 1961, within months of his arrival, 'Ethnology' was dropped from the department's name, Goodwin's jumbled, diorama-filled museum displaying artefacts was converted into an analysis-oriented teaching laboratory, the fieldwork element in Archaeology I and II was increased, and students taking the former course were advised that the emphasis 'will be on method and scope of archaeology rather than narrative prehistory and facts'.[215]

His lucid, lively, well-organised lectures – he had been a school teacher before studying archaeology – captivated students. 'His enthusiasm really was catching', remembered one,[216] while Wilson described him as a 'conspicuously able teacher … [who] creates such enthusiasm that they [his students] spend the greater part of their vacations and weekends on the work'.[217] 'His passion for the subject was such that there seemed to be no other way to lead our lives than to follow his direction and become archaeologists', testified one of several of his students who went on to make a name abroad as an archaeologist.[218]

For all the *esprit de corps* fostered by Inskeep's pedagogy, his lightly worn erudition, and the intellectual and social appeal of fieldwork, the intake of students remained small: 58 was the maximum reached in any one year in this era, as job prospects in South Africa were still few and far between. However, what blanket student numbers like this do not reveal is the fact that an unusually high percentage of these students were postgraduates. For example, of the 58 enrolled in 1966, five were registered for an Honours degree, two for MA degrees and three for doctorates. Clearly, a cohort of locally trained African archaeologists was beginning to be nurtured at UCT, not abroad as in most other disciplines, just as African archaeology was starting to take off, and in this Inskeep played a decisive part. 'Southern Africa is a magnificent field for archaeological research', gushed Wilson with unwonted fervour. 'The material available in bones and stones is enormous.'[219]

This is what Inskeep recognised and proceeded to exploit with a combination of fieldwork of exemplary quality and meticulous analysis back in the departmental laboratory. His magnum opus on the Later Stone Age site at Nelson's Bay Cave was 'a rich compendium of information and inference' which spawned a host of other studies,[220] while, though he was no theoretician, his ability to synthesise the growing body of evidence generated by his burgeoning discipline from the 1960s onwards is evident in his path-breaking chapter on 'The Archaeological Background' in volume 1 of the *Oxford History of South Africa* and in his book *The Peopling of South Africa*.

As fieldworker, teacher, mentor and builder of archaeology in southern Africa – he edited the *South African Archaeological Bulletin*, established the South African Association of Archaeologists and the South African Society for Quaternary Research, and lobbied museums and other universities to create posts for archaeologists – Inskeep was 'a pivotal figure in the development of South African archaeology',[221] who, by dint of his own example during his dozen years on the staff, unobtrusively made UCT a flagship of the discipline in the region. Appropriately, he became its first head when it gained independent departmental status in 1969.

Far less dynamic was the fourth constituent of the School of African Studies, the Department of Bantu Languages, a full department in its own right since 1935 and thus not part of the Anthropology Department, though obviously allied to it. Benefiting from UCT's paradoxical classification of indigenous African languages as 'foreign' languages, which met its requirement of one foreign-language course in every BA curriculum, it was able to attract a sufficient number of students to prevent questions about its viability and its *raison d'être* being posed, such as had led to its disestablishment in 1925.[222]

Strongly philological in orientation – its syllabus was replete with vocabulary, grammar, phonetics, morphology and syntax – until 1960 it focused on three languages, isiXhosa, South Sotho and Shona, but without putting them within a wider theoretical linguistic context. In that year, however, the departure of its Shona specialist, George Fortune, for a chair in Salisbury terminated the teaching of that language at UCT for some years, to the disappointment of the ten to fifteen students from Southern Rhodesia who regularly took his course in Shona every year. Although the head of the department since 1935, Gerard Lestrade, counted Shona among the 34 languages he spoke,[223] he was unwilling to add it to his existing teaching load.

Diligent but pedantic as a lecturer, Lestrade made little attempt to interact with his students. His heart was more into committee work both on campus and off, into writing minutely detailed studies of African folktales, language classification and ethnography, and into drafting school syllabuses and examination papers in all African languages, especially to meet the needs of the new Bantu Education system. Although he had difficulty seeing the wood for the linguistic trees and was unsympathetic to linguistic theory, his precise scholarship did help raise the status of local African languages as academic subjects, something which apartheid ideologues welcomed as confirmation of their standpoint that there were distinct 'Bantu cultures' in South Africa.

Fortune made a similar contribution with regard to Shona, his writings being crucial to the development of a standard Shona orthography, while his *Elements of Shona* is still regarded as a 'canonical text'.[224] With Lestrade, he therefore played a key role in establishing African linguistics as an academically acceptable field of study.

Integral to this overall linguistic achievement were two African lecturers in the department who completed doctorates under Lestrade's supervision, A.C. (Archibald) Jordan and D.P. (Daniel) Kunene. Only one other doctorate was awarded in the department – to Fortune – between 1948 and 1968. Appropriately known by his friends as 'Titshela' (i.e. teacher), Jordan was a former schoolmaster who had the knack of getting across to students the complexities of isiXhosa grammar while lacing his lectures with traditional folktales, wit and quotations from the Book of Proverbs. He was held 'in great esteem and affection by his students', testified Wilson,[225] one of them recalling how his 'inspiring and vital' lectures captivated the class.[226] Sometimes he even drew on his own novels and short stories to illustrate a grammatical point, thereby enhancing students' respect for him all the more.

Seventeen years his junior, Kunene was a conscientious teacher and author but, as Lestrade pointed out, 'very sure, but also very, very slow'.[227] Still, his pioneering work in the field of Sotho intonation was sufficiently impressive for him to be the runner-up to succeed Lestrade on the latter's death in 1962. By then he had already acted as head of the department for a year while Lestrade was on sick leave, during which time his juggling of both teaching and administration was judged to be 'phenomenal' by his ailing professor.[228] Personally, Wilson found him a delightful, alert and humorous colleague, with what she patronisingly called a 'gentleness and humanity that made him so essentially a civilised man'.[229] As in the case of Jordan two years earlier in 1962, it was the violation of this humanity by apartheid which led him in 1964 to leave the country. 'Every day we looked eagerly for some ray of hope in the darkness that covers South Africa like a shroud', he told Wilson. 'Yet the darkness seemed to grow thicker and yet thicker.'[230] Although he eventually gained a chair at the University of Wisconsin, 'I continue to think of UCT as one of the bright spots in that unfortunate land', he admitted.[231] In 2013, belatedly, UCT returned the compliment by awarding him an honorary degree at the age of 90.

The man who was appointed as Lestrade's successor in 1963 ahead of Kunene was the 44-year-old Ernst Westphal. Having grown up at a Lutheran mission station in Venda, he spoke Tshivenda with mother-tongue fluency and came to UCT from a lectureship at the School of African and Oriental Studies (SOAS) in London where he had gained a PhD for a thesis on 'The Sentence in Venda'. However, since then he had broadened his linguistic range to include several other Bantu languages and also Khoi and San click languages after proceeding on a year-long research tour to regions where they were still spoken. 'He has the inner urge to undertake the essential type of personal investigation, without which it is impossible to stimulate others in this direction', believed his head of department at SOAS.[232]

With the same energy as Inskeep displayed in reviving Archaeology – but without the same lightness of touch, bonhomie or ability to enthuse students – Westphal quickly had the department's name altered to 'African' Languages so as to be able to include non-Bantu languages like Nama and !xû in the syllabus, widened the range of Bantu languages in which courses might be given (including, once again, Shona), added a third course in African languages (now incorporating comparative Bantu studies too) to the existing two courses, set up a language teaching laboratory in the department, and made provision for occasional, non-degree courses in lesser-known Bantu languages. These were intended 'to aid missionaries, teachers, anthropologists, administrative officials … in the study of the available material on given pre-literate and undocumented languages'.[233]

Consequently, by 1968 the department was beginning to shed its outdated character, which had seen Fortune candidly admit in 1962 that 'Work done [there] according to methods valid enough twenty years ago would receive little recognition today'.[234] In 1966 it attracted its first postgraduate student in many years and by 1968 four more had followed in her path.

The one feature that did not change from Lestrade's time was the extensive power exercised by the head of the department over the predominantly African contract staff engaged annually to conduct the department's conversational classes and to do marking. Entirely dependent on him to be re-employed each year, they did not dare step out of line. How much more than just employment at UCT hung on this in high-apartheid South Africa is apparent from the rider to a UCT advertisement for a lectureship in the department in 1964. It read, 'African applicants must please note that it will be necessary for the University to obtain residential permits for the Cape Peninsula area before the appointment can be finalized.'[235]

It was not only subjects within the School of African Studies about whose academic respectability doubts were expressed on campus. In the case of Speech Training and Dramatic Art, however, such questioning was muted because Donald Inskip, a recent Dean of Arts and professor of French since 1932, strongly supported the idea that drama was a university-worthy subject. His own thespian inclination and his position as Director of UCT's Little Theatre[236] only added to his conviction.

Accordingly, in 1947 his proposal to introduce a single course in Drama in the Faculty was approved, while two years later, also at his initiative, the Speech Training and Elocution section of the Faculty of Music was shifted to Arts and, tellingly, renamed Speech Training and Dramatic Art. It provided the practical component (i.e. subjects like diction, production, costuming and lighting) for Inskip's Drama course, while his lectures on Western European Drama, given by five language departments, in turn doubled as part of the Speech Training and Dramatic Art course. This mutually supportive arrangement sustained these two arms of the discipline as each proceeded to establish its own academic credentials in the Faculty of Arts, something which, individually, they probably would have struggled to accomplish. Even when Drama II was added in 1965, thereby making it a majoring subject, the mutual dependency remained in place; indeed, from 1967, students intending to major in Drama were required to attend classes in the Speech Training and Dramatic Art Department in their first year.

As is so often the case in universities, the basis for this productive cross-departmental collaboration was not only intellectual, but also personal. Inskip spoke warmly of his long co-operation with Rosalie Van der Gucht, the head of Speech Training and Dramatic Art from 1946.[237] It was, he beamed, a relationship 'during which moments of strain were almost entirely absent'.[238] While his only involvement in actual teaching was to give the lectures on French drama in the Drama course, his main contribution to drama at UCT was as planner and facilitator, custodian of the Little Theatre and, as one student put it, 'godfather to the Drama Department'.[239]

For her part, Van der Gucht applied her training as an elocutionist in London to a range of practical, voice-related diploma and certificate courses offered by her department, which aimed to turn out speech therapists, speech teachers, actors, actresses and professional backstage staff. She was an oral educator par excellence, who employed the vibrant, artful and arresting methods of her own discipline to deliver its contents with an enthusiasm so infectious that it was 'caught by everyone working with her', noted a journalist who had sat in on rehearsals.[240]

Nowhere were her skills more in evidence than when it came to directing plays, which was the ultimate expression of her knowledge of the voice and its effective use on stage. To the 33 plays by European and American playwrights which she directed at the Little Theatre between 1946 and her retirement at the age of 62 in 1971, she brought a deep insight which she communicated with ease to her largely student casts. Whether it was a play by Shakespeare or Chekhov, Lorca or Euripides, 'she understood the thought behind the words and all its meaning … [and made us aware of] the music of the language which actually took the words', recognised an ex-student of hers astutely.[241] There was 'a clarity, a deliberateness of thought to her speech', confirmed a professional actor whom she directed; 'it was almost as if she etched the words in your mind'.[242]

With a precise idea in her own mind about what should be seen or heard on her stage, she placed exacting demands on her students. 'She was trying to make the best of each of us', reflected another former student. 'She tried to draw from you what your potential was. Her techniques were not experimental but she stretched you … [With] Van you had to think – she worked on your creative ability. It was not comfortable.'[243]

Van der Gucht's combination of rigorous professionalism, precision in speech and stagecraft, and a perceptive grasp of the text became the hallmark of the department under her direction and, consequently, of its thespian products who stood out for this on the stages of Cape Town and the country at large from the

1950s onwards. As she accurately observed about herself, 'Directing students … is a teaching practice in a way … [and] teaching is my thing.'[244] Even so, the fact that, though the head of a university department – only one of two women in such a position at UCT in these years – she was not raised to the rank of associate professor until the eve of her retirement suggests that not all of the doubts about her discipline had disappeared, especially as she herself held no degree.

Three of the six tenured members of her department in these years – all women – also had no degrees and were in the same mould as Van der Gucht, i.e. trained and diploma'd in England, with specialisations in fields allied to elocution, like articulation, gesture and movement. The three others were local products, two of them, Robert Mohr and Mavis Taylor, having gained university degrees before securing speech and drama qualifications in London. Both were later to become professors of drama at UCT.

Mohr, who started teaching in the department in 1960, was more intellectually adventurous and imaginative than Van der Gucht, and it showed in his more cerebral engagement with students and in his choice of plays for them to perform. 'I make an absolute principle of overseas visits … in order to keep myself well informed about all trends in the teaching and practice of my subject', he declared.[245] Nowhere was the fruit of this decision more apparent than in his production of a play in Japanese Kabuki style and of Ann Jellicoe's radical *The Sport of My Mad Mother* just three years after its premiere in London. 'The play's impact is as startling as a slap in the face, and it is quite unlike anything yet brought to the stage', wrote a shaken critic in *The Argus*.[246]

Reviewers of Mavis Taylor's productions were equally struck by her flair for innovative staging, the result perhaps of her original specialisation as set and costume designer and her keen interaction with students off as well as on stage. As she herself put it, 'I find establishing good rapport with students extremely gratifying and their co-operation rewarding. This may be why the critics seem to detect in my productions a special understanding of the problems of youth and of the modern scene.'[247] This may also help to explain why, depending on the decade, student memories recall her as looking and behaving as, in succession, a beatnik, a hippie and as 'a punk rocker before her time'.[248]

Typically, she would draw on her students' ideas to shape her own conception of a play and then implement the result with zeal. 'With her students she was a hard task-master', judged a colleague. Student tales about her mixed the 'humorous, [the] risqué and [the] profound.'[249] Although Van der Gucht had carefully nurtured Taylor when she first joined the department in 1952 at the age of 28, it is clear that by the time she succeeded Mohr as head of the department in 1988 she had long since put

# THE ARTS

*A sign of things to come? Pieter-Dirk Uys (left) and Peter Kruger in a Japanese Kabuki play directed by Robert Mohr at the Little Theatre in 1968* (Cape Argus, 14 April 1968).

the Van der Gucht model of teaching and directing far behind her. As one of her referees observed, 'She has a strong and independent personality based on a vital response to the life around her.'[250]

Around her, her fellow lecturers and the department's home alongside the Little Theatre on the UCT's Hiddingh campus, aspirant actors, actresses and speech teachers found an environment which one remembered as vibrant, 'a very nurturing place', characterised by 'camaraderie, familiarity and support'.[251] Within this self-contained, close-knit, 40–50-strong, face-to-face drama community, lively exchanges and engagement were the order of the day, the results of which often found their way onto the stage. 'That was what was so super about [the] drama school', recalled a former student, 'we did everything', from acting to stage-managing, from devising lighting plots to costuming.[252] As attested by one of the most outstanding beneficiaries of this holistic training, in which the very discipline was the medium of education, Pieter-Dirk Uys believed that, while student stage-manager at the Little Theatre, he had gained 'a total understanding of the stage on every technical level. That was the best training in the world.'[253] In every sense of the word, these students inter-acted, the enhancing results of which were to be applauded by many a theatre audience in Cape Town and beyond for decades.

Another field which long faced doubts as to its academic bona fides was librarianship. Even though a School of Librarianship had been set up at UCT under the Library's auspices in 1939,[254] it was not until 1951 that it was listed as a distinct department in the Faculty of Arts prospectus – until then it had merely been mentioned among the diplomas on offer in the Faculty – and not until 1976 that it acquired a chair and not until 1982 that it offered an undergraduate degree over and above a certificate or diploma.

In part, this was because librarianship in South Africa was slow to develop a distinctive professional philosophy or image – one member of UCT's Library Committee was still of the opinion in the 1940s that 'library work was after all only a useful way for a poor man to supplement his meagre earnings after his regular daily work was done'.[255] A second reason was that, to many, the School seemed to be merely an arm of UCT's Library by virtue of both its physical location in the Library's basement and the fact that many of its lecturers and tutors were members of the Library staff, who taught only part-time in the School. Not the least of these was the School's director, René Immelman, who was simultaneously the University Librarian.[256]

Wearing his director's hat, from the early 1950s Immelman determinedly sought to address these impediments to librarianship's academic status. In 1951 the School was moved out of the Library building, first to an ex-army hut on University Avenue and in 1957 to the Hiddingh campus. In 1951 too, the School's staffing establishment was reconfigured so as to replace most of the nine part-timers from the Library with two lecturers employed full-time by the School. Immelman argued that the School had to become 'a more distinct and self-contained unit … [and therefore] a further degree of separation [from the Library] was imperative … If the connection be too close, both teaching and the work of the Library suffer.'[257]

With the same overall aim in mind he also raised the level of the School's premier qualifications, the Higher Certificate and the Diploma in Librarianship. From 1952 an undergraduate degree became a prerequisite for admission to these courses, while their content henceforth focused not as narrowly on technical skills like cataloguing, classification and compiling bibliographies and a little more on training librarians to 'interpret books in relation to readers', as he put it.[258] To achieve this, he tried to give individual research and seminars more emphasis in the syllabus, partly at the expense of 'how to do it' courses and fact-filled lectures 'which the student then memorises'.[259] These reforms, Immelman summed up, were designed to give the student 'a more professional outlook on his future work, and to instil into him a sense of professional responsibility'.[260]

The use of 'his' and 'him' in this mission statement was wholly misleading, for of the 430 certificates and diplomas in librarianship awarded between 1948 and 1968, 88% were to women. 'There are so few men doing it', explained one woman graduate, that 'if you are a woman, it's the profession in which men do not keep you out of all the best jobs, because there are not enough of them.'[261] Most had pursued these qualifications in response to the rising demand in South Africa for librarians after World War II, both in the new provincial library services and in libraries being started by commercial, industrial and financial firms as the country's economy prospered. As, until 1958, UCT was the only university outside the Transvaal offering such training, a significant minority of these students were white Afrikaners. Between 1952 and 1965 some 17% of UCT's librarianship students were Afrikaans-speaking;[262] indeed, for a short while, some lectures were even given in both English and Afrikaans, while until 1986 students could take oral tests in both languages in order to gain a 'bilingual' endorsement of their qualification. Less likely to win kudos from the National Party Government was the fact that, until the 1960s, when courses in librarianship were begun at the new ethnic university colleges, a handful of 'coloured' and African students were trained as librarians at UCT. Though few in number, they became influential role models in the libraries where they subsequently worked. Not least among these was Vincent Kolbe, whose distinctive style of community librarianship went on to earn him the label of 'the people's librarian' in Cape Town.[263] In 2017 UCT named the Knowledge Commons of its main library, appropriately, after him.[264]

For all of these students UCT's Jagger Library was their practical training ground, while its five branches (at Hiddingh Hall and in the Faculties of Medicine, Law, Music and Architecture) served as sites for month-long periods of compulsory practical work. From 1953, when it was established, their training also included a visit to Immelman's pet project, the Special Collections Department, in which were housed manuscript collections which he himself, as a scholar-librarian, had zealously begun to collect, along with irreplaceable runs of government publications. Together, they betokened the emergence of an additional role for the Library, that of a repository for primary research material. With collections like the Bleek and Lloyd Archive of Bushman Folklore and the papers of Louis Leipoldt and Olive Schreiner on its shelves thanks to Immelman's energetic initiative and persuasive powers, UCT Library was moving beyond being just an undergraduate library to becoming a research library too. Thereby both the Library and its associated School began to gain in academic credibility.

Yet, academic credibility was not acquired just by virtue of healthy student numbers, though undoubtedly this helped to strengthen any such claim. UCT's Michaelis School of Fine Art learnt this fact by dint of its experience with the novel university subject of commercial art. Its introduction in 1933 of a certificate in this field (which included topics like the design of posters and advertisements, ceramics, and book and magazine illustration) had raised more than one academic eyebrow at the time, but did achieve its intended purpose of increasing student enrolments in the School. Indeed, by 1947 more students were enrolled for this certificate than for all four of the qualifications offered in the more traditional field of fine art.

Nevertheless, UCT's Senate refused the School's request in 1951 to change the label 'commercial art' to the more intellectually resonant 'graphic design', even though the School argued that the former had 'unpleasant associations … and suggests that all graphic work done by non-fine art students is commercial in character and lacking in taste'.[265] Nor was the UCT Senate alone in its disapproval of commercial art or (as some disparagingly dubbed it) 'crafts' as part of a university curriculum. A Government commission of inquiry in that year recommended that the only art course which should count for state grant purposes was history of art.[266] The School's rejoinder, that 'the practice of Art and Design is as much an intellectual activity as many other activities at the university',[267] fell on deaf ears, however, and it was some years before the recommendation was shelved, as by then graphic design had risen in the estimation of the academy locally and abroad and, thus, finally, of academics at UCT. In 1964 the label 'commercial art' was finally dropped in favour of 'graphic art'; henceforth, the School described itself as consisting of two departments, Fine Art and Graphic Art.

Ironically, this formal acceptance of graphic art came just after its main champion, the professor of fine art and Director of the School since 1948, Rupert Shephard, resigned to return to England for family reasons. The reserved but determined Shephard, although a painter trained at London's Slade School of Art, had subsequently broadened his artistic horizons through stints as an industrial draughtsman, a book illustrator, a poster designer and a potter. 'He has quite a strong feeling for recent developments in Art … and has done commercial art work of a high class', UCT's selection committee had pointed out.[268]

Accordingly, it is unsurprising that, within three years of assuming the chair at the age of 39, he had gradually – 'beneath a … benign and ingenuous avuncularity'[269] – introduced more art theory and history into the Fine Art courses to complement their concentration on closely supervised studio work and 'crit' classes and to 'knock it [the Michaelis School] into shape'[270] after the desiccating tenure of his predecessor, Edward Roworth.[271] Shephard's innovations also aimed to give the Fine Art course greater depth, although his bid to establish a purely Bachelor of Fine Art degree was turned down by the Senate on the grounds that such a degree would not be sufficiently academic.

To expand the range of what was offered in the sphere of commercial art, he appointed several professional designers as part-timers. By 1958 their practical skills had added to the syllabus silk-screen painting, lithography, mosaic work, murals, blockmaking, typesetting, and metal and cement casting. In effect, if not on paper, Shephard was transforming what had been primarily a fine art academy whose core business was the teaching of drawing and painting into a school of arts and crafts 'more into line with the contemporary art school model', as he proudly stated.[272] By 1958, 67 of the School's 144 students were enrolled for the Certificate in Commercial Art. An art historian has described Shephard's aim as wanting to move the School in the direction of German schools like the Bauhaus and the Stuttgart State Academy of Art and Design.[273]

Among the designers he appointed were the sensitive and exact lithographer, typographer, and book designer and illustrator Katrine Harries, whose feel for the effect of line and form was, he believed, 'an inspiration to all students that have contact with her';[274] the muralist, mosaicist and tapestry designer Eleanor Esmonde-White, who taught students not only these artistic skills but also how to negotiate contracts that utilised them, thus providing 'a lasting basis for one's own professional practice', as a successful former student of hers testified;[275] and the fine draughtsman Russell Harvey, whose experience as both a teacher of drawing and as a freelance designer at an advertising firm 'has done a great deal … to bridge the gap between commercial art and fine art', judged Shephard,[276] who was equally pleased that to the rather staid teaching of commercial art Harvey brought 'vigour and taste and inventiveness … imparting enthusiasm in their work to students & … getting the best from strong & weak students'.[277] Into whichever category a student might fall, however, she or he had impressed on them during Shephard's tenure that modern art was de rigueur and the style to follow. One student who sought instead to imitate Vladimir Tretchikoff's romantic realism claimed that she was told that she would fail if she did so. She did – and she did.[278]

Shephard's innovative appointments were not limited just to the field of graphic art and design. In 1950 he persuaded the progressive modernist sculptor 'Lippy' Lipshitz to join the staff on a part-time basis, thereby adding an Expressionist dimension to the country's only university-based sculpture department, which, under Ivan Mitford-Barberton since 1937, had been rigidly realist in its teaching until then. 'Students should be given a traditional training so that they can make … an exact likeness and carry it out in workmanlike manner', Mitford-Barberton averred … [They] should not be allowed to let their imaginations run riot, make ugly, fantastic stunts under the pretence of being modern. They can try these tricks after leaving the University.'[279]

Inevitably, the two men soon clashed and remained at chisels drawn for the rest of their shared time on the staff. But, to his students, Lipshitz was 'a kind of apostolate of wood and stone', as the Director of the South African National Gallery described him.[280] 'He encourages ... [their] vision and ... taste ... without forcing ideas on them, and can fire them with enthusiasm which is the mark of a great teacher', Shephard observed.[281]

On the face of it, another appointment by Shephard in the 1950s was an even greater departure from the School's tradition of employing mainly British-trained staff. Maurice van Essche had learnt the art of painting in his native Belgium and in France under Matisse, so he brought to the School a Continental approach to art and art training quite different from the English style which had been dominant there since its inception. His early students were quick to appreciate what one described as a 'fresh, broad vision and discipline' from an Expressionist artist to whom painting 'was a form of worship'.[282] Selected as a South African exhibitor for three successive Venice Biennales and the 1958 Brussels World Fair, he gained a reputation as a white artist who, unusually for that time, filtered 'African subject-matter through his modernist prism'.[283] The Dean of the Faculty of Fine Art and Architecture (of which the School was, for historical reasons, a component) deemed him to be 'an artist of international repute and financial success, an inspiring teacher'.[284]

Yet, by the time Van Essche succeeded Shephard in the chair of fine art in 1963 at the age of 57, he was increasingly out of sympathy with the experimentalist approach to fine art and sculpture essayed by a younger generation of staff, like the action sculptor Richard Wake and the architect turned often astringent art critic, art theorist and historian Neville Dubow, or by older staff like the colourist May Hillhouse, upon whom Van Essche cast aspersions for her apparent readiness to accept 'any progressive mad ideas from young artists' in a bid 'to remain young'.[285] 'People are sick & tired of this so called abstract & pop & op Art, [which is] so very ephemeral', fumed Van Essche. 'I am more and more convinced of the validity of my approach to Art.'[286] 'There must be blood in my painting ... I must remain human at all costs. I am decidedly a figurative painter, and my message must be clear.'[287]

Especially unsettling to a man who believed that 'an unbroken thread ... links the present with the past'[288] was the effect of such lecturers on the School's students. The latter 'are now encouraged in superficial vocabulary' by the former, whose roots, he railed, 'cannot be traced because they do not exist'.[289] 'If we go on in this way, students will have no academic training in the True sense of the word', he warned. 'They will be unable to produce a figure and one day when fashions will disappear they will be technically poor.'[290]

Disagreement about what was (and was not) taught and how this should or should not be done thus escalated among both staff and students at the School. Things began to 'turn nasty', recalled one member of the staff.[291] 'It is possible that I do not fit any more in this crazy world', despaired Van Essche. 'I cannot face the dishonesty & ignorance of our younger lecturers any more & I am tired of fighting.'[292] In 1970 he took early retirement on account of ill-health. After a protracted selection process, the committee's second choice, the urbane and articulate 37-year-old Dubow, was chosen to succeed him.

It is difficult to know how much the intellectual turmoil within the School in these years affected the technically adept, hands-on training which students received. Calls by younger staff for explicit attention to be given to the latest in art theory and research received short shrift from the likes of Van Essche. 'Michaelis had no seminars in all the time I was there', recalled a Graphic Design student of the mid-1960s. 'The closest we came to it was the general crit classes in which opinions were expressed about the visual solutions students brought to projects.'[293] Yet, maybe a sign that the students were not untouched is a review in *Die Burger* in 1967 of that year's annual exhibition of student work. Its well-informed and perceptive art critic wrote that 'Over-stimulation and over-intellectualising in their training has, in my opinion, caused certain aspects [of art] to be neglected. The result is plenty of noise but little music.'[294]

Ever since its inception in 1927, the annual end-of-year exhibition of student work had been the 'acme of the year', *Varsity* reported. 'Prestige is in proportion to the number of works [you have] on exhibition, so the rivalry is fantastic.'[295] If such competitiveness among students grew more marked each December, for the rest of the year a sense of being members of a small, intimate and collegial artistic community, separate from the rest of UCT, pervaded the School. Not only was it located on the Hiddingh campus, which made it a city-focused institution, ten kilometres away from the main campus, but its links with the one other department in its Faculty of Fine Art and Architecture, the School of Architecture, were purely administrative. Physically, the two schools had not been on the same campus since 1942 and had even issued separate prospectuses from 1944. They had little in common.

Michaelis students had therefore developed a distinct culture and ethos of their own, largely uninfluenced by their Varsity peers, who 'just thought we were weird'.[296] Recognisable by their colourful dress, behaviour and speech, they prided themselves on being sensitive, avant-garde aesthetes. Tongue-in-cheek, *Varsity* described how they 'sit in [Kloof Street] cafes and take themselves very seriously, discussing [even] the blue designs on the cups'.[297]

Over 80% of the 342 recipients of the School's eight different qualifications between 1948 and 1968 were women, many of them clad while on campus in paint-spattered smocks and, in the 1960s, in 'bright red and blue and black cat suits'.[298] Male

*Calculated bohemianism. A student cartoonist caricatures Michaelis students* (Varsity, 24 June 1964)

students were most often found in the commercial art courses, presumably with an eye to a career in advertising and printing. Most other students planned to become art teachers or seek jobs in the then burgeoning graphic design industry or work in art galleries or museums. All but four or five of the students were white-skinned.

For all their claimed sensitivity and progressive leanings, almost all of these students were as blind as their lecturers to the crude racism practised on their very doorstep in the 1940s and 1950s, which stipulated that 'coloured' students had to have their life-drawing classes separately from whites, lest they see a white-skinned model naked. Accordingly, remembered one, 'We were led into a separate room where a "coloured" model posed for the two of us in the nude. When I told my mother, she was aghast, not so much because of the segregation but because she thought that for her son to see nudes of any colour was immoral!'[299] In the context of apartheid South Africa, where only UCT and Witwatersrand University admitted black students to full fine art training, such compromised instruction was obviously deemed preferable to no instruction at all by these students. In the 1960s, however, when 'coloured' models were employed to pose for all students, such overt segregation became a thing of the past. 'We only think of colour in terms of paint', joked one student breezily.[300]

Most staff and students were blind in a second way too, since, for all of their awareness of contemporary, avant-garde artists and sculptors from the Global North, like David Hockney, Henry Moore, Jackson Pollock and Claes Oldenburg, the names and works of African artists and sculptors like Ernest Mancoba, Gerard Sekoto, Selby Mvusi and Sydney Kumalo were unknown to most. The characteristic colonial paradox of esteeming distant objects above local ones – a left-wing student trenchantly referred to 'the flatulent reverence of the colonial lecture-room'[301] – was as well developed on UCT's Hiddingh campus as it was at Groote Schuur.

In the Faculty of Arts on the Groote Schuur campus a similar combination of long- and short-sightedness prevailed in most departments in these years. While at least some of their members might strive to keep up with the latest ideas and approaches from abroad, they all had impaired vision when it came to seeing the full range of what lay around them. They were in South Africa but not of South Africa. That the most notable exceptions to this – the departments in the School of African Studies – were also fields whose academic bona fides had to be proven is not, perhaps, a coincidence, given UCT's overwhelmingly Eurocentric mindset in these years. Yet, at the same time, it is to the credit of the Faculty of Arts that it provided a nurturing environment in which each of them was given the opportunity to grow and prove itself, and thereby enter the academic canon.

*A delicate balance. Assistant lecturer in ballet, David Poole, lends a hand at a student rehearsal in 1962.*

*'This great stage of fools' (King Lear, Act IV, scene 6). An enthusiastic Mavis Taylor, lecturer in drama and producer of 'King Lear' at the Little Theatre in 1962, explains the set for this production to her cast of students and professionals.*
(Cape Times, 20 October 1962)

*Blank check. Professor Monica Wilson of Social Anthropology shows blank pages in her co-edited Oxford History of South Africa in 1971. The publisher had resorted to this strategy to prevent the book from being banned on account of its inclusion of banned material in its chapter on African nationalism.* (Cape Times, 26 June 1971)

*Tending his flock. Professor Rupert Shephard of Fine Art (centre, near the door) gives practical advice to art students at the Michaelis School of Fine Art in 1952.*

*At the pitface of prehistory. Ray Inskeep of Archaeology and two postgraduate students who went on to become distinguished archaeologists in their own right (Carmel Schrire above and Janette Buckland below) noting the stratigraphy of their excavations at the Oakhurst cave near Wilderness in 1961.*

*A multi-purpose library. The many uses to which Jagger Library was put are evident in this photograph taken in 1963: note-taking, studying, social interaction and, between the first and second pillars on the right, as a source of reserved books in high demand for essay writing.*

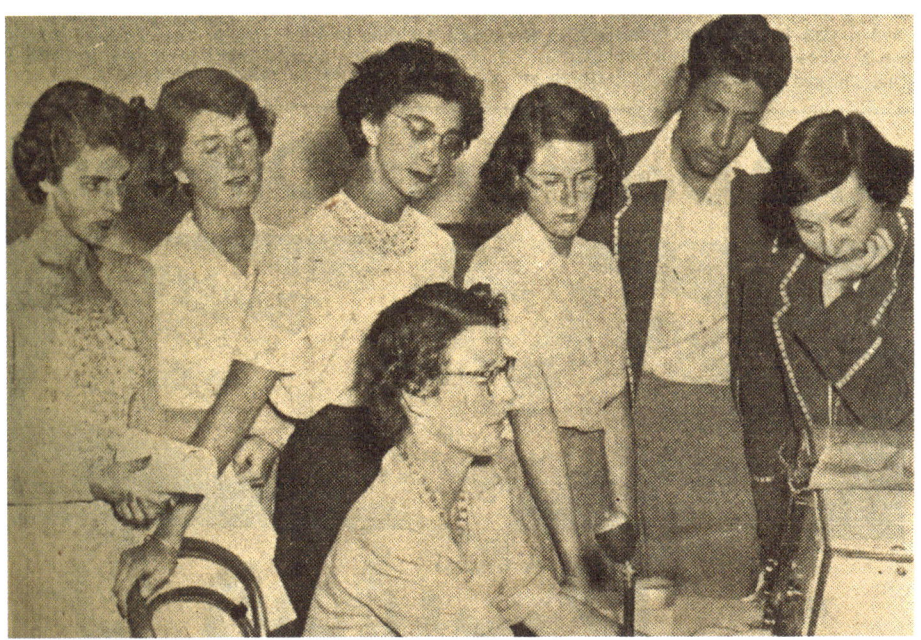

*Speak into the mike, I: Students watch Rosalie Van der Gucht, head of the Drama Department, demonstrate the technique of broadcasting, 1950.* (Cape Argus, 25 March 1950)

*Speak into the mike, II: Ku!wa, a Bushman/San from Gobabis, clearly enunciates a word in !Xu so it can be precisely recorded for inclusion in a guide to that language being compiled by Professor Ernst Westphal of African Languages (left) and the Rev. Philippus van der Westhuizen (right), a Dutch Reformed Church missionary in that area. The picture was taken in 1970.*

# CHAPTER 9

# Reaching Out: UCT and the Wider Community

Teaching and research on its campuses may have been UCT's core business, but from its inception the University had recognised that it was also part of wider society, especially in the Peninsula, to which it had close ties and obligations that had to be nurtured and maintained. Diplomatically its Registrar admitted that 'On our hill, we are as a rule rather inaccessible to the man in the street but … we are hoping to bring the University home to the people, [to] whom after all, it belongs.'[1] The way it did so was by what today is known as 'outreach'.

In 2019, outreach and engagement are standard and explicit elements in many universities' mission statements. The exact meaning of these two terms varies, but, typically, they include what one such institution describes as research that is 'useful beyond the academic community', teaching that 'enables learning beyond the campus walls', and service that 'directly benefits the public'.[2]

In 1948, however, such comprehensive, clear-cut aims were not the norm at Western universities, and certainly not at any of South Africa's nine university institutions. Providing occasional extension lectures on the British university model was about as far as any of them went. Indeed, the *Oxford English Dictionary* indicates that the use of the word 'outreach' with the above meaning dates from no earlier than 1967.[3]

At UCT, as this chapter will show, its limited interwar extension lecture activity did certainly burgeon into full-blown extra-mural lecture programmes in the 1950s, but its outreach and engagement with the wider community went far beyond this, as the University greatly expanded its existing activities in the fields of learning, culture, welfare, research on behalf of industry, business and government, and its production of graduates to serve potential employers.

Not that an examination of UCT's interaction with the wider community should be limited to just formal outreach of this sort. Informal contact with Capetonians via its Lodgings Bureau, which sought to secure accommodation for students whom it could not place in its residences, gave it a close connection with many householders in its environs, while 'Varsity' events like Rag, *Sax Appeal* day, Intervarsity and other sporting occasions contributed to taking it and the image it projected far beyond its walls. As the *Cape Times* formulated this idea, 'higher learning is not something segregated from life. It is part of life.'[4] Or as T.B. Davie neatly expressed it, 'We are not merely a university in Cape Town, but the University *of* Cape Town.'[5]

Of the four areas of formal outreach and engagement already mentioned, learning was closest to UCT's core activity of teaching. Its new Board of Extra-Mural Studies thus assumed the lead in taking learning beyond its creeper-covered walls when it replaced the existing Extension Lectures Committee in 1949. Whereas that committee had been organising public lectures only on an ad hoc basis since 1921,[6] the Board of Extra-Mural Studies came into being on a wave of World War II-induced zeal for extensive, well-organised adult education as crucial for the creation of an informed and responsible citizenry to uphold freedom. 'We should go out into the highways and byways and find out what the public wants and needs and then take steps to provide it', enthused Davie to the Board, under the inspiration of Bruce Truscot's vision of the new British 'redbrick' university 'with its doors flung open, its lights blazing and its great halls filled on wellnigh every night of the week – yes, and sometimes even on Sundays'.[7]

To this end, from 1950 it began to move beyond the occasional, one-off lecture of old to arranging courses of lectures, for the first time in South Africa, on particular subjects aimed at either specific audiences (e.g. on 'Management Problems' for business executives) or a keen-to-know-more general public (e.g. on 'Southern Africa in Perspective'). The success of the latter course given in 1954 – 500 people attended the final session – ensured that its format became the norm for that epitome of UCT's learning outreach initiative, Summer School, a label first used in 1951 to describe the second 'Management Problems' course, but one which soon became synonymous with UCT's two-week programme of integrated lectures on particular themes, which took an 'approach of which only a University is capable', as the chair of the Board of Extra-Mural studies put it.[8]

True to its origin in a desire to make up-to-date knowledge widely available to a wide array of the country's citizens, the Department of Extra-Mural Studies (into which the Board was upgraded in 1952) saw itself as having something of a missionary purpose. But this was an ambition which it struggled to fulfil in practice, as doing so required going beyond the ambit of predominantly white, middle-class audiences. Certainly, its one-off lectures were free, but its Summer School was not, nor were the School's weekday times and venues convenient for workers dependent

*Not missing a note. A rapt audience at Gunter Pulvermacher's Summer School lecture on 'Music', 1963.*

on public transport. Occasional lectures held in Langa were no substitute. With no little irony, in 1962 the *Cape Times* reported the Deputy Principal's opening speech at the Summer School to an overflowing audience of 200 whites and one African: 'The University', he declared, 'regarded the school as an opportunity for extending into the community its interests, and for showing its solidarity with our fellow citizens.'[9]

That 201-strong audience was, like many of that era which benefited from the economic boom of the 1950s and 1960s, filling larger and larger venues year by year. Total attendance at the annual Summer School in these years rose by leaps and bounds, from 697 in 1962 to 1000 in 1968,[10] but the audiences consisted largely of older whites seeking not only knowledge but also social interaction with their peers during the Cape summer. Politically uncontentious topics like 'Modern Trends in Art', 'Verdi', 'Men's Health', 'Biology in Modern Thought' and 'Cape Dutch Architecture' were the norm and, along with related outings, easily met attendees' desire for both enlightenment and social intercourse.

Alongside these increasingly popular Summer Schools to which the local press gave extensive coverage, the Department of Extra-Mural Studies also helped several academic departments to organise refresher courses for professionals like doctors, school teachers and accountants. Most participants found the 'process of "mental stretching'", as one described it,[11] quite salutary and, as a result, such courses were repeated several times during the 1950s and 1960s – in the case of the GPs' refresher course, nineteen times between 1951 and 1965. Throughout these decades, too, one-off public lectures continued to be arranged, but with mixed results, yielding both near-empty halls and also venues packed to the rafters with those eager, for instance, to view film footage of the recent Apollo 11 moonwalk or to hear Sir Julian Huxley speak on '100 Years of Evolution'.

Less directly, UCT also fostered non-student learning – and the positive institutional ties which came with it – by making its library facilities available to a wide range of professional bodies and its lecture halls and residences to those attending academic and professional conferences, symposia and workshops on its campus. It assisted kindred academic institutions like Unisa, the Carinus Nursing College and the Peninsula Technical College too by renting office, teaching and examinations space to them when they were hard pressed for such accommodation. Its spatial largesse, especially on its underutilised Hiddingh Hall campus, even extended to long-term leases for bodies like the South African Institute of International Affairs, the Cape Education Department's Guidance Service and the Oceanographic Division of the National Physical Research Laboratory. In very special cases, where there was a close match between the interests of UCT and two outside organisations, the Fishing Industry Research Institute and the Western Province Blood Transfusion Service's Laboratory, it even permitted them to occupy buildings on UCT property.[12] Clearly, at an official level at least, the University was an integral part of the local establishment which dominated not only education in the Peninsula, but also its professions.

One mark of this was the intimate connection which existed between UCT's Faculty of Education, the Cape Department of Education and local schools, in particular over arranging practical teaching undertaken by student teachers in over fifty schools every year. This was a relationship mutually beneficial to all three parties and one which, the Faculty recognised, imprinted a positive image of UCT on many minds off campus, both young and old. To that end, strict dress and conduct rules were laid down for student teachers, both on and off campus.

Other UCT students – usually not from the Faculty of Education – spread learning beyond campus in a far less straitjacketed manner. Spurred by their social conscience and an idealistic sense of mission akin to that which created Extra-Mural Studies – one spoke of it filling 'a deep void in our psyche'[13] – such students readily volunteered to teach in the night schools which the Cape Non-European Night School Association (as it became known) began to set up from 1945. By 1950 they – and recent UCT graduates – formed the bulk of the 75 teachers teaching in the

Association's five night schools on the Cape Flats. Though left-wing students 'did not like what we were doing … helping to placate blacks by giving them a few crumbs', as a committed volunteer recalled,[14] and though university examinations and vacations interfered with the continuity of teaching, a sufficient number of students kept coming forward, with the encouragement of NUSAS and SHAWCO, to run two of the schools almost by themselves until the apartheid state closed them down in the mid-1960s. The Government believed that these teachers, 'many of whom had been at the University of Cape Town, were sabotaging the minds of the pupils', explained a former National Party MP earnestly.[15] It is unlikely, however, that any of these adult 'pupils' would have agreed. Instead, they carried away with them a positive image of 'Ntabeni', the place on the mountain, and particularly of its students.

A third category of students who taught off campus, adding yet another aspect to UCT's contact with the wider community, were those who, from 1961 onwards, responded to the SRC's initiative to provide one-on-one coaching to pupils struggling with particular subjects at school. However, unlike the night school teachers, who were unpaid volunteers, these students were paid ten shillings per hour by parents, thus restricting the market to better-off families. That they were happy with the coaching and the reputation for success which it quickly gained is attested by the growing demand for these 'Varsity coaches': between 1962 and 1965 the number of pupils seeking such tutors, especially in mathematics and Afrikaans, jumped from 44 to 300.[16] But perhaps improved grades were not the only attraction; as the director of the SRC's scheme pointed out, 'Some of our most successful tutors have been amongst the best and most well-known sporting figures on the Campus at UCT.'[17]

If students teaching 'pupils' of various ages enhanced UCT's standing significantly in non-apartheid circles in the wider community in one way, their involvement in community welfare went even further in this direction. Chief among such initiatives was the Students' Health and Welfare Centres Organization (SHAWCO), founded in 1953 to co-ordinate and steer the activities of three student-run clinics-cum-social welfare centres that had been set up amidst the shacks of Kensington-Windermere, Retreat and Elsies River between 1943 and 1951, and fuelled by the same idealism as had created Extra-Mural Studies. T.B. Davie strongly supported this step as it provided an opportunity for all students (not just medics) to participate in an organised way and, in doing so, to gain practical professional, administrative and financial experience. For this reason he pushed hard to ensure that students made up at least two-thirds of every SHAWCO committee, in line with his conviction that students should manage their own affairs. 'I have the firmest belief that the students can shoulder this', he insisted.[18] He therefore gave his full blessing to SHAWCO's proposal that henceforth it, and not the Peninsula's hospitals, should receive the

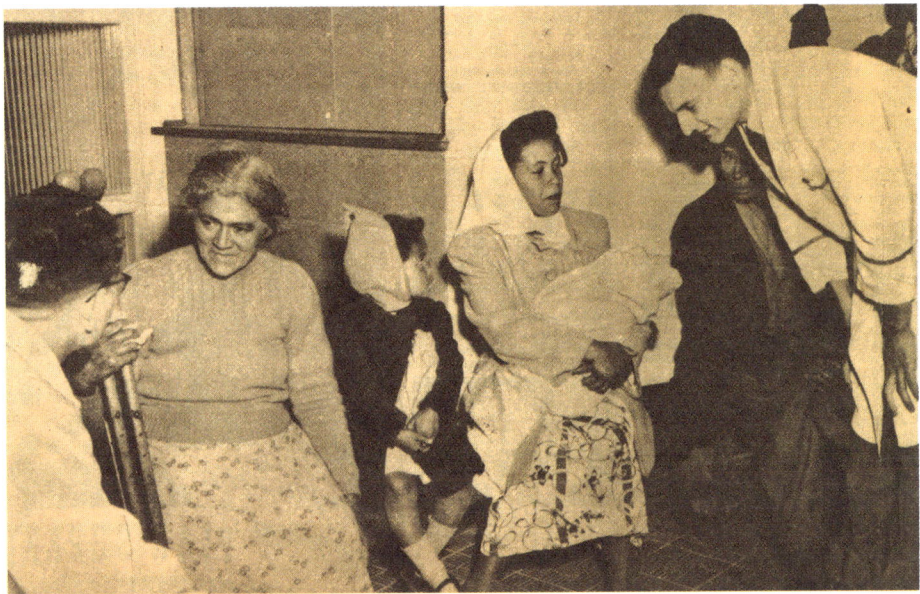

*A cramped waiting room consultation. A senior medical student hears a case-history at the student-run clinic in Kensington in 1952, the year before it became part of the new SHAWCO (Cape Times, 22 November 1952).*

lion's share of the proceeds of Rag.[19] This meant that, from 1954, it was assured of a finance stream which was both regular and sizeable, rendering it 'a colossus' among student societies,[20] able to employ staff, fund numerous activities, and purchase equipment and materiel. It was, in fact, unique among student welfare bodies in South Africa at that time, and possibly beyond the country too. The Director of the London School of Economics thought it 'the most beneficent example of what can be done by a student initiative that I have seen in any country in the world'.[21]

In practice, however, SHAWCO's scope and diversity made it unwieldy and difficult to run, especially if student involvement and commitment were sporadic, which they usually were. In the critical opinion of its first chairman, Professor Edward Batson, the tasks it had taken on were ones 'for which in the ordinary course persons of the age and qualifications of undergraduate students would not be regarded as qualified'.[22]

That it was overreaching its own capabilities soon became evident in delayed decision-making, financial confusion and the frustration of student volunteers. 'We feel that the standard of service to the community, considering the budget, has been very low', they declared, 'and that SHAWCO should consider modifying its objects and methods of obtaining them.'[23]

It consequently amended its modus operandi by appointing three full-time professionals to head, respectively, its Windermere clinic, the welfare services operating at the community centre there, and its overall administration, of which a retired British colonial administrator, A.B. Matthews, became first warden in 1958. To keep an informed eye on its finances, UCT's professor of accounting was made its honorary financial adviser. Greater efficiency followed, allowing SHAWCO to incorporate the still-autonomous student clinic and community centre in Retreat into its fold fully in 1961.

Despite its considerable teething problems – its original organisation was 'basically unsound', concluded its new chairman in 1957[24] – and with all of its shortcomings of discontinuity and racialised, paternalistic and patriarchal do-goodery – SHAWCO did provide three deeply impoverished black communities with basic health, educational, social and legal services, which would otherwise not have been available to them. That some 15,000 residents queued to see the student doctors every year, that SHAWCO-initiated health, sports, ballet and cultural clubs did not want for members until African residents were removed from the area, that the classes run in the SHAWCO community centres by the Cape Non-European Night School Association were filled to capacity as long as they were allowed to operate, that SHAWCO social workers never lacked clients, and that the student-staffed Legal Aid Society flourished during its short life, all point to how far SHAWCO's institutions met vital needs in these bereft areas. Half a loaf certainly seems to have been better than no bread in the eyes of many residents, and that it bore a 'Varsity' label gave UCT kudos in communities very far removed – in every sense – from its campus.

To be sure, especially on that campus, SHAWCO attracted criticism from those who charged that it was practising first aid when radical surgery was required, that, as one 'coloured' student charged, it was mainly about white students 'having a ball under the pretext of Non-White Welfare',[25] and that it was inhibiting the emergence of community initiative and leadership. But it was only in the 1970s that such views began to be openly expressed by the communities themselves, as their make-up changed because of Group Areas Act removals, from African and 'coloured' shack-dwellers to 'coloured' residents of a model municipal township. Before then, the only outright public objection in principle to the presence of SHAWCO came at the height of the Langa unrest in 1960, when some African residents said 'they simply don't want Europeans in Windermere – and SHAWCO is a European institution'.[26]

For the most part, however, UCT students and supervisory staff felt quite welcome while on SHAWCO duty. Identifiable by their white coats, medical students and professional social workers were usually quite safe. 'If your car gets stuck in the sand, people will gather round and pull it out. They know we are there to help', explained one social worker self-assuredly.[27]

For students it was an opportunity for hands-on practice of their chosen profession, which was the great reward. Being able to do so under the guidance of a senior student was 'enormously helpful … an interactive experience', remembered a then junior medical student. 'We benefited greatly from the instruction so given.'[28] Even when student involvement was less vocationally oriented, there were positive spin-offs to be gained. For instance, a white student who helped run a predominantly black African rugby club in Windermere remarked: 'All the things I learnt, the conversations and the fun I've had but most especially the friends I've made in that cheerful slum have more than compensated for what has sometimes seemed to be a thankless, frustrating and purposeless task…'[29] Clearly SHAWCO offered both lessons and laurels, the first to students and residents, the second to UCT.

The most notable absence from SHAWCO centres was a regular contingent of social work students, to attend to the welfare of residents in the same way as medical students saw to their health. In part this was because (as already hinted) the Dean of the Faculty of Social Science, Edward Batson, had grave doubts about the competence of a student-dominated organisation to operate effectively – students' lack of appropriate training (such as his Faculty provided) and experience in administration 'render[ed] them unqualified to have authority over senior employees or to control public money or have the care of property', he sniffed dismissively.[30]

To some extent, too, the small number of social work students at SHAWCO centres also stemmed from their Faculty assigning them to other social work agencies in Cape Town for their fieldwork. Until the early 1950s the Hyman Liberman Institute in District Six[31] was a major such agency, as the staff of the Faculty of Social Science had a dominant voice in its operation, prompting one harsh critic to dub it 'a guinea-pig for the aggrandisement and glorification of the Department of Social Science of the University of Cape Town'.[32] Weekday afternoons would see earnest young social work students descend on the Institute, intent on measuring social ills, setting them right and uplifting locals culturally, all in the space of a few hours. 'Whites with understanding in their eyes showed us how to play table-tennis', recalled a resident, Richard Rive, tongue-in-cheek.[33]

But by the mid-1950s, as the scope of social work expanded, so the Faculty opted for securing experience for its students in a wider array of agencies. It therefore began to place them elsewhere, reducing UCT's links with the Institute, and thus its high-profile presence in District Six. In 1958 this disengagement culminated in the total handover of the Institute to the Cape Town City Council and its absorption therein.

The presence of UCT medical students at the Peninsula's hospitals as an integral part of their clinical training yielded no such problems, however, and in many ways Groote Schuur, Red Cross, Somerset, Peninsula Maternity, Mowbray Maternity and Valkenberg Hospitals became extensions of UCT's Faculty of Medicine. UCT medical staff treated their patients, hundreds of UCT medical students learnt their trade there hands-on during their clinical years, and most of those in their beds welcomed the added attention that students being taken on ward rounds produced. Confirming this, a survey in 1969 showed that 92% of Groote Schuur's patients 'felt it a pleasure to help students', one declaring that she was 'privileged to help them learn better'.[34]

By extension, UCT stood equally high in the estimation of the hospitalised and their families. For UCT, the hospitals and those being treated there, it was a mutually beneficial relationship. With their state-of-the-art knowledge and confidence, and surrounded by a cluster of eager students in white coats (with a green stripe on the cuff to signify their status), UCT's clinicians projected a very positive image of their university. Of course, the presence of so many young male students in the wards – and in this era most medical students were men – had a further positive effect. As one young Groote Schuur nurse put it, 'Daily routine becomes *so much* [her emphasis] more interesting when medical students make their welcome appearance on the wards.'[35]

Even closer to the University's Groote Schuur campus, in Mowbray, another institution bearing UCT's stamp provided a similar combination of opportunities for clinical work, teaching and research, but in the specific area of child behaviour change. The Child Guidance Clinic had been established in 1932 by the Department of Psychology to help remedy the behaviour of so-called 'problem children'.[36] By 1953 it was treating 150 children a year, whose cases were also woven into the department's teaching to senior students. Assisted by the Cape Education Department and private funders, it was soon able to add remedial teaching in arithmetic, reading and spelling to the services it offered to schools free of charge and to broaden the range of students able to undertake clinical practicals in its new, custom-built premises opened in 1957. By 1967 it was seeing 220 cases a year. The relief and gratitude of anxious parents at how once-a-week sessions in the clinic after school could help 'unproblematise' their children or assist their 'backward' offspring to move forward were heartfelt and won this unique facility in the Cape Peninsula much favour in this segment of the wider community. Of course, given the times, this segment was almost certainly 99% white.

The third area of formal outreach and engagement by UCT was the cultural, in which the Little Theatre on the Hiddingh campus and the Faculty of Music were at the forefront. This was the result of an openness at UCT (then unusual in universities in the Western world) to the idea of its first professor of music, William Bell, that their performing arts departments should include opera, ballet and drama and that the University should have a theatre for public performances by both students and invited outsiders.[37]

By 1948 the Little Theatre's role as Cape Town's foremost venue for serious drama, opera and ballet was well established. While most of those on its stage were students, outside companies were also able to perform occasionally as 'guests'. Thus, between them, UCT's Speech and Drama Department, the Cape Town Repertory Society, the Kaapstadse Afrikaanse Toneelvereniging, the Bantu Theatre Company, the Royal Flemish Players, the Eoan Group and the Cambridge Shakespeare Group put on plays there by playwrights as diverse as Aeschylus, Shakespeare, Molière, Goethe, Ionesco, Lorca, Brecht, Beckett, A.C. Jordan and D.J. Opperman in the 1950s and 1960s. Accurately, one theatre critic praised the Little Theatre for fulfilling 'the true function of a university theatre – to offer us also, and perhaps above all, not only classics, but the unusual and the contemporary play'.[38]

To this theatrical feast put before the elite theatre-going public of the Peninsula, UCT's Opera and Ballet Schools added their own seasons of equally enriching productions on the Little Theatre's stage, though, in the case of the Ballet School, after 1950 it had to seek a venue with a bigger stage so as to accommodate its increasingly ambitious repertoire.

As for the Opera School, the twenty years after 1948 saw over 35 operas staged at the Little Theatre, from modest one-acters to full-scale productions of *Don Giovanni* and *Tosca*. Nor did the School's public performances end there. Some of its productions it sent on tour to other cities in southern Africa, while in 1957 it even took three operas to Britain. *The Times*'s music critic sang its praises: 'I know of no English Schools of Music which could offer a comparable standard of concerts and operas',[39] while South Africa's cultural attaché in London over-enthused, 'I would suggest that no cultural incursion into this country has made a greater impression since the visit of the Russian Bolshoi ballet.'[40]

To such acclaimed status the College of Music did not have to play second fiddle, however. Under Professor Erik Chisholm's driving leadership, the College orchestra regularly gave concerts of baroque, classical and contemporary music in public, at schools and on the air. 'The University Orchestra has developed into a vigorous workmanlike little body of strings, a few wind and percussion', commented a reviewer, while *Die Burger* lauded it for giving 'wonderful concerts … of works never before heard in our country'.[41]

For its part, still guided by Dulcie Howes's dictate that feet-on-the-stage experience was essential for every ballet student,[42] the School of Ballet's student company performed regularly in Cape Town and other cities and towns in the subcontinent, often with the commercial collaboration of African Consolidated Theatres. These near-professional productions served as effective image builders and recruiting tools not only for the School, but also for the University itself. To that end, an impeccable dress code was stipulated for the students. One remembered how 'the girls were expected to disembark from the train wearing hats and gloves, with the men in jackets and ties. This made a marvellous impression on the locals who had come to meet the train.'[43]

Along with these performances, four all-inclusive UCT Arts Festivals and a separate Golden Jubilee Music Festival, all featuring students and staff, constituted UCT's substantial official addition to highbrow culture in Cape Town and beyond from the 1940s to the 1960s. 'We are fortunate indeed to have in our midst an institution which has contributed so much to the cultural, spiritual and national life of our community as the University of Cape Town', proclaimed the *Cape Times*.[44]

However, with the establishment of professional, state-funded arts councils like CAPAB (the Cape Performing Arts Board) in 1963 and the construction of the Nico Malan Theatre on the Foreshore in 1971, UCT's premier role in the performing arts began to wane. Yet, as is particularly clear from the fact that the newly established CAPAB Ballet Company and Opera Company were largely expanded versions of the respective UCT companies, behind the scenes UCT's facilities and students continued to be a mainstay of serious performing art in the Western Cape.

To this, UCT was able to add a visual dimension too when, in 1968, it accepted the house of the recently deceased artist Irma Stern for use as an art gallery to display the works of Stern and others. With the financial backing of the Stern Trust, the house was converted for this purpose and opened in 1971 as UCT's Irma Stern Museum, which still operates as such adjacent to UCT's lower campus.

UCT's engagement with private industry and commerce and science-dependent state departments constituted a fourth aspect of its outreach beyond its walls. With the runaway growth of secondary industry in South Africa after World War II – the contribution of such industries to the country's GDP rose from 23% to 30.8% between 1948 and 1970[45] – the demand for industry-related research grew by leaps and bounds, as was shown by the creation by the Government of the Council for Scientific and Industrial Research in 1945. For such research UCT attracted significant funding, particularly from chemical, engineering, mining and fishing companies. As mentioned above, the last-mentioned even sponsored the establishment of the Fishing Industry Research Institute with a building of its own on campus.[46]

A second way in which UCT interacted with the private sector to their mutual benefit was by allowing professional associations to supplement the salaries of some

*Corps de packers. Members of the UCT Ballet Company pack stage props before embarking on their tour of southern Africa in 1950* (Cape Argus, 12 April 1950).

senior staff in faculties like Engineering, Science and Commerce. This meant that UCT was able to attract and keep very able academics on its staff, the transfer of whose knowledge to the next generation of graduates was thus ensured. In turn, to help steer these graduates towards these firms, in 1968 UCT set up a professional Careers Office, among other things to facilitate meetings between would-be employers and those about to graduate. 'One of its functions is to bring the university closer to industry', acknowledged its head,[47] and this it certainly did, to the advantage of both.

Not that this service to the private sector in any way diminished UCT's embrace of the rest of the city around it, for, to no small degree, it relied on Cape Town for students, their off-campus housing, supplementary funding, infrastructure and resources, institutional collaboration and goodwill. To help secure these and project a favourable image of itself, in 1951 UCT appointed its first public relations officer, who quickly took the lead in organising the University's annual open day to commemorate its foundation, two public expositions under the labels of 'Meet Your University' and 'You and UCT', and UCT stalls at several vocational guidance and industrial exhibitions. He also sought to promote UCT in the press and, until an alumni officer was appointed in 1961, to liaise with former students. To the latter end, in 1953 he started publication of *UCT*, a biannual magazine for 'alumni and friends of the university', carrying news of their alma mater and of its former students. It was intended to make them feel part of the University in such a way, a confidential report recommended, that 'they will be more easily approachable when the time comes for a full scale Fund Appeal'.[48]

A far more direct way of generating funds was, of course, students' annual Varsity Rag,[49] which probably did more than any organised initiative to win the hearts, minds and coins of ordinary Capetonians. The procession through central Cape Town of witty and titillating floats alongside garishly costumed students endeared UCT to the throngs of families who filled the streets and the students' collection boxes. Despite the predictable criticism of the accompanying high jinks and antics and of the skimpy dress of women students by both female and male Mother Grundys, the Rag procession was an eagerly anticipated highlight of Cape Town street life in these years, almost rivalling the Minstrels' Carnival at New Year in popularity. For most Capetonians, the fun and free entertainment which it offered epitomised the *joie de vivre* of UCT's students, leaving them with a positive image of 'Varsity'.

However, other celebratory processions in which UCT's students participated (or were invited to do so) were more politically contentious. In 1952 the SRC debated long and hard the pros and cons of students taking part in a procession at the Van Riebeeck Festival marking the tercentenary of the start of European settlement in South Africa. After an indecisive mass meeting in Jameson Hall, those in favour of participating won the day, thereby enabling the University's official presence at the festival on Cape Town's Foreshore to include student floats depicting 'Africa Dark and Unknown/Africa Awakes' and 'Higher Education', and the performance of music and plays. Despite this formal approval of the festival, a small number of progressive students demonstrated their opposition to what it symbolised by refusing to contribute to or sell the Rag magazine, *Sax Appeal*, because it bore a Van Riebeeck festival logo on the cover.

Eight years later, with the implementation of university apartheid still very fresh in everyone's mind on campus, opposition to the Union Jubilee Festival was far more widespread. Anxious not to be associated with a racially exclusive event which could be hijacked to serve party political ends and still smarting from having been 'dealt a mortal blow by the Government' through the Extension of University Education Act,[50] UCT's Senate gave a conditional answer to an invitation to participate in the planning leg of the festival. However, UCT's Council overrode Senate's reservations and fully committed UCT to helping plan the programme, which seems to be as far as its lukewarm involvement went, apart from granting special leave to one of its lecturers in opera to sing at the festival in Bloemfontein.

Twelve months down the line found UCT more resolute in its unwillingness to be associated with the 1961 Republic Festival. It played no part in the celebrations, but drew the line at heeding a call by the Radical Students' Society for UCT to close in sympathy with the appeal by an off-campus anti-apartheid front for the creation of the Republic to be marked by a national stay-at-home. UCT's response to the Radical Students' Society's call not to 'lose this opportunity to show that we are on the side of freedom and equality against racialism and poverty'[51] was, to use a Duminy-like expression, a dead bat: UCT expected all activities on those days, he announced, 'to be carried on in the normal way'.[52] As far as the records reveal, only one UCT academic, Associate Professor Jack Simons in the Department of Comparative African Government and Law, rescheduled his classes on the designated stay-away days to other days of the week. 'I am in sympathy with those students who on grounds of conscience or for other reasons wish to absent themselves from my classes on the days specified, and should not like them to be penalised', he told Duminy. On the letter Duminy, ever alive to legal niceties, noted, 'Dr Simons did not instruct his students to stay away from classes. The work of his Department is proceeding to my entire satisfaction.'[53]

In the eyes of the pro-apartheid public, however, UCT's less-than-enthusiastic response to the coming of the Republic, and its high-profile opposition to university apartheid before this,[54] merely confirmed its longstanding reputation for being unsympathetic to Afrikaners and for being slightly to the left of what passed for the centre of white politics in South Africa. Indeed, to them, as to the Government and its supporting press, UCT seemed to be moving further to the 'liberalistic' left. As chapter 10 shows, such charges escalated and became shriller all through the 1960s, in response to growing protests against apartheid by politically conscious students. This popular image of UCT as liberal, even radical, began to affect its interaction with some beyond its walls too. In 1965 Barkly Training College withdrew from involvement in Rag because of UCT's reputation 'as a political hotspot',[55] while conservative parents began to think twice about sending their children to UCT. One such father explained in 1967 that 'he did not wish to subject his sons to communistic influences' by sending them there.[56]

On the other hand, to some black South Africans, faced every day by the deepening discrimination and oppression of apartheid, even UCT's timid brand of liberalism seemed comparatively enlightened. Despite its inbuilt social discrimination against black students, it did – unlike all other residential universities in the country save Wits – admit them. This prompted Wits and UCT to proudly proclaim themselves to be the 'open universities', a label which stood them in as good stead abroad as it did not in pro-apartheid circles at home. Indeed, so convincing was the liberal image of itself which it projected internationally that in 1963 the president of the Organization of African Unity, Emperor Haile Selassie, invited UCT, 'as a progressive and anti-apartheid institution', to nominate someone for the OAU's new Africa Award.[57]

As with all multi-sided objects, which particular corner catches the eye of the beholder can shape their perception of the whole decisively.

*Crossing the apartheid divide. The former president of the ANC, Dr A.B. Xuma, participating in a discussion during a UCT Summer School course on 'Southern Africa in Perspective' in 1954*

*UCT as a conference centre. The opening of the national congress of Chartered Accountants (SA) in Beattie Theatre in 1966. Perhaps a glimpse of their future for the 'Accountancy Types' shown in the cartoon on page 147 (Cape Argus, 25 April 1966)*

*UCT's two floats at the Van Riebeeck Festival in 1952 depicted Higher Education (in front) and 'Africa Dark and Unknown/Africa Awakes'.* (Cape Times, 5 April 1952)

*Professor Erik Chisholm in full flight as he conducts the UCT Choir and the Cape Town Municipal Orchestra in a performance of 'Gaudeamus Igitur' to open the College of Music's Golden Jubilee Festival in 1960. At his request the audience in the house-full City Hall stood.* (South African Panorama, February 1961)

*UCT on display, I: Associate Professor Chris Barnard explains the working of the artificial heart valve to the Administrator of the Cape, Nico Malan, alongside him. The occasion was an exhibition of surgical research held at the Medical School in 1963.* (Cape Times, 22 January 1963)

*UCT on display, II: 'You and UCT' public exhibition held at the Old Drill Hall in 1963. The popular appeal of films showing open-heart surgery is obvious.*

*UCT Ballet's production of Coppélia at the Little Theatre, 1949.*

*The all-student Dramatic Society's production of Euripides' Bacchae on the dramatically lit Jameson Hall steps in 1961.*

# CHAPTER 10

# Colliding and Colluding: UCT and the Apartheid State

To apartheid South Africa, UCT brought not inconsiderable segregationist baggage, even though it and the University of the Witwatersrand (Wits) were the only two residential universities in the country which admitted black students to most of their classes without formally imposing racial restrictions on them. While UCT prided itself on practising such 'academic non-segregation' (to use its label) in the academic realm, unspoken social segregation by race remained the norm on campus, as it had been since the 1920s. As the SRC explained in 1954, 'sport, and social functions of the nature of dances … are not officially barred to them ['Non-European' students], but they have always refrained voluntarily from participating in them'.[1] Sanctimoniously, UCT's Chancellor, Albert Centlivres, claimed that the two universities 'believe that the advantages enjoyed by their non-White students under the policy of academic non-segregation far outweigh any disadvantages resulting from social segregation'.[2] Critics within the 'coloured' community differed sharply, however, calling the resultant academic non-segregation-cum-social segregation 'a shabby compromise'[3] and no more than 'the colour bar self-righteously decked out'.[4]

In the twenty years after 1948, UCT was therefore pulled in two directions as it strenuously sought to defend its academic non-segregation against the state's burgeoning policy of university apartheid, while at the same time allowing informal social segregation to remain in place. In the early days of apartheid T.B. Davie could hope that, in time, social relations on campus would evolve towards social integration 'neither impeded nor enforced by external influences'.[5] However, by the late 1950s, the juggernaut of apartheid was making it difficult to maintain such a laissez-faire approach, and it became a serious bone of contention between those at the top of the University's administration who wanted social segregation to be formalised and those more progressive students on campus who sought to abolish it. As *Die Transvaler* chortled about the similar situation at Wits, 'the University falls between the two stools of apartheid and integration'.[6] It is these contrary pressures on UCT as apartheid was rolled out from 1948 which this chapter will explore.

From what has been said, it might be surmised that relations between UCT and successive National Party governments were mutually antagonistic across the board throughout these years. But that would be to ignore the considerable areas where their interests overlapped or complemented each other, for instance, in the production of professionals, the operation of public facilities like hospitals, and the pursuit of critical research. Nowhere is the extent of the state's consequent support for UCT more evident than in its financial contribution to the running of the University. From 1954, when it introduced a new funding formula for universities, its subsidy to UCT rose to just over 60% of the University's annual income in most years, compared to 40–50% before 1948. Indeed, the University became quite accustomed to receiving an annual increment to its state subsidy 'almost as a matter of course, rightly or wrongly', admitted Deputy Principal Inskip frankly.[7] More than once provincial congresses of the National Party urged the Government to withhold part of this subsidy to force UCT and Wits to toe the apartheid line and 'honour and uphold the colour bar',[8] but it never did, though, on occasions, it probably was sorely tempted to do so.

It did, of course, have the statutory means to make UCT comply, and this it did not refrain from employing, albeit strictly in accordance with the letter of laws painstakingly piloted through Parliament. Accordingly, it was in the House of Assembly that the new National Party Prime Minister, D.F. Malan, first pointed a finger at UCT, which lay just 500 metres from his official residence at Groote Schuur. Speaking within weeks of coming to power in 1948, he ominously declared, 'We want apartheid as far as our educational institutions are concerned, more particularly our universities. An intolerable state of affairs has arisen here in the past few years … a state of affairs which gives rise to friction, to an unpleasant relationship between Europeans and non-Europeans.'[9]

What Malan felt was 'intolerable' was the presence at UCT of 127 'coloured', Indian and African students. Although they constituted just 3% of the University's entire student intake in 1948, the mere fact that they shared the same lecture rooms, laboratories, refectories and toilets was enough to raise the hackles of bigoted white fellow students, who were quick to report their outrage to *Die Burger* and National Party MPs in Parliament in Cape Town. Response to their outcry was shrill: the Afrikaner Studentebond called on the new government to end these 'prevailing conditions' at UCT and Wits forthwith,[10] while some Afrikaners railed against '*saamboerdery*' (mixed farming) at the two universities.[11] National Party congresses even demanded a cut in the state's grant to universities that disregarded the colour bar.

Nor did these rumblings remain only verbal. In 1950 the country's universities were forbidden to admit Africans from outside South Africa, despite protests by, among others, UCT that this would compromise its right to decide whom it admitted, while in the following year it could do no more than officially distance itself from the Department of Health's decision to close its conference in Jameson Hall to those who were not white. However, when it came to the state's requirement that to receive a subsidy towards the running of the Little Theatre, the audience had to consist of whites only, UCT turned the grant down.

A series of public speeches by Malan in 1951–2, warning that 'mingling of Europeans and non-Europeans at the two largest universities of South Africa would have to be eliminated as soon as possible … [as it] is directly opposed to the principle of apartheid',[12] drove home the fact that the Government was in earnest in its intention to impose apartheid on the entire university system, and so UCT prepared itself to oppose this. In 1954 it briefed a high-powered team to give evidence to a commission of inquiry appointed by the Government to look into the question of racially separate universities. Led by Principal Davie, it systematically demolished the notion that creating such separate universities might be practicable or affordable; nor did it omit to point out that the commission's narrow terms of reference had not allowed the prior question of whether separate universities were even desirable to be addressed. Davie argued powerfully that were such apartheid-conceived institutions set up, they would resemble universities 'of the Nazi and more recently the Communist regimes in which the University is regarded as an organisation for training for the state in academic work and at the dictates of the state…'[13] 'The danger of separate universities is the inevitability of indoctrinated teaching', he added.[14] 'In spelling out the attributes of a "proper" university', Davie 'lectured them as if they were schoolchildren and they hung on his every word', recalled the obviously impressed president of the SRC, who was present.[15]

Such evidence by UCT and other English-medium universities convinced the commission that creating separate ethnic universities would indeed be too costly and that, if segregated universities were needed, Fort Hare and Durban should instead cater only for Africans and Indians respectively. At the same time, the 'open universities' (as UCT and Wits tactically labelled themselves) should remain open to all for the foreseeable future.

However, for the Minister of Native Affairs, H.F. Verwoerd, ideology was more important than finance. He was adamant that apartheid had to be established 'regardless of cost',[16] and so had a second investigation into separate universities appointed, this time simply into what funding was required to set them up. Its compliant recommendations were incorporated into the uncompromising Separate

*Opposition in principle by a Principal. T.B. Davie (second from left) rejecting the concept of university apartheid before the Holloway Commission of Inquiry into Providing Separate Training Facilities for Non-Europeans at Universities, May 1954. Alongside him are the Registrar, A.V. Carter (first from left), a senior member of the UCT Council, A.F. Stephen (third from left), Professor W.H. Hutt (fourth from left) and Professor D.V. Cowen (fifth from left).* (Cape Argus, 12 May 1954).

University Education Bill, which was tabled early in 1957.

By then, bearing in mind the failure of German universities to oppose Nazification, UCT and many of its students had determined to take a stand against the legislation on the basis, not that it infringed on the right of admission of black students, but, perhaps with an eye to drawing as much public support as possible, on the grounds that it encroached on the University's autonomy to decide on whom it admitted. Bitterly, a 'coloured' critic remarked, 'Their defence of the principle of university autonomy is also a defence of apartheid because what is important to them is "autonomy" and not the right of every person, irrespective of race or colour, to enter any university.'[17]

Unabashed, UCT's Chancellor, Albert Centlivres, told a public protest meeting in the Cape Town City Hall, 'We pride ourselves on our great heritage from the past which has been handed down to us by our ancestors from Holland, Great Britain and France after centuries of struggle.'[18] For universities like UCT and Wits, a seminal element of this heritage was their academic freedom to decide on their own admission policies. In the ringing words of a declaration put out by the two universities after a joint conference on the looming legislation in 1957, 'Legislative enforcement of academic segregation on racial grounds is an unwarranted interference with university autonomy and academic freedom. These are values which should not be interfered with, save with the utmost circumspection.'[19]

But, rather than utmost circumspection, single-minded determination to impose apartheid characterised the Government's response. Playing on then dominant tropes in white politics, the new Prime Minister, J.G. Strijdom, inveighed against UCT and Wits for spreading doctrines 'that were perilous to the life and future of the white race',[20] while Verwoerd warned that the two universities were trying to make 'the Bantu … into a black Englishman … [to] be used against the Afrikaner, and that was the reason why the University Bill had come before Parliament [and therefore] … Cape Town and Witwatersrand would on no account be allowed to remain "open"'.[21] 'They are not concerned about the freedom of the university or the Bantu or the Coloured', he charged, 'but about the political domination of the heirs of imperialism.'[22] 'The Universities Bill is quite incredible, isn't it', fumed a UCT professor. 'Our lords & masters are beginning to do things so blatantly they are even giving up their habitual hypocrisy.'[23]

As a result, whatever opposition UCT raised in private or in public – the creation in 1957 of a dedicated Academic Freedom Committee to advise the University on the defence of academic freedom, the organisation of pickets outside Parliament and the symbolic dousing of the torch of academic freedom there, mass protest meetings on and off campus, vigils on the road passing the University, a solemn march by staff and students through central Cape Town, letters and articles in the press, a request to be heard at the Bar of the House of Assembly, priming Opposition MPs to counter the Government's arguments, and lobbying support from abroad for its stand – achieved little besides the repackaging of the bill under the less egregious title of the Extension of University Education Bill, which was finally enacted in 1959. 'Our University left no stone unturned in its endeavours to avert the disastrous course which has now been taken', concluded a disappointed Centlivres. 'It is difficult to see what more could have been done.'[24] What Verwoerd thought of these endeavours to uphold one of T.B. Davie's four pillars of academic freedom is evident from his one-sentence reply to the question of how he would respond to the deluge of protestation: 'All of these cables and telegrams will go the way of all wrong things – straight into the wastepaper basket.'[25]

Such disdain, supplemented by copious quantities of rhetorical hostility and affronts like refusing visas to lecturers invited to UCT from abroad,[26] thereafter became the hallmark of the Government's attitude to UCT, which was itself just one manifestation of its increasing authoritarianism and repression of dissent during the 1960s. Together, these 'profoundly reconstituted the political and legal terrain' of the country in this decade.[27] As the National Party consolidated its hold on the white electorate, appointing commissions of inquiry and receiving deputations, as in the 1950s, became a thing of the past. Ideologically, politically and socially, UCT was seen by the Government as a thorn in its flesh deserving of surveillance by informers, a breeding ground for liberalism and even that Cold War bogey, communism, and a haven for critics of apartheid who spoke out in very public ways against the sought-after hegemony of apartheid. It was a university 'to which a Christian can no longer send his children because of the liberal elements [there]', asserted a delegate to a National Party congress,[28] while a Cabinet Minister declaimed melodramatically that it was an institution with whom the leaders of the African National Congress and the Pan Africanist Congress were 'in league'. It was 'busy sharpening the assegai with which the White man was to be stabbed in the back'.[29]

And yet, for reasons already suggested, this self-same government did not think of closing UCT or penalising it financially for its 'heinous misdemeanours'. Instead, it began to target individuals on campus whom it had labelled as 'communists' and 'liberalists', a neologism echoing the Afrikaans *liberalis* but also, as Centlivres observed, because it allowed the word to be pronounced 'with a contemptuous snarl … [and] because it rhymes with communist'.[30] Thereby the Government showed itself quite willing to assail a third of Davie's four pillars of academic freedom, who shall teach. Its banning of books like Marx and Engels's *Collected Works*, John Reed's *Ten Days That Shook the World*, Erskine Caldwell's *Tobacco Road* and Nadine Gordimer's *A World of Strangers* (which were thereafter kept in a locked cupboard in Jagger Library) had already eroded the second pillar, what shall be taught.

In pursuit of politically suspect lecturers, therefore, between 1960 and 1968 the Government banned or restricted three academics (Jack Simons of Comparative African Government and Law, Gillian Jewell of French and 'Bill' Hoffenberg of Medicine), refused passports or residence visas to four (Hoffenberg before he was banned, A.C. Jordan of African Languages, Judy Bishop of Sociology and Kurt Danziger of Psychology), jailed two (Simons before his banning, and May Katzen of History) and barred one from working in a state hospital (Ralph Ger in Surgical Anatomy). Most of them, along with at least a dozen other members of the academic staff identified as 'leftists', were also at the receiving end of nocturnal attacks on their property, threatening phone calls or suspicious burglaries. At least 25 students were also jailed, banned or denied passports between 1955 and 1968, though possibly this was more because of their off-campus activities.

In the case of those jailed – whether staff or student – UCT was supportive in terms of providing textbooks and lecture notes for them in their cells. Philip Kgosana, a BCom student who had led the march on Cape Town from Langa in March 1960 before being arrested, wrote to Principal Duminy from the Roeland Street Prison expressing gratitude to the University for being 'so kind to send me some reading matter to keep myself busy. It was a surprise for me and I thank you

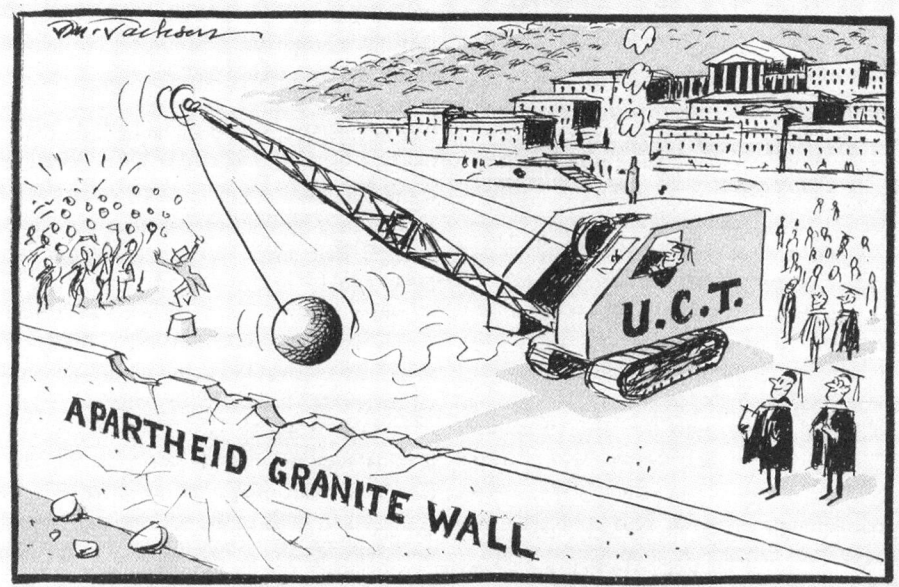

*UCT's desired public image of being a committed opponent of apartheid. A cartoon from the* Cape Argus, *reproduced in* UCT, *December 1961.*

for that. Although I have been completely cut off from my studies but these notes are definitely useful. They make useful reading.'[31]

Behind the scenes, Davie, Duminy and Luyt were also active in trying to persuade the Government to reverse its decisions to withhold passports. 'Please be so kind as to speed up the handling of his [Archie Mafeje's] application for a passport', Duminy requested the Minister of the Interior in 1964. Mafeje had submitted 'outstanding work … and has the talent to attain even greater achievements'.[32] As a result, the ministry's original reluctance to issue the passport was overruled and Mafeje was able to proceed to Cambridge to begin his doctorate in social anthropology.[33]

Both Davie and Duminy also sought to have the terms of banning orders on two full-time UCT students eased on academic grounds so that they might complete their studies. In the case of Albie Sachs, Davie's 'gutsy and supportive' intercession secured him permission to attend lectures,[34] but in the case of Amy Rietstein eleven years later, a now intractable Department of Justice was unbending.

Appeals to withdraw banning orders imposed on its own academic staff were made by UCT far more publicly. Again the example of what had happened in Nazi Germany was in everyone's mind. As a member of UCT's Academic Freedom Committee put it, echoing Pastor Martin Niemöller's haunting poem,[35] the list of '"communist" banned today can well be the "liberal" list of tomorrow, the "progressives" list of the day after and so on'.[36]

Consequently, the unilateral bans on Simons in 1964 and Hoffenberg in 1967 elicited extensive protests in the press by UCT, mass meetings on campus, petitions and deputations to try to persuade the Minister of Justice to change his decision. In the case of Simons, UCT even put before the Minister letters from an array of his students testifying to his unbiased teaching as proof that he should therefore be removed from the list of 'named' communists. However, 'In the face of these submissions the Minister remains polite, silent and inflexible', reported the chair of Council forlornly.[37]

UCT's protests against the banning of Hoffenberg were led by his departmental head, the venerable Professor John Brock, leaving the about-to-retire Duminy to play catch-up amid doubts that he was completely convinced of Hoffenberg's innocence. 'Dr Duminy could have handled the situation more effectively', commented Brock diplomatically.[38] On the other hand, Brock's very public stand – in contrast to the silence of the Dean of Medicine and most professors in his faculty – won ardent praise from many students. Hoffenberg himself was 'deeply moved … [by] your very fine statement … [and] your courageous defence of decent principles'. He would have been hard put, he told Brock, to find 'a chief more fair, more loyal and more resolute'.[39]

Duminy's extreme wariness in the Hoffenberg affair – a member of the SRC criticised his 'conspicuous absence from the protests at the time of the banning'[40] – is perhaps indicative of his growing reluctance to query Government decisions after 1964, in comparison with his earlier stance. For instance, in 1961 he had openly backed an appeal for a cross-party National Convention to address the country's critical racial problems and had signed a public declaration to that effect when it was circulated on campus. UCT could not be involved in party politics he assured an MP, 'but there is … nothing to prevent individual members of staff from collaborating with any other citizens of like mind in taking such steps as they deem necessary for the calling of such a meeting, should they wish to do so'.[41] Three years later, in 1964, he had publicly called on the Government to charge or release those arrested for their suspected involvement in the African Resistance Movement's bombing of pylons and railway cables. 'In the estimate of their friends and colleagues, [the UCT staff and students arrested] are unlikely to lend themselves to subversive activities of any kind', he stressed in a letter to the Minister of Justice.[42] When confessions by some of the accused showed the contrary to be the case, Duminy was pilloried for his gullibility. A National Party Senator accused him of being 'extremely weak and not capable of giving his students direction',[43] while *Die Burger* crowed about how 'the prevailing feelings about the University ... [had been] dimmed ... by the revelation in the courts of what certain students and lecturers perpetrated against the order and safety of the state. These revelations did the University great damage, which has not been repaired by what has so far been said [by Duminy] or done in public to put it right. A true leader ... [would] not be kept from ... an essential clean-up by the charge that he is doing the work of the opponents for them.'[44] Dismayed, Duminy deplored 'the ridicule and the vituperation that descended on our heads when our well-intentioned pleas on behalf of certain members of our University were completely misconceived and used against us'.[45] Thereafter, his readiness and that of his Council to contest actions by the Government seem to have wilted even more.

In 1966, in the face of threats by the Minister of Education, Jan de Klerk, to introduce legislation that would force the University to recognise a student society which restricted its membership to whites only,[46] Duminy and Council, despite the outright opposition of UCT's SRC, resolved that the SRC's existing constitution be replaced by one that allowed Council to override the SRC's decisions on student societies. *Varsity* lambasted this as no less than an 'Academic Munich',[47] and spoke of 'the malignant tumour of appeasement'.[48] The university authorities were 'doing the Government's dirty work in social matters', it charged.[49]

Eighteen months later, in 1968, even without Duminy, who had just been succeeded as Principal by Luyt, Council again succumbed to De Klerk's intimidation, this time over a decision to appoint Archie Mafeje as senior lecturer in social anthropology. De Klerk warned Luyt of the Government's 'intense displeasure at the decision [to appoint an African] which is tantamount to flouting the accepted traditional outlook of South Africa ... Should your Council ... disregard my appeal and give effect to the decision, the Government will not hesitate in taking such action as it may deem fit to ensure that the tradition referred to above is observed.'[50]

According to Luyt, he and Council acceded to this demand (by a vote of twelve to eight) as they feared that government action might produce a retrospective ban on the employment by UCT of any academic whose skin was not white; this would have required it to dismiss a 'coloured' member of the Department of English, John van der Westhuizen.[51] Luyt rationalised the rescinding of Mafeje's appointment by arguing that disobeying the Government's fiat would have been a double blow to the University: the non-appointment of Mafeje and the sacking of Van der Westhuizen. 'This would have been too high & too selfish a price to pay for a moment of glorious defiance and for an endeavour to uphold UCT's principle', he minuted.[52]

Council sought to clothe its third surrender in four years to a Government decision on who might teach with a self-exculpatory statement that it had reversed the decision to appoint Mafeje 'at his [the Minister's] request and in the light of his statement that steps would otherwise be taken to invalidate the appointment'.[53] The only flicker of open criticism of the Government's action by Council was a rider, carried by fourteen to seven, expressing 'its dismay and regret that its decision in this matter should have been challenged by the Minister'.[54] Mafeje's mentor and champion, Professor Monica Wilson, was far more forthright in her remarks to UCT's Senate: 'It is no use pretending to ourselves that we can now keep or choose the men [*sic*] best qualified to teach here. We have lost two first-rate teachers [Simons and Hoffenberg] through direct government action. We are told not to appoint a third. The pattern is like that of the Soviet Union, China, Nazi Germany, Spain and certain newly independent African states.'[55] Moreover, UCT lost a further member of staff as a result, Professor Maurice Pope of Classics, who resigned because he did not wish to owe his position to 'job reservation' for whites, which the Mafeje Affair indicated would henceforth be the case with regard to academic appointments at UCT. Staying on, he explained years later, 'would mean accepting and therefore giving my tacit agreement to this new racialist condition'.[56]

'We can only conclude that the University Council's spirit … (if not that of the students) has been broken by the Government's repeated attacks in recent years', concluded *Varsity* generously,[57] but most comment on campus about its decision was less forgiving. One student leader told a mass meeting that 'Council should not do the Government's dirty work',[58] while NUSAS declared that UCT was 'guilty of disloyalty to the principles of academic freedom and university autonomy'.[59] As demonstrated by the student sit-in that followed, many UCT students agreed.

Colluding – as in the title of this chapter – is an allusion not only to UCT's high-profile submission to the state's apartheid project, particularly after 1964. It refers, too, to the University's in-house maintenance or tightening after 1948 of numerous pre-apartheid segregationist practices on campus. Deliberately or otherwise, these complemented the more rigid apartheid measures introduced by the National Party Government. As early as 1949 a Non-European Unity Movement mouthpiece bitingly forecast that UCT would 'adapt itself willingly to the Procrustean bed provided for it by the government of the day'.[60]

For instance, the University's residences remained a whites-only preserve, even though the SRC had in 1954 requested that an additional residence be built which would be open to all races. With the Group Areas Act recently promulgated, *Die Burger* labelling the very idea of mixed hostels 'a revolutionary novelty, in conflict with its [UCT's] tradition of social segregation',[61] and many white alumni up in arms at such a prospect, UCT's Council played a dead bat and merely 'noted' the request. It was another fifteen years before the matter was officially raised again, and then only in relation to admitting a handful of Chinese students to a University residence.

Until the 1970s UCT was equally disinclined to call into question longstanding segregationist practices at state institutions on which its teaching relied but where apartheid ruled. Thus, 'coloured' and Indian medical students were restricted to the 'Non-European' wards of Groote Schuur Hospital and to 'Non-European' municipal clinics and were permitted to attend demonstrations and post-mortems of black patients only. Indeed, successive Deans of Medicine warned them, 'You are registered as a medical student subject to your continued compliance.'[62] Similarly, black trainee teachers continued to be barred from practice teaching at white schools or from visiting white 'special needs' schools without eliciting so much as a public murmur from the Faculty of Education, while only white students were allowed to go on the Zoology Department's field trips to Langebaan Lagoon because their accommodation there was at a Defence Force camp. This, *Varsity* observed, came as a rude surprise 'to many who think that this university has been honest in its attempt to live up to its ideals of academic non-segregation'.[63] With bitter humour it spoke of UCT's claim to be an 'open university' as 'a mere fiction, useful for political arguments. It is by no means "open" – it is "half closed".'[64]

Even on its own campus UCT was reluctant to rock white-created segregationist conventions. 'They have lived so long and so comfortably … in the stifling and insidious atmosphere of traditional segregation', sneered the Non-European Unity Movement-aligned *Educational Journal*.[65] Away from the academic eye, separate toilets were demarcated for white, 'coloured' and African staff working in UCT's Maintenance Department and the Library, a separate entrance was built at Smuts Hall for African employees so that, on their way to their quarters, they would not use the same staircase as white women staff, while in 1962 two separate ceremonies were held, an hour apart, to mark the roof-wetting of Bremner Building, the first for blacks and the second for whites. Even racial segregation practised by other institutions was accommodated. Unisa was allowed to hold its Cape Town examinations in two separate venues at UCT to which it assigned students by racial category, while, when Stellenbosch University hosted the annual rugby Intervarsity, those black Ikeys who did attend were forced to sit apart from their fellows. Even the UCT SRC was unwilling to challenge this arrangement in public. 'It would be political suicide to ban inter-varsity at this stage', argued a prominent member in 1961.[66]

Indeed, so acquiescent was UCT in observing apartheid regulations that when, in 1965, its long-standing oasis of theatrical multi-racialism, the Little Theatre, was included in the newly proclaimed white Group Area covering the central city, it dutifully applied for this venue to be exempted. Having to provide the segregated seating and refreshment bar which such an exemption required was avoided only because the University was able to persuade the Department of Community Development that what was performed on stage was not entertainment 'in the sense of popular artists' performances … or popular plays like "My Fair Lady"'. Attending a performance of Aristophanes' *The Birds* at the Little was enough to convince the Group Areas inspectors that 'possibly we did not fall under the concept of entertainment as envisaged by proclamation R26', reported UCT's liaison officer, 'nor [would] their colleagues be interested in these productions like "The Birds"'.[67] This cultural loophole allowed the Little Theatre to continue operating as an unsegregated theatrical enclave a kilometre away from the very Parliament where the Group Areas Act had been passed.

Not that UCT missed opportunities elsewhere on the public stage to counter suggestions that it was less than patriotic because of its resistance to university apartheid. Thus, despite dissenting student voices, it took an active part in the 1952 Van Riebeeck Festival[68] and even floodlit its campus for the occasion.[69] 'As the most truly national University in the country, it was our right and duty to participate in such a Festival', insisted the SRC.[70] In 1959 UCT readily agreed to its name being attached to a Citizen Force regiment set up as one of the Defence Force's new university regiments. About half of its members were UCT students, while its second commanding officer was D.C. Robertson of the Civil Engineering Department. One of the first operations which this new UCT Regiment undertook was to help cordon off Langa township during the state of emergency in 1960. The possibility that, in these circumstances, an armed, white-skinned UCT student clad in a khaki uniform may have confronted a black-skinned fellow UCT student wearing civvies is a scenario worthy of the pen of Nadine Gordimer.

However, by mid-year, the Government had crushed the opposition and the UCT Regiment engaged in less hazardous activities like parading behind a military band at the Union Festival, while in 1961 it marched to a different tune at the celebrations in Pretoria to inaugurate the Republic of South Africa. 'The officers of the regiment are definitely doing their utmost to foster a "varsity spirit" in the regiment', wrote one student magazine breezily.[71]

With an eye on its place on the national stage, UCT thereupon invited the country's first State President to the Principal's annual garden party. When he retired as State President and his successor was installed in Cape Town in 1968, UCT cancelled lectures so that its students might attend the ceremony on the Grand Parade. Few did.

Far more confrontational was the reaction of a progressive minority of students to UCT's efforts to keep social activities on campus by its black students in alignment with the standard, 'petty' racial segregation practised both before and after 1948 in the wider society.

Until UCT's campaign to resist the introduction of full university apartheid had heightened student awareness of segregation on campus, the participation of black students in organised social events like sports, dances and outings arranged by the University clubs and societies was minimal as a result of their small numbers, the common pattern of social relations between races off campus, and the boycott and abstentionist tradition fostered in local black circles by the influential Non-European Unity Movement. Yet, the University's authorities chose to believe that the main reason was that a 'gentleman's agreement' [*sic*] was in place, in terms of which these students, though not formally debarred from such social activities, would not in fact engage in them. In the words of one alienated 'coloured' student in the Faculty of Medicine, 'We had to pay fees for sport etc. but it was tacitly agreed that "coloured" students would not participate in sport, or join clubs and societies. We were sort of advised that we should not participate. We did not even attend social functions … For us, UCT was just a place to do medicine – we were not made to feel welcome.'[72] A contemporary of his in the Faculty of Science 'felt we were there on sufferance. We didn't take kindly to their social events, there was no genuine interaction … It was all fake.'[73]

However, in 1958, in the midst of UCT's high-profile campaign to stay university apartheid, a racially mixed party of conscientised students attended a fund-raising dance in Jameson Hall just as the enacting legislation was before Parliament. They wished to challenge UCT's unspoken bar on inter-racial dancing on campus in order, as they put it, 'to show the world where we stand [on segregation on campus]'.[74]

Against a backdrop of banner headlines in the press – *Die Burger* led with 'Mixed Dancing Stirs Row at UCT'[75] – UCT's new Principal, J.P. Duminy, expressed the University's disapproval of such flouting of 'the conventions observed by the community in which it exists',[76] and took the matter to Council for direction. By a vote of ten to two it went no further than recording 'its conviction that it is most desirable and also in the best interests of the University … [that it] abide by the customs and convictions of the community in which it exists'.[77] In effect, therefore, it left Duminy to decide how best to execute its restrained mandate.

Guided by a stereotypical white South African abhorrence of physical contact between the races on the dance floor or sports field, by a wish not to antagonise the Government further so that it closed the loophole in the pending legislation allowing a small number of black students to still study at UCT if given special Government permission, and by a concern not to outrun white public opinion, Duminy forbade the holding of several high-profile dances on campus over the next few years because their organisers refused to restrict them to whites only. 'We do not believe it to lie within the province of the University to be the spearhead in a move to change this custom [of social segregation]', he explained. 'Any departure from it will involve the University in the gravest and most tragic consequences.'[78] As far as he was concerned, 'Ballroom dancing has no place whatsoever in the fabric of a University … It would be totally unfair, inappropriate and illogical to expect the University to fight a battle on a ground which is completely foreign to its function.'[79]

Not surprisingly, these bans soured relations at several levels on campus. A number of societies shifted their dances to unsegregated venues off campus, only to see Duminy forbid such dances to be identified as UCT-linked. The liberal majority on successive SRCs very publicly contested his decisions. 'We are of the opinion that in attempting to fight one manifestation of apartheid, while practising another, the University Council is undermining the very basis of its case against University apartheid', declared the SRC indignantly.[80] In 1965 it went on to refuse any student club or society permission to hold whites-only dances on campus, as Duminy had stipulated in terms of Council's mandate, producing a de facto suspension of all such dances on campus.

These 'dance wars', along with other restrictions on the social activities of black students on campus, were grist to the mill of the Government and its press as they gleefully called out what *Die Transvaler* had earlier described as the 'scandalous hypocrisy' of the open universities for earnestly campaigning against university apartheid while at the same time not allowing black students 'to participate fully in university life'.[81] UCT's 'so-called academic freedom is hypocritical and false', charged one National Party MP in Parliament.[82] Demeaningly, *Die Burger* spoke of blacks at UCT as undertaking 'non-white sharecropping' when on campus.[83] So striking was this paradox that even those at the other end of South Africa's political spectrum could not keep quiet. The liberal *Rand Daily Mail*, for instance, observed that it was 'a thin sort of academic freedom that can be high-minded about academic freedom while insisting on apartheid in all activities outside the lecture room and the library … The Nationalists have every justification for pointing to the anomaly.'[84]

Indeed they did, for UCT, like many who thought of themselves as liberal in early apartheid South Africa, was caught between protest and privilege. It vigorously opposed high-profile apartheid policies if these threatened its own vested interests and the world it had fashioned for itself at Groote Schuur, but at the same time it was oblivious to or deliberately ignored inequities built into that very world already well before 1948. For all of UCT's belief that it and Wits were liberal institutions (which they were, compared to every other university in the country) and its claim that it subscribed to the Western ideal of academic freedom, the reality is that it was at the same time willy-nilly rooted in white-dominated South Africa, atop a racially structured hierarchy which, wittingly or unwittingly, it helped to maintain. As an SRC

*Not Moscow on the hill. State President Jim Fouché takes the salute as the UCT Regiment marches past him on the UCT rugby field in 1970. On the dais with him are the gowned chair of the UCT Council, Clive Corder, and the commander of the regiment. Like earlier Governor-Generals, the State President automatically filled the honorific position of Visitor to the University* (Die Burger, 25 February 1970).

of more progressive-minded students less steeped in UCT's segregationist heritage spelt out to Council in 1962, 'Any attempt to consider social segregation acceptable while at the same time attempting to justify Academic Freedom is both inconsistent and fundamentally incompatible.'[85]

With this indictment of UCT's partial (in both senses of the word) liberalism, these students were just beginning to grasp what a political sociologist was able to put into wider perspective forty years later: 'The separation of academic from social commitment is what ultimately constituted the crisis of liberalism in South Africa. It was a form of evasion, a literal academic-paying lip service to the social conditions that exist outside university environs. White liberals continued to mouth their opposition to racism while continuing of course to enjoy the privileges it bestowed on them. This is … the kind of compromised liberalism which was to come under attack from the black consciousness movement from the late 1960s.'[86] Or, as Rick Turner put it more pithily, white liberals were 'white first and liberals second'.

*Student opposition to university apartheid, I. Members of the Government-appointed Commission of Inquiry into Providing Separate Training Facilities for Non-Europeans at Universities were faced by organised student disapproval when they arrived at UCT for a sitting of the commission in May 1954.* (Cape Argus, 11 May 1954)

*Student opposition to university apartheid, II. Three student speakers at a mass meeting in Jameson Hall in 1956 to re-affirm students' opposition to university apartheid – left to right, Neville Alexander, Neville Rubin and Denis Worrall. Their subsequent political careers took them in very different directions, respectively to the National Liberation Front and Robben Island, the Liberal Party and the Defence and Aid Fund in exile, and the National Party, Parliament and South Africa House in London.* (Cape Argus, 4 October 1956)

*Student opposition to university apartheid, III. Flanked by other students, Neville Rubin (right) lights a torch on the steps of Jameson Hall in protest against the Separate University Education Bill then before Parliament, 1957* (Cape Times, 28 May 1957)

*UCT's official opposition to university apartheid, I. Preceded by two students, a procession of UCT staff and students marches up Adderley Street on 7 June 1957 to protest publicly against the Separate University Education Bill then being debated in Parliament. At the head of the procession are (left to right) Duncan Baxter, the chair of Council, Albert Centlivres, the Chancellor, and R.W. James, the Acting Principal. In the row immediately behind them are Professors John Day (far left) and Denis Cowen (far right).*

*UCT's official opposition to university apartheid, II. With the beat of three drums added as it passed Parliament, the procession turns into Queen Victoria Street. Now visible to the right of the third row is Dr A.C. Jordan, the only permanent black member of the academic staff.*

*Taking note(s). A policeman records details of one of the protesters against university apartheid outside Parliament in 1959.*

*A second protester outside Parliament in 1959, Adrian Leftwich, is given support by the president of the ANC, Chief Albert Luthuli. Leftwich (who was later to become president of NUSAS, a leader of the African Resistance Movement in the Cape and the man who betrayed it under harsh police interrogation) is holding the now extinguished torch of academic freedom.* (Varsity, 9 May 1962)

# COLLIDING AND COLLUDING

*Student protest against further incursions on academic freedom, I. The banning of Associate Professor Jack Simons, 1965*

*Student protest against further incursions on academic freedom, II. Hundreds of medical students honour Dr Bill Hoffenberg on his departure into exile from the incongruously named D.F. Malan Airport in Cape Town in March 1968.*

# CHAPTER 11

# Learning in (and out of) Class: Student Life

Students constituted the single largest component of the UCT community, but also its least permanent, as a new wave of 18-year-olds arrived on campus every year, many of them to leave the university as graduates and diplomates three to four years later. This meant that, like all student communities, UCT's student body was in a constant state of regeneration, annually feeding into the university the latest in youth culture, concerns and conduct, all within the churning container of late adolescence, that stage in cognitive, psychosocial and sexual development which an author of young adult books has called 'the most Technicolor time in our lives'.[1] Characteristics of this stage are idealism, ardour, an assertion of independence, a search for novelty, the exploration of ideas and the testing of boundaries. 'In no other phase in human lifespan', observes a modern educationalist, 'does the combination of … intellectual exploration, moral investigation and physical maturation provide such a remarkable time of personal development.'[2] Such factors doubtless influenced the conduct of many a UCT student in these years and this fact – though not quantifiable – should not be lost sight of throughout what follows.

There was, however, one notable exception to this situation in the student body between 1946 and about 1951, the ex-servicemen and ex-servicewomen who flooded into the University in the aftermath of World War II. Already well past adolescence – indeed, some were married and had children – by the time they first registered at UCT or re-registered there after having broken off their studies to volunteer for active service, in 1948 these mainly male war veterans still constituted nearly 33% of the total student body. However, this proportion fell rapidly thereafter, graduation by graduation; by 1951 they made up just 8% of all UCT students and two years later less than 2%.

Accordingly, their effect on student life was most marked at the very beginning of the period covered by this book, giving it a more masculine and more goal-directed character, both in class and out, as they sought to make up for time lost to the war. 'They are eager to learn, attend all their classes with the utmost regularity, and not only do the work they are asked to do but a great deal of other work as well', commented one professor approvingly.[3] They were a 'steadying influence' on younger students, judged a senior administrative official. 'They brought the spirit of the army with them, and the University benefited enormously from their stay',[4] a reference not only to their academic and social impact, but also to their beneficial effect on UCT's sports teams. While UCT went out of its way to assist them in their studies and their readjustment to civilian life,[5] younger students who had not seen active service regarded them with a mixture of awe, admiration and sympathy as they told their tales of the war, some still sporting items of uniform like bomber jackets 'to attract the girls'.[6] Being in their company was both 'very sad and very exciting', remembered one such student as she recalled that a number of them still showed signs of the physical, emotional and psychological damage which they had suffered on battlefields all over the world.[7] Nonetheless, if contemporary reports are anything to go by, most war veterans were much taken by the manner in which UCT went the extra mile for them. One spoke warmly of how he had been made to feel that 'we were like sons living in our father's home ... We know this experiment in family life to have been a successful and happy one.'[8]

With most ex-service students having left by 1951, prompting the ex-servicemen's residence, Driekoppen,[9] to change its house badge from an unsheathed to a sheathed sword, the student body dipped to its lowest total since 1946, 4007; yet this was still one and a half times larger than in the last year before the war. The intense pressure on facilities imposed by the flood of military veterans may have eased with their departure, but it certainly did not vanish.

Year by year from then on such pressure grew, as student numbers rose steadily, largely as a result of the escalating demand for professional graduates to meet the needs of the country's booming economy. By 1959 the total number of students had topped 5000, by 1966 6000 and in 1968 7000. In the last-mentioned year 7392 students were registered, an increase of 84% over the total in 1951. Most of them were white, from English-speaking homes and schools in the Cape, particularly the South African College School (SACS), Diocesan College (Bishops), Rustenburg Girls' High, Rondebosch Boys' High, Herschel Girls' School, and Wynberg Boys' and Girls' High. In the 1960s two new coeducational schools in the Peninsula, Westerford and Herzlia, joined this list of UCT's chief feeder schools.

Throughout this period male students regularly outnumbered female students by a ratio of at least two to one, the male proportion of the student body never dropping below 65% of the total number of students. Masculinity thus suffused almost every aspect of student life, from male-dominated SRCs, clubs, societies and student newspapers to the way in which males holding office in student bodies, without so much as a second thought on either side, directed women students into subordinate, gender-determined roles as drum majorettes at Rag, champagne-bearers at Intervarsity, debutantes, and Rag Queens and Princesses.

Nor was it unknown for male academics to treat female students as intellectually inferior, especially in faculties like Medicine, Commerce and Engineering, while male gibes were often heard about 'chicks' being on campus to do a 'BA Marriage' degree[10] in the 'Faculty of Hearts'[11] or being 'merely husband-hunters or frigid bluestockings'.[12] In keeping with the male chauvinist ethos widespread on campus, in 1961 *Varsity* began to include a photograph of 'Girl of the Week' in every edition. Sexual harassment of women students by their male peers was common, from wolf whistles and suggestive remarks to 'squaw' parades of newcomers to Fuller Hall in front of senior Smuts Hall men, and American-style 'panty raids' on the women's residences. One of the very few women studying in the Faculty of Engineering in the 1960s recalled that her first lecture there in 1963 'was the worst. I came late. The lecture room was packed solid and the students were transformed into a whistling, stamping mob ... The lecturers were all very helpful, some even went through their notes to cut out the risqué jokes. One lecturer apologised for his language, but pointed out that he only used words that I should have heard before.'[13]

Given the sexist nature of South African society as a whole then, in which male dominance was the norm, it is not surprising to find little evidence in these pre-feminist years of women students challenging their subservient, second-class status and objectification on campus. Indeed, there was usually keen competition among them to be chosen as Rag Royalty or as drum majorettes or as debutantes. 'We were so unaware of that sort of thing [gender discrimination]', mused a student of the early 1960s with hindsight, 'women hadn't seen the light yet',[14] a sentiment echoed by a contemporary of hers who, though sharply politically aware at the time, observed that 'we just accepted' gender discrimination, 'we were not conscious of it'. But then she added self-reflectively as an afterthought, 'the political issues and the racial issues [then] were so prominent that it tended to overshadow gender issues'.[15] An even more politically active student explained retrospectively that she had a gut feeling as a student that the 'beauty queen culture' was not for her and so she refused nomination to run for Rag Queen, but her discomfort ended there as 'gender was hardly spoken of or recognised as an issue'.[16] Instead, she became deeply involved in fighting apartheid.

In these years the bastions of promoting 'proper' female behaviour were UCT's two chief women's residences, New Women's Residence (renamed Fuller Hall in

1950) and Baxter Hall (opened in 1958). That the latter was named after a man (W.D. Baxter, chair of UCT Council from 1945 to 1960) does not seem to have struck anyone as anomalous. That it also contained a specially designed 'swain's room' alongside the entrance foyer for 'visiting male escorts' – where they could be seen at all times by the duty portress – was meant to mark it out as a modern residence, up with the times; at the older Fuller Hall, male escorts were not permitted beyond the porch.

Other restrictions in force at Fuller all through this period reflected UCT's belief that it should be acting *in loco parentis* for the women in its residences. Thus, they were barred from visiting bedrooms in any male residence, they had to be in the Hall by a stipulated time at night unless they had a 'per' (permit) from the warden or they would be gated, they had to wear an academic gown to dinner, they might not put on slacks or jeans if going out unless they climbed straight into a waiting car, and they were subject to spot fines for petty, in-house transgressions like walking on the grass. Fed up, in 1969 one anonymous Fuller resident described the residence as 'like a little island of Victorian standards. It does not fit in with a modern university atmosphere … Have we not outgrown the school prefect system?'[17] Going by numerous interviews years later, the answer from many of her fellow residents would have been an unapologetic 'no'. As one explained, 'I was aware that there were others who felt that our lives were over-regulated and they would have liked to have had more freedom … [but] the structure that all this provided for us allowed for comfortable and predictable living conditions, and a secure environment in which to study'.[18] Another student agreed, declaring that all the rules 'provided a helpful framework and routines for both studying and relaxing'.[19]

Far less comfortable at UCT was a smaller minority within the student body, black students both male and female. Encompassing mainly those classified as 'coloured' and 'Indian' by the apartheid state – the number of Africans on campus in this period was tiny – most were registered in the Faculties of Arts, Science, Medicine or Education. Between 1948 and 1959 (when the paradoxically titled Extension of University Education Act was passed[20]), their total number grew steadily, from 127 to 633 (i.e. from 2.98% of all students to 12.4%); after 1959, the enforcement of the Act systematically reduced these numbers from 563 in 1960 to 411 in 1968 (i.e. from 11.8% of all students to 5.5%[21]) as it required all black applications to 'white' universities like UCT first to be approved by an apartheid state intent on creating uniracial universities. Almost certainly the later figures would have been even lower if the state had not decided to grant admission permits to black students wanting to take degrees or courses not offered by the new, exclusively 'coloured', Indian or African university colleges opened in 1960. Thanks to this loophole, which a number of black students took advantage of by deliberately choosing courses not on offer at the new ethnic institutions, UCT was not quite reduced to a whites-only institution, even at the height of apartheid, a feature which it was not shy to publicise, especially abroad.

For most black students at UCT the campus was not a congenial environment, neither before nor after 1959. Not permitted to live in the whites-only University residences or white 'Group Areas' close by from about 1960, they had to travel long distances to reach the Groote Schuur campus from homes where study space was usually at a premium, especially if they were out-of-towners lodging with local relatives or friends. Daily commuting to and from UCT thus ate deeply into many a budget, in extreme cases at the cost of food. In only a few cases was the well-intentioned Non-European Students' Fund, set up by sympathetic academics in 1950, able to alleviate this plight. In one such case a 22-year-old student was lent the full cost of his one-year course, as he explained that 'it is to me a daily task to keep body and soul together'.[22] About one of his very few African students a sympathetic professor had 'the impression that he has often been short of food, while I gather that he has had some very unsatisfactory accommodation, sharing with some very doubtful characters'.[23] Another African student in a similar boat admitted that, throughout his time at UCT, he was dogged by worries as to where his next meal would come from. 'I was depressed, suppressed and too poor to buy books', he remembered. 'I used to drink lots of water on campus, just to fill my stomach.'[24]

Given the explicit racial discrimination systematically practised in the Faculty of Medicine[25] and, until 1960, in the Michaelis School of Fine Art,[26] the more sporadic but no less hurtful racial segregation and slights evident in classes given by some other departments,[27] and the unspoken bar to black student participation in sport and dances on campus – so-called 'social segregation' – it is little wonder that few black students felt at ease or even welcome at the University. 'We never felt part and parcel of the social setting, we never felt that we belonged to the "UCT family"', admitted one medical graduate years later,[28] a feeling echoed by a near contemporary who 'felt we were only tolerated there, [and were not] part of the institution'.[29] A third added that he always 'felt like an outsider'.[30] Even more alienated was a former student of similar vintage in the Faculty of Engineering who, in retrospect, did not hide his rancour – 'we regarded UCT as enemy territory', he stated plainly, 'a hostile environment for a student coming from a different political perspective to that dominating the campus ... I was determined to show white society that we didn't have to take second place academically, so I worked hard ... and passed with a first-class pass in all my four courses.'[31]

Social exclusion and a determination to give the lie to any hint of intellectual inferiority prompted some to concentrate single-mindedly on their studies. 'We became disillusioned with the reality of life at UCT and we just focused on the academic component of the place, and nothing else', explained another Engineering graduate.[32] Other black students adopted the same stance on explicitly political grounds, following closely the tenets of the rigid policy of the Non-European Unity Movement (NEUM) of no participation in or collaboration with any organisation which was not utterly non-racial.[33] Many of these students hailed from UCT's main black feeder schools in the Peninsula,[34] where the NEUM's ideas had a powerful hold. Moreover, to enforce its doctrine, any black student straying from this hard line of boycott and abstention was likely to be actively blackballed and labelled a Quisling. In one such case, just socialising with white students was enough to produce frowns of disapproval. 'A cool greeting or slight rebuff … [met] me when I rejoined my [coloured] group … [causing me] hurt and emotional turmoil', remembered a medical student who had spent time in the company of his white peers.[35]

General alienation from UCT and the prospect of such ostracism were further reasons for the very limited involvement of black students in official student affairs in these years. The few who did sell *Sax Appeal* or participate in Rag or Intervarsity were scorned as 'collaborators', though, paradoxically, not those who volunteered to work at a SHAWCO clinic in the predominantly 'coloured' area of Kensington. Participation in SRC elections, whether as candidate or voter, was, of course, quite beyond the pale. The SRC was nothing less than 'a tool to implement the dictates of the ruling class', preached a campus affiliate of the NEUM, the Cape Peninsula Students' Union (its telling acronym was CPSU), and it therefore should be boycotted at all costs as 'The struggle against segregation at UCT cannot be advanced through the SRC'.[36] In the light of this outlook, it is instructive to notice that five of the seven black students elected to the SRC in the 1950s and 1960s either did not hail from the Peninsula or had alternative social networks, and so were not as tied to local communities where NEUM ideology was predominant. Indeed, one of them, Elizabeth Thaele, even accepted the position of UCT's head woman student in 1962.

Turning their backs on mainstream social and political activities on campus in this way intensified a sense of group identity among 'coloured' and Indian students. 'We bonded, we socialised together, played cards in the Student Union [together]. Our group sort of formed a buffer against the rest of UCT', elaborated a student of that period. 'My bonds with the group largely cocooned me from overt racial discrimination … We were there for each other. We were all different: atheists, Muslims, Christians, but none of that made a difference to our bond.'[37]

However, from the late 1950s onwards, the more politically conscious and articulate left-wingers were emboldened to air their views in public by engaging

*'Not my bus!' A student picket against the introduction of racially-segregated buses on the UCT route, 1959* (Varsity, 3 September 1959)

in robust political debates on their home turf, 'Freedom Square', a patch of lawn alongside the Arts Block, which one contemporary labelled, tongue-in-cheek, 'the HQ for the darkies'.[38] Here leftists of all political and dermatological hues crossed verbal swords with ardour, honing their rhetorical and political skills as they did so. Looking out of the window of her office in the Arts Block, a lecturer described seeing the Square 'packed with knots of excited conspirators representing every shade of non-white political opinion from the Fourth International to the Liberal Party'.[39] Other black students either kept their political opinions within their own circle on campus so as not to give informers a chance to jeopardise their study permits or they voted – only with their feet – by joining a boycott of City Tramway buses to campus in 1959 when segregated seating was introduced on board or by not attending classes during the country-wide stay-aways called by the African National Congress and the Pan Africanist Congress in 1960 and 1961.

In 1968 those who did not dismiss the sit-in at Bremner Building as 'a white thing' in which they refused to participate,[40] and who bucked the Unity Movement line and visited Bremner Building, soon withdrew in the face of police warnings that they were putting their study permits at risk, or worse. One such student recalled that 'Two tough-looking white cops in civilian dress came to my house to warn me that if I put a foot on campus close to the Administration Building, I would disappear into a prison cell. So I sneaked into the Administration Building under the cover of darkness for just one night to show my solidarity with my [white] colleagues.'[41]

His reference to 'white colleagues' indicates that not every black student was estranged from UCT and its white students. Indeed, several like him recalled cordial personal relationships on campus, particularly with Jewish students, who were also a minority group at UCT subject to a measure of social discrimination. 'Some even sat alongside us', one remarked with a wry smile.[42] However, few contacts of this sort could be sustained for long off campus in the midst of an apartheid society. 'Once we were outside class,' regretted another black student, 'the veil went up and they acted as if they didn't know me'.[43]

No statistics of the number of Jewish students at UCT in these years are available, but an analysis of the surnames of graduates in these years points to the likelihood that they were especially numerous in the Faculties of Medicine (over 25% of all graduates), Law (a similar figure) and Commerce (almost 40%). On the SRC their presence rose steadily from the mid-1950s; in 1962 students believed to be Jewish made up 60% of its membership, evoking anti-semitic remarks on campus like 'too many bloody Jews' and 'out of all proportion to the number enrolled'.[44] In response, the newly elected SRC unanimously passed a motion condemning any form of anti-semitism at UCT. A later SRC rebuked a Government minister for making statements 'not in the best interests of maintaining friendly relations between groups'[45] when he called on the local Jewish community to 'put their hand in their own bosom' on account of the large number of 'students of Jewish extraction' whom he listed as being involved in the 1968 sit-in.[46]

Already the year before, UCT had officially shown its sympathy for its Jewish students when, with the particular support of Jewish members of Senate and Council, it had readily given generous leave of absence to 77 Jewish students who wished to volunteer to help Israel in the Six Day War. One member of Senate thought that this infringed on South Africa's declared policy of neutrality in Arab–Israeli matters but refrained from raising this 'in the light of the strong Jewish representation in the Senate'.[47] Israel's swift victory in this war produced elation in the Students' Jewish Association and corresponding anguish in the ranks of the Islamic Society. A debate between a rabbi and an imam and a teach-in on the Middle East conflict packed the New Science Lecture Theatre to capacity, the teach-in lasting all of eight, intense hours. Jewish students were 'walking on air and you could feel that on campus', noticed a non-Jewish lecturer. 'Among them 'there was a feeling of euphoria'.[48]

If the number and influence of Jewish students waxed markedly in these decades, that of another minority, white Afrikaners, waned. Whereas in 1953 they constituted some 13% of the student body, by 1968 the figure was less than half of this. Chief among the reasons for this was the opening at Stellenbosch University of faculties of Engineering (in 1942) and of Medicine (1956), which attracted many Afrikaners to that university instead of to UCT, which, until then, had had the only such faculties in the Cape Province. Moreover, as UCT geared up to defend its version of academic freedom against the National Party Government's policy of university apartheid, so did many Afrikaners begin to feel more and more uncomfortable on campus. They saw disrespect towards them and their language in the mangled Afrikaans of UCT's printed annual report for 1954, in the disappearance of articles in the language and of an Afrikaans editor of *Varsity* after 1961, and in the publication of an all-English *Sax Appeal* in 1955; contempt for Afrikaner heroes in the laughter of SRC members when an appeal for funds to erect a statue of General De Wet was under discussion; and blatant anti-Afrikanerism in the disparaging asides and ethnic jokes which were common among their English-speaking fellow students. The existence of an Afrikaans-language campus newspaper, *Die Afrikaner-Ikey*, and articles in Afrikaans in *Varsity* did little to assuage such hurt. Anyway, *Die Afrikaner-Ikey* ceased publication in 1953 and *Varsity* published its last editorial in Afrikaans in 1961. Only the Afrikaner Studenteklub survived as a cultural home on campus for the diminishing number of Afrikaners.

Politically, Afrikaners also felt increasingly ill at ease at UCT. In 1955 two of the three Afrikaners on the SRC resigned because of the ongoing political hostility of the rest of the Council – *Die Burger* was quick to speak shrilly of UCT's growing 'suppression' of Afrikaners' political views.

In 1964 the former Dutch Reformed Church chaplain at UCT lamented the declining number of Afrikaner students in his old congregation. Fewer and fewer Afrikaners were going to UCT, he believed, 'as the atmosphere of liberalism [there] increases. The spirit of the Ikeys is not the spirit which the Afrikaner can support.' Particularly after the revelations about links between UCT students and staff and the African Resistance Movement in 1964, many Afrikaner parents made known their 'disquiet at the spirit prevalent at UCT", he averred.[49] As a result, both parents and children were voting with their feet when it came to choosing a university.

Unlike the Afrikaners on campus, the not inconsiderable contingent of white students from the then Rhodesias (today Zimbabwe and Zambia) fitted easily into the preponderantly English-speaking culture and outlook at UCT, which, in fact, they complemented. Rising in number from 231 to 661 between 1950 and 1963 (i.e. from 5.6% of all students to a high of 11.3%), they shared most English South Africans' Anglophilia, their sense of superiority towards blacks and antipathy to Afrikaners, their love of sport and the outdoors, and their propensity for a robust and hearty social life. Where their upbringing did differ significantly was in their schooling, where the British O- and A-level system in the Rhodesias prepared them for university far better than did South Africa's state education system. Enviously, a product of one of the Peninsula's top state schools recalled that in Applied Mathematics I the Rhodesians were 'streets ahead of us – they often got over 100% in the weekly tests'.[50]

Notwithstanding their shared cultural values, on one issue the bulk of Rhodesian students disagreed sharply with liberally inclined English-speakers on campus. Following Southern Rhodesia's white minority Unilateral Declaration of Independence in 1965, UCT's SRC initially refrained from endorsing the condemnation by the National Union of South African Students (NUSAS) of the step, as it had its hands full trying to cope with undoing a Rag stunt which had seen the sons of Rhodesia's Prime Minister and its British-appointed Governor – both UCT students – held hostage until their fathers had met to discuss the Rhodesian issue over a glass of beer. After the Rag convenor had been interviewed by the South African Police, the said two sons were released. Two years later, however, in 1968, a new SRC reversed its predecessor's decision and backed the earlier NUSAS stand, unleashing a storm of criticism against it in a rowdy mass meeting, led by UCT Rhodesians bearing a large Rhodesian flag. Nailing their colours to the mast in this ostentatious way did not meet with success, for the meeting backed the NUSAS line. This only strengthened the SRC's commitment to NUSAS, which the anti-NUSAS faction among students had hoped to overturn with the backing of outraged Rhodesian students. 'So Rhodesia was not the goose that laid the golden egg [for the anti-NUSAS group]', gibed a NUSAS supporter.[51]

In UCT's residences Rhodesian students were more influential since a large percentage of them were concentrated there during term. Given that residence students were generally ready participants in university societies because of their proximity to campus and the central role it played in their social lives, it was not unusual to find Rhodesian students much involved in Rag, Intervarsity and social societies. As the secretary of the Smuts Hall House Committee pointed out proudly, 'Many societies and clubs have their headquarters in Residence, and Rag activities are run to a large extent from within its doors.'[52]

This was so even though residence students made up not much more than 20% of all UCT's students until 1964, and even less than this thereafter as the student body grew more rapidly. To accommodate these numbers UCT purchased or built four new residences on or adjacent to the newly acquired Rosebank Showgrounds, to add to the huts hastily erected as Driekoppen and Protem residences in 1945 for ex-service students. By locating the new College House, University House and

Baxter Hall there in 1951–8[53] and the new, custom-built Driekoppen there in 1965, it effectively turned the area into a hub of UCT residential life, which was reinforced by the construction and acquisition of more residences there in the 1970s and beyond. The long-cherished scheme to give UCT a large presence on the Main Road was becoming concrete.

Within a formal framework deliberately redolent of an Oxbridge college, the seven residences in operation by 1958 – four male, two female and one mixed (a residence near Groote Schuur Hospital, only for senior medical students) – offered their all-white occupants a well-ordered but closely monitored existence: three meals a day usually served by black waiters and waitresses, serviced bedrooms, common rooms and games rooms, clothes laundered and tutorial assistance provided. Indeed, a warden of one of the men's residences carped that his charges 'have so much done for them by menials that they tend, unconsciously, to be self-centred, conceited, inconsiderate and ungrateful'.[54] Nor was the monetary cost of such privilege excessive – the residences were house-full every year, with long waiting lists – but the psychological and physical price which 'freshers' and 'freshettes' (to use contemporary labels) had to pay in their first term, especially in the more tradition-bound male residences like College House and Smuts Hall, was often high because of the time-honoured practice of initiation.

All too easily this longstanding residence *rite de passage*, originally intended to foster cohesion, conformity and loyalty among schoolboys, turned into crude bullying and humiliation: parades in which new men were subjected to verbal abuse; obligatory deference to seniors in word and deed; the enforcement of a strict dress code requiring the wearing of, inter alia, brightly coloured ties by men and bows by women; and the compulsory sale of Rag raffle tickets across the Peninsula. 'Demeaning',[55] 'degrading',[56] and 'absurdly barbaric'[57] were words used years later to describe the practice by some of those at its receiving end. Supporters, on the other hand, laid stress on its important 'socialising and acculturating objective'[58] and its role in 'weld[ing] individuals into a corporate whole'.[59] Unapologetically, one of its foremost proponents argued that new men 'come to the University still wet behind the ears from school. It [initiation] won't harm them and it will help them to mature – it toughens one up.'[60]

In the face of such deeply entrenched support among senior students – not a few of them wished to do unto others as had been done unto them in their first year – and with wardens not opposed to some form of initiation, both Davie and Duminy struggled in vain to curb it. Davie's belief that he could persuade house committees to regulate it of their own accord proved wrong, while Duminy's annual notices spelling out unacceptable forms of initiation (or 'induction' as it was rebranded) went largely ignored. For every exposé of abuse by *Varsity* and every student who withdrew from a residence to escape such treatment, there was an answering chorus backing it. In 1966, for instance, a group signing itself as '74 Smuts Hall Newmen' proudly proclaimed that 'Initiation is responsible for upholding the strong esprit de corps associated with these residences … which is so sorely lacking throughout the rest of the campus'.[61] However, to Duminy's successor, Luyt, it was soon evident that initiation could not be reformed – it was all or nothing. Accordingly, in 1970 he persuaded a not wholly enthusiastic Council to ban it across the board in all UCT residences.

A newer, residence-related practice which got out of control in the 1950s was the raiding of each other's residences by UCT and Stellenbosch students in the run-up to the annual Intervarsity rugby match. Here the heightened political rivalry between English- and Afrikaans-speaking whites nationally may have been an exacerbating factor. Initially aimed at capturing their opponents' mascots, trophies, cups and banners, this escalated into kidnapping high-profile participants on or off the field. In 1954, in retaliation for a successful raid by College House men on one Stellenbosch residence – including humiliating some Maties by forcibly shaving their heads – over 180 Stellenbosch students staged a counter-attack on College House, in which fixtures, furniture and faces were seriously damaged. Police had to be called in to stop the mayhem. A repeat attack four years later found the residents' defences better prepared: 'The entire courtyard became a seething Matie mass', reported *Varsity* with glee. 'Any of them approaching the doorways were dragged inside and shaved, bathed and painted.'[62] Tragically, in their desperation to escape the College House men pursuing them after this clash, three Maties were killed. Belatedly, both universities henceforth outlawed such macho, gung-ho raiding entirely.

Residence students played a prominent part too in the merrier UCT frolics of Rag and the animated sale of the Rag magazine, the wittily named *Sax Appeal*. By 1950, the 25-year-old annual Varsity Rag procession through the central city had become an eagerly awaited part of Cape Town's outdoor public entertainments.[63] Costumed students on and alongside decorated, punningly labelled floats paraded up and down the main streets with gusto, beseeching the throngs of Capetonians lining the route to fill their jingling collection boxes with coins. Preceded by the SACS cadet band, marching drum majorettes and the Rag Queen in an open-topped car, the parade produced a good-humoured, distinctly carnivalesque atmosphere conducive to giving.

Although the appropriateness of the beneficiaries of this exuberant fund-raising was never doubted – from 1954 it was solely SHAWCO and, before that, an array of local charities and hospitals[64] – questions were invariably asked every year by those who, revealingly, found the students' displays morally objectionable. 'Women students paraded three-quarters naked in Adderley Street … Words fail me, for once', wrote a shocked South African College old boy,[65] while another's racialised fears went even deeper: 'Very skimpily adorned female students [parading] through the streets for the gaze of the lecherous', he believed, 'is not commendable, least of all in a coloured country.'[66] A student publication felt that the amount of space *Die Burger* gave to such expressions of moral outrage deliberately aimed to discredit UCT to readers 'who are prepared to believe anything about the University of Cape Town, as long as it is unfavourable'.[67]

Other elements of Rag's fund-raising initiative attracted criticism from within UCT: that compelling first-years in residences each to sell 320 tickets all across the Peninsula for a car raffle ate unduly into their study time, that float-building was an excuse for getting drunk, and that the cancellation of lectures on the day that *Sax Appeal* was sold by students to the public was, as one professor put it, 'contrary to the purposes for which the University was established and serves only to damage the good name and academic standing of the University in the eyes of the community'.[68]

Not that criticism of *Sax Appeal* from outside UCT was lacking. It did not take more than a year after its reappearance in 1948 – it had been suspended in 1941 on grounds that it was pornographic[69] – for it again to be in the firing line. In 1949 several Christian organisations expressed outrage at its inclusion of a parody of Psalm 23, while 'Parent' found its portrayal of semi-clad women on the cover 'vulgar and undignified'.[70] With a sigh, a student noted that such criticism of the deliberately spicy magazine 'happens with … clockwork-like regularity, year after year'.[71] Nevertheless, Principal Davie deemed it prudent to announce that future editions would be vetted before publication, a precaution which prevented further public outcries on moral or religious grounds, at least for the next few years. Unanticipated, however, was the call in 1952 by left-of-centre students for a boycott of the magazine because it carried the logo of the controversial Van Riebeeck Tercentenary Festival on its cover. Strongly opposed by the SRC, the appeal did not seem to affect sales.

It took longer for the third grand UCT showpiece of this era, the Intervarsity rugby match against Stellenbosch University, to draw similar political scrutiny. Probably conscientised by UCT's high-profile campaign against university apartheid, in 1957 the SRC debated a motion that Intervarsity be suspended until there were no barriers to participation by black students on or off the field. Narrowly defeated, the motion was subsequently endorsed by two campus societies, but it was not until 1968 that the SRC took up the issue in earnest again, culminating in the suspension of Intervarsity from 1973 to 1976, when Stellenbosch agreed to withdraw its opposition to multi-racial teams and spectator seating.

Successive SRCs' reluctance to confront head-on Intervarsity's racially discriminatory character speaks to the central place which it occupied in UCT's popular, male-moulded culture of this period.[72] 'By pushing this issue the grip on leadership will be lost', warned a former SRC president in 1961. 'From an evolutionary point of view the student body is not ready to ban inter-varsity.'[73] The SRC 'cannot dare' to insist on Intervarsity being desegregated, scoffed a left-wing student journal, 'because of the unpopularity it would cause them'. It had to allow 'the student body to have its cake and eat it – to be non-racialists [in academic matters] and play racial sport'.[74]

For most white students rugby and politics were 'almost separate, you never connected the two', explained a 1st XV player.[75] For the UCT Rugby Club, Intervarsity was 'the highlight of our rugby year, not only for the players but also for the supporters', enthused a devotee. 'It was a social highlight as much as a sporting event.'[76] While the players trained assiduously on the field for the great day, off the field the three-week run-up involved rituals like fervent singsong rehearsals in Jameson Hall, raids on the other university's residences (until these were banned in 1958[77]), an intervarsity singing competition, the 'Groot Brag', broadcast on the radio 'as a means of preparatory psychological stiffening',[78] and the sale of a special Intervarsity brochure, *Vuga SACS*. The mounting excitement on campus – and not just among students either – reached a riotous climax on the Saturday of the match, held one year at Newlands and one year at Stellenbosch. Clad in distinctively coloured outfits, students from the two universities, under the baton of cheerleaders, strove, amid sporadic exchanges of flour bombs, to out-sing and out-taunt their rivals. Typical was a gibe by a UCT cheerleader after the Ikeys had opened the score in the 1948 match: 'The first blood to us, Maties. By the end of the day, you'll need a transfusion.'[79]

The end-of-match whistle was the signal for the final act in the day's spectacle, dancing and more drinking, either to celebrate a victory or to lift the spirits after a defeat. Between 1948 and 1968 UCT students did the former six times and the latter twelve; the remaining Intervarsities were drawn.

Although by far paramount, rugby was just one of over 20 sports played at UCT in 1948, a figure that rose to 32 by 1968. To cater for the most popular of these, a set of squash courts was built and a soccer field laid out and floodlit, but it was not until UCT bought a large tract of land in Pinelands in 1959 that the prospect of an extensive UCT sports ground became feasible. Part was taken into use in 1963 and, to this, additional facilities were added over the next few years. However, its distance from campus made it unappealing to student clubs, and so, from 1993, some of its land began to be turned into a retirement village.

Which codes were added in this period and which disappeared reflected the changing sporting culture among UCT's students. The addition of karate and judo in the 1960s owed a great deal to, respectively, the popularity of martial arts films and the deep impression which images of judokas at the Tokyo Olympics had on the Western world, of which UCT was eagerly part. The surfing and underwater clubs, on the other hand, owed their establishment at UCT in the late 1960s to influences emanating from the United States, especially from California. From the US too came exposure to other new codes, which saw, for instance, basketball and volleyball introduced in 1960 and 1968 respectively.

The two sporting clubs which expired in the same period did so for quite different but equally telling reasons: the Golf Club because its idiosyncratic golf course behind Jameson Hall was appropriated for new academic buildings in the mid-1950s, and the Jukskei Club because of the move of its chief pool of members, Afrikaners, to Stellenbosch University at the same time. For their comings, goings and stayings, UCT's sport clubs have a revealing tale to tell of student culture both local and international, and of the interaction between the two.

The same is true of student societies. The creation of thirteen new faculty- or department-centred societies in this period reflects either a new discipline's emergence on campus (e.g. chemical engineering) or its maturation (as in the case of archaeology) to a point where enough students were keen to commit to it out of class; while the flowering of six political societies (several as fronts for the youth wings of political parties, which were, at least officially, not allowed to operate at UCT) coincided with the heightened political consciousness among students as apartheid was rolled out both on and off campus. For example, the Student Fellowship Society was founded in 1960 specifically for 'fostering inter-racial contact among, and co-operation between, students',[80] while the Radical Students' Society was launched in the same year 'to encourage a radical approach' to South Africa's social, economic and political affairs[81] and 'to encourage non-racial thinking on the campus'.[82] At the opposite end of the white political spectrum were the short-lived, unashamedly pro-apartheid Conservative Students' Association set up in 1964 and its apparently milder rival, the Independent Student Union, which portrayed itself as moderate, rational and 'opposed to any form of extremism', by which it understood, tellingly, universal suffrage, communism and the Bantustan system.[83]

If even university apartheid after 1959 did not prevent the inception of a Students' Islamic Society in 1962 – evidence of a slightly increasing Muslim presence at UCT, especially in the Faculties of Medicine and Engineering – the policy of apartheid did derail attempts at Christian ecumenism on campus. Under pressure from its Afrikaner members within and from the Government without, in 1965 the 69-year-old Students' Christian Association (SCA) split into four autonomous, racially based bodies. Triumphant, Afrikaner members rejoiced at the achievement of their long-cherished aim that no longer would the 'outlook of the one [denomination] … be forced upon the other … We believe in unity through diversity.'[84] Thereby the SCA was reduced to a whites-only, English-speaking, Protestant organisation – collaboration with the Catholic Kolbe Society was a bridge too far for it – its interdenominational claims a shadow of what they had once been. Henceforth, it consequently lacked that drawcard which had previously attracted students hesitant about its evangelism. This showed in its falling membership.

Declining membership was also responsible for the demise of several other societies in these years, as enthusiasm for their subject matter proved transient, unable to survive either a department's indifference (as in the case of the Education Society) or the absence of a fixed constituency, as the short-lived International Relations Society discovered. On the other hand, what did thrive were new cultural societies in which artistic, photographic, film, broadcasting, musical and ethno-nationalist focuses provided sustained appeal. For this reason, new societies founded in this period for students of German, French, Italian or Greek descent flourished as did the longstanding Students' Jewish Association, while the appreciation and promotion of a wide array of musical genres, new and old, held consistent appeal. The Jazz Appreciation Society even took upon itself, on its inception in 1951, the missionary task of dispelling 'the aura of misunderstanding, distastefulness and ridicule which surrounds the music'.[85] Despite this ebb and flow of student societies, their number trended upwards in these years, the 27 societies in existence in 1950 rising to 43 in 1967.

All these societies fell under the authority of the SRC, the supreme organ of student self-government at UCT. Elected annually in terms of a constitution approved by the University's Senate and Council, from 1949 to 1967 it consisted of fifteen members chosen by students, although briefly (1953–9) this number was raised to seventeen to lighten the workload of individual office-bearers. Until 1951 the student electorate was divided into overlapping constituencies consisting of residence students, day students and students-by-faculty, but in that year these cumbersome categories were replaced by an open system in which any student might vote for any candidate. That this meant that no SRC member represented an officially demarcated constituency made candidates' political or social views as important to voters as their personal knowledge of particular faculties or residences. This often produced, as an unanticipated consequence, what one student labelled 'ideological block representation',[86] which intensified the politicisation of successive SRCs, something that was to irk the UCT authorities to the point of confrontation in the 1960s. Out of the consequent constitutional crisis[87] there emerged in 1968 a larger, 21-member SRC, elected by a combination of faculty constituencies and a single, open constituency.

In general, therefore, the SRCs of the 1950 and 1960s had a left-of-centre orientation (at least on the white South African political spectrum), though middle-of-the-road and conservative opinions were never without a voice or three on the SRC. Marginalised, they complained of 'ideological tub-thumpers'[88] and 'political mongers'[89] on the SRC. In this vein, a *Varsity* columnist, having read the earnest election manifestos of all the candidates in the forthcoming election, commented that many candidates were 'prematurely preparing to shoulder the problems of Africa rather than the University'.[90] Despite such political grandstanding, voter turnout averaged 44%, even in the politically charged 1960s.

Although, officially, candidates for the SRC were not permitted to identify themselves with a national political party, the reality was that many inclined to the United Party until the 1950s, and thereafter to the Liberal and the Progressive parties. A few stood even further to the left, sympathising with the Congress of Democrats and the banned South African Communist Party. The NEUM's non-collaboration doctrine meant that no one on the SRC espoused its views.

Women and black[91] members of the SRC were few and far between; indeed, the SRCs of 1956–8 were exclusively male. Not surprisingly, Law, Arts and Medical Faculty students were the most numerous on the SRCs; at the other end of the scale, there were very few SRC members from the geographically distant Faculties of Music and of Fine Art and Architecture, or from Education, many of whose students spent weeks at a time practice-teaching off campus.

On Senate and Council the SRC had no representation. The closest it came to this was the informal arrangement instituted in 1943 whereby a professor and a Council member nominated by the SRC would consult with it on student-related matters due to come before Senate and Council respectively. Attempts to go beyond this were rejected by Council – including the SRC's request to be represented on its Student Affairs Committee created in 1962[92] – while a joint staff–student discussion group initiated by Duminy was short-lived. 'There is a regrettable lack of sympathy and rapport between students and those in authority over them', regretted one SRC president. 'This is far more noticeable in the case of Council than in the case of Senate.'[93] A candid private comment by the chair of Council, Allan Stephen, confirms this tellingly. 'I must say that my feeling towards these people is one of complete contempt', he told Duminy in 1964. 'For some years I have had scant respect for the SRC as a body … The control of that important institution has been in the hands of a poor type of student.'[94]

Yet, until the mid-1960s, there did remain in place several less public forums at UCT, constituted on the basis of Davie's conviction that students should have a significant voice in decisions affecting their out-of-classroom activities. In 1952 he had given form to this more inclusive idea by creating – albeit not without encountering resistance from some on Senate and Council – an overarching Student Amenities Finance Committee (SAFC) to assume responsibility for the allocation and oversight of expenditure by committees dealing with non-academic matters like student clubs and societies, student health, refectories, visits by eminent lecturers, Rag, and the health and welfare outreach programme run by SHAWCO.[95]

What was revolutionary about the SAFC and the committees financially dependent on it was that their membership was dominated by students nominated by the SRC, usually in a staff–student ratio of one to two. It was, Davie proudly announced, an 'experiment in delegation of major control of funds for student amenities to students themselves',[96] so that they could gain hands-on experience of administration and management as part of their being at UCT. By 1957 the SAFC was handling a budget of close to £60,000 annually. 'This is a considerable responsibility for a Committee composed mainly of undergraduates', noted a senior professor.[97] Moreover, in subsequent years, this sum grew even larger, for, as the number of students rose, so did the funding allocated to their amenities. By 1963 its budget exceeded the sum of all the maintenance grants made to UCT departments, to the concern of both the University's accountants and its auditors. At the same time, the burgeoning committees answerable to it felt that they had outgrown its authority. Thus, one by one, they sought independence from it. With Duminy and the University Council increasingly at odds with student leaders too (as will be seen below), in 1968 the SAFC was disbanded and replaced by a new Student Affairs Administration Department located in Bremner Building. Unlike its predecessor, its controlling Student Affairs Committee consisted of members of Council and Senate 'and of Student Representatives who attend meetings of the Committee by invitation'.[98] After sixteen years, Davie's far-sighted experiment had been terminated.

Another student-related innovation to win Davie's backing was the creation by the SRC of a Day Students' Council in 1951 to try to draw more fully into campus life those who actually made up the bulk (75–80%) of students. Elected by students living in eight constituencies across the Peninsula, the new council tried hard to foster a sense of identity among its charges by publishing a dedicated campus newspaper and by arranging social and sporting events for those whom it defined, with unwitting sexism, as 'daymen'. But the array of students falling into this category was too scattered around the Peninsula, too diverse in their interests, and lived too far away from the Groote Schuur campus to get there easily after hours for these efforts to succeed. Even subsidised transport and supper could not draw more than a handful onto campus at night to attend specially arranged society meetings. 'The relative isolation of the campus has made the organisation of daymen quite a headache', admitted the SRC,[99] and so in 1967 the Day Students' Council was allowed to die unmourned.

Even shorter-lived (1961–5) was the fruit of another SRC initiative aimed at being inclusive, the Hiddingh Hall Council. However, its ambition to turn students there into a distinct community with its own identity was quickly overwhelmed by its inability to provide basic amenities and parking for the part-time students who flocked to that city campus in the late afternoon or to draw them into any activity other than lectures and tutorials, which to them were 'an end, and not a means to their participation in the affairs and activities of the University'.[100] Hiddingh Hall 'plays the role of a Technical College, not of a University', judged a disapproving inquiry into conditions there. It is 'a travesty of a University'. There reigned on that campus 'an attitude of complete indifference and disinterest towards the University and its activities on the part of part-time students'.[101] Thinking back to his years at Hiddingh, a former student confirmed this outlook among his fellow students. 'I can't remember ever feeling part of UCT', he recalled. 'There was no social hub at Hiddingh. When I wanted to play rugby, I joined an outside club, Hamiltons, not UCT.'[102] No wonder that one student labelled it 'Hidden Hall' when it came to SRC elections,[103] even though the students there constituted about 15% of the entire electorate.

Far more influential, lasting and significant an initiative by the SRC was the founding of a student newspaper, *Varsity*, in 1942.[104] Although, formally, it was responsible to the SRC, which appointed a new editor each year, he (no woman filled this position until the 1980s[105]) enjoyed almost complete editorial freedom. '*Varsity* is not a barrel-organ, with the SRC turning the handle and *Varsity* playing the tune', insisted one SRC president in a striking metaphor.[106] Usually leftward-leaning in its political and social sympathies, *Varsity* aimed 'not only to reflect campus opinion, but [to] attempt to lead it forward', acknowledged one of its editors.[107]

To that end, in addition to campus and sporting news and film and music reviews, it included editorials, special articles, features and exposés which challenged mainstream white thinking. From such critiques UCT and its top decision-making bodies were not exempt, especially during Duminy's principalship. Twice, in 1966 and 1967, *Varsity* was temporarily suspended for what he and his Council felt were excessively critical comments about them. 'The slurs which it cast on the University Council were the last straw in a big load of hay which has been accumulating over the last few months', explained Duminy.[108] In addition, publishing articles which were deemed to be immoral or blasphemous saw two editors removed; subsequently, one was barred from membership of any UCT club or society and the other effectively rusticated. The latter held that Duminy's action was an 'attempt to disguise political censorship in the form of a morals charge [and] will fool no one'.[109] 'We always assumed Duminy didn't like *Varsity* because of its relentlessly left line', he recounted nearly fifty year later.[110]

How widely read by students *Varsity* was it is difficult to know. Its price of 3d certainly was no barrier to its being purchased. One editor recalled how, on publication day, 'stacks of papers were placed on tables at the top of Jameson Hall steps and most students picked up copies'.[111] By 1963 each edition was running to 1850 copies (for a student body of 5853). It had become a weekly only recently, in 1958; until then it had been what one SRC president slightly described as 'an irregularly produced, tatty broadsheet, the private hobby-horse of the editor'.[112] This situation was transformed by the switch to a weekly publication, streamlining every aspect, from reporting and editing to advertising, management and distribution. Already by 1960 the UCT delegation to NUSAS's annual congress was praising 'what excellent effects' the new-style *Varsity* was having on campus;[113] indeed, at the request of the University of the Witwatersrand, a special airmail edition was being sent there every week.

*Varsity*'s left-of-centre political and social viewpoint was, of course, not just the result of individual editors' personal politics. Having been chosen by the SRC, he was *ipso facto* in broad sympathy with the dominant views on that body. This dominance was, in turn, the product of effective electoral organisation and caucusing by successive cohorts of liberal-minded students, who, in the 1950s and 1960s, occupied the centre stage of student politics at UCT and Witwatersrand University in particular. On them the ideas circulating within NUSAS had a marked influence, for in the South Africa of those decades NUSAS became an increasingly prominent voice of left-of-centre political views, especially as dedicated political parties and organisations expressing such sentiments were banned by the Government or forced to disband.

With NUSAS, successive SRCs at UCT had a very close relationship. Except for a short period in 1948–9 when the then middle-of-the-road SRC was at odds with NUSAS and moved to withdraw its membership over the latter's too radical stance on racial equality on campuses, the two bodies were usually in accord with each other. A member of the SRC who was also a leading member of the local NUSAS branch at UCT recalled that the SRC saw itself 'almost as a franchise of NUSAS. There was certainly much overlap of people and views.'[114] It is therefore no surprise to find that seven NUSAS presidents between 1948 and 1969 had previously served on UCT's SRC, i.e. more than from any other South African university.

Because of this congruity and the presence in Cape Town of NUSAS's head office, UCT's SRCs tended to echo at a local level what NUSAS was saying and doing nationally, and also to attract similar invective from the Government and its media on the right and from the political left at the other extreme. NUSAS was in the 'grip of small groups of almost fanatical leftist-liberals not to mention communists', proclaimed the state radio service in McCarthyite tropes, and they were being 'helped and encouraged ... by lecturers and professors of the same rosy complexion'.[115] As far as the then Minister of Justice, B.J. Vorster, was concerned, NUSAS was obviously 'communist-inspired, and was a much greater force in our universities than ... realise[d]; it controlled SRC elections and dictated policies of student societies',[116] he told a delegation of university principals.

From the other end of the political spectrum, NUSAS and the SRC at UCT were tarred with the same brush by a radical member of both who blasted each as 'a middle class group trying to salve its political conscience by passing motions deploring actions of the Government, but doing nothing except trying to change the attitudes of white students, asking them to undergo a change of heart'.[117]

As state repression escalated and the country's political temperature rose from 1960, NUSAS adopted a more overt political stance, advocating a socially engaged position for students (the so-called 'student-in-society' stance) which went well beyond focusing narrowly on only students' immediate needs (the 'student-as-student' position). Occasionally, in this highly charged environment, even its relationship with UCT's SRC was put under strain, as it had been in 1948–9. In 1964 a kite flown by NUSAS's president, Jonty Driver, suggesting that the organisation become the 'avant-garde of the people ... the student wing of the liberation movement ... on the basis of an African majority membership, of African decision-making ... and of non-racialism',[118] elicited a motion by the SRC to dissociate itself from such a view and the resignation of over 170 UCT students from NUSAS. Along with the conviction shortly afterwards of several former NUSAS office-bearers (including a recent president, Adrian Leftwich) for their part in the African Resistance Movement's sabotage attacks on state facilities, this tilted the balance against NUSAS on campus. To try to mitigate this negative effect, in 1965 NUSAS agreed to revise its formal relationship with UCT's SRC to head off the University authorities' bid to secure complete disaffiliation. Whereas previously all students had automatically been members of NUSAS by virtue of the SRC's membership of that organisation, henceforth the SRC's centre-only membership applied to it only and did not bind UCT students to NUSAS's decisions. Tendering his emphatic resignation from 'the pseudo-political organisation called NUSAS', a disaffected mechanical engineering student invoked a standard stereotype of the organisation, jeering, 'If ever Nusas

*Reaching rhetorical heights: Senator Bobby Kennedy delivering the NUSAS Annual Day of Affirmation Address in Jameson Hall, 6 June 1966. Alongside him sits the SRC President Charles Diamond behind whom sits the Acting President of NUSAS, Margaret Marshall. The chair to Kennedy's left was left empty to mark the enforced absence of NUSAS President, Ian Robertson, who had been banned in May.*

considers the interest of students of science or engineering, instead of such subjects as political science, African studies or conditions in prison, kindly advise me, in which case I shall consider re-applying for membership.'[119]

Fearing more such resignations, NUSAS quickly sought to thaw its cooled relations with UCT by organising inclusive folk-singing sessions on campus on Sundays, by starting publication of a thought-provoking local NUSAS journal to improve its public image on campus, and by collaborating with the SRC to stage its 1966 Day of Affirmation of Academic and Human Freedom Address by the spellbinding Senator Robert Kennedy in Jameson Hall.[120] When, only weeks before the high-profile Kennedy spectacle, the president of NUSAS, Ian Robertson, was suddenly banned by the Government under the Suppression of Communism Act, the wave of indignation among UCT students produced a mass protest meeting, a staff–student march to the Cape Town Magistrate's Court, and two night vigils, the one on campus and the other on the steps of St George's Cathedral in the city. UCT and NUSAS were once again singing from the same hymn sheet. As a result, in 1967 the SRC finally persuaded the UCT Council to pay NUSAS the affiliation fees which the Council had been withholding since 1965 because of its reservations about the new form of UCT's centre-only membership of NUSAS.

Mild liberalism may have constituted the governing ideology in student politics at UCT in the 1950s and 1960s, but it must be borne in mind that it occupied this position only because the bulk of students were little involved in such matters, except perhaps when mobilised by pulse-quickening events like arrests, bannings, deportations and clashes with Council and the Principal or by bread-and-butter issues like transport and food. What the politically active readily condemned as 'debilitating political apathy [which] has hung over UCT'[121] probably arose in part from the demands of academic work, scorn for politics as 'a dirty game which is played too often on this campus' (in the words of a student magazine[122]), being warned to steer clear of politics by parents,[123] a conservative reluctance to confront critiques of their privileges, and a failure or unwillingness to see a link between what activists were saying and their own daily lives. As the official magazine of the Radical Students' Society put it scathingly, 'Reclining comfortably on the mattress of "white supremacy", they dream their idle dreams while the foundations of their way of life are crumbling, unnoticed, beneath them.'[124]

Other ideologies had their proponents on campus too, but in even smaller numbers. To liberals' right, the National Party-funded Conservative Students' Association was set up in 1964 'to break NUSAS and its liberal ideas'[125] by fostering support for apartheid. To this end it won control of the Day Students' Council and its newspaper so as to propagate its standpoint, printed hundreds of resignation-from-NUSAS forms, and even tried to challenge the SRC's authority on its home turf by declaring itself to be a 'whites-only' society in 1965. The SRC's rejection of this step was reluctantly approved by Duminy and the University Council, only for the latter, under pressure from the Government,[126] to revise the SRC's constitution in 1967 so that Council might, in special circumstances, override SRC decisions on the legality of any UCT club or society. By then, however, the cadre of conservatives who had started the Conservative Students' Association had left UCT, disheartened at their failure to force the SRC at a stroke to accept a racially segregated society on its campus. 'Taking a conservative line in the absence of a national or trans-campus body in support was akin to pushing a giant ball uphill', their leader mused years later.[127]

Chastened, a more circumspect group of conservatives pitched their Independent Students' Union as a society committed to the cause of moderation, equally opposed to NUSAS and its Afrikaner opposite number, the Afrikaner Studentebond. Tactically shrewd, it sought to win support on campus by, among other things, opposing the stand by NUSAS and the SRC against the Rhodesian Unilateral Declaration of Independence and by pledging itself to bringing white English- and Afrikaans-speakers together to maintain 'Western civilised standards in South Africa'.[128] However, alerted by *Varsity* and the liberal grapevine, too many students saw through the ploy for it to succeed.

To liberals' left, even smaller clusters of radical liberals, socialists and communists of various persuasions gathered in one of two loose-knit societies with fluid memberships. The older, the Modern World Society, had been established in 1949 as a front for the Students' Socialist Party, but in the 1950s it aligned itself with the Congress of Democrats. Priding itself on matching its deeds with its words, in 1959 it took a leading part in organising the boycott of buses with segregated seating running on the UCT route and of items made by companies with National Party connections; in the co-ordination in 1961 of a mixed-race lunch counter sit-in at a whites-only restaurant in the city and a pro-Cuba demonstration outside the US embassy; and in 1962 in the protests on campus against the Sabotage Bill. Nor did it hold back in its criticism of the choice of Harry Oppenheimer as T.B. Davie lecturer in that year, distributing leaflets at the lecture decrying his unsuitability and lambasting UCT's motives for inviting him as being 'as mercenary and hypocritical as those of Mr Oppenheimer himself'.[129] Its *Modern World Journal*, begun a year later, was marked by what *Varsity* described as 'dogmatic, somewhat fervid "The people shall overcome" tone',[130] a reflection of the earnest intensity of its members.

Passionate zeal of this sort saw several of them involved in the African Resistance Movement off campus; that movement's destruction in 1964 and the banning of the editor of the *Modern World Journal* tarnished its name and took the wind out of its sails. Accordingly, the next cohort of progressive-minded students took over a small, liberal, anti-communist rival to the Modern World Society, the Radical Students' Society, and gave it a makeover into a Modern World Society under another name so as to continue promoting leftist debate on campus. It scornfully dismissed the liberal establishment on the SRC and in NUSAS as 'sell-outs' and 'Bishops old boys';[131] they 'sham their liberalism … [and] mouth the clichés of the left … [but] forget what these clichés are really about', inveighed its chair.[132] A talk on Vietnam at UCT by the American ambassador was given a very hostile response and Robert Kennedy's Affirmation Day speech was boycotted in protest at his earlier backing for the South Vietnamese Government. That it had also taken over the Modern World Society's commitment to action to match its words would be demonstrated very clearly in 1968.

A yearning for action beyond words also characterised the African Resistance Movement (ARM), whose Cape Town cadre consisted of several current or ex-

UCT students and tutors formerly connected with NUSAS and the Liberal Party. 'ARM does not only talk. ARM acts ... ARM has declared itself and will declare itself through action', announced its 1964 manifesto defiantly.[133] Disillusioned by the inability of opponents of apartheid to check the policy's roll-out, these liberals-turned-radicals resorted to the use of sabotage to challenge the regime and to try to spark resistance to it. However, a dire lack of caution allowed the police to arrest several of its leaders in 1964, including the former vice-president of the SRC and NUSAS president, Adrian Leftwich, who proceeded to incriminate a slew of its members by revealing their names under torture and then ignominiously turning state witness against them.

Held by the white public to be guilty by association, NUSAS and the liberal cause on campus were rocked by these revelations, which provided grist to the mills of their detractors to both the left and the right. 'Hang De Keller, Leftwich. NUSAS = HIGGS = MURDERER' ran graffiti painted on Jameson Hall, referring to Leftwich, David de Keller, an SRC member implicated in ARM, and Denis Higgs, the leader of ARM in Johannesburg,[134] while Justice Minister Vorster angrily proclaimed NUSAS to be 'a detestable and damnable organisation' under cover of which 'young people were being abused by leftist saboteurs'.[135] To him, recent NUSAS presidents were 'the offspring of vipers'.[136] With a dose of heavy-handed humour, prison officers asked three UCT students working as bar stewards at a Prison Officers' Fund dance, 'You want to buy some detonators cheap?'[137]

At the opposite end of the political spectrum, Unity Movement members felt vindicated by the way that Leftwich had acted, as this demonstrated decisively what they had always maintained, that white '*herrenvolk* liberals' could not be trusted to act selflessly when the chips were down.[138] Not that they themselves were an example of opposition to apartheid which went much beyond the verbal. Wedded to the doctrine of non-participation in white-led student protests lest they be co-opted by organisations, like the SRC and NUSAS, which were less than impeccably non-racial and which were not committed to total desegregation, they infuriated passionate but uncomprehending white student leaders by their stance. One sounded off against the 'series of cliché-ridden diatribes to which we are regularly subjected by Non-European spokesmen ... If he is to get anywhere, he should ... accept all genuine support for his cause, without raising completely unnecessary barriers ... The refusal of Non-European students to ally themselves with ... support ... can only be a sign of infantile logic and mental immaturity.'[139]

The sense of superiority and hubris evident in such a statement was not uncommon among white students in their attitude to their black peers on campus. Nor, given the deep-rooted racial hierarchy in the country, is this surprising. In the opinion of a postgraduate in the Psychology Department, UCT's ethos might be 'superficially liberal', but, at bottom, even those who protested against racial discrimination were, in the main, racially prejudiced to some degree. 'They can keep up liberal appearances politically, but on the social level they are afraid of revealing their prejudices'; hence they did not mix with blacks socially.[140]

For their part, the black minority on campus kept largely to themselves. For instance, black tennis players using the UCT courts 'always played amongst themselves', reported the secretary of the Tennis Club, while over tea at the end of Geography Society meetings, black students 'stand together and chat among themselves, but such groups are easily broken and individuals drawn into free conversation'.[141] On the other hand, some black students were not willing to socialise with whites at all. 'White people didn't exist for me at UCT', recalled one. 'I socialised only with black students. I didn't join any clubs or societies etc. … because I assumed that any socialising afterwards would have been awkward because of apartheid as many facilities were segregated.'[142]

Those black students who did join campus clubs and societies often found themselves patronised by well-intentioned white members. The UCT Film Unit, for example, made sure that it screened only films which were not classified 'Whites only', even though, it noted, 'This does … considerably restrict the choice of films for screening',[143] while a racially mixed UCT table tennis first team did play unofficial matches against black clubs, but did not publicise these widely 'as we felt certain objections might have been raised by some students at the university'.[144] Indeed, so anxious was the UCT Mountain Club about the fact that its sole black member participated freely in climbs that it requested an SRC-initiated commission of inquiry into social, sporting and academic discrimination at UCT to keep this information confidential. In the end, the well-meaning commission decided that, so widely did the treatment of black members differ among clubs and societies, that it would not publish its findings lest 'the publicity … cause a more rigid limitation of existing practice'.[145]

However, racially mixed dances did attract intense publicity, as mentioned in the preceding chapter, and so became a sharp bone of contention between successive SRCs and Duminy and his Council, especially if the programme included partner-swapping 'Paul Joneses'. In the end, most whites' acute sensitivity to inter-racial physical contact – recalling Bernard Shaw's definition of dancing as 'a perpendicular expression of a horizontal desire' – won the day and such dances were officially barred between 1958 and 1965, when a stalemate was reached and all dances forbidden. As one professor had observed perceptively, 'Dancing can be regarded as raising emotions in its own right, [so] it is in a class of its own as far as integration is concerned.'[146]

Potentially far more distressing to white sensitivities was racially mixed swimming in the UCT pool; however, when this did now and again take place, it did so without publicity. This meant that the few occasions when white swimmers actually requested black students to leave the pool went unreported by the press and so did not turn into a high-profile issue on campus.

On the other hand, there was no racial friction over the use of non-sporting amenities on campus like toilets, common rooms and the cafeteria in the Students' Union. Indeed, the poor quality of food and drink on sale at the Union – the coffee there was notorious, being popularly known as 'the yellow peril'[147] – united customers of all hues in 1962 in a mass boycott, which quickly yielded a new manageress and the consequent improvement in what was served. A racial division noticeable in the cafeteria was in the groups gathered around the tables, for these clusters were usually racially and ethnically exclusive. 'Where is all this business of multiracialism and integration?' asked a Stellenbosch graduate who had come to study further at UCT. 'There is, as far as I can see, a more natural apartheid in operation here … At UCT in the Union you can see apartheid every day.'[148]

As the only cafeteria on the Groote Schuur campus was in the Students' Union, this was the bustling centre of students' social life. With a capacity of 400, by the 1960s it was heavily overcrowded until after lunchtime. Installing automatic snack and beverage machines did little to ease the pressure on the kitchen and serving staff in what students dubbed the 'cattle trough'.[149] Looking in there at lunchtime, observed Deputy Principal Inskip drily, 'will confirm opinion that cattle are, if anything, somewhat better behaved and accommodated in the modern world'.[150] Accordingly, in 1962 a bell was installed there which the manageress could ring to summon a member of the SRC if an exasperated customer became abusive to the cafeteria staff.

By default, therefore, other spaces on the Groote Schuur campus became the focus of social interaction. One was the Reserved Books reading room in Jagger Library, which one student angrily described as 'a Union without tea-cups'.[151] Many undergraduates seemed to regard it 'as an ideal rendezvous to discuss last night's dance or exchange dress patterns, essays, lecture notes and social information', complained a *Varsity* feature-writer.[152] More than once a stern-faced librarian had to warn readers there to be silent or the room would be cleared.

In dry weather the other prime site of social interaction was the Jameson Hall steps. Step-sitting was, to use a paradoxical phrase, a very longstanding activity at UCT, going back to the construction of the steps in 1931–2. 'There folks enjoy a chat,' rhapsodised one student, 'especially in autumn and spring when the sun's rays are nice and warm, and you know for sure that the next lecture will be dead boring [and should therefore be missed].'[153] The views it offered of the passing parade and of the landscape as far as the Hottentots Holland Mountains were hard to ignore. Such iconic status did step-sitting enjoy at UCT that a campus wit suggested the introduction of a full-time degree, the B.S-St (Bachelor of Step-Sitting), whose recipients 'will have indisputable knowledge concerning the best legs, figures, etc. on the Campus'.[154] Evidently the author was male.

Although step-sitters may have relished these distant and not-so-distant views, they were clearly uncaring about or unaware of their immediate environment, as the growing quantity of litter they left on the steps from the mid-1960s testified. Cool-drink bottles, cans, lunch-wrap and cigarette stubs were strewn about the steps by the end of every lunchtime, adding the new task of 'steps-clearing' to the cleaners' chores. Other users of the steps – protesters bearing placards, teams of residence students competing in 'toboggan' races down the stairs using wooden shower-duckboards as sleds, actors performing Classical plays at night, and vendors selling magazines – were more considerate and took their paraphernalia with them.

The cigarette stubs on the steps were evidence of the widespread popularity of smoking among students in those days before the association between tobacco and cancer was well known. Regular advertisements in student newspapers and magazines, sales of cigarettes in the cafeteria, contemporary photographs, and the ban on smoking in lecture rooms in 1964 (on account of damage to desks and floors by matches and butts) all point to the pervasive nature on campus of this habit, which was globally portrayed as a means for late adolescents and young adults to attain their aspirations – ruggedness and manliness for men and elegance and sexiness for women. Of particular appeal to students, especially at exam time, was the depiction of cigarette smoking as a source of stress relief. A study of spending by UCT students in 1967 concluded that 72.7% of male and 61.3% of female students smoked; on average, male smokers smoked 16.5 cigarettes per day, female 13.6.[155] Even if these figures appear unusually high, they do indicate that the 1950s and 1960s at UCT were clouded in a haze of tobacco smoke.

For the source of smoke from other substances there are, alas, no such hard statistics. Anecdotal evidence suggests that dagga was used by students, but not on a large scale,[156] though the quantity of dagga found jammed into the weep holes of the new Driekoppen Residence in 1966 would have kept more than one resident on a high for many a week.

Far more widely available – though not on campus, where its sale was banned except at formal dinners and dances – was alcohol. Permitted by law to drink liquor once they had turned 18, students often did so 'as a matter of bravado to assert their right to drink', thought Davie.[157] Occasions like float-building night before Rag, the lead-up to and aftermath of Intervarsity, and the Freshers' Hop were notorious for being accompanied by excessive drinking, which was perceived as part and parcel of being a student – and not just at UCT. As a recovered American alcoholic recently acknowledged, 'In college, we can wear our alcohol abuse as proudly as our university sweatshirts; the two concepts are virtually synonymous.'[158] In the 1967 survey of student spending, only 4.6% of men and 25.8% of women students identified themselves as teetotallers.[159] The two watering holes close to campus, the Pig 'n Whistle in Rondebosch and Foresters' Arms in Newlands, went out of their way to draw students by offering them specials, which in effect made them extensions of UCT's social life. The Pig 'n Whistle was 'the best place to practise insobriety', announced one student unapologetically,[160] an opinion more than confirmed by another's admission that she could not 'recall a single visit to the Pig 'n Whistle that didn't culminate in [a] strategic retreat more-or-less out of our skulls … all it took was R1.'[161]

For those wanting food only, Rondebosch and Rosebank contained several restaurants and tearooms, like the Evergreen, the Rob, the Gay Hussar and Lerici, which became institutions among students because of their cheap specials. When combined with inexpensive drinks at the Pig 'n Whistle, they could provide a filling night out for a hungry residence-dweller. 'At 2 bob [i.e. 20 cents] a pint [of draught beer] I could buy 4 pints and have 2 bob left to buy a hamburger at the Evergreen', recalled a student of the 1960s with nostalgia.[162]

These restaurants, tearooms and pubs were just some of the shops in Rondebosch, Rosebank, Mowbray and Observatory that took full advantage of their proximity to UCT. To these should be added boarding houses and digs accommodation within easy reach of both the Groote Schuur and Medical School campuses. In most cases such accommodation had first been approved by the Students' Lodging Bureau, which was set up in 1955 by an altruistic professor and his wife with UCT's co-operation to help students find suitable accommodation if they could not secure a place in a UCT residence.

Banks went even further to make their services accessible to students. Although Standard and Barclays operated branches in Rondebosch, in 1965 they both reopened dedicated agencies on the Groote Schuur campus too, to provide limited but on-the-spot banking for students.[163] Even though running such agencies may have been uneconomic in the short term, the banks recognised the long-term potential of such an investment in student clients. For the students and staff who required the resources of a post office, from 1964 a mobile post office visited the main campus for an hour every morning.

# LEARNING IN (AND OUT OF) CLASS

*Three student haunts. As the adverts make very clear, the owners of these establishments more than recognised the importance of student patronage.*

For their part, two clothing shops in Rondebosch identified what they thought would be an elegant way to attract student customers. Noting the growing tendency among students (except those in the Faculties of Medicine and Education) to dress casually as the clothing revolution of the 1960s in the Western world reached UCT, in 1968 they sponsored a 'Best Dressed Man' and a 'Best Dressed Woman' competition on campus. However, the tide of the fashion revolution was too strongly against them and only a few competitors came forward to participate before a student audience clad largely in jeans, slacks, stovepipes, open-necked shirts and miniskirts.

Try as the university authorities might to hold the line against this clothing revolution among the baby boom generation, they were bound to fail in the face of young white South Africans' eager imitation of the latest Western dress and behaviour codes. Duminy's formal notice in 1963 asking students to 'dress in a manner befitting the dignity and the prestige of the University'[164] drew a refusal from the SRC to assist in enforcing this request, while a *Varsity* columnist sneered at the Principal's 'frigid little notes about undesirable student dress that dot the notice-boards'.[165] In vain did Duminy rail in a graduation address at 'the impertinence of strange characters presenting themselves in our offices of administration and our halls of learning in a state which suggests that they had just come in from the Rag Procession, or been pulled by the feet out of a rugby scrum!'[166]

Though at heart Luyt shared Duminy's ideas on appropriate student dress, he was able to recognise the way that the fashion wind was blowing and its strength. Consequently, he soon eased the dress requirements for students wanting to be attended to at Bremner Building but did insist that men still had to wear a tie or cravat and shoes, 'even in this age of new fashions and freedoms'.[167] Yet, he knew that the fashion writing was on the wall for his idea of appropriate dress. To a former UCT professor who bemoaned the disappearance of gowns among students, he admitted with self-awareness that, with regard to student dress, 'I am in this matter regarded by staff and students alike as being more than a little old-fashioned and unreasonable!'[168]

Luyt's readiness to adapt his thinking to changing circumstances is apparent too in his readiness to accept that a student's well-being involved mental as well as physical health and that the University bore a responsibility for both. Whereas the Students' Health Service, which had been initiated jointly by progressive staff and students in 1952, was slow to incorporate a psychological dimension into the services it offered – its highest priority was preventing communicable diseases like TB and polio and treating adolescent conditions like acne, period pains and allergies – Luyt strongly backed the expansion of its scope. When the Students' Health Service was reorganised in 1969, its brief was spelt out as 'to meet the needs of an adolescent

*Not getting through. A student cartoonist's regret at the barrier between staff and students* (Varsity, 24 June 1970)

student population [in terms of] … the physical, social, preventative, promotive and psychological aspects of student health'.[169] 'This is becoming a necessary adjunct of every large university', UCT acknowledged,[170] at the same time as Luyt rejoiced that 'We … have struck a real enthusiasm for this [expanded] kind of work'.[171]

On contraception and the prevalence, treatment and prevention of sexually transmitted diseases among students, the UCT archives are almost entirely silent. Suggestions in *Varsity* that contraceptive pills be provided by the Students' Health Service elicited no official response, yet it is clear that the topic was much discussed on campus. Symposia in 1966 on 'Sex before Marriage' and 'Birth Control' attracted audiences of over a thousand students, while *Varsity*'s 'Campus Sex Survey', modelled on one undertaken by a Cambridge University student newspaper, carried articles with titillating titles like 'How Much Woman, How Much Student?' and 'Readers on Sex'. However, in the censorious South Africa of the time, their stolid content did not match these enticing headlines.[172]

One of the questions in this survey asked about attitudes towards male homosexuality, an issue which two student symposia at UCT took up in 1968, mainly because of pending government legislation to increase the penalties against it. In the

*'But not us'. A tart comment on Duminy's official ban on racially mixed dancing* (Trend, 12 May 1964)

oppressive environment of high-apartheid South Africa, however, there was little scope for free expression of opinion. Gay liberation in the country lay far in the future.

Luyt's adaptability stood in marked contrast to Duminy's social and political conservatism and stiff formality when dealing with students. His personality aside, this formality was a reflection too of the hierarchical structure then prevailing at UCT and at most of the older universities in Britain, Europe and the British Commonwealth. Again and again members of UCT's SRC appealed for greater personal contact between students and the academic staff beyond lectures – 'Staff don't know students … and students don't know staff … [from which] arises misunderstanding, intolerance and, on occasions, antagonisms', regretted the SRC's secretary in 1964[173] – but the gap between those who taught and the swelling numbers of those who were taught remained, with a few notable exceptions,[174] firmly in place. In almost all departments, knowledge was transmitted in one direction only, from the top down. Telling of this barrier of aloofness was another SRC member's admission that 'many students have not the nerve to approach their lecturers on academic matters which disturb them'.[175]

When added to the growing political consciousness of students engendered by opposition to apartheid, the increasing cultural and social gap between the baby boom generation and their seniors, and the spreading influence of the international 'Youthquake' of the 1960s, this was to produce a rising feeling among many students of alienation from the UCT establishment and, indeed, of antagonism towards its top decision-making bodies and their members, culminating in the sit-in of August 1968.

The paths between the SRC and the UCT authorities began to diverge in 1958 when a new, more conservative Council and a new, more conservative Principal (Duminy) adopted a less flexible stance on UCT's hitherto easy-going approach to social segregation in respect of out-of-class activities on campus by black students. The particular trigger was (as indicated earlier[176]) that hyper-sensitive issue for white South Africans, racially mixed dances on campus. Duminy's request that Council's wish should be respected, that in all non-academic or social affairs UCT should 'abide by the customs and conventions of the community in which it exists', created a sharp bone of contention and conflict between successive SRCs and the powers that be at UCT for the next ten years. 'How can the authorities expect to retain the loyalty and respect of the students when the ban [on a racially mixed medical students' ball] is enforced in spite of, and regardless of, expressed views of the majority of the students?' asked *Varsity* indignantly in 1962 when Duminy turned his request into an instruction.[177]

A year later the SRC and many more students were antagonised again by Council, this time over an anything-but-political issue, hitch-hiking. Until 1963, a large number of students had regularly hitched rides from cars passing UCT on Rhodes Drive, which ran in front of its rugby fields. In that year, however, Rhodes Drive was rebuilt as a highway along which hitch-hiking would be too dangerous in the opinion of the city's traffic authorities. Dismayed at the prospective loss of this popular student transport facility, the SRC took up the issue with the City Council, putting forward an alternative scheme on which the University Council indicated it had taken no particular position.

The sense of betrayal felt by the SRC can be imagined when its members read in the press that the UCT Council in fact supported the City Council's decision. 'You will agree with me', wrote an aggrieved SRC president to Duminy, 'that it is extremely unfavourable to find out Council's policy, especially when it affects students to such a large extent, by reading the newspaper … I am deeply disappointed that … the UCT Council did not see fit to support the students in their vital struggle to retain hitch-hiking.'[178]

At a seething mass meeting on the issue, an even angrier member of the SRC accused the UCT Council of having 'gone behind the students' backs in this matter'.[179] The meeting noted that Council had 'persistently disregarded the desires of the student-body' and specifically 'mentioned the issues of hitch-hiking and social practice [i.e. dances]' as cases in point.[180] In short, Council's track record 'leaves much to be desired'.[181] Exercising more restraint, the SRC president reported that the matter had 'left a certain amount of resentment among students'.[182]

Exacerbating this resentment was Council's overreaction in 1964 to the publication in *Varsity* of a mildly suggestive article entitled 'How to Seduce a Freshette', lifted from an interwar American bestseller.[183] The editor, Morris Sheftel, had been promptly charged with obscenity by a state determined to enforce its moral code on the country (and perhaps keen to show up the immorality rampant at UCT), but when the magistrate found him not guilty, UCT's Council acted to reassure parents that at least its moral compass was set right. It hauled him before the University's Court of Discipline (on which Council members and Duminy formed a majority) on a charge of bringing UCT into disrepute and, when he was found guilty there, insisted that he be removed as editor and barred from membership of any UCT club or society in perpetuity. Allan Stephen, the chair of Council, felt that Sheftel had been 'treated considerately and, in fact, somewhat lightly. He is fortunate in that he was not rusticated', he told Duminy privately.[184]

Outraged at the severity of the punishment, a mass meeting of students decried it as 'symptomatic of ... yet again the extent to which members of that august institution [i.e. Council] are out of touch with student body desires and opinion'.[185] A petition which they had drafted calling for a revision of the sentence was presented to Duminy at Bremner Building by a group of students bearing placards reading 'Please Consult Us' and 'Please Inform Us'. In this ad hoc fashion, the shape of what was to become the stage and the rituals for student protest at UCT began to materialise. 'There is no doubt ... that at present the attitude of the student body is not favourable to the University Council', the president of the SRC solemnly told Duminy and the Council.[186]

Nor did Council's clash with Sheftel's successor-but-one as editor of *Varsity*, Nick Irvine, do anything but strengthen its image among students of being unsympathetic, authoritarian and determined to keep the whip hand over them. Having judged that several articles appearing in *Varsity* in the first half of 1966 defamed or abused Council, Duminy and Deputy Principal Inskip suspended publication of the newspaper until it agreed to print in its next edition a full apology as dictated by Council. Irvine refused to do so and was forced to resign as editor by the SRC, which then tried to find a compromise solution by coming up with an apology it had drafted. A 'highly emotionally charged' mass meeting[187] rejected this and, amid furious denunciations of Council's high-handed approach, voted for Irvine's reinstatement. A newly elected

SRC was able to manage this without attracting further Council sanctions by deftly rewording the statement of apology. Yet it was obvious that, as a political scientist on campus elucidated, 'huge suspicion … [still] exists on either side' between Council and the student body, causing their respective stances to 'ossify as various issues come up i.e. conflict is built into the [University's] organisational structure'.[188]

He was not wrong. In September 1966, against the background of Minister De Klerk's threat to pass legislation allowing segregated societies to operate at UCT,[189] a demonstration by a few students against the presence on campus of another Cabinet Minister to open a new building incurred a rough and abusive response from a University official and a member of the academic staff to their posters reading 'Students Reject Campus Apartheid', 'Students Reject Neo-Nazi Bills' and 'Why Not Really Open the University?'

In the wake of this protest, charges and counter-charges were traded by students and the two UCT staff members, but Council decided to pursue neither, judging both sides to have behaved inappropriately. Dismayed at this failure to uphold students' right of protest on their very own campus, the SRC told Council that it was 'very disappointed that no conclusion was reached one way or the other since, as we saw it, the issues were quite clear cut'.[190]

By this time, the ongoing contestation over social segregation had decided Duminy and his Council to clip the SRC's wings once and for all, both to enshrine their supreme authority on student matters in law and to use this to convince De Klerk that his proposed legislation was not necessary to keep the SRC in line. For Duminy the last straw had been the SRC's insistence during the 1965 round of the 'dance wars' that it and not he as the Principal had the final say over the terms on which Jameson Hall might be used for social functions organised by students.

Accordingly, in 1966 Council appointed an inquiry into the SRC's constitution, fuelling what *Varsity* described as 'a rebellious mood' among students and the distribution on campus of leaflets headed 'Protect Your SRC'.[191] Nor was such foreboding misconceived, for the commission of inquiry recommended that the SRC's constitution be comprehensively revised so as to trim the SRC's authority significantly. As its chair, a conservative member of Council, told his fellow councillors, 'The powers and duties of the SRC must … be strictly circumscribed.'[192] This the revised constitution, along with a rewritten Statute of Discipline, did, although the SRC was able to mitigate their effect to some extent through negotiation. The one clause on which Council refused to budge, however, related to allowing student societies (like the Conservative Students' Association[193]) to restrict their membership racially. On this right Council insisted, minuted the president of the SRC, 'whether the SRC wanted it or not', thereby arousing 'many suspicions against

*Guarding UCT's (good?) name. UCT janitorial staff lined up willy-nilly to block a Cabinet Minister's view of a student demonstration against him outside the newly-opened Snape Civil Engineering Building* (Varsity, 28 September 1966)

Council which many accused of "doing a deal" with Senator De Klerk'.[194] The fact that very soon after this De Klerk announced that he would not proceed with his threatened legislation suggests that student opinion was not wrong. 'I am satisfied that a repetition of the students' unpleasantness of the past years at the University of Cape Town can in future be prevented', De Klerk predicted confidently.[195]

Yet such a prediction was premature. Faced by a constitutional fait accompli, in March 1967 the SRC refused to operate under the new constitution, a stand strongly supported by a mass meeting where a march to picket Bremner Building was mooted but eventually not pursued. Instead, inspired by the president of the SRC's description of UCT students as now 'the custodians of a tradition [of non-racialism]',[196] the meeting voiced its 'deep regret at the University Council's unilateral action, inconsistent with the freedom within a University, in which it failed to give safeguards for the retention of such freedom'.[197]

Emboldened, the SRC formally rejected the new constitution and announced that it would continue to function according to its previous constitution under which it had been elected, prompting the headline 'SRC Declares UDI'.[198] The constitutional

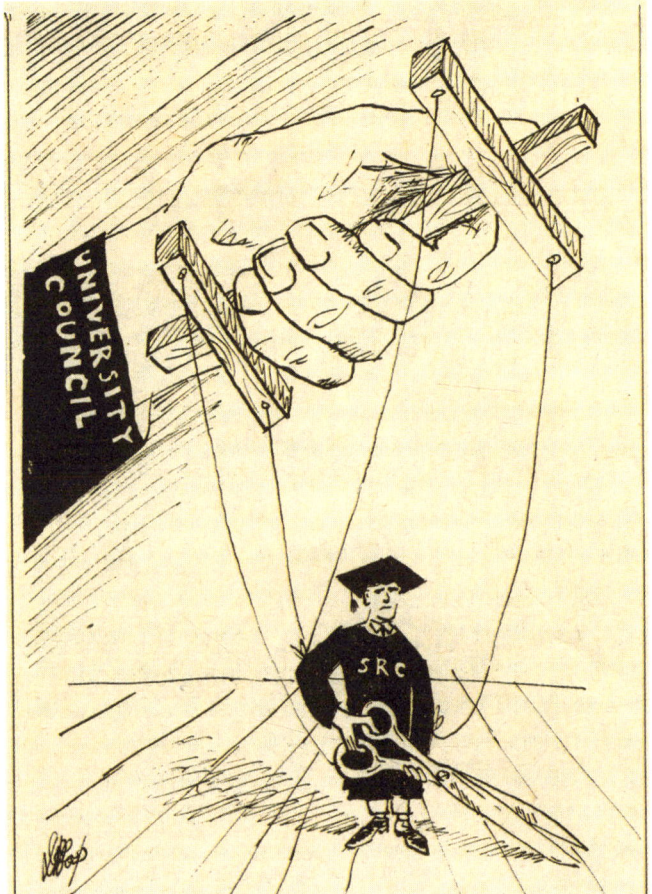

*Cutting ties? A student cartoonist's view of a likely outcome of the ongoing clash between the SRC and the University Council* (Varsity, 30 March 1967)

deadlock which ensued strained Council–SRC relations even further: a group of young lecturers publicly referred to 'the present unhappy state of relations between the SRC and the University Council … [which lay behind these student] reactions to authoritarianism',[199] while the SRC president warned of 'the imminence of a very wounding rupture' between the two.[200] Exercising discretion, Council did not take up the SRC's challenge head-on, but instead bided its time until the current SRC's term of office expired in August 1967. Then Duminy acted on behalf of Council against their two bugbears, the SRC and *Varsity*, those whom he called in private 'a comparative handful – vociferous, misguided and publicity-seeking'.[201]

The fifteen students elected under the old constitution to succeed the intransigent

*See no evil, hear no evil and definitely print no evil. A student cartoonist's view of the ban on* Varsity *in September 1967* (Trend, 11 October 1967).

outgoing SRC were told that *ipso facto* their election was invalid. At the same time *Varsity* was again suspended and its editor, Chris Pritchard, summoned before UCT's Court of Discipline on grounds of publishing articles which were blasphemous and disrespectful. Duminy explained that *Varsity* had been allowed 'to exceed the bounds of decency' and so he 'had taken it upon himself to ban the newspaper'.[202] In the last few issues the editor had 'overstepped all the bounds of propriety'.[203]

With indignation running high among students, a mass meeting condemned this 'invasion into student life'[204] amid renewed talk of a march to picket Bremner Building and even to stage a sit-in there following the example of civil rights and student protesters in the United States. The banning of *Varsity* was 'another action to throttle the voice of students', claimed one speaker, 'undertaken with the sole purpose of rendering the student body impotent'.[205] To overcome this enforced silence, a special issue of the University of the Witwatersrand's student newspaper, *Wits Student*, was printed and distributed at UCT, providing a student perspective on the events. 'I am convinced that it will have a tremendous impact on this campus', wrote a UCT leader to the president of the Wits SRC gratefully, 'particularly as feeling is very high at the moment'.[206]

Yet such righteous indignation had little palpable effect on the University authorities. Pritchard was found guilty, sent down for the rest of 1967 and barred from ever holding any office at UCT again. Years later he described the Court of Discipline as a 'kangaroo court' dominated by Duminy and members of Council.[207] To cement Council's dominant position, a Code of Ethics for Student Publications was adopted, explicitly safeguarding the reputation of University officers from disrespectful attacks on them. The Administration has acted 'as though student opinion did not exist', lamented the organ of the Day Students' Council,[208] while a student quipped, 'The University is in a shambles. We have no "official" SRC, no newspaper, no nothing.'[209] In one week, pointed out a student leader, 'Council has systematically attempted to destroy all effective student participation in our University affairs'.[210]

However, the University authorities could not dispense with an SRC as easily as it could with *Varsity*, for the SRC filled a central role in the administration of student affairs. Consequently, Duminy and his Council decided to bypass the constitutional deadlock by creating an Interim Students' Council (ISC) under the Principal's explicit authority and by appointing to it the same fifteen students who had been elected in the recent SRC elections. In effect, this ISC would perform the SRC's routine administrative tasks, but without the capacity to act in ways contrary to the wishes of the Principal and his Council. It would be a domesticated dog, able to bark but not bite without its master's approval.

Having consulted widely with student clubs and societies, the fifteen students agreed to their appointment as the ISC, their leader, Duncan Innes, reasoning that this was a strategic concession as they knew that Duminy would be retiring in three months' time and that his successor, Luyt, was likely to be more flexible. Even so, Innes entered into this arrangement with many reservations as president of an ISC 'whose rights, powers, privileges and duties are to be decided by the Principal'.[211] Around them on campus, student anger smouldered at what a member of the ISC called 'the rift which exists between the students of this University and their authorities'.[212] Accurately, the *Sunday Times* wrote that relations between the Council and the student body had 'gone sour', with the Council 'in a state of deadlock with the students',[213] and spoke of how the 'UCT malaise has split Council and students'.[214]

The looming rupture came in 1968, the year of global student rebellions which challenged university and other establishments around the world in a variety of ways, ranging 'from Counterculture to Molotov Cocktails', as a Uruguayan historian put it pithily.[215]

The trigger for the contestation at UCT was Council's decision in June 1968 to reverse the University's appointment of Archie Mafeje as senior lecturer in social anthropology solely because the National Party Government had made it known that it did not want a black academic teaching white-skinned students.[216] This blatant kowtowing to the Government yet again incensed many students, convincing them that, even with a new Principal, Sir Richard Luyt, in office, Council could not be trusted to uphold in practice one of the basic tenets of academic freedom to which it publicly subscribed, viz. who shall teach. Students were saying that they 'could not sympathise with a body that did not have the courage of its convictions', reported *Varsity*. 'Students feel more strongly about this issue than they have over any others for some time', it editorialised. 'It is obvious to all that a flagrant injustice has been done, and students feel that they must show their feelings in some way.'[217] A petition and numerous flyers were circulated on campus, calling on Council to reverse its reversal of Mafeje's appointment. Of these, that issued by the Radical Students' Society (RSS) was, characteristically, bluntest. 'For our Council to demean themselves by doing the Government's foul work is a shame or a disgrace', judged one of its flyers uncompromisingly.[218]

Both the RSS and the SRC quickly recognised that, although the extent of student indignation might be unusually wide, for any action they contemplated to bear fruit, it would have to be such as to maximise support across the board, from moderates and liberals to left-wing radicals. The sense of protest had to be 'massified' to secure a 'swelled resistance' on campus, explained the chair of the RSS years later.[219] In short, a popular front had to be fashioned.

Accordingly, the SRC and the RSS first confirmed that some kind of action did in fact have broad backing by holding a mass meeting at which, among others, Luyt spoke, criticising the Government's interference with UCT's freedom to choose its academic staff. It climaxed in the thousand present being asked to read in unison a general statement committing them to do all in their power 'to restore our university to its full independence, strength and dignity',[220] followed by a dramatic intervention by the chair of the RSS, the highly articulate zealot Raphie Kaplinsky, who leapt onto the stage and condemned the vague pledge as 'nothing but a salve to conscience and ritual', slated Council for 'doing the Government's dirty work',[221] and called for a follow-up mass meeting a week later to decide on more effective measures. 'Feeling was running high', he told Luyt in justification, 'and students were anxious to do something more effective than merely pass protest resolutions in the Jameson Hall. This had been done so often before to no avail.'[222]

As anticipation mounted over the next week, suggestions that had already been aired at a NUSAS congress in July did the rounds, to the effect that a sit-in along the lines of those at Columbia University and the Sorbonne earlier in the year was the best way to force Council to act. Consequently, when the second mass meeting was held on 14 August, to the already tabled motion that an SRC delegation meet Council members in Bremner Building to discuss the 'Mafeje incident', Kaplinsky added a last-minute amendment that those attending the mass meeting should accompany the delegation 'as a sign of solidarity … [and] sit in there until the student demands are met'.[223] It was a classic example of the RSS's commitment to deeds matching words.

Of the 854 students present 81.6% approved the amendment and, bearing already prepared banners and posters tactically calling on Council to 'Join Us', they followed the SRC president, Duncan Innes, down the Jameson Hall steps towards Bremner Building. 'I didn't know if there was anyone behind me as I marched down the steps and I didn't want to turn round and show doubt', he recalled nearly half a century later, 'so I said to Phil van der Merwe, the vice-president, who was alongside me, "Is there anyone else marching?" He looked back and then said to me, "About a thousand."'[224]

To the astonishment of the Bremner administrative staff and the Deputy Principal – Luyt had left for a conference in Sydney a few days earlier – over 600 surged into the building to the strains of 'We Shall Overcome' on a guitar and the sound of Kaplinsky's injunction to male students, 'No jackets and ties'. That Innes kept his on while Kaplinsky was in an open-necked shirt symbolises more than just the differing sartorial preferences of the two leaders; it spoke of their and their followers' very different attitudes to the UCT establishment and its regulations on dress and much else.

The student-occupied Senate Room became the hub of the sit-in, with coffee being brewed at one end and lively debates under way at the other as students waited to hear the outcome of the meeting between the SRC delegation and Council representatives. When it became apparent that Council was in no hurry to respond, the sitters-in realised that they would not be there just for the afternoon (as many had anticipated) and began to set up an alternative, democratic, student-run learning and living community, what Kaplinsky later proudly described as a 'counter-university'.[225] For their part, the UCT authorities clearly decided to sit out the sit-in, letting boredom and purposelessness erode student commitment.

At first, boredom and a lack of purpose were the last things that the sitters-in felt. Teach-ins on topics like student power led by charismatic intellectuals like the political philosopher Rick Turner who had completed a doctorate at the Sorbonne, lectures by outsiders like the earnest anti-apartheid activist William Nkomo, symposia on subjects like homosexuality and non-violence, and discussions of telling films like

*Battleship Potemkin* and *The Battle of Algiers* excited many, not only because of the novelty of the issues they focused on, but also because of the different, interactive ways of learning they offered. 'We discovered intellectual liberation', enthused one participant in retrospect. 'In one fell swoop we had thrown off our mental shackles. At last we were not just some isolated racist outpost of empire, but part of an international student movement. And the times – they really were a-changing.'[226]

Moreover, extensive local and international press coverage, interviews with TV and radio teams from abroad, the arrival of a comradely delegation from the University of the Witwatersrand to offer support, and the receipt of congratulatory telegrams from student organisations across the globe heightened this heady sense of excitement at being in the public eye. Hundreds of students from elsewhere on campus looked in at Bremner Building for an hour or two to witness the social and academic experiment in operation. 'I was motivated solely by social enjoyment and social curiosity', admitted one,[227] while more than a few sitters-in grumbled that too many visitors came 'thinking it is merely a social at Admin, and not a protest'.[228] Even schoolchildren came visiting to see what the sit-in was all about. Two fifteen-year-olds were 'astonished to see the orderly manner in which the sit-in is being conducted, contrary to the report one hears from all sides'.[229]

Such negative reports emanated, in the first instance, from the Government and its media and from indignant parents of UCT students. Allegations abounded of the sit-in as having been orchestrated by communists and of it being an excuse for indulging in immoral sexual behaviour, alcohol abuse and dagga smoking. 'We send our children to university to learn, not to muck about … not to participate in petty party political games – and, above all, not to make demands against their university authorities', thundered the father of two students whom he had warned, 'If you have anything to do with this thing your allowances will be stopped.'[230]

Other opponents of the sit-in went beyond mere words, setting off a smoke bomb inside Bremner Building, phoning the police with a hoax warning that a bomb had been placed in the building, hanging a human effigy on a nearby tree, keeping the building under surveillance from a police car parked within easy sight, gathering in a group in front of the building demanding entry, and, as one inebriated medical student did, smashing some of its windows with stones and milk bottles. As a result, the SRC hired extra security personnel and guard dogs, while all residence students were sternly warned by their wardens not to interfere with the sit-in.

Not that all responses to the sit-in were hostile. Public donations of food and magazines poured into Bremner Building in the first few days of the sit-in; three petitions by over 200 academic staff expressed support for it and requested a teach-in on the role of the university in society; some sympathetic lecturers repeated their on-campus lectures and tutorials at Bremner; while a number of parents did publicly approve of their children's participation in the sit-in. 'Perhaps our offspring has learnt more during this week than he would have learnt by attending a set of formal lectures', opined his mother. 'The justice of the cause is as indisputable as it is noble.'[231]

Notwithstanding this backing, by the end of a week inside what was already being informally dubbed the 'Archie Mafeje Room' the occupants had little to show for their willingness to sleep on the floor, to have hotdogs yet again for supper, and to debate and re-debate the same contentious issues for the umpteenth time. 'You've thought of all the thoughts you are going to have, you've talked all the talk you are going to have; it just becomes dull after a while, frankly', recalled a student who had been the epitome of ardour a week earlier.[232] Council continued to temporise, saying it would meet only once Luyt had returned from Australia; Senate had turned down the request for a 24-hour shutdown of UCT; the handful of black sitters-in had withdrawn because of intimidation by the police;[233] the Prime Minister, B.J. Vorster, had warned ominously that if universities like UCT and Wits did not 'end this trouble … then I will do it myself and I will do it thoroughly';[234] and the chair of UCT's Council had strongly urged that the sit-in be suspended to avoid an outbreak of violence, prompting an emotional debate among the occupants in which Innes argued that it was time to leave Bremner Building. Dismayingly too, in an interview in Britain, Mafeje had labelled the sit-in 'a farce [which was] … meaningless and futile',[235] suggesting that 'My case might have been the peg some students were looking for to demonstrate their own feelings of unrest with authority in the same way that students in many parts of the world have been doing lately'.[236]

Although Innes's call for the sit-in to end then was unsuccessful, it is clear that the popular front of moderates, liberals and radicals sustaining the sit-in was splintering. Numbers began to thin as commitment waned amid disagreement, loss of purpose and confidence, and a growing concern about falling too far behind academically. The sit-in's four-man Steering Committee was itself split and so was unable to provide decisive direction. 'Interminable policy meetings floundered unfruitfully', complained the SRC's secretary,[237] who was critical that the Committee had 'no end-game plan' to bring the sit-in to a conclusion if Council remained unyielding.[238] In short, the sit-in was unravelling in the face of pressure from both within and without.

On 21 August 1968, the same day on which Warsaw Pact troops invaded Czechoslovakia, sweeping the sit-in in Cape Town off the front pages of newspapers, the 221 remaining sitters-in voted by 128 to 93 to end their occupation of Bremner Building on the evening that Luyt returned from Australia. However, on the night before this, a mob of about a thousand Stellenbosch University students – to whose preparations for this foray that university turned a blind eye – tried to invade Bremner Building to drive out the UCT students sitting in there. Chanting 'Kom uit, Ikeys' and lustily baying Intervarsity war cries, they sought to force their way past UCT's two Deputy Principals, a few academic and administrative staff, and the dog-handlers at the entrance. Had it not been for the suspiciously well-timed arrival of forty policemen with dogs, they would probably have succeeded too, even if those inside the building had been able to direct jets of water from fire-hoses onto them, as was their plan. However, the policemen forced the Stellenbosch students to withdraw, which they did, shouting '*Bangbroeke*' and making dire threats that they would return. UCT staff and students inside and outside the building were left mopping their brows in relief. Having been told by the wryly-smiling police colonel in charge that his men had protected UCT students once but would be hard put to do so a second time, an overwrought Deputy Principal Inskip adjured those sitters-in still in occupation, in words recalling Cromwell's 1653 injunction, 'In God's name, bugger off tomorrow morning!' At 8 am next day they did so in what Innes described as 'a rather dejected and despondent state'.[239]

That night Luyt returned to Cape Town, thereby making possible the holding of a full Council meeting to discuss the 'Mafeje Affair' and the consequent sit-in. Though some members of the SRC hoped to win him to their position by going to the airport to get his ear first, his opinion on the 'dis-appointment' of Mafeje remained unchanged. Indeed, he proposed the motion which Council approved to reaffirm its June decision not to appoint Mafeje to UCT's staff. Disillusioned, Innes, now president of NUSAS, told the chair of UCT's Council that NUSAS believed that, 'in capitulating to the Minister's threats, [Council] had been guilty of a betrayal of the principles of academic freedom and university autonomy'.[240]

As a seasoned political tactician, Luyt concluded that, in his absence, the UCT authorities' policy of 'quietly containing, rather than forcibly terminating, the sit-in' had worked well in the end: 'there are no martyrs ... no allegations of brutality or unreasonable force, and ... the students were at sixes and sevens amongst themselves when the whole thing finally petered out.'[241] In private, however, he admitted that, though 'I cannot approve the method of protest that my students chose ... I am quietly proud of their finding the spirit and courage to protest against what they see as morally wrong. They may be scruffy and there may be a few extremists among them, but basically this was a demonstration against what most young people at this University believe to be evil. One can live and work contentedly in such an atmosphere.'[242] When compared to how the now-retired Duminy thought the sit-in should have been handled – he regarded it as 'a very, very lamentable and blameworthy breach of discipline ... and ... would have dealt with it in that way ... Shower the whole lot of them with hosepipes [to clear the building] or something like that'²⁴³ – then it is clear that, under Luyt, UCT was entering an era in which relations between students and Principal would not be as inimical, and could be almost mutually co-operative, as in Davie's day.

For the crestfallen sitters-in there was little by way of public achievements to celebrate. Having lasted nine days, the sit-in seemed destined to be akin to the proverbial wonder associated with that span of time. Mafeje never returned to UCT in any capacity; a plaque later set up in the Library foyer marking UCT's loss of freedom to select its staff was incomprehensible to most passers-by as the wording was in Latin, as if UCT was in Europe; a Mafeje Visiting Fellowship did not come into being for lack of funds; while a proposal to create a UCT Freedom Research Award suffered the same fate. 'Believe you me, to get our Senate and Council to do anything is some achievement in this day and age', fumed a frustrated Innes.²⁴⁴

Rather, it is at the personal level that the long-term impact of the sit-in is to be found. Especially among diehard sitters-in there is a firm conviction that they had their politics pushed to the left by the experience. It served to 'open me to ideas that I'd never really thought about', testified one who went on to become a leading human rights lawyer,²⁴⁵ while a peer of his who made his career in the South African trade union movement believes it 'put me on a new trajectory by forcing me to recognise the extent of state power and how strategic one had to be to challenge it'.²⁴⁶ It was 'a seminal moment in my political development', attested a sitter-in who became Deputy General Secretary of the South African Communist Party.²⁴⁷ For a member of the Anti-Apartheid Movement in Sweden who had cut her political teeth at the sit-in, it 'clarified many things for us [about opposition to apartheid] and many of us tried to continue on the road we took at the sit-in'.²⁴⁸ It was 'a defining moment for many of us', concluded Innes,²⁴⁹ who subsequently made a career for himself as a labour analyst in Johannesburg. Kaplinsky, who went into exile in Britain after his passport was withdrawn in the wake of the sit-in, went further, insisting that 'a whole cohort of individuals' were radicalised by the sit-in, people 'who subsequently came to play important roles in the [South African] liberation movement … [or] key progressive social roles in South Africa and abroad'.²⁵⁰ He himself taught at universities in England as a development economist. Moreover, he holds that the willingness of some UCT sitters-in to try to visit Fort Hare University to support a sit-in there in September 1968 opened the way for Steve Biko to engage with them subsequently to help crystallise his ideas on Black Consciousness; this bore fruit with the foundation of the South African Students' Congress in 1969.²⁵¹

Beyond the proud memories of these ageing veterans of 1968, the sit-in later found a place in UCT's own institutional memory by means of displays, articles in

*Varsity*, and word of mouth across student generations on account of the dramatic challenge it posed to apartheid. This was no mean paradox given the institution's official position in 1968, and speaks of changes in the University's official self-perception from the 1970s onwards. As such, the sit-in occupied an honoured place in UCT's 1998 exhibition, '5 Decades of Protest', which quoted Nelson Mandela's tribute when receiving an honorary doctorate at UCT in 1990: 'It was the student body that led the entire university community in mounting consistent and determined resistance [to university apartheid]', he pointed out.[252] As such too, the well-trodden path of protest from Jameson Hall to an occupation of Bremner Building which the 1968 sitters-in had pioneered was again followed in 2015 by the Rhodes Must Fall campaigners. Many a conflicted, 70-something veteran of 1968 gave a bitter-sweet smile at the parallel.

If, as Philip Altbach, the veteran historian of student protests globally, argues, 'Students learn as much outside the classroom as in it during their university years',[253] then the sit-in accomplished this comprehensively for a whole cohort of conscientised students. Moreover, if one applies this insight to more than just political education, it is apparent that in the twenty years after 1948, the out-of-class learning opportunities which UCT provided or facilitated for many of its students were generous, wide-ranging and often transformative.

Left, right or centre? Two first-year students try to determine where to register, March 1965.

Newmen line up apprehensively to face initiation at Smuts Hall, 1948 (National Library of South Africa)

Evening gowns, Baxter Hall-style. Dinner at Baxter Hall in the late 1960s. Wearing an academic gown at dinner was compulsory.

*What a student magazine called 'a B.A. prac' in the Students' Union, with B.A. being short for 'Bridge Addict'. A photograph taken in the late 1960s*

*The attraction of step-sitting on Jameson Hall steps is evident. A photograph taken in 1951* (Cape Argus, 31 July 1951)

*The descent of man. One of the many precursors to Rag, a toboggan race on shower duckboards down Jameson Hall steps, c. 1960*

*Two male instructors put thirty would-be Rag drum majorettes through their paces in front of Jameson Hall in 1965.* (Varsity, 5 May 1965)

*The Varsity Rag in full swing in a packed Adderley Street, 1965.*

*An ebullient Intervarsity cheerleader getting into his stride at the 1958 Intervarsity rugby match at Stellenbosch* (Varsity, 12 June 1968)

*In the wake of Rag. A cartoonist's sharp comment on the overlooked purpose of Rag, 1970* (Varsity, 25 March 1970)

*Thumbs up. Students hitch-hiking on Rhodes Drive in front of UCT, 1954.*

*Thumbs down. The effect on hitch-hiking of the conversion of Rhodes Drive into a highway, 1963.*
(Varsity, 5 September 1963)

*Choices, choices, choices. SRC election posters, 1966* (Cape Argus, 17 August 1966)

*The result of such choices. The 1966 SRC in session, with Charles Diamond, the SRC president, standing and the head woman student, Pru MacRobert, on the left, alongside SRC minutes secretary, David Katz. Other SRC members at the table are (left to right) Pete Withers, Raymond Suttner and Gert van Zyl.* (Varsity, 30 March 1966)

*Davie's legacy. SRC member and head woman student, Elizabeth Thaele, leads the academic procession into Jameson Hall for the annual T.B. Davie Memorial Lecture in 1962. She carries the torch of academic freedom extinguished in 1959 on the passing of the Extension of University Education Act. The lecture – on a topic linked to academic freedom – was initiated in 1959 by UCT students to commemorate Davie's attempts to uphold academic freedom against apartheid.* (Cape Argus, 6 September 1962)

*Coping with the pressure of exams. Differing student responses as they await the chief examiner's 'You may now start writing' in Jameson Hall, 1969.*

*The culmination of a student's years at UCT: A formal graduation ceremony in Jameson Hall, circa 1961*

*The student sit-in of 1968: The march to Bremner Building begins, 14 August 1968.*

*The student sit-in of 1968. The arrival at Bremner Building, watched by astonished Bremner administrative staff from the balcony.*

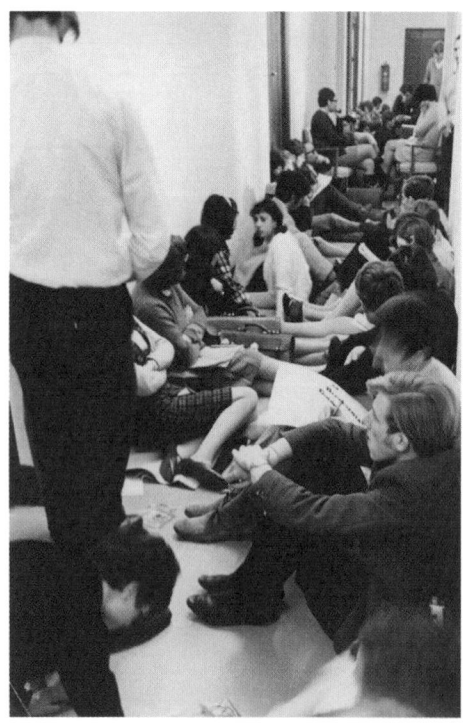

*Sitting-in in a Bremner corridor*

*The student sit-in of 1968. An address to sitters-in inside the Senate Room in Bremner Building by a prominent black community leader, Dr W.F. Nkomo. On his right sits the SRC President, Duncan Innes, and on his left the Vice-President, Phil van der Merwe, cigarette in hand. The two notices on the wall behind them tellingly request, 'Please Don't Put Your Feet On Tables or Chairs' and 'Please Use Ash Trays. Please Don't Scratch The Tables'.* (National Library of South Africa)

*The student sit-in of 1968. A teach-in by Dr Rick Turner outside Bremner Building* (Varsity, 28 August 1968)

*The student sit-in of 1968. The attempted invasion of Bremner Building on 22 August 1968 by baying Stellenbosch University students wanting to end the sit-in by force*

*In a sequel to the UCT student sit-in in August, a demonstration outside St George's Cathedral in central Cape Town on 13 September 1968 by UCT students in support of a sit-in at Fort Hare University was roughly broken up by South African Navy servicemen wearing mufti, as shown here.* (Cape Times, 14 September 1968)

# CHAPTER 12

# UCT and the World in 1968

No less for the world and South Africa than for UCT, the twenty years between 1948 and 1968 were partially transformative. At the global level this was the product of processes like the unfolding of the Cold War, the emergence of the United States as a world power, the decolonisation of Asia and much of Africa, revolutions in communications, technology and transport, and the long post-war economic boom and baby boom. In South Africa it flowed from the escalating roll-out of apartheid and the expansion of state power to crush all opposition to this. At UCT it was the result of changes in the institution's physical and human size, in its disciplinary range and syllabuses, and in its stance in relation to the state, often for reasons not unconnected with the wider processes mentioned above. However much the University might picture itself as an ivory tower on the mountainside above the city, it was both directly and indirectly connected to the world around it.

The first two areas of transformation were in its size and academic scope. In 1948 UCT was still primarily a teaching university – the second largest in South Africa after Wits in terms of enrolment – concentrated in fifteen tuitional buildings across three campuses; twenty years later, research had joined teaching as a strongly supported element in its expanded *raison d'être*, the two activities together filling 27 buildings. The number of individual departments had grown from 59 to 105, the greatest increase being in those faculties where veritable revolutions were under way like Medicine, Science, Engineering and Commerce; its staff complement had risen from 521 to 893, most of whom were now locally born academics who had gained their first degree in South Africa; and the size of its student body had swelled by 73%, from 4258 to 7392 as a result of booms both economic and demographic, though this increase was significantly smaller than those at the universities of South Africa, Pretoria, Stellenbosch and the Witwatersrand. Consequently, by 1968 UCT had dropped to being the country's fourth-largest university.

With the waning of the ex-servicemen's presence at UCT soon after 1948, the percentage of women students on campus had risen and then stabilised at about a third, where it remained until the 1980s. The racial and ethnic composition of the student body had changed far more, with the number of white Afrikaners steadily falling in the 1950s because of the introduction of engineering and medical training at the University of Stellenbosch and because of a sharpening political climate at UCT, which made many of them feel ill at ease there. At the same time, the number of black students (predominantly those classified as 'coloured' and 'Indian') peaked at 633 in 1959 (i.e. 12.4% of all students), whereafter it declined year by year because of restrictions imposed by apartheid. In 1968 it stood at 411 (i.e. 5.5% of all students). The student body in 1968 thus differed markedly from that of 1948 in both size and composition as a result of economic, demographic and political pressures.

It was these political pressures which were responsible too for the third of UCT's transformations in this period, that of its relationship with the state. In 1948 this had largely revolved around finance; by 1968, to this pivotal issue had been added the question of the racial identity of its students and teachers, issues which pitted it increasingly against the Government. If in the 1950s it was the University authorities who initiated this opposition in a very proper, formal manner, in the 1960s it was students who, taking full advantage of their university's location within reach of Parliament, set the pace in far more confrontational ways, even to the extent of challenging UCT itself. In the next two decades such protests were to gather pace on campus, giving rise to the tag for UCT as 'Moscow on the Hill' from critics. This was a very far cry from its image in 1953 as 'a credit to the city … a symbol of an ideal youth which works and plays in a spirit which is infectious', as *Varsity* portrayed it.[1]

The fourth transformation between 1948 and 1968 – in how departments taught their syllabuses – was limited to a small minority only. A few academics introduced interactive Socratic teaching methods into their classes and consequently became well known on campus for their exciting, challenging pedagogy. The majority of their colleagues remained wedded to traditional didactic lectures, however, which provided the recipients of the 5039 undergraduate and 1762 postgraduate degrees and 4713 diplomas and certificates which the University awarded between 1948 and 1968 with a solid rather than critical grounding in their disciplines. Thus trained, they made their way into professions locally and abroad. In some, UCT graduates made up a very high percentage of new entrants each year between 1948 and 1968: in South Africa 40% of architects, ballet dancers and opera singers, 36% of medical doctors, 35% of land surveyors, 25% of quantity surveyors, 25% of civil, mechanical and electrical engineers, 24% of librarians, 20% of accountants, 19% of town planners, 18% of advocates, and 10–12% of high and primary school teachers, social workers and physiotherapists. They – along with others whose subsequent careers are more difficult to determine – constituted UCT's primary contribution to South Africa

'I have the honour to present to you ….' Sir Richard Luyt and three of UCT's honorary graduates at UCT's Golden Jubilee dinner, August 1968. From left to right they are Clive Corder (chair of UCT's Council), Luyt, Eric Walker (professor of history at the South African College and then UCT from 1911 to 1936) and Archbishop Owen McCann (a UCT old boy).

and its pre-eminent *raison d'être*. Unhappily, a not insignificant proportion of these new professionals soon emigrated from the country, mainly for political reasons, and made careers and homes for themselves in English-speaking countries like the United Kingdom, Australia, the United States, Canada and New Zealand. 'We have become as great an exporter of brains as the Scottish nation', lamented a senior UCT professor in 1966.[2] Since then, this diaspora of UCT graduates has grown hand over fist because of an accelerating brain drain.

Those who did remain at UCT contributed to the fifth transformation at the University in these years, its growing research output. By 1968, with the University of the Witwatersrand, UCT was the top research university in the country. In some fields, the impact of its research was even of world import or, one might say bearing in mind Chris Barnard's pioneering cardiac surgery, cutting-edge. For a university which still regularly looked over its shoulder for affirmation from First World institutions, this was no mean achievement. It may have prided itself on being what one student of that era described as 'an English university transported to South Africa',[3] but beneath this exterior, innovative local shoots were growing up.

# UCT UNDER APARTHEID

On 27 August 1968, just four days after the headline-grabbing Mafeje sit-in ended, UCT's new Chancellor, Harry Oppenheimer, awarded thirteen honorary doctorates to scholars with whose achievements the University sought to identify to mark the 50th anniversary of its creation as an independent university.[4] Almost 70% of them were locals who had taken their degrees at a South African university. Thirty-nine years earlier, in 1929, when UCT had marked the centenary of the establishment of the South African College with the conferral of honorary degrees, just 28% of the recipients had been locally trained. The difference is telling of the vast strides made by the South African higher education system in the intervening years, to which UCT was no mean contributor. UCT had been transformed into 'a distinguished centre of learning and research', Oppenheimer declared proudly.[5] Yet, for all of this academic transformation, other features of UCT remained as they had been. Not least is the fact that, like the 1929 list of recipients, the 1968 list included just one woman and no blacks. Plus ça change.

# NOTE ON SOURCES

In the main, this book draws on three types of evidence, viz. the written word, the spoken word and the visual image. What this note does for those wanting to delve beyond the text is to identify these sources and briefly indicate their contents and location. Those wanting detailed information about the sources used should consult the book's endnotes.

## Written sources

At the foundation of this volume is the material to be found in UCT's two archival repositories, its Administrative Archives in Meulenhof Building in Mowbray and the Special Collections Division of its Library. The former contains the University's official administrative records – minutes of its Council, Senate, Faculty Board, committee and SRC meetings, its official circulars and correspondence, and the personal and appointment files of its staff. This collection of typed, roneoed, printed and handwritten (sometimes scrawled) documents constitutes a treasure trove of information on every aspect of UCT's past, making it an invaluable resource for the historian. It is to the University's credit that it has preserved and inventoried this material, giving it a prime place among university archives in South Africa and perhaps beyond.

The Special Collections Division of UCT Library complements the holdings of the Administrative Archives. Its collections are more varied, encompassing the private papers of individuals or organisations associated with the University such as its Principals, several of its academic staff, and organisations like NUSAS and the Students' Christian Association; departmental, society and student journals, magazines and leaflets; the student press, in particular *Varsity* and *The Day Student/Trend*; official magazines and news-sheets like *UCT* and *UCT Staff News*; annual prospectuses and handbooks; and press clippings from Cape Town newspapers, to be found in the BUZV folders and in 'Press Cuttings' albums.

A sub-department of the Special Collections Division, Government Publications, holds a complete run of the printed annual reports of the Department of Education under which UCT fell, of Hansard and of several state-appointed commissions of inquiry dealing with university affairs. The annual reports are laden with pertinent statistical data, not just on UCT but about the entire South African university sector, allowing UCT to be seen, to some degree, in comparative perspective.

Behind these printed state documents lie the unpublished records of government departments like Education, Public Works, Justice, Trade and Industry, and the National Council for Social Research held by the State Archives in Pretoria. These shed light on behind-the-scenes state policy-making in relation to UCT and sometimes provide assessments of the University and individual members of its staff, in some instances by campus spies. In a number of cases, these archives also hold copies of the verbatim evidence given to government commissions of inquiry into universities or into particular professions. This testimony is often frank and uninhibited, a far cry from what finally appeared in such commissions' published reports.

Two other repositories, the National Library of South Africa's Cape Town campus and the Archive for Contemporary Affairs at the Free State University, also hold collections of press clippings on universities; the latter's strength is that the newspapers it clipped include the non-Cape Town press too.

Also written, but not contemporary with the events they describe, are a range of secondary works, some published (like biographies, autobiographies, journal articles, and institutional, departmental, society and club histories) and some unpublished (especially theses and typescript memoirs). Although coloured by hindsight, these quite often significantly expand on official versions by viewing them through very particular lenses. The endnotes in this book mention many of these works.

## Oral sources

However rich the written records referred to may be, inevitably they tell only part of UCT's many-sided history. A useful complement to them were almost 200 interviews conducted with erstwhile UCT staff and students as part of this book's research project, which provided rich personal perspectives and experiences of UCT from a variety of angles. These complement and to some extent offset the voices that otherwise dominate UCT's written record.

## Visual source

UCT's splendid BUZV collection in the Special Collections Division of its Library holds abundant images of the many sides of university life through posed and action photographs, snapshots, press photographs and cartoons. Only a tiny selection of these appear in this book, alas. Where no other source is mentioned in a caption, the original will be found in this BUZV Collection.

# NOTES

**Preface**

1. B.K. Murray, *Wits, the Early Years: A History of the University of the Witwatersrand, Johannesburg, and its Precursors, 1896–1939* (University of the Witwatersrand Press, Johannesburg, 1982); B.K. Murray, *Wits, the 'Open' Years: A History of the University of the Witwatersrand, Johannesburg, 1939–1959* (University of the Witwatersrand Press, Johannesburg, 1997); H. Phillips, *The University of Cape Town, 1918–1948: The Formative Years* (UCT and UCT Press, Cape Town, 1993); P. van der Schyff, *Wonderdaad …! Die PUK tot 1951: wording, vestiging en selfstandigheid* (Paarl Print, Paarl, 2003); E.S. van Eeden (ed.), *In U lig. Die PU vir CHO: van selfstandigwording tot samesmelting, 1951–2004* (University of the North West, Potchefstroom, 2006); Universiteit van die Vrystaat, *Van sink tot sandsteen tot graniet. Die eerste 100 jaar van die Universiteit van die Vrystaat* (Universiteit van die Vrystaat, Bloemfontein, 2006); E. Brink, *The University of Johannesburg: The University for a New Generation* (University of Johannesburg, Johannesburg, 2010); D. Massey, *Under Protest: The Rise of Student Resistance at the University of Fort Hare* (Unisa Press, Pretoria, 2010); B. Guest, *Stella Aurorae: The History of a South African University, vol. 1: Natal University College, 1909–1949* (Natal Society Foundation, Pietermaritzburg, 2015); B. Guest, *Stella Aurorae: The History of a South African University, vol. 2: The University of Natal, 1949–1976* (Natal Society Foundation, Pietermaritzburg, 2017); B. Guest, *Stella Aurorae: The History of a South African University, vol. 3: The University of Natal, 1976–2003* (Natal Society Foundation, Pietermaritzburg, 2019); P. Maylam, *Rhodes University, 1904–2016: An Intellectual, Political and Cultural History* (Institute of Social and Economic Research, Grahamstown, 2017); A. Manson, *Unisa 1873–2018: The Making of a Distance Learning University* (Unisa Press, Pretoria, 2018); A. Grundlingh and H. Oosthuizen (eds.), *Universiteit Stellenbosch 100, 1918–2018* (Universiteit Stellenbosch, Stellenbosch, 2018).
2. J. Botha, 'Down Memory Lane – The Economic Society of South Africa: Past Presidents, 1925–63', *South African Journal of Economics*, Special Issue, September 2002, p. 74. Available at https://www.essa.org.za/memory_lane.pdf .
3. *Goethe's Faust* (translated by W. Kaufmann; Doubleday Anchor, New York, 1961), part 1, line 1237.

**Chapter 1 – UCT and the World In 1948**

1. Union of South Africa, *Debates of the House of Assembly*, 16 August 1948, col. 219.
2. UCT Libraries, Special Collections Division, BUZV Collection – Staff, T.B. Davie: 'Inaugural Address on the Occasion of the Installation of T.B. Davie as Principal, 1 March 1948'.
3. UCT Administrative Archives, 11.1.2, box 2008, Principal's Out-Letters, vol. 7: Falconer to Davie, 15 September 1947.

**Chapter 2 – Running UCT**

1. H.-D. Meyer and B. Rowan (eds.), *The New Institutionalism in Education* (SUNY Press, New York, 2006), p. 6.
2. The Senate consisted of the Principal, 45 professors, two Council members and two lecturers' representatives who, at this stage, could speak but not vote.
3. On his selection for this position, see H. Phillips, *UCT 1918–1948: The Formative Years* (UCT and UCT Press, Cape Town), p. 175.
4. *Cape Argus*, 6 April 1951.

5. UCT Administrative Archives [henceforth UCTAA], 16.1.5, box 1975, folder SEN/1, 'Albert van der Sandt Centlivres, Chancellor UCT: Memorial Ceremony, Jameson Hall, 13 October 1966', pp. 7–8.
6. *The Guardian* (London), 21 August 2000.
7. UCT Libraries, Special Collections Division, BC 1072 (Luyt Papers), A4: 'Inaugural Address of H.F. Oppenheimer, Chancellor, 30 May 1967', p. 2.
8. Ibid., p. 1.
9. UCTAA, 9A.1.2, box 1730: Statements by Dr J.F. Mountford, 12 June 1947 and by Sir Arnold McNair, 17 June 1947.
10. UCTAA, 14.1.1, box 1990, folder SEN/10: Davie to B. Gurzynski, March 1954.
11. UCTAA, 13.3.3, box 1995, folder STU/7a: Davie to Mrs Grubb, 24 April 1954.
12. UCTAA, 13.3.3, box 1994, folder STU/5: Davie to L. Walker, 27 September 1949.
13. UCT Libraries, Special Collections Division, BC 1041 (Brock Papers), box 18, folder D4: Obituaries.
14. UCTAA, 20a.1.2 (old Principal's files), Davie to Ashby, 25 March 1950.
15. *Varsity*, 26 March 1956, p. 6.
16. UCTAA, 13.3.3, box 1994, folder STU/5: J.M. Didcott to Davie, 18 August 1954; E.M. Wentzel to Principal, 11 December 1954.
17. UCT Libraries, Special Collections Division, BUZV Collection – Staff, T.B. Davie: 'Inaugural Address on the Occasion of the Installation of T.B. Davie as Principal, 1 March, 1948'.
18. Ibid., 'Address by T.B. Davie on Occasion of the University of the Witwatersrand Graduation Ceremony, 6 December 1950', p. 7.
19. T.B. Davie and E.F. Harris, *The Idea of a University: A Symposium* (SA Institute of Race Relations, Johannesburg, 1954), p. 18.
20. UCTAA, 14.1.2, box 1993, folder STU/1: 'Freshers' Week: The Meaning of a University Education', p. 2.
21. Interview with Emeritus Professor Edward Batson, 15 August 1996.
22. C.W. de Kiewiet, *Academic Freedom* (Second T.B. Davie Memorial Lecture, 26 July 1960) (UCT, Cape Town, 1960), p. 1.
23. Interview with D.V. Cowen, 7 August 1996.
24. UCT Libraries, Special Collections Division, BC 1041 (Brock Papers), D4: Obituary for T.B. Davie by L. Eales and M. van den Ende.
25. UCT Libraries, Special Collections Division, BC 7 (Davie Collection), folder 1: Professor J.F. Brock to Mrs Davie, 17 December 1955.
26. On James's academic career until then, see Phillips, *UCT 1918–1948*, pp. 343–4.
27. Interview with Sir Frank Berman, 17 February 2016.
28. UCT Libraries, Special Collections Division, R.W. James Papers: TS of speech at Cape Town City Hall meeting, 7 May 1957.
29. See Phillips, *UCT 1918–1948*, p. 5 for a photograph of him as a student in 1918.
30. Duminy was not UCT's first choice for the position of Principal. He was selected only after the two front-runners, the distinguished South African-born scientist Basil Schonland and the noted biochemist Professor F.G. Young of Cambridge University, had indicated that they would not accept the post. 'We … are left with a list of six or seven names which at best are second rate', revealed a member of Council indiscreetly – UCT Libraries, Special Collections Division: BC 1072 (Luyt Papers), B19: F.C. Robb to F.G. Young, 18 March 1957.
31. UCTAA, 14.2.1, box 1944, Speeches 1963: Speech by Duminy to Association of Universities of the British Commonwealth, 6 September 1963, p. 1.
32. Interview with Sir Frank Berman, 17 February 2016.

# NOTES

33. *Varsity*, 12 April 1961, p. 4.
34. *Varsity*, 22 March 1961, p. 2.
35. UCT Libraries, Special Collections Division, BC 133 (Duminy Papers), box 7 (Personal Correspondence M-S): Duminy to A.F. Stephen, 13 October 1964.
36. UCTAA, 14.2.1, box 1944: Graduation Address, 30 June 1967.
37. *Varsity*, 4 April 1962, p. 12.
38. *Varsity*, 13 March 1963, p. 6.
39. UCTAA, 18.1.5, box 1941, folder on 'Freshette Case': Statement by Duminy, 9 April 1964.
40. UCTAA, 14.2.1, box 1944: Graduation Address, 8 December 1966.
41. UCTAA, 14.2.1, box 1944: Draft III of speech to Institute of Citizenship, 26 November 1964.
42. UCT Libraries, Special Collections Division, BC 1072 (Luyt Papers), A4: 'Profile – Sir Richard Luyt', p. 16.
43. UCT Libraries, Special Collections Division, BUZV Collection – Staff: J.P. Duminy, 'Inaugural Address', 4 March 1958, p. 7.
44. UCTAA, 13.3.3, box 1994, folder STU/5: Duminy to W.A. von Holdt, 2 May 1966.
45. UCTAA, 14.2.1, box 1944: Graduation Address, 8 December 1966, p. 3.
46. UCTAA, 15.3.1, box 1940, folder 'Social Activities, 1957–65': A. Powell to Duminy, 8 June 1960.
47. UCTAA, 14.2.1, box 1944: Graduation Address, 30 June 1967.
48. *Varsity*, 1 June 1966, p. 4.
49. *Cape Argus*, 3 January 1968, p. 11.
50. Interview with Dr Duncan Innes, 7 January 2016.
51. *Varsity*, 7 June 1967, p. 3.
52. UCT Libraries, Special Collections Division, BC 1072 (Luyt Papers), B18: Luyt to C.L. Newton Thompson, 13 September 1966. Luyt's Oxford contemporary and South Africa's Minister of Foreign Affairs in 1966, Dr Hilgard Muller, advised Luyt not to accept the position as he was 'too out of touch' with the situation in the country (Interview with Sir Richard Luyt, 17 August 1991).
53. UCT Libraries, Special Collections Division, BC 1072 (Luyt Papers), A4: O.D. Wollheim to Luyt, 4 February 1982.
54. UCT Libraries, Special Collections Division, BC 880 (Wilson Papers), Correspondence G-H: Wilson to D. Hammond-Tooke, 6 December 1968.
55. *Rand Daily Mail*, 12 October 1968.
56. UCT Libraries, Special Collections Division, BC 1072 (Luyt Papers), B20: Tribute by L.G. Abrahamse.
57. UCTAA, 10.2.5, box 768, folder AR/20: Luyt to Professor Batson, 5 March 1968.
58. UCT Libraries, Special Collections Division, BC 1072 (Luyt Papers), A4: 'Inaugural Address of Sir Richard Edmonds Luyt, Principal and Vice-Chancellor, 19 March 1968'.
59. See p. 318
60. UCT Libraries, Special Collections Division, BC 1072 (Luyt Papers), B20: 'A leave-taking tribute to … A COMPLETE MAN, Richard Edmonds Luyt … Tribute by Sarah Cullinan, November 1980'.
61. On Inskip's earlier career at UCT, see Phillips, *UCT 1918–1948*, pp. 268–9.
62. UCT Libraries, Special Collections Division, BC 1244 (Inskip Papers), box 3, folder 1: Morris [Broughton] to Inskip, 30 June 1960.
63. See chapter 3.
64. On Carter's earlier career, see Phillips, *UCT 1918–1948*, p. 215.
65. UCTAA, 17.1.5, box 1967, folder MISC/18: Acting Principal's Report, 11 December 1953.
66. The constituencies which were represented and the number (in brackets) of members they returned were: Senate (2), the Government of the day (5), Convocation (6), the City Council of

Cape Town (2), Past Students and Life Governors (i.e. large donors) (3) and Diocesan College (1).
67. UCT Libraries, Special Collections Division, BC 1081 (Simons Collection), unnumbered box, folder C1.4 (Correspondence: Julius Lewin, 1942–84): D. Welsh to Lewin, 5 October 1967.
68. The post of associate professor had been created in 1954 to provide a promotion opportunity for high-achieving senior lecturers in departments where there was only a single professorial post.
69. See Phillips, *UCT 1918–1948*, pp. 11–12, 139–40 and 216.
70. *New York Times*, 18 March 1962.
71. UCTAA, Minutes of Senate meeting, 21 March 1961, Attachment: Confidential Memorandum to Deans' Committee by Professor Price, 16 January 1961.
72. UCTAA, Minutes of Senate meeting, 20 November 1962, Attachment: Memorandum by Professor Hutt on 'Staff Replacement', August 1961.
73. See p. 283.
74. E. Batson, 'A Reorganisation of the Academic Government of a University: A South African Sociological Study', *Sixth World Congress of Sociology, 1966: Transactions*, vol. 3 (1966), p. 357. My thanks to Hugh Amoore for this reference.
75. UCTAA, Minutes of Council meeting, 4 June 1958, p. 7.
76. UCTAA, Minutes of Senate meeting, 14 November 1960, p. 57.
77. UCTAA, 14.2.3, box 1949, folder EXT/9: Memorandum by Duminy in reply to Principal of the University of the Witwatersrand, 7 October 1965, p. 1.
78. Ibid., Duminy to I.D. MacCrone, 26 October 1965.
79. Ibid., Memorandum by Duminy in reply to Principal of the University of the Witwatersrand, 7 October 1965, p. 4.
80. UCTAA, Minutes of Senate meeting, 19 November 1963, Attachment: 'Lecturers' Association Memorandum on the New Scheme of Administration, on Promotions and on Salaries', 28 October 1963.
81. The number of these representatives finally was raised to four in 1971 and to eight in 1974.
82. UCTAA, Minutes of Council meeting, 4 August 1965, Attachment: 'Proposed Programme of Work in USA and Britain – P.G. McDonald to Principal, 14 July 1965'.
83. National Archives of South Africa, Pretoria, TES 2169, file F8/167 vol. 2: Secretary of Education, Arts and Science to Secretary of Finance, 19 December 1949.
84. UCTAA 14.2.3, box 1948, folder EXT/3a: Davie to Secretary for Education, Arts and Science, 16 January 1950.
85. National Archives of South Africa, Pretoria, TES 2169, file F8/167, vol. 2: Copy of 'Onderhoud, Vrydag 18 April 1952. Verteenwoordigers van die Komitee van Prinsipale van Universiteite en Universiteitspersoneel', p. 4.
86. UCTAA, Minutes of Senate meeting, 14 September 1959, p. 5.
87. UCTAA, Minutes of Senate meeting, 21 March 1960, Attachment: 'Announcement – A 25-Year Development Plan', 4 March 1960.
88. UCTAA 14.2.1, box 1944: Graduation Address, 15 December 1961.
89. UCTAA, Minutes of Council meeting, 5 May 1965, Attachment: Report of the Finance and General Purpose Committee, 2 June 1965, p. 7.
90. National Archives of South Africa, Pretoria, K263 (Kommissie van Ondersoek na Universiteitswese, 1968–72), box 25, Verrigtinge … 19 May 1969, vol. 3, p. 9: Evidence of Professor D.P. Inskip.
91. UCTAA, Minutes of Council meeting, 12 February 1969, Attachment E: 'Brief Summary of Financial Position for the Years 1968/9' by J.G. Finlay, 28 January 1969.
92. National Archives of South Africa, Pretoria, K263 (Kommissie van Ondersoek na Universiteitswese, 1968–72), box 25, Verrigtinge … 19 May 1969, vol. 3, p. 13: Evidence of Sir

Richard Luyt.

**Chapter 3 – Building a Second UCT**

1.. *UCT General Prospectus and Calendar*, 1948–9, p. 18.
2. This number does not include the hotel on the Main Road in Rosebank which UCT purchased for use as a residence – see p. 386, note 53.
3. UCT Administrative Archives [henceforth UCTAA], Minutes of Council meeting, 4 June 1969, p. 11.
4. UCTAA, Minutes of Council meeting, 30 July 1951, Attachment: Rhodes Trust – Rosebank Showground, Ref. no. 08985.
5. See H. Phillips, *UCT 1918–1948: The Formative Years* (UCT and UCT Press, Cape Town, 1993), p. 219.
6. Dates in brackets in this chapter indicate when a particular building was first taken into use.
7. UCTAA, Minutes of Council meeting, 29 October 1952, Attachment: New Residence for Women Students: Rhodes Trust – Report to Council from the Principal, 7 October 1952.
8. UCTAA, Minutes of Council meeting, 30 July 1951, Attachment: E.R. Syfret and Company to UCT, 16 July 1951.
9. UCT Libraries, Special Collections Division, BC 353 (Thornton White Papers), box 18, folder B27: Thornton White to Professor Price, Acting Principal, 29 January 1959.
10. UCTAA, 18.3.5, box 865, folder 'Anatomy and Radiology Building': Extract from Building Committee Report 164, D. Shipley to H.L. Kennedy, 13 February 1967; and J.D.P. van der Merwe to Deputy Finance Officer, UCT, 22 February 1967.
11. Ibid., Shipley to Kennedy, 17 February 1967.
12. On the acquisition of the Rosebank Showgrounds, see Phillips, *UCT 1918–1948*, pp. 220–1.
13. UCTAA, 14.2.1, box 1943, folder of Principal's Correspondence 1951–67: Graduation Address, 9 December 1960.
14. Ibid., 14.1.1, box 1989, folder SEN/5f: Typescript of article by Duminy for December 1967 edition of *UCT*.
15. On Thornton White, see Phillips, *UCT 1918–1948*, pp. 310–11.
16. UCT Libraries, Special Collections Division, BC 353, box 17, folder B26: Thornton White to Howell, 4 August 1964.
17. UCTAA, Minutes of Senate meeting, 20 November 1962.
18. UCTAA, Minutes of Senate meeting, 19 October 1959, Attachment: Memorandum on the Proposed New Administration Building, 19 September 1959.
19. Bremner Building was named after Mary Frances Bremner (1873–1959), the widow of a manager of Standard Bank who had left his picture collection to UCT on his death in 1938. Childless, she bequeathed the residue of her very substantial estate to UCT, perhaps having been influenced to do so by a friend, UCT's Chancellor Albert van der Sandt Centlivres. Council decided to commemorate her 'magnificent bequest' by naming its new Administration Building after her (UCTAA, Minutes of Council meeting, 7 October 1959, p. 13; UCTAA, Minutes of Senate meeting, 18 April 1961, p. 5; *Varsity*, 16 August 1961, p. 4; personal information from Neil Veitch, March 2015).
20. See Phillips, *UCT 1918–1948*, pp. 311–12.
21. UCT Libraries, Special Collections Division, BC 353, box 18, folder B26: Thornton White to Longstreth Thompson, 11 November 1959.
22. *Varsity*, 4 June 1959, p. 4.
23. *Varsity*, 13 August 1959, p. 2.
24. This widening of Rhodes Drive meant that the statue of Cecil John Rhodes perched on its edge

# UCT UNDER APARTHEID

since 1934 had to be removed, which it was in 1962, to the steps above UCT's rugby fields where it remained until the advent of #RhodesMustFall in 2015.

25. UCTAA, Minutes of Council meeting, 2 June 1965, Attachment: Report 84 of Building Committee, 30 April 1965, p. 6.
26. *UCT Redevelopment Survey 1964* (n.p., Cape Town, 1964), p. 254.
27. UCT Libraries, Special Collections Division, BC 353, box 17, B26: Thornton White to D. Harper, 8 July 1964.
28. UCTAA, Minutes of Council meeting, 4 August 1965, Attachment: Honorary Secretary, UCT Staff Association, to Registrar, 14 June 1965.
29. *Varsity*, 13 March 1963, p. 2.
30. *Cape Times*, 2 December 1958.
31. UCTAA, Minutes of Council meeting, 13 December 1967, Attachment: Report 201 of Building Committee, 8 December 1967, Uytenbogaardt to Inskip, 27 November 1967. Uytenbogaardt himself won the contract with his design for the Sports Centre. In 1970 he succeeded Strauss Brink as head of the School of Architecture.
32. UCT Libraries, Special Collections Division, BC 1217 (Jack Barnett Papers), box 27, folder D2.4.1: Barnett to L. Read, 15 May 1968.
33. Solomon Morris had graduated with a BSc (Civil Engineering) from UCT in 1933.
34. See p. 28.
35. See p. 311.
36. Other than the name University Avenue, which dated from 1929, these names were given in 1959 (UCTAA, Minutes of Council meeting, 4 November 1959, p. 11). Sports Avenue was renamed Rugby Road in 1962 (*UCT Principal's Circular* no. 33, 6 June 1962, p. 24).
37. UCTAA, Minutes of Senate meeting, 17 April 1951, Attachment: 'Memorandum on Siting of the New School of Architecture' by Thornton White, February 1951, p. 2.
38. *UCT Redevelopment Survey, 1964*, p. 113.
39. UCTAA, Minutes of Senate meeting, 17 June 1952, Attachment: letter from Lecturers' Association, 28 May 1952.
40. UCTAA, Minutes of Senate meeting, 16 April 1963, Attachment: Memorandum 'Parking at Orange Street' by Professor Hutt; UCTAA, Minutes of Senate meeting, 7 June 1966, Attachment: Letter from G. van Dyk (Vice-Chairman of Cape Chartered Accountants Students Society) to Registrar, 11 May 1966; UCTAA, Minutes of Council meeting, Attachment: Building Committee Report no. 84, 30 April 1965.
41. The SACS classrooms were renamed the Ritchie Building after the long-serving professor of Classics, William Ritchie (Phillips, *UCT 1918–1948*, pp. 14–15); the SACS hostel building remained known as Rosedale; and other halls were turned into mini-theatres or rehearsal rooms. However, the Paddock on the other side of Government Avenue was transferred to Cape Town High School.
42. UCT Libraries, Special Collections Division, BC 353, box 18, folder B 26: Thornton White to J.H. Stewart-Munn, 17 July 1965.
43. D. Greig, *A Guide to Architecture in South Africa* (Timmins, Cape Town, 1971), pp. 215–16.
44. UCTAA, Minutes of Council meeting, 5 November 1969, p. 2.

**Chapter 4 – Teaching, Learning and Researching: UCTs Academic Project**

1. That teaching in universities should be guided by current research was one of the revolutionary ideas propounded by the Prussian educational theorist and policy-maker, Wilhelm von Humboldt (1767–1835). From the University of Berlin where he began to implement it from 1810, it spread

throughout Europe, its settler colonies and North America in the next 150 years. According to him, universities should treat science 'as a problem which is never completely solved and therefore [they should be] engaged in constant research' (cited in *Prospects: The Quarterly Review of Comparative Education*, XXIII, 3/4 (1993), p. 620).
2. See H. Phillips, *UCT 1918–1948: The Formative Years* (UCT and UCT Press, Cape Town, 1993), p. 223.
3. Between 1961 and 1968, 177 doctorates, 391 Master's degrees and 552 Honours degrees were awarded, compared to 150 doctorates, 254 Master's degrees and 112 Honours degrees between 1951 and 1960.
4. UCT Administrative Archives [henceforth UCTAA], Minutes of Senate meeting, 21 March 1950, p. 111.
5. *CSIR Annual Report*, 1965, p. 33.
6. On the Bremner Bequest, see p. 347, note 19.
7. J. Scrivener, *Learning Teaching: A Guidebook for English Language Teaching* (Macmillan Education, Oxford, 2nd edition, 2005), p. 17.
8. *Varsity*, 7 September 1961, p. 5.
9. Interview with M. Fielding, 14 April 2016.
10. *Varsity*, 16 May 1962, p. 5.
11. Interviews with Dr E. Sapire, 22 October 2015 and with Dr C. le Grange, 18 April 2016.
12. *Varsity*, 27 August 1969, p. 3.
13. UCTAA, 18.4.3, box 830: Education '70 Survey, pp. B1, B2 and A3.
14. Interview with S. Bottcher, 7 March 2016.
15. Interview with Mr Justice Albie Sachs, 9 May 2016.
16. Interview with B. Rabinowitz, 1 April 2016.
17. Interview with Emeritus Professor G. Branch, 27 June 2016.
18. Address by Emeritus Professor Arderne Forder at Gala Dinner at 2007 Medical Graduation Reunion, 8 December 2007 at http://web.uct.ac.za/old/health/alumni/reunions/2007/1957/roundup_1957.htm.
19. J. Lawrence, *Past Imperfect* (Gryphon Press, Cape Town, 2014), p. 80.
20. Interview with Dr N. Rubin, 2 March 2016.
21. Cited in H. Beukes, *Long Road to Liberation: An Exiled Namibian Activist's Perspective* (Porcupine Press, Johannesburg, 2014), p. 40.
22. Interview with K. Pay, 14 March 2016.
23. UCTAA, 33.6.3, UCT Graduation Programme, 25 June 1982: Citation for Distinguished Teacher Award to Kathleen Irene Pay.
24. Phillips, *UCT 1918–1948*, p. 259.
25. UCTAA, Minutes of Council meeting, 27 October 1954, p. 76.
26. Interview with Emeritus Professor George Branch, 27 June 2016.
27. UCTAA, 14.2.3, box 1949, folder EXT/3b, University Finance Commission 1951–4: UCT Replies to Questionnaire U/1 … March 1952.
28. UCT Libraries, Special Collections Department, BC 689 (Mackie Notebooks), box 3: Conference of University Teachers of English … 10–12 July 1946.
29. *The Friend*, 23 July 1958.
30. UCTAA, 18.4.3, box 830: Education '70 Survey, p. C1.
31. *Varsity*, 27 March 1958, p. 3.
32. UCT Libraries, Special Collections Department, BC 290 (Goodwin Papers), box 23, folder F1.3.1: Goodwin to Glyn Daniel, 13 December 1948.
33. UCTAA, *UCT Principal's Circular*, no. 126, 8 February 1967, Appendix: Extract from *Sunday Times*,

2 October 1966.
34. Republic of South Africa, Department of Education, Arts and Science, *Report of Commission of Inquiry into Method of Training for University Degrees in Engineering (Straszacker Report)*, Part I & Part II, p. 97, #473.
35. *Trend*, 4 April 1967, p. 3.
36. Interview with Emeritus Associate Professor John Atkinson, 1 September 2015.

**Chapter 5 – Pure Science: The Faculty of Science**
1. UCT Administrative Archives [henceforth UCTAA], Minutes of Senate meeting, 17 March 1952, Appendix: Replies to Questionnaire from University Finances Commission, March 1952, pp. 3–7.
2. UCTAA, Minutes of Senate meeting, 11 November 1969, Appendix C: Memorandum by Warren, 26 September 1969.
3. UCTAA, Minutes of Senate meeting, 19 August 1957, Appendix: Memorandum by Schaffer, 25 August 1957, Staffing of Physics Department.
4. See p. 7.
5. On his earlier career at UCT, see H. Phillips, *UCT 1918–1948: The Formative Years* (UCT and UCT Press, Cape Town, 1993), p. 345.
6. On James's distinguished work in this field, see ibid., pp. 343–4.
7. E. Derman, *My Life as a Quant: Reflections on Physics and Finance* (Wiley, Hoboken, 2004), p. 18.
8. National Archives of South Africa, Pretoria, K 213, Archives of Commission of Enquiry into Method of Training for University Degrees in Engineering (Straszacker Commission), box 251, file marked 'South African curricula', transcript of tape 279: Evidence of Professor Schaffer, 18 November 1965, p. 3.
9. UCTAA, 14.1.1, box 1990, folder SEN/8 (Staff), sub-file 'Staff Promotions: Associate Professorships': James to T.B. Davie, 14 October 1954.
10. A. Buffler, 'Frank Brooks, 1931–2012' at http://www.phy.uct.ac.za/sites/default/files/image_tool/images/281/history/frank-brooks-obituary-ab.pdf.
11. UCTAA, 12.3.1, Chair of Theoretical Physics, 1963: F.R.N. Nabarro to Acting Registrar, UCT, 12 August 1963.
12. P.E. Spargo, *A Brief Account of the Faculty of Science at the University of Cape Town* (UCT, 1989), p. 11.
13. Max Born, *My Life and My Views* (1968), cited at https://todayinsci.com/B/Born_Max/BornMax-Quotations.htm.
14. National Archives of South Africa, Pretoria, K 213, Archives of Commission of Enquiry into Method of Training for University Degrees in Engineering (Straszacker Commission), box 251, file marked 'South African curricula', transcript of tape 279: Evidence of Professor Schaffer, 18 November 1965, p. 2
15. Interview with Emeritus Professor George Branch, 27 June 2016.
16. Interview with Emeritus Professor David Aschman, 24 October 2016.
17. Originally this copper-domed observatory had been mounted on the top of the old Physics–Mathematics Block to mark the 1957 International Geophysical Year. It was moved to the new James Building in 1966.
18. UCTAA, Minutes of Senate meeting, 16 November 1959, Appendix: Qualifying Course in Astronomy – A Report of the Subcommittee, 8 October 1959.
19. Interview with Emeritus Professor Marian Jacobs, 23 May 2015.
20. UCTAA, Minutes of Senate meeting, 14 April 1964, Appendix: Memorandum on Staffing by Professor E.C. Leisegang, n.d.
21. UCTAA, Minutes of Senate meeting, 16 April 1963, Appendix: Department of Chemistry, Memorandum on Staffing, March 1963.

22. *Trend*, 4 October 1966, p. 3.
23. Interview with Emeritus Professor Luigi Nassimbeni, 17 May 2016.
24. UCTAA, 13.1.2 (Chair of Chemistry 1920–1949): F.G. Mann to Registrar, UCT, 8 February 1949.
25. UCTAA, Minutes of Senate meeting, 16 November 1965, Appendix: Report of Subcommittee on Establishment of Chair and Department of Biochemistry, n.d.
26. L. Bohm, 'Claus von Holt 1925–2009' in *South African Journal of Science*, 105, 5/6 (May/June 2009), p. 170.
27. UCTAA, 13.1.2 (Chair of Chemistry, 1955, 1961; Chair of Organic Chemistry, 1961): L.R. Wager to Registrar, UCT, 29 July 1955.
28. S.R. Taylor, 'Memorial of Louis H. Ahrens, 1918–1990' in *American Mineralogist*, 80 (1995), p. 411.
29. O. Illner-Paine, 'South Africa Struggles to Keep Abreast' in *New Scientist*, 12 July 1973, p. 87.
30. *The Argus*, 4 September 1969.
31. L.H. Ahrens Scrapbook, 1970–1: SRC to Professor Louis Ahrens, 1971. My thanks to Mrs Y. Trainor, Ahrens's daughter, for giving me access to this volume.
32. *Cape Times*, 30 April 1963.
33. On Walker, see Phillips, *UCT 1918–1948*, pp. 357–9.
34. *UCT Staff Newsletter*, October 1958, p. 18.
35. UCTAA, 13.1.4, Chair of Geology, 1938, 1956, 1974: Confidential Report by F. Walker, 31 August 1956.
36. A.C. Brown, 'Some Royal but Unmentioned Fellows' in *Transactions of the Royal Society of South Africa*, 69, 1 (2014), p. 53.
37. Interview with Emeritus Professor Frank Shillington, 9 November 2016.
38. On her earlier career at UCT, see Phillips, *UCT 1918–1948*, p. 358.
39. H. Swingler, 'Doyenne of Geology Celebrates 100th Birthday' in *UCT Daily News*, 22 May 2013 at http://www.uct.ac.za/dailynews/?id=8455.
40. Davie had come to UCT from the University of Liverpool, which had pioneered the teaching of oceanography already in the 1920s. Tellingly too, one of Davie's staunchest allies in this initiative was Professor John Day of the Zoology Department, who had gained at doctorate in Liverpool's Department of Oceanography.
41. *Cape Times*, 31 October 1951.
42. On Gilchrist, see Phillips, *UCT 1918–1948*, pp. 56–7.
43. UCTAA, Minutes of Senate meeting, 15 August 1960, Appendix: Day to Registrar, 15 June 1960.
44. See Phillips, *UCT 1918–1948*, pp. 354–7.
45. Interview with Jennie Jarvis, 5 September 2016.
46. Interview with Emeritus Professor Charles Griffiths, 15 November 2016.
47. A.C. Brown, 'Reminiscences of John Day', *Transactions of the Royal Society of South Africa*, 47, 4 & 5 (1991), p. 779.
48. J.H. Day, *A Monograph on the Polychaeta of Southern Africa*, parts I and II (British Museum, London, 1967).
49. 'John Hemsworth Osborne Day 1909–1989' in *South African Journal of Marine Science*, 8, 1 (1989), p. 2.
50. A.C. Brown, 'Reminiscences of John Day', *Transactions of the Royal Society of South Africa*, 47, 4 & 5 (1991), p. 779.
51. Ibid.
52. A.C. Brown, 'Centennial History of the Zoology Department, UCT, 1903–2003: A Personal Memoir', *Transactions of the Royal Society of South Africa*, 58, 1 (2003), p. 17.
53. Interview with Mike Jarvis, 25 October 2016.
54. Anon., 'An Appreciation of Alexander Claude Brown', *Transactions of the Royal Society of South*

*Africa*, 58, 1 (2003), p. 23.
55. UCTAA, 33.5.6, Graduation Programmes 1980–5: Graduation Programme 26 June 1981, citation for Distinguished Teacher Award – Professor Alexander Claude Brown.
56. On Broekhuysen's early career, see Phillips, *UCT 1918–1948*, p. 355.
57. Sir James Percy FitzPatrick (1862–1931) was a politician, mining magnate, agricultural entrepreneur and author of *Jock of the Bushveld*. The Percy FitzPatrick Memorial Trust donated £15,000 to UCT in 1959 to establish an avian research institute in his memory. Dr Jack Winterbottom was its first director, from 1960 to 1971, during which time it began to put ornithology in South Africa onto a professional, scientific footing with its pioneering surveys of avian geography and ecology and detailed studies of individual bird species. 'Ornithology is becoming academically respectable', Winterbottom proudly declared in 1964, 'and bird-watching is ceasing to be regarded as an occupation for cranks' (J.M. Winterbottom, 'South African Ornithology To-day', *Lantern*, 14, 1 (September 1964), p. 8).
58. *Nature*, 190 (17 June 1961), p. 1058.
59. C. Helman, *Suburban Shaman: A Journey through Medicine* (Double Storey, Cape Town, 2004), p. 9.
60. Ibid.
61. Interview by e-mail with Sandra Fowkes, 10 March 2016.
62. Interview by e-mail with Aletta Loopuyt, 23 November 2015.
63. E-mail from Anthony Hooper, 24 November 2015.
64. Interview by e-mail with Sandra Fowkes, 10 March 2016.
65. Interview with Emeritus Professor George Branch, 27 June 2016.
66. On Adamson's career at UCT before 1948, see Phillips, *UCT 1918–1948*, p. 350.
67. UCTAA, 13.2.1, Chair of Botany 1961: M.R. Levyns to J.P. Duminy, 23 September 1961.
68. Ibid., N.P. Badenhuizen to J.P. Duminy, 2 October 1961.
69. Ibid., R.A. Dyer to J.P. Duminy, 25 September 1961.
70. UCTAA, Minutes of Senate meeting, 21 March 1955, Appendix: Memorandum by W.E. Isaac on Increased Maintenance Grant for the Botany Department, 2 March 1965.
71. Interview with Dr John Rourke, 1 December 2016.
72. On the Bolus Herbarium under 'Ma' Bolus, see Phillips, *UCT 1918–1948*, pp. 351–2.
73. Interview with Dr John Rourke, 1 December 2016.
74. A. Hooper, 'It was all about belonging – UCT in the early 1960s', p. 8 (e-mail to author, 8 December 2015).
75. Interview with Dr John Rourke, 1 December 2016.
76. J. Rourke, 'Hedley Brian Rycroft FRSSAf, 1918–90', *Transactions of the Royal Society of South Africa*, 50, 1 (August 1995), p. 105.
77. Interview with Professor Tim Hoffman, 18 November 2016.
78. E-mail from Aletta Loopuyt, 23 November 2015.
79. UCTAA, 13.2.1, Chair of Botany 1961: N.P. Badenhuizen to J.P. Duminy, 2 October 1961.
80. M.R.B. Levyns, *Insnar'd with Flow'rs: The Memoirs of a Great South African Botanist* (Botanical Society of South Africa, Kirstenbosch, 1977), p. 135.
81. A.A. Forder, 'Address to Gala Dinner, 8 December 2007' at http://web.uct.ac.za/old/health/alumni/reunions/2007/1957/roundup_1957.htm .
82. Ibid.
83. That UCT was willing to accept such breaching of the almost sacrosanct walls between departments, let alone between faculties, speaks volumes of the perceived importance of the new field.
84. W.J. Lütjeharms, 'Erfenis en Roeping', *Die bult. Oudstudenteblad van die UOVS* (1960), p. 82. Translation from Afrikaans by the author.

85. On Talbot and the early history of the Geography Department, see Phillips, *UCT 1918–1948*, pp. 360–2.
86. M.E. Meadows and R.F. Fuggle, 'Environmental and Geographical Science on the Slopes of Devil's Peak' in G. Visser, R. Donaldson and C. Seethal (eds.), *The Origin and Growth of Geography as a Discipline in South African Universities* (SUN Press, Stellenbosch, 2016), p. 121.
87. National Archives of South Africa, Pretoria, NRSN 32, file N/R/6/59: Director Trigonometrical Survey to Government Printer, 13 May 1953.
88. *Journal of Science Society*, 3 (1960), p. 10.
89. National Archives of South Africa, Pretoria, NRSN 32, file N/R/6/59: Secretary for Lands to Secretary for the Treasury, 12 October 1954. Translation from Afrikaans by the author.
90. UCTAA, 12.1.1, Lecturer in Geography 1958: Talbot to Registrar, 13 September 1957.
91. Ibid.
92. R. Fuggle, 'Visualising Information in the Pre-Digital Age' at http://www.digitalcollections.lib.uct.ac.za/humanitec/talbot.
93. Ibid. Today the African maps in this Talbot Collection have been digitised; see http://www.digitalcollections.lib.uct.ac.za/special-collections-maps.
94. Interview by e-mail with Rosemary Wailes (née Sharland), 26 November 2015.
95. UCT Libraries, Special Collections Division, BC 1079 (Talbot Papers), D3.1 (Departmental Information): Cyclostyled sheet, 1974.
96. Interview by e-mail with Rosemary Wailes (née Sharland), 26 November 2015.
97. UCTAA, 45.4.2, box 1, K.O. Househam personal file: Report on Study and Research Leave, 19 July 1976 – 18 July 1977.
98. National Archives of South Africa, Pretoria, K 213, Archives of Commission of Enquiry into Method of Training for University Degrees in Engineering (Straszacker Commission), box 251: Transcript of tape 279, p. 5, Evidence of Professor D.G. Parkyn.
99. *UCT Principal's Circular*, 158 (4 September 1968), p, 7.
100. UCTAA, Minutes of Senate meeting, 16 April 1963, Appendix: Departments of Pure Mathematics and Applied Mathematics – Request for Additional Cleaner by K.O. Househam and D.C. Parkyn, 12 March 1963.
101. Interview by e-mail with Professor Aaron Sloman, 29 January 2016.
102. Though Hales had taken his first degrees and his doctoral degree (1936) at UCT.
103. See Phillips, *UCT 1918–1948*, pp. 364–5.
104. UCTAA, 13.2.4, Chairs of Mathematics: Confidential memorandum by Professor Sears, 21 August 1961, p. 1.
105. *UCT Faculties of Arts and Science Prospectus*, 1967, p. 67.
106. UCTAA, 18.4.2, box 828, Computer Facilities 1966–78: Househam to Luyt, 5 April 1969.
107. UCTAA, Minutes of Senate meeting, 14 April 1964, Appendix: Memorandum of Renaming of Department of Pure Mathematics by Professor Househam, 10 March 1964.
108. J.M. Coetzee, *Summertime: Scenes from Provincial Life* (Vintage, London, 2010), p. 88. The tutor was the later Nobel Prize winner for Literature, John Coetzee, of whom the course convenor wrote, 'for calm competence he is very hard to beat, and he has been a most patient and helpful demonstrator to the most fatheaded of first-years' (cited in J.C. Kannemeyer, *J.M. Coetzee: A Life in Writing* (Jonathan Ball, Johannesburg, 2012), p. 105).
109. UCTAA, 13.1.1, Pure Mathematics Chair, 1948: Copy of Titchmarsh to Secretary of Association of Universities of the British Commonwealth, 4 March 1949.
110. UCTAA, 13.2.4, Chairs of Mathematics 1959–61: Confidential memorandum by Sears on Chairs of Applied and Pure Mathematics, 21 August 1961.
111. UCTAA, 45.4.2, box 1, K.O. Househam personal file: Househam to Registrar, 10 August 1961.

112. UCTAA, 13.2.4, Chairs of Mathematics 1959–61: Schaffer to Registrar, 15 August 1961.
113. UCTAA, 45.4.2, box 1, K.O. Househam personal file: Househam to Luyt, 3 November 1971.
114. UCTAA, 13.2.4, Chairs of Mathematics 1959–61: Confidential memorandum by Sears on Chairs of Applied and Pure Mathematics, 21 August 1961.
115. Interview with Emeritus Professor Ronnie Becker, 21 December 2016.
116. See p. 18.
117. UCTAA, 45.4.2, box 1, K.O. Househam personal file: Househam to Registrar, 21 January 1964.
118. On Skewes's career at UCT before 1948, see Phillips, *UCT 1918–1948*, p. 364.
119. On Pollard's career at UCT before 1948, see ibid., pp. 362–3.
120. UCTAA, 14.1.1, box 1990, folder SEN/8, sub-file 'Staff Promotions – Associate Professorships': Memorandum on Promotions to Senior Lecturers and Associate Professorships by D.B. Sears, 12 October 1954.
121. Interview with Kathleen Pay, 14 March 2016.
122. *UCT Principal's Circular*, 75 (8 July 1964): Memorandum for Applicants for Senior Lectureship in (Pure) Mathematics, 6 July 1964.
123. UCTAA, 14.1.1, box 1990, folder SEN/8 (Staff), sub-file 'Ad hoc promotions 1955 & 1956': Memorandum by D.B. Sears, 14 September 1956.
124. 'Research News' in *Journal of Science Society*, 6 (1963), p. 9.
125. Interview with Emeritus Professor David Aschman, 24 October 2016.
126. National Archives of South Africa, Pretoria, K 213, Archives of Commission of Enquiry into Method of Training for University Degrees in Engineering (Straszacker Commission), box 251: Transcript of tape 279, p. 6, Evidence of Professor D.G. Parkyn.
127. UCTAA, Minutes of Senate meeting, 14 April 1964, Appendix: 'Comments on proposed changes in syllabuses in Applied Mathematics for Engineers' by K.O. Househam, 5 March 1964.
128. On Reyburn's career at UCT, see Phillips, *UCT 1918–1948*, pp. 29–30, 282–4.
129. UCTAA, Minutes of Senate meeting, 18 November 1952, Appendix: Letter by J.G. Taylor, 24 October 1952.
130. K. Danziger, *Confessions of a Marginal Psychologist*, p. 1 at http://www.kurtdanziger.com/autobiogms.pdf.
131. J. Louw, 'South Africa' in D.B. Baker (ed.), *The Oxford Handbook of the History of Psychology: Global Perspectives* (OUP, Oxford, 2012), p. 497.
132. UCT Libraries, Special Collections Division, BC 880 (Wilson Papers), unnumbered box marked 'Correspondence G, H': Report by Professor Monica Wilson to Center for Advanced Study in Behavioral Sciences, Stanford University, 28 October 1960.
133. UCTAA, 4.2.5, box 354, K. Danziger personal file: O.A. Oeser to Registrar, UCT, 24 July 1957.
134. K. Danziger, *Confessions of a Marginal Psychologist*, p. 12 at http://www.kurtdanziger.com/autobiogms.pdf.
135. K. Danziger, 'Ideology and Utopia in South Africa: A Methodological Contribution to the Sociology of Knowledge', *British Journal of Sociology*, 14, 1 (1963), p. 76.
136. K. Danziger, *Confessions of a Marginal Psychologist*, p. 20 at http://www.kurtdanziger.com/autobiogms.pdf.
137. *Varsity*, 24 June 1964, p. 2.
138. *Varsity*, 1 September 1965, p. 3.
139. *Cape Times*, 11 August 1965.
140. R.W. Bieber (ed.), *Encyclopedia of the History of Psychological Theories*, part 4 (Springer, New York, 2012), pp. 142–3; K. Keith (ed.), *Encyclopedia of Cross-Cultural Psychology* (Wiley, Hoboken, 2013), p. 634.
141. *Cape Argus*, 13 December 2004.

142. UCTAA, 13.1.6, Chair of Psychology 1966: S.P. Jackson to Principal and Vice-Chancellor UCT, 2 May 1966.
143. Interview with Emeritus Professor Don Foster, 22 December 2016.
144. On their earlier work in the department, see Phillips, *UCT 1918–1948*, pp. 30, 283 and 316. A senior lecturer in the department, Dr Elise Botha, a disciple of Taylor, also acted as head of the department, but just for six months when Grover was on sabbatical leave in 1966.
145. UCTAA, 13.1.6, Chair of Psychology 1951: Taylor to Registrar, UCT, 2 September 1952.
146. Ibid., J.F. Foster to Registrar, UCT, 3 May 1951.
147. J.G. Taylor, *The Behavioral Basis of Perception* (Yale University Press, New Haven, 1962).
148. N. Sheehy, A.J. Chapman and W.A. Conroy (eds.), *Biographical Dictionary of Psychology* (Routledge, London and New York, 1997), pp. 559–60.
149. See p. 248.
150. UCTAA, Minutes of Council meeting, 4 October 1967, Appendix: Report of the Ad Hoc Promotions Committee, 12 September 1967.
151. It was renamed the Chair of Intellectual Disability in 2007.
152. Interview by e-mail with Benjamin Pogrund, 29 November 2015.
153. Ibid.
154. Interview by e-mail with Professor Andrew Colman, 26 March 2016.
155. H.A. Reyburn, *An Introduction to Psychology* (2nd edition, Maskew Miller, Cape Town, 1924), p. 169.
156. UCT Libraries, Special Collections Division, BC 133 (Duminy Papers), box 26, file marked 'Speeches, Addresses 1959–61': Principal's Address at Graduation Ceremonies, December 1959.
157. *Trend*, 4 October 1966, p. 3.

**Chapter 6 – The Applied Sciences: Engineering and Medicine**

1. M. Young and G. Whitty (eds.), *Society, State and Schooling* (Falmer Press, Brighton, 1977), p. 23.
2. National Archives of South Africa, Pretoria [hereafter NASA], K 213 (Commission of Inquiry into the Method of Training for University Degrees in Engineering – Straszacker Commission), box 150, envelope marked 'Visit to the Univ. of CT', Interviews by Commission with Staff Members, p. 8: Comment by D.P.J. Retief, 2 November 1961.
3. UCT Administrative Archives [henceforth UCTAA,] Minutes of Council meeting, 3 April 1963, Attachment: Report on the Building Requirement of Electrical and Mechanical Engineering by L.W. Thornton White, February 1963.
4. D. Goldberg, *The Mission: A Life for Freedom in South Africa* (STE Publishers, Johannesburg, 2010), p. 46.
5. *Varsity*, 28 August 1963, p. 6.
6. NASA, K213 (Straszacker Commission), box 150, 'Visit to the Univ. of CT', Interrogation of Students, 3 November 1959, p. 10: Evidence of J. Connold.
7. Ibid., 'Interviews by Commission with Staff Members', p. 16: Evidence of Dr Einhorn, 5–6 November 1959.
8. Interview with P. Naylor, 17 May 2016.
9. Interview with E.J. Robertson, 9 November 2015.
10. NASA, K213 (Straszacker Commission), box 148, 'Replies to Questionnaire Submitted by Commission of Inquiry (Memorandum U)', Questionnaire in *Government Gazette*, 3 January 1958, EC/QU/3.58: Reply to Questionnaire (Universities) Submitted by D.C. Robertson, p. 1.
11. See H. Phillips, *UCT 1918–1948: The Formative Years* (UCT and UCT Press, Cape Town, 1993), pp. 77–8. This description last appeared in the *UCT Faculty of Engineering Prospectus*, 1956, p. 2.
12. *UCT Faculty of Engineering Prospectus*, 1957, p. 2. Stoicheiometry is the branch of chemistry dealing with chemical combination in very precise proportions.

13. NASA, K 213 (Straszacker Commission), box 151, file on 'SA curricula', Interviews with UCT Staff, tape 277, p. 4: Evidence of A.D. Carr.
14. UCT Registry, Bremner Building, Personal file of A.D. Carr: E.T. Woodburn to Registrar, UCT, 4 March 1965.
15. NASA, K213 (Straszacker Commission), box 150, 'Visit to the Univ. of CT', Interviews by Commission with Staff Members, p. 25: Evidence of R.G. Robertson, 5–6 November 1959.
16. Ibid., p. 6: Evidence of D.C. Robertson.
17. See Phillips, *UCT 1918–1948*, pp. 75–7.
18. NASA, K213 (Straszacker Commission), box 150, 'Visit to the Univ. of CT', Interviews by Commission with Staff Members, p. 6: Evidence of R.G. Robertson, 5–6 November 1959.
19. Ibid., p. 22: Evidence of R.G. Robertson, 5–6 November 1959.
20. UCTAA, 12.3.4, 'Senior Lecturer in Civil Engineering, 1950': J.F. Foster to T.B. Davie, 7 April 1949.
21. Ibid., 77.1.4, box 11, personal file of F.A. Kilner: Robertson to Registrar, 4 October 1963.
22. *CSIR Scientiae*, 3, 1 (January 1962), p. 8.
23. UCTAA, 44.1.8, box 1, personal file of M.F. Kaplan: N. Stutterheim to J.R. Benfield, Registrar, UCT, 26 March 1965.
24. Kaplan's multi-sided ability and capacity for clear thinking saw him fill the chair for only five years before being appointed Deputy Principal of UCT in 1972.
25. *Cape Argus*, 20 December 1966, letter from M.F. Kaplan.
26. See Phillips, *UCT 1918–1948*, pp. 73–4.
27. NASA, K213 (Straszacker Commission), box 150, 'Visit to the Univ. of CT', Interviews by Commission with Staff Members, pp. 10–11: Evidence of G.G. Elliott, 5 November 1959.
28. UCTAA, 13.2.4, Chair of Mechanical Engineering, 1956: Handwritten comment on the list of applicants [almost certainly by T.B. Davie].
29. UCT Registry, Bremner Building, Personal file of P. Metcalf: A. Fogg to Registrar, UCT, 30 May 1961.
30. NASA, K213 (Straszacker Commission), box 150, 'Visit to the Univ. of CT', Interviews by Commission with Staff Members, p. 12: Evidence of G.G. Elliott, 5–6 November 1959.
31. NASA, K213 (Straszacker Commission), box 150, 'Visit to the Univ. of CT', Interrogation of Students, 3 November 1959, pp. 2, 4: Evidence of C. Malan.
32. UCTAA, Minutes of Senate meeting, 14 April 1964, Appendix: Memorandum by P. Metcalf, 13 September 1963, 'Additional Post of Senior Lecturer'.
33. UCT Registry, Bremner Building, Personal file of P. Metcalf: Elliott to Registrar, UCT, 2 June 1961.
34. See Phillips, *UCT 1918–1948*, pp. 299–300 on Goodlet's earlier career at UCT.
35. See Phillips, *UCT 1918–1948*, p. 300 on Guelke's early career at UCT.
36. Interview with Professor Adrian Guelke, 19 September 2016.
37. NASA, K213 (Straszacker Commission), box 150, 'Visit to the Univ. of CT', Inspection of Various Depts, 2 November 1959, p. 2: Evidence of R. Guelke.
38. UCTAA, 13.1.3, Chair of Electrical Engineering 1971: Guelke to Registrar, 16 March 1971. On another long-serving member of the department who did not receive promotion, Heinz Einhorn, see Phillips, *UCT 1918–1948*, p. 300 and above p. 142.
39. NASA, K213 (Straszacker Commission), box 150, 'Visit to the Univ. of CT', Interrogation of Students, 3 November 1959, p. 2: Evidence of E. Malan.
40. Ibid., p. 6: Evidence of C. Guelke [the professor's son].
41. Ibid., p. 3: Evidence of W. de Beer.
42. NASA, K213 (Straszacker Commission), box 150, 'Visit to the Univ. of CT', Inspection of

Various Depts, 2 November 1959, p. 2: Evidence of G. Menzies.
43. On the early history of Land Surveying at UCT and on Menzies, see Phillips, *UCT 1918–1948*, pp. 301–2.
44. NASA, K213 (Straszacker Commission), box 150, 'Univ. of Cape Town': Memorandum by G. Menzies, 2 November 1959, p. 4.
45. UCTAA, 4.2.4, box 352, personal file of B. Chiat: Reference by J. Packer, 18 October 1947.
46. UCTAA, 12.1.3, Lecturer in Land Surveying, 1967: P.L. Meadows to Registrar, UCT, 28 August 1967 (referring to L. Eekhout).
47. *Impact (Journal of the Engineering Society)*, 1963, p. 7.
48. Interview with Emeritus Professor D. Cooper, 10 February 2017.
49. Interview with Professor B. Turok, 10 November 2016.
50. *Varsity*, 20 June 1962, p. 7.
51. *Impact (Journal of the Engineering Society)*, 1963, p. 7.
52. *Journal of the UCT Engineering and Scientific Society*, VI, 4 (1950), p. 1.
53. NASA, K213 (Straszacker Commission), box 150, 'Visit to the Univ. of CT', Interrogation of Students, 3 November 1959, p. 10: Evidence of J. Brakeridge.
54. Cited in J.V. Reid and A.J. Wilmot (eds.), *Medical Education in South Africa* (Natal University Press, Pietermaritzburg, 1965), p. 377.
55. UCTAA, Minutes of Senate meeting, 16 May 1955, Appendix: Minimum Medical Curriculum – Preamble to Reply to SAMDC, n.d.
56. Cited in Reid and Wilmot (eds.), *Medical Education in South Africa*, p. 151.
57. Union of South Africa, *Report of the Commission of Enquiry into Facilities at Hospitals for Medical and Dental Training, 1950*, p. 26, #69.
58. C. Illingworth, 'Medical Education: A Plea for Initiative and Experiment', *Lancet*, I (8 February 1964), p. 286.
59. To these were added the Princess Alice Orthopaedic Hospital in 1955 and Red Cross Children's Hospital in 1956. In 1958 the teaching role of the Lady Michaelis Home was transferred to the new Faculty of Medicine at Stellenbosch University.
60. Province of the Cape of Good Hope, *Third and General Report by the Groote Schuur Hospital Committee of Inquiry*, p. 9, #42.
61. J.H. Louw, *In the Shadow of Table Mountain: A History of the University of Cape Town Medical School and Its Associated Teaching Hospitals up to 1950, with Glimpses into the Future* (Struik, Cape Town, 1969), p. 301.
62. Cited in A. Digby and H. Phillips, with H. Deacon and K. Thomson, *At the Heart of Healing: Groote Schuur Hospital 1938–2008* (Jacana Media, Johannesburg, 2008), p. 45.
63. Louw, *In the Shadow of Table Mountain*, p. 318.
64. UCTAA, Minutes of Senate meeting, 17 August 1948, Appendix: Memorandum from Standing Committee of Faculty of Medicine arising out of the suggestion of a public appeal for funds, June[?] 1948.
65. Ibid., 21 May 1956, Appendix: Memorandum from the Departments of Anatomy and of Physiology & Pharmacology, n.d.
66. UCTAA, Minutes of Council meeting, 3 July 1968, Appendix 'R': Memorandum on the Eligibility of Staff of Pre-Clinical Departments for the Merit/Service Awards … 24 June 1968.
67. On the history of the department in the eras of Jolly (1912–38) and Irving (1939–54), see Phillips, *UCT 1918–1948*, pp. 86–7, 325–7.
68. A.W. Sloan, 'Physical Fitness of Young South Africans' (PhD thesis, UCT, 1966), p. 156.
69. On the reasons for this, see Phillips, *UCT 1918–1948*, pp. 326–7. He was finally promoted to the new rank of associate professor in 1954.

70. W. Gevers, 'Henri (Harry) Zwarenstein', *Transactions of the Royal Society of South Africa*, 52, 2 (1997), p. 434.
71. *Cathartic*, 15, 1 (1966), p. 11.
72. A.W. Sloan, 'The Place of Physiology in Medical and Lay Education', *South African Medical Journal*, 20 (August 1955), p. 789.
73. Interview with Dr H. Dajee, 30 November 2015.
74. *UCT Staff Newsletter*, 15 (December 1965), p. 12.
75. On the history of the Department of Pharmacology in this period, see Phillips, *UCT 1918–1948*, pp. 94–5.
76. UCTAA, Minutes of Senate meeting, 16 May 1955, Appendix: Memorandum by Professor A.W. Sloan of the Department of Physiology and Pharmacology, 20 April 1955. Eight years later Sloan made the same case in exactly the same words with exactly the same, negative result – UCTAA, Minutes of Council meeting, 1 May 1963, Appendix: Memorandum on the Status of Pharmacology, 22 February 1963.
77. *UCT Principal's Circular* [PC] 62, 6 November 1963, Appendix: Report on Study Leave, 1963 by N. Sapeika.
78. N. Sapeika, 'The Teaching of Pharmacology Today' in Reid and Wilmot (eds.), *Medical Education in South Africa*, p. 61.
79. UCTAA, 11.9.3, box 70, Personal File of N. Sapeika: Circular re 'Appointment to Chair of Pharmacology', 31 March 1965.
80. Sapeika was the lecturer referred to on p. 41 whose lectures consisted of his reading notes taken verbatim from his textbook. See too Phillips, *UCT 1918–1948*, pp. 331–2.
81. *Cathartic*, XIV, 3 (1965), p. 15.
82. Interview with Emeritus Professor P. Folb, 17 March 2017.
83. D.J. Coetzee, *Living with the Dead: Impressions of Some Years with Professor M.R. Drennan, Medical School, Mowbray, Cape* (Sartorius, Observatory, 1954), p. 59.
84. However, his labelling did not gain support among archaeologists or physical anthropologists. Today it is believed that the remains belong to a forerunner of *Homo sapiens*. My thanks go to Emeritus Professor Alan Morris for this information.
85. *Inyanga*, 1955, p. 4.
86. Lecture by Singer in Chicago, 12 April 1960 at https://www.youtube.com/watch?v=JbUOq-wLDE8.
87. UCTAA, 13.1.1, Chair of Anatomy, 1955: copy of letter to Mr Carter from J.F. Foster, Secretary, Association of Universities of the British Commonwealth, 9 November 1955.
88. Interview with Emeritus Professor W. Pick, 29 April 2016.
89. Interview with Emeritus Professor P. Folb, 17 March 2017.
90. C. Helman, *Suburban Shaman: A Journey through Medicine* (Double Storey, Cape Town, 2004), p. 10.
91. Oral testimony suggests that this racial and gender segregation was not entirely rigid. White male 'repeats' who could not be accommodated in the large dissection room were sometimes assigned to the 'non-white' male students' room, while sometimes the number of 'non-white' females was so small that they were permitted into the white females' dissection room (Interviews with Emeritus Professors W. Pick and M. Jacobs, 29 April 2016 and 23 May 2016 respectively, and with Dr C. le Grange, 18 April 2016).
92. Interview with Dr C. le Grange, 18 April 2016.
93. Interview with Emeritus Professor M. Jacobs, 23 May 2016. The original comment was made in Afrikaans (perhaps by W.S. Hall) and has been translated above by the author.
94. UCTAA, 13.1.1, Chair of Anatomy, 1955: Memorandum on Chair of Anatomy, June 1955.
95. Coetzee, *Living with the Dead*, p. 25.

96. Cited in W. Pick, *The Slave Has Overcome* (W. Pick, Table View, 2007), p. 68.
97. Interview with Dr C. D'Arcy, 18 February 2016.
98. On the Department of Pathology under Ryrie, see Phillips, *UCT 1918–1948*, p. 92. In 1947 Ryrie had argued that the pathologist should become 'a clinician concerned with patients directly' and not remain a practitioner of 'pathology at a distance' (UCTAA, 14.2.4, box 1952, file MED/23, Teaching Hospitals and Medical School Planning, 1939–1949: Memorandum on Laboratory Services, December 1947 (?)).
99. D. Uys, 'Pranks and Pathology' in R. Kirsch and C. Knox (eds.), *UCT Medical School at 75* (Department of Medicine, UCT, Cape Town, 1987), p. 117.
100. *Cathartic*, 13, 1 (1964), p. 20.
101. *Inyanga*, 1969, p. 105.
102. UCTAA, 13.2.5, Chair of Pathology 1970: J.G. Thomson to Registrar, 20 January 1970.
103. UCT Registry, Bremner Building, Personal File of C.J. Uys: Application for Chair of Pathology, UCT, 19 December 1969, pp. 3–4.
104. UCTAA, 13.2.5, Chair of Pathology 1970: J.F. Murray to Registrar, UCT, 20 January 1970.
105. UCT Libraries, Special Collections Division, UCT Citation for Honorary Degrees: Award to Golda Selzer of the Honorary Degree of Doctor of Medicine, 6 October 1987.
106. UCTAA, 13.2.5, Chair of Pathology 1970: J.G. Thomson to Registrar, 20 January 1970.
107. For Linder's earlier career in the department, see Phillips, *UCT 1918–1948*, p. 331.
108. UCTAA, 45.3.2, box 5, Personal File of G.C. Linder: Testimonial from Professor F.R. Fraser, 25 September 1929.
109. M.C. Berman, 'Excitement and Fascination in Medical Science' (UCT Inaugural Lecture, 1977), p. 5.
110. UCTAA, 74.2.3, box 29, Personal File of J.E. Kench: R. Platt to Registrar, UCT, 29 July 1957.
111. R. Kirsch, 'The Fifties and Sixties: Years of Transition' in Kirsch and Knox (eds.), *UCT Medical School at 75*, p. 232.
112. Berman, 'Excitement and Fascination in Medical Science', p. 5.
113. UCT Registry, Bremner Building, Personal File of M.C. Berman: Report of Committee of Review, 30 April 1979.
114. On Van den Ende's early career, see Phillips, *UCT 1918–1948*, pp. 329–30.
115. Interview with Dr H.-R. Sanders, 13 October 2015.
116. F.G. Holliman in *Inyanga*, 1957, p. 7.
117. Interview with Mrs T. Davey, 8 June 2017.
118. *Lancet*, 269, 6982 (22 June 1957), p. 1306.
119. *British Medical Journal* (22 June 1957), p. 1477.
120. Kirsch, 'The Fifties and Sixties' in Kirsch and Knox (eds.), *UCT Medical School at 75*, p. 230.
121. UCTAA, UCT Graduation Ceremony Programme, 13 December 1985: Citation for Distinguished Teacher Award, A.A. Forder. In keeping with his wit and delight in words, students referred to him as the 'chief of staph' because of his energetic campaigns against hospital bacteria (Interview with Dr P. Cruse, 17 April 2017).
122. Cited in Digby and Phillips, *At the Heart of Healing*, p. 194.
123. On their early years in the department, see Phillips, *UCT 1918–1948*, pp. 333–5. The responsibilities of the headship were divided between hospital work (Forman) and academic work (Brock).
124. Concrete testimony to this was the publication in 1984 of a volume of recollections of Forman by former colleagues and students: R. Kirsch (ed.), *The Forman Years* (Department of Medicine, UCT, 1984).
125. Interview with Emeritus Professor I. Sakinofsky, 24 April 2013.
126. P. Jacobs, 'History and Achievements of Haematology at UCT: A Confluence of Ideologies', *Transactions of the Royal Society of South Africa*, 66, 3 (2011), p. 204.

127. UCTAA, 14.2.4, box 1953, Med/23, Teaching Hospitals and Medical School Planning 1950–4: Brock to the Principal, 8 August 1951.
128. J.F. Brock, 'The Teaching of Comprehensive Medicine', *South African Medical Journal*, 45, 2 (9 January 1971), p. 39.
129. Interview with Emeritus Professor D. Dent, 18 May 2017.
130. J.D.L. Hansen, 'John Fleming Brock', *Journal of Nutrition*, 117, 11 (1 November 1987), p. 816.
131. Both were excellent researchers too, Saunders on liver disease and Dowdle on porphyria and thrombosis, and both went on to occupy chairs at UCT, Saunders that of Medicine in succession to Brock in 1971, and Dowdle that of the new discipline, clinical science and immunology, in 1970. Saunders subsequently (1981) succeeded Sir Richard Luyt as UCT's Principal and Vice-Chancellor.
132. UCTAA, UCT Graduation Programme 1996: Citation for Honorary MD, Dr Helen Brown.
133. Interview with Dr A. James, 15 August 2016.
134. *PC*, 131, 10 May 1967, Appendix: Report on an eight-month stay in South Africa on an exchange scholarship by Heiko Iven, 10 December 1966.
135. Interview with Dr C. D'Arcy, 18 February 2016.
136. Interview with Dr S. Parbhoo, 28 September 2016.
137. UCT Libraries, Special Collections Division, BC 880 (Wilson Papers), box 52, folder J6.1 (Open University 1962–3): 'Interim Report to Academic Freedom Committee … on the Subject of Racial Discrimination' by T(hornton) W(hite), April 1963, p. 2. In the 1990s it was shown that this belief had no statutory basis.
138. E-mail from Dr R. Kester, 6 November 2016.
139. Cited in Digby and Phillips, *At the Heart of Healing*, p. 198.
140. Cited ibid.
141. Interview with Dr B. Madhoo, 23 October 2016.
142. C. Johnson, 'Unpublished Memoirs', p. 143.
143. On the flamboyant Cole Rous's brief term as professor before ill-health forced him to resign, see Phillips, *UCT 1918–1948*, pp. 321, 336.
144. On Saint's approach, see ibid., pp. 98–100.
145. Interview with Dr S. Parbhoo, 28 September 2016.
146. Kirsch, 'The Fifties and Sixties', p. 242.
147. UCTAA, 12.3.1, Chair of Surgery, 1955: Erasmus to Principal and Vice-Chancellor, UCT, 5 May 1955.
148. Interview with Dr A. James, 15 August 2016.
149. UCTAA, 12.3.1, Chair of Surgery, 1955: Erasmus to Principal and Vice-Chancellor, UCT, 5 May 1955.
150. *South African Medical Journal*, 81, 12 (20 June 1992), p. 629.
151. A. Millar, 'Surgery for Children: In Search of Perfection' (UCT Inaugural Lecture, 2008), p. 2.
152. UCT Libraries, Special Collections Division: Honorary MD citation, J.H. Louw, 1982. The former colleague was A.J. Walt, professor of Surgery at Wayne State University in Detroit.
153. UCTAA, 12.3.1, Chair of Surgery, 1955: Erasmus to Principal and Vice-Chancellor, UCT, 5 May 1955.
154. Louw, *In the Shadow of Table Mountain*; J.H. Louw, 'The History of Medicine in South Africa', *Transactions of the Colleges of Medicine of South Africa*, 20, 2 (September 1976); J.H. Louw, 'Somerset Hospital Centenary', *South African Medical Journal*, 36, 33 (18 June 1962).
155. On Goetz and his research at UCT since 1937, see Phillips, *UCT 1918–1948*, pp. 335–6.
156. J.H. Louw and H.S. Myers, 'Research in the Cape Town Medical School, 1912–62', *South African Medical Journal*, 37, 3 (19 January 1963), p. 55.

157. Cited in C. Logan, *Celebrity Surgeon: Christiaan Barnard, A Life* (Jonathan Ball, Johannesburg and Cape Town, 2003), p. 116.
158. Interview with Emeritus Professor I. Sakinofsky, 25 April 2013. Senior students received more hands-on training in transplant surgery in the animal surgical laboratory from Barnard's deft laboratory technician, Hamilton Naki, to whom UCT awarded an honorary MSc in Medicine in 2003 in recognition of his surgical teaching skills.
159. Logan, *Celebrity Surgeon*, p. 110.
160. Ibid., p. 154.
161. J.H. Louw, 'Ex Unitate Vires', *South African Medical Journal*, 41, 48 (30 December 1967), p. 1257.
162. Ibid., p. 1258
163. UCT Libraries, Special Collections Division, BC 1163 (Chris Barnard Papers), box 58, folder B1.4.3 (Correspondence Medical): Barnard to Professor D. State, 19 February 1963.
164. Interview with Dr E.S. Benjamin by R. Cramer, 12 August 2009, cited in R. Cramer, 'The Department of Dermatology at Groote Schuur Hospital' (unpublished BA Honours thesis, Department of Historical Studies, UCT, 2009), p. 7.
165. J.C. de Villiers, 'Perspectives in International Neurosurgery: Neurosurgery in South Africa', *Neurosurgery*, 13, 5 (1983), p. 610.
166. I.M. Viljoen, *The History of Urology in South Africa* (South African Urological Association, Cape Town, 2006), p. 57.
167. The endowment for this chair emanated from two sources, the Pieter Moll Fund and the Nuffield Fund for Cripple Care. Pieter Moll (1889–1934) had been appointed as the first clinical lecturer in orthopaedic surgery at UCT in 1931. On his death in a car accident in 1934, a fund was created in his memory. The Nuffield Trust had donated £40,000 in 1940 via the Cripple Care Association for the teaching of orthopaedic surgery.
168. A.A. Forder, 'Address to Gala Dinner for UCT Medical Graduates, 8 December 2017' at http://web.uct.ac.za/old/health/alumni/reunions/2007/1957/roundup_1957.htm.
169. G.F. Dommisse, *To Benefit the Maimed: The Story of Orthopaedics and the Care of the Crippled Child in South Africa* (South African Orthopaedic Association and the National Council for the Care of Cripples in South Africa, Johannesburg, 1982), p. 179.
170. J. Tribelhorn, *The Challenge and the Triumph: The True Story of a Woman Who Overcame the Loss of a Leg* (Tafelberg, Cape Town, 1962), p. 9.
171. M. Barnard, *Defining Moments: An Autobiography* (Zebra Press, Cape Town, 2011), p. 82.
172. Department of Ophthalmology, UCT: R.L.H. Townsend, 'The Department of Ophthalmology in Cape Town' (unpublished MS, March 1962).
173. Cited in C.E. Knoetze, 'The History of the Department of Obstetrics and Gynaecology at the University of Cape Town, 1952–1975' (unpublished BA Honours dissertation, UCT, 2013), p. 22.
174. *UCT Faculty of Medicine Prospectus*, 1962, p. 55.
175. Pick, *The Slave Has Overcome*, p. 93.
176. Interview with Dr A. James, 15 August 2016.
177. UCTAA, Minutes of Senate meeting, 15 April 1957, Appendix: Proposed reply to letter from Director of Hospital Services Concerning Occupancy of Proposed Maternity Block, n.d.
178. Interview with Emeritus Professor D.A. Davey, 8 June 2017.
179. On Crichton's career at UCT, see Phillips, *UCT 1918–1948*, pp. 100–2.
180. UCTAA, Minutes of Senate meeting, 17 April 1962, Appendix: South African Medical and Dental Council, Report by Dr R. Lance Impey on the Inspection of the Examinations in Obstetrics and Gynaecology, UCT, October–December 1962.
181. A.A. Forder, 'Address to Gala Dinner for UCT Medical Graduates, 8 December 2017' at http://web.uct.ac.za/old/health/alumni/reunions/2007/1957/roundup_1957.htm.

182. *Inyanga*, 1964, p. 114.
183. Louw told UCT that Jordaan's main responsibility would be to teach obstetrics and gynaecology pathology to 'non-white' students, but that white students who wished to attend his classes – 'and I am sure the wise will do so – would be welcome' (UCTAA, Minutes of Senate meeting, 18 August 1958, Appendix: Louw to Dean of Medicine, 24 July 1958). Jordaan continued in this part-time appointment until his departure for the US in 1977.
184. UCTAA, Minutes of Senate meeting, 21 March 1955, Appendix: Copy of letter from Louw to Professor Van den Ende, Dean of the Faculty of Medicine, 7 December 1954.
185. Interview with Dr A. James, 15 August 2016.
186. Interview with Emeritus Professor Dennis Davey, 8 June 2017.
187. UCT Libraries, Special Collections Division, Groote Schuur Hospital Archives: F. Ford, 'UCT Paediatrics 1953–1969' (unpublished TS, 7 June 1971).
188. UCTAA, Minutes of Senate meeting, 12 April 1949, Appendix: Memorandum on Proposed Chair of Child Health, April 1949. At this stage there were ten chairs of Child Health in Britain and one in South Africa, founded in 1943 at Pretoria University.
189. *Inyanga*, 1969, p. 29.
190. *UCT Staff Newsletter*, 9 (November 1962), p. 10.
191. Ford, 'UCT Paediatrics 1953–1969'.
192. *South African Medical Journal*, 83 (20 February 1993), p. 156.
193. Ibid., p. 154.
194. Cited in A. Bull, 'From Rag and Bottle to Pharmacokinetics' in Kirsch and Knox (eds), *UCT Medical School at 75*, p. 47.
195. Ibid., p. 49.
196. Louw, *In the Shadow of Table Mountain*, p. 380.
197. PC, 49, 3 April 1963, Appendix: Report from Dr S. Galloon of Cardiff Royal Infirmary, 27 February 1963.
198. *Cape Times*, 18 December 1966.
199. Obituary for Professor A.B. Bull at http://www.anaesthesia.uct.ac.za/staff/ripbull.
200. Interview with Dr S. Parbhoo, 28 September 2016.
201. Obituary for Professor G.G. Harrison at http://www.anaesthesia.uct.ac.za/staff/ripharsn.htm.
202. G.G. Harrison, 'Anaesthetics: A Great Safety Record', *Medical Chronicle* (October 1987), p. 12.
203. A citation classic is a highly cited publication as identified by the *Science Citation Index*. Harrison's co-authored paper, 'Anaesthetic-induced Malignant Hyperpyrexia and a Method for Its Prediction' appeared in *British Journal of Anaesthesia*, 41 (1969), pp. 844–55.
204. Cited in N. Parbhoo, 'The Department of Anaesthesia, UCT 1920–2000: A History' (MD thesis, UCT, 2002), p. 74.
205. Groote Schuur Hospital Group, *Report*, 1967, p. 45.
206. C.N. Barnard and C.B. Pepper, *Chris Barnard: One Life* (Timmins, Cape Town, 1969), p. 275.
207. On the early history of the Radiology Department, see Louw, *In the Shadow of Table Mountain*, pp. 381–4.
208. PC, 81, 31 March 1965, Appendix: Acting Dean, Faculty of Medicine to Registrar, 21 January 1965.
209. Werbeloff was the go-to radiologist who served as acting head of the department whenever the headship of Radiodiagnosis fell vacant, which it did thrice in this unstable period, in 1952–6, 1959–63 and 1969–72.
210. PC, 89, 31 March 1965, Appendix: Palmer to the Registrar, 11 January 1965.
211. UCTAA, 13.2.6, Chair of Radiology, 1973, Referee's report on B.J. Cremin: Palmer to P.G. McDonald, 6 November 1972.

212. *PC*, 89, 31 March 1965, Appendix: Palmer to Medical Superintendent, GSH, 26 November 1964.
213. R. Kottler, 'Radiology and the Territorial Imperative' in Kirsch and Knox (eds.), *UCT Medical School at 75*, p. 203.
214. *Inyanga*, 1966, p. 44.
215. 'Obituary: Philip Palmer', *South African Medical Journal*, 103, 4 (2013), p. 222.
216. UCT Libraries, Special Collections Division, GSH Archives: R. Kottler, 'An Informal History of the Radiology Department, Groote Schuur Hospital – The Last Fifty Years' (unpublished TS., 30 April 2003), p. 4.
217. http://www.phy.uct.ac.za/phy/history/amcormack.
218. UCTAA, Minutes of Senate meeting, 21 March 1955, Appendix: Report of Sub-Committee Appointed to Consider the Teaching of Psychiatry, 28 January 1955.
219. *PC*, 150, 7 April 1968, Appendix: Memorandum in Support of a Chair of Psychiatry within the Faculty of Medicine, 1 February 1968.
220. L.S. Gillis, 'Psychiatry in General Hospitals: Developments and Prospects' in *South African Medical Journal*, 38, 40 (12 December 1964), p. 932.
221. UCTAA, Minutes of Senate meeting, 14 April 1964, Appendix: Memorandum in Support of the Creation of a Chair of Psychiatry within the Faculty of Medicine, 10 March 1964.
222. W. Gevers, 'From DNA to District Six' in Kirsch and Knox (eds.), *UCT Medical School at 75*, p. 211.
223. Groote Schuur Hospital Group, *Report*, 1964, p. 9.
224. UCTAA, 13.1.6, Chair of Psychiatry, 1969: L.A. Hurst to Registrar, UCT, 3 April 1969.
225. Ibid., G.A. Elliott to Registrar, UCT, 9 April 1969.
226. Interview with Dr A. Robins, 28 March 2017.
227. Interview with Emeritus Professor L. Gillis, 4 July 2017.
228. Ibid.
229. *Inyanga*, 1963, p. 239.
230. J.L. Burton, *Essentials of Dermatology* (Churchill-Livingstone, Edinburgh, 1979), p. 1.
231. Cited in Cramer, 'The Department of Dermatology at Groote Schuur Hospital', p. 39.
232. Cited ibid., p. 46.
233. Interview with Dr A. Robins, 28 March 2017.
234. Pick, *The Slave Has Overcome*, p. 92.
235. R. Lang, 'The Department of Dermatology, UCT, 1922—1962' in *South African Medical Journal*, 67, 26 (29 June 1985), p. 1066.
236. Cited in Reid and Wilmot (eds.), *Medical Education in South Africa*, p. 139.
237. Louw, *In the Shadow of Table Mountain*, p. 254.
238. See p. 110.
239. UCTAA, Minutes of Senate meeting, 18 April 1961, Appendix: Redesignation of Department of Public Health – Expansion of Teaching in Promotive and Preventive Medicine, 7 March 1961.
240. Cited in Reid and Wilmot (eds.), *Medical Education in South Africa*, p. 154.
241. The blanket labels used by the medical profession to bracket together these professions from the 1950s to the 1980s ('auxiliary services', 'ancillary services', 'professions allied to medicine', 'allied health professions') all bear testimony to the manner in which they were seen as primarily supportive of medicine. That most of their practitioners were female at a time when most medical practitioners were male merely confirmed this subordinate status.
242. Reid and Wilmot (eds.), *Medical Education in South Africa*, p. 173.
243. UCTAA, Minutes of Senate meeting, 14 September 1948, p. 14.
244. Reid and Wilmot (eds.), *Medical Education in South Africa*, p. 175.
245. Cited in Digby and Phillips, *At the Heart of Healing*, p. 230.
246. Cited ibid., p. 225.

247. *UCT Faculty of Medicine Prospectus*, 1960, p. 32.
248. Interview with D. Goodley, 3 July 2016.
249. E-mail from S.K., 16 November 2016.
250. *UCT Faculty of Medicine Prospectus*, 1961, p. 25.
251. This explains why the four, first-year pre-medical courses were offered in Afrikaans too until 1957.
252. *Varsity*, 4 September 1951, p. 4.
253. *Varsity*, 1 April 1949, p. 3. Translated from the Afrikaans original by the author.
254. *Varsity*, 20 September 1950, p. 8: letter from E.T.
255. An earlier attempt by the Medical Students' Council in 1952 to have a distinctive Medical School badge approved had been vetoed by the SRC amidst charges that medical students were 'isolationists' (*Inyanga*, 1952, p. 7).
256. Interview with Emeritus Professor J.C. de Villiers, 30 October 2015.
257. *Varsity*, 19 May 1949, p. 7.
258. *Varsity*, 26 April 1951, p. 6: 'Materia Medica' by Tarsus.
259. UCTAA, Minutes of Senate meeting, 16 May 1955, Appendix: UCT Faculty of Medicine, Minimum Medical Curriculum, n.d.
260. Louw, *In the Shadow of Table Mountain*, p. vii.
261. *PC*, 111, 4 May 1966, Appendix: Report on Study Leave, April–October 1965 by Dr R. Hoffenberg.

**Chapter 7 – The Professional Faculties: Commerce, Law, Education, Architecture and Social Science**

1. UCT Administrative Archives [henceforth UCTAA], 20A.4.6, box 1727: Republic of South Africa, Department of Education, Arts and Science, National Bureau of Education and Social Research, *An Investigation of the Matriculants of November–December 1961 and March 1962 Considered as Potential University Study Material* (Research Series, no. 10, 1963), preface.
2. D. Hobart Houghton, 'Economic Development, 1865–1965' in M. Wilson and L.M. Thompson (eds.), *Oxford History of South Africa, vol. 2: South Africa 1870–1966* (OUP, Oxford, 1971), p. 32.
3. UCTAA, Minutes of Senate meeting, 19 November 1956, Appendix: Memorandum by Prof. H. Greenwood on 'The Training of Accounting Students', 26 October 1956.
4. UCTAA, Minutes of Senate meeting, 17 August 1959, Appendix: Memorandum on the Appointment of a Full-time Lecturer in the Accounting Department, n.d.
5. For the history of the Department before 1948, when its relationship with the accounting profession fluctuated sharply, see H. Phillips, *UCT 1918–1948: The Formative Years* (UCT and UCT Press, Cape Town, 1993), pp. 107–9, 308–9.
6. Interview with K. Penkin, 10 March 2016.
7. UCTAA, 13.1.1, Chair of Accountancy 1947: Application by H. Greenwood, 27 October 1947.
8. UCTAA, Minutes of Senate meeting, 19 November 1956, Appendix: Memorandum by Prof. H. Greenwood on 'The Training of Accounting Students', 26 October 1956.
9. Ibid.
10. *UCT Faculty of Commerce Prospectus*, 1948, pp. 1–2. This outline (which dated from 1925) remained unchanged in the prospectus until the purpose of the BCom degree was fundamentally altered in 1968.
11. For Hutt's career before 1948, see Phillips, *UCT 1918–1948*, pp. 306–8.
12. J. Botha, 'Down Memory Lane: The Economic Society of South Africa – Past Presidents 1925–63', *South African Journal of Economics*, Special Issue, (September 2002), p. 35.
13. R. Ackerman as told to D. Pritchard, *Hearing Grasshoppers Jump: The Story of Raymond Ackerman* (David Philip, Cape Town, 2001), p. 38.

## NOTES

14. UCTAA, 12.4.4, Commerce Lectureship 1956: Hutt to J. Benfield, 15 May 1956.
15. UCTAA, 13.2.2, Chair of Commerce 1964: Hutt to J.G. Benfield, 19 August 1964.
16. UCTAA, 13.2.2, Chair of Commerce 1964: Handwritten 'Notes on Dept. of Commerce' by J.P. Duminy, October 1964.
17. *UCT Faculty of Commerce Prospectus*, 1969, p. 26.
18. *Cape Times*, 1 September 1967.
19. Interview with Dr B. Boland, 16 March 2016.
20. *UCT Faculty of Commerce Prospectus*, 1964, p. 19.
21. UCTAA, 23.1.4, box 1404, personal file of R.G.A. Boland: J.B. Fox to Registrar, UCT, 15 July 1964.
22. Interview with Boland, 16 March 2016.
23. Today the hutments have long since gone and the site is occupied by Graça Machel Hall.
24. Interview with Boland, 16 March 2016.
25. UCT Libraries, Special Collections Division, BC 1117 (GSB Archives), Folder A1.2: 'The First Year of the Graduate School of Business at the University of Cape Town' by N. Lindhard, October 1966, pp. 7–8.
26. Interview with Dr T. Berkow, 23 March 2016.
27. Interview with 'Tiger' at GSB '69 Reunion 2014 at http://www.gsb69.com/.
28. Interview with Boland, 16 March 2016.
29. Interview with Berkow, 23 March 2016.
30. The first black student to register for the MBA course was discreetly admitted in 1972.
31. Interview with Boland, 16 March 2016.
32. Interview with F. Kleinman in *Turnover*, 4, 1 (February/March 1970), p. 1.
33. Interview with C. Hudson, 10 August 2016.
34. *Cape Times*, 28 May 1966.
35. UCTAA, Minutes of Senate meeting, 11 April 1967, Appendix: UCT GSB Director's Report for 1966, p. 2.
36. Interview with C. Hudson, 10 August 2016.
37. On the history of the Faculty up to 1945, see Phillips, *UCT 1918–1948: The Formative Years*, pp. 66–70, 304–5 and D. Cowen and D. Visser, *The University of Cape Town Law Faculty: A History 1859–2004* (Siber Ink, Claremont and UCT Faculty of Law, 2004), pp. 24–51.
38. T.W. Price, *The Future of Roman-Dutch Law in South Africa* (UCT, Cape Town, 1947), p. 14.
39. B. Beinart, *Roman Law in South African Practice* (UCT, Cape Town, 1952), p. 25.
40. *Butterworth's South African Law Review*, I (1954), preface.
41. UCTAA, 13.2.4, Chair of Law 1946: copy of letter from Dr Loveday, 29 December 1945.
42. Interview with J. MacFarlane, 8 September 2016.
43. Interview with Dr N. Rubin, 2 March 2016.
44. W. de Vos et al. (eds.), *Essays in Honour of Ben Beinart* (Juta, Cape Town, 1978), p. xv.
45. D. Davis, 'Social Power and Civil Rights: Towards a New Jurisprudence for a Future South Africa', *South African Law Journal*, 108, 3 (1991), p. 453.
46. Beinart, *Roman Law in South African Practice*, p. 25.
47. UCT Libraries, Special Collections Division, BC 1081 (Simons Collection), unnumbered box, folder C2.1 (Correspondence – Academic): R. Suttner to Jack Simons, 14 September 1969.
48. Interview with Mr Justice Albie Sachs, 9 May 2016.
49. A. Sachs, 'Freedom of Thought and Its Expression' in S. Cowen (ed.), *Cowen on Law: Selected Essays* (Juta, Cape Town, 2008), p. 184.
50. Interview with Mr Justice Ian Farlam, 15 August 2017.
51. UCTAA, 13.1.6, Chair of Public Law 1967: J.C. de Wet to Registrar, UCT, 24 November 1966.

52. Ibid., Lord Chorley to Registrar, UCT, 8 December 1966. The volume went through five editions in Cowen's lifetime.
53. Cited in J. Gauntlett, 'Since the Law Makes the King' in Cowen (ed.), *Cowen on Law*, p. 52. The essay was *Parliamentary Sovereignty and the Entrenched Sections of the South Africa Act* (Juta, Cape Town, 1951).
54. L. Ackermann, 'Introduction' in Cowen (ed.), *Cowen on Law*, p. xxii.
55. See p. 262.
56. UCTAA, 13.1.6, Chair of Public Law 1967: J.C. de Wet to Registrar, UCT, 24 November 1966.
57. Ibid., Professor T.B. Smith to Registrar, UCT, 25 November 1966.
58. Cowen and Visser, *The UCT Law Faculty*, p. 61.
59. J. Lotz and D. Visser, 'Wouter de Vos: A Tribute' in *Acta Juridica* (1992), p. vii. This seminal book, *Verrykingsaanspreeklikheid in die Suid-Afrikaanse reg*, went into three editions, the last in 1987.
60. Interview with Advocate D. Kawalsky, 16 November 2015.
61. Apart from De Vos and Molteno who began their time at UCT as senior lecturers, Solly Leeman, a product of J.C. de Wet's critical rationalist school at Stellenbosch, and the Irish maritime lawyer Derry Devine joined the Faculty as senior lecturers in the early 1960s. Both were later appointed professors there.
62. Cowen and Visser, *The UCT Law Faculty*, p. 63.
63. Interview with Sachs, 9 May 2016.
64. UCTAA, 13.2.4, Chair of Law, 1962: R.M. Lee to Registrar, UCT, 7 June 1962 re: Application by Advocate J.D. Thomas.
65. These 397 constituted 18% of all South Africa's LLB graduates between 1948 and 1968. Of the 397, about 383 were white.
66. UCTAA, Minutes of Senate meeting, 20 June 1960, Appendix: De Vos to Dean of Faculty of Law, 8 June 1960.
67. http://blogs.sun.ac.za/responsa/files/2013/07/Guest-Editorial-Helen-Scott-Douglas-Scott.pdf .
68. For the history of the Faculty before 1948, see Phillips, *UCT 1918–1948: The Formative Years*, pp. 79–83, 314–15.
69. It should be borne in mind that until the 1980s women teachers in white state schools were compelled to resign when they married, with the result that there was a constant demand for unmarried female teaching graduates.
70. National Archives of South Africa, K195 (Kommissie van Ondersoek na die Opleiding van Onderwysers), box 2, Getuienis, p. 563: Evidence of W.T. Ferguson, 16 September 1968.
71. Ibid., p. 555: Evidence of Professor R.E. Lighton, 16 September 1968.
72. Republic of South Africa, *Report of Commission of Inquiry into the Training of White Persons as Teachers*, R.P. 29/69, p. 28.
73. B. Nasson, 'The Unity Movement: Its Legacy in Historical Consciousness', *Radical History Review*, 46, 7 (1990), p. 190.
74. P. Randall, 'From Orthodoxy to Orthodoxy: The Study of Education at UCT 1910–1980', *Paedagogica Historia*, 3, Supplementary Series (1998), p. 164.
75. P. Randall, 'The Role of the History of Education in Teacher Education in South Africa' (unpublished PhD thesis, University of the Witwatersrand, 1988), p. 251.
76. *Varsity*, 21 August 1963.
77. UCT Libraries, Special Collections Division, BC 641 (Smit Collection), box 28, folder marked 'Fac. Circulars UCT 1963': 'A Few Comments on Education Courses at the University' [1962].
78. E-mail from Aletta Loopuyt, 23 November 2015.
79. *Varsity*, 19 June 1958.

80. *Varsity*, 6 May 1964.
81. UCT Libraries, Special Collections Division, BC 641 (Smit Collection), box 28, folder marked 'Fac. Circulars UCT 1963': 'A Few Comments on Education Courses at the University' [1962].
82. C.J. Driver, 'Memoir of South African Years' (unpublished memoir, 2015), chapter 12, p. 26.
83. On their pre-1948 careers, see Phillips, *UCT 1918–1948*, pp. 314–15.
84. Pells died suddenly in 1958 at the age of 56. For his earlier career, see Phillips, *UCT 1918–1948*, pp. 316–18.
85. Olivier was appointed as the first rector of the University College for Indians in Durban in 1961 after filling the UCT chair from 1957, while Smit became Superintendent-General of Education in the Cape Province in 1964 after just two years at UCT.
86. UCT Libraries, Special Collections Division, BC 1206 (Lighton Papers), box 3, Diary 1968–70: Synopsis of 1964.
87. Throughout the period at least three of the lecturers were women, but only one, Ida Hart, rose above the rank of lecturer. Hart herself was eventually appointed professor of education (Methodology) in 1971 at the age of 55. The part-time staff (seven in 1948 and ten in 1968) were all female. They were responsible for teaching subjects like needlework, physical drill, arts and crafts, singing and hygiene.
88. 'Thinking about Teaching: A Festschrift in Honour and Appreciation of Professor Clive J. Millar' at http://www.cfce.org.za/downloads/research/staff/Thinking_About_Teaching_-_festschrift_in_honour_of_Prof_Clive_Millar.pdf , Afterword: Personal Reflections by Colleagues and Students, p. 247.
89. A lively applicant for a lectureship who challenged the curricular status quo in 1966 with a proposal to introduce a sociological dimension to the study of education was firmly told that he 'would have to work within the framework of the curriculum offered by the Faculty of Education (pages 13, 15 and 16 of the Faculty of Education Prospectus enclosed herewith' (UCTAA, 12.3.5, Education – Lecturer, 1966: J.P. Duminy to C.J. Millar, 7 November 1966).
90. UCTAA, 13.1.3, Chair of Education (English Medium), 1971: Lighton to Registrar, UCT, 15 May 1971.
91. UCTAA, 13.1.3, Chair of Education (English Medium), 1969: Smit to Registrar, UCT, 13 June 1968.
92. National Archives of South Africa, K195 (Kommissie van Ondersoek na die Opleiding van Onderwysers), box 2, Getuienis, pp. 554–5: Comments by Lighton, 16 September 1968.
93. UCTAA, 13.1.3 Chair of Education (English Medium), 1968: Lighton to Registrar, UCT, 8 June 1968.
94. UCTAA, 13.1.3 Chair of Education (English Medium), 1969: Lighton to Registrar, UCT, 25 August 1969.
95. For the earlier history of the School, see Phillips, *UCT 1918–1948*, pp. 109–11, 310–11.
96. UCT Libraries, Special Collections Division, BC 353 (Thornton White Papers), box 17, folder B26 (E): Thornton White to Eaton, 18 July 1965.
97. UCTAA, 13.2.1, Chair of Architecture 1964: Hanson to Registrar, UCT, 22 April 1964.
98. *South African Architectural Record*, March 1966, p. 35.
99. UCTAA, 13.2.1, Chair of Architecture 1964: Memorandum by Thornton White, 14 May 1964.
100. UCTAA, 12.4.2, Architecture – Lecturers and Studio Masters 1954: Memorandum of the Conditions of Employment Applying to Studio Masters in the School of Architecture, 27 January 1955.
101. See p. 27.
102. J.P. Duminy, 'Leonard William Thornton-White', *South African Architectural Record*, (March 1966), p. 35.

103. UCT Libraries, Special Collections Division, BC 353, box 18, folder B27 (University folder): Thornton White to T.B. Davie, 10 January 1955.
104. Interview with F. Todeschini, 16 October 2017.
105. Interview with D. Parenzee, 20 June 2016.
106. See p. 34. About one of his Medical School buildings, the Medical Library, the much-travelled professor of medicine, John Brock, commented, 'I do not know a medical library in the English-speaking world which combines more satisfactorily internal function and aesthetics.' (UCTAA, 13.2.1, Chair of Architecture 1964: Brock to Registrar, UCT, 22 April 1964).
107. UCT Libraries, Special Collections Division, BC 353, box 16, folder B26 (A): Thornton White to Alex, 5 January 1961.
108. UCTAA, 12.4.2, Architecture – Lecturers and Studiomasters 1957: Thornton White to Benfield, 9 January 1957.
109. UCTAA, 13.2.1, Chair of Architecture 1974: Pryce Lewis to Registrar, UCT, 8 February 1974.
110. UCT Libraries, Special Collections Division, BC 353, box 16, folder B26 (F): Confidential Report by Thornton White, 9 September 1960.
111. http://www.artefacts.co.za/main/Buildings/archframes.php?archid=2099.
112. UCTAA, Chair of Architecture 1965: Thornton White to Benfield, 18 April 1964.
113. E-mail from W. Lederle to author, 5 August 2016.
114. http://www.artefacts.co.za/main/Buildings/archframes.php?archid=2952.
115. C. Strauss Brink, 'The Inspiration of Italy', *UCT*, 3, 8 (December 1969), p. 2.
116. Interview with F. Todeschini, 16 October 2017.
117. The Diploma in Architecture differed from the BArch degree only in the fact that a matriculation exemption was not a pre-requisite for enrolment; the content was exactly the same.
118. *UCT School of Architecture Prospectus*, 1960, p. 20.
119. Interview with F. Todeschini, 16 October 2017.
120. E-mail from W. Lederle to author, 5 August 2016.
121. E-mail from P. Cazalet, 15 September 2016.
122. *UCT Staff Newsletter*, 1 (October 1958), p. 9.
123. Interview with D. Parenzee, 20 June 2016.
124. Ibid.
125. E-mail from P. Cazalet, 15 September 2016.
126. *Varsity*, 13 October 1949, p. 6.
127. *Varsity*, 6 September 1962, p. 8.
128. *Varsity*, 4 June 1964, p. 2.
129. http://www.artefacts.co.za/main/Buildings/archframes.php?archid=2952.
130. On the beginning of QS at UCT, see Phillips, *UCT 1918–1948*, p. 314.
131. *Property Argus*, 7 September 1973.
132. UCTAA, Minutes of Senate meeting, 20 June 1961, Appendix: Memorandum on 'Proposed Re-arrangement of Diploma Course in Quantity Surveying', 9 May 1961.
133. UCT Libraries, Special Collections Division, BC 353, box 18, folder B28 (Architectural Affairs): Thornton White's 'Private and Confidential Notes on the Applicants for the Chair of Architecture in the University of Cape Town', 24 April 1964.
134. UCTAA, 12.3.1, Chair of Town and Country Planning 1964: Kepes to Registrar UCT, 14 April 1964.
135. Of the 708 architects awarded qualifications by UCT, about 95% were male and 99.2% white. As for quantity surveyors, all 151 appear to have been white males.
136. For Batson's career at UCT before 1948, see Phillips, *UCT 1918–1948*, pp. 278–80.
137. UCTAA, 20a.1.2, unnumbered box marked 'Old Principal's files', folder titled 'Dr Davie –

Personal': Davie to Baring, 18 April 1951.
138. *Cape Argus*, 5 August 1950.
139. UCTAA, Minutes of Council meeting, 12 September 1947, Appendix.
140. UCTAA, Minutes of Senate meeting, 22 May 1963, Appendix: Report of Sub-committee on Inter-racial Studies, 22 February 1963, p. 25.
141. Interview with Emeritus Professor D. Welsh, 26 June 2016.
142. Interview with Emeritus Associate Professor J. Atkinson, 1 September 2015.
143. *Varsity*, 30 March 1967, p. 3.
144. UCTAA, *Principal's Circular* [*PC*], no. 136, 9 August 1967, p. 35.
145. UCTAA, Minutes of Senate meeting, 20 April 1967, Appendix: Helm to Principal, 13 April 1967.
146. This was not acted upon, however, probably because it was feared that doing so would have made registration of UCT's social work graduates difficult in terms of the new National Welfare Act of 1965.
147. UCTAA, Minutes of Council meeting, 11 October 1967, p. 3.
148. *Varsity*, 13 March 1968.
149. UCTAA, 13.1.1, Chair of Applied Sociology in Social Work, 1969: H.T. Chabot to Registrar, UCT, 10 February 1969.
150. UCTAA, 74.1.7, box 20, personal file of W.B. Francis: Hare to Registrar, 13 March 1974.
151. G. Davie, *Poverty Knowledge in South Africa: A Social History of Human Science, 1855–2005* (Cambridge University Press, Cambridge, 2015), p. 174.
152. UCTAA, 63.6.1, box 4, SRC Correspondence, Minutes and Agenda, January to June 1958: Bromberger to Gunther, 22 January 1958.
153. Interview with G. Robins, 5 November 2017.
154. *UCT Faculty of Social Science Prospectus*, 1962, p. 6.
155. Interview with M. Turok, 19 August 2016.
156. UCTAA, 14.2.1, box 1942, Van der Riet Commission of Enquiry into Department of Sociology, 1967: Report of the Commission of Enquiry, p. 23.
157. Cited in D.G. Davie, 'Quantifying Poverty in the Era of Liberal Reform: Edward Batson and the Limits of the Scientific Persuasion, 1939–1953' (paper presented at Workshop on South Africa in the 1940s, Kingston, September 2003), p. 23, note 116.
158. UCTAA, 14.2.1, box 1942, Van der Riet Commission of Enquiry into Department of Sociology, 1967: Van der Riet to J.P. Duminy, 12 October 1967.
159. Ibid., Report of the Commission of Enquiry, p. 16.
160. UCT Libraries, Special Collections Division, BC 880 (Wilson Papers), unnumbered box, Correspondence 'C': Wilson to Carstens, 5 November 1971.

**Chapter 8 – The Arts: Musical, Liberal and Fine**

1. Cited in H. Phillips, *UCT 1918–1948: The Formative Years* (UCT and UCT Press, Cape Town, 1993), p. 14.
2. On Chisholm's earlier career, see Phillips, *UCT 1918–1948*, pp. 288–90.
3. UCT Administrative Archives [henceforth UCTAA], 58.4.5, box 6, personal file of Erik Chisholm: Reference by E.J. Dent, 13 February 1938.
4. D.P. Inskip, *Forty Little Years: The Story of a Theatre* (Timmins, Cape Town, 1972), pp. 56–7.
5. On Paganelli, see Phillips, *UCT 1918–1948*, pp. 36, 205, 253.
6. D. Talbot, *For the Love of Singing: 50 Years of Opera at UCT* (Oxford University Press, Cape Town, 1978), p. 31.
7. G. Fiasconaro, *I'd Do It Again* (Books of Africa, Cape Town, 1982), pp. 66, 67.
8. Ibid., p. 82.

9. Cited in Talbot, *For the Love of Singing*, p. 35.
10. UCTAA, Minutes of Council meeting, 13 April 1966, Appendix N: Report by Fiasconaro, 9 March 1966.
11. Talbot, *For the Love of Singing*, p. 38.
12. See p. 249.
13. Mosco Carner in *Time and Tide* cited in UCT Libraries, Special Collections Division, BC 129 (Chisholm Papers), box 130, doc. 31.262.4 (1): 'History of University Opera in Cape Town' (n.d.)
14. See pp. 190, 250.
15. UCTAA, Minutes of Senate meeting, 14 April 1958, Appendix: Memorandum by Chisholm to Chairman of Staffing Committee re: Upgrading of Junior Lectureship to Lectureship, 19 March 1958.
16. UCTAA, Minutes of Senate meeting, 14 April 1964, Appendix: Memorandum from Chisholm on 'Additional Lecturer in Piano', 6 March 1964.
17. UCTAA, Minutes of Finance Committee meeting, 13 August 1947, Appendix.
18. *New York Times*, 7 November 1986 at http://www.nytimes.com/1986/11/07/obituaries/lili-kraus-hungarian-pianist.html.
19. UCTAA, 13.1.5, Chair of Music, 1973: Alfred Brendel to P.G. McDonald, 17 February 1973.
20. Glasser also composed some of the music for the African musical *King Kong* (1959), for which production he was musical director.
21. *The Argus*, 11 March 1987.
22. Interview with D. Pritchard, 25 January 2016
23. UCTAA, 13.1.5, Chair of Music 1965: Confidential Report on Mr G. Pulvermacher by T.W. Price, 21 March 1966.
24. He was appointed Dean of the Faculty of Music only in 1968, presumably to spare him the full weight of the administrative burdens associated with filling all three posts at once.
25. Ibid., Gruber to J.G. Benfield, 9 January 1966.
26. Interview with D. Pritchard, 25 January 2016.
27. For the school's history before 1948, see Phillips, *UCT 1918–1948*, pp. 290–3.
28. UCTAA, Minutes of Senate meeting, 17 March 1952, p. 22.
29. R. Glasstone, *Dulcie Howes, Pioneer of Ballet in South Africa* (Human and Rousseau, Cape Town, 1996), p. 18.
30. Interview with S. Chisholm, 5 September 2016.
31. Ibid.
32. Cited in Glasstone, *Dulcie Howes*, p. 12.
33. Cited ibid., p. 44.
34. Ibid., p. 29.
35. Ibid., p. 45.
36. Interview with J. Mosaval, 17 November 2016.
37. UCT Libraries, Special Collections Division, BC 1101 (Dulcie Howes Papers), unnumbered box, folder C (Professional Career): D. Howes, 'The Future of the Cechetti Method – The University' (1976), p. 8.
38. M. Grut, *The History of Ballet in South Africa* (Human and Rousseau, Cape Town, 1981), p. 103.
39. *UCT Monday Paper*, 10, 27 (September 1991), p. 2.
40. Cited in Glasstone, *Dulcie Howes*, p. 73.
41. Fiasconaro, *I'd Do It Again*, p. 98.
42. UCT Libraries, Special Collections Division, BC 129 (Chisholm Papers), box 16A, folder 129, document 16.129.4: Howes to Brodie, c. 9 June 1965.
43. *Varsity*, 13 October 1949, p. 6. This description was not original, however. It was plagiarised from

an editorial in *Varsity*, 6 August 1943. See Phillips, *UCT 1919–1948*, p. 262.
44. *Varsity*, 17 September 1969, p. 7.
45. UCTAA, Minutes of Senate meeting, 10 June 1969, Appendix 'R': Memorandum for Commission of Inquiry into Universities, 12 June 1969, p. 12.
46. Ibid., p. 14.
47. UCTAA, Minutes of the Senate meeting, 16 May 1960, Appendix: Application for renewal of part-time post of Secretary to the Dean of the Faculty of Arts after 1960 as a post on the permanent establishment, 10 March 1960.
48. Cited in M.C. Penrith, 'A Historical and Critical Account of the Teaching of English Language and Literature in English-Medium Universities in South Africa, with Particular Reference to the University of Cape Town and the South African College' (MA thesis, UCT, 1972), p. 148.
49. J.M. Coetzee, *Youth* (Secker and Warburg, London, 2002), p. 26.
50. Cited in A. Lennox-Short, 'Remedial English at UCT' in *ELTS Occasional Papers*, I (Department of English Language, UCT, 1970), pp. 4–5.
51. On her career before 1948, see Phillips, *UCT 1918–1948*, p. 264.
52. A. Lennox-Short, *Effective Expression: A Course in Communication* (Evans Bros., London, 1970), p. 1.
53. On the department under Mackie, see Phillips, *UCT 1918–1948*, pp. 16–17, 264–5.
54. UCTAA, 13.2.3, Chair of English Language 1951: W.R. Halliday to J.R. Foster, 21 September 1950.
55. UCTAA, Minutes of Senate meeting, 16 September 1952, Appendix: 1952 enrolments.
56. Phillips, *UCT 1918–1948*, p. 265.
57. J. Cope, 'The World of Contrast', *English in Africa*, 7, 2 (September 1980), p. 18.
58. R.G. Howarth, *The Life of Literature* (UCT Inaugural lecture, 1956), pp. 6–7.
59. Ibid., p. 20.
60. Cited in J.C. Kannemeyer, *J.M. Coetzee: A Life in Writing* (Jonathan Ball, Johannesburg, 2012), p. 99. Given this sentiment, Coetzee would have been gratified by a review in *Varsity* of one of his published poems, which praised it as showing 'a maturity, a sensitivity and in parts a genuine profundity that gives it real stature' (*Varsity*, 27 August 1959, p. 4).
61. Howarth, *Life of Literature*, p. 20.
62. J. Crewe, 'Arrival: J.M. Coetzee in Cape Town', *English in Africa*, 40, 1 (May 2013), p. 24.
63. On Segal's career at UCT before 1948, see Phillips, *UCT 1918–1948*, p. 264.
64. Interview with B. Rabinowitz, 1 April 2016.
65. B. Busch, L. Busch and K. Press (eds.), *Interviews with Neville Alexander: The Power of Languages against the Language of Power* (UKZN Press, Pietermaritzburg, 2014), p. 40.
66. *New Nation*, 22 September 1973.
67. UCT Libraries, Special Collections Division, BC 977 (Philip Segal Papers), folder B2.3 (Correspondence M–Z): D. Wilkinson to Gerda Segal, 22 December 1970.
68. E-mail from Dr Jeff Opland, 17 October 2016.
69. UCTAA, 4.4.2, box 382, Personal file of A.G. Woodward: Letter by W. Bayley, 6 April 1958.
70. L. Gordon, *Shared Lives* (David Philip, Cape Town, 1992), p. 131.
71. B. Cooper, *A Boat, a Mask, Two Photographs and a Manticore: African Fiction in a Global Context* (UCT Inaugural lecture 2000), p. 1.
72. Cited in Kannemeyer, *J.M. Coetzee*, p. 90.
73. Cited in Kannemeyer, *J.M. Coetzee*, p. 106.
74. Interview with Professor Adam Small, 2 November 2015.
75. On Scholtz's pre-1950 career at UCT, see Phillips, *UCT 1918–1948*, p. 266.
76. A.P. Grové (compiler), *D.J. Opperman: dolosgooier van die woord; saamgestel … by geleentheid van die digter se sestige verjaarsdag* (Tafelberg, Cape Town, 1974). Tellingly, the two other greats of Afrikaans

poetry in the 20th century, N.P. van Wyk Louw and Breyten Breytenbach, also were at UCT, Van Wyk Louw as a lecturer in the Faculty of Education (1929–50) and Breytenbach as a student in, inter alia, the Department of Nederlands and Afrikaans (1958–9).

77. On Van der Merwe's earlier career at UCT, see Phillips, *UCT 1918–1948*, pp. 266–7.
78. Wium van Zyl cited at www.litnet.co.za/dj-opperman-1914-1985/.
79. Lisbé Smuts cited at www.litnet.co.za/merwe-scholtz-1924-2005/.
80. Louise Viljoen cited ibid. As in the preceding two footnotes, the translation is by the author.
81. J. du P. Scholtz, 'Afrikaans, Internal History of' in *Standard Encyclopedia of South Africa*, vol. I (Nasou, Cape Town, 1970), p. 89.
82. UCTAA, *Principal's Circular* [*PC*], 117 (17 August 1966), Appendix: Scholtz to Assistant Registrar, 25 May 1966. Translation by the author.
83. J.C. Kannemeyer, *D.J. Opperman: 'n biografie* (Human and Rousseau, Cape Town and Pretoria, 1986), pp. 174, 302.
84. Pieter Fourie cited at www.litnet.co.za/merwe-scholtz -1924-2005/.
85. The University College of the Western Cape, which was opened in 1960 as an institution for 'coloureds' only, was initially dominated by white Afrikaners sympathetic to apartheid.
86. Vernon February cited in H. Willemse, 'Apartheid, Afrikaans en ballingskap in die biografie van Vernon February', *Stilet*, XVII, 1 (March 2005), p. 38.
87. Interview with J. Jessop, 21 December 2016.
88. On Inskip's earlier career at UCT, see Phillips, *UCT 1918–148*, pp. 268–9.
89. See above chapter 2.
90. *PC*, 33 (6 June 1962), Appendix: Request for Appointment of a Junior Lecturer in French by Prof. M. Shackleton, 7 May 1962.
91. *PC*, 130 (19 April 1967), Appendix: Application for the Post of Lecturer in French, by Prof. M. Shackleton, 7 September 1966.
92. J. Robertson (ed.), *Mélanges de littérature française offerts à M. Shackleton et C.J. Greshoff par leurs collègues et amis* (UCT, Cape Town, 1985), p. xi. Translation by the author.
93. On Rosteutscher's career a UCT before 1948, see Phillips, *UCT 1918–1948*, p. 268.
94. See entries on him in C. König (ed.), *Internationales Germanistenlexicon* (De Gruyter, Berlin and New York, 2003), p. 1531 and W. Killy and R. Vierhaus (eds.), *Deutsche biographische Enzyklopädie* (Saur Verlag, Munich, 2007), vol. 8, p. 556.
95. *Varsity*, 7 August 1963, p. 8.
96. Busch, Busch and Press, *Interviews with Neville Alexander*, p. 46.
97. Ibid., p. 44.
98. http://www.serfontein.org/education.html.
99. Interview with Professor Adam Small, 2 November 2015.
100. Interview with Emeritus Professor M. Shackleton, 21 October 2015.
101. For Abrahams's career at UCT until 1948, see Phillips, *UCT 1918-1948*, p. 269.
102. UCTAA, Minutes of UCT Senate meeting, 14 November 1967, Appendix: Report of Sub-committee … 17 October 1967.
103. Thomas Jefferson in 'Virginia Board of Visitors Minutes', 1824. ME: 19-444, consulted at http://rotunda.upress.virginia.edu/founders/default.xqy?keys=FOEA-print-04-02-4598.
104. UCTAA, Minutes of Senate meeting, 7 December 1948, Appendix: Memorandum on Staffing of the Classics Department by Professors Rollo and Baldry, 29 November 1948.
105. E-mail from Dr Jeff Opland, 17 October 2016.
106. Classical Culture I had been introduced in 1931. By 1948 it had 63 students, prompting the department to introduce Classical Culture II in 1950. See Phillips, *UCT 1918–1948*, pp. 262–3.
107. H.C. Baldry, *The Classics in the Modern World* (UCT Inaugural Lecture, 1949).

# NOTES

108. C.J. Driver, 'Memoir of South African Years' (unpublished TS), chapter 12, p. 9.
109. On Baldry's pre-1948 career at UCT, see Phillips, *UCT 1918–1948*, p. 263; Goold went on to a stellar career as a Latinist, eventually becoming editor of the prestigious Loeb Classics Library.
110. On Rollo's career at UCT, see Phillips, *UCT 1918–1948*, p. 263.
111. UCTAA, 4.3.4, box 371, personal file of M.W.M. Pope: Application by Pope, 6 June 1957.
112. E-mail from Dr J. Opland, 17 October 2016.
113. L. Baumbach, 'The Impact of the Development of the Linear B Script on Linguistic and Historical Studies' (UCT Inaugural lecture, 1977).
114. M. Pope (compiler), *Saecula Latina: From the Beginnings of Latin Literature to Sir Isaac Newton* (UCT, Cape Town, 1962).
115. E-mail from Dr J. Opland, 17 October 2016.
116. UCTAA, 13.2.2, Chair of Classics, 1969: T.J. Haarhoff to Registrar, UCT, 6 January 1969.
117. UCTAA, Minutes of Senate meeting, 16 April 1956, Appendix: Memorandum by Professor G.P. Goold, to Dean of Faculty of Arts, 21 March 1956.
118. Interview with Emeritus Associate Professor J.E. Atkinson, 1 September 2015.
119. On Mandelbrote's career at the South African College and UCT since 1916, see Phillips, *UCT 1918–1948*, pp. 33, 275.
120. On Thompson's career at UCT since 1946, see Phillips, *UCT 1918–1948*, p. 275.
121. R. Oliver, *In the Realms of Gold: Pioneering in African History* (Cass, London, 1997), p. 223.
122. T.R.H. Davenport, 'Memoirs' (unpublished TS, 2012), p. 29.
123. The most notorious rejection of African history as a respectable academic subject at this time came from the Regius Professor of Modern History at Oxford, Hugh Trevor-Roper, who in 1963 proclaimed, 'Perhaps, in the future, there will be some African history to teach. But at present there is none, or very little: there is only the history of Europeans in Africa. The rest is largely darkness … And darkness is not a subject for history' (H. Trevor-Roper, 'The Rise of Christian Europe', *The Listener*, LXX, 1809 (28 November 1963), p. 871).
124. E-mail to author from A.R. Goodwin, 18 April 2017.
125. On her earlier career at UCT, see Phillips, *UCT 1918–1948*, p. 276.
126. C.C. Saunders, 'Jean van der Poel, Historian', *Quarterly Bulletin of the South African Library*, 41, 2 (December 1986), p. 65.
127. Ibid. p. 66.
128. Interview with Sir Frank Berman, 17 February 2016.
129. Interviews with Associate Professor R. Mendelsohn and Dr E. van Heyningen, 23 September 2002.
130. UCTAA, 13.2.4, Chair of History 1962: Mandelbrote to Registrar, UCT, 30 September 1961.
131. N. Southey, 'Interview with T.R.H. Davenport' in *South African Historical Journal*, 26 (1992), p. 26.
132. E-mail from A.R. Goodwin, 18 April 2017.
133. *UCT Staff Newsletter*, July 1965, p. 8.
134. UCTAA, 13.2.4, Chair of History 1962: Referee's report by Professor W.A. Maxwell, 13 September 1961.
135. The original apophthegm by the celebrated economist Kenneth Boulding is: 'Mathematics brought rigor to economics. Unfortunately it also brought mortis' (https://www.goodreads.com/author/quotes/132729.Kenneth_E_Boulding).
136. On Robertson's career at UCT from 1930 to 1950, see Phillips, *UCT 1918–1948*, p. 276.
137. J. de V. Graaff, 'Obituary: H.M Robertson (1905–1984)', *South African Journal of Economics*, 52, 3 (1984), p. 312.
138. Interview with Brian Kantor, 28 March 2018.
139. E-mail to author from Melvyn Drummond, 9 October 2015.

140. Interview with Emeritus Professor Robert Schrire, 20 June 2016.
141. UCTAA, Senate minutes 19 August 1957, Appendix: Additional memorandum by Professor H.M. Robertson regarding the Institution of a Second Chair in the Department of Economics, 1 August 1957.
142. On her pre-1948 career, see Phillips, *UCT 1918–1948*, p. 277.
143. See p. 150.
144. UCTAA, 13.1.3, Chair of Economics 1969: Robertson to Benfield, 11 September 1969.
145. Interview with Emeritus Professor Francis Wilson, 16 March 2018.
146. S. Archer and J. Heywood, 'Obituary: Sheila van der Horst (1909–2001)', *South African Journal of Economics*, 71, 1 (2003), p. 212.
147. Interview with Emeritus Professor Francis Wilson, 16 March 2018.
148. T. Jenkin, *Inside Out: Escape from Pretoria Prison* (Jacana Media, Johannesburg, 2003), p. 17.
149. UCTAA, 45.2.2, box 4, personal file of M. Kooy: Kooy to Principal, UCT, 6 May 1976.
150. Interview with Emeritus Professor Robert Schrire, 20 June 2016.
151. For the prior history of these departments, see Phillips, *UCT 1918–1948*, p. 282.
152. *UCT Faculties of Arts and Science Prospectus*, 1952, p. 104.
153. On Murray's early career at UCT, see Phillips, *UCT 1918–1948*, pp. 281–2.
154. *Cape Times*, 20 June 1950.
155. UCTAA, Minutes of Council meeting, 5 November 1958, Appendix: Murray to Registrar, 2 October 1958.
156. Ibid.
157. *Cape Times*, 7 May 1956 and 10 May 1956.
158. T. Barnes, '"Apartheid's Professor": A.H. Murray, a Liberal University and the Fight for Transformation in South Africa, 1950–2015' (unpublished TS), chapter 1, p. 5.
159. On his pre-1948 career at UCT, see Phillips, *UCT 1918–1948*, p. 282.
160. UCTAA, 36.4.5, box 35, Citations 1976–1994: UCT honorary degree citation for Marthinus Versfeld, 1987, p. 2.
161. H. Sheehan, 'Interview with Jeremy Cronin, 17 April 2001', p. 2, consulted at http://webpages.dcu.ie/~sheehanh/za/cronin-aah01.htm.
162. Interview with Dr Duncan Innes, 7 January 2016.
163. M. Versfeld, *Pots and Poetry, and Other Essays* (Protea, Pretoria, 2000), p. 90.
164. J. Gaffney SJ, 'Review of *The Mirror of Philosophers*', *Woodstock Letters*, 90, 1 (1961), p. 77.
165. Interview with Dr Denis Worrall, 18 November 2015.
166. Thereby they maintained a distinctive feature of the department since its inception in 1920, for Murray's predecessor in the chair was G.H.T. Malan, whose connection with the department continued into the 1950s, as he was Murray's temporary substitute while the latter was involved in the Treason Trial in 1958.
167. *PC*, 150 (7 April 1968), Appendix: Application for lectureship, 6 March 1968, p. 2.
168. Interview with Dr Peter Knox-Shaw, 15 November 2016.
169. B. Keniston, *Choosing to Be Free: The Life Story of Rick Turner* (Jacana Media, Johannesburg, 2013), p. 148. See too p. 17.
170. On the pre-1948 history of the School, see Phillips, *UCT 1918–1948*, pp. 21–9 and 270–1.
171. UCTAA, Minutes of Senate meeting, 19 April 1960, Appendix: Memorandum on Expansion in African Studies by Professors H.M. Robertson, M. Wilson and L.M. Thompson, n.d.
172. *PC*, 130, 19 April 1967: Westphal to Registrar, 21 February 1967.
173. Comment by Deputy Vice-Chancellor Professor Eric Axelson to author, 10 November 1974.
174. UCT Libraries, Special Collections Division, BC 880 (Wilson Papers), unnumbered box marked 'Correspondence H–I', Wilson to R.R. Inskeep, 22 November 1966 (?).

175. Gordon, *Shared Lives*, p. 126.
176. P. Reynolds, 'Gleanings and Leavings: Encounters in Hindsight' in A. Bank and L.J. Bank (eds.), *Inside African Anthropology: Monica Wilson and Her Interpreters* (International African Institute London and Cambridge University Press, New York, 2013), pp. 315–16.
177. Cited in S. Morrow, *The Fires Beneath: The Life of Monica Wilson, South African Anthropologist* (Penguin, Cape Town, 2016), p. 249.
178. UCT Libraries, Special Collections Division, BC 880, box 48, folder J1 (UCT Social Anthropology Department – Information re: staffing … 1953–64): Memorandum by Wilson, 'Dept of Anthropology, 1953'.
179. Ibid., Memorandum by Wilson, 12 August 1963.
180. *PC*, 60, 9 October 1963: Memorandum by Wilson, 12 August 1963.
181. UCT Libraries, Special Collections Division, BC 880, B6.14: Audrey Richards to Rhodes University Appointments Committee, 15 June 1946.
182. A. Bank, 'Introduction' in Bank and Bank (eds.), *Inside African Anthropology*, p. 1.
183. For its path to this status under Radcliffe Brown and Schapera, see Phillips, *UCT 1918–1948*, pp. 22–5, 271–3.
184. *PC*, 78, September 1964: Report on Special Leave by Professor M. Wilson, 27 May 1964.
185. Cited in Morrow, *The Fires Beneath*, p. 275.
186. Neville Alexander cited in S. Morrow and C. Saunders, '"Part of One Whole": Anthropology and History in the Work of Monica Wilson' in Bank and Bank (eds.), *Inside African Anthropology*, pp. 295–6.
187. Interview with Professor Carmel Schrire, 14 August 2015.
188. UCT Libraries, BC 880, box 49, folder J 3 (Examinations 1953–69), Whisson to Professor J. Blacking, 12 February 1969.
189. Cited in S.R. Barrett, 'Peter Carstens (1929–2010)', *Anthropologica*, 52 (2010), p. 389.
190. UCTAA, 13.2.6, Chair of Social Anthropology 1973–7, Professor M. Fortes to Registrar, UCT, 30 May 1973.
191. UCT Libraries, Special Collections Division, BC 880, unnumbered box marked 'Correspondence H–I': Wilson to Inskeep, 22 November 1966 (?).
192. Cited in Morrow, *The Fires Beneath*, p. 259.
193. See pp. 267–8.
194. UCT Libraries, Special Collections Division, BC 1072 (Luyt Papers), B2.1 (UCT Mafeje Affair, 1968: Documents): J. de Klerk to Principal and Vice-Chancellor, UCT, 3 May 1968.
195. On Simons's career at UCT before 1948, see Phillips, *UCT 1918–1948*, pp. 274–5.
196. A diploma course in Native (later African) Administration was offered until 1968, but it attracted very few takers. Only 15 such diplomas were awarded between 1948 and 1968.
197. J. Lawrence: *Past Imperfect* (Gryphon Press, Cape Town, 2014), p. 80.
198. UCTAA, 18.1.5, box 941, folder 'Dr H.J. Simons – Restriction Order 1964/5': Letter from G.D. van Schalkwyk, 12 October 1964.
199. UCTAA, 14.2.3, box 1948, folder EXT/2, 'National Council for Social Research 1942–54', T.B. Davie to H. v.d. Walt, 30 April 1954.
200. UCT Libraries, Special Collections Division, BC 1081 (Simons Collection), box 1, folder A1.1: Interview with J.F., p. 17.
201. Cited in H. Macmillan, *Jack Simons: Teacher, Scholar, Comrade* (Jacana Media, Johannesburg, 2016), p. 7.
202. National Archives of South Africa, Pretoria, MJU 139, file J. 21/22/2/41: Memorandum on Dr Harold Jack Simons attached to letter from Commissioner of the South African Police to Minister of Justice, 2 June 1954 (translation from Afrikaans by the author).

203. National Archives of South Africa, Pretoria, NRSN 61, file N/R/6/395/1 – 'UCT. African Communities in the W. Province': Gloss by Dr Olckers (?), dated 11 April 1957, for Minister of Education, Arts and Science on K. Henshall to Dr Robbertse, 3 April 1957 (translation by author from Afrikaans).
204. UCT Libraries, Special Collections Division, BC 1081, unnumbered box, folder C 2.1: R. Suttner to Jack Simons, 13 April 1969.
205. See Phillips, *UCT 1918–1948*, p. 25.
206. UCTAA, 4.2.6, box 358, personal file of A.J.H. Goodwin: Wilson to Registrar, 27 July 1959.
207. C. Schrire, 'Obituary: H. J. Deacon' in *South African Journal of Science*, 106, 11 & 12 (2010), p. 466. On Goodwin's pre-1948 career at UCT, see Phillips, *UCT 1918–1948*, pp. 25, 27, 273–4.
208. UCT Libraries, Special Collections Division, BC 826 (School of African Studies, UCT: Papers): R.R. Inskeep, 'Can Archaeology Write History for the Pre- and Non-Literate Societies of Africa?' (seminar paper, October 1961), p. 1.
209. UCT Libraries, Special Collections Division, BC 290 (Goodwin Papers), box 14, folder D5: Goodwin to Oakly [*sic*], 30 August 1952. On the involvement of members of the Anatomy Department, see pp. 100–1.
210. UCT Libraries, Special Collections Division, BC 290, box 8, folder D5, Goodwin to Gracie, 31 July 1952.
211. Interview with Emeritus Professor John Parkington, 18 April 2018.
212. Interview with Dr J. Deacon, 7 July 2016.
213. *PC*, 130 (19 April 1967), Appendix: 'Future Development of Archaeology in the University of Cape Town' by R.R. Inskeep, 16 October 1964.
214. J. Deacon, 'The Cinderella Metaphor: The Maturing of Archaeology as a Profession in South Africa', *South African Archaeological Bulletin*, 48, 158 (1993), p. 77.
215. *UCT Faculties of Arts and Science Prospectus*, 1961, p. 45.
216. E-mail from A.R. Goodwin to author, 18 April 2017.
217. UCT Libraries, Special Collections Division, BC 880, unnumbered box marked 'Correspondence H–I': Confidential reference by Professor Monica Wilson, 12 August 1968.
218. C. Schrire, 'In Memoriam: R.R. Inskeep', *South African Archaeological Bulletin*, 58, 178 (2003), p. 100.
219. *PC*, 150 (7 April 1968), Appendix: Memorandum on 'Chair in Archaeology' by Wilson, 1968.
220. Schrire, 'In Memoriam: Raymond Robert Inskeep', p. 101.
221. P. Mitchell, 'Ray Inskeep 1926–2003', *Azania: Archaeological Research in Africa*, 38, 1 (2003), p. 218.
222. See Phillips, *UCT 1918–1948*, pp. 23–4.
223. On his career at UCT up to 1948, see Phillips, *UCT 1918–1948*, p. 271.
224. http://ufdc.ufl.edu/fortune.
225. UCT Libraries, Special Collections Division, BC 880, unnumbered box marked 'Correspondence C.D.': Carnegie Corporation – Referee's report by Professor M. Wilson, 18 March 1960.
226. http://en.wikipedia.org/wiki/Archibald_Campbell_Jordan .
227. UCTAA, 13.2.1, Chair of Bantu Languages, 1963: G.P. Lestrade – Referee's report on D.P. Kunene, c. June 1962.
228. UCTAA, 13.2.1, Chair of Bantu Languages, 1963: G.P. Lestrade to Registrar, 20 May 1962.
229. Cited in Morrow, *The Fires Beneath*, p. 274.
230. UCT Libraries, Special Collections Division, BC 880, unnumbered box with 11f on top, 'Correspondence K': Kunene to Wilson, 3 April 1964.
231. Ibid., Kunene to Wilson, 25 September 1974.
232. UCTAA, 13.2.1, Chair of Bantu Languages, 1963: Professor M. Guthrie to J.G. Benfield, UCT, 2 August 1962.
233. *UCT Faculties of Arts and Science Prospectus*, 1965, p. 56.

234. UCTAA, 13.2.1, Chair of Bantu Languages, 1963: Professor G. Fortune to Registrar, UCT, 8 August 1962.
235. *PC*, 77 (19 August 1964), Appendix: Memorandum on 'Lectureship in African Languages', 18 August 1964.
236. On the Little Theatre, see pp. 248–9.
237. On Van der Gucht's career at UCT before 1948, see Phillips, *UCT 1918–1948*, pp. 294–6.
238. D.P. Inskip, *Forty Little Years: The Story of a Theatre* (Timmins, Cape Town, 1972), p. 53.
239. Interview with Robin Malan, 12 September 2016.
240. *Sunday Chronicle*, 11 July 1965, as cited in G. Morris, 'A Critical Biography of Rosalie Van der Gucht: Investigating Her Contribution to Education in South Africa with Special Reference to Speech and Drama' (MA thesis, UCT, 1989), p. 159.
241. Interview with Pieter-Dirk Uys, 11 August 2016.
242. Ronald France cited in Morris, 'A Critical Biography of Rosalie Van der Gucht', p. 229.
243. Helen Houghton cited ibid., pp. 56, 47.
244. Cited in Morris, 'A Critical Biography of Rosalie Van der Gucht', pp. 224, 230.
245. UCTAA, 58.5.4, box 28, personal file of Robert Mohr: Application by Mohr, 1 September 1971.
246. Cited in Inskip, *Forty Little Years*, p. 96.
247. UCTAA, 12.3.1, Chair of Speech Training and Dramatic Art, 1971: Taylor to Registrar, UCT, 2 September 1971.
248. Interview with Pieter-Dirk Uys, 11 August 2016.
249. 'A Tribute to Mavis Taylor' in *UCT Monday Paper*, 16, 34 (10–17 November 1997), p. 6.
250. UCTAA, 12.3.1, Chair of Speech Training and Dramatic Art, 1971: Professor E. Sneddon to Registrar, UCT, 10 September 1971.
251. Interview with Erin Bates, 19 September 2016.
252. Elizabeth Coates cited in Morris, 'Rosalie Van der Gucht', p. 152.
253. Interview with Pieter-Dirk Uys, 11 August 2016.
254. On the origin and early development of the School, see Phillips, *UCT 1918–1948*, p. 283.
255. R.F.M. Immelman, 'The University of Cape Town Scheme of Education in Librarianship', *South African Libraries*, 8 (1941), p. 152.
256. On Immelman's early career at UCT from 1935, see Phillips, *UCT 1918–1948*, pp. 283–5.
257. UCTAA, Minutes of Senate meeting, 17 April 1951, Appendix: School of Librarianship Annual Report for 1950, p. 2 – C. Changes in Organisation and Curriculum Proposed for 1951.
258. UCTAA, Minutes of Council meeting, 30 April 1952, Appendix: School of Librarianship Annual Report for 1951, p. 3 – C. Curriculum Changes.
259. UCTAA, Minutes of Senate meeting, 17 April 1951, Appendix: School of Librarianship Annual Report for 1950, p. 2 – C. Changes in Organisation and Curriculum Proposed for 1951.
260. Ibid.
261. Cited in L. Wertheimer, 'The University of Cape Town's School of Librarianship: A Survey of Its Ex-Students, 1939–1959', *South African Libraries*, 28, 4 (1961), p. 132.
262. D. Ivey, 'School of Librarianship of the University of Cape Town, 1939 to 1988: Overview', *South African Journal of Libraries and Information Science*, 57, 3 (1989), p. 292.
263. https://www.news.uct.ac.za/article/-2017-03-29-renamed-knowledge-commons-honours-struggle-librarian.
264. In 2002 it had awarded him an honorary MA degree.
265. UCTAA, Minutes of Senate meeting, 20 November 1951, Appendix: Memorandum by Professor Shephard, 'Proposed Alteration of the Title of the Certificate in Commercial Art to the Certificate in Graphic Design', 1 November 1951. For Senate's refusal, see UCTAA, Minutes of Senate meeting, 18 March 1952.

266. Union of South Africa, *Report of the Commission of Inquiry into University Finances and Salaries, 1951*, p. 177.
267. UCTAA, Minutes of Senate meeting, 22 August 1955, Appendix: Memorandum from Professor Shephard to the Faculty of Fine Art and Architecture, 'A Review of Recommendations of the Holloway Report on University Finances in Respect of the Teaching of Fine Art in the University of Cape Town', n.d.
268. UCTAA, 13.2.3, Chair of Fine Art 1948: Report on Applicants for the Chair of Fine Art, UCT, 17 December 1947.
269. Obituary by a former student, Bruce Arnott, *Cape Times*, 30 April 1992.
270. Cited in L. Raymond, *Eleanor Esmonde-White* (Main Street, Paarl, 2015), p. 33.
271. On Roworth's tenure from 1937 to 1948, see Phillips, *UCT 1918–1948*, pp. 285–6.
272. UCTAA, Minutes of Senate meeting, 19 May 1958, Appendix: Memorandum by Professor Shephard on Staffing at Michaelis Art School, 5 May 1958.
273. A. Tietze, 'The Art of Design: Curriculum Policy and the Fine Art vs. Design Debate at Michaelis School of Fine Art, 1925–1972', *de arte*, 91 (2015), p. 13.
274. UCT Libraries, Special Collections Division, BC 667 (Harries Collection), box 2, B41.21.3: Testimonial by R. Shephard, 19 November 1959.
275. Cited in Raymond, *Eleanor Esmonde-White*, p. 46.
276. UCTAA, Minutes of Senate meeting, 22 March 1954, Appendix: Michaelis School of Fine Art – 'Memoranda on Staff: Application for Rise in Salary for Mr Russell Harvey' by Professor R. Shephard, n.d.
277. UCTAA, 4.3.1, box 360, personal file of R. Harvey: Professor R. Shephard to Registrar, UCT, 20 November 1957.
278. J. Campbell, *I Adore Red* (Contemporary Art Publishers, Cape Town, 2008), p. 13.
279. UCTAA, 13.2.3, Chair of Fine Art 1963: Mitford-Barberton to Duminy, 5 May 1963.
280. UCTAA, 58.5.2, box 23, personal file of I. Lipshitz: J. Paris to Registrar, UCT, 31 July 1959.
281. UCTAA, Minutes of Senate meeting, 17 March 1953, Appendix to meeting of Senate Executive Committee, 19 January 1953: Memorandum by R.N. Shephard on 'Michaelis School: Increase in Honoraria', n.d.
282. Clipping from *Cape Times*, July 1977 in UCTAA, 58.6.2, box 46, personal file of M. van Essche.
283. http://www.Revisions.co.za/biographies/maurice-van-essche//#.Wvl.
284. UCT Libraries, Special Collections Division, BC 353 (Thornton White Papers), box 18, folder B26 ('S'): Thornton White to Sutton, 27 April 1957.
285. UCT Libraries, Special Collections Division, BC 856 (Lippy Lipshitz Papers), box 6, folder D5 (Letters from Van Essche): Van Essche to Lipshitz, 11 May 1966.
286. Ibid., Van Essche to Lipshitz, 2 November 1966.
287. Cited in C. Büchner, *Van Essche* (Tafelberg, Cape Town, 1967), p. 3.
288. Ibid., p. 1.
289. UCT Libraries, Special Collections Division, BC 856 (Lippy Lipshitz Papers), box 6, folder D5 (Letters from Van Essche): Van Essche to Lipshitz, 30 May 1966.
290. Ibid., Van Essche to Lipshitz, 2 November 1966.
291. Cited in Raymond, *Eleanor Esmonde-White*, p. 49.
292. UCT Libraries, Special Collections Division, BC 856 (Lippy Lipshitz Papers), box 6, folder D5 (Letters from Van Essche): Van Essche to Lipshitz, 29 November 1966.
293. E-mail to author from Gavin Jantjes, 31 May 2018.
294. Undated clipping from *Die Burger* (December 1967?) in BC 667 (Harries Collection), box 6, D1.98). Translation by the author.
295. *Varsity*, 11 April 1962, p. 8.

296. E-mail from Gavin Jantjes to author, 31 May 2018.
297. *Varsity*, 11 April 1962, p. 8.
298. *Varsity*, 13 April 1960, p. 5.
299. Interview with Professor Adam Small, 2 November 2015.
300. *Varsity*, 19 April 1961, p. 3.
301. R. Segal, *Into Exile* (McGraw Hill, New York and Toronto, 1963), p. 96.

**Chapter 9 – Reaching Out: UCT and the Wider Community**
1. *Cape Times*, 1 October 1949.
2. Statement by Ohio State University's Office of University Outreach and Engagement, 30 June 2016 at http://outreach.osu.edu/about-us/faq.html.
3. http://www.oed.com.ezproxy.uct.ac.za/view/Entry/133882?rskey=5hBEg1&result=12#eid32784731.
4. *Cape Times*, 8 June 1962.
5. *Cape Times*, 25 April 1952.
6. See H. Phillips, *UCT 1918–1948: The Formative Years* (UCT and UCT Press, Cape Town, 1993), pp. 167–8.
7. UCT Administrative Archives [hereafter UCTAA], 14.1.1 (box 1990), folder 'EMS 1948–53': Extra-Mural Studies – General Policy, pp. 2, 3.
8. UCTAA, Minutes of Council meeting, 24 June 1953, Appendix: Memorandum on the Extension of the Post of Director of Extra-Mural Studies … by T.W. Price.
9. Cited in Centre for Extra-Mural Studies, *Celebrating Fifty Years of Adult Learning* (UCT, Cape Town, 2000), p. 7.
10. Ibid.
11. *Education*, XLVII, 7 (July 1957), p. 19.
12. The Fishing Industry Research Institute building was erected on the slope above Jameson Hall in 1957 while the Western Province Blood Transfusion Service's Laboratory rented accommodation on the Medical campus from 1961.
13. Cited in D.M. Wilson, *Against the Odds: The Struggle of the Cape African Night Schools 1945–1967* (Centre for African Studies and Department of Adult Education and Extra-Mural Studies, UCT, 1991), p. 161.
14. Cited ibid., p. 66.
15. Cited ibid., p. 142.
16. UCTAA, 63.6.2 (SRC box 7), SRC Daily File: G. McIntosh to 'The Wanderer', *Cape Argus*, 26 June 1962; and UCTAA, 63.1.1 (SRC box 11), SRC Correspondence, Minutes, Agenda, July–September 1965: SRC President's Report.
17. UCTAA, 63.1.1 (SRC box 9), SRC Daily File, 1963–4: G. McIntosh to 'The Wanderer', *Cape Argus*, 5 March 1964.
18. Cited in E.B. van Heyningen, *The History of SHAWCO 1943–1975* (SHAWCO, Cape Town, 1975), p. v.
19. Rag was thereby converted from being the 'Hospital Rag' to the 'Varsity Rag': see Phillips, *UCT 1918–1948*, p. 240.
20. UCTAA, Minutes of Council meeting, 7 October 1959, Appendix: 'A Review of the Position of the Student Amenities Finance Council, 1957' by Professor Edward Batson, p. 15.
21. UCTAA, Minutes of Senate meeting, 19 June 1962, Appendix: Draft for University's General Prospectus, 3 May 1962.
22. UCTAA, Minutes of Council meeting, 7 October 1959, Appendix: 'A Review of the Position of the Student Amenities Finance Council, 1957' by Professor Edward Batson, p. 18.

23. Cited in Van Heyningen, The *History of SHAWCO*, p. 37.
24. UCTAA, Minutes of Council meeting, 5 June 1967, Appendix: Associate Professor L.M. Thompson to Acting Principal, 13 May 1957.
25. *Varsity*, 2 April 1964, p. 7.
26. Cited in Van Heyningen, *The History of SHAWCO*, p. 52.
27. Cited ibid., p. 47.
28. Interview with Emeritus Professor William Pick, 6 May 2016.
29. Cited in Van Heyningen, *The History of SHAWCO*, p. 73.
30. UCTAA, Minutes of Council meeting, 7 October 1959, Appendix: 'A Review of the Position of the Student Amenities Finance Council, 1957' by Professor Edward Batson, p. 19.
31. See Phillips, *UCT 1918–1948*, p. 207 for the history of the earlier links between the Institute and UCT.
32. *Cape Argus*, 1 February 1955.
33. R. Rive, 'The Liberal Tradition in South African Literature', *Contrast*, 55 (1983), p. 20.
34. A. Digby and H. Phillips, *At the Heart of Healing: Groote Schuur Hospital, 1938–2008* (Jacana Media, Johannesburg, 2008), p. 355, note 39 and p. 149, note 39.
35. Cited ibid., p. 202, note 49.
36. On the Clinic's earlier history, see Phillips, *UCT 1918–1948*, p. 207.
37. On Bell and the early years of the Little Theatre, see Phillips, *UCT 1918–1948*, pp. 204–5 and 290.
38. Cited in D. Inskip, *Forty Little Years* (Howard Timmins, Cape Town, 1972), p. 104.
39. UCTAA, Minutes of Senate meeting, 21 October 1957, Appendix: Memorandum by Professor Chisholm, 12 October 1957.
40. Cited in J. Purser, *Erik Chisholm, Scottish Modernist, 1904–1965: Chasing a Restless Muse* (Boydell Press, Woodbridge and Rochester, NY, 2009), p. 165.
41. Two undated press clippings in UCT Libraries, Special Collections Division, BC 129 (Chisholm Papers), box 121, folder 157. Translation from *Die Burger* by the author.
42. On the foundation and early history of the Ballet School, see Phillips, *UCT 1918–1948*, pp. 253–4, 290–2.
43. R. Glasstone, *Dulcie Howes: Pioneer of Ballet in South Africa* (Human and Rousseau, Cape Town, 1996), pp. 87–8.
44. *Cape Times*, 5 August 1953.
45. C. Feinstein, *An Economic History of South Africa: Conquest, Discrimination and Development* (Cambridge University Press, Cambridge, 2005), p. 144.
46. See pp. 243 and 379, note 12.
47. N. Lindhard, 'The Careers Office Opens Its Doors', *UCT*, 6 (1969), p. 28.
48. UCTAA, Minutes of Council meeting, 12 December 1956, Appendix: Report of Sub-Committee on the Publication of *UCT* and Maintenance Grant for Public Relations Department, 29 November 1956.
49. On the origins and development of Rag, see Phillips, *UCT 1918–1948*, pp. 125, 193–4, 239–40.
50. UCTAA, Minutes of Senate meeting, 14 September 1959, Appendix: Memorandum on Union Jubilee 1960.
51. UCTAA, 16.1.5, box 1975, folder SEN/3 (Discipline 1949–66): Leaflet issued by Radical Students' Society, 25 May 1961.
52. UCTAA, 16.1.5, box 1975, folder SEN/3 (Discipline 1949–66): Notice by J.P. Duminy, 22 May 1961.
53. Ibid., Note by Duminy on letter from Simons to the Principal, 25 May 1961.
54. See chapter 10.
55. UCTAA, 63.1.1, SRC box 11, SRC Correspondence, Minutes and Agenda, July–September 1965:

Rag 1965 – Report of Outgoing Chairman to SRC, V. Carruthers, 8 June 1965.
56. UCTAA, Minutes of Council meeting, 1 February 1967, Appendix: Kempen & Kempen to Registrar, 27 January 1967.
57. UCT Library, Special Collections Division, BC 353 (Thornton White Papers), box 16, folder B26: Thornton White to Ian Leslie, 5 November 1963.

**Chapter 10 – Colliding and Colluding: UCT and the Apartheid State**

1. UCT Administrative Archive [hereafter UCTAA], 63.6.1, box 3 (SRC 1954–1956): Evidence Submitted on Behalf of the Students of UCT by the SRC of that University to the Government Commission of Enquiry into the Provision of Separate University Facilities for Non-European Students, March 1954, p. 2.
2. Cited in UNESCO, *Apartheid: Its Effects on Education, Science, Culture and Information* (UNESCO, Paris, 1967), p. 84, note 5.
3. *Educational Journal*, XXVII, 8 (April 1956), p. 1.
4. *Educational Journal*, XXXVII, 7 (March 1957), p. 1.
5. T.B. Davie, 'The Function of a University in a Multi-Racial Society' in T.B. Davie and E.E. Harris, *The Idea of a University: A Symposium* (S.A. Institute of Race Relations, Johannesburg, 1954), p. 16.
6. UCTAA, 63.6.1 (SRC box 5), SRC Miscellaneous Correspondence, January–June 1959: NUSAS Newsletter, 22, 6 June 1959, p. 9, citing *Die Transvaler*, 12 May 1959.
7. National Archives of South Africa, K263 (Kommissie van Ondersoek na Universiteitswese, 1968-72), box 25, Verrigtinge van die Kommissie … Betoë ten Behoewe van die Univ. van Kaapstad, 19 Mei 1969, vol. 3, p. 9: Evidence of Prof D.P. Inskip.
8. Cited in M.A. Beale, 'Apartheid and University Education 1948–1970' (PhD thesis, University of the Witwatersrand, 1998), vol. 1, p. 116.
9. Union of South Africa, *Debates of the House of Assembly*, 16 August 1948, col. 219.
10. Cited in Beale, 'Apartheid and University Education 1948–1970', vol. 1, p. 128.
11. Cited ibid., p. 70.
12. UCTAA, 63.3.2 (SRC box 24), Ac/5.1, Protests – Confidential: Cited in 'The Universities and the State 1959–1969'.
13. UCT Libraries, Special Collections Division, [uncatalogued] Cowen Papers, 'Apartheid & Univs' – Davie's file: Handwritten notes by T.B. Davie, 1954.
14. National Archives of South Africa, Pretoria, E 53/94, part I, Kommissie i.s. Afsonderlike Universiteite –Opleidingsgeriewe vir Nie-Blankes, Meeting of Commission at UCT, 12 May 1954: Evidence by UCT [T.B. Davie].
15. E.M. Wentzel cited in interview with Dr N. Rubin by the author, 2 March 2016.
16. UCT Libraries, Special Collections Division, BC 345 (Ballinger Papers), box 20, doc. D12.66: Correspondence between NUSAS and the Minister of Education … 21 January 1957, p. 3.
17. *Educational Journal*, XXVIII, 8 (April 1957), p. 10.
18. UCT Libraries, Special Collections Division, [uncatalogued] Cowen Papers, folder on 'Sep Univ Educ Bill, Speeches Against'. City Hall Meeting, 1957: Cyclostyled copy of speech of the Chancellor of the Univ. of Cape Town at the meeting in the City Hall on May 7, 1957, p. 2.
19. *The Open Universities in South Africa* (Witwatersrand University Press, Johannesburg, 1957), p. 5.
20. Cited in *Varsity*, 16 May 1958, p. 5.
21. Cited in *Varsity*, 19 June 1958, p. 2.
22. *Die Burger*, 18 March 1959 (translation by author).
23. UCT Libraries, Special Collections Division, BC 1263 (Axelson Papers), box 13: H.M. Robertson to Axelson, 22 March 1957.
24. UCT Libraries, Special Collections Division, BC 283 (Centlivres Papers), box 3, folder XVI

(Reports, speeches, MSS, notes etc.): Address by Chancellor of UCT in Jameson Hall on 29 July 1959, p. 3.
25. *Cape Times*, 18 March 1959.
26. The most notable instance of this was the denial of a visa to Clark Kerr, a leading American university administrator who had been invited to deliver the T.B. Davie Memorial lecture in 1967. Two other would-be T.B. Davie lecturers had been similarly treated three years earlier, while the overseas academic who did eventually give the 1967 Lecture was interrogated by a police colonel in his hotel.
27. M. Fullard, 'State Repression in the 1960s' in South African Democracy Education Trust, *The Road to Democracy in South Africa*, vol. 1, 1960–1970 (Zebra Press, Cape Town, 2004), p. 341.
28. *Cape Argus*, 18 August 1965.
29. *Cape Times*, 2 May 1960.
30. UCT Libraries, Special Collections Division, BC 283 (Centlivres Papers), box 4, folder marked 'Speeches etc.': Speech by Centlivres, 19 February 1964, 'A Further Onslaught on Academic Freedom'.
31. UCTAA, 13.3.3, box 1996, folder STU/8, Students – General, 1957–60: P. Kgosana to J.P. Duminy, 23 May 1960.
32. National Archives of South Africa, Pretoria, BAO 3536, file 100/6/1479, part 1 – 'Passport. A.B.M. Mafeje': Duminy to Minister of the Interior, 3 March 1964 (translation from Afrikaans by the author).
33. Ibid., Note by M.D.C. de Wet Nel, 20 March 1964 on copy of Secretary for Bantu Administration and Development to the Minister, 19 March 1964. The Minister noted, 'I have been informed that he is a good student and is searching for the truth – perhaps he will be disillusioned.' (Translation from Afrikaans by the author)
34. Interview with A. Sachs, 9 May 2016. See too UCTAA, 14.2.3, box 1949, folder EXT/4a (Ministries – Other 1948–65): Davie to A. Sachs, 3 October 1955; Secretary for Justice to Principal and Vice-Chancellor, UCT, 8 November 1955.
35. Niemöller's preferred version of the poem ran: 'When the Nazis came for the communists / I remained silent; I was not a communist. / When they locked up the social democrats, / I remained silent, / I was not a social democrat. / When they came for the trade unionists, / I did not speak out, / I was not a trade unionist. / When they came for the Jews, / I remained silent, / I wasn't a Jew. / When they came for me, / There was no one left to speak out.'
36. UCTAA, 18.1.5, box 1941, folder 'Dr H.J. Simons 1964/5: Restriction Order': Memorandum to Academic Freedom Committee by Professor Thornton White, 11 September 1964, in Agenda for Meeting of Academic Freedom Committee, 21 October 1964.
37. UCTAA, Minutes of Senate meeting, 13 April 1965, Appendix: Statement by Chairman of Council on 'The Case of Dr Simons', 9 April 1965.
38. UCT Libraries, Special Collections Division, BC 1041 (Brock Papers), box 8, B3.1.2 (Raymond Hoffenberg Correspondence, September to December 1967), Brock to Sir Harold Harmsworth, 26 February 1968.
39. Ibid., B 3.1.1 (Raymond Hoffenberg Correspondence 1957–1967): Hoffenberg to Brock, 2 August 1967.
40. *Cape Times*, 21 September 1967, letter from P. van der Merwe.
41. UCTAA, 14.2.1, box 1944, folder 'National Convention & Declaration by UCT Staff': J.P. Duminy to C.W. Eglin, 22 May 1961.
42. UCTAA, 15.3.6, box 1972, folder Misc. 39 (Detention of Students): J.P. Duminy to B.J. Vorster, 25 August 1964.
43. Cited in *Varsity*, 19 May 1965, p. 1.

44. *Die Burger*, 11 December 1964 (translation in *Cape Times*, 12 December 1964).
45. UCTAA, 18.1.5, box 1941, folder 'Ian Robertson Banning Order 1966': Duminy to SRC President, 13 May 1966. Duminy made this retrospective comment in 1966, after he had publicly stated that the recent banning of the president of NUSAS just ahead of Senator Kennedy's visit might not have been without justification. His statement elicited strong condemnation from a number of students and staff, including Professor Brock.
46. See p. 300.
47. *Varsity*, 10 May 1967, p. 7.
48. *Varsity*, 23 August 1967, p. 2.
49. Ibid.
50. UCT Libraries, Special Collections Division, BC 1072 (Luyt Papers), B2.1 (UCT Mafeje Affair 1968: Documents): J. de Klerk to Principal and Vice-Chancellor, UCT, 3 May 1968. Of course, the tradition that De Klerk referred to was that of white South Africans only, i.e. of 17% of the country's population.
51. See p. 197.
52. UCT Libraries, Special Collections Division, BC 1072 (Luyt Papers), B2.1 (UCT Mafeje Affair 1968: Documents): Aide Memoire – Senior Lectureship Social Anthropology Department, 3 June 1968, p. 5.
53. UCTAA, *Principal's Circular* [PC], 156 (7 August 1968), Appendix.
54. UCTAA, Minutes of Council meeting, 5 June 1968, p. 3.
55. UCTAA, Minutes of Senate meeting, 11 June 1968, p. 2.
56. E-mail from Maurice Pope to author, 22 August 2015.
57. *Varsity*, 7 August 1968, p. 2.
58. UCT Libraries, Special Collections Division, BC 1072 (Luyt Papers), B2.1 (UCT Mafeje Affair 1968: Documents): The Mafeje Case – Student Reaction, 11 August 1968.
59. National Archives of South Africa, Pretoria, K263 (Kommissie van Ondersoek na die Universiteitswese, 1968–72), box 49, file Univ. 1/11/5, Hoër Onderwys – Kommissie van Ondersoek na die Universiteitswese, Studente-Aangeleenthede: Memorandum on 'Die Rol van Studente-Organisasies: Die Nasionale Unie van S.-A. Studente', B5.4 (ii), p. 5.
60. *Educational Journal*, XX, 13 (March 1949), p. 1. On the Non-European Unity Movement, see p. 283, note 33.
61. *Die Burger*, 8 July 1954.
62. UCTAA, Cowen Papers, 'Apartheid and Universities – Davie's File': Copy of Circular from Dean of Faculty of Medicine, March 1954.
63. *Varsity*, 27 April 1960.
64. *Varsity*, 7 April 1961.
65. *Educational Journal*, XXVII, 8 (April 1956), p. 2.
66. UCT Libraries, Special Collections Division, BC 1502 (Rubin Papers), box 51, folder B1.248 (Correspondence with Melmed): Minutes of Meeting … 4 December 1961, p. 4.
67. UCTAA, 15.3.6, box 1972, folder MISC. 40 (Mixed Audiences), Report of Principal's Liaison Officer to Principal, July 1965, p. 2.
68. See p. 252.
69. A year later, acknowledging its English heritage, it used the same floodlights to illuminate the campus in honour of the coronation of Queen Elizabeth II.
70. *Varsity*, 17 September 1951, p. 1.
71. *Day Student*, 17 April 1961, p. 1.
72. Interview with Dr C. D'Arcy, 18 February 2016.
73. Interview with F. v.d. Horst, 13 May 2018.

74. UCTAA, 15.3.1, folder 'Social Activities 1957–65': Memorandum on 'Facts Concerning Mixing of Races at UCT Dances' [late 1959?], p. 2.
75. *Die Burger*, 13 August 1958. (Translation by the author from the Afrikaans, 'Gemengde dansery wek twis aan U.K.')
76. *Cape Times*, 13 August 1958.
77. UCTAA, Minutes of meeting of Council, 3 December 1958, p. 1.
78. UCTAA, 15.3.1, folder 'Social Activities 1957–65': Draft memorandum on 'Social Segregation', 21 November 1958.
79. Ibid., Draft memorandum on 'Social Amenities', 14 January 1960.
80. UCTAA, 63.3.1 (SRC box 22), P/R 1.3, 'Academic Freedom – Social Practice': Memorandum by H. Melmed on behalf of the SRC 1961–2 on Social Practice at UCT, 25 May 1962, p. 2.
81. *Die Transvaler*, 22 January 1957 (translation by the author).
82. Union of South Africa, *Debates of the House of Assembly*, 8 April 1958, col. 3203.
83. *Die Burger*, 20 December 1956.
84. *Rand Daily Mail*, 10 August 1962.
85. UCTAA, 63.3.1 (SRC box 22), P/R 1.3, Academic Freedom – Social Practice: Memorandum on Social Practice at the University of Cape Town, 25 May 1962, p. 6.
86. X. Mangcu, 'Reflections on the Revolution of Our Times' (2006), p. 7 as cited in F. Hendricks, 'The Mafeje Affair: The University of Cape Town and Apartheid', *African Studies*, 67, 3 (December 2008), p. 426.

**Chapter 11 – Learning in (and out of) Class: Student Life**

1. Interview with Ned Vizzini, 10 January 2012 at https://www.wired.com/2012/10/other-normals.
2. M.S. Garrison, 'The Cognitive Development of Collegiate Students: A Brief Literature Review', *Campbellsville Review*, 4 (2009), p. 87 (http://moodle.f.bg.ac.rs/file.php/151/Resursi_-_Opsta_andragogija_/Literatura_za_vezbe_/Garrison_M._S._The_Cognitive_Development_of_Collegiate_Students_-_A_Brief_Literature_Review.pdf).
3. Cited in H. Phillips, *UCT 1918–1948: The Formative Years* (UCT and UCT Press, Cape Town, 1993), p. 230.
4. Cited ibid.
5. For a fuller account of this and other aspects of the war veterans' life at UCT, see Phillips, *UCT 1918–1948*, pp. 229–30.
6. Interview with V.M. Stein, 18 August 2016.
7. Interview with P.S. Hare, 17 December 2015.
8. UCT Administrative Archives [hereafter UCTAA], 20a.1.2 (unnumbered box), old Principal's files, folder marked 'Dr. Davie – personal letters': H.R.B. Wilson to T.B. Davie, 8 April 1951.
9. With dark humour the residence was informally dubbed 'Belsen' by its first ex-servicemen residents. See Phillips, *UCT 1918–1948*, p. 227.
10. *Varsity*, 19 June 1958, p. 1.
11. *Sax Appeal*, 1960, p. 15.
12. *Varsity*, 8 September 1966, p. 4.
13. *Varsity*, 14 April 1965, p. 3.
14. Interview with B.E. Greene, 11 August 2016.
15. Interview with R. Fischer Rice, 14 August 2016.
16. Interview with S. K., 14 November 2016.
17. *Varsity*, 17 September 1969, p. 7: Letter from 'Fuller House Resident'.
18. E-mail to author from A. Loopuyt, 23 November 2015.

19. Interview with B.M. Boxall, 3 June 2015.
20. See p. 263.
21. It was widely believed by black students in the Faculty of Medicine that their number there was deliberately limited to a quota of 10% of all medical students both before and after 1959. Documentary support for this contention has not been found. Indeed, the Dean did aver privately to the Principal in 1963 that 'The selection of students is based entirely on academic merit, the race of applicants does not receive any consideration what-so-ever' (UCTAA, 14.1.6, box 1954, folder MED/29 (Medical Training of Non-Whites 1949–64): Bromilow-Downing to Duminy, 29 March 1963).
22. UCT Libraries, Special Collections Division, Non-European Students' Fund Collection: Applicants' file A–L: Application by P. Bestenbier, 6 March 1950.
23. UCTAA, 13.3.3, box 1996, folder STU/8 (Students – General 1957–60): Statement by Professor H.M. Robertson, n.d.
24. Interview with P. Kgosana, 31 March 2016.
25. See pp. 102, 104, 112, 269.
26. See p. 234.
27. See p. 269.
28. Interview with Dr Pat Lawrence, 16 May 2016.
29. Interview with Emeritus Professor William Pick, 6 May 2016.
30. A.M. Perez, N. Ahmed and L. London, 'Racial discrimination: Experiences of Black Medical School Alumni at the University of Cape Town, 1945–1994' in *South African Medical Journal*, 102, 6 (2012), p. 575.
31. Interview with Eugene Cairncross, 30 July 2016.
32. Interview with Patrick Naylor, 17 May 2016.
33. The NEUM was established in 1943 as a doctrinaire Trotskyist organisation for national liberation. It drew most of its support from the Western Cape. In 1960 it rebranded itself the Unity Movement of South Africa.
34. Harold Cressy High School, Trafalgar High, Livingstone High and South Peninsula High.
35. Clary Johnson, 'Autobiography' (unpublished), p. 115.
36. *Varsity*, 7 September 1961, p. 3.
37. Interview with Dr Pat Lawrence, 16 May 2016.
38. Interview with Emeritus Professor Marian Jacobs, 23 May 2016.
39. D. Levinson, *Five Years: An Experience of South Africa* (Deutsch, London, 1966), p. 93.
40. Interview with Dr B. Brown, 29 February 2016.
41. E-mail from Gavin Jantjes to author, 31 May 2018.
42. Interview with Emeritus Professor William Pick, 6 May 2016.
43. H. Dajee with P. Apodaca, *A Boy Named Courage: A Surgeon's Memoir of Apartheid* (Cynren Press, Malvern, PS, 2018), p. 44.
44. *Varsity*, 29 August 1962, p. 1.
45. UCTAA, 62.5.1 (SRC box 33), SRC minutes 1968–9: Minutes of SRC meeting, 3 September 1968, p. 6.
46. *Cape Times*, 29 August 1968.
47. National Archives of South Africa, Pretoria, OKW 7, file O4/3/1, Universiteite. Stigting van Universiteite. Aansoek en Algemeen. Universiteit Kaapstad: C.J. von Hirschberg pp. Secretary for Foreign Affairs to Secretary for Education, Arts and Science, 27 June 1967.
48. Interview with Emeritus Professor L. Nassimbeni, 17 May 2016.
49. *Cape Argus*, 8 August 1964.
50. Interview with Norman Bromberger, 26 November 2016.

51. *Varsity*, 19 June 1968, p. 2.
52. UCTAA, Minutes of Council meeting, 25 September 1950, Appendix: Letter from Honorary Secretary, House Committee, Men's Residence, 25 August 1950.
53. The original College House near UCT's Hiddingh Hall campus in town had been closed in 1954 because of declining numbers. After two years in temporary accommodation in Rosebank – in the ex-servicewomen's residence, Protem – it had found a permanent home in 1958 in a former private hotel bought by UCT in that suburb. When College House moved out of its temporary premises at Protem, the huts became the home of a revived University House Residence, which had been in hibernation since its closure in 1937 (Phillips, *UCT 1918–1948*, p. 187). In 1965 it moved into the huts previously occupied by Driekoppen, where it remains today (ibid., p. 387 note 1).
54. UCTAA, 14.1.1, box 1989, folder SEN/7 (Residences): Report by Professor Pells, 24 February 1949.
55. C.J. Driver, 'Unpublished Memoir', chapter 12, p .5.
56. Interview with Brian Marquard, 15 December 2016.
57. Interview with John Clare, 19 September 2016.
58. E-mail from Tony Hooper to author, 8 December 2015.
59. UCTAA, 14.1.1, box 1989, folder SEN/7 (Residences): Report by Professor Pells, 24 February 1949.
60. *Cape Times*, 8 March 1963.
61. *Varsity*, 23 March 1966, p. 6.
62. *Varsity*, 6 June 1962, p. 5.
63. On the origins and early history of Rag, see Phillips, *UCT 1918–1948*, pp. 124–5, 239–40.
64. See pp. 244–5.
65. *Cape Times*, 6 June 1958: Letter from M. Leendertz.
66. UCTAA, 63.6.2, SRC box 6, SRC Correspondence & Minutes & Agenda, April–June 1960: L.G. Ballard to F. Berman, 19 April 1960.
67. *Trend*, 8 April 1964, p. 2.
68. UCTAA, *Principal's Circular [PC]* 156, 7 August 1968, p. 29: Objection by Professor Househam.
69. See Phillips, *UCT 1918–1948*, p. 240.
70. *Cape Times*, 1 April 1949.
71. *Cape Times*, 11 April 1949.
72. For the history of this event, see Phillips, *UCT 1918–1948*, pp. 126–7, 239.
73. UCT Libraries, Special Collections Division, BC 1502 (Rubin Papers), box 51, folder B1.248 (Correspondence with Melmed): Minutes of meeting, 4 December 1961, p. 4. Telling of the key role of rugby in student popular culture at UCT, as against other student social activities, is the fact that in 1960 the UCT Debating Society was able to cancel the Intervarsity debate with Stellenbosch without eliciting a murmur on campus because the latter's Debating Society had refused to participate against a UCT team that was not all white.
74. *Modern World Journal*, 1, 1963, editorial.
75. Cited in F. Swanson, '"Die SACS kom terug": Intervarsity Rugby, Masculinity and White Identity at the University of Cape Town, 1960s–1970s' in S. Field, R. Meyer and F. Swanson (eds.), *Imagining the City: Memories and Cultures in Cape Town* (HSRC Press, Cape Town, 2007), p. 225.
76. I. Nurick, *Hooked on Varsity* (UCT Rugby Club, 2009), p. 12.
77. See p. 289.
78. *Varsity*, 28 May 1959.
79. Cited in L. Babrow and R.K. Stent, *The Varsity Spirit: The Story of Rugby Football at UCT 1883–1963* (Johnson and Neville, Cape Town, 1963), p. 122.

# NOTES

80. UCT Libraries, Special Collections Division, BC 1231 (Modern World Society Collection): Constitution of Students' Fellowship Society.
81. UCTAA, 13.3.3, box 1994, folder STU/4 (Societies & Clubs 1955–61): Secretary of the Radical Students' Society to Principal, 2 August 1960.
82. *The Radical: Official Magazine of the Radical Students' Society*, I (August 1960), p. 2.
83. *Trend*, 1 October 1965, p. 1.
84. UCT Libraries, Special Collections Division, BC 1473 (Student Christian Association Archives), box 55, folder C8.1.4.2 (Correspondence relating to constitutional controversies, 1948–53): Memorandum on SCA Affairs, with special reference to the Afrikaans-speaking students submitted to the SCA Committee of the UCT Branch, p. 2, II (c), (a).
85. *Varsity*, 17 September 1951, p. 3.
86. UCTAA, Minutes of Senate meeting, 20 October 1958, Appendix: Petition to the Senate and Council of UCT by H.B. Steer et al., September [?] 1958.
87. See pp. 313–4.
88. *Varsity*, 4 September 1958, p. 5.
89. *Varsity*, 28 August 1963, p. 2.
90. *Varsity*, 27 August 1959, p. 2.
91. See p. 283.
92. Only when Luyt became Principal in 1968 were two SRC representatives invited to join this Committee.
93. UCTAA, 63.6.2, SRC box 7 (SRC Miscellaneous Correspondence, Minutes & Agenda, April–June 1961): F. Berman to Professor Ahrens, 26 June 1961.
94. UCT Libraries, Special Collections Division, BC 133 (Duminy Papers), box 7, Personal Correspondence M–S: Allan [Stephen] to J.P. Duminy, 1 September 1964.
95. See pp. 244–6.
96. UCTAA, Misc/18, Report of Principal 1948–57: Report dated 12 December 1952, p. 4.
97. UCTAA, Minutes of Council meeting 7 October 1959, Appendix: 'A Review of the Position and Problems of the Students Amenities Finance Committee, 1957' by Professor Edward Batson, p. 3.
98. *UCT General Prospectus*, 1969, p. 123.
99. UCTAA, 63.6.1, box 3, SRC Correspondence, Minutes …, 1955: Report of UCT Delegation to Annual NUSAS Congress, July 1955, p. 4.
100. UCTAA, 13.3.3, box 1996, folder STU/8 (Students General 1952–6): Hiddingh Hall Commission Report plus Annexures, May 1956.
101. UCTAA, 13.3.3, box 1996, folder STU/8 (Students General 1952–6): Hiddingh Hall Commission: Synopsis of Conclusions and Recommendations, May 1956.
102. Interview with Kenneth Penkin, 10 March 2016.
103. *Varsity*, 4 September 1951, p. 5.
104. See Phillips, *UCT 1918–1948*, p. 232 for the troubled circumstances in which it was established.
105. However, two women, Juliana du Toit and Daphne van Rooyen, did fill the secondary position of Afrikaans editor in 1956 and 1958 respectively.
106. *Varsity*, 19 September 1962, p. 2.
107. UCTAA, 63.6.2, SRC box 6, SRC Correspondence & Minutes & Agenda, January–March 1960, SRC Publications, Correspondence, December 1959–1960: C.J. Driver to Secretary SRC, 12 September 1959.
108. UCT Libraries, Special Collections Division, BC 1206 (Reg Lighton Papers), box 11, folder B1.6.3: Duminy to Professor Lighton, 6 September, 1967.
109. *Trend*, 7 September 1967, p. 3.

110. E-mail from C. Pritchard to author, 8 March 2016.
111. E-mail from C. Pritchard to author, 29 February 2016.
112. *Varsity*, 19 September 1962, p. 2.
113. UCTAA, 63.6.2, SRC box 6, SRC Correspondence & Minutes & Agenda, January–March 1960: UCT Delegation Report, 28 June 1960.
114. E-mail from Professor Andrew Colman to the author, 26 March 2016.
115. UCTAA, 63.1.1, SRC box 11 (SRC Correspondence, Minutes & Agenda, January–March 1965), Cornell University International Conference of Students, February 1965, 'The University Education – A Student Perspective': Views of J.H. Levenstein, UCT, 'What Is the Role of the Student inside and outside the University?', p. 3.
116. UCTAA, 18.1.5, box 1941, folder 'Ministerial Attacks on English-Language Universities 1963–5': 'Notes on Interview with Mr J.B. [*sic*] Vorster in Pretoria, 22 September 1964' by J.P. Duminy.
117. *Varsity*, 8 September 1960, p. 2.
118. UCTAA, 63.6.2, SRC box 8 (SRC Correspondence, Minutes and Agenda, July–October 1963): Speech by Jonty Driver … at NUSAS seminar … Botha's Hill, 29 April 1964 to 3 May 1964, p. 8.
119. UCTAA, 63.1.1, SRC box 11 (SRC Correspondence, Minutes & Agenda, July–September 1965): G.G. Ledgerwood to Secretary SRC, 12 August 1965.
120. A record of his inspiring, superbly crafted speech was subsequently sold by the SRC. It can be heard at https://www.youtube.com/watch?v=yp81OYCjXtU.
121. *Radical*, 1965, 1, p. 3.
122. *The Radical*, I, August 1960, p. 2.
123. The anxious mother of one student activist feelingly bemoaned how, in her view, 'politics were interfering with [academic] progress, delaying degree awards, causing friction in erstwhile happy homes, saddening and darkening happiness for the more sensitive and serious-minded young' (cited in *Varsity*, 23 June 1965, p. 1).
124. *The Radical*, I, August 1960, p. 1.
125. *Trend*, 10 March 1964, p. 5.
126. See p. 313.
127. E-mail from Melvyn Drummond to author, 9 October 2015.
128. UCTAA, 18.3.3, box 887, Societies Constitution: Independent Students' Union Constitution, 17 May 1968.
129. UCTAA, 14.1.2, box 1992, folder SEN/16a (T.B. Davie Memorial Lecture 1959–1969): Flyer issued by Modern World Society, [September 1962].
130. *Varsity*, 14 April 1965, p. 14.
131. A reference to a number of them being products of the elite, Anglocentric Diocesan College, a boys' school in Cape Town, which saw itself as the Harrow or Eton of South Africa.
132. R. Kaplinsky, in *Dialogue*, II, April, p. 23.
133. https://www.sahistory.org.za/topic/african-resistance-movement-arm1969ARM: Announcement, 12 June 1964.
134. UCTAA, 63.1.1, RC box 10, SEC Daily File, September 1964 to November 1965: Unsigned note to President, SRC, 4 September 1964.
135. *Varsity*, 9 June 1965, p. 3.
136. Cited in C.E.A. McKay, 'A History of the National Union of South African Students (NUSAS): 1956–1970' (DLitt et Phil thesis, Unisa, 2015), p. 352.
137. *Trend*, 18 August 1964, p. 1.
138. McKay, 'A History of the National Union of South African Students (NUSAS): 1956–1970', p. 351.
139. *Varsity*, 19 June 1958, pp. 2, 5.

140. *Varsity*, 11 September 1963, p. 5.
141. UCTAA, 63.6.1, SRC box 5 (SRC Miscellaneous Correspondence, Minutes & Agenda, July–December 1959): Replies to Questionnaire from Commission on Social, Sporting and Academic Discrimination, 1959.
142. Interview with D. Goodley, 3 July 2016.
143. UCTAA, 63.6.1, SRC box 5 (SRC Miscellaneous Correspondence, Minutes & Agenda, July–December 1959): Replies to Questionnaire from Commission on Social, Sporting and Academic Discrimination, 1959–Reply by Chairman, UCT Film Unit, 22 September 1959.
144. Ibid., Reply by Secretary UCT Table Tennis Club, 6 October 1959.
145. UCTAA, 63.6.2, SRC box 8 (SRC Correspondence, Minutes & Agenda, April–June 1962): Professor M. Wilson to President SRC, 22 May 1962.
146. UCTAA, 15.3.1, box 1940, folder 'Social Activities 1957–65': Holliman to Duminy, 29 August 1958.
147. *Varsity*, 31 August 1960, p. 2.
148. *Trend*, 4 April 1967, p. 2.
149. *Varsity*, 10 March 1965, p. 4.
150. *Cape Times*, 25 February 1966.
151. *Varsity*, 16 September 1954, p. 3.
152. *Varsity*, 13 June 1962, p. 7.
153. *Die Afrikaans-Ikey*, I, 1 (Winter 1952), p. 4. Translation from Afrikaans by the author.
154. *Varsity*, 1 April 1949, p. 5.
155. 'Students Spending Habits Probed', *Turnover: UCT Commerce Magazine*, I, 2, June 1967, p. 9.
156. In 1967 a newspaper report claimed that about 3% of UCT students had smoked dagga (*Cape Times*, 3 October 1967).
157. UCTAA, 13.3.3, box 1996, folder STU/8 (Students: General 1952–6): Davie to Dr Simpson Wells, 2 March 1954.
158. K. Zailckas, *Smashed: Story of a Drunken Girlhood* (Penguin, New York, 2016), p. 111.
159. 'Students Spending Habits Probed', *Turnover: UCT Commerce Magazine*, I, 2, June 1967, p. 9. Beer was males' drink of choice, with wine a distant second; women preferred wine and sherry.
160. https://www.facebook.com/groups/2781637321/: Posting by Rory Harman, 29 January 2009.
161. Ibid., Posting by Anne Snyders, 22 January 2016.
162. Ibid., Posting by Ian Bradburn, 14 October 2014.
163. Both banks had operated agencies on the Groote Schuur campus from 1930, but had closed these down during World War II: see Phillips, *UCT 1918–1948*, p. 203.
164. UCTAA, Minutes of the Board of Faculty of Social Science meeting, 8 May 1963, Appendix: 'Student Dress – Notice Circulated by the Principal, UCT', 13 March 1963.
165. *Varsity*, 11 March 1964, p. 4.
166. UCTAA, Principal's Correspondence Files 1948–68, box 1944: Graduation Address, 13 December 1963.
167. UCTAA, Principal – Correspondence File and Speeches 1968–80, box 1337: Graduation Address, 10 December 1970, p. 4.
168. UCT Libraries, Special Collections Division, BC 649 (Doughty Papers), box 1, document A4.4: Luyt to Doughty, 15 September 1969.
169. *UCT General Prospectus*, 1969, p. 124.
170. UCTAA, Minutes of Senate meeting 10 June 1969, Appendix 'R': Memorandum for Commission of Inquiry into Universities … 12 June 1969, p. 17.
171. National Archives of South Africa, Pretoria, K 263 (Kommissie van Ondersoek na Universiteitswese 1968–72) [Van Wyk de Vries Commission], Verbatim Getuienis, box 27:

Verrigtinge van die Kommissie, vol. 16, p. 110: Evidence by Sir Richard Luyt [1969?].
172. *Varsity*, 8 September 1966, pp. 4–5.
173. UCT Libraries, Special Collections Division, BC 1231 (Modern World Society Collection), Folder 'D' (Miscellaneous): Minutes of UCT Student Affairs Committee, 14 September 1964.
174. See p. 42.
175. UCTAA, 62.2.2, SRC box 57, folder 'Staff/Student Relations 1964–1966': Memorandum on Student–Staff Relationship at UCT by L. Lurie, 10 March 1964.
176. See pp. 271–2.
177. *Varsity*, 16 May 1962, p. 2.
178. UCTAA, 13.3.3, box 1994, folder STU/5 (SRC 1964–1967): J.H. Levenstein to Duminy, 4 December 1963.
179. UCTAA, 62.2.2, SRC box 57, folder '*Varsity* 1951–66': Memorandum on Hitch-Hiking on De Waal Drive, 7 August 1964.
180. *Varsity*, 12 August 1964, p. 1.
181. UCTAA, 62.2.2, SRC box 57, folder '*Varsity* 1951–66': Memorandum on Hitch-Hiking on De Waal Drive, 7 August 1964.
182. Ibid.
183. Jack Harley, *Let's Make Mary: Being a Gentleman's Guide to Scientific Seduction in Eight Easy Lessons* (Phoenix Press, 1937).
184. UCT Libraries, Special Collections Division, BC 133 (Duminy Papers), box 7, Personal Correspondence M–S: Stephen to Duminy, 1 September 1964.
185. *Varsity*, 5 August 1964, p. 4.
186. UCTAA, Minutes of Council meeting, 2 September 1964, Appendix: Memorandum to the Principal and University Council by J. Levenstein on behalf of the students of UCT, 7 August 1964.
187. UCTAA, 62.2.2, SRC box 57, folder '*Varsity* 1951–66': Minutes of Mass Meeting, 16 August 1966, p. 4.
188. UCT Libraries, Special Collections Division, BC 587 (Leo Marquard Papers), folder D, document D2.67: David [Welsh] to Marquard, 17 June 1966.
189. See p. 267.
190. UCTAA, 63.1.2, SRC 12, SRC Daily File, September 1966 to August 1967: I. Hume to Chairman of UCT Council, 6 December 1966.
191. *Varsity*, 9 March 1966, p. 1.
192. UCTAA, Minutes of Council meeting, 21 December 1966, p. 2.
193. See pp. 292, 300.
194. UCTAA, Minutes of Council meeting, 14 December 1966, Appendix: 'A Synopsis of the SRC Constitution Revision', 20 April 1967, p. 3.
195. *Cape Times*, 20 February 1967.
196. *Trend*, 18 April 1967, p. 1; UCTAA, 18.1.5, box 1941, folder 'SRC Constitution': Minutes of mass meeting, 23 March 1967, p. 5.
197. Ibid., p. 4.
198. *Trend*, 18 April 1967, p. 1.
199. *Cape Times*, 17 May 1967.
200. *Varsity*, 7 June 1967, p. 4.
201. UCT Libraries, Special Collections Division, BC 133 (Duminy Papers), box 35, file marked 'General': Duminy to W.A.P. von Holdt, 19 December 1967.
202. UCTAA, 63.1.2, SRC 12 (SRC Daily File, August–December 1967): Synopsis by Duncan Innes, 8 September 1967, p. 2.

203. UCTAA, 14.2.1, box 1942, folder 'Interim Students' Council, 1967': Duminy to Alan Paton, 29 September 1967.
204. *Wits Student*, 14 September 1967, p. 1.
205. *Trend*, 13 September 1967, p. 1; *Wits Student*, 14 September 1967, p. 2.
206. UCTAA, 63.1.2, SRC 12 (SRC Daily File, August–December 1967): D. Innes to J. Kane-Berman, 14 September 1967.
207. E-mail from C. Pritchard to author, 9 March 2016.
208. *Trend*, 20 September 1967, p. 2.
209. Ibid., p. 1.
210. UCTAA, 14.2.1, box 1942, folder 'Interim Students Council 1967': Memorandum by D. Innes on Constitutional Crisis, 11 September 1967.
211. UCTAA, 63.1.2, SRC 12, SRC Daily File, August–December 1967: Innes to J. Kane-Berman, 14 September 1967.
212. UCTAA, 24.1.7, box 3, folder C. 7/3 (Commission of Enquiry into Allegations against Dept of Sociology and Administration), A. Clarke to C. Corder, 23 October 1967.
213. *Sunday Times*, 1 October 1967.
214. *Sunday Times*, 8 October 1967.
215. V. Markarian, *Uruguay, 1968: Student Activism from Global Counterculture to Molotov Cocktails* (University of California Press, Berkeley, 2017).
216. See pp. 267–8.
217. *Varsity*, 14 August 1968, p. 2.
218. UCT Libraries, Special Collections Division, BC 1072 (Sir Richard Luyt Papers), A1.6 (Letters to be retained): undated flyer issued by Radical Students' Society.
219. Interview with Professor Raphie Kaplinsky, 14 December 2016.
220. UCTAA, 62.5.1, SRC box 33, SRC Minutes 1968–9, Attachments to Agenda of Extraordinary Meeting of SRC, 19 November 1968, Appendix C: Minutes of Mass Meeting, 7 August 1968.
221. *Varsity*, 14 August 1968, p. 1.
222. UCTAA, Minutes of UCT Council meeting 26 August 1968, Appendix C: Memorandum by Luyt on the Mafeje Case: Student Reaction, 11 August 1968.
223. UCTAA, 18.3.4, box 890, Mafeje – SRC Action: Handwritten amendment by Raphie Kaplinsky and Tony Shapiro, [14 August 1968].
224. Interview with Duncan Innes, 7 January 2016.
225. R. Kaplinsky, 'Little Acorns and Big Oaks: 40 Years On from the UCT Sit-in' (unpublished paper, 14 August 2008), p. 1.
226. M. Plaut, 'South African Student Protest, 1968: Remembering the Mafeje Sit-in', *History Workshop Journal*, 69 (2010), pp. 201–2.
227. UCT Libraries, Special Collection Division, BC 1072 (Luyt Papers), B16 (Foreign Students 1968): Affidavit by M.C. Galaun, n.d.
228. *New Trend*, 20 August 1986, p. 1.
229. *Varsity*, 21 August 1968, p. 4.
230. *Cape Argus*, 17 August 1968.
231. *Cape Times*, 23 August 1968.
232. Interview with Martin Plaut, 7 June 2016. Compare this sentiment with his earlier enthusiasm – see his statement in note 226 above.
233. See pp. 284–5.
234. *The Star*, 17 August 1968.
235. *The Star*, 21 August 1968.
236. *Rand Daily Mail*, 17 August 1968.

237. *New Trend*, 10 September 1968, p. 1.
238. Interview with Advocate David Kawalsky, 16 November 2015.
239. UCTAA, 62.5.1, SRC box 33, SRC Minutes 1968–9: Official report-back of SRC President – Mass meeting, 12 September 1968.
240. UCTAA, 18.3.4, box 890, Mafeje – SRC Action: Innes to Corder, 15 September 1968.
241. UCT Libraries, Special Collections Division, BC 1072 (Luyt Papers), B2.3 (Mafeje Affair 1968: Subsequent Correspondence etc.): Luyt to E.G. Malherbe, 23 September 1968.
242. Ibid., Luyt to Professor Wilson, Bristol University, 23 September 1968.
243. National Archives of South Africa, Pretoria, K263 (Kommissie van Ondersoek na Universiteitswese 1968–72) [Van Wyk de Vries Commission], Verbatim Getuienis, box 28, Verrigtinge van die Kommissie, vol. 25, p. 51: Evidence of J.P. Duminy.
244. UCTAA, 62.5.1, SRC box 33, SRC Minutes 1968–9: Official report-back of SRC President – Mass meeting, 12 September 1968. Years later, however, a post-apartheid UCT conferred a posthumous honorary doctorate on Mafeje (2008), renamed its Senate Room, the hub of the 1968 sit-in, after him (2008), and established the Archie Mafeje Scholarship in African Studies (2016) and the Archie Mafeje Chair in Critical and Decolonial Humanities (2017).
245. Advocate Geoff Budlender cited in R. Erbmann, 'Conservative Revolutionaries: Anti-Apartheid Activism at UCT 1963–1973' (Hons dissertation, University of Oxford, 2005), p. 9.
246. Speech by Jan Theron at the Sit-in Symposium at the Centre for African Studies, UCT, 8 August 2018.
247. Jeremy Cronin cited in I. Macqueen, 'Richard Turner, the New Left and Nationalism, 1968–1977' (Unpublished paper, South African Historical Society 25th Biennial Conference, 2015).
248. Speech by Madi Gray at the Sit-in Symposium at the Centre for African Studies, UCT, 8 August 2018.
249. 'Reunion Reflections', e-mail from Duncan Innes to Sit-in Veterans, 30 August 2008.
250. R. Kaplinsky 'Little Acorns', p. 3
251. Ibid.
252. *5 Decades of Protest @ UCT* (1998), p. 5.
253. P. Altbach, 'Student Political Activism' in L.R. Sherrod (ed.), *Youth Activism: An International Encyclopedia*, vol. 2 (Greenwood Press, Westport, 2006), p. 629.

**Chapter 12 – UCT and the World in 1968**

1. *Varsity*, 9 October 1953, p. 2.
2. UCT Libraries, Special Collections Division, BC 1041 (Brock Papers), box 8, folder B 3.1.1, Raymond Hoffenberg Correspondence 1957–67: draft of Brock to Minister of Justice, B.J. Vorster, 4 May 1966.
3. Interview with Brigid Erin Bates, 19 September 2016.
4. The thirteen recipients of honorary doctorates were R.H. Compton, C.S. Corder, J.C. de Wet, N.P. van Wyk Louw, O. McCann, C.K. Niven, H. Olivier, S.F. Oosthuizen, A. Plant, F.C. Robb, R. van der Riet Woolley, J.T. van Wyk and E.A. Walker.
5. *Cape Times*, 28 August 1968.

# INDEX

Note: Numerical indicators in **bold** refer to pages containing illustrative material.

## A

Abrahams, Israel 203
academic freedom 4, 6, 7, 10, 262–4, 268, 272, 276–7, 286, 299, 318, 322, 332
Academic Freedom Committee 263, 265
academic year 44, 119–20
academics
    division between different ranks of 17, 32, 45–6, 69
    effect of political conditions on 53, 69, 74–5, 77
    liberal 11, 13, 155, 206, 209
    recruitment of 14, 69, 97, 176, 190, 251
    salaries 14–5, 19, 65, 73, 97, 149, 139, 250–1
    shortage of 53, 69, 160
    *see also* associate professors; black academics; chairs; deans; lecturers; Jewish academics, lecturing style; part-time academics; professors; teaching assistants; tutors; women academics
accommodation, students, *see also* Lodgings Bureau; residences
Accounting, Department of 147–9
    part-time staff 147–8
Ackerman, Raymond 149
*Acta Juridica*, 154
Adams, Perseus 196
Adamson, Robert 60
administration 15, 285, 298, 317
    *see also* Bremer Building
administrative staff 13, 17–8, 319, **334**
African History 206, 215, 373n.123
African Languages, Department of 215, 222–4, **239**, 264
African National Congress 264, 284

African Resistance Movement (ARM) 10, 266, **276**, 286, 298, 301–2
African students *see* black students
African Studies, School of 214–5, 218, 224, 235
    *see also* African Languages, Department of; Archaeology, Department of; Comparative African Government and Law, Department of; Social Anthropology, Department of
Afrikaans and Nederlands, Department of 197–9, 372n.76
*Afrikaner-Ikey, Die* 286
Afrikaner Studentebond 286, 300
Afrikaner Studenteklub 286
Afrikaners 13, 139, 161, 164, 197–9, 229, 253, 260, 264, 285–6, 292, 338, 372n.85
Ahrens, Louis 53–4, **81**
alcohol and drug consumption 94, 287, 305–6, 320, 389n.159
Alexander, Neville 74, **274**
Allan, Colin Lewer 118–11
Allison, David 70
Alma, Joanna 70
Alumni Office 251
Ames, Frances 134
Anaesthetics, Department of 124–7, 134
Anatomy Building 25, 34
Anatomy, Department of 97, 100–3, 140, 144n.220, 264
Anglo American Corporation 53, 125
Anglophilia 197, 286
anti-semitism 285
apartheid *see also* racial discrimination; racism; spatial apartheid; social discrimination; university apartheid
apartheid, opposition to 199, 206, 210, 214, 253, 264, 286, 319
    *see also* African Resistance Movement (ARM)
Applied Mathematics, Department of 50, 66–7, 70

Applied Sociology in Social Work, Department of 175–7
   *see also* Social Work, Department of
Archaeology, Department of 43, 215, 220–223
Architectural Students' Council 168
architecture and design of UCT 20, 24–9, 166–7, 169, 171, 190, 250
   *see also* Groote Schuur campus; Hiddingh Hall campus; Lower campus, Medical School campus; *and under the names of specific buildings*
Architecture, School of 26–7, 166–70, 233, 368n.117
   students 27–9
   *see also* Building Science; Centlivres Building; Fine Arts and Architecture, Faculty of; Quantity Surveying, Department of
Arkin, Marcus 210
Arts Block 160, 214, 284
Arts, Faculty of 40–2, 45, 66, 72, 146, 159, 160, 175, 183, 191–2, 207, 209, 211, 215, 224, 228, 235, 281, 294
   *see also under names of departments and units*, eg, Classics, Department of
Assistant Principal *see* Beinart, Ben-Zion; Schaffer, Walter
associate professors 14, 70, 91, 116, 226, 253, 346n.68
Astronomy, Department of 50
Atkinson, John 205
Atomic Energy Board 40, 55
Axelson, Eric 206, 208

**B**

Bacteriology, Department of 104, 108–9
Baillie, Peter 122
Baldry, H.C. **39,** 204
Ballet Company 185, 189–90, 250, 251
   *see also* Cape Performing Arts Board (CAPAB)
Ballet School 184, 188, 190–1, 249
   *see also* Cape Performing Arts Board (CAPAB)
banking services on campus 306, 389n.163
Bantu Education Act 163

Barnard, Chris **115**, 116–7, 145
Barnett, Jack 30
Barrett, Peter 48
Batson, Edward, 174–5, 180
Batson, Helen 176
Baumbach, Lydia 205
Bax, Dirk 200
Bax-Botha, Marie 198
Baxter, W. Duncan 13, **23**, 30, **275**
Baxter Hall 25–6, 281, 288, **325**
Beattie, J. Carruthers 183
Beattie Building and Theatre **38**, 66, 175, **194**, **255**
Becker, Ronnie 70
Becker, Walter 108–9
Beinart, Ben-Zion 13, 154–5, 157
Beinart, Julian 29, 172
Bell, William 249
Benfield, John 13, **81**
Berman, Mervyn 107–8
Berman, Sam 133
Besseling, Louis 91
Biko, Steve 323
Biochemistry, Department of 47, 51–3, 99
black academics 121, **276**, 318
   *see also* Jordaan, Harold; Jordan, A.C.; Kunene, Daniel; Van der Westhuizen, John
black staff 15, 50, 62, 66
black students 10, 16, 102, 104, 112, 135, 138–9, 162, 199, 212, 229, 234, 246, 259–60, 263–4, 269, 271–2, 282–4, 338, 356n.91, 362n.183, 365n.30, 385n.21
   admission permit required by 261
Board of Extra-Mural Studies, 241
Boland, Bob 150–1
Bolt, Robin **78**
Bolus, Louisa 61
Bolus Herbarium 24, 60–1
Botany, Department of 43, 56, 60–3, **64**, **80**
Botha, Elise 355n.144
Botha, Joubert, 210
Bowie, Malcolm 124
boycotts, academic 14–15
boycotts, student 112, 271, 283–4, 290, 301, 304

Bremner Bequest 41
Bremner Building 17–8, 27–8, 269, 284, 295, 308, 314, 316, 319–22, 324, 334–6, 347n.19
Bremner Building *see also* administration; Sit-in of 1968
Breytenbach, Breyten 198, 372n.76
Brink, Christiaan Strauss 168, 171
British universities as model 3, 44, 85, 111, 138, 183, 240
British universities as model *see also* Cambridge University; London tertiary educational institutions; Oxford University
Brock, John, 109–110, 266
Broekhuysen, Gerry 59
Bromilow-Downing, Bromilow 94–104
Brooks, Alan 218
Brooks, Frank 49
Brown, Alec 58
Brown, Helen 111
Brummer, Guillaume 71
Buhr, Heinrich 87
building and development programmes *see under* architecture and design
Building Committee 29, 34
Building Science degree 171
Bull, Arthur 125–7
Burger, Johannes F. 164, 181
bursaries, Government 161, 201
bus service *see* traffic and transport
Business Science, Department of 150
*see also* Commerce, Department of
Butt, Jack 172
Butterworth, Douglas 70

### C

Cambridge University, influence on lecturing style, etc, 41, 67, 71, 216, 288
campuses *see* Groote Schuur campus; Hiddingh Hall campus; Lower campus; Medical School campus
Cape Non-European Night School Association 243, 246
Cape Performing Arts Board (CAPAB) 185, 190–1, 250
Cape Provincial Administration (CPA) 5, 30, 96–7, 116, 121, 128, 133, 137–8
Cape Society of Attorneys 160
Cape Town Municipal Orchestra 185–6
Carinus Nursing College 139
Carr, Donald 87
Carstens, Peter 217
Carter, Albert V., 7, 13, **81, 262**
Casson, Leslie 193, 195
Cavers, Dorothy 193
Centlivres, Albert van de Sandt as Chancellor 3–4, 15, **22, 23, 39,** 259, 262–4, **275**
Centlivres Building 27, **39,** 166, 168–9, 174
Centre for Organ Transplantation and Heart Disease Building 27, 34
chancellorship *see* Centlivres, Albert van de Sandt; Oppenheimer, Harry; Smuts, Jan
Chamber of Mines 53–5
Chapter of South African Quantity Surveyors 171–3
Chemical Engineering, Department of, 85–7, 292
Chemical Engineering buildings 27, 87, 166
Chemical Pathology, Department of 99, 104, 106
Chemistry, Department of, 50–3, 81, **86**
Chemistry Building *see* P.D. Hahn Building
Cherry, Robin 48–50
Child Guidance Clinic 26–7, 76, 248
Child Health, Department of 123-4
*see also* Institute of Child Health
Chinese students 268
Chisholm, Erik 183–4, **186,** 249, **256**
Chrimes, Pamela 190
City Infectious Diseases Hospital 136
Civil Engineering Building *see* Snape Building
Civil Engineering, Department of 56, 84, 87–90, 92, **142,** 270
students 142
Civil Rights League 12, 155
Classics, Department of, 204–5, 372n.107
Clinical Nutrition Research Unit 110
Clinical Virology, Department of 109
Coetzee, Daan 103
Coetzee, John M. 194, 196–7, 371n.60
Cold War 1, 195, 337
College House 287–9, 386n.53
Colleges of Medicine of South Africa 95

colour bar 259–260
    see also under apartheid
'coloured' students see black students
'coloured' vote case 155–6
Commerce, Department of 146–7, 149–50
    see also Business Science, Department of;
        part-time students
Commerce, Faculty of 45, 47, 66–7, 146–7, 153,
    178, 191, 193, 251, 280, 285, 337
Commercial Law, Department of 158
Committee of Deans 16, 50, 175
Community Medicine, Department of 110
Comparative African Government and Law,
    Department of 159, 375n.196
Computer Centre **18**, 70
Computer Science, Department of 68
Congress of Democrats 294, 309
Conservative Students' Association 292, 300, 313
Convocation 4, 315n.66, 345n.55
Cooper, Ed 136
Corder, Clive 13, **22**, **145**, **273**, **339**
Cormack, Allan 48–49, 130
Council 8, 11–13, 16–7, 24, 30, 156, 175, 212,
    252, 281
    composition of 13, 14, 345n.66
    conservatism of 13, 31, 311, 313
    Finance Committee 20–1
    relations with government 266–8, 271–3, 286
    and *Varsity* 296, 312–3, 315-6
Council for Scientific and Industrial Research
    (CSIR), 49, 52, 56–7, 81, 88–9, 108, 119, 143
    provides funding for research 40–1, 53,
        55–6, 107, 110–11
Court of Discipline 312, 316-7
Cowen, Denis 154–7, **178**, 180, **262**
Crichton, Cuthbert 121
Crowson, Lamar 186
Cullinan, Sarah 12
cultural societies 293
    see also under names of specific societies, eg,
        Students' French Society, etc.
culture, UCT's contribution to 240, 248, 250
    see also cultural societies; student culture
curriculum 169, 172, 197, 209, 222, 230, 378
    Engineering 85, 87, 90–1

Law 159, 160, 218
matriculation 43, 95–6
Medical School 96, 109, 119–20, 123, 130,
    134, 357, 364

**D**
Dall, George 119
dances/dancing 272, 291, 303–4, 306
    racial integration of 10, 259, 271–2, 282,
        303, **310**, 311
Darbyshire, Jack 56
Davenport, Rodney 208
Davey, Dennis 122
Davie, T.B. 1–2, 4–9, 11–12, 14, 19, 21, **22**–**3**, 25,
    **39**, 48, 56, 156, 173, 219–20. 241, 244, 259,
    261, **262**, 265, 288, 290, 295, 301, 306
Davies, David Hywel 65
Day, John 56–8,60, **82**, **275**, 351n.40
*Day Student/Trend* 341
Day Students' Council 295–6, 300, 317
Day of Affirmation of Academic and Human
    Freedom Address 299, 310
De Beers Consolidated Mines Ltd 125, 193
Debating Society 386n.73
degrees see postgraduate degrees; undergraduate
    degrees; honorary degrees
De Groot, Herman 122
De Keller, David 302
De Klerk, Jan 267, 313–4, 383n.50
De la Cruz family 15
Deputy Principal see Inskip, Donald
Dermatology, Department of 134
Deutsche Studentebund 120
Development Fund Appeal 5, 19
Devine, Derry 366n.61
De Vos, Wouter 157, 366n.61
Deyzel, Wynand 29
discrimination see gender discrimination;
    racial discrimination; social discrimination
Distinguished Teacher Award 58
Diocesan College (Bishops) 279
Donald, Ian 122
donations and loans from private sector 20, 85,
    87, 146, 250–1
Doughty. O., 195

Dowdle, Eugene 111, 144, 360n.131, 386n.73
Drama, Department of 33, 43, 224–5, 239, 249, 377n.240
Drennan, Matthew 100–1, 103
Driekoppen 279, 287–8, 305, 386n.53
Driver, Jonty 196, 298
Dryding family 15
Du Preez, Peter 75
Dubow, Neville 232–3
Duminy, J.P. 4, 9-13**, 22, 23, 38,** 125, 168, 266, 294, 300, 310-11, 315, 344n.30

E

Eales, Lennox 110–1
Economic History, Department of 209–10
Economics, Department of 149, 209–11, 374
Education, Faculty of 45, 66, 72, 146, 161–5
  part-time staff 367n.87
Education Society 293
Education Survey 1969 44
*Educational Journal* 269
Einhorn, Heinz 142
Electrical Engineering, Department of 91–2, 126
Elliott, George 89–90
Endocrine Research Group 111
Engineering, Faculty of 71–2, 87, 93–4, 280, 282
  see also Chemical Engineering, Department of; Civil Engineering, Department of; Electrical Engineering, Department of; Mechanical Engineering, Department of
Engineering students 51, 70, 72, 85, 93–4, **142,** 192
Engineering Students' Association 93
English Language and Literature, Department of 192–97
English Language Tutorial Scheme (ELTS) 193
Enslin, Nicholas 91
Erasmus, Jan 114–6
Erasmus, Ockert 164
Erlank, Tony 54
Esmonde-White, Eleanor 231
examinations 44, 118, 123, 148, 193, 200, 243-4
  *see too* British universities as model
ex-service students 5, 18, 139, 191, 278–9, 287, 337
Extension of University Education Act 252, 281, **332**

Extra-Mural Studies, Department of 241–3
  lectures 19, 240
  Summer School 202, 219, 241–2, 255
  *see also* Board of Extra-Mural Studies

F

faculties *see under* Architecture; Arts; Commerce; Education; Engineering; Law; Medical School, Music; Science; Social Science
faculty boards 17, 27
failure rate 43–44, 47, 69, 72, 84 *see also under* first-year students; Science, Faculty of
Falconer, A.W. 2
Falmouth Building 27, 34
February, Vernon 196
Fehrsen, Fred 136
Feldberg, Meyer 179
Ferguson, William 165
Fernie, John 50
Feros, Christie 70
Fiasconaro, Gregorio 184, 187
financial management of UCT, 20–21, 246
Fine Arts *see* Michaelis School of Fine Arts
Fine Arts and Architecture, Faculty of 27, 45, 146, 166, 170–1, 178, 183, 229, 232–3, 294
first-year students 5, 25, 43–4, 48, 51–2, 59, 62–3, 68, 77, **79,** 84, 207, 211, 290, **325,** 353n.108, 364n.251
  failure rate 47, 69, 72
Fishing Industry Research Institute 40, 243, 250, 379n12
Floyd, Hugh 167
Folb, Peter 145
Ford, Findlay 123–4
Forman, Frank 109–10
Forsyth, Malcolm **186**
Forsyth, Robert 117
Fortune, George 222, 224
Frahn, Wilhelm 49
Francis, Bill 176
Francis family 15
French, Department of 12, 155, 200–2
freshers/freshettes *see* first-year students
Freshers' Hop 306
Freshers' Week 5

Fullard, Catherina **81**
Fuller, Tom 124
Fuller Hall 280
funding 107, 110, 149, 151–3, 199–200, 202–3, 206, 208
    *see also* government subsidy
fund-raising 189–90
    *see also* Development Fund Appeal; Rag; UCT Foundation

**G**
gender discrimination 280, 282–3
gender segregation 358n.91
'gentleman's agreement' 271
Geochemistry, Department of 43, 53–4
Geochemistry Research Unit 53
Geography, Department of 55, 63–64
Geography Society 303
Geology, Department of 43, 53–4, 56, **79**
Geology Building 25, 66
Ger, Ralph 264
German, Department of 200, 202–3
Gerstman, Blanche 186
Gibson, Jimmy 158
Gillis, Lynn 132–3
Glasser, Stanley 186–7, 370n.20
Glasstone, Richard 190
Goetz, Robert 116
Golf Club 292
Goodlet, Brian 91
Goodwin, John 220–1
Goold, George 204, 373n.109
Gordon, Hymie **145**
Gordon, Walter 135
government subsidy 65, 191
    funding formula
    under National Party 19–20
    under Smuts 19
Graduate School of Business 147, 151–3 *see also* Postgraduate School of Business Administration and Applied Economics
graduation ceremony 18, 29, 95, 191, 278, 308, **333**
Grant, Willie 164
Gray, Stephen 196
Greenwood, Herbert **19**, 148

Greshoff, Kees 201
Grieve, James Muir 129–30
Groote Schuur (homestead) 24–25
Groote Schuur Campus 24–26, 28, 30–**35,** 44, 153, 160
Groote Schuur Estate 24–6
Groote Schuur Hospital (GSH) 24–6, **36**, 96, 105, 109, 111–2, 114, 116–7, 121–2, 125–7, 129–31, 133–5, 137–8, 140–1, 144–5, 209, 288
Grover, Vera 75–6, 355n.114
Guelke, Roland **81**, 91-2
Gunn, John, 99
Gynaecology *see* Obstetrics and Gynaecology, Department of

**H**
Hales, Anton 68–9, 352n.102
Hall, Anthony 61
Hall, Kenneth 73–6, **82**
Hallett, Robin 206
Hampton, John 150, 179
Hansen, John 124
Hardie, Keith 71
Haresnape, Geoffrey 196–7
Harold Cressy High School 162, 281, 385n.34
Harries, Katrine 231
Harris, Sandy 57
Harrison, Gaisford 126
Harrison, Paddy 139
Hart, Ida 367n.85
Harvey, Russell 231
heart transplant operation, 1967 127
Hebrew, Department of 200, 203
Heese, 'Boet' 124
Helm, Brunhilde 175, 180
Herschel School 279
Herzlia School 203, 279
Heselson, Jack 117
Heyns, Isak 'Tinkie' 165
Hiddingh Hall campus 26, 33, 153, 180, 200
Hiddingh Hall Council 296
History, Department of, 206–9, 217, 264
    *see also* African History
hitch-hiking 31, 36, 311–2, **330**
Hoffenberg, Raymond 111, 141, 264, 266, 268, 277

Hofmeyr, J.H. **23**
Holliman, Fred 52
honorary degrees **2**, 75, 117, **145**, 219, 223, 324
Honoré, Jasmine 190
Horwitz, Ralph **179**
Househam, Keith, 67–70, 72
Howarth, Guy 194–5
Howes, Dulcie 188–9, 191
Hutt, W.H. 149, **179**, **262**
Hyman Liberman Institute, District Six 247

## I

Ikeys 269, 286, 291, 322
Immelman, R.F.M. 14, **39**, 228
Impey, Laurence 65
initiation 288–9, **325**
Independent Student Union 292
Indian students *see* black students
Innes, Duncan 11, 317, 319, 321–3, **335**
Inskeep, Raymond 220–3, **238**
Inskip, Donald 22, 38, 145, 200
Institute of Child Health 124
Institute of South African Architects 171
Interim Students' Council 10–11
International Relations Society 293
Intervarsity 94, 241, 269, 280, 282, 287, 289–91, 322, **329**
    debate 386n.73
    Law 160
Irma Stern Museum 250
Irvine, Nick 312
Isaac, William Edwyn 60–1
Islamic Society 285, 292

## J

Jacobs family 15
Jacobs, Abel 62
Jacobson, Jack 128
Jagger Library 202, 264, 228–9, **238**, 264, 269, 302, 304, 323
James, Reginald William, 4, 7-8, 12–13, **39**, 48, 52, **275**
Jameson Hall 30, 174, 252, **258**, 261, 271, **274**, **275**, 291–2, 297, **299**, 302
janitorial staff 15, **314**

*Janitors' Staff News* 15
Jazz Appreciation Society 293
Jewell, Gillian 264
Jewish students 139, 285
Jewish staff 285
*John D. Gilchrist* (research vessel) 56
Johnson, Samuel, 66
Joint Staff Agreement 96–97 *see also* Cape Provincial Administration
Jordaan, Harold 121, 362n.183
Jordan, Archibald Campbell 215, 222–3n.249, **275**–6
Jukskei Club 292
Juritz, John 50, **78**

## K

Kahn, Louis 168
Kannemeyer, John 198
Kantor, Brian 210
Kaplan, Maurice 88–9
Kaplinsky, Raphie 318–9, 323
Katzen, May 209, 264
Keen, Ted, 103
Keet, Marina 190
Kench, James 106–7
Kennedy, Robert 299, 301
Key, Gordon 130
Kgosana, Philip 264–5
King, W.H. **142**
Kipps, Arthur 108
Kipps, Helene 70
Klug, Aaron 48
Kolbe, Vincent 229
Kolbe Society 293
Kooy, Marcelle 210
Kotzé, Wesley 71
Kraus, Lili 186
Krijgsman, Bob 59
Kritzinger, Leon 153

## L

laboratory and technical staff 15, 62, 66, 100, 102–4, 114, 176, 361 n. 158
Lady Michaelis Orthopaedic Hospital 96, 357n.59

Lamb, Archie 103
Lamchen, Max **81**
Land Surveying, Department of 50, 56, 66, 92–3, **143**
Lang, Richard 135
Langhout, Jan 148
Law, Faculty of 153–161 *see also under names of departments*, eg, Commercial Law, Department of
Law Students' Council 160
lecturers 186–7
    junior 10, 32, 78, 99, 128, 194, 197, 201, 207, 211, 213–4, 214, 218
    salaries 15
    senior 53, 55, 57, 68–9, 90–1, 101, 110, 157–8, 165, 169, 192–4, 205, 217–8, 251, 267, 318, 346n.68, 364n.68, 366n.61
    students' complaints about 71, 77
    visiting 151–2, 319
Lecturers' Association 15
lecturing style 41–3,124, 155
    in Architecture 166–8
    in Commerce 149–152
    in Education 163–5
    in Engineering 87, 90–2
    in Law 154–158, 160, **180**
    at Medical School 98–102, 105, 108–9, 111, 114–5, 118, 122–3, 126, 128–9, 134–5
    in Science 43, 49–50, 52, 55, 58, 61–2, 67, 69–71, 74
    in Social Science 174–6, 178
    at the South African College of Music 184, 187, 189
    *see also* Socratic style *and under* Cambridge University; London tertiary educational institutions; Oxford University
Leeman, Solly, 366n.61
Leftwich, Adrian 218, **278**, 298, 302
Lennox-Short, Alan 193
Levine, Gerald 145
Liberal Party 155, 284, 302
liberalism 11, 253, 264, 273, 286, 300–1
Librarianship, School of 228–9
    part-time staff in 228
Library *see* Jagger Library; University Libraries

Lighton, Reg 164–5
Linder, Geoffrey 106
Lipshitz, Lippy 231–2
Little Theatre 188, 190, 225, 227, **236**, 248–9, **258**, 261, 269–70
Livingstone High School 162, 281, 385n.34
Lodgings Bureau 241, 306
Logic and Psychology, Department of *see* Psychology, Department of
Louw, James 121–2
London tertiary education institutions, influence on lecturing style, etc. 119, 122, 132, 166, 169, 170, 192
Louw, Jannie **113**–6, 140
Louw, N.P. van Wyk 198, 372n.76
Lower Campus 26, 28, 250
Lütjeharms, Wilhelm 60–1, 63
Luyt, R.E. 4, 21, **23**, 215, 267, 289, 309, 319, 321–2, **339**
    and government 265, 267, 318
    and students 11, 308, 317, 327
    *see also* Mafeje Affair

**M**
Mabbutt, Jack 65
McArthur, Ian 70
MacGregor, Jim 134
Macintosh, Robert 125
Mackie, William 193
McMillan, Duncan 189–90, **143**
Madden, 'Helmie' 117
Mafeje, Archie 218, 265, 267–8, 318, 321–3, 399n.244
Mafeje Affair 12, 218, 268, 322
    *see also* Sit-in of 1968
Malan, D.F. 250, 260–1
Malan, G.H.T. 374n.166
Mallory, John 57
Mandela, Nelson 324
Mandelbrote, Harry 206, 208
Mansergh, Brian 27
Marais, Gerrit 89
Mark, Myra 211
Marine Geological Research Group 55
marking 83, 87, 163, 177, 201, 214, 216, 224

mass meetings 171, 252, 268, 274, 287, 311–2, 314, 316, 318–9
Massey, Patricia 121–2
Master's degree *see* postgraduate degrees
Mathematical Statistics, Department of 47, 67
Mathematics Block **18**, 350n.17
Mathematics, Department of 66–72
mathematics, undergraduate teaching of 42, 47–8, 67, 69–72, 90–1, 93, 192
Mathias, Morna 55
Maties (Stellenbosch University students) 289, 291
matriculation examination 43–44, 47, 203
Matthews, A.B. 246
Mauerberger Foundation 119
Mechanical Engineering, Department of 86, 89, 91
Medical campus 26–7, 34, 167, 379n.12
   *see also* Medical School
Medical consultants 118
   *see* part-time staff *under* Medical School
Medical Library **39,** 112
Medical Research Council 40
Medical Residence 288
Medical School **36,** 42–43
   black students quota 385n.21
   curriculum 95–6
   effects of apartheid on 101, 141
   growth of 33, 95
   part-time staff 124, 126, 130, 134–5, 362n.183
   research funding 97
   *see also* Joint Staff Agreement; *and under names of departments or units,* eg, Anatomy, Department of; Medicine, Department of, etc
Medical School buildings, *see under names of buildings,* eg, Falmouth Building, etc
medical students 43, 51, 59, 62, 83, 103–4, 106–7, 118, 137, 139–40, 246–8, 269, 277, 288, 311, 364n.255, 385n.21
medical staff, treatment of patients by 109, 11–2, 115, 124, 127–9, 132–3, 138, 248, 359n.98
Medical Students' Council, 140, 364n.255
medical technology 106, 111, 122, 137
medical training, growth of 95–6
Medicine, Department of 109–12, 118, 120, 123, 130, 134, 136
Men's Residence *see* Smuts Hall
Mental Handicap, chair of 76
Menzies, George 92–3
Metcalf, Peter 90
Michaelis School of Fine Art 229–33, **237,** 282
   part-time staff 231
   racism in 234
   students 234, **237**
Microbiology, Department of 47, 52, 63
Mitford-Barberton, Ivan 231
*Modern World Journal* 301
Modern World Society 301
Mohr, Robert 226
Moll, Pieter 361 n.167
Molteno, Donald, 157, 366n.61
Mosaval, Johaar 189
Mowbray 248, 306
Mowbray Maternity Hospital 96, 120, 248
Murray, Andrew 212–4,
Music, Faculty of 29, 183–4, 190, 370n.24
   *see also* Ballet School; Opera School; South African College of Music
Muslim students 283, 292

## N

Naki, Hamilton 361n.158
National Council for Social Research 65
National Physical Research Laboratory 56
National Party 1, 19, 155, 190, 212, 229, 260–1, 263–4, 266–8, 272, 286, 300–1, 318
National Union of South African Students (NUSAS) 12, 244, 297–9, 302, 308, 322
   and academic freedom **276**
   opposition to 287, 297–8
   resignation of members 298–9
   and UCT 244, 268, 287, 299, 322
Native Law and Administration, Department of *see* Comparative African Government and Law, Department of
Nederlands and Afrikaans, Department of *see* Afrikaans and Nederlands, Department of
Nederlandse Kultuurgeskiedenis, Department of 199–200
Neurology, Department of 130, 133–4

Neurosurgery, Department of 317
New Science Lecture Theatre **78**, 166
Newlands 33, 291
Nkomo, William 319, **335**
non-academic staff *see* administrative staff; black staff; janitorial staff; laboratory and technical staff; library staff
Non-European Staff Association *see* UCT Workers' Association
Non-European Unity Movement (NEUM) 162, 268–9, 271, 283, 385n.33
Non-Europeans *see under* black
Nursing Tuition, Department of 138–8
NUSAS *see* National Union of South African Students

O

O'Dowd, Clodagh 207
Observatory 306
Obstetrics and Gynaecology, Department of 121–3
Oceanography, Department of 43, 47, 55–7
   research vessels 56–**7**
Olivier, Dorothea 63
Olivier, Stephanus, 164, 367n.85
Opera School 184–5, 250
Opera School Company
   *see also* Cape Performing Arts Board (CAPAB)
Ophthalmology, Department of 117–9
Oppenheimer, Harry 4, 11, **22–3,** 145, 301, 340
Opperman, D.J. 198–9
Orthopaedic Surgery, Department of 118–9
Otorhinolaryngology, Department of 117–118
outreach 240–1, 248, 250, 295
   *see also* Students' Health and Welfare Centres Organization (SHAWCO); Extra-Mural Studies, Department of
Oxford University, influence on lecturing style, etc. 41, 43, 67, 119, 172, 193, 197, 288
Ozinsky, Joe 127

P

Paap, Anton 204
P.D. Hahn Building 27–8, 51
Paediatrics, Department of 122-3

Palmer, Philip 128–9
Pan Africanist Congress 264, 284
parking *see under* traffic and transport
Parkyn, Dennis 67–8, 71–2
Parsons, Talcott 176
part-time staff 117–8, 122, 126, 134–5, 153, 158, 167, 185, 228, 231
   *see also under* Architecture, School of; Law, Faculty of; Medical School; Michaelis School of Fine Art; Music, Faculty of; *and under* Librarianship, School of
part-time students 147–8, 152–3, 172, 188, 209, 296
Pathology, Department of 108–9
Pathology, Division of 104, 107
patients, treatment by medical staff 109, 111–2, 115, 124, 127–9, 132–3, 138, 248, 359n.98
Pay, Kathleen 42, 70
pedagogic style/pedagogy *see* lecturing style
Pells, Eddie 164
Peninsula Maternity Hospital 96, 120, 248
Percy FitzPatrick Institute for African Ornithology 59, 352n.57
Pett, Douglas 167
Ph.Ds *see* postgraduate degrees
Pharmacology, Department of 97, 99–100
Philosophy, Department of 42, 72, 211–214
Physical Medicine Department *see* Rheumatology, Department of 137
Physics, Department of 7, 13, 48–52
Physiology and Medical Biochemistry, Department of 26, 97–9
Physiology block 99
Physiotherapy, Department of 95, 136–9
Plant, Arnold 150
Plastic Surgery and Maxillo-Facial Surgery, Department of 117–8
Poliomyelitis Research Foundation 108
political societies 292
Pollard, Martin 70
Poole, David 190, **236**
Pope, Maurice 204–5
postgraduate degrees 40, 47, 349n.3
   doctorates 49, 177, 221, 223
   Master's 47–9, 50, 61, 63, 89–90, 167, 172,

177, 216
Postgraduate School of Business Administration and Applied Economics, 151
  see also Graduate School of Business
postgraduate students 40, 47, 49, 54, 58–9, 61, 69–70, 90, 99, 107, 109, 116, 119, 124–5, 134, 150, 160, 177, 192, 202, 207–8, 221, 349n.3
Potgieter, Gideon 107
Price, Tom 154, 155, 156, 157, 159, 241
Pritchard, Chris 316–7
Princess Alice Orthopaedic Hospital 118
Principal's Circular 16–7
Principalship and Vice-Chancellorship 4
  see also Assistant Principal; Davie, T.B.; Deputy Principal; Duminy, J.P.; Falconer, A.W; James, R.W; Inskip, Donald; Luyt, R.E.
Professional Communications Unit 193
professoriate, composition of 13, 14
professors 17, 45–6, 70, 267, 295, 339, 366n.61, 367n.85
professors see also associate professors
Protem residence 151, 287, 386n.53
protests 29, 74, 171, 218, 262–3, 272, **275**, **277**, 299, 312–3, 318, 322, 324
  see also mass meetings
Prout, Ernest 52
Pryce Lewis, Owen 167
Psychiatric Day Hospital 132–3
Psychiatry, Department of 76, 130, 133–4
Psychology, Department of 72–7, **82**, 185, 248, 264, 303
public displays and exhibitions 251, **257**
Public Accountants' and Auditors' Board 149
Public Health, Department of 135–6
Public Law, Department of 157
public relations officer 251
Pulvermacher, Gunther 186–7
Pure Mathematics, Department of see Mathematics, Department of

## Q

Quantity Surveying (QS), Department of 171

## R

Rabie, James 172
racial discrimination 9, 253, 259, 262, 268–71, 282, 284
  see also social discrimination
racial segregation 102, 104, 112–3, 135, 138, 267, 358n.91, 366n.183
racialism 253, 269, 298
racism 135, 138, 152, 234, 274
  see also racial discrimination; racial segregation
Radical Students' Society (RSS) 253, 292, 300–1, 318
Radiodiagnosis, Department of 127–9, 362n.209
Radiology, Department of 127–8, 134
Radiotherapy, Department of 129–30, 366n.209
Radloff, Peter 75
Rag 94, 241, 245, 252–3, 280, 283, 287–8, 295, **327**, **329**, 379n.19
  floats 60, 170, 188, 252, 289, 308, **328**
  see also *Sax Appeal*; Students' Health and Welfare Centres Organisation (SHAWCO)
Raidt, Edith 198
Radical Students' Society (RSS) 323
Red Cross War Memorial Children's Hospital 123–4, 248, 357n.59
Renal Metabolic Research Group 111
Republic of South Africa Festival, 1961 253, 270
research groups 55, 71, 87, 111
research vessels 56, 57
Residence Avenue 31
residences 26, 29, 93, 152, 154, 156, 268–9, 287–9, 293, 305–6, 320
  see also initiation *and under* names of residences, eg, College House; Smuts Hall; University House
*Responsa Meridiana* 160
Reyburn, Hugh 72–3, 76–7
Rheumatology, Department of 137
Rhodes, Cecil John 24, 36, 347n.24
Rhodes Drive 28–31, **36**, 311, **330**, 347n.24
'Rhodes Must Fall' Movement (2015) 324, 348n.24
Rhodes Scholarship 8, 11

403

Rhodes Trustees 25, 27
Rhodesian students 93–4, 286
Rhodesian Unilateral Declaration of
    Independence, Rag stunt 287
Rietstein, Amy 265
Robbins, Lionel 150
Robertson, D.C. 270
Robertson, H. M. 209–10
Robertson, Ian 299
Robertson, Reginald 88
Rollo, William 204
Roman-Dutch Law, Department of 157
Rondebosch 123, 131, 306, 308
Rondebosch Boys' High School 279
Roper, Margaret 137
Rosebank 26, 29–30, 306
Rosebank Showgrounds 5, 26, 287
Rosteutscher, Joachim 202–203
Roworth, Edward, 230
Rubens, Harold 186
Rubin, Neville 218, **274–5**
Rugby Road 348n.36
rugby 291, 295, 385n.73
rugby fields 32, 170, 273, 311, 348n.24
Rustenburg Girls' High School 279
Rycroft, Brian 61,
Ryrie, Ben, 94

S
Sachs, Albie 265
Sacks, George 117
St Monica's Home 96, 120
Sakinofsky, Isaac 132
Sapeika, Norman 99–100
Sarkin, Teddy 119
Saunders, Stuart 111, 360n.131
*Sax Appeal* 241, 252, 283, 286, 289–90
Schach, Stephen 70
Schaffer, Walter 13, 48–50
Schapera, Isaac 215
Schelpe, E.A.C.L.E. 61, **80**
Schlagbauer, Hartmut 71
Scholtz, Johannes du Plessis 198
Scholtz, Merwe 198–9
Schonland, Basil 344n.30

school culture 165
schools 162, 203, 279, 281, 385n.34
Schrire, Velva 111
Schulze, Bill 117
Science, Faculty of 43, 45, 60, 67, 77, 271
    failure rate 47
    medical students in 47, 49, 51, 59, 62, 112,
        140
    staff–student ratio, 48
Sealy, Rossall 129–30
Searle, Laura, 186–7
Sears, Douglas 68–70
Segal, Philip 196
segregation 234–5, 262, 283
    *see also* gender segregation; racial segregation;
        social segregation
Selzer, Golda 105–6
Senate 16, 52, 172, 175, 203, 239, 268, 323
    composition and role of 13–14
    and Mafeje Affair 321
    meetings 16–17
    minutes 43–4
    and SRC 203, 294–5
Senate Building Advisory Committee 27–8
Senate Expenditure and Development
    Committee 15
Senate General Purpose Committee 16
Sevel, David 119
Shackleton, Mitchell 200–1, 203
Sharp, Ruby 121
SHAWCO *see* Students' Health and Welfare
    Centres Organisation
Sheftel, Morris 312
Shell South Africa 151
Shephard, Rupert 230–2, **237**
Silber, Bill 117
Simons, Jack (H.J.) 42, 214–5, 218–20, 253, 264,
    266, 268, **277**
Simons, Ray Alexander 219
Simpson, Eric 54–56
Singer, Martin 119
Singer, Ronald 101, 103
Sit-in of 1968 218, 268, 284–5, 311, 316, 318–
    24, **333–336**, 340
Skewes, Stanley 70

# INDEX

Sloan, Archie 97–99, 358n.76
Smit, Gideon, 164–5
Smuts, Jan **23,** 208
Smuts Hall 287–9
Snape, Alfred 88
Snape Building 84, 88, **314**
Social Anthropology, Department of 215–6, 218, 237
social discrimination 259, 268. 272–3, 282, 311, 313, 358n. 91 *see also* racial discrimination
social segregation 102, 112, **144**, 214, 259, 262–3, 272–3, 282, 311, 313
Social Medicine Research Unit, 110
Social Science, Department of 183, 247
Social Science, Faculty of 16, 42, 45, 72, 146, 173–8, 183, 191, 211, 215, 247
Social Survey of Cape Town 173, 175, 177
Social Work, Department of 43, 175–7
    *see also* Applied Sociology in Social Work, Department of; Sociology and Administration, Department (School) of 173–5
Socratic style of teaching 42, 156, 213, 218, 338
Solomon, J.M. 24, 26–7
Somerset Hospital 96, 120, 126
South African Bureau of Standards 108
South African College 4, 9, 89, 290, 340
South African College of Music (SACM) 183–8, 190–1
    part-time staff 184–5
    *see also* Ballet School; Music, Faculty of; Opera School
South African College School (SACS) 33, 279
South African Communist Party 218, 294, 323
South African Institute of International Affairs 243
South African Institution of Town Planners 172
South African Institute of Race Relations 155, 210
South African Institute of Refrigeration 90
South African Medical and Dental Council (SAMDC) 95, 121, 361, 127, 361, 364
*South African Medical Journal* 117, 129
South African Society of Anaesthetists 125
South African Teachers' Association 165
South Peninsula High School 162, 281, 385n.34
spatial apartheid 169

Sports Avenue 32, 348n.36 *see also* Rugby Road
Sports Centre 30
sports clubs and activities 291–2 *see also* under name of specific club, eg, Golf Club; Jukskei Club, etc
SRC 41–2, 139, 159, 269, 272, 282–3, 286–91, 265–6, 299
    black members 281, 283
    composition of 293
    and Council 294, 313–4
    and Davie, T.B. 4–5, 8–9, 26, 205, 295
    and Duminy, J.P. 9–11, 266, 294, 300, 310–11
    elections 188, 283, 331
    finances 295
    and Intervarsity 29, 209, 291
    Jewish members 285
    and Luyt, R.E. 11–12, 308, 310
    male domination of 280, 294
    NUSAS 287, 297–302
    Rhodes Drive development 311, 315
    and Van Riebeeck Festival 252, 270, 290
    *see also* Innes, Duncan, Mafeje Affair; Sit-in of 1968
staff benefits 15
Staff Research Fund 40
staff-student ratio 44, 48, 51
Statistics and Operations Research Laboratory 67
Stegen, Reino 90
Stellenbosch University 160 *see also* Maties
Stephen, Alastair, 52
Stephen, Allan Farquhar 13, **38, 262**
Stoy, Richard 50
Straszacker Commission 83, 88–9, 92
Strijdom, J.G. 263
Student Affairs Committee 294, 295
Student Affairs Administration Department 295
Student Amenities Financial Council (SAFC) 295
student adviser 192
student clubs 272, 297, 300, 312
student clubs *see also* sports clubs
student culture 90, 233, 278, 286–7, 291–2
student publications 290, 317 *see also under names* of publications, eg, *Afrikaner-Ikey, Die; Varsity*; etc
student societies *see also* cultural societies;

405

political societies; sports clubs and activities; students' clubs and societies *under the names of specific societies*, eg. Afrikaner Studentebond; Deutsche Studentebund; Students' French Society, etc.

students
    political consciousness of 162, 292, 298, 310–1
    *See also under* faculty or department *and* Afrikaners; alcohol and drug consumption; black students; Chinese students; conservative students; Jewish students; Ikeys; Muslim students; part-time students; Rhodesian students

Student Fellowship Society 292
Students' Christian Association (SCA) 292–3
Students' French Society 292, 294
Students' Geographical Society 66
Students' Health and Welfare Centres Organisation (SHAWCO) 247, 283, 289, 295
Students' Health Service 308–9
Students' Jewish Association 285, 293
Students Representative Council *see* SRC
Students' Science Society 65
Sturrock, Jack 167, 182
Surgery, Department of 116–117, 119–20, 123

**T**
Talbot, Anne-Marie 64
Talbot, William 64–5
Taute, Bill 167
Taylor, James 75–6
Taylor, Mavis 226–7, **236**
Taylor, Ross 53–4
*T.B. Davie* (research vessel) 56, 57
T.B. Davie Memorial Lecture 382n.26
Teaching Methods Research Unit 43
Teachers' League of South Africa 162
teaching style *see* lecturing style
technical staff *see* laboratory and technical staff
Tennis Club 303
Thaele, Elizabeth 281, **332**
Thompson, Leonard 206, 208
Thomson, Jim 104–5
Thornton White, Leonard 26–7, 29, 34, 166–9, 172–3

Tober, Karl 202-203
Topology Research Group 71
Trapido, Stanley 218
Trafalgar High School 162, 281, 385n.34
traffic and transport 32, 296, 300, 311
    bus service 31
    hitch-hiking 31, **36**, 311–2, **330**
    parking 28, 32, **33**, 296
    public transport 34, 120, 242
    road system 30–1
Traffic Court 32
traffic officer 32
Treason Trial 374n.166
Trigonometry Survey 92–3
Troskie, Cas 67
Trotti, Leopoldo 56
Truscot, Bruce 241
Tugwell Hall 29–30
Turner, Rick, 214, 273, 319, **355**
tutorial system, overhaul of 69, 211
tutorials 42–3, 47, 67, 105, 150, 166, 197, 201, 207, 211, 320
    small-group 42, 128, 133, 160, 214
tutors 5, 69, 197, 218, 228, 302

**U**
UCT Citizen Force regiment 270, **273**
UCT Foundation 172, 193
*UCT* (magazine) 251–2
UCT Mountain Club 303
*UCT Redevelopment Survey* 28–29
UCT Staff Association 15
UCT-Witwatersrand University conference 156
UCT Workers' Association 15–6
undergraduates 43–44, 54, 73, 77, 87, 92, 109, 111, 114, 116, 121, 124, 127, 134–5, 153, 162, 174, 183, 202, 208, 210, 218, 295, 304
Union Jubilee Festival 252
Unisa 243, 289
university apartheid 4, 7, 74, 112, 156, 252–3, 259, 262, 270–2, 274–6, 268, 286, 290, 292, 324
university autonomy *see* academic freedom
University Avenue 26, 29, 31–2, 228, 348n. 26
University of Cape Town Act (1916) 3
University House 25, 287
University Librarian *see* Immelman R.F.M.

University Libraries 92, 148, 200–1, 226, 228, 243
Special Collections Department 229
    *see also* Architecture Library; Hiddingh Hall Library; Jagger Library; Law Library; Medical Library; Music Library
University Orator 156
Urban and Regional Planning, Department of, 172, 298
Urology, Department 117
Utian, Wulf 122
Uys, Dirk 105
Uytenbogaardt, Roelof, 30, 168

### V

Valkenberg Mental Hospital 130, 133
Van den Ende, Marinus, 107–8
Van der Horst, Sheila 210, 211, 215
Van der Merwe, A.J. 145
Van der Merwe, Hannes 34
Van der Poel, Jean 208
Van der Merwe, I.W. 198
Van der Westhuizen, John 197, 267
Van Heerden, Helena 186-187
Van Riebeeck Festival (1952) 252, **256**
Van Ryswyk, Willem 213
Van Wyk, Arnold 186
*Varsity* 6, 10, 28, 44, 140, 163, 174–5, 202, 233, 233, 267–9, 280, 289, 294, 297, 301, 304, 308, 318, 338
    Afrikaans edition 286
    circulation 311, 315
    and Council 312, 315, 317
    and Duminy, J.P 311, 315
    founding of 296
    see also Irvine, Nicholas; Pritchard, Chris; Sheftel, Morris
Versfeld, Martin 42, 213
Verwoerd, H.F. 261, 263
Virus Research Unit 107–8
Von Holt, Claus 53, **81**
Vorster, B.J. 298, 303, 321
*Vuga SACS* 291

### W

Walker, Eric **339**
Walker, Fred 54–55
Walton, Henry 132
Warren, Frank 47–48
Water Resources and Public Engineering, chair of 89
Weaver, William 89
Webb, John 70
Webster, Gilbert, 91–2
Wells, Lawrence 102
Welsh, David 219
Werbeloff, Leslie 128
Western Province Blood Transfusion Service's Laboratory 379n.12
Westerford High School 279
Whitaker, Marie 201–2
Whiteman, Michael 70
Williams (later Maud), Marie 207
William Slater Rehabilitation Hospital 131
Wilson, Francis 210
Wilson, Monica 215–21, 223, **237**, 268
Winterbottom, Jack 342n.57
Wives' Club 152
women academics 63–4, 70, 75–76, 106–7, 111, 121, 139, 198, 355n.144
women, status of 363n.241
Women's Residence *see* Fuller Hall
Woodward, Anthony 196
Woolsack Drive **37**
World Health Organisation 108, 110
World War I (1914–1918) 26
World War II (1939–1945) 2, 27, 48, 55, 58, 63, 91, 96, 99, 107, 132, 140, 202, 229, 241, 250, 278–9
    *see also* ex-service students
Wynberg Boys' High School 279
Wynberg Girls' High School 279

### X

Xuma, A.B. **255**

### Y

Young, F.G. 344n.30

### Z

Zoology, Department of 43, 56–9, 61, **78**, **82**, **269**, 351n.40
Zwarenstein, Harry 97–9

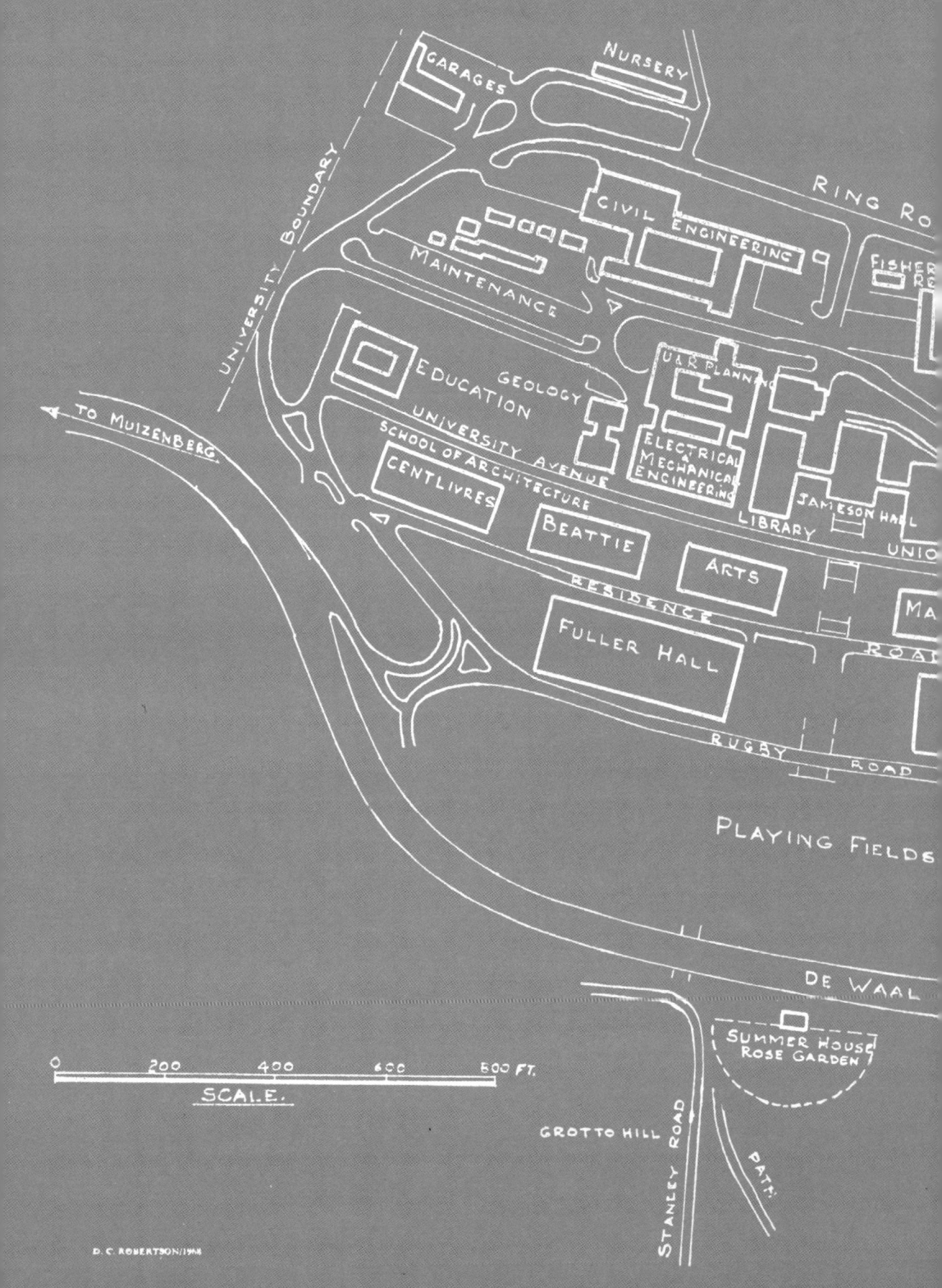